Cases and Materials
on
Evidence

CASES AND MATERIALS ON EVIDENCE

by

J. D. HEYDON, M.A., B.C.L. (Oxon.),

*of Gray's Inn and the New South Wales Bar, Barrister, Professor of Law,
University of Sydney, sometime Fellow of Keble College, Oxford.*

LONDON
BUTTERWORTHS
1975

ENGLAND:	BUTTERWORTH & CO. (PUBLISHERS) LTD. LONDON: 88 Kingsway, WC2B 6AB
AUSTRALIA:	BUTTERWORTHS PTY. LTD. SYDNEY: 586 Pacific Highway, Chatswood, NSW 2067 MELBOURNE: 343 Little Collins Street, 3000 BRISBANE: 240 Queen Street, 4000
CANADA:	BUTTERWORTH & CO. (CANADA) LTD. TORONTO: 2265 Midland Avenue, Scarborough M1P 4S1
NEW ZEALAND:	BUTTERWORTHS OF NEW ZEALAND LTD. WELLINGTON: 26/28 Waring Taylor Street, 1
SOUTH AFRICA:	BUTTERWORTH & CO. (SOUTH AFRICA) (PTY.) LTD. DURBAN: 152/154 Gale Street

ISBN—Casebound: 0 406 59485 6
Limp: 0 406 59486 4

Preface

This collection of cases and materials is intended to be suitable for use in all University courses on the law of evidence and in preparing for professional examinations. English cases and statutes form the basis of the book. But American, Australian and Scots cases have been used where relevant; the leading American writers have often been relied on, and other Commonwealth materials are occasionally mentioned. In selecting materials I have chosen those which seem to me to have merit as expositions of the fundamental but sometimes conflicting principles that run through the law. Most recent House of Lords cases dealing with the subject therefore appear; so do the views of writers, who have often been able to discuss fundamental questions more fully than harassed criminal appellate courts. Apart from the usual apparatus of questions, notes and suggestions for further reading, there is a very full commentary on the materials. It is thought the commentary is sufficiently full to make the book an independent guide to the subject in any jurisdiction substantially based on English law, though it can equally be used as a supplement to a text book.

Evidence is a subject which has proved resistant to rational or agreed organization, and there is even some doubt about its proper province. What this book contains is a mixture of matters united by one or more of the following links. Some matters are particularly interesting to the modern undergraduate (e.g. the protection of the accused). Some are of fundamental theoretical importance (e.g. the rules about hearsay and the burden of proof). Some matters have received or require the attention of law reformers acting on some consistent principle. The book is a full guide to the present law; and it appears at an important moment in the development of the law of evidence. After much waiting, we can now see the future shape of the law, at least mistily. The civil law has been radically changed; the criminal law may soon be changed even more. But if these changes turn out to be unsatisfactory, there may be a second chance to consider them when the entire law of evidence is codified. Hence the present student generations will not know for a decade or two what the precise evidentiary rules of their maturity will be. Throughout this book I have accordingly presented both the present law and the proposals for reforming it in a critical spirit.

Some consider that there ought to be no law of evidence. It is a view quite incompatible with the use of juries or lay magistrates, and indeed not easy to reconcile with rational modes of thought. Others agree with C. P. Harvey's forceful characterization of the subject: "Founded apparently on the propositions that all jurymen are deaf to reason, that all witnesses are presumptively liars and that all documents are presumptively forgeries, it has been added to, subtracted from and tinkered with for two centuries, until it has become less of a structure than a pile of builders' debris" (*The Advocate's Devil* (London, 1958) p. 79). At the opposite extreme, we might note the view of Lord Kenyon that "the rules of evidence have been matured by the wisdom of the ages and are now revered from their antiquity and the good sense in which they are founded" (*R. v. Inhabitants of Eriswell* (1790), 3 Term. Rep. 707, at p. 711). There is more to be said for Lord Kenyon's position than commonly is now said, and this book attempts to investigate both the necessity for and the hazards of reform.

Some matters treated in the fullest works on evidence have been omitted here. Sometimes this is because of lack of space. Sometimes it is because they are arguably not truly part of the subject—pretrial procedure, formal admissions, the parol evidence rule, estoppel. Sometimes it is because they are not much to undergraduate tastes—estoppel, documentary evidence, judicial notice. Other matters have been dealt with more briefly than might be thought desirable. In some cases this is because they depend more on the instinct and experience of practitioners and the discretion of different judges than on the application of precise or predictable rules. Two major examples would be the law of opinion evidence and the course of the trial. In other cases it is because the present law has reached a very sterile and complicated state of learning, and to rehearse it fully is likely to be otiose because of its imminent demise. The rules of competence and compellability, and many of the hearsay exceptions in criminal cases, are examples.

I owe thanks to Mr. Mark Weinberg, Miss Jenny Wily and Mr. G. D. Woods for their valuable comments on parts of the manuscript; to Mr. Geoffrey Flick and Mrs. Margaret Nesci for research assistance; to Miss Jo Bury, Miss Jenny Littman and in particular Mrs. Pauline Browning for typing the manuscript.

The staff of Butterworths have shown their usual skill and courtesy. Finally I owe an older debt to Sir Rupert Cross and Mr. L. H. Hoffmann, at whose feet I first learnt something of the subject.

J.D.H.

April 1975

Acknowledgements

The Publishers and Author make acknowledgement to the following for permission to quote copyright material:

The American Law Institute: E. M. Morgan, Introduction to the American Law Institute's *Model Code of Evidence*, 1942, pp. 3–4 and 27.

Butterworths & Co. (Publishers) Ltd.: *All England Reports*; *Journal of the Society of Public Teachers of Law*.

Butterworths Pty. Ltd.: *The Australian Law Reports*.

Butterworth & Co. (SA) (Pty.) Ltd.: L. H. Hoffmann, *The South African Law of Evidence*, 2nd Edn., 1970, pp. 34, 38–9, 348, 353, 421 and 437–41.

Cambridge University Press: *The Pollock-Holmes Letters* Vol. II, 1942, pp. 284–5.

Canada Law Book Co.: *Dominion Law Reports*.

Carswell Co., Ltd.: Kaufman, *The Admissibility of Confessions*, 2nd Edn., 1974, pp. 16–17.

Collins & Sons & Co., Ltd.: S. Bedford, *The Best We Can Do*, 1958, p. 249.

Council of Law Reporting in Victoria: *Victorian Law Reports*, *Victorian Reports*.

David Higham Associates Ltd.: C. H. Rolph, *Personal Identity*, Michael Joseph, 1957, pp. 120–2.

Faculty of Advocates: *Session Cases and Justiciary Cases*.

W. Green & Son, Ltd.: *Scots Law Times*.

Harvard Law Review Association: Sutherland, 79 Harv. L.R. 21 (1965).

Her Majesty's Stationery Office: *11th Report of the Criminal Law Revision Committee*, Cmnd. 4991, 1972.

Incorporated Council of Law Reporting for England and Wales: *Law Reports* and *Weekly Law Reports*.

Incorporated Council of Law Reporting for Ireland: *Irish Reports*.

Incorporated Council of Law Reporting for Northern Ireland: *Northern Ireland Reports*.

John Wiley & Sons Inc.: J. H. Skolnick, *Justice Without Trial*, 1966, p. 217.

Law Book Co., Ltd.: *Australian Law Journal*, *Australian Law Journal Reports*, *Commonwealth Law Reports*, *NSW State Reports*, *South Australian State Reports*.

Little, Brown & Co.: Maguire, *Evidence of Guilt*, 1959, para. 3.062 n. 9; Wigmore, *A Treatise on Evidence*, 3rd Edn., 1940, paras. 822–3, 851, 857–8, 866–7, 924a, 1745, 1767, 2033, 2059, 2061, 2251.

Macmillan (London and Basingstoke): H. R. Trevor-Roper, *The European Witch Craze of the 17th and 18th Centuries*, Penguin Edn., 1969, p. 44.

Oxford University Press: Devlin, *The Criminal Prosecution in England*, 1960, pp. 30–1, 38–46, and 48–9; D. Karlen, *Anglo-American Criminal Justice*, 1967, p. 98.

Stevens & Sons Ltd.: *English Reports*; *Law Quarterly Review*, Williams, *The Proof of Guilt*, 3rd Edn., 1963, pp. 88, 109–10, 113, 120–2.

Sweet & Maxwell Ltd.: *Criminal Appeal Reports*; Cross, [1973] Crim.L.R. at p. 332; Salmond, *Torts*, 16th Edn., 1973, p. 241; Williams, [1973] Crim.L.R. at pp. 76–7.

The Times: Times Law Reports.

U.S. Government Printing Office: U.S. Reports.

West Publishing Co.: *Atlantic Reporter*; *Federal Reporter*; W. T. Fryer (ed.), *Selected Writings on the Law of Evidence and Trial*, 1957, p. 846; McCormick, *Evidence*, 1st Edn., 1954, para. 109.

Williams & Wilkins & Co. and Fred E. Inbau: Inbau & Reid, *Criminal Interrogation and Confessions*, 2nd Edn., 1967, contents page.

Yale Law Journal and Fred B. Rothman & Co.: Morgan, 31 Yale L.J. 229.

Acknowledgement is also made of permission from the following to use material written by the author:

Stevens & Sons Ltd. and the Editors of the *Law Quarterly Review* and *Modern Law Review*: 87 L.Q.R. 214 (1971); 89 L.Q.R. 552 (1973); 37 M.L.R. 601 (1974).

Sweet & Maxwell Ltd. and the Editor of the *Criminal Law Review*: [1973] Crim.L.R. 264 and 603.

Table of Contents

A*

x *Table of Contents*

PART FIVE: WITNESSES

PART SIX: THE COURSE OF THE TRIAL

Table of Statutes

References in this Table to *"Statutes"* are to Halsbury's Statutes of England (Third Edition) showing the volume and page at which the annotated text of the Act will be found. Page references printed in bold type indicate where the Act is set out in part or in full.

List of Cases

Page references printed in bold type indicate where a case is set out.

List of Cases

Table of Abbreviations

Baker—R. W. Baker, *The Hearsay Rule* (London, 1950).

Bentham—J. Bentham, *A Rationale of Judicial Evidence* (*Works*, ed. Bowring), Vols. VI and VII.

Best—W. M. Best, *Principles of the Law of Evidence* (London, 1911, 11th Edn.).

Cowen and Carter—Z. Cowen and P. B. Carter, *Essays in the Law of Evidence* (Oxford, 1956).

Criminal Law Revision Committee—11th Report of the Criminal Law Revision Committee, Evidence (General), 1972, Cmnd. 4991.

Cross—A. R. W. Cross, *Evidence* (London, 1974, 4th Edn.).

Glass—H. H. Glass (ed.), *Seminars on Evidence* (Sydney, 1970).

Hoffmann—L. H. Hoffmann, *The South African Law of Evidence* (Durban, 2nd Edn., 1970).

McCormick—C. T. McCormick, *Handbook of the Law of Evidence* (St. Paul, Minn., 1954).

Maguire—Maguire, *Evidence: Common Sense and Common Law* (Chicago, 1947).

Nokes—G. D. Nokes, *An Introduction to the Law of Evidence* (London, 1947, 4th Edn.).

Phipson—S. L. Phipson, *Evidence* (London, 1970, 11th Edn.).

Taylor—Pitt Taylor, *Treatise on the Law of Evidence* (London, 1931, 12th Edn.).

Thayer—J. B. Thayer, *Preliminary Treatise on Evidence at the Common Law* (Boston, 1898).

Wigmore—J. H. Wigmore, *Treatise on the Anglo-American System of Evidence in Trials at Common Law* (Boston, 1940, 3rd Edn.).

Williams—Glanville Williams, *The Proof of Guilt* (London, 1963, 3rd Edn.).

PART ONE

Introduction

I

Introduction

I THE NATURE OF THE SUBJECT

The Anglo-American law of evidence began to assume a modern form two centuries ago, though some of its rules are much older. Most of its principles reveal it as a child of our traditional system of adversary trial before a lay jury as opposed to inquisitorial trial by professional judges. These principles have survived into an age in which juries scarcely sit outside serious criminal cases and which, in legal procedure as in economics, says it prefers etatist intervention to competition.

The rules of evidence state what matters may be considered in proving facts and what weight they have. They are largely ununified and scattered, existing for disparate and sometimes conflicting reasons: they are a mixture of astonishing judicial achievements and sterile, inconvenient disasters. There is a law of contract, and perhaps to some extent a law of tort, but only a group of laws of evidence.

A large part of the subject consists of rules excluding relevant and often weighty information—rules based on "calculated and supposedly helpful obstructionism" (Maguire, p. 11). A small part of it consists of rules giving greater relevance and weight to facts than common sense would always suggest. Now in ordinary life the only limitations on the matters which we take into account in proving facts are those imposed by logic and common sense. Why does law differ in this respect from ordinary life? This question can be partly answered by surveying the character and main rules of the subject.

Much evidence is excluded because there is a risk of it being untrue or of unreliable inferences being drawn: hearsay evidence, confessions, the silence or misconduct of a party. Other defective evidence is admitted but requires corroboration before the court can safely act on it, e.g. evidence of accomplices, children and complainants in sex cases. Some evidence is excluded by reason of particular witnesses having a privilege not to speak in certain matters. Thus a lawyer's client is privileged not to reveal communications between himself and the lawyer, and the lawyer cannot reveal them without the client's consent; in this way full disclosure in the seeking of legal advice will be encouraged. A witness need not give answers which may incriminate him because there is a risk he will lie and will be induced not to testify at all. Certain statements made in the course of negotiating to settle disputes without prejudice are excluded to encourage recourse to frank negotiation rather than litigation.

3

Some evidence is excluded because it would be injurious to the public interest. The burden of proof rules state who must begin adducing evidence and how much is necessary to prove certain points. Some facts are so notorious as not to require proof: the judge will take "judicial notice" of them. Special rules govern the right and duty of different classes of person to testify. There are rules governing the course of the trial—the order in which evidence is admitted. The prior good or bad conduct and character of a party raises special problems of relevance and weight. Confessions and improperly obtained evidence are excluded partly to encourage a high standard of police behaviour.

Morgan: Introduction to the American Law Institute Model Code of Evidence
(1942) Pp. 3–4

Thoughtful lawyers realize that a lawsuit is not, and cannot be made, a scientific investigation for the discovery of truth. The matter to be investigated is determined by the parties. They may eliminate many elements which a scientist would insist upon considering. The court has no machinery for discovering sources of information unknown to the parties or undisclosed by them. It must rely in the main upon data furnished by interested persons. The material event or condition may have been observed by only a few. The capacities and stimuli of each of these few for accurately observing and remembering will vary. The ability and desire to narrate truly may be slight or great. The trier of fact can get no more than the adversaries are able and willing to present. The rules governing the acceptable content of the data and the methods and forms of presenting them must be almost instantly applied in the heat and hurry of the trial. Prompt decision on the merits is imperative, for justice delayed is often justice denied. Sometimes a wrong decision quickly made is better than a right decision after undue procrastination. "Some concession must be made to the shortness of human life." The trier must assume that the data presented are complete, and the litigants must be satisfied with a determination of the preponderance of probability. If the data leave the mind of the trier in equilibrium, the decision must be against the party having the burden of persuasion. No scientist would think of basing a conclusion upon such data so presented. The court is not a scientific body. It is composed of one or more persons skilled in the law, skilled in the general art of investigation, but not necessarily skilled in the field which the dispute concerns, acting either alone or with a body of men not necessarily trained in investigation of any kind. Its final determination is binding only between the parties and their privies. It does not pronounce upon the facts for any purpose other than the adjustment of the controversy before it. Consequently there must be a recognition at the outset that nicely accurate results cannot be expected; that society and the litigants must be content with a rather rough approximation of what a scientist might demand. And it must never be forgotten that in the settlement of disputes in a court room, as in all other experiences of individuals in our society, the emotions of the persons involved—litigants, counsel, witnesses, judge and jurors—will play a part. A trial cannot be a purely intellectual performance.

All this is not to say that the rules for conducting the investigation of the facts cannot be, or need not be, rational. Quite the contrary. In such a setting it is especially important that artificial barriers to logically persuasive data be removed. With such a tribunal acting in such circumstances the exercise of superlative psychological powers is not to be expected. Rules calling for nice intellectual discriminations and unusual intellectual and emotional controls are impossible of application. Speaking generally, the tribunal should hear and consider those data which reasonable men confronted with the necessity of acting in a matter of like importance in their everyday life would use in making up their minds what to do.

In the last decade there has been some movement towards Morgan's ideal. Many reforms have been achieved and many more proposed. The writer thinks that much of the current law is worth retaining, but throughout we will seek not merely to discover and explain the law, but to test each rule against its purpose and each purpose against modern needs. We will not consider, save briefly in this chapter, certain matters which are not much debated or taught (e.g. judicial notice, documentary evidence) or which relate more to procedure or substantive law (e.g. formal admissions, estoppel, the parol evidence rule).

In the remainder of this chapter it is proposed to discuss certain matters of terminology, classification, and arrangement (see generally Nokes, Chaps. 1–3 and 5; Cross, Chaps. 1–3).

II TERMINOLOGY

A. Facts in issue and collateral facts

The law of evidence governs the proof of "facts in issue". These are all the facts which the plaintiff or prosecutor and the defendant must prove to succeed. What they are in a given case is determined partly by whatever substantive rules of law apply and partly by reference to the charge and plea in criminal cases or the pleadings in civil cases. Facts in issue are distinguishable from "subordinate" or "collateral facts". These are facts which affect the proof of facts in issue, either because they affect the credibility of a witness testifying to a fact in issue (e.g. proving his bias, bad eyesight or bad character), or because they affect the admissibility of an item of evidence tending to prove a fact in issue (e.g. police misconduct affecting the voluntariness of a confession).

B. Direct testimony, hearsay, documents, real evidence and circumstantial evidence

"Direct testimony" is the assertion of a witness about a fact of which he has direct knowledge offered as evidence of the truth of that which is asserted. "Hearsay" or "indirect testimony" is the assertion of a person, other than the witness who is testifying, offered as evidence of the truth of that asserted, rather than as evidence of the fact that the assertion was made (the latter being called "original" evidence). There is a general rule against the admissibility of hearsay evidence which is now riddled with many common law and statutory exceptions (see Chap. 12, *post*). The contents of a document are admissible provided the original is produced; "secondary evidence" by means of copies is admitted in many cases by way of exception (e.g. where the document is public, or lost, or impossible to produce; or where an opponent has failed to produce it after a notice to do so). "Real evidence" is admitted when a court draws an inference from its own observation of some material object rather than relying on that of witnesses, e.g. the physical condition of a document or other physical object, the appearance of handwriting, photographs or films, the intonation of the voices on a tape recording, the appearance and demeanour of persons. Usually the admission of real evidence must be accompanied by the testimony of a witness to identify or explain it. In general neither views of the scene nor reconstructions of past events should be held without the consent and in the presence of the parties; but opinions differ on whether they are real evidence or merely an aid to the understanding of the evidence (cf. *Salsbury* v. *Woodland*, [1970] I Q.B. 324; [1969] 3 All E.R. 863 C.A., with *Scott* v. *Numurkah Corporation* (1954), 91 C.L.R. 300, and see Solomon (1960), 34 A.L.J. 46). "Circumstantial evidence" is any fact ("fact relevant to the issue") from which the existence of a fact in issue may be inferred. An item of circumstantial evidence may be proved by any other evidence, including circumstantial evidence. Circumstantial evidence is sometimes contrasted with other ("direct") evidence in that facts in issue are *indirectly inferred* rather than *directly perceived*. The inferences drawn from circumstantial evidence are often stated in presumptive form (see Chap. 4, *post*).

It should be noticed that the above forms of evidence need not always be relied on, for facts which are formally admitted or of which judicial notice is taken need not be proved. Formal admissions may be made in civil cases by a party to save his opponent the trouble of proving them and to avoid the risk of having to pay his opponent's costs of so doing. Unlike informal admissions, admitted under an exception to the hearsay rule (see Chap. 13, *post*), they cannot be contradicted, they are only binding for the purposes of the instant proceedings, and they are made as part of the proceedings, not before them. Formal admissions were permitted in criminal cases as well as civil for the first time by the Criminal Justice Act 1967, s. 10. Judicial notice is taken of facts so generally known that they cannot be seriously disputed or capable of speedy and accurate discovery. Sometimes judicial inquiry is necessary first, e.g. where the status of foreign sovereigns, historical details, customs, or the reliability of technical instruments are concerned. Sometimes statute provides for judicial notice to be taken of particular facts. The doctrine is applied tacitly much more often than it is expressly.

C. Relevance, admissibility, weight, discretion

All evidence relevant to prove or disprove a fact in issue is admissible unless one of the exclusionary rules which make up so much of the law of evidence applies. What is admissible depends on rules of law which are supposed to be based on special considerations such as avoiding jury bias, deterring police misconduct, protecting state security and so forth. What is relevant is largely a matter of common sense (but see Eggleston, J., in Glass, pp. 53–89). However, some presumptions based on circumstantial evidence remind us of what is relevant, and some rules remind us what may not be relevant (e.g. proof of bad past conduct different from that with which the accused is charged). Prior decisions on relevance may sometimes be strongly persuasive from the viewpoint of later courts. Matters which are marginally relevant may be excluded because it would take too long to investigate them, or because they would distract the jury from the main issues, or because they raise the risk of further evidence on new issues being called, leading to decisions which may be unfair to parties not before the court. The difficulties of relevance usually arise in the areas of similar fact and *res gestae* evidence (see Chaps. 10 and 13, *post*).

It should be noted that evidence may be admissible for one purpose but not for another: a hearsay statement is admissible if the issue is whether it was made, but not if the issue is whether it is true. This rule of "multiple admissibility" (Wigmore, para. 13) may be dangerous, particularly in jury cases, but prevents too great a tension between paternalism and commonsense. A further notion is "conditional admissibility". Because evidence comes out by degrees at a trial, the relevance of some evidence may be conditional on later evidence which may or may not be given. If the earlier evidence is admitted, it is said to have been admitted conditionally or "*de bene esse*".

Like relevance, weight is a common-sense notion: our law has "no orders for the reasoning faculty" (Thayer (1900), 14 Harv.L.R. 139, at p. 141). Unlike admissibility, it is a question of fact for the jury. Evidence of doubtful weight—because of a risk of bias, or imperfect observation—may be excluded by the judge from the jury's consideration.

Recently it has been recognised in a number of areas that the judge has a discretion (probably only in criminal cases) to exclude relevant evidence if its probative force would be exceeded by its prejudicial effect. This applies to similar fact evidence (Chap. 10, *post*), evidence of the accused's bad record put to him in cross-examination (Chap. 11, *post*), and statements made in the presence of the accused to which he gives no answer (Chap. 7, *post*). Another related and possibly identical discretionary power is to exclude evidence which would operate unfairly against the accused: this applies to confessions (Chap. 8, *post*) and illegally or improperly obtained evidence (Chap. 9, *post*; see generally Weinberg, (1975), 21 McGill, L.J.). A further kind of discretion applicable to both civil and criminal cases is a discretion to disallow hectoring questions in cross-examination and to absolve a witness from answering particular relevant questions even though no privilege exists (e.g. questions to a priest about a penitent's confession). But at common law there is no discretion to include relevant but inadmissible evidence.

Harris . DPP [1952]
Selvey v. DPP [1970]

III   THE FUNCTION OF JUDGE AND JURY

The division between the functions of judge and jury, and the merits and dangers of jury trial, have profoundly affected the modern law of evidence even as it applies in cases without a jury. Indeed, one of the most striking features of English law, which differentiates it from American, is the extent to which the judge controls the jury.

In general the judge decides issues of law, including admissibility of evidence, and directs the jury as to the meaning of the legal rules they must apply to the facts; the jury decides on questions of fact. But the operation of formal admissions, some presumptions and the evidence of judicial notice limits the jury's competence to find facts. Further, the judge decides whether there is any evidence fit to go to the jury on any fact in issue (see Chap. 2, *post*); what the ordinary meaning (but not any peculiar meaning) of words used by the parties is, save in defamation cases; what foreign law provides; whether the defendant in a malicious prosecution suit had reasonable and probable cause for prosecuting; whether a covenant in restraint of trade is unreasonable; whether facts precedent to the admissibility of items of evidence are proved. A "trial within the trial" called the *voir dire* is used for this latter purpose, particularly in the case of confessions (see Chap. 8, *post*). Since it is often impossible to decide issues of admissibility without considering the evidence to be admitted, the jury is generally absent from the *voir dire* and from arguments about the admissibility of evidence. But the jury's absence during the *voir dire* may hamper them in determining the weight of later evidence, and they may think that the more often they are ordered out of the court the more likely the accused is to be guilty. Hence they should be present unless there is a risk of prejudice (cf. *R. v. Reynolds;* [1950] I K.B. 606; [1950] I All E.R. 335, C.C.A.). Judges have differed on whether a full *voir dire* without the jury as well as the same testimony in the jury's presence should be permitted where the disputed fact preliminary to the admissibility of evidence is identical with the fact in issue (cf. *Doe d. Jenkins v. Davies* (1847), 10 Q.B. 314, with *Hitchins v. Eardley* (1871), L.R. 2 P. & D. 248).

Judicial control over the jury in practice appears most strongly in the judge's summing up. It is usually undesirable for the judge simply to state the law without giving any guidance on how to apply it to the precise facts. Further he may give the jury, expressly or impliedly, his views on the credibility of witnesses and the evidence generally. However, it should be made clear to them that they are not bound by these views (*Broadhurst v. R.*, [1964] A.C. 441; [1964] I All E.R. 111, P.C.). A conviction may be set aside on appeal as being unsafe or unsatisfactory, or because of a wrong decision of law, or because there was a material irregularity in the course of the trial; but the appeal may be dismissed if the court's view is that no miscarriage of justice actually occurred even though the appellant's ground of appeal was soundly based (Criminal Appeal Act 1968, s. 2 (1)). This dissuades counsel from unsuccessful objections and appeals which though meritorious are technical in the sense that they would not affect the outcome. An appeal against a civil jury verdict may be based on it being against the weight of the evidence, but it must be "almost perverse" (*Metropolitan Rail Co. v. Wright* (1886), 11 A.C. 152, at p. 153; [1886–90] All E.R. Rep. 391, H.L., *per* Lord Selborne).

The judge has wide discretionary powers in conducting the trial. However, these are controllable on appeal, particularly if he intervenes so much as to prevent parties or their counsel conducting the case properly (see *Jones v. National Coal Board*, [1957] 2 Q.B. 55; [1957] 2 All E.R. 155, C.A.). The judge must act only on the evidence put before him by the parties, for each side has a right to comment on what the other says and neither can do this if the judge acts on secret information.

IV EVIDENTIARY GHOSTS

There are two principles which once had, or were thought to have, much more importance in the law of evidence than they do now. It is important not to be misled by references to them.

Lord Hardwicke said: "the judges and sages of the law have laid it down that there is but one general rule of evidence, *the best that the nature of the case will admit*" (*Omychund v. Barker* (1745), I Atk. 21, at p. 49). But it is not now true either that a party cannot introduce an item of evidence if better is available, or that he can introduce an item of evidence if, though it is defective, there is none better: much inadmissible hearsay would be admitted if the "best evidence" rule were law. The rule that in general the original of a private document must be produced to prove its contents is usually said to be the sole survival of the rule (cf. Thayer, Chap. 11), except that evidence which is not the best evidence may be ignored because it lacks weight and may even be excluded on this ground (e.g. *R. v. Quinn*, [1962] 2 Q.B. 245; [1961] 3 All E.R. 88, C.C.A.).

Many of the rules of evidence are said to be justified by the maxim *res inter alios acta alteri nocere non debet*, which is intended to mean that a party to litigation should not be prejudiced by transactions between strangers. These include similar fact evidence (Chap. 10, *post*), hearsay evidence (Chap. 12, *post*) and judgments in earlier proceedings (Chap. 15 *post*). We shall see that these rules rest on other bases. Invocation of the maxim tends to beg questions as to the relevance and weight of evidence; its only real importance is in providing an historical explanation of some modern rules.

V SPECIAL FORMS OF EVIDENCE

Tape recordings are sometimes admitted under exceptions to the hearsay rule if the words are relied on as evidence of their truth, sometimes as original evidence if the words are relied on simply as proof of the fact they were uttered, and sometimes as real evidence, where the intonation of the words is important. There is controversy over whether only the original is admissible (cf. *R. v. Stevenson*, [1971] 1 All E.R. 678; [1971] 1 W.L.R. 1; and *R. v. Matthews*, [1972] V.R. 3), but no further special rules or problems exist other than unreliability. Fingerprint evidence is very weighty circumstantial evidence: judicial notice is taken of the fact that each person's fingerprints are unique. Blood tests are real evidence (if the sole issue is the percentage of blood alcohol) or circumstantial evidence (e.g. if the issue is fitness to drive, or paternity). There are special statutory procedures for the sampling of blood (and breath and urine). Evidence of the behaviour of tracker dogs which follow a scent to the accused, may, if exceptionally reliable, be admissible circumstantial evidence. Sufficiently reliable photographs and films of places and people, identified by a witness as such, are admissible; and a film of radar reception made without human intervention has been admitted (*The Statue of Liberty*, [1968] 2 All E.R. 195; [1968] 1 W.L.R. 739). Evidence of a person's behaviour under the influence of a truth drug is inadmissible for a number of technical reasons but principally because it is so unreliable (*R. v. McKay*, [1967] N.Z.L.R. 139). The same is true of lie detector evidence (in America as well as England, contrary to common belief).

VI WRITERS AND JUDGES

Something should be said briefly of those who have helped to develop the law of evidence or who have shown a peculiar mastery of its exposition. The great judges have usually revealed their greatness in evidence law as in other areas. But perhaps unfortunately the importance of jury trial has made the contributions of equity judges relatively slight and those of criminal judges preponderant, particularly in modern times. The subject began to take on coherent form in the time of Lord Mansfield, and since then Lord Ellenborough C.J., Parke, B., Willes, J., Bowen, L.J., Lord Sumner, Lord Devlin and Lord Denning, and in Australia Jordan, C.J. and Dixon, C.J., have made notable contributions. The shortage of appellate authority until this century has made writers unusually unimportant. Bentham's great potential influence was limited by a crabbed style and a tendency to excessive drawing of distinctions; of other nineteenth century writers, Best and Taylor remain very stimulating; and Stephen's Indian Code did much to reduce the subject to order. Among Americans Thayer revealed a masterly historical understanding and Wigmore an unrivalled knowledge in detail of the modern law and its rationale: both have had considerable influence on judicial and legislative developments in America and outside. The same is true of the modern masters, Morgan and McCormick in America and Cross in England.

VII ARRANGEMENT

No two books on Evidence are laid out in the same way. The plan we shall adopt is rather like our subject in having no single basis. In the next part we discuss certain basic problems that pervade the entire law: on whom the burden of proof rests, what standard must be achieved, and how certain presumptions operate. In Part III we discuss those rules of evidence which, though they sometimes also arise outside criminal cases or serve other purposes, have as their principal aim the protection of the accused from wrong conviction or other forms of maltreatment by the State. These rules constitute perhaps the largest single part of the law of evidence in practice and to many students they are the most interesting. In Part IV we discuss the rule against hearsay, which used to be the major technical rule of evidence in the sense that much of the law could be stated in terms of the rule and its exceptions, but which is now of diminishing importance as a result of extensive actual and proposed reforms. It retains fundamental theoretical interest. In Part V we discuss who can testify as a witness, who can be forced to testify and which particular questions need not be answered by witnesses because of private or state privilege. In Part VI certain miscellaneous rules are briefly considered, such as the admissibility of opinion evidence, character evidence, and earlier judicial findings. Finally, in Part VII we discuss the rules governing the course of the trial.

PART TWO

Burdens and Presumptions

2

The Burden of Proof

I INTRODUCTION

The phrase "burden of proof" has two senses to which a variety of different names are given. The first sense refers to the duty of a party to persuade the trier of fact by the end of the case of the truth of certain propositions. What these propositions are depends on substantive rules of law and pleading. This first burden is variously called the "legal burden", the "persuasive burden", "the burden of proof on the pleadings", "the fixed burden of proof", "the risk of non-persuasion" (Wigmore), and "the burden of proof".

The second sense of "burden of proof" refers to one party's duty of producing sufficient evidence for a judge to call on the other party to answer. The incidence of this duty is determined by particular rules of evidence. This task of producing evidence fit to be considered by a jury is called the "evidential burden", the "burden of adducing evidence", or the duty "of passing the judge". As the Privy Council pointed out in *Jayasena v. R.*, [1970] A.C. 618, at p. 624; [1970] 1 All E.R. 219, at p. 222, H.L., it is misleading to call this a burden of proof when it is capable of discharge by evidence falling far short of proof. Failure to discharge the first burden will cause the trier of fact to decide against the proponent on that issue; failure to discharge the second will cause the judge to decide against the proponent without calling on his opponent or letting the case go to the trier of fact at all.

A luxuriant terminology has characterized and caused confusion in the general area of burden of proof, and this part of it is no exception. Plainly, some of these names are better guides to meaning than others; but the case-law is insufficiently settled to permit dogmatism. So long as the reasonably simple distinction stated is made clear, it matters little what names are used. We will use the names "legal" and "evidential" burden.

The same evidence may serve both purposes. It is in fact misleading to suppose that some evidence is introduced to jump the "evidential burden" hurdle and then other evidence to jump the "legal burden" hurdle. On a given issue, the proponent will put in all his evidence. It will be for the judge to decide whether he has satisfied the evidential burden. The same evidence will, after the opponent has put his case, then be considered by the trier of fact, perhaps strengthened by the opponent's failure to answer it, or by the poor performance under examination-in-chief and cross-examination of the opponent or his witnesses. Even if the opponent says nothing and calls no evidence, the proponent may fail to satisfy the legal burden, for the judge may think he has made out a case to answer while the trier of fact finds his case not sufficiently weighty to satisfy the higher legal burden.

The evidential burden must be known when there is doubt as to who should or may begin calling evidence; and when there is a submission at the close of the proponent's case that he has not made out a case to answer. The legal burden must be known when the trier of fact is in doubt at the close of the evidence and when the judge is directing the trier of fact about this. A further occasion exists when either burden must be known: this is when an appellate court is hearing an appeal alleging some mistake respecting the first four occasions when the burden is relevant.

II HOW CAN THE INCIDENCE OF THE TWO BURDENS OF PROOF BE DETERMINED?

A common test for the incidence of the legal burden on a particular fact in issue is, "Who would lose on that issue if the evidence is equally balanced at the end of the case?" A similar test for the evidential burden is "Who would lose if no evidence at all were given?" But these questions merely restate the problem of working out which factors influence the formulation of the rules which answer the questions.

The general rules are that the evidential burden normally lies in the same place as the legal burden, and that the legal burden of proving facts lies on him who asserts them. The rule as to the legal burden exists because he who involves the state's aid through its judicial system, with consequent trouble and expense to others, should justify his conduct by assuming the initial difficulty it entails. The rule tends to avoid harrassing and vexatious litigation.

The rule as to the evidential burden exists in order to prevent a man being forced to justify his past conduct without a colourable case having been made against him. It protects the privacy of individuals against the state and their enemies or busybodies. It also partially controls capricious jury verdicts. Though these can be upset on appeal, they are better prevented by a directed verdict than cured retrospectively by the action of the appellate court. Another function arises in those criminal cases where an evidential burden is on the accused. Here the burden tends to force the accused to testify if he wishes to deny facts (particularly relating to a state of mind) which would be inferred from the prosecution's case. In these cases the rule also saves the prosecution from having to rebut a large number of defences some of which may not in fact be relied on or have any basis. There are statutory exceptions to the above rule (see Williams, *Criminal Law: The General Part* (2nd Edn.), para. 292, n. 1). Further, the parties in a civil case may vary the burden of proof by agreement, express or implied; normally the agreement will be taken to relate to the legal burden of proof.

But the general rule may be qualified by the operation of numerous other factors.

One is the difficulty of proving a negative. The prosecution must sometimes prove a negative (e.g. absence of consent in rape); so must the proponent in a civil case (e.g. non-performance of a contract). But the fact that a negative might have to be proved by one party is sometimes a reason for placing the burden of proof on the other (*Joseph Constantine Steamship Line, Ltd.* v.

Imperial Smelting Corporation Ltd., [1942] A.C. 154; [1941] 2 All E.R. 165, H.L.).

Another exception to the general rule that the legal and evidential burdens are borne by the same party, i.e. he who asserts a fact, arises with certain defences in criminal cases. The Crown has the legal burden of proving murder and thus of negativing facts which justify or excuse homicide, but the accused bears the evidential burden of raising such issues as provocation (*Mancini* v. *D.P.P.,* [1942] A.C. 1; [1941] 3 All E.R. 272, H.L.), self-defence (*R.* v. *Lobell,* [1957] 1 Q.B. 547; [1957] 1 All E.R. 734, C.C.A.; *Bullard* v. *R.,* [1957] A.C. 635; [1961] 3 All E.R. 470 n., P.C.), sane automatism and drunkenness (*Bratty* v. *A.-G. for Northern Ireland,* [1963] A.C. 386; [1961] 3 All E.R. 532, H.L.). The same applies to mechanical defect on a charge of dangerous driving (*R.* v. *Spurge,* [1961] 2 Q.B. 205; [1961] 2 All E.R. 688, C.C.A.); a reasonable excuse on a charge of failure to provide a specimen for a laboratory test in connection with possible traffic offences (*R.* v. *Clarke,* [1969] 2 All E.R. 1008; [1969] 1 W.L.R. 1109, C.A.); duress (*R.* v. *Gill,* [1963] 2 All E.R. 688; [1963] 1 W.L.R. 841, C.C.A.; *R.* v. *Smyth,* [1963] V.R. 737); necessity (*R.* v. *Trim,* [1943] V.L.R. 109); alibi (*R.* v. *Johnson:* [1961] 3 All E.R. 969; [1961] 1 W.L.R. 1478); but not the prosecutrix's consent in rape (cf. *R.* v. *Donovan,* [1934] 2 K.B. 498, C.C.A.; [1934] All E.R. Rep. 207). It is misleading to refer to these issues as "defences" for this may suggest the accused bears a legal burden (*R.* v. *Wheeler,* [1967] 3 All E.R. 829, C.A.; [1967] 1 W.L.R. 1531; *R.* v. *Abraham,* [1973] 3 All E.R. 694, C.A.; [1973] 1 W.L.R. 1270). They should be put to the jury if there is some evidence of them whether or not the accused relies on them; defence counsel may have made a wrong choice of the issues on which to fight, or may think it tactically unwise to raise partly conflicting issues (*Mancini* v. *Director of Public Prosecutions* [1942] A.C. 1; [1941] 3 All E.R. 272, H.L.; cf. *R.* v. *Gill,* [1963] 2 All E.R. 688; [1963] 1 W.L.R. 841, C.C.A.). An evidential burden may be discharged without the party bearing it having to give evidence, e.g. because of what the other side's witnesses say. This is an important practical point where the accused bears an evidential burden; the burden by no means completely undermines his right to silence.

It would be unfair for the Crown to have to rebut every possible fact which might be relied on by the defence. It would be difficult to do without some understanding of what form the issue might take; it would lengthen the trial and confuse the jury with a multiplicity of irrelevant questions.

However, the legal burden of proving insanity (*Sodeman* v. *R.,* [1936] 2 All E.R. 1138, P.C.) or insane automatism (*Bratty* v. *A.-G. for Northern Ireland,* [1963] A.C. 386; [1961] 3 All E.R. 532, H.L.) or unfitness to plead (*R.* v. *Podola,* [1960] 1 Q.B. 325; [1959] 3 All E.R. 418, C.C.A.; *R.* v. *Robertson,* [1968] 3 All E.R. 557; [1968] 1 W.L.R. 1767 C.A.) or diminished responsibility. (Homicide Act 1957, s. 2 (2); *R.* v. *Dunbar,* [1958] 1 Q.B. 1; [1957] 2 All E.R. 737, C.C.A.) is on the accused on the balance of probabilities if he raises the issue; otherwise the Crown bears the legal burden of proving the defective mental state beyond reasonable doubt. The general rule that he who asserts a fact must prove it applies in this case because of the inherent unlikelihood of a defective mental state, because the accused knows far more about his state of mind than the prosecution, because such a state is very difficult to disprove "in the air", without some evidence of it to be refuted and because it is desirable to prevent these defences being raised frivolously. Indeed, if the prosecution bore the burden too many accused might be acquitted.

Other relevant factors are that a fact is peculiarly within one party's knowledge, that it forms one of a number of possible excuses or qualifications, and that if the onus of proof rested on the other party he would have to prove a negative. If all three are present, the legal burden may be on the opponent of one who affirms (*R.* v. *Turner* (1816), 5 M. & S. 206; [1814–23] All E.R. Rep. 713; p. 25, *post*). The factor of peculiar knowledge alone is unlikely to alter the legal burden (*R.* v. *Spurge*, [1961] 2 Q.B. 205; [1961] 2 All E.R. 688, C.C.A.). However, it may be relevant in determining how much evidence discharges the evidential burden and the legal burden. In the latter connexion Lord Mansfield once remarked: "It is certainly a maxim that all evidence is to be weighed according to the proof which it was in the power of one side to have produced, and in the power of the other to have contradicted" (*Blatch* v. *Archer* (1774), 1 Cowp. 63, at p. 65).

In England peculiar knowledge and the need to avoid making a party prove the negative have often been held, without express statutory words, to put an evidential burden on the accused: this commonly arises in crimes of carrying on some activity without a licence or certificate (e.g. *John* v. *Humphreys*, [1955] 1 All E.R. 793; [1955] 1 W.L.R. 325; cf. *McGowan* v. *Carville*, [1960] I.R. 330 and *Everard* v. *Opperman*, [1958] V.R. 389). It is justified by the triviality of these offences and the desirability of lightening the prosecution burden in respect of them. However, the cases constitute an anomalous exception to the general coincidence of legal and evidential burdens; indeed since the weight of the two burdens in this area in practice tends to be the same, they virtually place the legal burden on the accused, which is very anomalous. Further, it is unclear that it is more onerous for the prosecution to produce a witness who says the accused did not on a former occasion produce his licence when asked, than for the witness to come to court to produce his licence or explain his failure to.

Another factor was enunciated by Lord Mansfield thus: "It is a known distinction that what comes by way of proviso in a statute must be insisted on by way of defence by the party accused; but, where exceptions are in the enacting part of a law, it must appear in the charge that the defendant does not fall within any of them" (*R.* v. *Jarvis* (1756), 1 East. 643 n.). This factor may be taken into account not only in statutes but also in agreements affecting the burden of proof. This is not a logically sound test but a formalist one, for there is no logical difference between a class cut down by an exception and a smaller class which excludes crimes covered by the exception. There is no difference, as regards those not punished, between not punishing "licensed persons" and punishing "all mankind save those with a licence". However, the test is justifiable if it genuinely does correspond with the intent of the legislator. This seems doubtful, because the test is not applied in any systematic way, and the cases reach different results on whether the legal burden as well as the evidential is affected. A principle similar but more sensible in not depending on the accident of word order has been enacted in the Magistrates' Courts Act 1952, s. 81, which provides that "where the defendant to an information or complaint relies for his defence on any exception, exemption, proviso, excuse or qualification, . . . the burden of proving the exception, exemption, proviso, excuse or qualification shall be on him". It applies only to summary offences. It may well affect the legal burden (*Roberts* v. *Humphreys* (1873), L.R. 8 Q.B. 483; *Taylor* v. *Ellis*, [1956] V.L.R. 457; *Gatland* v. *Metro-*

politan Police Commissioner, [1968] 2 Q.B. 279, at p. 286; [1968] 2 All E.R. 100, at p. 103.

Another relevant factor is whether the fact alleged is common or uncommon; for if it is uncommon, it will be harder to prove, and he who alleges should prove; while if it is common, it is not unfair to expect that he who denies its existence should disprove it. This is one reason why the burden of proving insanity is on the accused. It also justifies the result in the *Constantine* case p. 22, *post*) which held that the burden of proving that frustration is self-induced rests on the party who denies frustration. In many frustration cases it is difficult to prove the cause, and in most (reported) cases frustration is not caused by the fault of the parties. "A rule requiring the defendant pleading frustration to negative fault will then *ex hypothesi* do injustice to the great majority of defendants. While on the other hand, a rule requiring the plaintiff to prove fault will *ex hypothesi* do injustice to only a small minority of plaintiffs. . . . Moreover, in those cases where the circumstances do not make proof impossible the rule laid down . . . is preferable on the ground taken by some of the Lords that an affirmative is easier to prove than a negative. For there will be proportionately less cases of injustice through failure of proof among plaintiffs required to prove the affirmative, than there would be among defendants who had to prove the negative" (Stone (1944), 60 L.Q.R. 262, at p. 278).

In practice the incidence of the burden of proof is well settled in most cases. The particular rules are, as Wigmore says, based on "broad reasons of expedience and fairness" (para. 2486). The basic rule, that he who invokes the State's aid must prove his case, answers most questions; exceptions grow up in a piecemeal way which cannot be investigated in a detailed way here.

It might be noted that the 11th Report of the Criminal Law Revision Committee recommends that in general, statutory burdens placed on the accused should be evidential only, and that the same should be true of insanity (paras. 137–42). The reasons were that such burdens frequently entail proof of a negative (i.e. proof of lack of blameworthy intent), and that they are anomalous exceptions to the general common law rule and the principle of such statutes as the Theft Act 1968, s. 25 (3) (which places only an evidential burden of proving that potential instruments of crime in the accused's possession were not for the purpose of committing certain crimes). The Committee considered that any useful purpose behind the placing of any burden on the accused was sufficiently served by making it evidential only; and they felt that the need to direct the jury as to the difference between the burden on the prosecution of proving a matter beyond reasonable doubt and the burden on the accused of proving a matter on the balance of probabilities should be avoided.

Abrath v. North Eastern Rail. Co.
(1883), 11 Q.B.D. 440; [1881–5] All E.R. Rep. 614, C.A.

This was an action for malicious prosecution in which an issue arose as to whether the burden of proving absence of reasonable and probable cause as well as the prosecution lay on the plaintiff. The Court of Appeal, in allowing an appeal from a Queen's Bench Divisional Court order for a new trial, decided that it did.

BOWEN, L.J.: Whenever litigation exists, somebody must go on with it; the plaintiff is the first to begin; if he does nothing, he fails; if he makes a *prima facie* case, and nothing is done to answer it, the defendant fails. The test, therefore, as to the burden of proof or onus of proof, whichever term is used, is simply this: to ask oneself which party will be successful if no evidence is given, or if no more evidence is given than has been given at a particular point of the case, for it is obvious that as the controversy involved in the litigation travels on, the parties from moment to moment may reach points at which the onus of proof shifts, and at which the tribunal will have to say that if the case stops there, it must be decided in a particular manner. The test being such as I have stated, it is not a burden that goes on for ever resting on the shoulders of the person upon whom it is first cast. As soon as he brings evidence which, until it is answered, rebuts the evidence against which he is contending, then the balance descends on the other side, and the burden rolls over until again there is evidence which once more turns the scale. That being so, the question of onus of proof is only a rule for deciding on whom the obligation of going further, if he wishes to win, rests. It is not a rule to enable the jury to decide on the value of conflicting evidence. . . . Now in an action for malicious prosecution the plaintiff has the burden throughout of establishing that the circumstances of the prosecution were such that a judge can see no reasonable or probable cause for instituting it. In one sense that is the assertion of a negative, and we have been pressed with the proposition that when a negative is to be made out the onus of proof shifts. That is not so. If the assertion of a negative is an essential part of the plaintiff's case, the proof of the assertion still rests upon the plaintiff. The terms "negative" and "affirmative" are after all relative and not absolute. In dealing with a question of negligence, that term may be considered either as negative or affirmative according to the definition adopted in measuring the duty which is neglected. Wherever a person asserts affirmatively as part of his case that a certain state of facts is present or is absent, or that a particular thing is insufficient for a particular purpose, that is an averment which he is bound to prove positively. It has been said that an exception exists in those cases where the facts lie peculiarly within the knowledge of the opposite party. The counsel for the plaintiff have not gone the length of contending that in all those cases the onus shifts, and that the person within whose knowledge the truth peculiarly lies is bound to prove or disprove the matter in dispute. I think a proposition of that kind cannot be maintained, and that the exceptions supposed to be found amongst cases relating to the game laws may be explained on special grounds.

. . . Who had to make good their point as to the proposition whether the defendants had taken reasonable and proper care to inform themselves of the true state of the case? The defendants were not bound to make good anything. It was the plaintiff's duty to shew the absence of reasonable care. . . .

BRETT, M.R. and FRY, L.J. concurred.

Woolmington v. Director of Public Prosecutions
[1935] A.C. 462; [1935] All E.R. Rep. I, H.L.

The accused was convicted of murder. His defence was accident. In his summing up to the jury Swift, J. said: "Once it is shown to a jury that somebody has died through the act of another, that is presumed to be murder, unless the person who has been guilty of the act which causes the death can satisfy a jury that what happened was something less, something which might be alleviated, something which might be reduced to a charge of manslaughter, or something which was accidental, or something which could be justified."

The accused appealed unsuccessfully to the Court of Appeal but successfully to the House of Lords.

VISCOUNT SANKEY, L.C.: If at any period of a trial it was permissible for the judge to rule that the prosecution had established its case and that the onus was shifted on the prisoner to prove that he was not guilty and that unless he discharged that onus the prosecution was entitled to succeed, it would be enabling the judge in such a case to say that the jury must in law find the prisoner guilty and so make the judge decide the case and not the jury, which is not the common law. . . . But while the prosecution must prove the guilt of the prisoner, there is no such burden laid on the prisoner to prove his innocence and it is sufficient for him to raise a doubt as to his guilt; he is not bound to satisfy the jury of his innocence.

. . . [W]here intent is an ingredient of a crime there is no onus on the defendant to prove that the act alleged was accidental. Throughout the web of the English Criminal Law one golden thread is always to be seen, that it is the duty of the prosecution to prove the prisoner's guilt subject to what I have already said as to the defence of insanity and subject also to any statutory exception. If, at the end of and on the whole of the case, there is a reasonable doubt, created by the evidence given by either the prosecution or the prisoner, as to whether the prisoner killed the deceased with a malicious intention, the prosecution has not made out the case and the prisoner is entitled to an acquittal. No matter what the charge or where the trial, the principle that the prosecution must prove the guilt of the prisoner is part of the common law of England and no attempt to whittle it down can be entertained. When dealing with a murder case the Crown must prove (*a*) death as the result of a voluntary act of the accused and (*b*) malice of the accused. It may prove malice either expressly or by implication. For malice may be implied where death occurs as the result of a voluntary act of the accused which is (i) intentional and (ii) unprovoked. When evidence of death and malice has been given (this is a question for the jury) the accused is entitled to show, by evidence or by examination of the circumstances adduced by the Crown that the act on his part which caused death was either unintentional or provoked. If the jury are either satisfied with his explanation or, upon a review of all the evidence, are left in reasonable doubt whether, even if his explanation be not accepted, the act was unintentional or provoked, the prisoner is entitled to the benefit of the doubt.

LORDS ATKIN, HEWART, C.J., TOMLIN, and WRIGHT agreed.

[The last five words were added by Lord Simon, L.C., with Viscount Sankey's consent in *Mancini* v. *Director of Public Prosecutions*, [1942] A.C. 1, at p. 13; [1941] 3 All E.R. 272, at p. 280, H.L., to cover the case of provocation, which does not entitle the accused to an acquittal but only to a conviction of manslaughter rather than murder.]

Hill v. Baxter
[1958] 1 Q.B. 277; [1958] 1 All E.R. 193

The defendant pleaded that he became unconscious as a result of a sudden illness in answer to charges of dangerous driving. No evidence of this was produced. The magistrates acquitted him and the prosecutor successfully appealed to the Divisional Court.

LORD GODDARD, C.J.: [U]ndoubtedly the onus of proving that he was in a state of automatism must be on him. This is not only akin to a defence of insanity, but it is a rule of the law of evidence that the onus of proving a fact which must be exclusively within the knowledge of a party lies on him who asserts it. This, no doubt, is subject to the qualification that where an onus is on the defendant in a criminal case the burden is not as high as it is on a prosecutor.

. . . I am content to rest my judgment on the ground that there was no evidence which justified the justices finding that he was not fully responsible in law for his actions. . . .

DEVLIN, J. [in agreeing with the order proposed]: I am satisfied that even in a case in which liability depended upon full proof of *mens rea*, it would not be open to the defence to rely upon automatism without providing some evidence of it. If it amounted to insanity in the legal sense, it is well established that the burden of proof would start with and remain throughout upon the defence. But there is also recognized in the criminal law a lighter burden which the accused discharges by producing some evidence, but which does not relieve the prosecution from having to prove in the end all the facts necessary to establish guilt. This principle has manifested itself in different forms; most of them relate to the accused's state of mind and put it upon him to give some evidence about it. Thus the fact that an accused is found in possession of property recently stolen does not of itself prove that he knew of the stealing. Nevertheless, it is not open to the accused at the end of the prosecution's case to submit that he has no case to answer; he must offer some explanation to account for his possession though he does not have to prove that the explanation is true: *R. v. Aves*, [1950] 2 All E.R. 330, C.C.A. In a charge of murder it is for the prosecution to prove that the killing was intentional and unprovoked, and that burden is never shifted: *Woolmington* v. *Director of Public Prosecutions*, [1935] A.C. 462, H.L.; [1935] All E.R. Rep. 1. But though the prosecution must in the end prove lack of provocation, the obligation arises only if there is some evidence of provocation fit to go to the jury: *Holmes* v. *Director of Public Prosecutions*, [1946] A.C. 588, H.L.; [1946] 2 All E.R. 124. The same rule applies in the case of self-defence: *R. v. Lobell*, [1957] 1 Q.B. 547, C.C.A.; [1957] 1 All E.R. 734. In any crime involving *mens rea* the prosecution must prove guilty intent, but if the defence suggests drunkenness as negativing intention, they must offer evidence of it, if, indeed, they do not have to prove it: *Director of Public Prosecutions* v. *Beard*, [1920] A.C. 479, H.L., at p. 507; [1920] All E.R. Rep. 21, at p. 31. It would be quite unreasonable to allow the defence to submit at the end of the prosecution's case that the Crown had not proved affirmatively and beyond a reasonable doubt that the accused was at the time of the crime sober, or not sleepwalking or not in a trance or black out. I am satisfied that such matters ought not to be considered at all until the defence has produced at least *prima facie* evidence. I should wish to reserve for future consideration when necessary the question of where the burden ultimately lies.

PEARSON, J.: I agree with the judgment of the Lord Chief Justice subject to the reservation and explanations which Devlin, J. has made with regard to the burden of proof in a case such as this.

Bratty *v*. A.-G. for Northern Ireland
[1963] A.C. 386; [1961] 3 All E.R. 523, H.L.

The accused was convicted of murdering an 18-year-old girl by strangulation. Two of his defences were insanity and insane automatism. An appeal to the Court of Criminal Appeal in Northern Ireland and the House of Lords against the judge's refusal to put the automatism defences to the jury failed. Some of their Lordships uttered dicta on the burden of proof of sane automatism.

VISCOUNT KILMUIR, L.C.: Where the defence succeeds in surmounting the initial hurdle (see *Mancini* v. *Director of Public Prosecutions*, [1942] A.C. 1; [1941] 3 All E.R. 272 H.L.), and satisfies the judge that there is evidence fit for the jury to consider, the question remains whether the proper direction is: (*a*) that the jury will acquit if, and only if, they are satisfied on the balance of probabilities that the accused acted in a state of automatism, or (*b*) that they should acquit if they are left in reasonable doubt on this point. In favour of the former direction it might be argued that, since a defence of automatism is (as Lord Goddard said in *Hill* v. *Baxter*, [1958] 1 Q.B. 277, at p. 282; [1958] 1 All E.R. 193, at p. 195) very near a defence of insanity, it would be anomalous if there were any distinction between the onus in the one case and in the other. If this argument were to prevail it would follow that the defence would fail unless they established on a balance of probabilities that the prisoner's act was unconscious and involuntary in the same way as, under the M'Naghten Rules, they must establish on a balance of probabilities that the necessary requirements are satisfied.

Nevertheless, one must not lose sight of the overriding principle, laid down by this

House in *Woolmington's* case, [1935] A.C. 462; [1935] All E.R. Rep. 1, H.L. that it is for the prosecution to prove every element of the offence charged. One of these elements is the accused's state of mind; normally the presumption of mental capacity is sufficient to prove that he acted consciously and voluntarily, and the prosecution need go no further. But if, after considering evidence properly left to them by the judge, the jury are left in real doubt whether or not the accused acted in a state of automatism, it seems to me that on principle they should acquit because the necessary *mens rea*—if indeed the *actus reus*—has not been proved beyond reasonable doubt.

LORD DENNING: . . . [W]hilst the *ultimate* burden rests on the Crown of proving every element essential in the crime, nevertheless in order to prove that the act was a voluntary act, the Crown is entitled to rely on the *presumption* that every man has sufficient mental capacity to be responsible for his crimes: and that if the defence wish to displace the presumption they must give some evidence from which the contrary may reasonably be inferred. Thus a drunken man is presumed to have the capacity to form the specific intent necessary to constitute the crime, unless evidence is given from which it can reasonably be inferred that he was incapable of forming it, see the valuable judgment of the Court of Justiciary in *Kennedy* v. *H.M. Advocate*, 1944 S.C.(J.) 171, at p. 177, which was delivered by Lord Normand. So also it seems to me that a man's act is presumed to be a voluntary act unless there is evidence from which it can reasonably be inferred that it was involuntary. To use the words of Devlin, J., the defence of automatism "ought not to be considered at all until the defence has produced at least *prima facie* evidence", see *Hill* v. *Baxter*, [1958] 1 Q.B. 277, at p. 285; [1958] 1 All E.R. 193, at p. 196; and the words of North, J. in New Zealand "unless a proper foundation is laid", see *R.* v. *Cottle*, [1958] N.Z.L.R. 999, at p. 1025. The necessity of laying the proper foundation is on the defence: and if it is not so laid, the defence of automatism need not be left to the jury, any more than the defence of drunkenness (*Kennedy* v. *H.M. Advocate*, 1944 S.C.(J.) 171, at p. 177), provocation (*R.* v. *Gauthier* (1943), 29 Cr. App. Rep. 113, C.C.A.) or self-defence (*R.* v. *Lobell*, [1957] 1 Q.B. 547; [1957] 1 All E.R. 734, C.C.A.) need be.

What, then, is a proper foundation? The presumption of mental capacity of which I have spoken is a provisional presumption only. It does not put the legal burden on the defence in the same way as the presumption of sanity does. It leaves the legal burden on the prosecution, but nevertheless, until it is displaced it enables the prosecution to discharge the ultimate burden of proving that the act was voluntary. Not because the presumption is evidence itself, but because it takes the place of evidence. In order to displace the presumption of mental capacity, the defence must give sufficient evidence from which it may reasonably be inferred that the act was involuntary. The evidence of the man himself will rarely be sufficient unless it is supported by medical evidence which points to the cause of the mental incapacity. It is not sufficient for a man to say "I had a black-out": for "black-out" as Stable, J. said in *Cooper* v. *McKenna, Ex parte Cooper*, [1960] Qd. R. 406, at p. 419, "is one of the first refuges of a guilty conscience and a popular excuse." The words of Devlin, J. in *Hill* v. *Baxter*, [1958] 1 Q.B. 277 at p. 285; [1958] 1 All E.R. 193, at p. 197, should be remembered: "I do not doubt that there are genuine cases of automatism and the like, but I do not see how the layman can safely attempt without the help of some medical or scientific evidence to distinguish the genuine from the fraudulent." When the only cause that is assigned for an involuntary act is drunkenness, then it is only necessary to leave drunkenness to the jury, with the consequential directions, and not to leave automatism at all. When the only cause that is assigned for it is a disease of the mind, then it is only necessary to leave insanity to the jury, and not automatism. When the cause assigned is concussion or sleep-walking, there should be some evidence from which it can reasonably be inferred before it should be left to the jury. If it is said to be due to concussion, there should be evidence of a severe blow shortly beforehand. If it is said to be sleep-walking, there should be some credible support for it. His mere assertion that he was asleep will not suffice.

Once a proper foundation is thus laid for automatism, the matter becomes at large and must be left to the jury. As the case proceeds, the evidence may weigh first to one side and then to the other: and so the burden may appear to shift to and fro. But at the end of the day the legal burden comes into play and requires that the jury should be satisfied beyond reasonable doubt that the act was a voluntary act.

LORD MORRIS OF BORTH-Y-GEST: The "golden" rule of the English criminal law that it is the duty of the prosecution to prove an accused person's guilt (subject to any statutory exception and subject to the special position which arises where it is given in evidence that an accused person is insane), does not involve that the prosecution must speculate as to and specifically anticipate every conceivable explanation that an accused person might offer.

[LORDS TUCKER and HODSON agreed with VISCOUNT KILMUIR, L.C. and LORD MORRIS.]

Joseph Constantine Steamship Line, Ltd. v. Imperial Smelting Corporation Ltd.
[1942] A.C. 154; [1941] 2 All E.R. 165, H.L.

Shipowners pleaded that an explosion on a ship, the cause of which was unascertained, had frustrated a charterparty for breach of which the charterers were claiming damages. Atkinson, J. held that the onus of proving that the frustration was induced by the shipowners' default was on the charterers. The Court of Appeal reversed him, and an appeal to the House of Lords against this decision succeeded.

VISCOUNT SIMON, L.C.: . . . The question here is where the onus of proof lies; i.e. whether, when a supervening event has been proved which would, apart from the defendant's "default" put an end to the contract, and when at the end of the case no inference of "default" exists and the evidence is equally consistent with either view, the defence fails because the defendant has not established affirmatively that the supervening event was not due to his default.

I may observe, in the first place, that, if this were correct, there must be many cases in which, although in truth frustration is complete and unavoidable, the defendant will be held liable because of his inability to prove a negative—in some cases, indeed, a whole series of negatives. Suppose that a vessel while on the high seas disappears completely during a storm. Can it be that the defence of frustration of the adventure depends on the owner's ability to prove that all his servants on board were navigating the ship with adequate skill and that there was no "default" which brought about the catastrophe? Suppose that a vessel in convoy is torpedoed by the enemy and sinks immediately with all hands. Does the application of the doctrine require that the owners should affirmatively prove that those on board were keeping a good look-out, were obscuring lights, were steering as directed, and so forth? There is no reported case which requires us so to hold. . . .

In this connection it is well to emphasize that when "frustration" in the legal sense occurs, it does not merely provide one party with a defence in an action brought by the other. It kills the contract itself and discharges both parties automatically. The plaintiff sues for breach at a past date and the defendant pleads that at that date no contract existed. In this situation the plaintiff could only succeed if it were shown that the determination of the contract were due to the defendant's "default", and it would be a strange result if the party alleging this were not the party required to prove it.

. . . Every case in this branch of the law can be stated as turning on the question whether from the express terms of the particular contract a further term should be implied which, when its conditions are fulfilled, put an end to the contract.

If the matter is regarded in this way, the question is as to the construction of a contract taking into consideration its express and implied terms. The implied term in the present case may well be—"This contract is to cease to be binding if the vessel is disabled by an overpowering disaster, provided that disaster is not brought about by the default of either party." This is very similar to an express exception of "perils of the seas", as to which it is ancient law that by an implied term of the contract the shipowner cannot rely on the exception if its operation was brought about either (*a*) by negligence of his servants, or (*b*) by his breach of the implied warranty of seaworthiness. If a ship sails and is never heard of again the shipowner can claim protection for loss of the cargo under the express exception of perils of the seas. To establish that, must he go on to prove (*a*) that the perils were *not* caused by negligence of his servants, and (*b*) were not caused by any unseaworthiness? I think clearly not. He proves a *prima facie* case of loss by sea perils, and that he is within the exception. If the cargo owner wants to defeat that plea it is for him by rejoinder to allege and prove either negligence or unseaworthiness. The judgment of the Court of Appeal in *The Glendarroch*. [1894] p. 226; (1891–4). All E.R. Rep. 484, C.A., is plain authority for this.

. . . The decision in *The Northumbria,* [1906] P. 292, involves the same conclusion. Another example, from the law of bailment, confirms this view. Assume a bailment of goods to be kept in a named warehouse with an express exception of loss by fire. Proof of destruction by fire would prima facie excuse the bailee. The bailor could counter by alleging either (*a*) fire caused by the negligence of the bailee or (*b*) goods when burnt were not stored in the agreed warehouse. But it would be for the bailor not only to allege but to prove either (*a*) or (*b*), though he might rely on facts proved or admitted by the bailee as establishing his proposition.

VISCOUNT MAUGHAM: It is, however, to be noted that it is often a mere accident, for instance the condition of the market, which decides the question which of two parties will desire to rely on the doctrine of frustration. Yet it follows that, if the Court of Appeal is right, there are cases in which frustration would be held not to apply if the party setting up the principle was unable to discharge the onus of proof held to be on him, while a different result would follow if the other party were relying on frustration and he was able to discharge the onus.

. . . My Lords, if the principle of frustration is that the contract automatically comes to an end irrespective of the wishes of either party, provided only that the event is "caused by something for which neither party was responsible" (see *Maritime National Fish, Ltd.* v. *Ocean Trawlers, Ltd.,* [1935] A.C. 524; at p. 531; [1953] All E.R. Rep. 86, at p. 90, P.C.) I can see no firm ground for the proposition that the party relying on frustration in an action or in arbitration proceedings must establish affirmatively that "the cause was not brought into operation by his default". (I am quoting from the judgment of Scott, L.J. in the present case.) Such a proposition seems to me to be equivalent to laying down that the determination of the contract by frustration is not the automatic result of the event, but is dependent on the option of the parties, for neither party can be compelled to call evidence to prove affirmatively that the cause was not due to his default. . . .

Other considerations seem to me to lead to the same conclusion. Frustration may occur, as I have already mentioned, in very different circumstances. First, in cases resembling the present where there has been the destruction of a specific thing necessary for the performance of the contract. Secondly, where performance becomes virtually impossible owing to a change in the law. Thirdly, where circumstances arise which make the performance of the contract impossible in the manner and at the time contemplated. Fourthly, where performance becomes impossible by reason of the death or incapacity of a party whose continued good health was essential to the carrying out of the contract. There may be other categories, and I have not forgotten the coronation and the review cases, of which *Krell* v. *Henry,* [1903] 2 K.B. 740, C.A. is the leading example, but they do not come within the same principle of impossibility, and I do not desire to express any opinion about them. Taking the four groups which I have mentioned, a consideration of the many different kinds of events leading to the impossibility of performance leads, I think, to the view that it would be unreasonable, if not absurd, to lay on the person relying on frustration the onus of proof that he was not responsible for the event. In the first category we have the case of fire. Destruction of a building by fire is generally due to someone's fault or negligence. If the owner of a large building, in which he employs many persons, sets up the doctrine of frustration on the ground of the destruction of the building by fire, it may be quite impossible for him to prove affirmatively that one of his employees who has left his service was not guilty of default. If both the plaintiff and the defendant have had duties to perform in the building under the terms of the contract, the cause of the fire may be due to either of them. It would not be reasonable to throw this heavy onus on the party setting up frustration, since, having regard to the fourth proposition above stated, it may be mere accidental circumstances which cause one party rather than the other to rely on the doctrine. If the destruction of the thing is due to earthquake, volcanic action, flood, storm, lightning, restraint of princes, change in the law and so forth, it would seem to be absurd to apply the suggested doctrine of onus except in very unlikely circumstances. This shows, at any rate, that the rule stated by the Court of Appeal requires some qualification. Where the contract is for personal services, the performance of which by one party depends on his health and life, no one has ever yet suggested that, if the person promising the personal service is alive and sets up frustration, he must show that his illness was not due to some rash act on his part. Nor, if the promisor is dead, would it, I think, be reasonable to expect his legal personal representative to prove absence of some default leading to the disaster.

My Lords, I also agree with the view expressed by Atkinson, J. that the term or condition which might reasonably be implied in relation to the destruction of the vessel in this case, or in any case of true frustration, does not throw on the plaintiff or claimant the burden of proving something which it may be impossible in practice to prove. The term or condition is not for the benefit of one party rather than the other. As I have already indicated, it is usually impossible at the date of the contract to know, if frustration of the adventure takes place, which of the two parties will desire to rely on the doctrine. In these circumstances I cannot see why a court should decide that the parties ought to be presumed to have intended that the ordinary rules as to onus of proof ought not to apply.

. . . In general the rule which applies is *"Ei qui affirmat non ei qui negat incumbit probatio"*. It is an ancient rule founded on considerations of good sense and it should not be departed from without strong reasons.

LORD WRIGHT: . . . The appeal can, I think, be decided according to the generally accepted view that frustration involves as one of its elements absence of fault, by applying the ordinary rules as to onus of proof. If frustration is viewed (as I think it can be) as analogous to an exception, since it is generally relied on as a defence to a claim for failure to perform a contract, the same rule will properly be applied to it as to the ordinary type of exceptions. The defence may be rebutted by proof of fault, but the onus of proving fault will rest on the plaintiff. This is merely to apply the familiar rule which is applied, for instance, where a carrier by sea relies on the exception of perils of the seas. If the goods owner then desires to rebut that *prima facie* defence on the ground of negligence or other fault on the part of the ship-owner, it rests on the goods owner to establish the negligence or fault.

Thus, on the view most favourable to the conclusion of the Court of Appeal I still reject it. In addition, the ordinary rule is that a man is not held guilty of fault unless fault is established and found by the court. This rule, which is sometimes described as the presumption of innocence, is no doubt peculiarly important in criminal cases or matters, but it is also true in civil disputes. Thus it was said in *Thomas* v. *Thomas* (1855), 2 K. & J. 79, by Wood, V.-C., "possession is never considered adverse if it can be referred to a legal title". I need not multiply citations for a principle familiar to lawyers. There is, for example, no presumption of fraud. It must be alleged and proved. So, also, of other wrongful acts or breaches of contract. If it is necessary, in order to defend a claim, to prove that it was a case of felo de se and not merely innocent suicide while of unsound mind, the full fact must be affirmatively proved. An illustration, perhaps more germane, is afforded by the rules as to the onus of proof in cases of unseaworthiness. If at the end of the case it is not ascertainable on the evidence that the real cause of the loss was unseaworthiness, the defence must fail.

[Lords Russell of Killowen and Porter agreed.]

R. v. Turner
(1816), 5 M. & S. 206; [1814–23] All E.R. Rep. 713

A statute of Anne made possession of game unlawful unless the accused brought himself within one of a number of qualifications listed in a statute of Charles II. An appeal against conviction on the ground that the prosecutor had not negatived the qualifications failed before the Court of King's Bench.

Lord Ellenborough, C.J.: The question is, upon whom the *onus probandi* lies; whether it lies upon the person who affirms a qualification, to prove the affirmative, or upon the informer, who denies any qualification to prove the negative. There are, I think, about ten different heads of qualification enumerated in the statute to which the proof may be applied; and, according to the argument of to-day, every person who lays an information of this sort is bound to give satisfactory evidence before the magistrates to negative the defendant's qualification upon each of those several heads. The argument really comes to this, that there would be a moral impossibility of ever convicting upon such an information. If the informer should establish the negative of any part of these different qualifications, that would be insufficient, because it would be said, *non liquet*, but that the defendant may be qualified under the other. And does not, then, common sense shew, that the burden of proof ought to be cast on the person, who, by establishing any one of the qualifications, will be well defended? Is not the Statute of Anne in effect a prohibition on every person to kill game, unless he brings himself within some one of the qualifications allowed by law; the proof of which is easy on the one side, but almost impossible on the other?

Bayley, J.: I am of the same opinion. I have always understood it to be a general rule, that if a negative averment be made by one party, which is peculiarly within the knowledge of the other, the party within whose knowledge it lies, and who asserts the affirmative is to prove it, and not he who avers the negative. And if we consider the reason of the thing in this particular case, we cannot but see that it is next to impossible that the witness for the prosecution should be prepared to give any evidence of the defendant's want of qualification. If, indeed, it is to be presumed, that he must be acquainted with the defendant, and with his situation or habits in life, then he might give general evidence what those were; but if, as it is more probable, he is unacquainted with any of these matters, how is he to form any judgment whether he is qualified or not, from his appearance only? Therefore, if the law were to require that the witness should depose negatively to these things, it seems to me, that it might lead to the encouragement of much hardihood of swearing. The witness would have to depose to a multitude of facts; he must swear that the defendant has not an estate in his own or his wife's right, of a certain value; that he is not the son and heir apparent of an esquire, &c.; but how is it at all probable, that a witness should be likely to depose with truth to such minutiæ? On the other hand, there is no hardship in casting the burden of the affirmative proof on the defendant, because he must be presumed to know his own qualification, and to be able to prove it. If the defendant plead to the information, that he is a qualified person, and require time to substantiate his plea in evidence, it is a matter of course for the justices to postpone the hearing, in order to afford him time, and an opportunity of proving his qualifications. But if the onus of proving the negative is to lie on the other party, it seems to me, that it will be the cause of many offenders escaping conviction.

[HOLROYD, J. agreed.]

R. v. Spurge
[1961] 2 Q.B. 205; [1961] 2 All E.R. 688, C.C.A.

The accused raised the defence of mechanical defect as a defence to a dangerous driving charge. His appeal against conviction failed because he was aware of the defect.

SALMON, J.: It has been suggested by counsel for the Crown that the onus of establishing any defence based on mechanical defect must be upon the accused because necessarily the facts relating to it are peculiarly within his own knowledge. The facts, however, relating to a defence of provocation or self-defence to a charge of murder are often peculiarly within the knowledge of the accused since often the only persons present at the time of the killing are the accused and the deceased. Yet once there is any evidence to support these defences, the onus of disproving them undoubtedly rests upon the prosecution. There is no rule of law that where the facts are peculiarly within the knowledge of the accused, the burden of establishing any defence based on these facts shifts to the accused. No doubt there are a number of statutes where the onus of establishing a statutory defence is placed on the accused because the facts relating to it are peculiarly within his knowledge. But we are not here considering any statutory defence.

Vines v. Djordjevitch
(1955), 91 C.L.R. 512

The Victorian Motor Car Act 1951, s. 47 (1), made provision for recovery against a nominal defendant of losses sustained in motor car accidents where the car's identity could not be established, provided "that no such judgment may be obtained unless such person as soon as possible after he knew that the identity of the motor car could not be established gave to the Minister notice of intention to make the claim and a short statement of the grounds thereof".

The High Court of Australia upheld the judgment of the Full Court of the Victorian Supreme Court to the effect that the proviso imposed a condition precedent to the cause of action, and the legal burden of proving compliance with it lay on the plaintiff.

DIXON, C.J., McTIERNAN, WEBB, FULLAGAR and KITTO, JJ.: It is said that the form of the sub-section places the burden of disproof on the defendant. For the requirement of prompt notice after the injured party becomes aware of the impossibility of identifying the car inflicting the injuries is expressed in the form of a proviso. "There is a technical distinction between a proviso and an exception, which is well understood. All the cases say, that if there be an exception in the enacting clause, it must be negatived: but if there be a separate proviso, it need not"—*per* Abbott, J. in *Steel* v. *Smith* (1817), 1 B. & Ald. 94, at p. 99. The distinction has perhaps come to be applied in a less technical manner, and now depends not so much upon form as upon substantial considerations. In the end, of course, it is a matter of the intention that ought, in the case of a particular enactment, to be ascribed to the legislature and therefore the manner in which the legislature has expressed its will must remain of importance. But whether the form is that of a proviso or of an exception, the intrinsic character of the provision that the proviso makes and its real effect cannot be put out of consideration in determining where the burden of proof lies. When an enactment is stating the grounds of some liability that it is imposing or the conditions giving rise to some right that it is creating, it is possible that in defining the elements forming the title to the right or the basis of the liability the provision may rely upon qualifications exceptions or provisos and it may employ negative as well as positive expressions. Yet it may be sufficiently clear that the whole amounts to a statement of the complete factual situation which must be found to exist before anybody obtains a right or incurs a liability under the provision. In other words it may embody the principle which the legislature seeks to apply generally. On the other hand it may be the purpose of the enactment to lay down some principle of liability which it means to apply generally and then to provide for some special grounds of excuse, justification or exculpation depending upon new or additional facts. In the same way where conditions of general application giving rise to a right are laid down, additional facts of a special nature may be made a ground for defeating or excluding the right. For such a purpose the use of a proviso is natural. But in whatever form the enactment is cast, if it expresses an exculpation, justification, excuse, ground of defeasance or exclusion which assumes the existence of the general or primary grounds from which the liability or right arises but denies the right or liability in a particular case by reason of additional or special facts, then it is evident that such an enactment supplies considerations of substance for placing the burden of proof on the party seeking to rely upon the additional or special matter.

The fact that in s. 47 (1) the requirement of notice takes the form of a proviso gives some support for the claim that the plaintiff need not affirmatively establish compliance and that the burden of proving non-compliance is upon the defendant. But the operative words express a negative co-extensive with the affirmative imposition of liability in the main provision. In terms the proviso makes it incumbent upon everybody claiming under the main provision to give the notice and to do so as soon as possible after knowledge of the impossibility of establishing the identity of the car responsible for his injury. It is expressed as a statement of a further requirement to be fulfilled by all before the main provision can be availed of. For the plaintiff, however, it is said that though the requirement is expressed as applicable to all coming within the main provision, it cannot so intend. For there are classes of people who could not be expected to comply with it, e.g. children of tender years or other persons rendered incapable of action or of knowledge by their injuries or by their mental or bodily condition. It is pointed out too that the remedy given by the main provision of s. 47 (1) is not confined to the injured person. If as a result of the death or injury of the victim of an accident, any other person becomes entitled to actionable rights against the driver of the unidentified car he may sue the nominal defendant under s. 47 (1). . . . In the case of young children and incapacitated persons it may be that the requisite "knowledge" under the proviso cannot be imputed to them and that they are not precluded by failure on the part of those who represent them, whether in the suit or generally, to give a notice as soon as possible after the representatives obtain knowledge of the impossibility of establishing the identity of the car causing the injury. But that is a matter that does not arise in this case and one about which no opinion need be expressed. There is, however, no reason to doubt that other intending plaintiffs may obtain such a knowledge and must then give notice.

In any case it is evident that the legislature did not mean that the necessity of notice should be exceptional and did not advert to the contingency of a plaintiff's having no knowledge of the very fact which the main provision of s. 47 (1) makes essential to his statutory cause of action.

The substance of the proviso and its general tenor show that it means to impose a condition precedent to the cause of action. Accordingly the burden of proof lies on the plaintiff.

III   THE BURDEN OF PROOF OF INSANITY

There is some controversy over whether this should be properly placed on the accused, as English and Commonwealth courts have. American courts have differed sharply on the question and continue to do so.

Davis v. U.S.
160 U.S. 469 (1895)

The effect of the trial court's direction to the jury was to suggest that the accused bore the legal burden of proving insanity. He successfully appealed against his conviction for murder to the U.S. Supreme Court.

HARLAN, J.: The plea of not guilty is unlike a special plea in a civil action, which, admitting the case averred, seeks to establish substantive grounds of defence by a preponderance of evidence. It is not in confession and avoidance, for it is a plea that controverts the existence of every fact essential to constitute the crime charged. [The accused's] guilt cannot in the very nature of things be regarded as proved, if the jury entertain a reasonable doubt from all the evidence whether he was legally capable of committing crime.

. . . In a certain sense it may be true that where the defence is insanity, and where the case made by the prosecution discloses nothing whatever in excuse or extenuation of the crime charged, the accused is bound to produce some evidence that will impair or weaken the force of the legal presumption in favour of sanity. But to hold that such presumption must absolutely control the jury until it is overthrown or impaired by evidence sufficient to establish the fact of insanity beyond all reasonable doubt or to the reasonable satisfaction of the jury is in effect to require him to establish his innocence. . . .

Strictly speaking, the burden of proof, as those words are understood in criminal law, is never upon the accused to establish his innocence, or to disprove the facts necessary to establish the crime for which he is indicted. It is on the prosecution from the beginning to the end of the trial, and applies to every element necessary to constitute the crime. Giving to the prosecution, where the defense is insanity, the benefit in the way of proof of the presumption in favor of sanity, the vital question, from the time a plea of not guilty is entered until the return of the verdict, is whether upon all the evidence, by whatever side adduced, guilt is established beyond reasonable doubt. If the whole evidence, including that supplied by the presumption of sanity, does not exclude beyond reasonable doubt the hypothesis of insanity, of which some proof is adduced, the accused is entitled to an acquittal of the specific offence charged.

State v. Quigley
58 A. 905 (1904)

The accused was convicted of murder after the court directed the jury that the burden of proof of insanity was on him. His appeal to the Supreme Court of Rhode Island failed.

DOUGLAS, J.: . . . Sanity is not an ingredient of crime. It is a condition precedent of all intelligent action, as well benevolent as nefarious. It is a quality of the actor, not an element of the act. It is incumbent upon the prosecution to show the commission of the act, and from this showing and its circumstances to sustain the inferences of malice and such emotions as the particular crime may include. But sanity is not one of these inferences. It is a pre-existing fact which may be taken for granted as implied by law and general experience. . . .

It is argued that criminal intent, malice, and premeditation are facts to be proven by the prosecutor; that these cannot exist in any insane mind; hence sanity must be proved by the prosecutor. But these are facts of mental condition and action, and they can only be proved by inference from material facts, circumstances, and acts. It is incumbent, therefore, upon the prosecution to prove such material facts, circumstances, and acts as would compel the inference of guilt in a sane person; and this is the limit of his burden. In murder the prosecution must establish the act, and either by inference or additional evidence, malice, and premeditation. If these ingredients of the crime cannot exist without sanity, sanity is presumed. All the ingredients of the crime must be proved, and as to these we agree the burden never shifts; but as to sanity it never attaches to the prosecutor. The plea of not guilty by itself does not put the sanity of the accused in issue. He must raise the question otherwise, as all agree, if not by special plea at least by introducing evidence, and this is confession and avoidance.

Thomas v. R.
(1960), 102 C.L.R. 584

WINDEYER, J.: The "golden thread that runs throughout the web of English criminal law" is broken by the defence of insanity. It is better to recognize this than to rationalize it. For there is really no logical answer to the rhetorical question of Harlan, J., asked in the course of delivering the impressive judgment of the Supreme Court of the United States in *Davis* v. *United Sates*, "How, then, upon principle or consistently with humanity can a verdict of guilty be properly returned if the jury entertain a reasonable doubt as to the existence of a fact which is essential to guilt, namely, the capacity in law of the accused to commit that crime?" 160 U.S. 469, at p. 488 (1895). Nevertheless, it is the firmly established rule of our law that when insanity is put forward as a defence to a criminal charge, it is for the defence to show that the accused was, in the relevant sense, insane.

Reference should be made to Williams, *Criminal Law: The General Part* (2nd Edn.), para. 288. He argues that the legal burden of proving insanity can only rest on the accused where the issue is whether the accused knew that what he was doing was wrong. It cannot rest on him where the issue is whether the accused knew the nature and quality of his act, for if he does not, he lacks *mens rea*, and the burden of proving *mens rea* rests on the prosecution.

IV SHIFTING THE BURDEN

It is often said that during a trial a "shifting" of the burden of proof occurs. It is doubtful whether the phrase has much utility. It is used in four senses, of which the first and fourth are otiose and ambiguous, the second unnecessary, and the third wrong.

One function of the phrase is to describe the answer given by the Court to the question whether the proponent on some issue has made out a case to answer. If there is a case to answer, the proponent has discharged the evidential burden; it has "shifted". In this sense the phrase is otiose since perfectly clear words already exist to make the point. It is also ambiguous. It may mean that the proponent's evidence has been weighty enough to entitle a reasonable man to decide in his favour, though not weighty enough to compel him to do so. The burden has shifted to the opponent in the sense that as a matter of prudence he should answer the case. If he fails to, he may, but will not necessarily, lose. Lord Denning calls this a "provisional burden" on the opponent. The other sense of shifting the evidential burden applies where the proponent's evidence is so weighty as to compel a reasonable man to decide in the proponent's favour unless it is answered. The burden that has shifted forces the opponent to call evidence or lose. Bridge calls the first kind of evidence "*prima facie*" and the second "presumptive" (12 M.L.R. 273, at p. 277); Lord Denning would call the first burden "provisional" and the second "compelling" (61 L.Q.R. 379, at p. 380). Cross calls the first shifting of the burden "tactical"; once it occurs it is important only to the parties. He calls the second "legal": it concerns more than a matter of tactics, and indicates failure or success in discharging the legal burden (pp. 74–5). The difference, which is one of degree, may be illustrated by the case of a ship sinking. If unseaworthiness is alleged and the proponent proves that it sank six months after leaving port, the evidential burden would have shifted so as to put a provisional burden on the other side: he may, but will not necessarily, lose without further evidence. But if it is proved that the ship sank ten minutes after leaving its berth, the evidential burden would have so shifted as to put a compelling burden on the other side: the latter's silence will cause him to lose (*Pickup* v. *Thames and Mersey Marine Insurance Co.* (1878), 3 Q.B.D. 594, C.A.).

During a trial there can be no other shifting of any evidential burden that is relevant for the judge or trier of fact. A party may have to make all kinds of sudden decisions about either putting in new evidence which may improve, or if disbelieved, worsen his position, or adopting new lines of cross-examination depending on his estimate of the changing strength of his case; but this can have no legal significance because the evidential burden is relevant to the judge on two occasions: when he decides who has the right to begin and whether there is a case to answer. However, we may say that a second function of the phrase "shifting the burden" is to state the truism that the state of convincing evidence on a given issue varies as the trial proceeds. The swinging back and forth of the evidential burden would only be legally significant if the trial was suddenly frozen at various stages. In fact the trial is only frozen at three points for particular purposes: the outset (who begins?), the end of the proponent's case (is there a case to answer?) and the end (who wins on that issue?). It is misleading to think of the trial as a tennis match and the evidential burden as a ball: "there are no points to be gained merely by sending the evidential burden back across the net, and what is more, no one is keeping score. . . . The shifting of the evidential burden during the trial is therefore . . . only part of a process of reasoning, sometimes convenient and sometimes dangerous, whereby the judge assesses the probabilities by dividing up the evidence into those facts which tend to support one party and those which his opponent has proved in reply" (Hoffman, p. 353).

A third sense in which the burden of proof is said to shift is when the legal burden is said to shift. However, this usage is probably not merely otiose or confusing, but wrong. Orthodoxy requires that the legal burden in fact never shifts (*May* v. *O'Sullivan* (1955), 92 C.L.R. 654). As Hoffman says (p. 348):

> "If the impression of shifting is given, it will always be found that there is really more than one issue. For as a matter of ordinary logic, if the plaintiff proves a fact which places upon the defendant, in order to avoid an adverse judgment, the burden of disproving X, then what the plaintiff proved must have been something other than X. One cannnot disprove a fact which is held to have been proved."

The problem may be illustrated by the problem of proving a child's legitimacy. He who bears the legal burden must prove a valid marriage between the parents and birth in wedlock. Some say the legal burden of proving illegitimacy by non-access then shifts. The orthodox say there is not one issue of legitimacy but three—a valid marriage, birth in wedlock and access. The legal burden of the first two rests on one side, the legal burden of proving non-access on the other. There is no shifting of the burden. "What shifts is the obligation; but it is an obligation to prove different facts" (Nokes, p. 480). This reasoning is not affected by occasional difficulty in correctly isolating the issues. Admittedly it makes no practical difference which view is correct. The only functions of the legal burden are to tell us who wins if the evidence is evenly balanced at the end of the case, and to suggest who should begin calling evidence (since the evidential burden and the legal burden usually lie in the same place). Orthodoxy and unorthodoxy produce the same result in both cases.

Our discussion now leads to the fourth meaning of "shifting the burden". In a criminal case, the Crown has the legal burden of proving all issues but insanity. If it produces sufficient evidence to convict the accused, the "ultimate burden" of proof can be said to have shifted to the accused, because he must prove insanity or lose. There has been no shifting of any legal burden, for a new issue has arisen; but the ultimate burden of winning the case has shifted. (See also *Medawar* v. *Grand Hotel Co.*, [1891] 2 Q.B. 11; [1891–4] All E.R. Rep. 571, C.A.) "Shifting the burden" in this sense is otiose language, for all it refers to is the necessity for a party to win on the case as a whole. It is also potentially confusing, for the ultimate burden may not be distinguished from the various legal burdens and may thus suggest there is only one legal burden, whereas in fact there is one legal burden for every issue in the case.

Further reading

Adams, *Criminal Onus and Exculpations* (Wellington, N.Z., 1968); Bridge 12 M.L.R. 273; Denning (1945), 61 L.Q.R. 379; Thayer, Chap. 9.

3

Standard of Proof

Miller v. Minister of Pensions
[1947] 2 All E.R. 372

DENNING, J.: . . . [T]he degree of cogency required in a criminal case before an accused person is found guilty . . . is well settled. It need not reach certainty, but it must carry a high degree of probability. Proof beyond reasonable doubt does not mean proof beyond the shadow of a doubt. The law would fail to protect the community if it admitted fanciful possibilities to deflect the course of justice. If the evidence is so strong against a man as to leave only a remote possibility in his favour which can be dismissed with the sentence "of course it is possible, but not in the least probable", the case is proved beyond reasonable doubt, but nothing short of that will suffice.

. . . [T]he degree of cogency . . . required to discharge a burden in a civil case . . . is well settled. It must carry a reasonable degree of probability, but not so high as is required in a criminal case. If the evidence is such that the tribunal can say: "We think it more probable than not," the burden is discharged, but, if the probabilities are equal, it is not.

I FORMULATION OF THE STANDARDS

After some doubt, it is now settled that in civil cases the standard of proof is the balance of probabilities; in criminal cases the prosecution must attain a standard of proof beyond reasonable doubt, and the accused need attain only the lesser civil standard (*R. v. Carr-Briant*, [1943] K.B. 607; [1943] 2 All E.R. 156, C.C.A.). What remains doubtful is precisely how a standard should be explained to the jury. Appeals are often successful against judicial explanations, and in the 1950s the Court of Criminal Appeal strongly criticized the use of the time-honoured "reasonable doubt" formula in criminal cases (*R. v. Summers*, [1952] 1 All E.R. 1059, C.C.A.). However, in ascending order of merit, it now seems permissible to say "beyond reasonable doubt", or "completely satisfied", or "feel sure" (*R. v. Hepworth*, [1955] 2 Q.B. 600, at p. 603; [1955] 2 All E.R. 918, C.C.A.). It is not clear that attempts to improve on "beyond reasonable doubt" can hope to succeed. Wigmore attacked the far wider range of American formulae as "useless refinements", "wordy quibbles" and "maunderings", calculated only to confuse the jury and entrap the judge into forgetfulness of some detail or precedent. "The truth is no one has yet invented or discovered a mode of measurement for the intensity of human belief. Hence there can be yet no successful method of communicating intelligibly to a jury a sound method of self-analysis for one's belief" (para. 2497).

R. v. Hepworth
[1955] 2 Q.B. 600; [1955] 2 All E.R. 918, C.C.A.

The only indication given by the recorder in his summing up to the jury of the standard of proof was use of the word "satisfied". This was criticized by the Court of Criminal Appeal.

LORD GODDARD, C.J.: It may be, especially considering the number of cases recently in which this question has arisen, that I misled courts because I said in R. v. *Summers*, [1952] 1 All E.R. 1059, C.C.A.—and I still adhere to it—that I thought that it was very unfortunate to talk to juries about "reasonable doubt" because the explanations given as to what is and what is not a reasonable doubt are so very often extraordinarily difficult to follow and it is very difficult to tell a jury what is a reasonable doubt. To tell a jury that it must not be a fanciful doubt is something that is without any real guidance. To tell them that a reasonable doubt is such a doubt as to cause them to hesitate in their own affairs never seems to me to convey any particular standard; one member of the jury might say he would hesitate over something and another member might say that that would not cause him to hesitate at all. I therefore suggested that it would be better to use some other expression, by which I meant to convey to the jury that they should only convict if they felt sure of the guilt of the accused. It may be that in some cases the word "satisfied" is enough. Then, it is said that the jury in a civil case has to be satisfied and, therefore, one is only laying down the same standard of proof as in a civil case. I confess that I have had some difficulty in understanding how there is or there can be two standards; therefore, one would be on safe ground if one said in a criminal case to a jury: "You must be satisfied beyond reasonable doubt" and one could also say: "You, the jury, must be completely satisfied," or better still: "You must feel sure of the prisoner's guilt." But I desire to repeat what I said in R. v. *Kritz*, [1950] 1 K.B. 82, at p. 89; [1949] 2 All E.R. 406, at p. 410: "It is not the particular formula that matters: it is the effect of the summing-up. If the jury are made to understand that they have to be satisfied and must not return a verdict against a defendant unless they feel sure, and that the onus is all the time on the prosecution and not on the defence," that is enough.

R. v. Onufrejczyk
[1955] 1 Q.B. 388; [1955] 1 All E.R. 247, C.C.A.

Oliver, J. said in summing up: "the fact of death should be proved by such circumstances as render the commission of the crime morally certain and leave no ground for reasonable doubt". The Court of Criminal Appeal criticized the use of the word "morally".

LORD GODDARD, C.J.: It is always a pity, when dealing with evidence, to use epithets either to increase or decrease its value; and when cases in the books use expressions such as "a high degree of certainty" or "strong evidence" and so on, they really add nothing to what the law requires. The law requires a case to be proved, and a jury is warned and told that its members have to be satisfied on the evidence that the crime is proved, that the prisoner is guilty of the crime; and they should be told that if when they have heard the evidence they are not satisfied, and do not feel sure that the crime has been committed or that the prisoner has committed the crime, their verdict should be "not guilty". Let us leave out of account, if we can, any expression such as "giving the prisoner the benefit of the doubt". It is not a question of giving him the benefit of the doubt, for if the jury are left with any degree of doubt that the prisoner is guilty, the case has not been proved.

Thomas v. R.
(1960), 102 C.L.R. 584

In the course of his summing up the trial judge said of the standard of proof: "There is no particular magic about the way you've got to consider it, no special rules, you consider it in an ordinary common sense manner and in the way you would consider the more serious matters which come up for consideration and decision in your lives, and if considering it in that way . . . you come to a feeling of comfortable satisfaction that the accused is guilty, then you should find him so guilty."

An appeal to the West Australian Court of Appeal failed but succeeded before the High Court of Australia.

McTIERNAN, J.: [T]here is a danger in venturing upon a novel elucidation of this principle of the criminal law. It is dubious advice to tell the jury that no particular magic is required to perform their duty. To assure them that they are not bound by any special rules is calculated to encourage them to believe they are chartered libertines. Surely they are bound to estimate the credit due to each witness and weigh the evidence and to deliberate in a judicial manner. The expression "the more serious matters which come up for consideration" is vague. It would include a wide range of matters of various grades of seriousness. Experience of such matters is invaluable in the jury room but it is not right to tell the jury that they may decide whether the accused is guilty or not guilty in the same sort of fashion as they decide serious matters that arise for their decision out of court.

FULLAGAR, J.: [W]hat is required to justify a conviction is proof beyond reasonable doubt: see generally *Brown* v. R. (1913), 17 C.L.R. 570, at pp. 584–6, 594–6. It may be noted that in this case Barton, A.C.J. said: ". . . one embarks on a dangerous sea if he attempts to define with precision a term which is in ordinary and common use with relation to this subject matter, and which is usually stated to a jury without embellishment as a well understood expression" (at p. 584). Then, "comfortable satisfaction" has perhaps gained a certain currency, but even in civil cases it has little, in my opinion, to recommend it. It was used by Rich, J. in *Briginshaw* v. *Briginshaw* (1938), 60 C.L.R. 336, at p. 350, in relation to the standard of proof in cases where adultery is in issue. But his Honour was careful to distinguish the standard conveyed by that expression from the standard required in criminal cases and conveyed by the words "proof beyond reasonable doubt". In truth, to "come to the feeling" referred to in his Honour's charge is by no means the same thing as being satisfied beyond reasonable doubt.

KITTO, J.: Whether a doubt is reasonable is for the jury to say; and the danger that invests an attempt to explain what "reasonable" means is that the attempt not only may prove unhelpful but may obscure the vital point that the accused must be given the benefit of any doubt which the jury considers reasonable.

WINDEYER, J.: [A]lthough the direction conveyed by the words taken as a whole and in relation to the rest of the charge must be said to be erroneous, I would point out that many of his Honour's phrases taken by themselves are not without precedent and approval. The reference to "the more serious matters that come up for consideration and decision in your lives" is, however, somewhat weaker than Pollock C.B.'s "that degree of certainty with which you decide upon and conclude your own most important transactions in life". And it is not without significance that the editors of Foster & Finlason's Reports wrote in 1867 that that direction "somewhat startled the profession" because it was a departure from "the old, safe, well-established rule" that the jury should be satisfied beyond all reasonable doubt of the prisoner's guilt: see footnote to R. v. *White* (1865), 4. F. & F. 383. Attempts by paraphrase and embellishment to explain to juries what is meant by satisfaction beyond reasonable doubt are not always helpful. And explanation is not always necessary. Wigmore's observations on this point are filled with good sense (*Wigmore on Evidence* (3rd Edn.), Vol. IX, § 2497, p. 316). I would add, although it does not arise from any omission by the learned judge in this case, that, in my view, it is not desirable that the time-honoured expression "satisfied beyond reasonable doubt" should be omitted and some substitute adopted. It is said that it was "invented by the common-law judges for the very reason that it was capable of being understood and applied by men in the jury box" (quoted in *Wigmore on Evidence* (3rd Edn.), Vol. IX, § 2497, p. 323). The expression proof beyond a doubt conveys a meaning without lawyers' elaborations. Othello's meaning was clear enough: ". . . so prove it, that the probation bear no hinge nor loop to hang a doubt on". For generations jurymen have been directed in terms of "reasonable doubt", "moral certainty" and "the benefit of the doubt". Now it has been suggested in England, mainly by Lord Goddard, that these phrases should be abandoned. With great respect for those whose great experience has led them to this view I think that it would be unfortunate if it were adopted in Australia. The House of Lords said in *Mancini* v. *Director of Public Prosecutions*, [1942] A.C. 1, at p. 13; [1941] 3 All E.R. 272, at p. 280, that a direction "as to reasonable doubt" must be "plainly given".

The best and plainest way to give it is, I venture to think, to tell the jury that they must be satisfied beyond all reasonable doubt. In the same case it was said that there is "no prescribed formula"—in *Bullard* v. R. it becomes "no magic formula" [1957] A.C. 635 P.C., at p. 645; [1961] 3 All E.R. 470, n. But that no particular form of words is prescribed does not mean that an old and well-known expression is to be proscribed.

Of course, if the trial judge thinks that, influenced by advocacy or for some other reason, the jury may conjure up mere chimeras of doubt, he may well emphasize that for a doubt to stand in the way of a conviction of guilt it must be a real doubt and a reasonable doubt—a doubt which after a full and fair consideration of the evidence the jury really on reasonable grounds entertain.

[TAYLOR, J. agreed.]

Dawson v. R.
(1961), 106 C.L.R. 1

DIXON, C.J.: [I]n my view it is a mistake to depart from the time-honoured formula. It is, I think, used by ordinary people and is understood well enough by the average man in the community. The attempts to substitute other expressions, of which there have been many examples not only here but in England, have never prospered. It is wise as well as proper to avoid such expressions.

Sodeman v. R.
(1936), 55 C.L.R. 192

STARKE, J.: English-speaking juries understand English words and phrases, as do most other English-speaking people, in their plain and ordinary signification. A phrase such as "the preponderance of probabilities" is grandiloquent enough, but would probably be less understood by a jury than the common English words that they must be satisfied of the insanity of the accused.

Fewer problems have arisen in formulating the civil standard, but the phrase "balance of probabilities" does have its dangers. It may suggest that to satisfy the standard one need only introduce enough evidence to disturb a balanced pair of scales. But in fact if one party gives a little evidence and the other none, the former will not necessarily succeed. The former's contention may be inherently improbable; and failure to contradict an assertion does not necessarily make it credible. As Hoffmann says (p. 365), "What is being weighed in

the 'balance' is not quantities of evidence but the probabilities arising from
that evidence and all the circumstances of the case.''

II JUSTIFICATION

The formulation of the different standards of proof is one thing; their
justification is another. The high modern criminal standard appears to have
originated at the end of the 18th century. Starkie adopted the test of ''moral
certainty, to the exclusion of all reasonable doubt'' in his treatise, published
in 1824. The courts finally accepted the higher criminal standard in *R. v.
Winsor* (1865), 4 F. & F. 363. It is sometimes said that two standards are
impossible: either a thing is proved or it is not. It is also said that the criminal
standard makes it too difficult to convict the guilty. Both points are put only
by a small minority, and may be doubted.

Sodeman v. R.
(1936), 55 C.L.R. 192

DIXON, J.: The difference between the two opposing degrees of persuasion cannot be
regarded as a matter of little or no importance. The daily experience of the administration of justice shows the powerful effect produced by the high degree of certainty
which the one demands. It also illustrates how a sensible preponderance of evidence
usually suffices to turn the scale when the lower standard prevails.

Stephen: *History of the Criminal Law*, I
pp. 354, 438

If it be asked why an accused person is presumed to be innocent, I think the true
answer is, not that the presumption is probably true, but that society in the present
day is so much stronger than the individual, and is capable of inflicting so very much
more harm on the individual than the individual as a rule can inflict upon society, that
it can afford to be generous. It is, however, a question of degree, varying according to
time and place, how far this generosity can or ought to be carried. . . .

[T]he saying that it is better that ten guilty men should escape than one innocent
man should suffer [is] an observation which appears to me to be open to two decisive
objections. In the first place, it assumes, in opposition to the fact, that modes of
procedure likely to convict the guilty are equally likely to convict the innocent, and
it thus resembles a suggestion that soldiers should be armed with bad guns because
it is better that they should miss ten enemies than that they should hit one friend. In
fact, the rule which acquits a guilty man is likely to convict an innocent one. Just as the
gun which misses the object at which it is aimed is likely to hit an object at which it
is not aimed. In the second place, it is by no means true that under all circumstances
it is better that ten guilty men should escape than that one innocent man should
suffer. Everything depends on what the guilty men have been doing, and something
depends on the way in which the innocent man came to be suspected. I think it probable that the length to which this sentiment has been carried in our criminal courts is
due to a considerable extent to the extreme severity of the old criminal law, and even
more to the capriciousness of its severity and the element of chance which . . . was
introduced into its administration.

Cross: The Right to Silence and the Presumption of Innocence—Sacred Cows or Safeguards of Liberty?

(1970), 11 J.S. P.T.L. 66

(i) The principal object of the criminal process is to ensure the conviction of the guilty and the acquittal of the innocent.

(ii) If this object cannot be achieved to perfection, it is better to err on the side of acquitting the guilty than on that of convicting the innocent. I won't weary you with pointless discussions about the magnitude of the permissible error. Is it better that two, ten or even a hundred guilty people should go free than that one innocent man should be punished? Clearly the line has got to be drawn somewhere, and the whereabouts of the drawing depends very much upon the nature of the offence, not to mention the nature of the punishment.

(iii) It is right that a heavy burden of proof should be borne by the prosecution. This particular dove-like assumption is of course only made for the purpose of my discussion of the right to silence . . .; but I would like to emphasize here and now that the assumption is a declaration of faith rather than a dictate of common-sense. In contemporary England common sense would place the burden of proving his innocence on the accused. The great majority of those put on trial is guilty; I say this simply because the majority of them plead guilty. Common sense would say that, if there is doubt on the question of guilt, it should be resolved in favour of the State because the mere fact that the accused is on trial is strong evidence of his guilt.

Question

Allen (*Legal Duties*, p. 286) says: "the acquittal of ten guilty persons is exactly ten times as great a failure to *justice* as the conviction of one innocent person". Do you agree? If so, is this relevant to the distinction between the criminal and civil standards of proof?

III HOW MANY STANDARDS?

Is there any intermediate standard between the normal criminal and civil standards? For some purposes this is so in America, but not in England (*Dingwall* v. *J. Wharton (Shipping), Ltd.*, [1961] 2 Lloyd's Rep. 213, at p. 216, H.L., *per* Lord Tucker). Certainly the existence of three standards would make jury direction even harder than the existence of two. However, depending on the issue, there may be within each standard variations in the amount of evidence required depending on the inherent likelihood or unlikelihood of the fact asserted.

Bater v. Bater

[1951] P. 35; [1950] 2 All E.R. 458, C.A.

A wife petitioned for divorce on grounds of cruelty. The commissioner said she had to prove her case beyond reasonable doubt. The Court of Appeal held that this was not a misdirection.

BUCKNILL and SOMERVELL, L.JJ. held it was correct to apply the criminal standard of proof.

DENNING, L.J.: The difference of opinion which has been evoked about the standard of proof in recent cases may well turn out to be more a matter of words than anything else. It is of course true that by our law a higher standard of proof is required in criminal cases than in civil cases. But this is subject to the qualification that there is no absolute standard in either case. In criminal cases the charge must be proved beyond reasonable doubt, but there may be degrees of proof within that standard.

As Best, C.J. and many other great judges have said, "in proportion as the crime is enormous, so ought the proof to be clear". So also in civil cases, the case may be proved by a preponderance of probability, but there may be degrees of probability within that standard. The degree depends on the subject-matter. A civil court, when considering a charge of fraud, will naturally require for itself a higher degree of probability than that which it would require when asking if negligence is established. It does not adopt so high a degree as a criminal court, even when it is considering a charge of a criminal nature; but still it does require a degree of probability which is commensurate with the occasion. Likewise, a divorce court should require a degree of probability which is proportionate to the subject-matter.

I do not think that the matter can be better put than it was by Lord Stowell in *Loveden* v. *Loveden* (1810), 2 Hag. Con. 1, at p. 3. "The only general rule that can be laid down upon the subject is, that the circumstances must be such as would lead the guarded discretion of a reasonable and just man to the conclusion." The degree of probability which a reasonable and just man would require to come to a conclusion—and likewise the degree of doubt which would prevent him coming to it—depends on the conclusion to which he is required to come. It would depend on whether it was a criminal case or a civil case, what the charge was, and what the consequences might be; and if he were left in real and substantial doubt on the particular matter, he would hold the charge not to be established: he would not be satisfied about it.

But what is a real and substantial doubt? It is only another way of saying a reasonable doubt; and a reasonable doubt is simply that degree of doubt which would prevent a reasonable and just man from coming to the conclusion. So the phrase "reasonable doubt" takes the matter no further. It does not say that the degree of probability must be as high as 99 per cent. or as low as 51 per cent. The degree required must depend on the mind of the reasonable and just man who is considering the particular subject-matter. In some cases 51 per cent. would be enough, but not in others. When this is realized, the phrase "reasonable doubt" can be used just as aptly in a civil case or a divorce case as in a criminal case. . . . The only difference is that, because of our high regard for the liberty of the individual, a doubt may be regarded as reasonable in the criminal courts, which would not be so in the civil courts. I agree therefore with my brothers that the use of the phrase "reasonable doubt" by the commissioner in this case was not a misdirection any more than it was in *Briginshaw* v. *Briginshaw* (1938), 60 C.L.R. 336.

If, however, the commissioner had put the case higher and said that the case had to be proved with the same strictness as a crime is proved in a criminal court, then he would, I think, have misdirected himself, because that would be the very error which this court corrected in *Davis* v. *Davis*, [1950] P. 125, C.A.; [1950] 1 All E.R. 40. I would be adopting too high a standard. The divorce court is a civil court, not a criminal court, and it should not adopt the rules and standards of the criminal court. I agree that the appeal should be dismissed.

The principle referred to by Denning, L.J. can also be illustrated by Lord Brougham's defence of Queen Caroline: "The evidence before us is inadequate even to prove a debt—impotent to deprive of a civil right—ridiculous for convicting of the pettiest offence—scandalous if brought forward to support a charge of any grave character—monstrous if to ruin the honour of an English Queen" (*Speeches*, Vol. I, p. 227). The question is one of probability. The character of certain persons will make it unlikely they will commit certain conduct; and the character of certain forms of conduct makes it unlikely that they will be committed, e.g. because there are moral and legal sanctions against it. Though standards of proof do not vary from issue to issue, the quantum of evidence needed to meet the standard may vary, because more evidence will be needed to prove the occurrence of an improbable event than a likely one. In Hoffmann's words, "To speak of variable standards of proof is . . . to confuse probabilities with the quantity of evidence needed to create them" (p. 367).

IV PROOF OF CRIMES IN CIVIL CASES

If a crime is alleged in civil proceedings, the standard is the civil one, not the criminal.

Hornal v. Neuberger Products, Ltd.
[1957] 1 Q.B. 247; [1956] 3 All E.R. 970, C.A.

The plaintiff sued for damages for breach of warranty or alternatively for fraudulent misrepresentation. He alleged that the director of the defendant company had said a used capstan lathe had been reconditioned by certain toolmakers. The defendants denied this. The judge held that he was satisfied on the blance of probabilities, but not beyond reasonable doubt, that the statement had been made. The Court of Appeal held that the former was the correct standard.

DENNING, L.J.: I must say that, if I was sitting as a judge alone, and I was satisfied that the statement was made, that would be enough for me, whether the claim was put in warranty or on fraud. I think it would bring the law into contempt if a judge were to say that on the issue of warranty he finds the statement was made, and that on the issue of fraud he finds it was not made.

Nevertheless, the judge having set the problem to himself, he answered it, I think, correctly. He reviewed all the cases and held rightly that the standard of proof depends on the nature of the issue. The more serious the allegation the higher the degree of probability that is required: but it need not, in a civil case, reach the very high standard required by the criminal law.

HODSON, L.J.: The comparative dearth of express authority on this topic is not surprising. No responsible counsel undertakes to prove a serious accusation without admitting that cogent evidence is required, and judges approach serious accusations in the same way without necessarily considering in every case whether or not there is a criminal issue involved. For example, in the ordinary case arising from a collision between two motor-cars involving charges of negligence, I have never heard of a judge applying the criminal standard of proof, on the ground that his judgment might involve the finding of one of the parties guilty of a criminal offence.

The judge took great pains to consider the cases in which the question he posed had been considered. I do not propose to follow him in their review, agreeing as I do with his conclusion. I agree with him that in most civil cases, where the standard of proof in cases involving crime has been mentioned, there has been no argument, and the heavier burden of proof has been accepted by counsel or assumed as necessary by the judge. I also think that it is impossible to find a satisfactory explanation of all cases where divergent views have been taken. For example, it seems to have been taken for granted in what may be called the third party cases that the crime of a person not concerned in the action may be established on a balance of probabilities: see, for example, *Boyce* v. *Chapman and Brown* (1835), 2 Bing. N.C. 222, and *Vaughton* v. *London and North Western Rail Co.* (1874), L.R. 9 Ex. Ch. 93. If the criminal standard were required in civil cases for the reason suggested in Taylor on Evidence (12th Edn., Vol. 1, p. 106), namely, that every man has a right to his character and not to have the presumption of innocence rebutted unless the strict standard were adopted, the third party cases would appear to be cases where the rule ought to be most strictly applied, since the third party may not even know of the charge which is being made against him in an action between two persons in whose dispute he is not interested, and even if he knows of it may have no opportunity of intervening in it.

Notwithstanding the existence of some cases where the point appears to have been argued and decided in a contrary sense, I think the true view, and that most strongly supported by authority, is that which the judge took, namely, that in a civil case the balance of probability standard is correct.

Morris, L.J.: He has said that if as to this he ought to be satisfied in the way in which a court or a jury would have to be satisfied before convicting in a criminal case, then in this case he was not so satisfied, but he was satisfied if he was entitled to decide the matter as issues in civil actions are decided, that is, according to the balance of probabilities. The precision of this revealed judicial heart-searching is impeccable from the point of view of its logical nicety. The question of fact which the judge had to decide was simply whether Mr. Neuberger spoke the two words in question. If he did, the words might have been a warranty or they might have been a representation, which in this case would be actionable because fraudulent. It would be strange if different standards of proof as to the speaking of the two words could be applicable according as to what civil legal rights followed. . . .

It is, I think, clear from the authorities that a difference of approach in civil cases has been recognized. Many judicial utterances show this. The phrase "balance of probabilities" is often employed as a convenient phrase to express the basis upon which civil issues are decided. It may well be that no clear-cut logical reconciliation can be formulated in regard to the authorities on these topics. But perhaps they illustrate that "the life of the law is not logic but experience". In some criminal cases liberty may be involved; in some it may not. In some civil cases the issues may involve questions of reputation which can transcend in importance even questions of personal liberty. Good name in man or woman is "the immediate jewel of their souls".

But in truth no real mischief results from an acceptance of the fact that there is some difference of approach in civil actions. Particularly is this so if the words which are used to define that approach are the servants but not the masters of meaning. Though no court and no jury would give less careful attention to issues lacking gravity than to those marked by it, the very elements of gravity become a part of the whole range of circumstances which have to be weighed in the scale when deciding as to the balance of probabilities. This view was denoted by Denning, L.J. when in his judgment in *Bater* v. *Bater*, [1951] P. 35, C.A., at pp. 36–37; [1950] 2 All E.R. 458, at p. 459, he spoke of a "degree of probability which is commensurate with the occasion" and of "a degree of probability which is proportionate to the subject-matter".

In English law the citizen is regarded as being a free man of good repute. Issues may be raised in a civil action which affect character and reputation, and these will not be forgotten by judges and juries when considering the probabilities in regard to whatever misconduct is alleged. There will be reluctance to rob any man of his good name: there will also be reluctance to make any man pay what is not due or to make any man liable who is not or not liable who is. A court will not be deterred from a conclusion because of regret at its consequences: a court must arrive at such conclusion as is directed by the weight and preponderance of the evidence.

Rejfek v. McElroy
(1965) 39 A.L.J.R. 177

The action was for damages for fraudulent misrepresentation. The judge applied the criminal standard of proof. The High Court of Australia reversed him.

Barwick, C.J., Kitto, Taylor, Menzies and Windeyer, JJ.: [T]he standard of proof to be applied in a case and the relationship between the degree of persuasion of the mind according to the balance of probabilities and the gravity or otherwise of the fact of whose existence the mind is to be persuaded are not to be confused. The difference between the criminal standard of proof and the civil standard of proof is no mere matter of words: it is a matter of critical substance. No matter how grave the fact which is to be found in a civil case, the mind has only to be reasonably satisfied and has not with respect to any matter in issue in such a proceeding to attain that degree of certainty which is indispensable to the support of a conviction upon a criminal charge.

V STANDARD OF PROOF OF MATRIMONIAL OFFENCES

There has been a sharp division of opinion among Commonwealth courts on the standard of proof of matrimonial offences. For reasons to be seen, the debate may now be academic. We will therefore only discuss it very briefly. The English Court of Appeal decided (*Ginesi* v. *Ginesi*, [1948] P. 179; [1948] 1 All E.R. 373, C.A.) and the House of Lords assumed ((*Preston-Jones* v. *Preston-Jones*, [1951] A.C. 391 [1951] 1 All E.R. 124, H.L.) that the standard of proof of adultery was beyond reasonable doubt. This was followed in New Zealand (*Macdonald* v. *Macdonald*, [1952] N.Z.L.R. 924; cf. *F.* v. *F.*, [1966] N.Z.L.R. 894). Indeed, some took the view that this standard applied to all matrimonial offences. However, the High Court of Australia (*Briginshaw* v. *Briginshaw* (1938), 60 C.L.R. 336) and the Canadian courts (*Smith* v. *Smith*, [1952] 3 D.L.R. 449) supported only the civil standard. One argument for the higher standard was that adultery was regarded as quasi-criminal by the ecclesiastical courts; but the House of Lords had earlier decided that divorce proceedings based on adultery were civil proceedings (*Mordaunt* v. *Moncrieffe* (1874), L.R. 2 Sc. Div. 374; [1874–80] All E.R. Rep. 288, H.L.). Another argument is that the charge of adultery and the consequences of dissolution of marriage are so serious that only proof beyond reasonable doubt would do. However, there is no public interest in continuing marriages where one spouse has probably though not certainly committed adultery and the other spouse objects. The arguments against the higher standard are various. In *Blyth* v. *Blyth*, [1966] A.C. 643; [1966] 1 All E.R. 524, H.L., Lord Denning attacked the higher standard and Lord Pearson apparently agreed. Court of Appeal *dicta* have expressed agreement (*Bastable* v. *Bastable*, [1968] 3 All E.R. 701, C.A.). Further, *Blyth* v. *Blyth* decided that condonation as a bar to matrimonial relief need not be disproved beyond reasonable doubt; it would be odd if the standard applicable to bars to divorce differed from that applicable to grounds. Further, the Family Law Reform Act 1969, s. 26, provides that the presumption of legitimacy may be rebutted by proof to the contrary on the balance of probability, and it would be strange if a court had to hold that a child was illegitimate though no divorce decree could be pronounced against its mother because the adultery which led to the birth was not proved beyond reasonable doubt.

The debate is now becoming academic because of legislative intervention. Thus the Australian Matrimonial Causes Act 1959, s. 96, provides that reasonable satisfaction is the standard of proof (see also Domestic Proceedings Act 1968 (N.Z.), s. 115). More importantly, the U.K. Divorce Reform Act 1969 (see now Matrimonial Causes Act 1973) poses issues that do not suggest that any possible difference in standards of proof could lead to a different result, e.g.

that a marriage has irretrievably broken down because the respondent has behaved in such a way that the petitioner cannot reasonably be expected to live with the respondent (s. 2 (1) (*b*)). Further, in *Pheasant* v. *Pheasant*, [1972] Fam. 202, at p. 208; [1972] 1 All E.R. 587, at p. 591, Ormrod, J. said: "It would be consistent with the spirit of the new legislation if this problem were now to be approached more from the point of view of breach of obligation than in terms of the now out-moded idea of the matrimonial offence."

For these reasons the above debate will tend to become dead as the U.K. legislation or something similar is enacted elsewhere.

Briginshaw v. Briginshaw
(1938), 60 C.L.R. 336

The Victorian Marriage Act 1928, s. 80 provides: "Upon any petition for dissolution of marriage, it shall be the duty of the court to satisfy itself, so far as it reasonably can, as to the facts alleged." Section 86 provides: "Subject to the provisions of this Act the court, if it is satisfied that the case of the petitioner is established, shall pronounce a decree nisi for dissolution of marriage."

The High Court of Australia, on a divorce petition on the ground of adultery, held, contrary to the trial judge's view, that the Act did not require a standard of proof beyond reasonable doubt.

LATHAM, C.J.: There is no mathematical scale according to which degrees of certainty of intellectual conviction can be computed or valued. But there are differences in degree of certainty, which are real, and which can be intelligently stated, although it is impossible to draw precise lines, as upon a diagram, and to assign each case to a particular subdivision of certainty. No court should act upon mere suspicion, surmise or guesswork in any case. In a civil case, fair inference may justify a finding upon the basis of preponderance of probability. The standard of proof required by a cautious and responsible tribunal will naturally vary in accordance with the seriousness or importance of the issue—See Wills: *Circumstantial Evidence* (5th Edn.), p. 267, note *n*: "Men will pronounce without hesitation that a person owes another a hundred pounds on evidence on which they certainly would not hang him, and yet all the rules of law applying to one case apply to the other and the processes are the same."

I am not prepared to adopt the view, which was suggested in argument, that the difference between the criminal and civil standards of proof is really only a matter of words.

RICH, J.: The phrase "satisfy itself, so far as it reasonably can" obviously reflects the influence of the common expression "reasonable satisfaction". In a serious matter like a charge of adultery the satisfaction of a just and prudent mind cannot be produced by slender and exiguous proofs or circumstances pointing with a wavering finger to an affirmative conclusion. The nature of the allegation requires as a matter of common sense and worldly wisdom the careful weighing of testimony, the close examination of facts proved as a basis of inference and a comfortable satisfaction that the tribunal has reached both a correct and just conclusion. But to say this is not to lay it down as a matter of law that such complete and absolute certainty must be reached as is ordinarily described in a criminal charge as "satisfaction beyond reasonable doubt". A petition for dissolution of marriage is not quasi-criminal, whatever the grounds. . . .

DIXON, J.: The truth is that, when the law requires the proof of any fact, the tribunal must feel an actual persuasion of its occurrence or existence before it can be found. It cannot be found as a result of a mere mechanical comparison of probabilities independently of any belief in its reality. No doubt an opinion that a state of facts exists may be held according to indefinite gradations of certainty; and this has led to attempts to define exactly the certainty required by the law for various purposes. Fortunately, however, at common law no third standard of persuasion was definitely developed. Except upon criminal issues to be proved by the prosecution, it is enough that the affirmative of an allegation is made out to the reasonable satisfaction of the tribunal. But reasonable satisfaction is not a state of mind that is attained or established independently of the nature and consequence of the fact or facts to be proved. The seriousness of an allegation made, the inherent unlikelihood of an occurrence of a given description, or the gravity of the consequences flowing from a particular finding are considerations which must affect the answer to the question whether the issue has been proved to the reasonable satisfaction of the tribunal. In such matters "reasonable satisfaction" should not be produced by inexact proofs, indefinite testimony, or indirect inferences. Everyone must feel that, when, for instance, the issue is on which of two dates an admitted occurrence took place, a satisfactory conclusion may be reached on materials of a kind that would not satisfy any sound and prudent judgment if the question was whether some act had been done involving grave moral delinquency. . . . It is often said that such an issue as fraud must be proved "clearly", "unequivocally", "strictly" or "with certainty". . . . This does not mean that some standard of persuasion is fixed intermediate between the satisfaction beyond reasonable doubt required upon a criminal inquest and the reasonable satisfaction which in a civil issue may, not must, be based on a preponderance of probability. It means that the nature of the issue necessarily affects the process by which reasonable satisfaction is attained. When, in a civil proceeding, a question arises whether a crime has been committed, the standard of persuasion is, according to the better opinion, the same as upon other civil issues. . . . But, consistently with this opinion, weight is given to the presumption of innocence and exactness of proof is expected.

. . . [I]t must very rarely happen that a tribunal of fact, upon a careful scrutiny and critical examination of the circumstances proved in evidence or of the testimony adduced, forms a definite opinion that adultery has been committed and yet retains a doubt, based upon reasonable grounds, of the correctness of the opinion. For the very practical reason that the decision of cases has not been found to depend upon the distinction the necessity has not arisen in England of attempting to define with precision the measure or standard of persuasion required before adultery is found in a matrimonial cause. At the same time, I think that the foregoing discussion of the authorities makes it clear that in England the high degree of persuasion exacted in the criminal jurisdiction has not been adopted as the standard where adultery is in issue in the matrimonial jurisdiction. It is a common experience that in criminal matters the great certainty demanded has a most important influence upon the result. The distinction between that and a lower standard of persuasion cannot be considered unreal.

[STARKE and McTIERNAN, JJ. delivered concurring judgments.]

VI STANDARD OF PROOF (EVIDENTIAL BURDEN)

The test is generally thought to be: "are there facts in evidence which if unanswered would justify men of ordinary reason and fairness in affirming the question which the plaintiff is bound to maintain?" (*Bridges* v. *North London Rail. Co.* (1874), L.R. 7 H.L. 213, at p. 233 H.L., *per* Brett, J.; and see *May* v. *O'Sullivan* (1955), 92 C.L.R. 654). Cross suggests that a lower standard applies where an evidential burden rests on the accused. No authority is cited in the 4th English edition (p. 107); the authorities cited in the Australian edition (p. 124 n. 85) do not support the proposition, and the statements of all the Law Lords in *Bratty* v. *A-G for Northern Ireland* [1963] A.C. 386, at pp. 406, 413 and 417, H.L. are against it. However, in practice it is doubtless easier for a plaintiff to discharge an evidential burden than a prosecutor, and easier still for the accused.

4

Presumptions

I INTRODUCTION

According to McCormick (1st Edn.), p. 639, "presumption is the slipperiest member of the family of legal terms, except its first cousin, 'burden of proof'..."

Presumptions are of two kinds. First, a presumption is a conclusion which may or must be drawn until the contrary is proved; that is, the opponent of the presumption bears some burden of disproving it. In this sense presumptions are simply another way of stating the effect of rules as to the burden of proof. To say that "an accused is *presumed* to be innocent" means only that the prosecution must prove his guilt; it is not a separate requirement; it is not in itself an item of evidence to put to the jury (cf. the strange case of *Coffin v. U.S.*, 156 U.S. 432 (1895)). To say that the accused is presumed to be sane means only that he bears the burden of proving himself insane. The second kind of presumption is a conclusion (the "presumed fact") which may or must be drawn if another fact (the "basic fact") is first proved. If a child is born in wedlock, it is presumed legitimate. Indeed, both kinds of presumption can be classified in terms of what quantum of evidence will suffice to rebut them and on whom the onus of producing this quantum rests. Cross, for example, states four categories of presumption—conclusive, persuasive, evidential and provisional. These terms do not correspond with those of the courts; but no agreed classification exists, and the terms used by Cross do indicate the differences between presumptions more accurately than any others. With conclusive presumptions, no evidence can rebut the truth of the presumed fact. With persuasive presumptions, the presumed fact can be disbelieved by the tribunal if sufficient evidence is adduced to persuade the tribunal of the non-existence of the presumed fact on the balance of probability (or in some cases beyond reasonable doubt). If no evidence is offered to rebut an evidential presumption, the fact presumed must be taken to exist. (Thus if the accused gives no evidence of duress, he is taken to have acted without duress; he bears the evidential burden of proving duress and there is an evidential presumption that men do not normally act under duress.) An evidential presumption can be rebutted by evidence which if uncontradicted might persuade a reasonable tribunal of the non-existence of the presumed fact; the case will then be determined by the legal burden of proof in the light of all the evidence. In the case of provisional presumptions, a reasonable tribunal is entitled to disbelieve the presumed fact even if no rebutting evidence

44

at all is adduced; however, in many circumstances failure to call rebutting evidence will cause the tribunal to hold the presumed fact to be true.

Conclusive presumptions (more traditionally called irrebuttable presumptions of law) are essentially not rules of evidence, since no evidence to rebut them is admissible; rather they are rules of substantive law misleadingly expressed in presumptive form. Hence it is a misnomer to call them "presumptions". An example is the "presumption" at common law that no boy under fourteen can be guilty of rape as a principal in the first degree; another is the presumption that every man knows the law.

A persuasive presumption (traditionally called a presumption of law) imposes a legal burden of disproof on the other side. The standard is sometimes the balance of probabilities (e.g. the presumption that a person who has been absent and not heard of for seven years by those who would be likely to hear of him is dead). Sometimes the standard is beyond reasonable doubt, e.g. the presumption of legitimacy at common law on proof of birth in wedlock (though where the accused has to disprove legitimacy the burden on him would only be evidential because the only legal burden borne by the accused at common law is proving his insanity). That is, the tribunal *must* make a finding that the presumed fact is true if insufficient rebutting evidence is adduced, and it *must* find the presumed fact to be untrue if sufficient rebutting evidence is adduced. The probative force of persuasive presumptions sometimes corresponds with the common sense inferences from the facts, and sometimes exceeds them. Even if there were no presumption of legitimacy, it is easy as a matter of common sense to infer legitimacy from birth in wedlock in the absence of other facts. This may be compared with the different presumptions of death. Where a person has been absent for seven years unheard of by those who would be likely to hear of him, he is presumed to be dead in the absence of contrary evidence on a balance of probabilities. But if such a person is absent for a day less than seven years, there is (depending on the circumstances) only an evidential or provisional presumption of death. This extra probative value in certain circumstances is usually imposed for some special reason of policy such as convenience (seven years' absence is a convenient period after which to presume death for the purposes of distributing property). Such reasons also explain the differences in standard of proof required to rebut persuasive presumptions: the criminal standard was imposed for the common law presumption of legitimacy because children should not lightly be bastardized. But sometimes, no doubt, the criminal standard is imposed simply because of the strong probative force of the basic fact. It would seem that where presumptions have an artificially enhanced probative value less evidence is needed to rebut them than where the presumption is intrinsically probable.

Evidential presumptions are traditionally lumped together with persuasive presumptions as "presumptions of law". An evidential presumption imposes an evidential burden of proof on the other side; that is, it can be rebutted by evidence which is capable of persuading a reasonable tribunal of its untruth, though the tribunal would not necessarily be bound to draw that conclusion. If *no* rebutting evidence is adduced the tribunal must find that the presumed fact is true. If rebutting evidence of the kind indicated is adduced, the tribunal *may* find it untrue, but whether it does depends on its view of the facts as a whole. An example is the presumption of testamentary capacity. A claimant under a will bears a legal burden of proving its validity and hence the testator's sanity. But on proof of a duly executed will, it will be held valid (i.e. the testator will be presumed sane) unless the claimant's opponent can produce enough evidence of insanity to entitle a reasonable tribunal to hold the testator insane. If such evidence is produced, it is for the actual tribunal trying the case to decide whether it is convinced of sanity or insanity (*Sutton* v. *Sadler* (1857), 3 C.B. N.S. 87). The evidence which destroys the evidential presumption of testamentary sanity that follows from due execution leaves the legal burden of proving sanity on the devisee; the tribunal then has to decide the matter on the facts without the aid of the evidential presumption.

Finally, there are provisional presumptions (traditionally called "presumptions of fact"). These impose a "tactical" burden of disproving their truth on the opponent. If he gives no rebutting evidence, he may win his case, because provisional presumptions are weak, and the tribunal may disbelieve them even without rebutting evidence. But he would be tactically wise to attempt to rebut any provisional presumption which may operate against him, because the court is entitled, though not bound, to find that the presumed fact is true; and sometimes it would be a perverse verdict if they did not. The leading examples of such presumptions are the inferences that can be drawn as a matter of common-sense from circumstantial evidence, e.g. the presumption that personal habit or the ordinary course of business has been followed in a given case.

Since these presumptions are simply based on circumstantial evidence it is wrong to cite examples of them as binding authorities; circumstantial evidence which rightly has probative force in one case may not in another. Provisional presumptions are often in fact much weightier and more difficult to rebut than their name suggests. The categories just discussed do not constitute an iron hierarchy; presumptions are essentially guides to probability, and presumptions vary in this respect, both intrinsically and on the facts of particular cases. More evidence may be needed to rebut an improbable persuasive presumption than a highly probable provisional presumption. It is therefore more important for courts to remember this than to work out an accurate hierarchy of presumptions, which is perhaps one reason why no clear classification has been developed or accepted. The courts have been wise to avoid any misleading or tyrannical scheme, though some courts have achieved the worst of both worlds.

II   THE REASONS FOR PRESUMPTIONS

Why do presumptions exist?

First, presumptions often accord with the preponderance of probability and are thus simply short-hand ways of expressing conclusions that can be independently reached as a matter of common-sense; or at least, the conclusion is so likely to be true that it ought to be reached in favour of one party unless the other disproves it. But this explanation cannot account for all presumptions. Some of them do not state intrinsically likely propositions, e.g. the presumption of innocence. Another example is the commorientes presumption: where two or more persons die in circumstances making it uncertain which survived, the deaths are presumed for property purposes to have occurred in order of seniority (Law of Property Act 1925, s. 184; p. 48, *post*). But it is by no means likely on the balance of probability that the deaths occurred in that order.

Another reason why some presumptions exist is to save time at the trial. It would be both absurd and unduly onerous for the prosecution to have to prove in every case that the accused was sane; it is easier to put the burden on the defence.

Thirdly, it is often easier for one party to prove a fact than for his opponent to prove the contrary; for example where the knowledge of a fact is wholly with one party.

Fourthly, presumptions are useful in settling a problem where the ordinary rules of evidence lead to an impasse. If X and Y leave their property to each other provided the beneficiary survives the donor, but otherwise X leaves his to A and Y his to B, then if X and Y die in circumstances rendering it doubtful who died first, A and B each bear a legal burden of proving that they succeed. A will want to prove Y died first; B will want to prove X died first. Both would fail, and the next of kin would take, except for the fact that the Law of Property Act 1925, s. 184 ensures that X is presumed to die first, if older than Y, so that all the property goes to B.

Fifthly, pressures of social policy have moulded some presumptions. It is undesirable that children be held illegitimate lightly, so there is a presumption of legitimacy. Ownership is inferred from possession because stability of title is desirable. The driver of a car is presumed to be driving with the owner's consent in order to give anyone injured by the driver a better chance of recovery and also to encourage road safety by giving an inducement to owners to select careful drivers. Deaths are presumed to be due to accident rather than suicide partly so that life insurance contracts for the deceased's family will be performed rather than avoided by the insurer. The accused is presumed innocent because it is thought important not to convict men wrongly and this is one way of ensuring that the trier of fact takes care.

Sixthly, presumptions often operate to promote convenience. The presumption that a man unheard of by those who would be likely to do so is dead enables affairs of property to be wound up in a reasonable time.

Seventhly, evidential and provisional presumptions serve a variety of procedural purposes. They tend to force the accused to testify if he raises certain issues as to which he knows more than the prosecution or if suspicious circumstances have been proved against him like the possession of recently stolen property. They tend to prevent the jury's time being wasted by considering issues unsupported by evidence. They thus shorten the trial by dispensing with the evidence of one party if the other had adduced no evidence to support a finding in his favour. They prevent perverse verdicts.

III PARTICULAR PRESUMPTIONS

We have Thayer's authority for the view that any comprehensive or detailed discussion of the hundreds of presumptions erected by the substantive law would be "an unprofitable and monstrous task" (p. 313). In particular, there is little point in discussing in detail what kinds of evidence can rebut presumptions, for these are essentially issues of fact and it is wrong to regard prior cases as establishing binding rules of law. But some points about a few presumptions should perhaps be made.

A. Persuasive presumptions

i *Commorientes*

Law of Property Act 1925, s. 184 (1): "In all cases where . . . two or more persons have died in circumstances rendering it uncertain which of them survived the other or others, such deaths shall (subject to any order of the court), for all purposes affecting the title to property, be presumed to have occurred in the order of seniority . . ."

Notes

1. This does not apply to deaths of husbands and wives intestate for the purpose of determining the benefits of spouses on intestacy: Intestate's Estates Act 1952, s. 1 (4) and 1st Schedule.

2. The relevant "circumstances" are not limited to a common disaster: s. 184 will apply if a husband dies at sea on an uncertain day and his wife dies about the same time in a nursing home (*Hickman* v. *Peacey*, [1945] A.C. 304, at pp. 314–15; [1945] 2 All E.R. 215, H.L., *per* Viscount Simon, L.C.).

3. In *Hickman* v. *Peacey*, [1945] A.C. 304; [1945] 2 All E.R. 215, H.L., the majority of the House of Lords held that s. 184 applied even where the deaths might have been simultaneous because it is not possible to be sure who, if anyone, survived. The minority view would have narrowed s. 184, for it would not be applied if the deaths were in fact consecutive. The minority view would also entail more litigation, to decide in each case whether the deaths were simultaneous or consecutive; and it would be difficult to formulate the test of simultaneity.

4. The standard of proof for rebutting the presumption is apparently the balance of probabilities, though the matter is a little obscure (*Re Bate, Chillingworth* v. *Bate*, [1947] 2 All E.R. 418).

5. The words in brackets do not entitle a court to apply or refuse to apply the presumption in its discretion (*Re Lindop, Lee-Barber* v. *Reynolds*, [1942] Ch. 377; [1942] 2 All E.R. 46, C.A.; *Re Brush*, [1962] V.R. 596).

ii *Presumption of death*

If a person is not heard of by those who would be likely to have done so, there is a provisional presumption (the strength of which depends on the circumstances) that he is dead. This presumption becomes persuasive if the person is unheard of for seven years.

Chard v. Chard
[1956] P. 259; [1955] 3 All E.R. 721

A woman who married her husband in 1909 was last heard of in 1917. She was of normal health. In 1933 she would have been 44. Her husband was frequently in prison. It was impossible to find anyone who since 1917 would naturally have heard of her. No evidence of registration of her death could be found. In 1933 the husband remarried and in these proceedings he and his second wife sought decrees of nullity. Sachs, J. granted the decrees, holding that there was no evidence of the first wife's death.

SACHS, J.: On the basis, which I have adopted, that any presumption of continuance of life is simply one of fact, the various decisions cited to me and the *dicta* therein become reconciled. Further, due weight can thus be given in each case to the different circumstances of any given individual, e.g. whether a friendless orphan or a gregarious man in public life, whether in good or in bad health, and whether following a quiet or a dangerous occupation. . . .

My view is thus that in matters where no statute lays down an applicable rule, the issue of whether a person is, or is not to be presumed dead, is generally speaking one of fact and not subject to a presumption of law.

To that there is an exception which can be assumed without affecting the present case. By virtue of a long sequence of judicial statements, which either assert or assume such an rule, it appears accepted that there is a convenient presumption of law applicable to certain cases of seven years' absence where no statute applies. That presumption in its modern shape takes effect (without examining its terms too exactly) substantially as follows. Where as regards "A.B." there is no acceptable affirmative evidence that he was alive at some time during a continuous period of seven years or more, then if it can be proved first, that there are persons who would be likely to have heard of him over that period, secondly that those persons have not heard of him, and thirdly that all due inquiries have been made appropriate to the circumstances, "A.B." will be presumed to have died at some time within that period. (Such a presumption would, of course be one of law, and could not be one of fact, because there can hardly be a logical inference from any particular set of facts that a man had not died within 2,555 days but had died within 2,560.)

Mr. Campbell has cogently argued that the greater regimentation and registration of our lives and deaths in 1955 now renders unrealistic any such general presumption, at any rate where a death certificate could be expected to be found but is not; and has suggested that as the *dicta* really originate from judgments of the first half of last century when the presumption of continuing life was also regarded as one of law, they too are now suspect. Further, it appears on examination that some of the above *dicta* derive either from some case . . . to which some statute applied, and that others . . . were based on earlier judgments in such cases. Against that, however, one can point to yet others, . . . where there is no apparent trace of such an origin. . . . It is, however, not necessary for me to deal further with the questions raised by Mr. Campbell because in the present case there is no one who has been shown to have been likely to have heard from the 1909 wife in the years 1917 to 1933 or, indeed, from 1933 to date and so such a rule could not operate.

The present case is thus one where there is no suggestion that in 1917 the 1909 wife was other than a woman of normal health, nor any evidence of any fact by reason of which her expectation of life could be regarded as greatly sub-normal. There are many factors which, as previously mentioned, might have led her not to wish to be heard of by the prisoner or his family, there is no one known who would naturally have heard of her, and there is no registration of a relevant death.

I accordingly approach the matter on the footing (1) that this is a case in which the court is put upon inquiry as to the validity of the 1933 marriage; (2) that once the husband was shown to have contracted the 1909 marriage it is for him (or his present wife) to prove facts from which a cessation before May 18, 1933, of the earlier marriage can be inferred before it can be said that the 1933 marriage is valid . . . (3) that there is in the present case no presumption of law either as to the continuance of life or as to death having supervened; (4) that this is thus one of the class of cases which has to be determined on its own facts.

Axon v. Axon
(1937), 59 C.L.R. 395

Mauro Herzich deserted his wife in 1923; she obtained a maintenance order against him. She heard no more of him, despite inquiries, and in 1932 she remarried. In these proceedings she sought maintenance against her second husband who pleaded that the marriage was void. At first instance this was granted, the court stating: "strict proof is required of the existence of Herzich if the defence set up . . . is to succeed, and the defendant has failed to discharge the onus which lies upon him in this regard to the satisfaction of the court". The husband's appeal to the Supreme Court of South Australia succeeded, and the High Court of Australia dismissed the appeal and remitted the matter to the magistrates for rehearing.

DIXON, J.: When it is proved that a human being exists at a specified time the proof will support the inference that he was alive at a later time to which, having regard to the circumstances, it is reasonably likely that in the ordinary course of affairs he would survive. It is not a rigid presumption of law. The greater the length of time the weaker the support for the inference. If it appears that there were circumstances of danger to the life in question, such as illness, enlistment for active service or participation in a perilous enterprise, the presumption will be overturned, at all events when reasonable inquiries have been made into the man's fate or whereabouts and without result. The presumption of life is but a deduction from probabilities and must always depend on the accompanying facts. "In England it is only a general supposition of continuance, applicable to everything which has once been proved to exist—to an orange as well as a man;—a presumption which serves, in reasoning, to relieve from the necessity of constantly re-proving, from minute to minute, this once-proved fact of existence" (The late Professor J. B. Thayer, *Preliminary Treatise* on *Evidence at Common Law* (1898), p. 348). As time increases, the inference of survivorship may become inadmissible, and after a period arbitrarily fixed at seven years, if certain conditions are fulfilled, a presumption of law arises under which a court must treat the life as having ended before the proceedings in which the question arises. If, at the time when the issue whether a man is alive or dead must be judicially determined, at least seven years have elapsed since he was last seen or heard of by those who in the circumstances of the case would according to the common course of affairs be likely to have received communications from him or to have learned of his whereabouts, were he living, then, in the absence of evidence to the contrary, it should be found that he is dead. But the presumption authorizes no finding that he died at or before a given date. It is limited to a presumptive conclusion that at the time of the proceedings the man no longer lives. In *Lal Chand Marwari* v. *Mahaut Ramrup Gir* (1925), 42 T.L.R. 159, at p. 160, Lord Blanesburgh, speaking for the Privy Council, said that there is only one presumption and that is that at the time when the suit was instituted the man there in question was no longer alive. "There is no presumption at all as to when he died. That like any other fact is a matter of proof." His Lordship observed as not a little remarkable that the contrary theory was still widely held, although so often shown to be mistaken. After stating how it reappeared in the case before the board, he continued: "Searching for an explanation of this very persistent heresy their Lordships find it in words in which the rule both in India and in England is usually expressed. These words, taken originally from *Re Phené's Trusts* (1870), 5 Ch. App. 139; [1861–73] All E.R. Rep. 514, run as follows: 'If a person has not been heard of for seven years, there is a presumption of law that he is dead: but at what time within that period he died is not a matter of presumption but of evidence and the onus of proving that the death took place at any particular time within the seven years lies upon the person who claims a right to the establishment of which that fact is essential.' Following these words, it is constantly assumed—not perhaps unnaturally—that where the period of disappearance exceeds seven years, death, which may not be presumed at any time during the period of seven years, may be presumed to have taken place at its close. This of course is not so. The presumption is the same if the period exceeds seven years. The period is one and continuous, though it may be divisible into three or four periods of seven years. Probably the true rule would be less liable to be missed, and would itself be stated more accurately, if, instead of speaking of a person who had not been heard of for seven years, it described the period of disappearance as one 'of not less than seven years'." It follows that in the present case the disappearance in 1923 of Mauro Herzich gives rise to no presumption that he was dead on 6th January 1932. In fact the conditions were not fulfilled for presuming his death at the hearing before the court of summary jurisdiction when the order now in question was made. For, in the circumstances in which he left his wife, she was not a person with whom he would be likely to communicate or who would be likely to hear of his whereabouts. He was, in effect, a fugitive from her.

But the question is not whether a positive finding that he was dead on 6th January 1932 is justified by proof or legal presumption. It was for the respondent to overcome the presumption in favour of the marriage celebrated on that date between himself and the appellant. He failed to obtain from the court of summary jurisdiction an affirmative finding that Mauro Herzich was then alive, and unless such a finding is made the marriage must be treated as valid. Richards, J., to whom *Monckton* v. *Tarr* (1930), 23 B.W.C.C. 504, does not appear to have been cited, set aside the decision because he considered that the court had erroneously placed upon the alleged husband, the now respondent, the burden of proving that Mauro Herzich survived until 6th January 1932. But, in my opinion, it was not erroneous to place that onus upon him, and, if in the end the court of summary jurisdiction were not satisfied upon a balance of probabilities that her previous husband was alive on that day, the marriage with the now respondent, the celebration of which was proved by his alleged wife, the now appellant, must be upheld as valid.

At the same time, in considering whether the higher degree of probability was in favour of the inference that Mauro Herzich was then living, the court was bound to weigh with the other circumstances of the case the presumption arising from the fact that in 1923 he was thirty-nine years of age and, so far as appears, was in good health. He had already deserted his wife, and the order for maintenance would afford a powerful motive for his hiding his identity and suppressing his whereabouts from her. The husband attempted to prove that a man bearing the name Herzog was in fact Mauro Herzich, and the reasons of the court of summary jurisdiction contain the statement that, after a full consideration of the evidence, a substantial doubt remained in the minds of the court as to whether the man Herzog was in fact identical with Herzich. The reasons proceed to say that "strict proof is required of the existence of Herzich". These observations suggest that, in arriving at its conclusion, the court did not give consideration, or, at all events, full weight, to the presumption of life as affording, in the general circumstances of the case, presumptive proof of Mauro Herzich's existence on 6th January 1932 on which the court was at liberty to act if, on all the facts, a sufficient degree of probability arose to produce a reasonable satisfaction of his survival to that date. The question must be treated as one of fact, and the court was not bound to draw such an inference. But it seems likely that the court demanded a stricter degree or heavier burden of proof than the law requires and treated the failure to prove to its complete satisfaction that Herzog and Herzich were one man and not two men as decisive against the husband.

[LATHAM, C.J. and EVATT, J. agreed in dismissing the appeal.]

Notes

1. It is a question of fact whether a person is likely to have heard of the propositus. A husband who has been constantly in jail is not such a person (*Chard* v. *Chard, supra*); similarly fugitives from the police or from creditors, or those who for some other reason have no wish to see their family, friends or neighbours again. In practice persons likely to have heard of the propositus are sought in the places he is known to have been in before ceasing to be heard from. It might be more logical to seek them in the places to which he went, but it would be more inconvenient, since such places may be unknown and even if they are known it may be hard to identify his likely circle.

2. The statutes referred to by Sachs, J. are as follows. The Cestui que Vie Act 1666 provides that if persons on whose lives estates depend remain beyond the seas or elsewhere absent themselves in this realm for the space of seven years they shall be accounted as naturally dead. The Offences against the Persons Act 1861 defines bigamy and provides that nothing in the section shall extend to any person marrying a second time whose husband or wife shall have been continually absent from such person for the space of seven years last past, and shall not have been known by that person to have been living within that time. The evidential burden of proving absence and lack of knowledge rests on the accused; the legal burden of proving lack of knowledge rests on the prosecution (*R.* v. *Curgerwen* (1865), L.R. 1 C.C.R. 1). *R.* v. *Bonner*, [1957] V.L.R. 227 suggests by analogy that the legal burden of proving absence rests on the accused but this may be doubted.

The Matrimonial Causes Act 1973, s. 19, permits the court, in proceedings brought by a married person, to make a decree presuming the death of the other spouse on reasonable grounds and dissolving the marriage. A rebuttable presumption of the propositus' death arises if he has been continually absent from the petitioner for seven years and the latter has no reason to believe that the propositus was living during that time. The reasons for believing in the continued existence of the propositus which prevent the presumption arising must be found in the seven-year period (*Thompson* v. *Thompson*, [1956] P. 414; [1956] 1 All E.R. 603). The fact that the propositus would have been unlikely to get in touch with the petitioner during the seven-year period is immaterial, so that this is wider than the common law presumption of death (*Parkinson* v. *Parkinson*, [1939] P. 346; [1939] 3 All E.R. 108).

3. Dixon, J. in saying that the presumption of death after seven years does not entail any conclusion as to *when* death occurred other than that it occurred before the proceedings, is adopting the strict view of *Re Phené's Trusts* (1870), 5 Ch. App. 139; [1861–73] All E.R. Rep. 514. That view is inconvenient in many instances where it is necessary not simply to prove that death has occurred (e.g. for life insurance purposes) but also to prove that it occurred before a certain time (e.g. a particular marriage). It has therefore not been followed in some cases, such as *Re Aldersey, Gibson* v. *Hall*, [1905] 2 Ch. 181; [1904–07] All E.R. Rep. 644, where for purposes of succession a child of the testator was presumed to have died seven years after he was last heard of. This lax view that death can be presumed after any seven-year period before proceedings, not simply the period ending in the date of proceedings, produces more convenient results. Where one person has died on a known date and another is presumed dead but his date of death is unknown, the equivalent of s. 184 of the Law of Property Act 1925 has been applied to hold that the deaths occurred in order of seniority, since two persons have died in circumstances producing uncertainty as to which survived (*Re Watkinson*, [1952] V.L.R. 123; *In the Estate of Dixon* (1969), 90 W.N. (Pt. 1) N.S.W. 469). But absurd results have been shown to follow from this argument (*Re Albert*, [1967] V.R. 875).

4. Is a person "heard of" if the only information received about him is unreliable? See *Prudential Assurance Co.* v. *Edmonds* (1877), 2 App. Cas. 487, H.L. If Sachs, J. in *Chard* v. *Chard* is correct in demanding that due enquiry be made, is it sufficient if fruitless inquiries are made just before proceedings or need they be made persistently during the period of absence?

5. The court will conclude that a man presumed dead died unmarried or childless on the strength of very little evidence, though there is no formal presumption to this effect (*Re Jackson; Jackson v. Ward*, [1907] 2 Ch. 354). The reverse is also true.

6. The amount of evidence which will rebut the presumption of death, both after less than seven and more than seven years, will vary depending on the circumstances. The fact that the seven-year presumption is usually stated as a persuasive presumption does not mean that in some cases it may not be easily rebutted.

7. The court may presume death after a short time if the circumstances in which the propositus disappeared warrant this, e.g. if he appeared to have committed suicide or accidentally drowned or perished in a snowstorm or died in battle. (Any motive the propositus has for feigning death will be considered.) In such cases there will rarely be any problem as to the time of death; if death is presumed at all, the time when it occurred will be indicated fairly exactly by the circumstances. The fact that the circumstances may allow death to be presumed quite soon after disappearance undermines the force of some of Wigmore's criticism of the rigidity of the seven-year rule (para. 2531 *b*).

Further reading

Treitel, "The Presumption of Death", (1954), 17 M.L.R. 530.

iii Presumption of legitimacy

A child is presumed legitimate on proof of birth or conception in lawful wedlock. Few problems remain. It is a persuasive presumption, now rebuttable on the balance of probabilities (Family Law Reform Act 1969, s. 26; *S. v. McC.*, [1972] A.C. 24, H.L.; [1970] 3 All E.R. 107). Its operation is unaffected by the fact that conception occurred before the relevant marriage was celebrated (*Cocks v. Juncken* (1947), 74 C.L.R. 277) or birth after it was terminated (*Re Overbury, Sheppard v. Matthews*, [1955] Ch. 122; [1954] 3 All E.R. 308). In the latter case the presumption is obviously easier to rebut than normal; but it is not rebutted simply by proof of remarriage before the child is born. The presumption does not apply where the husband and wife have been separated by judicial order, but it does apply where there is a maintenance order against the husband or the parties are living apart under a separation agreement or a decree nisi of divorce has been pronounced. These distinctions are artificial and ripe for review (see *Bowen v. Norman*, [1938] 1 K.B. 689; [1938] 2 All E.R. 776; *Ettenfield v. Ettenfield*, [1940] P. 96; [1940]; 1 All E.R. 293, C.A.; *Brown v. Brown* (1947), 64 W.N.N.S.W. 28).

The persuasive presumption of legitimacy should be distinguished from the provisional presumption that sexual intercourse between husband and wife is likely to have followed proved opportunities for it; the latter will generally be much weaker (see *Piggott v. Piggott* (1938), 61 C.L.R. 378, at p. 413, *per* Dixon, J.).

The presumption is rebuttable by such matters as the husband's impotence, his non-access, circumstances making it unlikely he would avail himself of access, blood group evidence, the colour or other features of the child, the conduct towards it of the wife and a putative natural father, or an admission by the latter. Proof of one or more acts of adultery will not necessarily rebut the presumption. A relevant factor may be the lapse of time between access and birth considered in relation to the maturity of the baby. Public reputation other than family reputation is inadmissible (*Re Osmand; Bennett* v. *Booty*, [1906] V.L.R. 455, at p. 467). Either spouse may state whether intercourse occurred at any time during the marriage (Matrimonial Causes Act 1973, s. 48 (1), abolishing the rule in *Russell* v. *Russell*, [1924] A.C. 687 and the matrimonial intercourse privilege). The presumed unlikelihood of a wife committing adultery wil be taken into account by the Court.

Problem

On January 1, H_1 who is married to W, dies. On January 3 W marries H_2. On September 30 a child is born. Discuss its legitimacy. (See Guttmann, "Presumptions of Legitimacy and Paternity Arising out of Birth in Lawful Wedlock" (1956), 5 I.C.L.Q. 217, at pp. 222–227.)

iv Presumption of formal validity of marriage

Where there is evidence of a ceremony of marriage which, on due compliance with the requisite formalities, is capable of producing a valid marriage by local law, the validity of the marriage will be presumed even though it cannot be proved that all the formalities were complied with. Indeed, the presumption arises whether the possible formal defects are trivial or extensive.

Whoever (other than an accused) attempts to rebut the presumption bears a legal burden, and there is authority for the standard being beyond reasonable doubt (*Mahadervan* v. *Mahadervan*, [1964] P. 233; [1962] 3 All E.R. 1108). But in fact the standard is probably only the balance of probabilities, for this is the normal standard in matrimonial causes (*Blyth* v. *Blyth and Pugh*, [1966] A.C. 643; [1966] 1 All E.R. 524, H.L.). "It would be both tragic and chaotic" if the standard were lower (*Russell* v. *A.-G.*, [1949] p. 391, at p. 394 *per* Barnard, J.).

There is also a presumption that the marriage is monogamous (*Ng Ping On* v. *Ng Choy Fung Kam*, [1963] S.R. (N.S.W.) 782; *Cheni (otherwise Rodriguez)* v. *Cheni;* [1965] P. 85, at p. 90; [1962] 3 All E.R. 873, at p. 877).

v Essential validity

It is presumed that a formally valid marriage is essentially valid, i.e. that its parties were capable of marrying and consented to do so. It is unclear whether a legal or only an evidential burden rests on whoever attempts to rebut the presumption (cf. *Axon* v. *Axon* (1937), 59 C.L.R. 395, at pp. 407 and 415 with *Re Peete, Peete* v. *Crompton;* [1952] 2 All E.R. 599 and *Re Peatling* [1969] V.R. 214, and see p. 50, *supra*). However, it is submitted that the same burden should apply here as with the presumption of formal validity, legitimacy, and valid marriage arising from cohabitation and repute, namely a legal burden. The fact that those who perform marriage ceremonies take great care about matters of form but do not have to inquire as to capacity and consent does not affect the undesirability of questioning the validity of marriages without good reason. The standard of proof in rebuttal ought to be the balance of probabilities. It will often be met by proof of a prior marriage and the absence of any reason to suppose the death of the former spouse.

vi Cohabitation and repute

There is a persuasive presumption that parties are validly married where they are proved to have lived together, holding themselves out as man and wife. It appears to be governed by the same rules as the presumption of formal validity; indeed the two often arise in the same case. It is difficult to rebut but may be rebutted by an admission.

vii Res ipsa loquitur

The details of this subject are best studied in books on torts, but one evidential problem it raises should be outlined here.

In *Scott* v. *London and St. Katherine Docks Co.* (1865), 3 H. & C. 596, at p. 601; [1861–73] All E.R. Rep. 246, at p. 248, the majority of the Court of Exchequer Chamber said: "There must be reasonable evidence of negligence; . . . where the thing is shown to be under the management of the defendant or his servants, and the accident is such as, in the ordinary course of things, does not happen if those who have the management use proper care, it affords reasonable evidence, in the absence of explanation by the defendants, that the accident arose from want of care." Heuston remarks that "it is characteristic of the great Victorian masters of the common law who framed these limpid sentences . . . that they should have avoided both lengthy elaboration of the obvious and the use of the Latin maxim *res ipsa loquitur*. These temptations have not always been resisted by their successors, with the result that the law on this topic is still curiously complex" (Salmond, *Torts* (16th Edn.), p. 241). The latter words are an understatement, for the maxim *res ipsa loquitur* "has not been allowed to speak for itself" (*Anchor Products, Ltd.* v. *Hedges* (1966), 115 C.L.R. 493, at p. 496 *per* Windeyer, J.).

It is clear that if the presumption applies the plaintiff is entitled to have his case left to the jury. Judges probably differ in their willingness to find proved the basic facts—a situation where the defendant has sole control and an accident which does not ordinarily happen if care is used; they also differ over what the *res* is which speaks, but the main controversy is about the effect of the presumption. There is authority for four views—that it is persuasive, or evidential, or provisional, or not a presumption at all. The bulk of English and some New Zealand authority favours one or other of the first two views; the bulk of authority elsewhere, particularly Australia, one or other of the latter two.

Barkway v. South Wales Transport Co., Ltd.
[1949] 1 K.B. 54; [1948] 2 All E.R. 460 (C.A.).

Asquith, L.J.: . . . (i) If the defendants' omnibus leaves the road and falls down an embankment, and this without more is proved, then *res ipsa loquitur,* there is a presumption that the event is caused by negligence on the part of the defendants, and the plaintiff succeeds unless the defendants can rebut this presumption. (ii) It is no rebuttal for the defendants to show, again without more, that the immediate cause of the omnibus leaving the road is a tyre-burst, since a tyre-burst *per se* is a neutral event consistent, and equally consistent, with negligence or due diligence on the part of the defendants. When a balance has been tilted one way, you cannot redress it by adding an equal weight to each scale. The depressed scale will remain down. . . . (iii) To displace the presumption, the defendants must go further and prove (or it must emerge from the evidence as a whole) either (*a*) that the burst itself was due to a specific cause which does not connote negligence on their part but points to its absence as more probable, or (*b*), if they can point to no such specific cause, that they used all reasonable care in and about the management of their tyres. . . .

The above view seems now to have been adopted by the House of Lords (*Henderson* v. *Henry E. Jenkins & Sons;* [1970] A.C. 282, H.L.; [1969] 3 All E.R.

756; and perhaps *Colvilles, Ltd.* v. *Devine*, [1969] 2 All E.R. 53, H.L.); the
Privy Council (*Swan* v. *Salisbury Construction Co., Ltd.*, [1966] 2 All E.R. 138,
P.C.); and the Court of Appeal (*Moore* v. *R. Fox & Sons*, [1956] 1 Q.B. 596,
C.A.; [1956] 1 All E.R. 182). Cf. *Ballard* v. *North British Rail. Co.* 1923 S.C. 43,
H.L., at pp. 54 and 56; *The Kite*, [1933] P. 154, [1933] All E.R. Rep. 234; *The
Mulbera*, [1937] P. 82; *O'Hara* v. *Central S.M.T. Co., Ltd.*, 1941 S.C. 363; *Woods*
v. *Duncan*, [1946] A.C. 401, at p. 434; [1946] 1 All E.R. 420, H.L.; the law of
South Africa: *Arthur* v. *Bezuidenhout and Mieny* 1962 (2) S.A. 566; the law of the
United States: *Sweeny* v. *Erving*, 228 U.S. 233 (1931) and the law of Canada:
Temple v. *Terrace Transfer Ltd.* (1966), 57 D.L.R. (2d.) 631. In New Zealand, the
decisions are divided: cf. *Watson* v. *Davidson*, [1966] N.Z.L.R. 853, at
p. 856, and *Hawke's Bay Motor Co., Ltd.* v. *Russell*, [1972] N.Z.L.R. 542 with
Frederic Maeder Pty., Ltd. (N.Z.) v. *Wellington City*, [1969] N.Z.L.R. 222.

Fitzpatrick v. Walter E. Cooper Pty. Ltd.
(1935), 54 C.L.R. 200

DIXON, J. (in the High Court of Australia): When damage is caused by some unusual
event which might reasonably be expected to happen only as the result of an omission
to take ordinary precautions, or of a positive act of negligence, and it arises out of
operations or the behaviour of inanimate things which are within the exclusive control
of a party, no more is required to support an allegation of negligence against him unless
and until some further facts appear which supply an explanation of the cause of the
accident and displace the ground for inferring negligence. The circumstances may be so
strong that a failure to be satisfied of negligence would be unreasonable. But, in my
opinion, it is not the law that a legal presumption arises under which the burden of disproving negligence rests upon the party denying it, so that unless evidence is forthcoming reasonably sufficient to support a positive finding that negligence was absent, the
party alleging negligence is entitled to a verdict as a matter of law. The distinction is
clear between, on the one hand, a rule of law which, as soon as given facts appear,
places the legal burden of proof upon the opposite party, and, on the other hand, a
presumption of fact arising from circumstances, even if the presumption be so strong
that, although the legal burden of proof is unchanged, a finding that the issue was not
established would be set aside as unreasonable. In the first case, the Court must direct a
verdict if the party upon whom the legal burden of proof is thrown fails to adduce
evidence sufficient to discharge it. For the sufficiency or insufficiency of evidence to
prove a fact or the absence of a fact is always a question of law for the Court. But, in the
latter case, the Court could never direct a verdict.

See also *Davis* v. *Bunn* (1936), 56 C.L.R. 246, at pp. 254, 260 and 267–72;
Anchor Products, Ltd. v. *Hedges* (1966), 115 C.L.R. 493; *Nominal Defendant* v.
Haslbauer (1967), 117 C.L.R. 448; *Piening* v. *Wanless* (1968), 117 C.L.R. 498.
But cf. *Fitzpatrick's* case at pp. 207–8. In *Ballard* v. *North British Railway Co.*,
1923 S.C. (H.L.) 43, at p. 56, Lord Shaw said of *res ipsa loquitur*, "If that phrase
had not been in Latin, nobody would have called it a principle."

Government Insurance Office of New South Wales v. Fredrichberg
(1968), 118 C.L.R. 403

BARWICK, C.J. (in the High Court of Australia): First, that the so-called "doctrine"
is no more than a process of logic by which an inference of negligence may be drawn
from the circumstance of the occurrence itself where in the ordinary affairs of mankind
such an occurrence is not likely to occur without lack of care towards the plaintiff on
the part of a person in the position of the defendant; or perhaps, as it might more

accurately, in my opinion, be expressed, where, in the opinion of the judge, the jury would be entitled to think that such an occurrence was not likely to occur in the ordinary experience of mankind without such a want of due care on the part of such a person. Second, that a case in which this can properly be said should be allowed to go to the jury whether or not there is evidence of specific acts or occurrences which could be found to be negligent but that no presumption of any kind in favour of the plaintiff thereby arises. That the occurrence affords evidence of negligence does not merely not alter the onus which rests on the plaintiff to establish his case on the probabilities to the satisfaction of the jury, but does not give the plaintiff any entrenched or preferred position in relation to the decision by the jury of that question. I quite realize that it may be attractive to the mind to conclude that, because the jury is allowed to draw an inference of negligence from the occurrence for the reason that they are at liberty to think that it was not likely to occur without a want of care on the part of the defendant, the inference of negligence must be drawn by them if the ground upon which it may be drawn is not displaced by other evidence explaining the occurrence. That line of thought seems to me to have found favour with English Courts and to have resulted in the creation by the decisions of those Courts of a presumption of fact in favour of a plaintiff in such circumstances. But this Court has been unable to accept such reasoning and the law is otherwise in Australia. In my opinion, the jury are not bound either to conclude that such an occurrence was unlikely to occur without negligence on the part of a person in the defendant's position or to draw the inference that it did in fact occur in the case before them because of the negligence of the defendant. All that has happened, in my opinion, at the point in the hearing of a case at which the judge rules that there is evidence of negligence on the part of the defendant furnished by the occurrence itself is that the judge is satisfied that a jury would be entitled to conclude that such an occurrence in the ordinary affairs of mankind is not likely to occur without negligence on the part of a person in the situation of the defendant. For the rest, it is a question for the jury whether they think the occurrence unlikely in this sense and, if so, whether in the particular case they will be satisfied that there was in fact relevant negligence.

We are not concerned in this case with the effect of any explanation of the occurrence which the defendant is able to give and as to the appropriate directions then to be given. What we are concerned with in this case is the question whether after it has been decided that there is evidence to go to the jury and there is no question of an explanation, the jury must be told not merely that on the evidence they may find against the defendant on the issue of liability without identifying any particular act of negligence but that the reason why they are at liberty so to find is because, in the ordinary affairs of mankind, the occurrence is not likely to occur without negligence on the part of the defendant. In my opinion, in general, the trial judge is not bound to explain to the jury the reason why he has ruled that there is evidence on which they may find a verdict for the plaintiff. To tell them that in the Court's opinion such an occurrence is unlikely to occur without relevant negligence would be an error for it is their opinion of what is likely or unlikely which is of consequence at that stage of the trial. If it is a case where the occurrence itself provides the evidence of negligence, they will usually as men of the world recognize that the occurrence itself speaks of the likelihood of negligence if that is the fact. But of course there may be cases in which the nature of the occurrence, because of its complexity or of some other feature, makes it necessary for the jury to be given a direction such as I shall later mention. But the present is not a case of that kind. Here, there being neither complexity in the occurrence nor any attempted explanation of it, a direction that the jury can find for the plaintiff although they are not able to identify the particular act or acts of negligence which caused or contributed to the impact is, in my opinion, a sufficient direction.

But, in my opinion, there can be no objection to the judge informing the jury that they *may* take the view that the occurrence was not likely to have taken place without some negligence on the part of the defendant, provided he properly identifies for them what was relevantly the occurrence and the facts in relation to it of which they should be satisfied, and makes it plain that though they may think that in the ordinary affairs of men such an occurrence is not likely to occur without negligence upon the part of a person in the place of the defendant, they must yet be satisfied in their minds that more probably than not the defendant was in fact negligent and that his negligence, even though they cannot identify the particular negligent act or omission, caused the plaintiff's injuries. As I have said, there may be cases in which these directions are not only permissible but, for the reasons above mentioned, necessary. I should mention in passing that my references to the defendant in the preceding paragraphs include, in cases where the defendant did not do the act or make the omission which is said to be in breach of duty, the person for whose acts or omissions the defendant is liable.

Thus there is, in my opinion, no room for counsel, as was claimed in this case, to discuss with the jury "the doctrine of *res ipsa* and its effects". Counsel can of course attempt to persuade the jury that, using their general knowledge of affairs, they should conclude that the occurrence because of its nature and circumstances was in all probability due to the defendant's negligence and in that connexion to urge that in point of fact they should take the view that the circumstances of the occurrence speak for themselves in that regard.

The English position has been explained as an accidental consequence of the virtual disappearance of civil juries in England. The judge has to decide both whether *res ipsa loquitur* applies and whether the plaintiff in the end succeeds in proving negligence. Once he decides that it does apply, i.e. that the facts suggest negligence, it is understandable that he requires persuasive proof in order to change his mind (Wright, *Cases on the Law of Torts*, (4th Edn., 1967), p. 246.)

But whether this historical explanation be correct, the merits of the differing views are a separate issue.

Sometimes the debate is conducted as though *res ipsa loquitur* must always be a presumption of the same kind. From this point of view the English approach deserves support because it often works well. Cross (p. 134) points out that there may be circumstances where accidents are typically caused by negligence. In cases where no evidence can be found of the cause, less injustice will be caused by a persuasive presumption because the defendant is more likely than not to be negligent. Any other rule would be harsh to more plaintiffs than the number of defendants who may be harshly treated by this rule. A more familiar justification for a persuasive presumption here is that in many modern cases, particularly those involving breakdowns in hospital or other institutional procedure, or defective machinery, or explosions during industrial processes, it will be far easier for the defendant to disprove negligence by proving, for example, the frequency of his inspection and maintenance and the quality of the methods used than for the plaintiff to prove the reverse. Further, the defendant is in a far better position to discover the precise cause of the accident than the plaintiff. The maxim also overcomes the problem common in medical cases where an inexpert plaintiff does not know what happened to him under an anaesthetic, and where there are several possible defendants who are reluctant to testify against each other. Thus a trend towards strict liability is disguised as negligence. Admittedly, in cases where these factors are not present the English view is defective in giving the plaintiff the benefit of the artificial weight attached to the presumption for no good reason.

But it is not necessary that *res ipsa loquitur* should always have the same effect; nor does it. Sometimes facts raising the presumption will be so weak that even if the defendant gives no evidence he may win and here the pre-sumption will only be provisional. Sometimes the facts will be stronger; if the defendant gives no evidence the trier of fact would be perverse if the plaintiff lost, but the presumption is rebuttable by evidence less than that satisfying a legal burden on the defendant. Sometimes the presumption will be raised by facts so convincing that only proof which convinces the particular tribunal of its untruth will rebut it. Dixon J. may be correct in *Fitzpatrick's* case in saying that the court would have no power to direct a verdict; but the certainty of a successful appeal against a finding for a dependant who has not answered the facts raising the presumption means that on the assumed facts *res ipsa loquitur* operates as a persuasive presumption in the long run: the chances of ultimate success of the parties govern their trial tactics. There is no practical difference between a "provisional" presumption which has the effect of a persuasive presumption, and a presumption technically called persuasive. In other words, the strength of the presumption will vary with the basic facts which bring it into play. The presumption here is different from that discussed in the pre-ceding paragraph: it has no artificial weight superior to its natural weight. It is therefore inappropriate to label it as either persuasive, evidential or provisional except as the facts of particular cases suggest.

The High Court of Australia in *Mummery v. Irvings Pty, Ltd.* (1956), 96 C.L.R. 99, at p. 121, said that the presumption could not be persuasive because "The rule . . . is merely descriptive of a method by which, in appropriate cases, a *prima facie* case of negligence may be made out and we can see no reason why a plaintiff, who is permitted to make out a *prima facie* case in such a way, should be regarded as in any different position from a plaintiff who makes out a *prima facie* case in any other way". But if the inference is stronger than a *prima facie* one, as it may be on the facts, then the argument to that extent fails. Just as the English view is sometimes defective in giving too much weight to the presumption, so the Australian view is defective in giving too little: if it is constantly referred to as a presumption of fact this obscures the possibility that it may be much stronger in the circumstances than such presumptions often are. Further, it is possible to imagine direct evidence which would have the effect of imposing a persuasive burden on the defendant, e.g. a witness who says "The explosion occurred because the defendant's servant lit a cigarette near the petrol tank." In these circumstances it will be hard for the defendant to succeed, though possible; and if he gives no evidence he will lose.

In *Mummery v. Irvings Pty, Ltd.* (1956), 96 C.L.R. 99 Dixon, C.J. said that where the plaintiff, instead of relying on mere proof of the occurrence, himself adduces evidence of the cause of the accident, the doctrine of *res ipsa loquitur* had no application, which is why it had no application when the defendant produced such evidence. But the doctrine will continue to apply, surely, if the evidence of the cause of the accident suggests negligence in the defendant. Such evidence would simply be part of the basic facts giving rise to the pre-sumption. On the other hand, Barwick C.J.'s view (*Fredrichberg's* case (1968), 118 C.L.R. 403, at p. 413), that it is not a presumption at all but merely "a process of logic by which an inference of negligence may be drawn" appears to overlook the fact that all provisional presumptions are of this kind, and that in particular cases a provisional presumption may be so convincing as to have the effect of an evidential or persuasive presumption.

The objection that *res ipsa loquitur* cannot shift the persuasive burden because that burden never shifts can be met in two ways. It might be said that the view that the persuasive burden never shifts is a useless dogma which can be ignored. A more orthodox reply would be that negligence is not the sole issue; in cases where the doctrine has the effect of shifting the persuasive burden there are really two issues. The plaintiff must prove facts which raise a persuasive inference of negligence; if he does, the defendant must prove non-negligence. The persuasive burden does not shift, but a different persuasive burden is imposed on the defendant after the plaintiff has discharged his.

Sometimes the English view produces a sensible result, and sometimes the Australian one does (*not* for converse reasons); but neither operating exclusively could do so in every case. We need two kinds of *res ipsa loquitur* rule. One would be a persuasive presumption in cases where it is difficult for the plaintiff to discover how the accident occurred and in cases where the accident is more likely than not to be caused by negligence. The other would be a possible inference of negligence the strength of which is infinitely variable depending on the facts. We have seen that the reasons for presumptions differ (p. 46, *supra*); the present law of *res ipsa loquitur* is a good example of the confusion that can be caused by failing to understand the different purposes a presumption may serve. Correspondence with reality is one aim; placing a burden on a defendant with means of knowledge is another and the avoidance of injustice arising from a lack of evidence a third. These aims cannot be achieved by a single verbally and substantively rigid rule. We need an artificial presumption and a natural one; there is perhaps little point in calling the latter a presumption because it would not add anything to the inferences of common sense which in any case arise outside the boundaries within which the maxim presently applies. *Res ipsa loquitur* would then simply cover those special cases where for some reason an artificial weight should be attributed to the basic fact, either to force the defendant to tell all he knows or because he is, on the law of averages, more likely to be negligent than not.

Further reading

Atiyah (1972), 35 M.L.R. 337; Lewis (1951), 11 C.L.J. 74; Morison in Glass (ed.), Chap. 2; O'Connell, [1954] C.L.J. 118; Prosser, *Handbook of the Law of Torts* (4th Edn., 1971), paras. 39–40.

viii *Omnia praesumuntur rite esse acta*

So far as appointments affecting the public at large are concerned, proof that someone acted in that capacity is evidence of his due appointment and capacity to act. This has been applied to state officials, companies and solicitors (though not in relation to any particular client). The presumption is probably persuasive, and so operates even against the accused (*R. v. Verelst* (1813), 3 Camp. 432, cf. *R. v. Martin*, [1967] 2 N.S.W.R. 523, at p. 525).

ix *Possession*

There is a persuasive presumption that the possessor of property is its owner, and that the possessor of some land owns adjoining and similar land. This is sometimes called a presumption of lawful origin.

B. Evidential and provisional presumptions

These two groups will be examined together because the major examples are of circumstantial evidence, and the courts have not been careful to state what the precise effect of such evidence is. This is partly because its weight varies greatly according to the particular facts and what common sense says. It can be very misleading. Mark Twain has pointed out that when a woman sharpens a pencil one would think she did it with her teeth (*Puddnhead Wilson;* Chap. 20). The basic fact alone may prove the presumption beyond reasonable doubt or on the balance of probabilities, or may only shift an evidential or provisional burden. The fact that nothing general can be said about these presumptions and that no weight attaches to them other than their inherent probative value suggests that in this area at least, the fashionable modern calls for the abolition of rules of evidence have some point. First, we have seen that a man's life is presumed to continue to exist (p. 50 *supra*), and a similar *presumption* of *continuance* applies to the continued existence of a man's opinions, his partnership, his agency, his ownership, his car's speed.

Secondly, subject to questions of relevance and to the rule prohibiting the admission of similar fact evidence (Chap. 10, *post*), evidence of a man's *habits* may be admitted to prove that he followed them in a particular instance. The same is true of practices within a household or business, e.g. that immediately after being copied into a letter-book all letters were posted, or that letters handed to a servant were usually given to his master. The habit must be indulged often enough and in a sufficiently similar way to make the inference likely as a matter of common sense.

A third group concerns motive, plan, intention, capacity, opportunity. The presence or absence of motive to do an act is relevant to whether it was done; it is presumed that men act in accordance with their motives. This "presumption", apart from being of even greater variation in terms of weight than normal, also often conflicts with the presumption of innocence. Further, "there is a great difference between absence of proved motive and proved absence of motive" (*R. v. Ellwood* (1908) 1 Cr. App. Rep. 181, at p. 182, C.C.A., *per* Channell, J.). But sometimes this presumption taken in conjunction with other circumstantial evidence has sufficed to prove guilt beyond reasonable doubt even though there is no evidence of any act of the accused causing the crime (*Plomp* v. *R.* (1963), 110 C.L.R. 234). A similar presumption arises from acts of planning and preparation, and sometimes the doing of an act may be inferred from statements of intention to do it admitted as hearsay exceptions, subject to the possibility of a self-serving statement by a party or the intervention of some factor preventing the completion of the act. (Cf. such cases as *Johnson* v. *Lyford* (1868), L.R. 1 P. & D. 546; *R.* v. *Buckley* (1873), 13 Cox C.C. 293 and *Mutual Life Insurance* v. *Hillmon* (1892), 145 U.S. 284 with *R.* v. *Wainwright* (1875), 13 Cox C.C. 171.) Similarly the existence of an intention to do a thing may be inferred from the fact it was subsequently done, as long as there is no risk of manufacture. Further, there is the presumption that a man intends the natural consequences of his acts; since he is usually able to foresee the latter, it is often but not always reasonable to infer that he did foresee and intend them (see Criminal Justice Act 1967, s. 8). Ability or inability to do a thing may raise a presumption that it was or was not done. The same is true of opportunity, particularly if the defence of alibi is not promptly raised so that the police cannot check it; indeed the alibi is inadmissible now under the Criminal Justice Act 1967, s. 11, in proceedings on indictment unless notice is given to the prosecution within seven days of the end of committal proceedings. The strength of the inference from opportunity varies, because it is much more likely that advantage will be taken of opportunities to commit some forms of conduct than others. The inference is strong in consensual sex cases. "Clodius and Pompeia are found naked in bed together. A sufficient time for sexual relations to have taken place has elapsed. He has been in love with the girl for some time, and has written letters inviting her to have intercourse with him. Who would hesitate to condemn them both for adultery? Who is so lacking in common sense that he would be unaware of the usual consequences of night, wine, love, and a girl and boy together?" (Matthaeus, *De Criminibus Ad. D.* 48, 15, 6; see Hoffmann, p. 369).

Fourthly, there is a presumption that the conduct and general practice of professional men or businessmen in one set of circumstances shows what objective standard should have been attained or *what terms were accepted* in the similar circumstances.

Fifthly, there is a presumption that *mechanical devices are in working order.* This applies to devices of a familiar and well-known kind like traffic lights, watches, speedometers, weighbridges, tyre pressure gauges, but not to strange ones, because if the machine is strange there is no basis for common sense and common experience to support the view that the machine normally works.

Sixthly, there is a presumption that the driver of a car is authorized to do so by the owner (*Barnard* v. *Sully* (1931), 47 T.L.R. 557; *Young* v. *Masci* (1932), 289 U.S. 253, at p. 259; *Hannan* v. *Jennings*, [1969] 1 N.S.W.R. 260). A similar principle that *what seems to be in order is in order* applies in a wide but uncertain way; it will be used only cautiously in cases where the accused challenges the fundamental procedural legality of the prosecution's conduct (*Scott* v. *Baker*, [1969] 1 Q.B. 659; [1968] 2 All E.R. 993).

Seventhly, under the spoliation doctrine, inferences may be drawn from any lying, fraud, fabrication or suppression of evidence, flight or interference with the course of justice by a party. Such conduct is seen as an implied admission of the weakness of his case.

Finally, a party's failure to give any satisfactory explanation of a *prima facie* case against him may suggest that the case is sound, either because silence is assent—an implied admission, or because it shows a consciousness of guilt or liability, or because inferences from the *prima facie* case, being unchallenged, are thereby strengthened. The presumption is the stronger where the facts are particularly within his knowledge. Hence silence is sometimes said to give rise to a provisional presumption. Special problems arise with the silence of the accused (p. 141, *post*). A similar presumption may arise from a party's delay in enforcing his rights (e.g. *Sellen* v. *Norman* (1829), 4 C. & P. 80). A party's failure to call a witness or produce a document ordinarily suggests that the absent evidence would not support him, and sometimes may suggest that it is actually hostile to his case. (See *Dilosa* v. *Latec Finance Pty., Ltd.* (1966), 84 W.N.N.S.W. 557.)

IV CONFLICTING PRESUMPTIONS

It is often said or assumed that though presumptions of different kinds cannot conflict, two presumptions of the same kind may do. The solution usually offered is to ignore them and decide the matter on the evidence as a whole, if necessary relying on an undischarged legal burden of proof. Thus in

Danyluk v. *Danyluk*, [1964] W.A.R. 124 W married H_1 in 1946 and H_2 in 1951, and alleged her first marriage was void because H_1 had married in 1937. There were persuasive presumptions that both the 1946 and the 1951 marriages were valid; but Hale, J. ignored these because they conflicted. He simply held that on the facts W was able to discharge the legal burden of proof resting on her that it was probable that H_1's spouse survived the war, with the assistance of the provisional presumption that life continues. The presumption of death after not being heard of did not arise because there was no evidence of inquiries about her. (See also *Monckton* v. *Tarr* (1930), 23 B.W.C.C. 504 where the plaintiff widow failed to discharge the legal burden of proving that a husband of an earlier wife of her deceased spouse had survived until the marriage between the earlier wife and the plaintiff's husband, in spite of assistance from the provisional presumption of continuance. And see *R.* v. *Willshire* (1881), 6 Q.B.D. 366; *Re Overbury, Sheppard* v. *Matthews*, [1955] Ch. 122; [1954] 3 All E.R. 308.)

This orthodox account of the problem seems wrong both in statement and solution. Presumptions may conflict, but this is not typical of, nor limited to presumptions of the same kind. But even two presumptions of the same kind need not conflict, because a presumption merely directs that a conclusion should or may be drawn in the absence of a certain amount of contrary evidence. How much contrary evidence depends on the degree of probability associated with the presumption and all the circumstances of the case. A conflict between two presumptions of the validity of marriage is almost always illusory, because one in fact will be more probable than the other, and the general facts of the case will resolve any conflict between them, or at least will cause the case to be decided in accordance with the legal burden of proof. Further, presumptions of different kinds—a persuasive presumption and a provisional presumption—may or may not conflict; but this will not depend on the formal hierarchy but on the intrinsic weight of the presumptions on the facts. The persuasive presumption of innocence in theory outweighs the provisional or evidential presumption of theft based on the possession of stolen property; but if the accused does not testify he may very well be convicted. If H marries W_1 (aged 70) in 1900, W_2 (aged 20) in 1930, and W^3 in 1931, the persuasive presumption of the validity of the 1930 marriage does not conflict with the provisional presumption of continuance of W_1's life because the latter is so weak. On the other hand, the presumption of validity of the third marriage is much weaker than the presumption of continuance of W_2's life.

Thus Dixon, J. in *Axon* v. *Axon* (1937), 59 C.L.R. 395 reasoned as follows. W, who claimed maintenance against H_2, bore the onus of proving that her marriage to him in 1932 was valid. She could rely on the presumption that her 1932 marriage was valid, thus placing a legal burden on H_2 of proving that H_1, whom W had married in 1911, survived until 1932. In the circumstances of the case, the presumption that H_1's life continued could be relied on by H_2 as being sufficient evidence in all the circumstances to discharge that burden. He held that the matter should be remitted to the justices because they appeared to hold erroneously that H_2 must prove H_1's survival beyond reasonable doubt rather than the balance of probabilities. (The judgments of Latham, C.J. and Evatt, J. are obscure on this point and it is submitted they do not destroy the authority of Dixon, J.; cf. Cross, (Aust. Edn.), pp. 134–5, 136, 146).

To look briefly at the matter another way, when two witnesses differ on a point, the Court does not regard them as cancelling each other out as in a mathematical equation; it attempts to discover which is the more credible. For presumptions no different process is adopted.

Whatever the correct approach to conflicting presumptions, it is thought that one recent solution is not likely to be helpful. In *Re Peatling*, [1969] V.R. 214, McInerney, J. acted on a suggestion of Morgan's (44 Harv. L.R. 906) that where presumptions conflict the solution depends on balancing the social policies underlying the presumptions. He held that in that case the presumption of validity of marriage and the presumption of innocence (i.e. against bigamy) should outweigh the presumption of continuance of life, because it was socially important that marriages be not lightly invalidated, and that persons be not lightly assumed guilty of bigamy. It is not clear that the same result could not have been reached simply by relying on the orthodox view that there was no conflict because the presumption of marriage is persuasive and the presumption of continuance on the facts only evidential or provisional; McInerney, J. rejected this because in his view, the presumption of marriage is not persuasive but only evidential. This is not the usual view and it is an odd one if the presumption is supported by such important social policies. The same result could also have been reached, if there is a conflict, by resorting to the legal burden of proof resting on the proponent of validity, which on the facts he might well have discharged. Further, the notion of balancing social policies is one which can only produce an uncertainty inappropriate in this area; if presumptions conflict it is better that parties fail for want of evidence than that they succeed after vague judicial speculation.

Further reading

Bridge (1949), 12 M.L.R. 273; Denning (1945), 61 L.Q.R. 379; Edwards (1969), Uni. of W.A.L. Rev. 169; Eggleston (1963), 4 Melb. U.L.R. 180; Thayer, Chap. 8; Williams, *Criminal Law, The General Part* (2nd Edn.), Chap. 23.

Questions

1. "Every presumption operates to satisfy the evidential burden" (Williams, *Criminal Law, The General Part* (2nd Edn.), p. 877). Do you agree?

2. Prosser says: (*Handbook of the Law of Torts* (4th Edn., 1971), para. 38): "a presumption, as a rule of law applied in the absence of evidence, is not itself evidence, and can no more be balanced against evidence than two and a half pounds of sugar can be weighed against half-past two in the afternoon". Do you agree?

Is Prosser's the same as the view that presumptions are "bats of the law flitting in the twilight, but disappearing in the sunshine of actual facts"? (*Mackowik* v. *Kansas City, St. J. & C.B.R. Co.*, 94 S.W. 256, at p. 262, *per* Lamm, J.)

PART THREE

The Protection of the Accused

5

Corroboration

I INTRODUCTION

Corroboration is evidence tending to confirm some fact of which other evidence is given. As a matter of common sense, the more corroboration is present the easier it is to prove a fact, and from this point of view a trier of fact will always look for corroboration. But sometimes English law *requires* that attention be paid to the issue of corroboration, and these corroboration requirements are of three kinds.

First, some facts cannot be proved without corroboration. These principally include perjury, driving a motor vehicle at an excessive speed, procuration of girls for prostitution and similar offences, facts testified to by unsworn child witnesses, and paternity testified to by the mother in affiliation proceedings. Here corroboration is a mandatory requirement in the sense that no matter how convincing the evidence requiring corroboration is, the party relying on that evidence will fail unless he adduces corroboration. A finding of fact must necessarily be set aside in its absence; and no question can arise of applying the proviso to s. 2 (1) of the Criminal Appeal Act 1968 (or its civil equivalent), which permits an appeal to be dismissed on the ground that "no miscarriage of justice has actually occurred", because of the absolute way the rules of law surrounding this corroboration requirement are framed.

Secondly, in some cases the judge *must* warn the jury (or himself, if he is sitting alone) of the dangers of reaching a conclusion without corroboration. This necessity arises where the evidence of accomplices, or sworn child witnesses, or the victims of sexual offences is concerned. Provided the warning is given, there is no objection to the trier of fact reaching a conclusion without corroboration, for he may well decide that the intrinsic worth of the evidence before him entirely justifies proceeding to a conclusion without corroboration. Failure to warn will be a ground of successful appeal unless the proviso is applied.

Thirdly, in some cases an appellate court may consider that on the particular facts of the case the trial judge ought, as a matter of discretion, to have given the jury or himself a warning as to the danger of reaching a conclusion without corroboration. There is no closed or definite list of cases where a corroboration warning of this kind may be required, but the main instances of appellate intervention have occurred in cases turning on identification, in claims against deceased estates, in cases of agent provocateur evidence, and in matrimonial causes. However, the discretion of the judge not to give such a warning is a fairly unfettered one, and only in a very clear case will an appeal against a failure to give it succeed.

Apart from perjury, the origins of corroboration requirements in English law are either statutory or very recent or both. In this respect the common law has traditionally differed from civil law systems; modern Scots law, for example, has at least a weak requirement that corroboration be looked for in every case. But the common law only set its face firmly against a general corroboration requirement in the seventeenth century; indeed the issue only arose on a substantial scale when the phenomenon of witnesses testifying in court in a characteristically modern way became widespread and the common law judges had to decide whether to follow the requirement of ecclesiastical and civilian systems of more than one witness. The triumphant view had to battle a persistent medieval line of contrary opinion to the effect that "the testimony of a single person is as the testimony of no one" (*Cressy v. Siward* (1312), Y.B. 5 Edw. I, Selden Society Vol. 33, p. 121, at p. 123; and see Wigmore, para. 2032).

The historical reason why the common law judges eventually took the view they did was that in the sixteenth century the jury were to some extent still regarded as witnesses themselves rather than open-minded triers of fact quite ignorant of the case before the trial. On this approach, any general demand for particular numerical requirements of witnesses would be considered otiose, because there were always twelve witnesses other than the one testifying. For the same reason, no judge could declare the evidence of any one witness insufficient. Apart from this historical reason, however, there is room for argument both about the sense of a general rule requiring or not requiring corroboration, and also about the justice of requiring corroboration in particular circumstances. The latter group of questions will be considered later (pp. 70–84, *post*).

A number of points have traditionally been made in favour of a general corroboration requirement. First, such a rule prevents a man of honour being destroyed by the assertions of a single rogue. But rogues sometimes tell the truth and honourable men sometimes commit crimes; in any event, the right to undermine a rogue's credibility by attacking his character affords some solution to an honourable man accused of crime. Further, as Napoleon said when he abolished a two-witness rule in the Rhineland, "one honourable man by his testimony could not prove a single rascal guilty; though two rascals by their testimony could prove an honourable man guilty" (Bonnier, *Traité des Preuves* (5th Edn., 1888), para. 293, cited in Wigmore, para. 2033, n. 3).

A second justification for a two-witness rule was advanced by Montesquieu: "Reason requires two witnesses: because a witness who affirms, and a party accused who denies, make assertion against assertion, and it requires a third to turn the scale" (see Bentham, IX, 6, c. 1., para. 1). The objection to this is that it is only a mechanical method of obtaining security, unrelated to the real forms and causes of unreliable testimony. In Bentham's words: "*Pondere, non numero.* From numbers (the particulars of the case out of the question) no just conclusion can be formed. . . . In many cases, a single witness, by the simplicity and clearness of his narrative, by the probability and consistency of the incidents he relates, by their agreement with other matters of fact too notorious to stand in need of testimony,—a single witness (especially if situation and character be taken into account) will be enough to stamp conviction on the most reluctant mind. In other instances, a cloud of witnesses, though all were to the same fact, will be found wanting in the balance.'' Further, the balance of opposed witnesses which supposedly has to be broken by an extra witness does not in fact generally exist. For example, the accused in a serious criminal charge has everything to gain and little to lose by lying, while a prosecution witness has much to lose and nothing to gain (except in special circumstances, as where he is an accomplice carrying out his side of a bargain by which the police will arrange for him to be leniently treated). It is more likely that the accused will lie than his accuser, and so Montesquieu's argument if anything suggests that the defence should always have to provide a plurality of witnesses.

A third point is that a general corroboration rule protects the innocent because ''it is hard for two or more so to agree upon all circumstances relating unto a lye, as not to thwart one another'' (Algernon Sidney's *Apologia*, 9 How. St. Tr. 916, at p. 927). This is particularly so where the lies are detailed and the witnesses who tell them are subject to skilful cross-examination. But such a rule causes hardships which outweigh its benefits. First, it will lead to many crimes going unpunished and will in fact encourage crime to be committed by persons aware of the difficulties of conviction. Bentham said that under a corroboration rule: ''those to whom, in consequence of the licence granted by this same rule, it might happen, and (if the rule were universally known) could not but happen, to suffer the same or worse punishment at the hands of malefactors, are altogether overlooked. The innocent who scarcely present themselves by so much as scores or dozens, engross the whole attention, and pass for the whole world. The innocent who ought to have presented themselves by millions, are overlooked, and left out of the account'' (*op. cit.*). Secondly, a corroboration rule tends to increase the likelihood of perjury and subornation of perjury on the part of litigants attempting to comply with it, and a consequential decline in public respect for the entire legal system. Roger North noted of a Turkish law to this effect that an English merchant ''will directly hire a Turk to swear that fact of which he knows nothing; which the Turk doth out of faith he hath in the merchant's veracity; and the merchant is very safe in it, for, without two Turks to testify, he cannot be accused of the subornation. This is not, as here, accounted a villainous subornation, but an ease under an oppression, and a lawful means of coming into a just right'' (Roger North, *Life of Sir Dudley North* (1744), p. 46, quoted Wigmore, para. 2033, n. 3). Thirdly, as Best said, corroboration rules may ''produce a mischievous effect on the tribunal, by their natural tendency to react on the human mind; and they thus create a system of mechanical decision, dependent on the number of proofs, and regardless of their weight'' (para. 598).

In sum, to use Wigmore's words: ''The probative value of a witness' assertion is utterly incapable of being measured by arithmetic. All the considerations which operate to discredit testimony affect it in such varying ways for different witnesses that the net trustworthiness of each one's testimony is not to be estimated, either in itself or in reference to others' testimony, by any uniform numerical standard. Probative effects are too elusive and intangible for that. The personal element behind the assertion is the vital one, and is too multifarious to be measured by rule. 'Testimony,' as Boyle well said, 'is like the shot of a long-bow, which owes its efficacy to the force of the shooter; argument [i.e. circumstantial inference] is like the shot of a cross-bow, equally forcible whether discharged by a giant or a dwarf' (quoted in 8 How. St. Tr. 1041). The cross-bow notion of testimony—the notion that one man's shot is as forceful as any other man's—can find no defenders to-day" (para. 2033).

These arguments suggest that any general corroboration requirement would be too wide. But experience has persuaded the legislature and the judges that sometimes corroboration should be looked for. This may be because of the *situation of the witness*—he may be very young, or he may have a motive to lie, for example, because he is an accomplice. Sometimes *the subject-matter of the case* carries dangers. Charges may be hard to disprove, for example, allegations of sexual offences, or paternity, or claims against deceased estates; or allegations may stir up prejudice against one party. Sometimes *the nature of what the testimony is about* carries dangers, for example, evidence of the speed of cars, or evidence of personal identification. Sometimes there is some *prudential reason unconnected with reliability* for requiring corroboration: the need for testimony of perjury to be corroborated is probably justified by the need to remove any factor which might prevent witnesses coming forward to testify; and this might occur were it possible to obtain a conviction for perjury on uncorroborated evidence.

II WHEN IS CORROBORATION NEEDED?

A. Mandatory cases

Corroboration is required in English law principally for the unsworn evidence of children (Children and Young Persons Act 1933, s. 38), the evidence as to paternity of the complainant in affiliation proceedings (Affiliation Proceedings Act 1957, ss. 4 and 8, as amended by the Affiliation Proceedings (Amendment) Act 1972), evidence as to the procuration of women to have unlawful sexual intercourse (Sexual Offences Act 1956, ss. 2–4, 22 and 23), evidence as to speeding in a motor vehicle (Road Traffic Act 1960, s. 4 (2), and perjury and kindred offences (Perjury Act 1911, s. 13).

The justification for the corroboration requirement regarding unsworn children, offences involving procuration, and affiliation proceedings will be discussed later (pp. 79–84, *post*). The obvious unreliability of a single witness's estimate of the speed of a car justifies the need for corroboration of his evidence. The justification for requiring corroboration of evidence as to perjury is that this removes one barrier to witnesses freely testifying, namely that they might run the risk of being convicted for perjury.

Best: Principles of the Law of Evidence
11th Edn. Para. 607

The legislator dealing with the offence of perjury has to determine the relative weight of conflicting duties. Measured merely by its religious or moral enormity, perjury, always a grievous, would in many cases be the greatest of crimes, and as such be deserving of the severest punishment which the law could inflict. But when we consider the very peculiar nature of this offence, and that every person who appears as a witness in a court of justice is liable to be accused of it by those against whom his evidence tells, who are frequently the basest and most unprincipled of mankind; and when we remember how powerless are the best rules of municipal law without the co-operation of society to enforce them,—we shall see that the obligation of protecting witnesses from oppression, or annoyance, by charges, or threats of charges of having borne false testimony, is far paramount to that of giving even perjury its deserts. To repress that crime, prevention is better than cure; and the law of England relies, for this purpose, on the means provided for detecting and exposing the crime at the moment of commission,—such as publicity, cross-examination, the aid of a jury, &c.; and on the infliction of a severe, though not excessive punishment, wherever the commission of the crime has been clearly proved. But in order to carry out the great objects above mentioned, our law gives witnesses the privilege of refusing to answer questions which tend to criminate, or to expose them to penalty of forfeiture; it allows no action to be brought against a witness, for words written or spoken in the course of his evidence; and it throws every fence round a person accused of perjury. Besides, great precision is required in the indictment; the strictest proof is exacted of what the accused swore; and, lastly, the testimony of at least two witnesses must be forthcoming to prove its falsity. The result accordingly is that in England little difficulty, comparatively speaking, is found in obtaining voluntary evidence for the purposes of justice; and although many persons may escape the punishment awarded by law to perjury, instances of erroneous convictions for it are unknown, and the threat of an indictment for perjury is treated by honest and upright witnesses as a *brutum fulmen*.

Notes

1. The law has changed slightly since Best's day. It is not true that two *witnesses* are necessary, since the corroboration can be found in non-testimonial evidence.

2. There are other illustrations apart from those given by Best of the general policy which encourages witnesses to come forward by protecting them; for example, it is a crime to intimidate witnesses. Indeed, the policy extends to advocates who are protected against actions for negligence respecting their conduct in court (*Rondel* v. *Worsley*, [1969] 1 A.C. 191; [1967] 3 All E.R. 993, H.L.).

B. The corroboration warning requirement

i Accomplices

In England the jury must be warned that though they may convict on the evidence of an accomplice it is dangerous to do so unless it is corroborated.

Davies v. Director of Public Prosecutions
[1954] A.C. 378; [1954] 1 All E.R. 507, H.L.

The accused and other youths attacked with their fists another group of youths, one of whom was stabbed and died. One of the first group, Lawson, who had been acquitted of murder but convicted of common assault, testified at the trial of the accused for murder that the accused had admitted possession of a knife. The trial judge did not treat him as an accomplice, and the Court of Criminal Appeal and House of Lords upheld this decision.

LORD SIMONDS, L.C.: The true rule has been, in my view, accurately formulated by the appellant's counsel in his first three propositions, more particularly in the third. These propositions as amended read as follows:
"*First proposition:*
"In a criminal trial where a person who is an accomplice gives evidence on behalf of the prosecution, it is the duty of the judge to warn the jury that, although they may convict upon his evidence, it is dangerous to do so unless it is corroborated.
"*Second proposition:*
"This rule, although a rule of practice, now has the force of a rule of law.

"*Third proposition:*

"Where the judge fails to warn the jury in accordance with this rule, the conviction will be quashed, even if in fact there be ample corroboration of the evidence of the accomplice, unless the appellate court can apply the proviso to s. 4 (1) of the Criminal Appeal Act, 1907."

The rule, it will be observed, applies only to witnesses for the prosecution.

The remaining questions, therefore, on the main issue are—(B) and (C)—What is an "accomplice" within the rule? And has the rule, on the proper construction of the word "accomplice" contained in it, any application to Lawson in the present case?

There is in the authorities no formal definition of the term "accomplice": and your Lordships are forced to deduce a meaning for the word from the cases in which X, Y and Z have been held to be, or held liable to be treated as, accomplices. On the cases it would appear that the following persons, if called as witnesses for the prosecution, have been treated as falling within the category:

(1) On any view, persons who are *participes criminis* in respect of the actual crime charged, whether as principals or accessories before or after the fact (in felonies) or persons committing, procuring or aiding and abetting (in the case of misdemeanors). This is surely the natural and primary meaning of the term "accomplice". But in two cases, persons falling strictly outside the ambit of this category have, in particular decisions, been held to be accomplices for the purpose of the rule: viz.:

(2) Receivers have been held to be accomplices of the thieves from whom they receive goods on a trial of the latter for larceny (R. v. *Jennings* (1912), 7 Cr. App. Rep. 242, C.C.A.; R. v. *Dixon* (1925), 19 Cr. App. Rep. 36, C.C.A.):

(3) When X has been charged with a specific offence on a particular occasion, and evidence is admissible, and has been admitted, of his having committed crimes of this identical type on other occasions, as proving system and intent and negativing accident; in such cases the court has held that in relation to such other similar offences, if evidence of them were given by parties to them, the evidence of such other parties should not be left to the jury without a warning that it is dangerous to accept it without corroboration (R. v. *Farid* (1945), 173 L.T. 68, C.C.A.).

In both of these cases (2) and (3) a person not a party or not necessarily a party to the substantive crime charged was treated as an accomplice for the purpose of the requirement of warning. (I say "not necessarily" to cover the case of receivers. A receiver may on the facts of a particular case have procured the theft, or aided and abetted it, or may have helped to shield the thief from justice. But he can be a receiver without doing any of these things.) The primary meaning of the term "accomplice", then, has been extended to embrace these two anomalous cases. In each case there are special circumstances to justify or at least excuse the extension. A receiver is not only committing a crime intimately allied in character with that of theft: he could not commit the crime of receiving at all without the crime of theft having preceded it. The two crimes are in a relationship of "one-sided dependence". In the case of "system", the requirement of warning within the special field of similar crimes committed is a logical application within that collateral field of the general principle, though it involves a warning as to the evidence of persons not accomplices to the substantive crime charged.

My Lords, these extensions of the term are imbedded in our case law and it would be inconvenient for any authority other than the legislature to disturb them. Neither of them affects this case. Lawson was not a receiver, nor was there any question of "system"; Lawson, if he was to be an accomplice at all had to be an accomplice to the crime of murder. I can see no reason for any further extension of the term "accomplice". In particular, I can see no reason why, if half a dozen boys fight another crowd, and one of them produces a knife and stabs one of the opponents to death, all the rest of his group should be treated as accomplices in the use of a knife and the infliction of mortal injury by that means, unless there is evidence that the rest intended or concerted or at least contemplated an attack with a knife by one of their number, as opposed to a common assault. If all that was designed or envisaged was in fact a common assault, and there was no evidence that Lawson, a party to that common assault, knew that any of his companions had a knife, then Lawson was not an accomplice in the crime consisting in its felonious use. . . .

My Lords, I have tried to define the term "accomplice". The branch of the definition relevant to this case is that which covers "*participes criminis*" in respect of the actual crime charged, "whether as principals or accessories before or after the fact". But, it may reasonably be asked, who is to decide, or how is it to be decided, whether a particular witness was a "*particeps criminis*" in the case in hand? In many or most cases this question answers itself, or, to be more exact, is answered by the witness in question himself, by confessing to participation, by pleading guilty to it, or by being convicted of it. But it is indisputable that there are witnesses outside these straightforward categories, in respect of whom the answer has to be sought elsewhere. The witnesses concerned may never have confessed, or may never have been arraigned or put on trial, in respect of the crime involved. Such cases fall into two classes. In the first, the judge can properly rule that there is no evidence that the witness was, what I will, for short, call a participant. The present case, in my view, happens to fall within this class, and can be decided on that narrow ground. But there are other cases within this field in which there is evidence on which a reasonable jury could find that a witness was a "participant". In such a case the issue of "*accomplice vel non*" is for the jury's decision: and a judge should direct them that if they consider on the evidence that the witness was an accomplice, it is dangerous for them to act on his evidence unless corroborated: though it is competent for them to do so if, after that warning, they still think fit to do so.

[LORDS PORTER, OAKSEY, TUCKER and ASQUITH agreed.]

a). Rationale.—Accomplice evidence has traditionally been thought to present several dangers.

The first is that even if a man is certain to be found guilty, he may seek the avoidance or reduction of his punishment as a reward, not on the ground that his role in the crime was a minor one—it may not be—but for enabling the crime to be brought home against the other criminals; and he may be tempted to curry favour with the prosecution by painting their guilt more blackly than it deserves. "The danger is, that when a man is fixed, and knows that his own guilt is detected, he purchases impunity by falsely accusing others" (*R. v. Farler* (1837), 8 C. & P. 106, at p. 108). In this connection Macaulay wrote of the trial of one of James II's victims in the persecutions after Monmouth's rebellion: "The witnesses against him were men of infamous character, men, too, who were swearing for their own lives. None of them had yet got his pardon; and it was a popular saying that they fished for prey like tame cormorants, with ropes round their necks" (*History of England* (Everyman Edn., London, 1906), Vol. I, p. 500).

The second danger is the most obvious and common: where a man wishes to suggest his innocence or minor participation and transfers the blame to others.

Thirdly, according to Maule, J., "it often happens that an accomplice is a friend of those who committed the crime with him, and he would much rather get them out of the scrape and fix an innocent man than his real associates" (*R. v. Mullins* (1848), 3 Cox C.C. 526, at p. 531).

Fourthly, a man may be informed against by an innocent witness; in spite and to revenge himself, he accuses the informer of in fact taking part in the crime. Pollock, C.B. once said it was "perilous . . . to convict a person as receiver on the sole evidence of the thief. This would put it in the power of a thief from malice or revenge to lay a crime on any one against whom he had a grudge'' (*R. v. Robinson* (1864), 4 F. & F. 43).

Fifthly, there is a notion found more in the older cases than today that depends on the ''moral guilt of the witness'': he should not be believed because he is a confessed or proved criminal.

The dangers inherent in all these cases will be increased by the fact that though the accomplice's evidence may be false in implicating the accused, it will usually have a seeming plausibility because the accomplice will have familiarity with at least some details of the crime. It is for this reason that the courts require that corroborative evidence implicate the accused in some material particular.

The English courts have been on the whole persuaded of the force of these points; but there is no doubt that sometimes the accomplice warning equipment operates unsatisfactorily. First, the questions of what corroboration is, the effect of its absence, what an accomplice is, and all the other matters about which a jury must be directed, can make a corroboration warning a complicated affair, difficult for a jury to understand, and a fertile source of appeal. The rule places ''in the hands of counsel a set of juggling formulas with which to practise upon the chance of obtaining a new trial'' (Wigmore, para. 2059). In avoiding this risk the court may go too far the other way and use as set forms of words summing-ups previously approved on appeal, or repeatedly stress the dangers of accomplice evidence; apart from not necessarily being comprehensible to the jury in the instant case, this may make them reluctant to convict when it would be both safe and their duty, had they been properly directed, to do so. This raises a second point: that a corroboration requirement automatically makes it harder to obtain convictions for certain crimes. If the women in crimes associated with prostitution and the partners in sex crimes, and such crimes as illegal bribery and illegal sales, are accomplices, it will be hard to convict for these crimes, because in their nature there will be little evidence about them except what proceeds from the parties to them. And it is thought that corroboration requirements make it particularly difficult to prosecute large-scale organized crime and racketeering. Lord Holt, C.J. once said that ''conspiracies are deeds of darkness as well of wickedness, the discovery whereof can properly only come from the conspirators themselves'' (quoted in *R. v. Despard* (1803), 28 State Tr. 346, at p. 489). Thirdly, the law is inconsistent in not demanding corroboration for evidence which may be weaker than accomplice evidence, e.g. evidence of identification: the warning as to the dangers of such evidence is only optional. Fourthly, the likelihood that the accomplice will lie must depend partly on a balance between the probable penalty for perjury and that for the crime in respect of which he is seeking to evade punishment. ''But the rule applies with equal force to the accomplice who may apprehend but a month's imprisonment for the most trifling petit larceny, and to him who may reasonably dread death for an atrocious murder'' (Joy, *The Evidence of Accomplices*, p. 4, quoted by Wigmore, para. 2057). Fifthly, the practical operation of the accomplice rule tends to determine in advance of the testimony, in ignorance of the particular facts of the case, and without paying attention to the witness's demeanour and general credibility, that an accomplice is not credible. In Joy's words, ''Why a fixed, unvarying rule should be applied to a subject which admits of such endless variety as the credit of witnesses, seems hardly reconcilable to the principles of reason.''

Apart from these general problems, there are particular comments to be made on the suggested dangers of accomplice evidence. First, the dangers arising from attempts to curry favour with the prosecution will seemingly depend partly on the witness's belief in an express or implied promise of immunity. Where this is absent, the rule pro tanto lacks a rationale, for "credibility is a matter of elusive variety, and it is impossible and anachronistic to determine in advance that, with or without promise, a given man's story must be distrusted" (Wigmore, para. 2057). Secondly, the dangers of a witness exculpating himself by blaming another are often obvious and do not demand a complicated warning. Thirdly, the role of revenge and spite as a motive, and indeed that of solidarity with friends, cannot be great compared with that of self-interest: "the extreme case of the wretch who fabricates merely for the malicious desire to drag down others in his own ruin can be no foundation for a general rule" (*ibid.*). And the "moral guilt of the witness" must surely vary with the type and seriousness of the crime committed. A sex criminal will not necessarily lack credit as much as one who commits a crime involving dishonesty.

This dispute may never be resolved. The Criminal Law Revision Committee considered that there was no need for an invariable warning about accomplices, but that the courts should have a discretion to warn in appropriate cases (para. 185).

b). What is an accomplice?.—The definition offered by Lord Simonds in *Davies v. Director of Public Prosecutions*, [1954] A.C. 378; [1954] 1 All E.R. 507 prevails in England. Arguments that it is too broad are unconvincing (see [1973] Crim. L.R. 264, at pp. 270–6) except as to the inclusion of accessories after the fact. The bulk of non-English authority is against this extension (e.g. *R. v. Ready*, [1942] V.L.R. 85; *Khan v. R.*, [1971] W.A.R. 44), and there is one good reason for this. The principal danger in an accomplice's evidence is that he will blame another to reduce his own responsibility; no such danger exists in the case of an accessory after the fact. The interest of an accessory after the fact is in establishing the innocence of the principal offender, not his guilt; any testimony as to his guilt bears the stamp of truth as being against interest. But the problem is not a simple one; Sholl, J. suggests "the possible and by no means improbable case of a witness seeking to minimize his own part in a crime, from which he cannot in the circumstances hope entirely to dissociate himself, by reducing it from that of principal or accessory before the fact to that of accessory after the fact, by falsifying or exaggerating in evidence the part played by his associates, or reversing his part and theirs" (*McNee v. Kay*, [1953] V.L.R. 520, at p. 530). The solution depends on a choice between not having a corroboration rule (on the ground that normally it will be unnecessary) or retaining a rule which sometimes produces unsatisfactory results (on the ground that it has the capacity to deal with occasional abnormal situations).

Lord Simonds' definition may be thought too narrow in not including thieves testifying at the trial of those who receive from them. As Cross points out, "there are undoubtedly cases in which it would be wrong to treat the thief as an accomplice. For example, if A and B steal something and C is charged with receiving it from B, there may be a good reason for treating B as C's accomplice at C's trial, but there would be no good reason for treating A as C's accomplice" (p. 177). But Lord Simonds did not expressly exclude thieves, and there is English authority for including them (*R. v. Crane* (1912), 7 Cr. App. Rep. 113, C.C.A.; *R. v. Reynolds* (1927), 20 Cr. App. Rep. 125, C.C.A.). In *R. v. Vernon*, [1962] Crim. L.R. 35, the Court of Criminal Appeal held that thieves were capable of being accomplices if they were participants in the crime of receiving, i.e. if they knew that the "receiver" knew the goods were stolen. This test seems a little narrow, for it can make no difference to the reliability of the thief's evidence that he knows or does not know that the receiver thinks the goods are stolen. A better test is whether the thief actually hands over the goods to the person charged with receiving; and there are authorities for the view that "the thief would be an accomplice because he is *particeps criminis* in a broad sense" (*R. v. Sneesby*, [1951] Qd. R. 26, at p. 29, *per* Philp, J.).

Wider definitions are sometimes advocated to take account of the vital factor that the witness has been involved in a series of events which the police regard seriously and which for all he knows will involve him in criminal liability. This may be reflected in Lord Simonds' definition of accomplice to include receivers because the crimes are "intimately allied in character" (*Davies v. Director of Public Prosecutions*, [1954] A.C. 378, at p. 401; [1954] 1 All E.R. 507, at p. 513, H.L.), or in the inclusion by Philp, J. of a thief as an accomplice at the receiver's trial "because he is *particeps criminis* in a broad sense" (*R. v. Sneesby*, [1951] Qd. R. 26, at p. 29).

This kind of approach has been persuasively put by Sholl, J. in *McNee v. Kay*, [1953] V.L.R. 520, at pp. 530–1. After noting that the risk underlying an accomplice's evidence was that he might blame another to curry favour with the prosecution or the court, he said:

"Such reasoning would seem to be equally applicable whether a witness who has taken part in activities which infringe the law is chargeable in connection therewith with the same offence as the accused, either as principal or as accessory, or with a different and distinct offence. The temptation to exaggerate or make false accusations would appear to be much more related to the nature and possible punishment of the offence of the witness than to its technical identity with that alleged against the accused. . . . I should consider the true principle to be that that person is an accomplice . . . who is chargeable, in relation to the same events as those founding the charge against the accused, with an offence (whether the same offence or not) of such a character, and who would be if convicted thereof liable to such punishment, as might possibly tempt that person to exaggerate or fabricate evidence as to the guilt of the accused."

In the answer to an argument that the corroboration warning rule only applied where the crime charged involved a *mens rea* to which the witness was party, Sholl, J. continued:

"If the true basis of the rule is the possible temptation to give false evidence in order to protect oneself as far as possible against the consequences of one's own infringement of the law in the course of the relevant events, it is his liability to successful prosecution, known to the witness, and existing when he gives evidence, or at least up to the time that he is offered immunity, that is material. Though in general offences to the establishment of which the proof of *mens rea* is necessary are more likely to be of a serious character, and to affect the testimony of an accomplice, common sense rejects the notion that a witness, who knows he may be convicted of an offence in relation to the same matters as found the charge against the defendant, notwithstanding that he had no *mens rea,* can never be tempted in such circumstances to falsify his evidence with a view to improving his own position."

The principal justification for this wide approach is stated by Sholl, J. to be that a narrower approach will exclude from the ambit of a warning many people who might be interested in testifying falsely against the accused; but there is another. On a narrower test, the need for a corroboration warning would vary capriciously depending on what crime was charged. If in a homicide case the accomplice's only knowledge was of intent to assault in furtherance of robbery rather than to kill, a corroboration warning would be needed on a charge of manslaughter, but not murder. That is, if the accused were convicted of a crime different from that actually charged on uncorroborated accomplice evidence without a warning, the conviction would stand on the *Davies* v. *Director of Public Prosecutions* test even though it would have to be set aside had the accused been charged with the actual offence of which he had been convicted (see *Khan* v. *R.,* [1971] W.A.R. 44, at pp. 49, 51). To put it another way, if Davies had only been charged with assault, the witness would have been an accomplice. It is odd that the accused should be worse protected when charged with murder than when charged with the less serious crime of assault.

As the Criminal Law Revision Committee have said, "there is an increasing tendency in favour of a practice that the judge should give a warning to the jury of the need for special care before convicting on the uncorroborated evidence of a witness, whether a co-accused or a witness for the prosecution, who may have some purpose of his own to serve in giving evidence against the accused, although the witness may not be an accomplice in the strict sense" (para. 183). This is commonly referred to as the doctrine in *R.* v. *Prater,* [1960] 2 Q.B. 464; [1960] I All E.R. 298, C.C.A. (and see *R.* v. *Russell* (1968), 52 Cr. App. Rep. 147, C.C.A.).

It tends to remedy various respects in which the accomplice rule is too narrow. One of them is that the evidence of *agents provocateurs* and traps falls outside it (*Sneddon* v. *Stevenson,* [1967] 2 All E.R. 1277; [1967] I W.L.R. 1051, D.C.; see [1973] Camb. L. J. 268). But such persons often have an interest of their own to serve, and a warning may be demanded by such particular circumstances as pecuniary interest, excessive zeal, the use of deceit (*R.* v. *Dowling* (1848), 3 Cox. C.C. 509, at p. 516), the trapper's poor character and record, the contradictory nature of his evidence, the unsatisfactoriness or absence of the evidence of persons allegedly accompanying him, the fact that he is a drug addict, or a probationary policeman whose promotion depends on getting convictions, or a person over whom the police have some hold if his evidence is not satisfactory to them.

Some miscellaneous points on the definition of "accomplice" should be noted. The definition of an accomplice is a matter of law. Whether a witness is capable of being an accomplice is a matter for the judge; whether he is in fact an accomplice is a matter for a properly directed jury. The burden of proof (beyond reasonable doubt) that a witness is not an accomplice rests on the Crown.

Lord Simonds said in *Davies* v. *Director of Public Prosecutions,* [1954] A.C. 378 H.L.; [1954] I All E.R. 507, H.L., that the corroboration warning need only be given when the accomplice testified for the prosecution, but the better view is thought to be that a co-accused testifying also attracts the warning (*R. v. Teitler*, [1959] V.R. 321). The dangers of self-exculpatory or spitefully motivated evidence seem even greater in the case of witnesses testifying on their own behalf than in the case of prosecution witnesses, for the fate of the latter is settled, but that of the former is still uncertain.

Evidence given by a witness who has already been convicted remains accomplice evidence (*Davies v. Director of Public Prosecutions.*, [1954] A.C. 378; [1954] 1 All E.R. 507, H.L.). The test is not whether the witness is subject to conviction at the time of testifying but whether he had become liable to prosecution as a result of the events in issue. The reason is that the accomplice's evidence at his own trial may have been tailored to inculpate the accused at the second trial, and he is likely to stick to it because of fears of a perjury charge, unpopularity with or reprisals from the police, and possible, albeit unreal, fears of further prosecutions arising from the events in question. Even if the witness has been acquitted he may be an accomplice, for the acquittal may have been wrong. In *Davies v. Director of Public Prosecutions* the witness had been acquitted of murder but he was not an accomplice because there was little evidence against him and the Crown had offered none.

The judge has a discretion not to give the corroboration warning if he thinks more harm would be done to the defence by giving it than not, for example, where the accomplice's evidence favours the accused (*R. v. Anthony*, [1962] V.R. 440; *R. v. Peach*, [1974] Crim. L.R. 245, C.A.), or where it partly favours the accused and partly injures him (*R. v. Royce-Bentley*, [1974] 2 All E.R. 347; [1974] 1 W.L.R. 535, C.A.).

One special rule that should be noted is that one accomplice cannot corroborate another (*R. v. Gay* (1909), 2 Cr. App. Rep. 327, C.C.A.). This is usually said to have been first decided in *R. v. Noakes* (1832), 5 C. & P. 326, but Littledale, J.'s judgment is obscure, and the rule against mutual corroboration has recently been disapproved by the House of Lords as regards children (*Director of Public Prosecutions v. Hester*, [1973] A.C. 297; [1972] 3 All E.R. 1056, H.L.; *Director of Public Prosecutions v. Kilbourne*, [1973] A.C. 729; [1973] 1 All E.R. 440, H.L.). Indeed in the latter case the witnesses who corroborated each other were within the third class of accomplices listed in *Davies v. Director of Public Prosecutions* [1954] A.C. 378; [1954] 1 All E.R. 507, H.L.

It is thought that the rule against mutual corroboration of accomplices, though more justifiable than such a rule generally, will not long survive. Its abolition has been recommended by the Criminal Law Revision Committee (para. 194).

The wife of an accomplice who is not called can corroborate an accomplice who does testify (*R. v. Willis*, [1916] 1 K.B. 933, C.C.A.). The wife of an accomplice may corroborate the accomplice (*R. v. Evans*, [1965] 2 Q.B. 295; [1964] 3 All E.R. 431, C.C.A., following *R. v. Tripodi* (1961), 104 C.L.R. 1 and not following *R. v. Neal and Taylor* (1835), 7 C. & P. 168); of course in many circumstances her evidence will not be very weighty because she may have an interest in supporting her husband.

Question

Why cannot accomplices corroborate each other? Do you agree with the view that "the factors rendering it dangerous to act on the evidence of children and accomplices differ. In each case there is a danger of invention, but the tendency of all accomplices is to tell the same kind of lie, i.e. one implicating the accused, while there is no reason why the over-imaginativeness of children should lead to coincidence in their untruthfulness. . . ."? (See Cross, *Evidence* (3rd ed.), p. 175.)

ii Sex cases

The rule making a corroboration warning mandatory in sex cases applies not only to offences against women but also against boys and men (*R. v. Burgess* (1956), 40 Cr. App. Rep. 144, C.C.A.). The reasons underlying the rule also apply to some extent to the procuration offences under the Sexual Offences Act 1956 and to affiliation proceedings. What are they?

Hale: Pleas of the Crown, I
Pp. 635–6

It is true, rape is a most detestable crime, and therefore ought severely and impartially to be punished with death; but it must be remembered that it is an accusation easily to be made and hard to be proved; and harder to be defended by the party accused, tho' never so innocent. . . .

[We must] be the more cautious upon trials of offences of this nature, wherein the court and jury may with so much ease be imposed upon without great care and vigilance; the heinousness of the offence many times transporting the judge and jury with so much indignation that they are over hastily carried to the conviction of the person accused thereof, by the confident testimony sometimes of malicious and false witnesses.

In *Conoway v. State* (1931), 156 S.E. 664 Russell, C.J. suggests that Hale's words should be disregarded since they "were expounded in a remote age when woman was considered but little more than a chattel, and presumed, unless she was corroborated, to have been willing to engage in sexual intercourse almost upon suggestion". Does this seem a correct account of seventeenth-century views?

Kelly v. U.S.
(1952), 194 F.2d 150

The U.S. Court of Appeals, District of Columbia Circuit considered an invitation to sodomy testified to by only a single witness.

PRETTYMAN, J.: The public has a peculiar interest in the problem before us. The alleged offence, consisting of a few spoken words, may be alleged to have occurred in any public place, where any citizen is likely to be. They may be alleged to have been whispered, or to have occurred in the course of a most casual conversation. Any citizen who answers a stranger's inquiry as to direction, or time, or a request for a dime or a match is liable to be threatened with an accusation of this sort. There is virtually no protection, except one's reputation and appearance of credibility, against an uncorroborated charge of this sort. At the same time, the results of the accusation itself are devastating to the accused. . . .

It follows that threatened accusation of this offence is the easiest of blackmail methods. . . .

. . . [T]he testimony of a single witness to a verbal invitation to sodomy should be received and considered with great caution.

Wigmore: Treatise on the Anglo-American System of Evidence
Para. 924a, 2061

1940

The unchaste (let us call it) mentality finds incidental but direct expression in the narration of imaginary sex-incidents of which the narrator is the heroine or the victim. On the surface, the narration is straightforward and convincing. The real victim, however, too often in such cases is the innocent man; for the respect and sympathy naturally felt by any tribunal for a wronged female helps to give easy credit to such a plausible tale. . . .

The modern realist movement having insisted on removing the veil of romance which enveloped all womanhood since the days of chivalry, it is now allowable for judges to look at the facts. The facts are that there exist occasionally female types of excessive or perverted sexuality, just as there are such male types; and that these are often accompanied by a testimonial plausibility which should not be taken at its face value. . . .

No judge should ever let a sex-offence charge go to the jury unless the female complainant's social history and mental make-up have been examined and testified to by a qualified physician.

. . . [A] rule of law requiring corroboration has probably little actual influence upon the jurors' minds over and above that ordinary caution and suspicion which would naturally suggest itself for such charges; and the rule thus tends to become in practice merely a means of securing from the trial judge the utterance of a form of words which may chance to be erroneous and to lay the foundation for a new trial. . . .

The fact is that, in the light of modern psychology, this technical rule of corroboration seems but a crude and childish measure, if it be relied upon as an adequate means for determining the credibility of the complaining witness. . . . The problem of estimating the veracity of feminine testimony in complaints against masculine offenders is baffling enough to the experienced psychologist. This . . . rule is unfortunate in that it tends to produce reliance upon a rule of thumb. Better to inculcate the resort to an expert scientific analysis of the particular witness' mentality, as the true measure of enlightenment.

Let us evaluate the usual arguments for and against the sex corroboration requirement. The first is that in the case of violent sexual attacks, the victim may be so overwhelmed by confusion and hysteria as to increase the chance of a wrong identification; and as we shall see, this is substantial even in normal circumstances. This is not seriously contested but it only applies as between strangers, and many sex crimes are committed between acquaintances.

Secondly, allegations of sexual crime may cause excessive sympathy for the victim among the jury. Such evidence as exists partly, but only partly, suggests this. Kalven and Zeisel (*The American Jury* (Boston 1966), pp. 249–54, 274–80) found in the cases they examined that the jury was more unwilling than the judge to convict of rape involving a single attacker with no extrinsic violence (i.e. non-aggravated rape) and where the defendant and the victim were not strangers; similarly with some forms of statutory rape and indecent exposure to adults. The jury was, however, more eager to convict for aggravated rape, indecent exposure to children, and statutory rape where the victim was young or some other fact made the crime seem more serious. Juries also tend to be lenient where the victim assumes the risk of rape by going to the accused's house or freely admitting him to hers. Rape trials are generally held before largely male juries unsympathetic to prosecutions of this particular kind and aware of the heavy penalties for the crime. It should be remembered that jury prejudice may not be the only reason for low conviction rates in non-aggravated rape and high conviction rates in aggravated rape; in aggravated rape carried out by more than one attacker, there is more likelihood of finding corroboration in the lies or admissions of each accused.

Thirdly, in affiliation cases corroboration is needed because women may have a desire "to shield their paramours or to impose burdens on some persons who are better able to bear them" (*Nichols* v. *Digney*, [1921] V.L.R. 513, at p. 515, *per* Irvine, C.J.). This is not of general application.

Fourthly, women may bring a false charge for a variety of special motives. A woman may wish to repudiate an act of which she is ashamed or which she fears will result in pregnancy with consequent criticism from her family and circle. A woman jilted by a man may revenge herself by falsely alleging rape. A false sex offence may be alleged as part of a blackmail scheme, particularly against persons who have much to lose by the revelation of sexual improprieties and ample opportunity for them, e.g. doctors and dentists. A spitefully motivated woman may allege a sex crime as the best way of destroying a man, particularly since sometimes unproved allegations are as damaging as proved ones. Thus a mother who hates a father may allege that he has committed incest with the children (*R.* v. *Phillips* (1936), 26 Cr. App. Rep. 17, C.C.A.). Then false accusations may proceed from all kinds of psychological neuroses and delusions. A woman who is frustrated and unconsciously desires sexual experience, or who is afraid of men may allege that sexual incidents happened to her. She may desire notoriety on the basis that it is better to be raped than ignored. Girls or boys passing through puberty may lie, imagine or exaggerate (*R.* v. *Gammon* (1959), 43 Cr. App. Rep. 155, at p. 159, C.C.A.). The danger here is that it is very difficult to detect when some bizarre motive of this kind is operating, and the supposed victim may have so high a social standing or so innocent-seeming an exterior as to disarm suspicion and attract sympathy (see Williams, pp. 173–8). The current improvement in the status of women is said to lessen the chance of such fantasy, but this is doubtful.

Finally, as many have followed Hale in pointing out, rape "is an accusation easily to be made and hard to be proved; and harder to be defended by the party accused, tho' never so innocent". Sexual crimes are usually alleged to have occurred in private, and they may leave no outward traces, so that proof depends on the accused's word against the accusers. This theory is probably exaggerated. Several factors discourage idle accusations of rape. The victim may feel humiliated and is often shunned as contaminated. (It is defamatory to say a woman has been raped: *Youssoupoff* v. *Metro-Goldwyn-Mayer Pictures* (1934), 50 T.L.R. 581, C.A.) The trial of a sex case is unpleasant for the complainant, with its publicity and the virtual certainty of a long and gruelling cross-examination attacking her character, following on repeated interrogations by the police. There may be a fear of retaliation by the accused and his friends. It is therefore sometimes said that if a rape is reported, the odium the victim has to bear guarantees the truth of what she says. But a woman strongly motivated by spite or fantasy may be inadvertent to or ignorant of these dangers or may feel that the odium the accused will suffer from even an unsuccessful prosecution will make her own ordeal worthwhile.

So much for the arguments in favour of the rule; we must now examine some drawbacks which are said to outweigh their merits, such as they are. First, rape is intrinsically difficult to prove, and the difficulties should not be added to by a corroboration requirement which reduces the number of reports of, and prosecutions and convictions for rape. There are unlikely to be eye-witnesses. Most rapes occur outside, so that there will not be the broken furniture or forced locks characteristic of violent indoor crime. If the victim sensibly submits to the threat of force there will be no physical injuries or torn clothing (Amir found that force was absent from 14·9 per cent of the 646 rapes he studied: *Patterns in Forcible Rape* (1971), p. 155). Since many victims douche after the assault, sperm traces will be removed. There is force in these points, but statistics do not entirely support them. One American study compared the prosecution and conviction figures for rape over the United States as a whole with those three states who have a mandatory corroboration requirement. In two of them (Georgia and Iowa) it found that both prosecutions and convictions were well above average ((1972), 81 Yale L.J. 1365, at p. 1370, n. 38). This may be explained by the fact that the police there put more energy into rape cases than others, or that fewer rapes are known to the police, or that these states have a higher than average rate of conviction for sex crimes generally or for all crimes. It may even be due to the corroboration requirement in that this focusses attention on a more careful analysis of the evidence overall, which tells against guilty accused persons (cf. Cornish, [1973] Crim. L.R. 208, at pp. 220–1). It may be that the effect of the corroboration requirement is to make accused persons as a whole worse off, though innocent accused are better off for having the facts more carefully considered by a jury directed to think about them harder as a result of the corroboration warning.

Secondly, the corroboration requirement is said to be "sexist"; since rape is committed on women, the difficulty of prosecuting the crime and hence of protecting women from it results in them being treated badly and in men rapists being treated with undue favour. But most criminals are men; is the accomplice warning rule, by making it harder for male co-accused to be convicted, therefore sexist as well?

Thirdly, it is asked whether the credibility of a victim of a violent sexual attack is so much less than that of a victim of a non-sexual attack as to justify requiring corroboration in one case but not the other. The answer is that in the case of non-sexual attacks, an optional corroboration warning may be given if identification is in issue, and such a warning may be given respecting any aspect of the facts which demands it. A mandatory warning is needed in sexual cases, however, because of the greater obscurity of the dangers they present.

A fourth objection is that there is no corroboration requirement for crimes carrying severer penalties than sex crimes. But these other crimes do not have the evidentiary dangers calling for a cautionary warning present in sex cases. Then it is said that assuming there are dangers in sex cases the really dangerous cases can be dealt with in the judge's discretion; a required warning is unnecessary. But the obscurity of sexually based unreliability is such that even a judge may be unaware of it.

Finally, it is said that the abolition of the corroboration requirement is needed as one method of controlling the increase in sex crimes. But it is very doubtful whether the rate of increase in sex crimes differs sufficiently from the rate of increase in all crimes to justify removing this established safeguard.

Wigmore made two principal attacks on the corroboration rule in sex cases which were quoted above and which are worth considering. One was that the rule did little good because the dangers were obvious; the other was that there were much better ways of checking credibility which the courts should utilize. The first point is questionable, though to some extent supported by Kalven and Zeisel's finding that the jury tends to acquit in non-violent cases if there is no corroboration. Wigmore cites certain guides as useful in estimating veracity—whether the victim made immediate complaint, whether she had prior knowledge of the accused, whether the crime occurred in a lonely place or in one to which help would quickly have come had the woman protested, whether her demeanour and consistency suggested she was telling the truth. But there are many cases where these tests might be passed and the complainant might still be lying.

Wigmore's second point was that the court should investigate the character and record of the complainant more thoroughly than is done at present. At the moment her credibility may be challenged in cross-examination; but her answers are final unless she denies prior intercourse with the accused or denies prostitution. He envisages the use of psychiatric examination. But the purpose of psychiatry is not to discover the truth, it is to cure. In any case, to be effective, the examination would have to be compulsory, and public opinion might well object to this. However a psychiatric examination can be ordered in some U.S. jurisdictions, e.g. California: *Ballard* v. *Superior Court of San Diego County* 410 (1966) P. 2d 838, at p. 849. Such a requirement would also deter victims from coming forward and adding to their ordeal even more than the current law does. The same comment might be made *a fortiori* regarding the compulsory use of truth drugs and lie detectors; in any event there are well-founded legal and scientific and indeed common-sense objections to the admissibility of evidence so obtained (*p. 9 supra*).

Some particular points

It has been said that in sexual cases where the corroboration warning has not been given the proviso to s. 2 (I) of the Criminal Appeal Act 1968 should not be applied (*R.* v. *Trigg*, [1963] I All E.R. 490; [1963] I W.L.R. 805, C.C.A.). This was a strong statement, for the facts of that case made it very suitable for the proviso. There was no question the victim had been raped; the only question was who had done it, and there was ample corroboration of the victim's identification of the accused. But the weight of *Trigg* on this point has been undercut by subsequent judicial readiness to apply the proviso in sex cases (*R.* v. *O'Reilly*, [1967] 2 Q.B. 722; [1967] 2 All E.R. 766, C.A.).

In cases where the evidence of the witness to be corroborated seems quite unlikely to suffer from the usual dangers it is more open to the jury than normal to act without corroboration, e.g. where the victim is 73 and her evidence is unlikely to be affected by hysteria or exaggeration (*R.* v. *Zielinski*, [1950] 2 All E.R. 1114 n., C.C.A.).

It has also been suggested that a jury should be readier to act on the uncorroborated evidence of a complainant than on that of an accomplice (*R.* v. *Crocker* (1922), 92 L.J.K.B., 428; [1922] All E.R. Rep. 775). This may be doubted, for the dangers in accomplice cases are far more obvious than in sex cases. In one respect there is a difference: where similar fact evidence is proved, accomplices in past acts fall within Lord Simonds' extended definition in *Davies* v. *Director of Public Prosecutions*, and hence require corroboration, but non-consensual victims of past offences do not. ''The position of a person who is supporting a charge by his evidence is . . . wholly different from the position of a person who merely comes to describe incidents, albeit incidents in every way similar to the charge, for the purpose of rebutting accident, or for any other purpose for which evidence of that kind is admissible'' (*R. v. Sanders* (1962), 46 Cr. App. Rep. 60, at p. 65). One may doubt this: there would appear in theory to be equal dangers for all sex cases. However, the law can perhaps be justified in this way. Accomplices in a number of separate cases even if they act independently will always tend to blame the accused. The danger is deliberate fabrication. But the danger with victims is generally of imagination or mistake; and large numbers of independent victims are most unlikely to be mistaken as to the accused's identity or to imagine the offence.

It is doubtful whether there is any merit in the suggestion that the child corroboration warning only applies when she is complainant rather than witness to a crime against another (*R. v. Cleal*, [1942] I All E.R. 203, at p. 205, C.C.A.; cf. *R. v. Mitchell* (1952), 36 Cr. App. Rep. 79, C.C.A.). Nor in general is there any distinction between the importance of the warning in sex cases as between children's evidence and that of adults: the dangers may be different but are equally great (*R. v. Dossi* (1918), 87 L.J.K.B. 1024, C.C.A.).

iii Sworn evidence of children

We have seen that the unsworn evidence of children *must* be corroborated; their sworn evidence requires only a corroboration warning. But why should a child's evidence be suspect?

First, a child's powers of observation and memory are less reliable than an adult's. Secondly, children are prone to live in a make-believe world, so that they magnify incidents which happen to them or invent them completely (*R. v. Dossi* (1918), 87 L.J.K.B. 1024, at p. 1026, C.C.A., *per* Atkin, J.) Thirdly, they are also very egocentric, so that details seemingly unrelated to their own world are quickly forgotten by them. Fourthly, because of their immaturity they are very suggestible and can easily be influenced both by adults and other children. One lying child may influence others to lie; anxious parents may take a child through a story again and again so that it becomes drilled in untruths. Most dangerously, a policeman taking a statement from a child may without illwill use leading questions so that the child tends to confuse what actually happened with the answer suggested implicitly by the question. A fifth danger is that children often have little notion of the duty to speak the truth, and they may fail to realize how important their evidence is in a case and how important it is for it to be accurate. Finally, children sometimes behave in a way evil beyond their years. They may consent to sexual offences against themselves and then deny consent. They may completely invent sexual offences. Some children know that the adult world regards such matters in a serious and peculiar way, and they enjoy investigating this mystery or revenging themselves by making false accusations.

In spite of its unreliability, unsworn evidence may be given in criminal cases by children who are sufficiently intelligent and understand the duty to tell the truth, and sworn evidence in civil and criminal cases by those who understand the nature of an oath. This constitutes a not entirely realistic attempt to distinguish grades of trustworthiness among children. It is thought wrong to exclude their evidence entirely, because such evidence is vital in the prosecution of many crimes, some of them serious.

The warning is mandatory, and does not depend on whether the child is an accuser (*R. v. Cleal*, [1942] 1 All E.R. 203, C.C.A.; cf. *R. v. Mitchell* (1952), 36 Cr. App. Rep. 79, C.C.A.).

The principal problem regarding the corroboration of children's evidence is whether an unsworn child can corroborate or be corroborated by a sworn child. The proviso to the Children and Young Persons Act 1933, s. 38, which permits the admission of the unsworn evidence of children in criminal cases, reads: "Provided that where evidence admitted by virtue of this section is given on behalf of the prosecution the accused shall not be liable to be convicted . . . unless that evidence is corroborated by some other material evidence. . . ." It has been held that unsworn children cannot corroborate each other (*R. v. Manser* (1934), 25 Cr. App. Rep. 18, C.C.A.); the phrase "some other material evidence" in the Children and Young Persons Act 1933, s. 38, is taken to mean evidence other than that of unsworn children. However, unsworn children can corroborate adults, and sworn children can corroborate each other (*R. v. Campbell*, [1956] 2 Q.B. 432; [1956] 2 All E.R. 272, C.C.A.). The issue of whether unsworn children can corroborate sworn children was settled in *Director of Public Prosecutions* v. *Hester*.

Director of Public Prosecutions *v.* Hester
[1973] A.C. 296; [1972] 3 All E.R. 1056, H.L.

The accused was charged with indecently assaulting a 12-year-old girl, Valerie, who testified against him on oath. Her 9-year-old sister, June, gave unsworn evidence to the same effect. The jury were directed that in law the evidence of an unsworn child could corroborate a sworn child. The Court of Appeal held this to be wrong and the Director of Public Prosecutions appealed.

LORD MORRIS OF BORTH-Y-GEST: The accumulated experience of courts of law, reflecting accepted general knowledge of the ways of the world, has shown that there are many circumstances and situations in which it is unwise to found settled conclusions on the testimony of one person alone. The reasons for this are diverse. There are some suggestions which can readily be made but which are only with more difficulty rebutted. There may in some cases be motives of self-interest, or of self-exculpation, or of vindictiveness. In some situations the straight line of truth is diverted by the influences of emotion or of hysteria or of alarm or of remorse. Sometimes it may be that owing to immaturity or perhaps to lively imaginative gifts there is no true appreciation of the gulf that separates truth from falsehood. It must, therefore, be sound policy to have rules of law or of practice which are designed to avert the peril that findings of guilt may be insecurely based. So it has come about that certain statutory enactments impose the necessity in some instances of having more than one witness before there can be a conviction. So also has it come about that in other instances the courts have given guidance in terms which have become rules. Included in such cases are those in which charges of sexual offences are made. It has long been recognized that juries should in such cases be told that there are dangers in convicting on the uncorroborated testimony of a complainant though they may convict if they are satisfied that the testimony is true. As this is no mere idle process it follows that there are no set words which must be adopted to express the warning. Rather must the good sense of the matter be expounded with clarity and in the setting of a particular case. Also included in the types of cases above referred to are those in which children are witnesses. The common sense and the common experience of men and women on a jury will guide them when they have to decide what measure of credence and dependence they should accord to evidence which they have heard.

All the rules which have been evolved are in accord with the central principle of our criminal law that a person should only be convicted of a crime if those in whose hands decision rests are sure that guilt has been established. In England it has not been laid down that such certainty ought never to be reached in dependence upon the testimony of but one witness. It has, however, been recognized that the risk or danger of a wrong decision being reached is greater in certain circumstances than in others. It is where those circumstances exist that rules based upon experience, wisdom and common sense have been introduced.

On the construction of the proviso to s. 38 (1) the further question arises whether the unsworn evidence of a child could be corroborated by the unsworn evidence of another child. The evidence of the first child would be "evidence admitted by virtue of" the section. Would the evidence of the second child (being evidence supporting that of the first and implicating the accused) be "some other material evidence" within the meaning of the proviso? It would be "other" evidence in the sense that the evidence of the second child would be other than the evidence of the first child. If the language permits of ambiguity it would seem to be more in accord with the intention of the proviso that the words "some other material evidence" should be regarded as denoting evidence other than "evidence admitted by virtue of this section". This would conform with the view which has been generally entertained. The decision in R. v. *Coyle*, [1926] N.I. 208 was to this effect.

Although it has been necessary to refer to the reports (many of them almost too brief to record statements of principle) of many decided cases, it is to those in the cases of R. v. *Manser* (1934), 25 Cr. App. Rep. 18 and R. v. *Campbell*, [1956] 2 Q.B. 432 that attention must chiefly be directed.

. . . In *Manser's* case, (1934), 25 Cr. App. Rep. 18 there was a conviction of carnal knowledge of a girl (Barbara) who was under 13 years of age. A sister of Barbara, Doris, aged nine years, gave evidence without being sworn; her evidence was substantially the only corroboration of the evidence of Barbara. One of the grounds of appeal was that there was no real corroboration of Barbara's story. It does not clearly appear from the report whether Barbara gave evidence on oath but my reading of the report leaves me with the impression that she did. On that basis the important part of the decision of the court lies in the following passage in the judgment, at pp. 20–1:

> "There is one further matter which is the most important of all and may indeed be regarded as conclusive. The story of the little child Doris, who was 9 years of age and had given evidence without taking the oath, was treated as corroborative of the evidence of the girl Barbara. Now by statute the evidence of the little child who had not been sworn was not to be accepted as evidence at all, unless it was corroborated. The argument for the prosecution is therefore an argument in a circle. Let it be granted that the evidence of Barbara has to be corroborated: it is corroborated by the evidence of Doris. She, however, also needs to be corroborated. The answer is that she is corroborated by the evidence of Barbara, and that is called 'mutual corroboration'. In truth and in fact the evidence of the girl Doris ought to have been obliterated altogether from the case, inasmuch as it was not corroborated. It clearly was not corroborated by the evidence of the girl Barbara."

It is the correctness or otherwise of the reasoning there set out that is central to the determination of the main issue in this appeal. The conviction was quashed in *Manser's* case not merely because the summing up failed sufficiently to direct the jury as to corroboration but also because (on the basis of the reasoning of the above passage) the "intrinsic evidence adduced on the part of the prosecution was deficient" (p. 21). It is to be noted that the headnote of the report was as follows:

> "Where the evidence of a young child requires corroboration as a matter of law or practice, the unsworn testimony of another child, which itself requires to be corroborated, cannot be treated as supplying the requisite corroboration."

In R. v. *Campbell*, [1956] 2 Q.B. 432; [1956] 2 All E.R. 272 there was a conviction on each one of seven counts in an indictment each one of which alleged an indecent assault on one of seven different boys under the age of 16. The seven boys, who were about 10 years of age, gave evidence. In some cases one boy gave evidence in corroboration of the evidence of another. As to four counts there was corroborative evidence given by three other children (two boys and one girl) who had not themselves been assaulted and who were not therefore involved in any of the charges. All the children gave evidence on oath. One of the chief points raised on appeal was whether the evidence of complaining children could be corroborated by the evidence of other children (being children not alleged to have been assaulted). The summing up had stressed the importance of having corroboration of the evidence of young boys and the danger of convicting in its absence though the jury had been told that if they fully appreciated the danger they could convict if they were absolutely certain that they were right in doing so.

In giving the judgment of the court dismissing the appeal, Lord Goddard, C.J. referred to R. v. *Manser* (1934), 25 Cr. App. Rep. 18 as authority for the proposition that unsworn evidence cannot be corroborated by other unsworn evidence. As I have indicated, I prefer to regard *Manser* as a case in which the evidence of Barbara was given on oath though that of Doris was not. Lord Goddard, C.J. proceeded, at p. 436:

> "Whether a child is of tender years is a matter for the good sense of the court, and though it may be difficult to decide whether a child understands the obligation of an oath, a court probably would have no difficulty in deciding whether he or she was of tender years. Where, then, such a child gives unsworn evidence, it must be corroborated by some other evidence, and we can see no reason why the corroboration should not be the evidence of another child who in the opinion of the court is capable of being sworn."

Lord Goddard, C.J. does not in this passage in terms deal with the question whether, accepting that the unsworn evidence of child A can be corroborated by the sworn evidence of child B, the corroboration of that sworn evidence of B may be found in the evidence of A.

Lord Goddard, C.J. did, however, consider the situation which arises where evidence is given by two people in circumstances where there is a danger in convicting unless the evidence is corroborated. He instanced the case of an indecent assault upon a mother in the presence of her son. He dealt with the matter thus, at p. 436:

> "It is true that for very many years the courts have always warned juries that it is dangerous to convict on the uncorroborated evidence of a child, whether of tender years or not, but so also is a similar warning given in all sexual cases. In a case where the complaining party is a grown woman the jury would be advised to look for corroboration and if the evidence is that of a child, that is, of one under the age of 14, but who in the opinion of the court can be sworn, we can find no reason for saying that such evidence could not be accepted by the jury as corroboration. To hold otherwise would mean that if a mother was indecently assaulted in the presence of her son, aged, say, 12 or 13, his evidence could not be accepted as corroboration if the jury believed him. Whether evidence that is legally admissible does corroborate is for a jury to determine. The court points out to them what can be corroboration, and then it is for the jury to decide whether it does corroborate and it is open to them to accept it or to reject it, it may be because they do not think it safe to act upon the evidence of one so young."

In my view, this passage, the principle of which I regard as acceptable, shows that the sworn evidence of A may corroborate the sworn evidence of B which may itself corroborate the sworn evidence of A. But if evidence which needs (following judicial utterances) to be corroborated can be corroborated by evidence which itself (for comparable reasons) needs to be corroborated so that each one of two witnesses may corroborate the other the question may be asked why the legally admitted but unsworn evidence of child A should not corroborate the legally admitted but unsworn evidence of child B and vice versa. The answer to that question must be found by considering the wording of the proviso to s. 38 (1)—a matter to which I have referred above. In the case of an accomplice who gives sworn evidence it must be accepted that there are special reasons which have guided the laying down of certain rules such as those in *Davies* v. *Director of Public Prosecutions,* [1954] A.C. 378; [1954] 1 All E.R. 507. I do not find it necessary to discuss those rules.

Though in *Campbell's* case, [1956] 2 Q.B. 432 the court was dealing with a case where only sworn evidence was given, it was expressly stated that the court was endeavouring to deal comprehensively with the evidence of children. At the end of the judgment, at p. 438, Lord Goddard, C.J. summed up the conclusions of the court. They may be stated as follows: (*a*) The unsworn evidence of a child must be corroborated by sworn evidence; if, then, the only evidence implicating the accused is that of unsworn children the judge must stop the case. (*b*) It makes no difference whether the child's evidence relates to an assault on himself or herself or to any other charge, for example, where an unsworn child says that he saw the accused person steal an article. (*c*) The sworn evidence of a child need not as a matter of law be corroborated, but a jury should be warned, not that they must find corroboration, but that there is a risk in acting on the uncorroborated evidence of young boys or girls though they may do so if convinced that the witness is telling the truth. (*d*) Such warning should also be given where a young boy or girl is called to corroborate the evidence either of another child whether sworn or unsworn or of an adult. (*e*) As the statute which permits a child of tender years to give unsworn evidence expressly provides for such evidence being given in any proceeding against any person for any offence, the unsworn evidence of a child can be given to corroborate the evidence of another person given on oath but in such case a particularly careful warning should be given.

Subject to my comment as to the last of these I consider that they correctly summarize the law. It is no part of our present province to express any opinion as to whether the law could be improved or should be altered. Nor does any question arise for discussion as to the nature of corroboration or its definition. By the wording of the proviso the unsworn evidence of a child of tender years must (before the accused is liable to be convicted) be "corroborated by some other material evidence in support thereof implicating" the accused. If the jury in the present case were prepared to accept the evidence of June that she saw the accused assault Valerie it could not be doubted that such evidence corroborated that of Valerie that she was assaulted by the accused: nor *per contra* could it be doubted that the evidence of Valerie corroborated that of June. The wording of the proviso to s. 38 (1) was, therefore, satisfied inasmuch as the evidence of June which was admitted by virtue of the section was corroborated by the evidence of Valerie which was not admitted by virtue of the section and was evidence in support of the evidence of June and was evidence which implicated the accused.

In my view, the discussion in *Campbell's* case, [1956] 2 Q.B. 432; [1956] 2 All E.R. 272 does not fully cover the point under consideration. I accept, as set out under (*e*) above, that unsworn evidence may be given to corroborate sworn evidence but, as the problem did not arise in *Campbell's* case, the court did not go on to consider the necessity for and the nature of the corroboration of the unsworn evidence itself. There was in *Campbell's* case no analysis or testing of the reasoning in *Manser's* case, (1934), 25 Cr. App. Rep. 18. It is to that that I now turn. I have quoted above the relevant words in the judgment of the court. On the basis that in that case the girl Barbara gave evidence on oath then the wording of the judgment if it were applied to the present case would be as follows: "Now by statute the evidence of the little girl who had not been sworn was not to be accepted as evidence at all, unless it was corroborated. The argument for the prosecution is therefore an argument in a circle. Let it be granted that the evidence of Valerie has to be corroborated: it is corroborated by the evidence of June. She, however, also needs to be corroborated. The answer is that she is corroborated by the evidence of Valerie, and that is called 'mutual corroboration'. In truth and in fact the evidence of the girl June ought to have been obliterated altogether from the case, inasmuch as it was not corroborated. It clearly was not corroborated by the evidence of the girl Valerie." But why, I ask, is this an argument in a circle? If child A gives evidence and says "I was assaulted by X" and if child B gives evidence and says "I saw X assault A" I would have thought that each corroborates the other. Each gives evidence implicating X. The evidence of each one is parallel with the evidence of the other. The evidence of A of having been assaulted by X is confirmed by the evidence of B of having seen X assault A. The evidence of B of having seen X assault A is confirmed by the evidence of A of having been assaulted by X. One of the elements supplied by corroborative evidence is that there are two witnesses rather than one. The weight of the evidence is for the jury—in cases where there is a trial by jury. It is for the jury to decide whether witnesses are creditworthy. If a witness is not, then the testimony of the witness must be rejected. The essence of corroborative evidence is that one creditworthy witness confirms what another creditworthy witness has said. Any risk of the conviction of an innocent person is lessened if conviction is based upon the testimony of more than one acceptable witness. Corroborative evidence in the sense of some other material evidence in support implicating the accused furnishes a safeguard which makes a conclusion more sure than it would be without such evidence. But to rule it out on the basis that there is some mutuality between that which confirms and that which is confirmed would be to rule it out because of its essential nature and indeed because of its virtue. The purpose of corroboration is not to give validity or credence to evidence which is deficient or suspect or incredible but only to confirm and support that which as evidence is sufficient and satisfactory and credible: and corroborative evidence will only fill its role if it itself is completely credible evidence. All of this emphasizes the importance of directing a jury that the evidence of children must be examined with special care. The need for such special care is manifest where vital issues fall to be determined only on the evidence of children.

If, then, the court, being satisfied that the requirements of s. 38 (1) are met, allows child A to give evidence not on oath and if child A gives evidence of having been assaulted by X there could be no conviction of X unless the evidence of A is corroborated by some other material evidence in support of it implicating X. If child B gives sworn testimony of having seen X assault A then I see no reason why there could not be a conviction. The weight to be given to the evidence of A and of B would be for the jury and undoubtedly a judge would have to warn a jury that they should consider the evidence of A and of B (both being children) with great care. If, however, the jury was satisfied that both A and B were telling the truth then there could be a conviction. This view was presumably adopted as long ago as 1932 in R. v. *Gregg* (1932), 24 Cr. App. Rep. 13. The accused was charged with indecently assaulting a girl aged 7 whose evidence was admitted without her being sworn. A girl aged 9 gave evidence on oath of having witnessed the indecent assault. At the trial the recorder omitted to tell the jury that by law the unsworn evidence of the child aged 7 required corroboration. The accused was convicted. His appeal was dismissed on the ground that there was corroboration of the unsworn evidence and that though the summing up was defective no injustice had been done.

If child A gave sworn evidence of having been assaulted by X then only if the jury, after having applied their minds to a proper warning, were absolutely sure could there be a conviction in the absence of the support of corroborative evidence. If child B was allowed to give evidence, not on oath, of having seen X assault A there could, in my view, be a conviction if the jury, regarding the evidence of A and of B with great care, were satisfied that each was telling the truth. It was argued that this conclusion would lead to the result that A would be corroborating himself. The argument is, in my view, fallacious. If A and B were independent of each other then clearly what B said would be separate from and independent of what was said by A. If A and B were not independent of each other either for the reason that they had agreed together to concoct a story or for some other reason such as that they had (though with no wrong motive) closely collaborated then their evidence would be either discredited or of little value. Any warning to a jury of the need to examine the evidence of children with care would no doubt in a suitable case include mention of any circumstances affecting the independence of their testimony. But as to this no general rule could be laid down. According to the infinite variety of differing sets of circumstances a judge would exercise his judgment as to the style and language of the guidance that it would be helpful and wise for him to give.

LORD DIPLOCK: Whereas at common law the jury if given adequate warning were entitled to convict upon the uncorroborated evidence of witnesses in the suspect categories, [s. 38 (1)] imposes an absolute prohibition upon conviction on the uncorroborated evidence of an unsworn child. Secondly, it expressly excludes as a permissible source of such corroboration the evidence of any other unsworn child.

In this latter respect it presents an analogy with the common law rule as to accomplices who are participes criminis in the actual offence charged. The practice of giving the warning as to the desirability of confirmation from another source when more than one accomplice gave evidence implicating the accused seems to have originated in the opinion expressed by Littledale, J. in his summing up in R. v. *Noakes* (1832), 5 C. & P. 326. It appears to have been based upon reason—though Littledale, J. himself gave none—rather than upon precedent which at that date had been confined to the evidence of a single accomplice. There is a continuing logical basis for the practice, for the reason which makes one accomplice a suspect witness, *viz.*, the natural temptation to exculpate himself or to minimize the part which he played in a common crime, applies also to any other accomplice in the same crime, and there is every reason for them to concert together to tell the same false story. But there was in 1832 a possible further justification which no longer subsists. The accused himself was not a competent witness and so was debarred from giving evidence to contradict that of any accomplices as to matters which might well be known only to him and them. Furthermore, had they too been charged in the same indictment, as, being accomplices, they might have been, they too would have been incompetent to give evidence. Common fairness, with which the judges sought to mitigate the rigour of the law which debarred the accused from giving evidence in his own defence, may well have influenced Littledale, J. and those who subsequently adopted the same practice to limit the advantage which the prosecution could obtain by choosing not to arraign accomplices in the same indictment as the accused.

This practice, as well as that relating to a single accomplice, was accepted as "virtually equivalent to a rule of law", in R. v. *Baskerville,* [1916] 2 K.B. 658, at p. 663. I would not wish to question it today, for although the possible historical justification for it has vanished the logical reason for it still remains. But the same reason does not apply where the reason for regarding each of the witnesses as suspect is different or, although the same, is not one which makes it likely that they will concert together to tell the same false story. There is no case in the books to support the practice of treating the evidence of one suspect witness as incapable in law of corroborating the evidence of another, except where both suspect witnesses are accomplices in the strict sense of being participes criminis with the accused in the crime with which he is charged. R. v. *Campbell,* [1956] 2 Q.B. 432; [1956] 2 All E.R. 272 is direct authority to the contrary.

I conclude, therefore, that there is not now, and a fortiori was not in 1885, any common law rule *of general application* that evidence of a witness which is itself suspect for a reason which calls for a warning of the danger of convicting on it unless it is corroborated is incapable in law of amounting to corroboration of the evidence of another witness whose evidence is also suspect for the same or any other reason which calls for a similar warning. It is, in my view, impossible to infer that Parliament, which expressly provided that the evidence of one unsworn child must be corroborated by some evidence other than that of another unsworn child before the jury could convict upon it, intended by an implication so clear that it goes without saying—for there are no words in the proviso which suggest it—to impose a further but unexpressed limitation upon the power of the jury to rely upon the evidence of an unsworn child in support of a conviction.

I would be content to say that there were a number of features of the case which in combination make it unsafe to allow the conviction to stand. There is one, however, which I would single out for comment, *viz*., the nature of summing up on the question of corroboration, for this I believe to be a frequent source of bewilderment to juries in cases of this kind.

To say this is no reproach to the learned deputy chairman. There is scarcely a phrase in his statement to the jury of the law upon this topic which has not at some time or other received the blessing of the Court of Criminal Appeal or the Court of Appeal. As is so often the practice even of very experienced judges in these cases, he followed the course of treating the jury to a general exposition of the law as to the corroboration of the evidence of children using for that purpose a succession of verbal formulae culled from decisions of appellate courts and hallowed by usage.

My Lords, to incorporate in the summing up a general disquisition upon the law of corroboration in the sort of language used by lawyers may make the summing up immune to appeal upon a point of law, but it is calculated to confuse a jury of laymen and, if it does not pass so far over their heads that when they reach the jury room they simply rely upon their native common sense, may, I believe, as respects the weight to be attached to evidence requiring corroboration, have the contrary effect to a sensible warning couched in ordinary language directed to the facts of the particular case.

Only too often the sort of direction given to the jury is to tell them at the outset that they must not convict unless they are satisfied beyond reasonable doubt by the evidence put before them that the accused is guilty of the offence with which he is charged. Then, as respects the unsworn evidence of a young child tendered by the prosecution, they are instructed that they are prohibited by statute from paying any regard to that evidence unless it is corroborated by some other evidence, and one of the *Baskerville* formulae—for there are several in that judgment (R. v. *Baskerville,* [1916] 2 K.B. 658)— is used to explain what "corroboration" means. Next they are told that it is for the judge to say whether there is other evidence *capable* of amounting to corroboration of the child's evidence and their attention is drawn to the evidence which falls within this category, but they are then told that it is for the jury, not the judge, to decide whether that evidence *does* amount to corroboration and that only if they do so decide are they entitled to pay any regard to the unsworn child's evidence in deciding to convict.

These complicated formulae about the concept of corroboration and the respective functions of judge and jury are, I believe, unintelligible to the ordinary laymen, even where only one witness whose evidence calls for corroboration is involved. But where the sworn evidence of a young child is tendered by the prosecution in the same case as that of an unsworn child the jury are told that the law as respects the sworn evidence is different. The judge, they are informed, is required by law to give them a solemn warning that it is dangerous to convict upon the sworn child's evidence unless it is corroborated, but that if, bearing in mind that warning, they are nevertheless convinced that the child is telling the truth they *are* entitled to convict upon that evidence alone.

It is common practice to sum up upon these lines and one cannot blame the deputy chairman for following that practice in the instant appeal. It contains no statement of the law that is incorrect but it is seldom of any assistance to the jury in any case, and in a case such as your Lordships are now reviewing where the only evidence inculpating the accused is that of two young children, one sworn and one unsworn, both of whom tell substantially identical stories either of which, if accepted, proves that the accused was guilty of the offence charged, a summing up on these conventional lines must positively bemuse the jury.

My Lords, if a summing up is to perform its proper function in a criminal trial by jury it should not contain a general disquisition on the law of corroboration couched in lawyer's language but should be tailored to the particular circumstances of the case.

It would be highly dangerous to suppose that there is any such thing as a model summing up appropriate to all cases of this kind. No doubt if there is unsupported evidence on oath of a child complainant fit to be left to the jury the judge should tell them that it is open to them to convict upon her evidence alone, though he should remind them forcibly of the danger of doing so. But there is no need for him to tell them of what kind of evidence *could* amount to corroboration of her story if in fact there is none at all.

LORDS DILHORNE, PEARSON and CROSS agreed.

Further reading

Tapper
(1973), 36 M.L.R. 541.

Question

Do you agree with the interpretation of s. 38 of the Children and Young Persons Act 1933 as a matter of statutory construction? Bearing in mind the difference between the tests for sworn and unsworn evidence, how much more unreliable do you think two unsworn children are compared to two sworn?

C. The discretion to warn

i Identification

It is convenient to discuss problems of identification evidence generally before turning to the corroboration rules.

Since an identification of the accused by a witness while he is in the dock is of only trifling value (*R. v. Cartwright* (1914), 10 Cr. App. Rep. 219, C.C.A.), it is common for evidence to be admitted of prior acts of identification of the accused. This evidence may be primary, i.e. proceeding from the identifier, or secondary, as where another witness testifies to the first's act of identification. One unresolved problem is whether the first witness must testify to his prior act of identification before the second witness can say he saw it. The problem arose in *R. v. Christie*, [1914] A.C. 545; [1914–15] All E.R. Rep. 63, H.L. where a boy gave evidence that he had been assaulted, identified the accused in court, but failed to mention an act of prior identification which was then sworn to by his mother and a policeman. The House of Lords held that their evidence was admissible as part of an admission by the accused, but there was a disagreement on the point under consideration. Lords Atkinson and Parker thought the evidence admissible. This is justifiable on grounds of common sense—it is important that evidence increasing faith in the boy's consistency should be put before the jury—and by analogy with other evidence admitted to show consistency, such as a complaint in a sexual case or a previous statement admitted in answer to a suggestion of recent fabrication. Statements of these kinds can be proved by a non-maker even though the maker did not mention them while testifying. Lord Moulton and Viscount Haldane, L.C. held the evidence inadmissible on the basis that it was secondary evidence where primary evidence was available. This seems a rather formalistic point, and there is South African authority for the first view (*R. v. Rassool* 1932 N.P.D. 112, at p. 124) which has also been adopted by the English Court of Appeal (*R. v. Osbourne*, [1973] Q.B. 678 [1973] 1 All E.R. 649, C.A.). Further, as Lord Atkinson said (p. 554), there was no violation of "the rule that the best evidence must be given. His [the boy's] evidence of what he did was no better in that sense than was their evidence as to what they saw him do.''

It would seem clear that in these circumstances if the identifying witness in fact fails to testify or to identify the accused in court proof of prior identification is impossible unless another ground for admission is found. It would be hearsay and there would be no relevant testimony of the identifying witness on which consistency could be shown.

It is improper to show the witness the accused alone or almost alone and ask "Is that the man?" (*R. v. Chapman* (1911), 7 Cr. App. Rep. 53, C.C.A.; *R. v. Cartwright* (1914), 10 Cr. App. Rep. 219, C.C.A.; *Davies v. R.* (1937), 57 C.L.R. 170). There is an obvious danger of the identification simply being based on the witness's assumption that the police have got the correct person. A conviction can be quashed if the accused is pointed out to the witness by the police before an identification parade (*R. v. Dickman* (1910), 5 Cr. App. Rep. 135, C.C.A.; *R. v. Bundy* (1910), 5 Cr. App. Rep. 270, C.C.A.).

If a witness is shown only a photograph before the arrest and identifies the accused from it, his later identification of the same person at a parade is inadmissible; it is otherwise if a series of photographs is shown (*R. v. Dwyer*, [1925] 2 K.B. 799, C.C.A.; [1924] All E.R. Rep. 272). It is also improper, and a ground for quashing any conviction, for the police to show a suspect's photograph *after* arrest to a witness before the identification parade (*R. v. Haslam* (1925), 19 Cr. App. Rep. 59, C.C.A.; *R. v. Seiga* (1961), 45 Cr. App. Rep. 220, C.C.A.).

What corroboration rule applies?

In *R. v. Williams*, [1956] Crim. L.R. 833 the Court of Criminal Appeal held that there was no obligation to warn of the danger of convicting on evidence of identification without corroboration; see also *R. v. Long* (1973), 57 Cr. App. Rep. 871, C.A. In *Arthurs v. A.–G. for Northern Ireland* (1971), 55 Cr. App. Rep. 161, the House of Lords left the question open in cases where the accused was not known to the witness. The following judgment is often commended as an ideal towards which English law should move.

The People v. Casey (No. 2)
[1963] I.R. 33

The conviction depended on an identification by two witnesses, both previously unacquainted with the accused. The Eire Supreme Court ordered a new trial.

KINGSMILL MOORE, J.: The category of circumstances and special types of case which call for special directions and warnings from the trial judge cannot be considered as closed. Increased judicial experience, and indeed further psychological research, may extend it. . . .

We are of opinion that juries . . . may not be fully aware of the dangers involved in visual identification nor of the considerable number of cases in which such identification has been proved to be erroneous; and also that they may be inclined to attribute too much probative effect to the test of an identification parade. In our opinion it is desirable that in all cases, where the verdict depends substantially on the correctness of an identification, their attention should be called in general terms to the fact that in a number of instances such identification has proved erroneous, to the possibilities of mistake in the case before them and to the necessity of caution. Nor do we think that such warning should be confined to cases where the identification is that of only one witness. Experience has shown that mistakes can occur where two or more witnesses have made positive identifications. . . .

[See also *Craig* v. *R.* (1933), 49 C.L.R. 429, at p. 449, *per* Evatt and McTiernan, JJ.; *Davies* v. *R.* (1937), 57 C.L.R. 170, at p. 182; *R.* v. *Preston*, [1961] V.R. 761; *R.* v. *Gaunt*, [1964] N.S.W.R. 864; *R.* v. *Boardman*, [1969] V.R. 151.]

Williams: The Proof of Guilt
[3rd Edn. Pp. 88, 109–10, 113, 120–2

[This experiment took place at the London School of Economics.] There was an altercation between an Englishman and a Welshman; each drew weapons and the Englishman "shot" the Welshman. When members of the audience were examined as to what had happened, they said that the Welshman had brandished his weapon first, whereas in actual fact both drew weapons at the same time. The reason for the mistake was that at the dramatic moment . . . all eyes were on the Welshman. . . .

In the experiment at the London School of Economics nine members of the audience were asked to try and identify the two actors at an identification parade held a week after the event. The parade consisted of thirteen persons. Only two students out of the nine were able to identify the Englishman and only four were able to identify the Welshman. The rest with varying degrees of assurance identified completely innocent men. Two innocent men were identified twice.

. . . Identification seems to be a matter on which personal pride has a strong effect: the witness often resents it when his ability to recognize someone is questioned. The women who identified Beck [a notorious victim of mistaken identification] became more sure of their identification under cross-examination. . . .

There is reason to suppose that persons continue to be falsely convicted as the result of identification parades. Juries are still given no adequate instruction on the limitations of these parades. It is the experience of the police that of the majority of such parades the witness picks out nobody, or the "wrong" man. If a witness fails in this way he may not be called at the trial, his evidence being useless. . . . It will be obvious that this fact seriously discounts the probative value of a positive identification. . . . [T]he danger of the identification parade is that the witness expects to find the guilty person present, and therefore points to the man who he thinks is most like the one he remembers. Thus all that an identification parade can really be said to establish is that the accused resembled the criminal more closely than any other members of the parade did, which is not saying very much. . . .

. . . If the witness "identifies" [a police photograph] as being that of the culprit, the person whose photograph is thus picked out is likely to be arrested . . .; he will be put in an identification parade, where he will again be "identified" by the witness; . . . at the trial evidence may be given that the witness identified him at the parade.

. . . When the witness is shown the photographs, he is likely to pick on the face that best accords with his recollection of the culprit. Thereafter, his recollection of the culprit and recollection of the photograph are likely to be so merged that he can no longer separate them. . . .

Hoffmann: The South African Law of Evidence
2nd Edn., Pp. 437–41

The accuracy of a witness's observation depends first, of course, upon his eyesight. Secondly, it will be affected by the circumstances in which he saw the person in question; the state of the light, how far away he was, whether he was able to see him from an advantageous position, how long he had him under observation. Thirdly, impressions of appearance may be distorted by the witness's prejudices and preconceptions. He may expect people who behave in a particular way or belong to a certain class to have some physical characteristic, which he will ascribe to such a person without having verified his belief by observation. Fourthly, his ability to form an accurate impression will be affected by his state of mind. Did he have any reason to take particular notice, or was his attention concentrated upon something else? Did he really see who was there, or did he think he was seeing the person whom he expected to be there? Was he in a state of mind to make a trustworthy observation of anything?... Fifthly, the distinctiveness of the person's appearance. The court will be able to observe whether the accused has any peculiar features, but some people look distinctive to one witness and not to another. Thus to a person of one race, everyone belonging to another race tends to look alike, and to a lesser extent the same is true of different age-groups. On the other hand, a person well known to the witness may register a distinctive impression even though the witness is unable to mention any peculiar features. . . .

[Recollection] depends, first, upon the strength of the witness's memory. Very young and very old people tend to forget more easily than others. Secondly, the nature of the original impression; for example, whether it was accompanied by any unusual incident which made it likely that the witness's impression would be preserved. Striking features are more likely to be remembered than ordinary ones, and if the person in question was known to the witness, he will be able to preserve the short-hand recollection "I saw X" better than he would remember X's individual features. The time-lag is of course important, and perhaps most crucial of all is the extent to which the witness's original impression had been overlaid by subsequent suggestion and imagination. If a witness is shown a person who is alleged to have been the criminal, he is very likely to make a subconscious substitution of that person's features for those which he actually observed. The more he sees of the accused, the more certain he will become that he is the person whom he actually saw. The same process can happen if the witness is shown a photograph of the accused, or if it is suggested to him that the person whom he saw had certain features. It is because the possibility of suggestion seriously diminishes the value of identification evidence that the courts have insisted upon the holding of identification parades subject to stringent precautions. [Convictions may be set] aside because, instead of holding an identification parade, the police . . . simply [take] the accused to the sole identifying witness and [ask] him whether he was [is] the right man. Evidence of identification in such circumstances can have very little value. The same may be said of the usual question "Do you see the man in court?" The witness would look very silly if he pointed to anywhere other than the dock. . . .

. . . An identification witness should be asked to give a detailed description of the alleged criminal at the earliest possible moment. If there is a delay he is not only likely to forget but may have an opportunity to compare notes with other witnesses, which would diminish the value of his evidence. For the same reasons, an identification parade should be held as soon as possible.

The procedure for the conduct of the parade is largely a matter of police practice, but judges have occasionally suggested rules which should be observed if the accused is not to be prejudiced and the parade is to have maximum probative value. The cardinal principle is fairness to the accused. . . .

The parade should consist of at least eight people who are similar to the accused in general appearance. In particular, the accused should not be dressed differently from the others or have any distinctive features which would inevitably attract attention. . . . Care should be taken that the witness does not see the accused in custody before the parade, or while the parade is being formed. Courts have commented adversely upon witnesses being put into a room with a window through which they might have seen the parade. . . . The prosecution should also eliminate, as far as possible, the chance that someone may have told the witness which man to pick out. It is therefore undesirable that the officer investigating the case should also take charge of the parade, and the person who conducts the witness to the place where the parade is held should not have seen it being formed or know who the accused is.

If there are several witnesses, they should be segregated or kept under supervision before the parade to prevent them from comparing notes about the criminal's appearance, and a witness who has completed his identification should not be allowed to rejoin the others.

... [T]he witness may think that the police are unlikely to have held a parade unless it contains someone whom they suspect. Another possible solution is to hold a "blank parade" before or after the one which includes the accused, the witness being told that more than one parades will be held.

If the witness fails to identify anyone, or picks out someone other than the accused, the prosecution should disclose this fact in evidence. ...

Circumstantial evidence of identity may be provided by any characteristic which the person before the court and the person to be identified are shown to have in common. Traces left behind, such as fingerprints, footprints and palm prints are commonly used to provide circumstantial evidence of identification. ...

Craig v. R.
(1933), 49 C.L.R. 429

EVATT and McTIERNAN, JJ.: An honest witness who says, "The prisoner is the man who drove the car," while appearing to affirm a simple, clear and impressive proposition, is really asserting:

(1) that he observed the driver,
(2) that the observation became impressed on his mind,
(3) that he still retains the original impression,
(4) that such impression has not been affected, altered, or replaced by published portraits of the prisoner, and
(5) that the resemblance between the original impression and the prisoner is sufficient to base a judgment, not of resemblance but of identity.

Further reading

Williams, [1955] Crim. L.R. 525 and *The Proof of Guilt* pp. 106–24; Williams and Hammelmann, [1963] Crim. L.R. 479, 545; 11th Report of the Criminal Law Revision Committee, paras. 196–203; Best, pp. 495–503; Rolph, *Personal Identity* (London, 1957), Chaps. 3, 6, 7 and 8.

Questions

1. If a man was picked out by more than one witness at an identification parade, how much more reliable would this make the conclusion that he was guilty?

2. Would you favour permitting the defence to call witnesses who failed to identify the accused?

ii *Other cases*

There are a number of other cases probably to be grouped with identification. These are claims against deceased estates and proof of matrimonial offences. It is difficult to say a warning is required here, since these cases are almost invariably tried without a jury; the rule is better formulated by saying the court will normally require corroboration though it is entitled to reach a conclusion without it. The reason for the rule in the case of deceased estates is the risk of false claims and in the case of matrimonial offences the serious consequences for the parties and their children as well as the extreme unreliability of one spouse's evidence alone. The matrimonial offences rule may fade away under the new English divorce law where the issue is the broad one of matrimonial "breakdown" rather than the narrow one of specific offences. Further, an Australian court has held that the public interest in marriage has changed from the later nineteenth century. Then it was a union for life to be dissolved only for limited reasons. The greater width of the grounds for divorce means its importance is less; so no corroboration rule need apply (*Hutton* v. *Hutton* (1972) 18 F.L.R. 228).

On deceased estates, see *Re Garnett, Gandy* v. *Macaulay* (1885), 31 Ch. D. 1, C.A.; *Re Hodgson*; *Beckett* v. *Ransdale* (1885), 31 Ch. D. 177, C.A.; [1881–5] All E.R. Rep. 931

Galler v. Galler
[1954] P. 252; [1954] 1 All E.R. 536, C.A.

The issue was whether adultery had been committed. The Court of Appeal held that the non-spouse's evidence should have attracted a corroboration warning.

HODSON, L.J.: [J]uries are to be directed that it is unsafe to act on uncorroborated evidence of this nature, although they are at liberty to do so if they feel sure. . . .

It has been my experience that, when evidence of this kind is given in divorce cases, it is treated with the caution which I have described for . . . the obvious reason that a charge of this kind is particularly difficult to rebut. Any man who is in the position of being alone in a house with or without children may have a nurse to look after the children or a housekeeper to look after him, and if that person chooses to make an accusation of this kind against him, it is a matter which he must find very difficult to deny by any affirmative evidence other than his own. A person who is making the accusation is putting forward her own wrongdoing and is in the same kind of position as that of an accomplice. . . .

Alli v. Alli
[1965] 3 All E.R. 480

SIR JOCELYN SIMON, P.: [There are] two classes of case. In the first—those alleging sexual misconduct and those where the evidence of adultery is that of a willing participant—experience has shown that there is such an exceptional risk of a miscarriage of justice unless the court has in mind the danger of acting on uncorroborated evidence that an appellate court will intervene unless the trial court has expressly warned itself of that danger. However, in other classes of case, the risk is less acute and the absence of an express indication that the desirability of corroboration was in mind will not of itself call for the intervention of the appellate court; though no doubt such absence may, together with other matters, convince the appellate court that the trial court must have proceeded oblivious of the rules of practice to which we have referred, and that it would not be safe to let the decision stand.

Do confessions require corroboration? After some disputes in the nineteenth century, the modern position seems to be that it is open to a jury to convict on an uncorroborated confession (see *R.* v. *Sullivan* (1887), 16 Cox 347, following *R.* v. *Unkles* (1874) I.R. & C.L. 50). However, circumstances may make a warning prudent. A case where the circumstances justified the warning which was in fact given is *R.* v. *Sykes* (1913), 8 Cr. App. Rep. 233, at p. 237, C.C.A., where "the murder was the talk of the countryside, and it might well be that a man under the influence of insanity or a morbid desire for notoriety would accuse himself of such a crime". But it is probably only in an extreme case that an appeal for want of the warning would succeed; a case, in fact, where an appeal on the ground that the verdict was against the weight of the evidence would also succeed. In America there is a fixed rule that corroboration is necessary, but this extension seems mistaken. It is wrong to elevate the common-sense consideration that in some circumstances an uncorroborated confession should be scrutinized cautiously into a rule of law requiring either actual corroboration or a universal corroboration warning. In practice it will be rare that the only evidence of guilt is a confession. In many cases the police will not prosecute because such confessions may be false (Chap. 8, *post*).

In general it may be said that there is no closed list of situations where a corroboration warning may be desirable and in any case where the facts justify it a suitable warning should be given.

III WHAT IS CORROBORATION?

A. General

Three views have struggled for recognition. One extreme view is that corroboration is independent evidence tending to verify any part of the suspect testimony. This was favoured by Joy, C.B.; his book, from which quotation is made below, was conceived as an attempt to reverse a trend apparent in his time towards the corroboration rules becoming more rigid. At the other extreme, there is the view that corroboration should amount to independent evidence of the whole of the suspect testimony. This has not been favoured since *R. v. Mullins* (1848), 3 Cox C.C. 526, for if the other testimony corroborated every part of the suspect testimony, the latter would be quite unnecessary. The middle view favoured by the courts since *R. v. Baskerville*, [1916] 2 K.B. 658; [1916–17] All E.R. Rep. 38, C.C.A. is that corroboration should not only show that some part of the suspect testimony is true, but also that it tends to prove the fact in issue. For example, in accomplice cases corroboration should be evidence implicating the accused. Joy, C.B.'s view was rejected as involving too much risk that a guilty man, knowing the details of the crime, could plausibly blame an innocent man.

Chief Baron Joy: Evidence of Accomplices
P. 8 (Wigmore, para. 2059)

The defect in the evidence is not in its *quantity,* but in its *quality.* The witness swearing directly to the prisoner's guilt, that guilt is established if the witness be credible. What, therefore, is required is to throw something, no matter of what nature, into the opposite scale, which will serve as a counterpoise to the impeachment of the witness' credit arising from the character in which he appears; something that will improve the *quality* of the proof which has been given by the accomplice; and *that* something may be anything which induces a rational belief in the mind of the jury that the narrative of the accomplice is in all respects a correct one.

R. v. Tidd
(1820) 33 State. Tr. 1483

GARROW, B.: [I]t may not be unfit to observe . . . that the confirmation to be derived to an accomplice, is not a repetition by others of the whole story of the accomplice and a confirmation of every part of it, that would be either impossible or unnecessary and absurd. . . .

R. v. Farler
(1837), 8 C. & P. 106

LORD ABINGER, C.B.: [C]orroboration ought to consist in some circumstance that affects the identity of the party accused. A man who has been guilty of a crime himself will always be able to relate the facts of the case, and if the confirmation be only on the truth of that history, without identifying the persons, that is really no corroboration at all. If a man was to break open a house and put a knife to your throat, and steal your property, it would be no corroboration that he had stated all the facts correctly, that he had described how the person did put a knife to the throat and did steal the property. It would not at all tend to shew that the party accused participated in it.

R. v. Birkett
(1839), 8 C. & P. 732

The accused was charged with receiving a stolen sheep. One of the thieves testified that the other thief gave the sheep to the accused. Patteson, J. ruled that there was sufficient evidence of corroboration to be left to the jury.

PATTESON, J.: If the confirmation had merely gone to the extent of confirming the accomplice as to matters connected with himself only, it would not have been sufficient. For example, the finding of the skins at the place at which the accomplice said they were would have been no sufficient confirmation of the evidence against the prisoner, because the witness might have put the skins there himself; but here we have a great deal more; we have a quantity of mutton found in the house in which the prisoner resides, and that I think is such a confirmation of the accomplice's evidence as I must leave to the jury.

R. v. Baskerville
[1916] 2 K.B. 658; [1916–17] All E.R. 38, C.C.A.

LORD READING, C.J.: [T]he better opinion of the law upon this point is that stated in R. v. *Stubbs* (1855), Dears. 555 by Parke, B., namely, that the evidence of an accomplice must be confirmed not only as to the circumstances of the crime, but also as to the identity of the prisoner. The learned Baron does not mean that there must be confirmation of all the circumstances of the crime; as we have already stated, that is unnecessary. It is sufficient if there is confirmation as to a material circumstance of the crime and of the identity of the accused in relation to the crime. Parke, B. gave this opinion as a result of twenty-five years' practice; it was accepted by the other judges, and has been much relied upon in later cases. . . .

We hold that evidence in corroboration must be independent testimony which affects the accused by connecting or tending to connect him with the crime. In other words, it must be evidence which implicates him, that is, which confirms in some material particular not only the evidence that the crime has been committed, but also that the prisoner committed it. The test applicable to determine the nature and extent of the corroboration is thus the same whether the case falls within the rule of practice at common law or within that class of offences for which corroboration is required by statute. The language of the statute, "implicates the accused", compendiously incorporates the test applicable at common law in the rule of practice. The nature of the corroboration will necessarily vary according to the particular circumstances of the offence charged. It would be in high degree dangerous to attempt to formulate the kind of evidence which would be regarded as corroboration, except to say that corroborative evidence is evidence which shows or tends to show that the story of the accomplice that the accused committed the crime is true, not merely that the crime has been committed, but that it was committed by the accused.

The corroboration need not be direct evidence that the accused committed the crime; it is sufficient if it is merely circumstantial evidence of his connection with the crime. A good instance of this indirect evidence is to be found in R. v. *Birkett* (1839), 8 C. & P. 732. Were the law otherwise many crimes which are usually committed between accomplices in secret, such as incest, offences with females, or the present case [homosexual misconduct], could never be brought to justice.

In *Thomas* v. *Jones*, [1921] I K.B. 22, at pp. 44–45; [1920] All E.R. Rep. 462, at p. 473, C.A., this decision was said to be generally applicable throughout the law of corroboration, i.e. it is not limited to accomplices; cf. Denning, L.J.'s view in *Fromhold* v. *Fromhold*, [1952] I T.L.R. 1522, at pp. 1526–7, C.A., that any confirmatory evidence is corroboration of cruelty in divorce.

It is often said that facts equally consistent with the truth or falsity of the evidence to be corroborated cannot be corroboration. This is correct but does not express the precise scope of the *Baskerville* doctrine, since it is true of all three positions stated above.

B. Examples of sufficient corroboration

corroboration?

According to Wigmore (para. 2059), decisions on the sufficiency of particular items of evidence as consideration are "mere useless chaff, ground out by the vain labour of able minds mistaking the true material for their energies". But some questions of legal interest surround this issue.

i To what extent can the person to be corroborated supply corroboration?

The requirement that corroboration be independent of the witness to be corroborated means that complaints and other statements consistent with the witness's testimony cannot be corroboration. But the witness's physical condition may be relevant, e.g. a small child suffering from the same venereal disease as the accused (*R.* v. *Gregg* (1932), 24 Cr. App. Rep. 13, C.C.A.; *R.* v. *Jones* (1939), 27 Cr. App. Rep. 33, C.C.A.); the injuries suffered by a rape victim (*R.* v. *Trigg*, [1963] I All E.R. 490; [1963] I W.L.R. 305, C.C.A.); or a distressed condition, though this can sometimes be simulated (*R.* v. *Redpath* (1962), 46 Cr. App. Rep. 319, C.C.A.; *R.* v. *Knight*, [1966] I All E.R. 647; [1966] I W.L.R. 230, C.C.A.) or be due to remorse, or simply be a consequence of rough handling during consensual intercourse (*R.* v. *Richards*, [1965] Qd. R. 354). Serious bruises or wounds may corroborate a sex victim's claim of non-consent; similarly if her clothes are blood-stained or badly torn. A medical examination for sperm traces and other signs may corroborate an allegation of intercourse if that is in issue.

ii Admissions

The defendant's admissions, in court or outside it, may corroborate the case against him. His admission must go to some issue which is relevant to what has to be corroborated. In indecent assault cases, an admission of indecency short of assault suffices (*R.* v. *Rolfe* (1952), 36 Cr. App. Rep. 4, C.C.A.), but an admission of platonic handling does not (*R.* v. *Tragen*, [1956] Crim. L.R. 332, C.C.A.; cf. *R.* v. *Dossi* (1918), 87 L.J.K.B. 1024, C.C.A.).

In paternity cases admissions of sexual intercourse or other familiarity at other times may be corroboration (*Cole* v. *Manning* (1877), 2 Q.B.D. 611; *Simpson* v. *Collinson*, [1964] 2 Q.B. 80; [1964] I All E.R. 262, C.A.). Sometimes the admission is implied, as where a man agrees to support a woman's child (*Thomas* v. *Jones*, [1921] I K.B. 22, at p. 39, C.A.; [1920] All E.R. Rep. 462, at p. 470).

iii False statements out of court

It is clear that these are capable of amounting to corroboration, as too are other attempts to subvert the course of justice, e.g. by suborning witnesses (*Mahoney* v. *Wright*, [1943] S.A.S.R. 61).

Moriarty v. London, Chatham and Dover Rail. Co.
(1870), L.R. 5 Q.B. 314

The plaintiff in a personal injury claim attempted to suborn false evidence. The Court of Queen's Bench held that evidence of his act was admissible.

COCKBURN, C.J.: The conduct of a party to a cause may be of the highest importance in determining whether the cause of action in which he is plaintiff, or the ground of defence, if he is defendant, is honest and just; just as it is evidence against a prisoner that he has said one thing at one time and another at another, as shewing that the recourse to falsehood leads fairly to an inference of guilt. Anything from which such an inference can be drawn is cogent and important evidence with a view to the issue. So, if you can shew that a plaintiff has been suborning false testimony, and has endeavoured to have recourse to perjury, it is strong evidence that he knew perfectly well his cause was an unrighteous one. I do not say that it is conclusive; I fully agree that it should be put to the jury, with the intimation that it does not always follow, because a man, not sure he shall be able to succeed by righteous means, has recourse to means of a different character, that that which he desires, namely, the gaining of the victory, is not his due, or that he has not good ground for believing that justice entitles him to it. It does not necessarily follow that he has not a good cause of action, any more than a prisoner's making a false statement to increase his appearance of innocence is necessarily a proof of his guilt; but it is always evidence which ought to be submitted to the consideration of the tribunal which has to judge of the facts; and therefore I think that the evidence was admissible, inasmuch as it went to shew that the plaintiff thought he had a bad case.

[BLACKBURN and LUSH, JJ. agreed.]

Popovic v. Derks
[1961] V.R. 413

The alleged father falsely denied on oath in affiliation proceedings that he was a frequent visitor to the complainant's house and that he often took her out in his car. Sholl, J. in the Supreme Court of Victoria held that the lie was capable of being corroboration.

SHOLL, J.: [C]orroboration is evidence rendering the *factum probandum* more probable by strengthening the proof of one or more *facta probabilia*. In an affiliation case the *factum probandum* is paternity. The most important *factum probabile* is intercourse at the material time. Corroboration may be of that *factum probabile* by evidence shewing that such intercourse was very likely, and thereby rendering more probable the complainant's evidence thereof.

In *Thomas v. Jones*, [1921] 1 K.B. 22; [1920] All E.R. Rep. 462, C.A. Scrutton, L.J., in a dissenting judgment, at pp. 39–40, very clearly analysed the position. He said: "What is meant by 'corroboration in some material particular' that is, in a material fact? The vital fact to be proved in a bastardy case is that a child has been born to the applicant as the result of sexual connexion with the man. From the nature of the case it is almost inevitable that there never will be any direct corroboration of sexual connexion. The evidence in corroboration must always be circumstantial evidence of the main fact, that is to say, evidence from which it may be inferred that the main fact happened. For instance, the fact that the man has had connexion with the woman and a child has resulted is sometimes inferred from evidence of previous affection, that they had been seen together shewing affection to each other. Sometimes it is inferred from the fact of subsequent affection—that the man and woman are seen together shewing signs of affection. Sometimes it is inferred from the fact that the man has done acts which may be treated as recognizing responsibility for the child as his child, statements that he will provide for the child, payments for the child, all facts from which as a matter of inference and probability it is more probable that the intercourse did take place than not. I quite agree with what Bankes, L.J. has said, that if the fact is such that the probabilities are equal one way or the other, an inference cannot legitimately be drawn from it one way or the other. It must shew, even only slightly, more probability that intercourse took place than not, and if there is that balance of probability it is not for the court to say that it is so slight that it would not have acted upon it. If there is evidence on which the justices could have come to that view, it does not matter that the court would have come to a different view. It is similar to the question as to when there is evidence for the jury; if there is evidence it is for the jury to decide, and not for the judge."

. . . [I]ntercourse is merely a material circumstance or particular,—that is to say, material to the allegation of paternity,—and . . . corroboration is evidence tending to render more probable circumstantially the complainant's allegation of intercourse. . . .

When an inference can be drawn that the defendant is falsely denying the circumstances because he fears that to admit them would appear inconsistent with his innocence, or throw suspicion upon himself, corroboration may be found. This is a kind of admission by conduct. That is to say, matters which otherwise might be ambiguous or colourless are rendered suspicious and corroborative by reason of the defendant's false denial—the inference open to the tribunal of fact being that, to him, the matter denied suggests guilt, so that, therefore, he is prepared falsely to deny it.

There is some analogy between this type of case and the case of flight rather than face interrogation or trial. . . .

. . . In *Credland* v. *Knowler* (1951), 35 Cr. App. Rep. 48, Lord Goddard, C.J. at pp. 54–5, when considering a false denial in a criminal case, said: "Most of the argument and, no doubt, much of the case has dealt with the lie which the appellant told and the question whether the fact that the appellant told a lie is in itself corroboration. I should be very sorry to lay down, and I have no intention of laying down and I do not think any case has gone the length of laying down, that the mere fact that an accused person has told a lie can in itself amount to corroboration. It may, but it does not follow that it must. If a man tells a lie when he is spoken to about an alleged offence, the fact that he tells a lie at once throws great doubt upon his evidence, if he afterwards gives evidence, and it may very good ground for rejecting his evidence, but the fact that his evidence ought to be rejected does not of itself amount to there being corroboration. In fact, I do not think we can put the proposition better than it was put by Lord Dunedin in *Dawson* v. *M'Kenzie*, 1908 S.C. 648, and the passage to which I am about to refer was approved by this Court in *Jones* v. *Thomas*, [1934] 1 K.B. 323, D.C.; [1933] All E.R. Rep. 535." And his Lordship then went on to quote the passage already cited in this judgment from *Dawson* v. *M'Kenzie, supra.* . . .

In *Pitman* v. *Byrne*, [1926] S.A.S.R. 207, at pp. 212–13, where a false denial was held to be capable of affording corroboration, the Full Court stated four principles which are relevant to the present problem; they were numbered (5) to (8) in that case: "(5) The weight to be attributed to a deliberately false denial or to false evidence must therefore depend on the facts of the particular case. Where it is the denial of a proved opportunity, it is evidence from which the Court may, if it thinks fit, infer guilt in relation to that opportunity. But in a proper case it would seem that false evidence might conceivably be of such a character as to lead to an inference definitely inconsistent with the innocence of the defendant without any independent evidence of opportunity (*Mash* v. *Darley*, [1914] 3 K.B. 1226, C.A.). (6) It is a question of degree. The admission by conduct is in every case evidence which goes to the jury in support of the other evidence upon the whole case, but its weight varies. It depends upon the strength of the other evidence and the degree of deliberation and the enormity of conduct manifested. A false answer on the spur of the moment under cross-examination is a relatively slender peg on which to hang an inference of guilt. A fabricated charge of unchastity, as in *Mash* v. *Darley, supra,* is stronger, but the subornation of perjured evidence to support a fabricated charge might afford an inference too strong to be reasonably explainable on any theory of innocence. . . .

It seems clear from the above review of the authorities that a false denial of opportunity or other fact need not be of an opportunity or other fact suspicious in itself, since it is the very false denial which may be used by the tribunal of fact to confer on the opportunity or other fact the suspicious or sinister character which makes it corroborative,—for example, in an affiliation case, corroborative of the complainant's evidence of intercourse. I, therefore, think that Mr. Shillito cannot be right in the present case, when he submits that the denials here relied on could not amount to corroboration, unless they were shewn to be denials of an opportunity independently proved to be suspicious. . . .

On the other hand, it cannot be right to say that a false denial of a fact is of no more significance than that fact would be if the respondent had, in the first instance, admitted it or not denied it; for there may be a world of difference between the effect of an admitted fact of a neutral character, such as the opportunity of intercourse, or presence at or near the scene of a crime at the material time, and the effect of that fact together with a false denial of it by the person alleged to be implicated. Dealing with this topic quite recently in *Tripodi's Case,* [1961] V.R. 186, in relation to criminal matters, the Full Court has recently said at pp. 193–4: "It rests, we think, not so much on the denial itself of the accused, as on the conduct which it betokens. A verbal admission by the accused of the commission of the offence would not only be admissible evidence, but if believed the strongest evidence of its commission. Conduct of the accused too which tended to shew incriminatory incidents of the crime could also be, and often is, the subject of admissible evidence, for example, that he once possessed and had got rid of, or attempted to get rid of, the weapon with which the crime had been committed; that he had been seen running away from the scene of the crime just after it had been committed; that he had been apprehended and broken away and escaped; and there may be many others. It is his conduct which is put before the jury, and they may think that he lies from a consciousness that, if he tells the truth, the truth will convict him. The lying statement must, of course, relate to incriminatory features of the crime; for if it were otherwise, any lying statement by the accused might convict him of any crime in the calendar, and such a result has only to be stated to be at once rejected as the law. We think that this view may explain why the courts have not discriminated between statements made by the accused out of court and in his evidence in court. In the latter case the jury themselves observe his conduct in giving evidence and, if they think he is lying, draw their own conclusions as to why he is lying; and no doubt the prosecutor, in inviting the jury to reject the accused's denial, will suggest the reason."

The rules governing the admissibility of out of court lies as corroboration are:

a. The statement must be material, e.g. a false denial of association with the victim (*Credland* v. *Knowler* (1951), 35 Cr. App. Rep. 48) or witnesses, or an accomplice; a false alibi; false accusations of impropriety against other suspects or against the victim (*Mash* v. *Darley,* [1914] 3 K.B. 1226, C.A.).

b. The statement must be false, without serious ambiguity.

c. The statement must be deliberately false, and prompted not by fear of a wrong judgment but by fear of the truth. It must not be due to panic, accidental error, attempts to terminate inquiries quickly, shame, resentment at officious questioning, or a desire to avoid the discovery of other misconduct.

d. The evidence of the falsity of the statement must proceed from some source independent of the witness to be corroborated. Thus in *R.* v. *King,* [1967] 2 Q.B. 338, C.C.A.; [1967] 1 All E.R. 379, the accused may have uttered certain lies, but the only testimony that they were lies proceeded from two boys who complained of the accused's sexual misconduct. The boys could not corroborate themselves directly and they could not be allowed to do so by this indirect means.

iv Can lies in court constitute corroboration?
English authority gives a negative answer.

R. v. Chapman
[1973] Q.B. 774; [1973] 2 All E.R. 624

The judge warned the jury that false evidence was capable of amounting to corroboration. The Court of Appeal criticized this.

ROSKILL, L.J.: In the view of this court the judge's direction was wrong, both on principle and on authority, to none of which was his attention drawn. It was wrong in principle for this reason: if the question is whether A's evidence or B's evidence is true, the mere rejection of B's evidence does not of itself mean that A's evidence must be accepted as true. B might have a separate and independent reason for lying or otherwise giving unreliable evidence or evidence which is for some reason incapable of belief. Mere rejection of evidence is not affirmative proof of the contrary of the evidence which has been rejected.

The most recent decision on this question is *Tumahole Bereng* v. R., [1949] A.C. 253, a decision of the Judicial Committee of the Privy Council which included both Lord MacDermott and Lord Reid. It is not necessary to relate the complex facts of that case. Lord MacDermott, delivering the opinion of the Board, said, at p. 270:

> "The circumstances that the appellants (other than No. 2) elected not to give evidence is equally incapable of constituting corroboration, though on more general grounds. Silence on the part of an accused person which is tantamount to an admission by conduct may, on occasion, amount to corroboration. But an accused admits nothing by exercising at his trial the right which the law gives him of electing not to deny the charge on oath. Silence of that kind—and it is the only kind relevant to this appeal—affords no corroboration to satisfy the rule of practice under consideration. Nor does an accused corroborate an accomplice merely by giving evidence which is not accepted and must therefore be regarded as false. Corroboration may well be found in the evidence of an accused person; but that is a different matter, for there confirmation comes, if at all, from what is said, and not from the falsity of what is said. It is, of course, correct to say that these circumstances—the failure to give evidence or the giving of false evidence—may bear against an accused and assist in his conviction if there is other material sufficient to sustain a verdict against him. But if the other material is insufficient either in its quality or extent they cannot be used as a make-weight. To hold [this is] as repugnant to the Proclamation of 1938 as to the common law of England."

That passage is, of course, not strictly binding on this court, but is the highest persuasive authority. For some reason that decision is not cited in *Archbold Criminal Pleading Evidence & Practice*, 37th Edn. (1969).

Two years later in *Credland* v. *Knowler* (1951), 35 Cr. App. Rep. 48, at pp. 54, 55, Lord Goddard, C.J. delivering the judgment of the Divisional Court, treated as axiomatic the proposition that the fact that a defendant's evidence ought to be rejected did not of itself amount to corroboration. Lord Goddard, C.J. went on to refer to a judgment of Lord President Dunedin in the First Division of the Inner House in *Dawson* v. *M'Kenzie* 1908, 45 Sc.L.R. 473, later approved by the Divisional Court in *Jones* v. *Thomas*, [1934] 1 K.B. 323.

Reference to the report of *Dawson* v. *M'Kenzie* 1908, 45 Sc.L.R. 473, at p. 474 shows that the Lord President was himself founding upon an earlier decision of the Second

Division of the Inner House in *Macpherson* v. *Largue* 1896, 23 R. (Ct. of Sess.) 785. This, like *Dawson* v. *M'Kenzie* and *Jones* v. *Thomas,* was a bastardy case. Corroboration was required by statute. The putative father's evidence had been rejected both by the sheriff's substitute and by the sheriff. There was other evidence capable of being corroboration. When the appeal in *Macpherson* v. *Largue* came before the Second Division of the Inner House the Lord Justice-Clerk said, at p. 790:

> "I agree that no corroboration can be derived from evidence of the defender which shows he is not speaking the truth. If his evidence is not to be believed it must be taken out of the case altogether, and the case must be treated as if he had not been examined."

Lord Trayner said, at p. 791:

> "On the other hand, the denial by the defender of material facts or circumstances (although not believed) does not corroborate the pursuer's statement. A false statement, or a statement not believed, by whomsoever made, is not corroboration of anything else. But if the pursuer is corroborated as to material statements made by her, and as to which she is contradicted by the defender, his denial, if proved false, or not believed, may give a complexion to the whole evidence, adverse to the defender, different from what it would have borne had his denial not been disbelieved or shown to be false."

Lord Moncreiff agreed. This is a clear Scottish decision that mere rejection of a defendant's evidence is not corroboration of the otherwise uncorroborated evidence against him. In the Lord Justice-Clerk's words, "if his evidence is not to be believed it must be taken out of the case altogether." Once so taken out it plainly cannot be used as corroboration.

In *Dawson* v. *M'Kenzie* 1908, 45 Sc.L.R. 473, Lord President Dunedin said, at p. 474: "The modern doctrine," that is plainly, in the context, the modern doctrine relating to corroboration, "—and the modern doctrine owed its introduction to the alteration of the old law under which the parties were not competent witnesses—was first laid down in the case of *M'Bayne* v. *Davidson* (1860), 22 Dunl. (Ct. of Sess.) 738, and perhaps the best expression of it was that given in a more recent decision by the Lord Justice-Clerk and Lord Trayner in the case of *Macpherson* 1896, 23 R. (Ct. of Sess.) 785, with which I entirely concur. The outcome of it is this, that there must be something more than the pursuer's own statement, and that that something must amount to corroboration. Now, the mistake which the learned sheriff has made here is in taking the mere proof or opportunity as amounting to corroboration. Mere opportunity alone does not amount to corroboration, but two things may be said about it. One is, that the opportunity may be of such a character as to bring in the element of suspicion. That is, that the circumstances and locality of the opportunity may be such as in themselves amount to corroboration. The other is, that the opportunity may have a complexion put upon it by statements made by the defender which are proved to be false. It is not that a false statement made by the defender proves that the pursuer's statements are true, but it may give to a proved opportunity a different complexion from what it would have borne had no such false statement been made. I am really only repeating in other words what was said by the Lord Justice-Clerk in the case of *Macpherson* 1896, 23 R. (Ct. of Sess.) 785."

The Lord President went on to quote the words that the Lord Justice-Clerk had used. Lord M'Laren, whose opinion followed, said, at p. 475:

> "I concur in your Lordship's opinion, and it is hardly necessary to add anything. It is a very common state of the evidence in such cases as this that the pursuer's case depends only upon her own evidence, with a certain amount of corroboration as to opportunities, and then the question of fact arises whether these opportunities were

such as to raise legal grounds of suspicion, or were merely of the nature of innocent meetings between man and woman. I think that in this class of cases the law laid down by the Lord Justice-Clerk in the case of *Macpherson* comes to be of importance, because I agree with his Lordship that it is not sufficient corroboration if you merely displace the evidence of the defender and show that he has made false statements. There must be corroboration of the pursuer's evidence; yet when the effect of the defender's false evidence, i.e., his denial of circumstances which are otherwise proved, is to show that there is something of which he is ashamed, or something the admission of which he conceived would throw suspicion upon himself, this will put a different complexion on what the court might otherwise be disposed to regard as innocent intimacy between the parties."

Lord Kinnear agreed. As already stated, Lord Dunedin's opinion was expressly adopted and approved by the Divisional Court in *Jones* v. *Thomas*, [1934] 1 K.B. 323.

Those two decisions of the Inner House are in precise accord with the passages from the opinion of the Board in *Tumahole Bereng* v. *R.*, [1949] A.C. 253, though neither decision nor *Jones* v. *Thomas* appears to have been cited in argument before the Judicial Committee and *Tumahole's* case does not appear to have been cited to the Divisional Court in *Credland* v. *Knowler* (1951), 35 Cr. App. Rep. 48. Curiously enough this point seems never to have arisen for direct decision by the Court of Appeal in this country either in a civil or criminal case. But this court has no doubt both on principle and authority that the statements quoted are correct and respectfully adopts them all.

As already mentioned, *Tumahole Bereng* v. *R.*, [1949] A.C. 253 finds no place in *Archbold*, but it is mentioned in *Cross on Evidence*, 3rd Edn. (1967), at p. 179. The learned author, after citing the passage already quoted from that case, goes on to say:

"There is nothing in the context which suggests that this dictum is only applicable to the testimony of an accomplice, and there can be no doubt that it is generally true of all cases in which corroboration must be sought."

This court respectfully agrees with and adopts that passage. The author then continues:

"There is, however, room for some debate whether it is universally valid. We shall see that demonstrable lies out of court may amount to corroboration of the case against the person who tells them, and there is no obvious reason why lies of a certain type told in the evidence of the defendant or accused should not have a similar effect. The contrivance of a falsehood can sometimes only be explained on the footing that its contriver is anxious to conceal his guilt, but this is not always so."

The author does not there mention the two Scottish decisions to which we have referred which, as we think, state the position with precise accuracy though he does cite *Dawson* v. *M'Kenzie* 1908, 45 Sc.L.R. 473 lower down on the same page in a different connection.

There is no doubt that a lie told out of court is capable in some circumstances of constituting corroboration, though it may not necessarily do so. There may be an explanation of the lie which will clearly prevent it being corroboration: see, for example, *R.* v. *Clynes* (1960), 44 Cr. App. Rep. 158, C.C.A., at pp. 163–4. But, in the view of this court, there is a clear distinction in principle between a lie told out of court and evidence given in the witness box which the jury rejects as incapable of belief or as otherwise unreliable. Proof of a lie told out of court is capable of being direct evidence, admissible at the trial, amounting to affirmative proof of the untruth of the defendant's denial of guilt. This in turn may tend to confirm the evidence against him and to implicate him in the offence charged. But a denial in the witness box which is untruthful or otherwise incapable of belief is not positive proof of anything. It leads only to the rejection of the evidence given, which then has to be treated as if it had not been given.

Mere rejection of evidence is not of itself affirmative or confirmatory proof of the truth of other evidence to the contrary.

This provokes several comments.

First, it is said that while an out of court lie is direct evidence affirmatively proving guilt, a lie in court is not positive proof of anything, it only leads to the rejection of the evidence given. But why is there a difference? It may be easier on the whole to prove that an out of court statement clearly is a lie, but if it can have probative value, why not in court statements which are clearly proved to be untrue? Similarly, not all lies in court can be said to proceed from a consciousness of guilt, but nor do all out of court lies. In either case appropriate jury directions will point out whether a lie merely destroys the liar's credit or is capable of going to prove that his case is weak.

Secondly, it is said that a man's silence in the face of a charge out of court can be corroboration if it operates as an admission by conduct, though silence in court cannot be corroboration because the law gives the accused a right not to testify. By analogy, out of court lies operate as an admission by conduct, but not in court lies, and any other rule would undermine the presumption of innocence. But why should the rules on lies be assimilated to the rules on silence? The existence of an optional right to silence cannot determine what should happen if it is not exercised and lies are told on oath. In any event, the present distinction between silence out of court and silence in court is irrational. A man may understandably be reluctant to speak out of court where he may be confused, unable to think clearly, in oppressive circumstances, alone, with what he says capable of being misunderstood or misrecorded. In court, however, he is protected by a lawyer and a judge, by the rules of evidence and procedure; there is less likelihood of panic, confusion and inadequate preparation and so the right to silence in court is harder to defend. The rules on silence are if anything the wrong way around, and should not be used as a model for the rules on lies.

Thirdly, it is said that though corroboration can be found in the evidence of an accused, this does not mean that lies can corroborate, for the corroboration that is found comes not from the falsity of what is said but from its truth. But this represents a misunderstanding of the probative nature of lies. They operate as implied admissions proceeding from the speaker's consciousness of guilt. There should be no difference in the rules for admissions whether express or implied.

Fourthly, Lord MacDermott said in *Tumahole Bereng* v. *R.*, [1949] A.C. 253, at p. 270, P.C. "It is, of course, correct to say that these circumstances—the failure to give evidence or the giving of false evidence—may bear against an accused and assist in his conviction if there is other material sufficient to sustain a verdict against him. But if the other material is insufficient either in its quality or extent they cannot be used as a make-weight." This theory that a lie can help prove a fact if the fact is proved by other means but has no probative value if the fact is otherwise uncertain seems odd. It makes for a difficult jury direction, and it has similarities with the notion, repudiated by the House of Lords in *Director of Public Prosecutions* v. *Kilbourne*, [1973] A.C. 729; [1973] 1 All E.R. 440, that some kinds of admissible similar fact evidence cannot be used as corroboration despite their tendency to implicate the accused in a material particular.

As a matter of authority, the Court of Appeal's position is open to question. It is suggested that *Jones* v. *Thomas*, [1934] 1 K.B. 323; [1933] All E.R. Rep. 535; *Credland* v. *Knowler* (1951), 35 Cr. App. Rep. 48, D.C.; *Macpherson* v. *Largue* 1896, 23 R. (Ct. of Sess.) 785 and *Dawson* v. *McKenzie* 1908, 45 Sc.L.R. 473 are misrepresented by Roskill, L.J. and do not support him. It is suggested that some English authority (*Thomas* v. *Jones*, [1921] 1 K.B. 22, at p. 37, C.A. per Bankes, L.J.; *Corfield* v. *Hodgson*, [1966] 2 All E.R. 205; [1966] 1 W.L.R. 590), and much other authority is against *Chapman* (Heydon (1973), 89 L.Q.R. 552; see *R.* v. *Boardman*, [1974] 2 All E.R. 958, at p. 963, C.A.; affirmed *sub nom. Boardman* v. *D.P.P.*; [1974] 3 All E.R. 887; [1974] 3 W.L.R. 673 at p. 680).

Pitman v. Byrne
[1926] S.A.S.R. 207

In affiliation proceedings the putative father falsely denied certain meetings with the mother. The South Australian Full Court held that this amounted to corroboration.

NAPIER, J.: If a party to litigation is shewn to have attempted to subvert the course of justice, this is a fact which may be used as circumstantial evidence tending to a conclusion adverse to his case. . . . The subornation of false testimony or the setting up of a false alibi, as distinct from the failure to establish it, are familiar instances; and the giving of wilfully false testimony stands on no other footing. [The Court must be able] to infer not merely that the testimony is false, but that it is deliberately false; and, further, that the motive which prompts the falsehood is not merely the fear of an unjust judgment, but a fear of the truth. If this inference is . . . reached, the result is in the nature of an admission by conduct.

v Silence out of court

The normal rule (p. 147, *post*) that silence can only exceptionally amount to assent to some proposition put to the accused means it will only exceptionally be corroboration, i.e. when a reply would be expected from an innocent man. This was so in *R.* v. *Cramp* (1880), 14 Cox C.C. 390 where a girl's father in effect accused the defendant of abetting her abortion and having in his possession material evidence of guilt. The normal rule is illustrated by *R.* v. *Tate*, [1908] 2 K.B. 680, C.C.A.; *R.* v. *Whitehead*, [1929] 1 K.B. 99; [1928] All E.R. Rep. 186, C.C.A.; *R.* v. *Keeling*, [1942] 1 All E.R. 507, C.C.A. *R.* v. *Feigenbaum*, [1919] 1 K.B. 431; [1918–19] All E.R. Rep. 489, C.C.A. is wrong, and some other cases state the rule perhaps too widely, e.g. *Bessela* v. *Stern* (1877), 2 C.P.D. 265, at p. 272.

Sometimes silence coupled with flight is corroboration (*R.* v. *Bondy* (1957), 121 C.C.C. 337). The failure of the defendant in affiliation proceedings to reply to a letter from the plaintiff's father (who was also the defendant's father-in-law) alleging paternity and stating that the matter would be put in a solicitor's hands if no reply were received was held corroboration in *Ex parte Freeman* (1922), 39 N.S.W.W.N. 73, at p. 75: "One might ignore the accusation of a busy-body stranger, but this was a family affair in which the honour of accuser and accused were equally at stake." Apart from cases where silence amounts to an admission, the only effect of silence will be to strengthen the opposing case and make the accused's less credible.

Wiedemann v. Walpole
[1891] 2 Q.B. 534, C.A.

LORD ESHER, M.R.: Now there are cases—business and mercantile cases—in which the Courts have taken notice that, in the ordinary course of business, if one man of business states in a letter to another that he has agreed to do certain things, the person who receives that letter must answer it if he means to dispute the fact that he did so agree. So, where merchants are in dispute one with the other in the course of carrying on some business negotiations, and one writes to the other, "but you promised me that you would do this or that", if the other does not answer the letter, but proceeds with the negotiations, he must be taken to admit the truth of the statement. But such cases as those are wholly unlike the case of a letter charging a man with some offence or meanness. Is it the ordinary habit of mankind, of which the Courts will take notice, to answer such letters; and must it be taken, according to the ordinary practice of mankind, that if a man does not answer he admits the truth of the charge made against him? If it were so, life would be unbearable. A man might day by day write such letters, which, if they were not answered, would be brought forward as evidence of the truth of the charges made in them. The ordinary and wise practice is not to answer them—to take no notice of them. Unless it is made out to be the ordinary practice of mankind to answer, I cannot see that not answering is any evidence that the person who receives such letters admits the truth of the statements contained in them.

[BOWEN and KAY, L.JJ. agreed.]

Thomas v. Jones
[1921] 1 K.B. 22; [1920] All E.R. Rep. 462, C.A.

SCRUTTON, L.J.: The question of not immediately repudiating an accusation is one of very considerable difficulty, and is, in my view, entirely a question of degree. If a charge of outrageous conduct is made against a person in public, and he says nothing, I have always thought that a jury would be entitled to treat his silence as an admission, if it was the class of accusation in respect of which, and the people in the neighbourhood were the class of people from whom, a repudiation of an untrue charge would be expected. But I do not think the same principle applies to accusations made by private letter. Lunatics write all sorts of letters to all manner of people, and if the receiver of a letter from a lunatic making a charge were bound to write at once and deny it, the time of judges, at any rate, would be fully taken up by answering the letters. I quite agree with what was said in *Wiedemann* v. *Walpole*, [1891] 2 Q.B. 534, C.A.

vi Silence in court

Although a party's failure to give evidence may strengthen the inferences to be drawn from the evidence against him, it is not a separate item of evidence and therefore is incapable of being corroboration.

The precise effect of silence here as elsewhere is obscure. In *R.* v. *Jackson,* [1953] 1 All E.R. 872, C.C.A., at p. 873, Lord Goddard, C.J. said, "It is a matter which the jury could very properly take into account and very probably would," but it was not corroboration. In *Cracknell* v. *Smith,* [1960] 3 All E.R. 569, at p. 571, D.C. Lord Parker, C.J. said, "If there is evidence against him, and some corroborative evidence, it may be that the justices are entitled to take into consideration the fact that he gave no evidence in considering the weight to be attached to the corroboration," but silence was not itself corroboration. Lord Parker, C.J.'s remark suggests silence strengthens the opposing case without being itself corroboration (*Jensen* v. *Ilka,* [1960] Qd. R. 274); it presumably also weakens the accused's own case, as with out of court silence. See also *R.* v. *Naylor,* [1933] 1 K.B. 685; [1932] All E.R. Rep. 152, C.C.A.; *R.* v. *Smith* (1935), 25 Cr. App. Rep. 119, C.C.A.; *R.* v. *Charavanmuttu* (1930), 22 Cr. App. Rep., 1. C.C.A. Thus the accused's silence may make it safe to convict without corroboration.

Failure to cross-examine does not corroborate evidence in chief (*Dingwell v. J. Wharton (Shipping), Ltd.,* [1961] 2 Lloyd's Rep. 213, at p. 219, H.L.).

Silence is sometimes held corroborative when coupled with special circumstances. Thus when a putative father told one story to the justices but did not repeat it at the trial on assize, its falsity could be inferred and this was corroboration (*Mash v. Darley,* [1914] 3 K.B. 1226, C.A.). An unexplained absconding from bail has been held to be corroboration (*R. v. McKenna* (1956), 73 N.S.W.W.N. 345). In these cases the court can imply an admission from conduct because there is something more than mere silence; hence these examples are not an exception to the general rule that silence alone is not corroboration.

The 11th Report of the Criminal Law Revision Committee proposes that silence before or during the trial should be capable of amounting to corroboration (para. 40–2).

vii Conduct on previous occasions

Let us assume the accused commits a series of crimes such that, under the similar fact evidence rules, evidence of one is admissible in respect to all the others because this is relevant to some issue (see Chap. 10, *post*). If the victims are different and independent, they corroborate each other (*Director of Public Prosecutions v. Kilbourne, infra; R. v. Mitchell* (1952), 36 Cr. App. Rep. 79, C.C.A.). If the victim is the same, any independent corroboration of one incident can constitute corroboration as to the others (e.g. *R. v. Hartley,* [1941] 1 K.B. 5, C.C.A.). Thus previous convictions of the accused for offences against the same victim may be corroboration (*R. v. Marsh* (1949), 33 Cr. App. Rep. 185, C.C.A.).

Director of Public Prosecutions *v.* Kilbourne
[1973] A.C. 729; [1973] 1 All E.R. 440, H.L.

The accused was convicted of various homosexual offences against two groups of boys. Four counts related to offences in 1970 against the first group of boys; three counts related to offences in 1971 against the second. The accused's defence was innocent association (i.e. the enjoyment of ordinary amusements and "sky-larking") coupled with a denial of those parts of the evidence incapable of any such construction. Lawson, J. told the jury they could take the uncorroborated evidence of the second group of two boys, or either of them if they believed it, as corroboration of the three boys in the first group, and vice versa. He also directed them that the evidence of one boy in a group could not be used to corroborate another boy in that group because of the risk of a concocted story between boys well known to each other.

LORD HAILSHAM, L.C.: The Court of Appeal whose judgment was given by Lawton, L.J. approached the matter in three stages.

Lawton, L.J. said, [1972] 3 All E.R. 545, at p. 548:

". . . we have to decide whether the evidence of one group of boys was admissible at all on the counts in which the other group of boys were named. If it was not, there was a misdirection as to the admissibility of evidence; but if it was admissible, the second and third stages have to be considered. The question at the second stage is whether such evidence if it had involved neither victims nor children could have been capable of being corroboration; and the third stage is whether, in the circumstances of this case in which child victims were involved, it was capable of being corroboration."

The Court of Appeal then held on the authority of *R. v. Sims,* [1946] K.B. 531; [1946]

1 All E.R. 699, C.C.A.; R. v. *Chandor*, [1959] 1 Q.B. 545; [1959] 1 All E.R. 702, C.C.A., and R. v. *Flack*, [1969] 2 All E.R. 784; [1969] 1 W.L.R. 937, C.A., that the evidence was admissible, and admissible because it was relevant to the matters in dispute and implicated the accused in the criminal conduct alleged in the indictment. The nerve of their argument is contained in the following short passage in the judgment of the court, [1972] 3 All E.R. 545, at pp. 548–9:

> "In the present case, with the exception of the penis touching incident involving the boy Kevin, each accusation bears a resemblance to the other and shows not merely that the appellant was a homosexual which would not have been enough to make the evidence admissible, but that he was one whose proclivities in that regard took a particular form. Further, the evidence of each boy went to rebut the defence of innocent association which the appellant put forward: this by itself made the similar fact evidence admissible: see R. v. *Chandor*, [1959] 1 Q.B. 545, at p. 550; [1959] 1 All E.R. 702, at p. 704, C.C.A. *per* Lord Parker, C.J. We have had no doubt that the evidence of one group of boys could properly be taken into account by the jury when considering the counts relating to the other group. But for what purpose since only relevant evidence is admissible? What, for example, did Gary's evidence prove in relation to John's on count 1? The answer must be that his evidence, having the striking features of the resemblance between the acts committed on him and those alleged to have been committed on him and those alleged to have been committed on John, makes it more likely that John was telling the truth when he said that the appellant had behaved in the same way to him."

The court went on to quote the passage of the judgment of the Court of Criminal Appeal in R. v. *Sims*, [1946] K.B. 531, at pp. 539–40; [1946] 1 All E.R. 697, at p. 701, C.C.A. when they say:

> "The evidence of each man was that the accused invited him into the house and there committed the acts charged. The acts they describe bear a striking similarity. That is a special feature sufficient in itself to justify the admissibility of the evidence; . . . The probative force of all the acts together is much greater than one alone; for, whereas the jury might think that one man might be telling an untruth, three or four are hardly likely to tell the same untruth unless they were conspiring together. If there is nothing to suggest a conspiracy, their evidence would seem to be overwhelming."

In spite of this reasoning, the Court of Appeal went on to say that nonetheless there was nothing mutually corroborative in testimony of this kind. They felt themselves constrained to come to this conclusion because of the later passage in R. v. *Sims* which says, at p. 544 [and p. 703]:

> "We do not think that the evidence of the men can be considered as corroborating one another, because each may be said to be an accomplice in the act to which he speaks and his evidence is to be viewed with caution;"

On this the Court of Appeal quoted with some relish, the comments of Professor Cross on *Evidence*, 3rd Edn. (1967), p. 182:

> ". . . it is difficult to see how admissible evidence of misconduct of the defendant or accused on other occasions could ever fail to corroborate the evidence relating to the question with which the court is concerned. If it is admissible at all on account of its relevance for some reason other than its tendency to show a propensity towards wrongdoing in general or wrongdoing of the kind into which the court is inquiring, the conduct must, it would seem, implicate the defendant or accused in a material particular in relation to the occasion into which the court is inquiring."

In quashing all the convictions on this ground the Court of Appeal went on to rely on the authority of *R. v. Campbell,* [1956] 2 Q.B. 432; [1956] 2 All E.R. 272, C.C.A., where it is said, at p. 438 [and p. 276]:

"... we may perhaps endeavour to give some guidance to courts who have from time to time to deal with cases of sexual assaults on children where the evidence of each child deals only with the assault on himself or herself. In such cases it is right to tell a jury that because A says that the accused assaulted him, it is no corroboration of his evidence that B says that he also was the victim of a similar assault though both say it on oath. At the same time we think a jury may be told that a succession of these cases may help them to determine the truth of the matter provided they are satisfied that there is no collaboration between the children to put up a false story. And if the defence is one of innocent association by the accused with the children, *R.* v. *Sims,* subsequently approved on this point by the House of Lords in *Harris* v. *Director of Public Prosecutions,* [1952] A.C. 694; [1952] 1 All E.R. 1044, shows that such evidence can be given to rebut the defence."

On this particular passage the Court of Appeal comment [1972] 3 All E.R. 545, at p. 550:

"Here Lord Goddard, C.J. is apparently distinguishing between evidence which can be used as corroboration and evidence which may help the jury in some way to determine the truth. A's evidence that the accused indecently assaulted him may not be used to corroborate B's evidence that B was indecently assaulted, but it may be used in some other way to help the jury to determine the truth of B's evidence; see *Cross on Evidence* at pp. 320 and 321, footnote 7, where he cites *Sims'* case as an authority for this difficult distinction."

Basing themselves on this state of the authorities, the Court of Appeal decided, at p. 551:

"Accordingly we must hold the direction to be defective, with whatever consequences may follow from this view."

The consequences, of course, involved the quashing of all the convictions.

We now have to determine at the invitation of the Court of Appeal how "evidence which can be used as corroboration, and evidence which may help the jury in some other way to determine the truth" can be validly distinguished, and the distinction explained to a jury.

The question certified by the Court of Appeal in the present case as of general public importance is:

"whether and in what circumstances the sworn evidence of a child victim as to an offence charged can be corroborated by the admissible but uncorroborated evidence of another child victim as to similar misconduct of the accused on a different occasion."

I may say at once that I regard the passage in *R.* v. *Campbell,* [1956] 2 Q.B. 432; [1956] 2 All E.R. 272, C.C.A. which attempts to draw a distinction between evidence which helps the jury to arrive at a conclusion about evidence requiring corroboration and evidence which is confirmatory or corroborative of evidence requiring corroboration as a valiant, but wholly unsuccessful, attempt to reconcile the two quoted passages in *R.* v. *Sims,* [1946] K.B. 531, at pp. 539, 544; [1946] 1 All E.R. 697, at pp. 701, 703, C.C.A. the second of which I believe to be wholly inconsistent with the first. The second passage may be based on what I believe to be a false analogy with the use which can be made by the prosecution of complaints by the alleged victim of a rape as evidence of consistency, but not corroboration, since a witness requiring corroboration "cannot corroborate herself". It may also be based to some extent on the rule about joint accomplices stretching back to *R.* v. *Noakes* (1832), 5 C. & P. 326 at p. 328 *per* Littledale, J. But this also, as I shall endeavour to show, is a false analogy.

In my view, there is no magic or artificiality about the rule of practice concerning corroboration at all. In Scottish law, it seems, some corroboration is necessary in every criminal case. In contrast, by the English common law, the evidence of one competent witness is enough to support a verdict whether in civil or criminal proceedings except in cases of perjury (cf. *Hawkins' Pleas of the Crown,* vol. 4, c. 46, .s 2; *Fosters' Crown Cases* (1762), 233). This is still the general rule, but there are now two main classes of exception to it. In the first place, there are a number of statutory exceptions. . . .

But side by side with the statutory exceptions is the rule of practice now under discussion by which judges have in fact warned juries in certain classes of case that it is dangerous to found a conviction on the evidence of particular witnesses or classes of witness unless that evidence is corroborated in a material particular implicating the accused, or confirming the disputed items in the case. The earliest of these classes to be recognized was probably the evidence of accomplices "approving" for the Crown, no doubt, partly because at that time the accused could not give evidence on his own behalf and was therefore peculiarly vulnerable to invented allegations by persons guilty of the same offence. By now the recognized categories also include children who give evidence under oath, the alleged victims, whether adults or children, in cases of sexual assault, and persons of admittedly bad character. I do not regard these categories as closed. A judge is almost certainly wise to give a similar warning about the evidence of any principal witness for the Crown where the witness can reasonably be suggested to have some purpose of his own to serve in giving false evidence (cf. R. v. *Prater,* [1960] 2 Q.B. 464; [1960] 1 All E.R. 298, C.C.A.; R. v. *Russell* (1968), 52 Cr. App. Rep. 147, C.C.A.). The Supreme Court of the Republic of Ireland has apparently decided that at least in some cases of disputed identity a similar warning is necessary (*People* v. *Casey* (*No. 2*), [1963] I.R. 33, at pp. 39–40.) This question may still be open here (cf. R. v. *Williams,* [1956] Crim. L.R. 833, C.C.A.; *Arthurs* v. *A.-G. for Northern Ireland* (1970), 55 Cr. App. R. 161, at p. 169, H.L.).

Since the institution of the Court of Criminal Appeal in 1907, the rule, which was originally discretionary in the trial judge, has acquired the force of a rule of law in the sense that a conviction after a direction to the jury which does not contain the warning will be quashed, unless the proviso is applied: see R. v. *Baskerville,* [1916] 2 K.B. 658; [1916–17] All E.R. Rep. 38, C.C.A.; *Davies* v. *Director of Public Prosecutions,* [1954] A.C. 378, at p. 398; [1954] 1 All E.R. 507, at p. 513, H.L. *per* Lord Simonds, L.C.

However, it is open to a judge to discuss with the jury the nature of the danger to be apprehended in convicting without corroboration and the degree of such danger (cf. R. v. *Price,* [1969] 1 Q.B. 541, at p. 546; [1968] 2 All E.R. 282, at p. 285, C.A.) and it is well established that a conviction after an appropriate warning may stand notwithstanding that the evidence is uncorroborated, unless, of course, the verdict is otherwise unsatisfactory: R. v. *Baskerville,* [1916] 2 K.B. 658. There is, moreover, no magic formula to be used: R. v. *Price,* [1969] 1 Q.B. 541; [1968] 2 All E.R. 282, C.A. . . . [I]t is wrong for a judge to confuse the jury with a general if learned disquisition on the law. His summing up should be tailormade to suit the circumstances of the particular case. The word "corroboration" is not a technical term of art, but a dictionary word bearing its ordinary meaning; since it is slightly unusual in common speech the actual word need not be used, and in fact it may be better not to use it. Where it is used it needs to be explained.

. . . Counsel for the respondent was in the end constrained to agree that all the evidence in this case was both admissible and relevant, and that the Court of Appeal was right to draw attention [1972] 3 All E.R. 545, at p. 549 to the "striking features of the resemblance" between the acts alleged to have been committed in one count and those alleged to have been committed in the others, and to say that this made it "more likely that John was telling the truth when he said that the appellant had behaved in the same way to him". In my view, this was wholly correct. With the exception of one incident

"each accusation bears a resemblance to the other and shows not merely that [Kilbourne] was a homosexual, which would not have been enough to make the evidence admissible, but that he was one whose proclivities in that regard took a particular form" [1972] 3 All E.R. 545, at pp. 548–9.

I also agree with the Court of Appeal in saying that the evidence of each child went to contradict any possibility of innocent association. As such it was admissible as part of the prosecution case, and since, by the time the judge came to sum up, innocent association was the foundation of the defence put forward by the accused, the admissibility, relevance, and, indeed cogency of the evidence was beyond question. The word "corroboration" by itself means no more than evidence tending to confirm other evidence. In my opinion, evidence which is (*a*) admissible and (*b*) relevant to the evidence requiring corroboration, and, if believed, confirming it in the required particulars, is capable of being corroboration of that evidence and, when believed, is in fact such corroboration.

As Professor Cross well says in his book on *Evidence*, 3rd ed. p. 316:

> "The ground of the admissibility of this type of evidence was succinctly stated by Hallett, J., when delivering the judgment by the Court of Criminal Appeal: 'If the jury are precluded by some rule of law from taking the view that something is a coincidence which is against all probabilities if the accused person is innocent, then it would seem to be a doctrine of law which prevents a jury from using what looks like common sense'." R. v. *Robinson*, [1953] 2 All E.R. 334.

That this is so in the law of Scotland seems beyond dispute, and it would be astonishing if the law of England were different in this respect, since one would hope that the same rules of logic and common sense are common to both. We were referred to the cases of *Moorov* v. *H.M. Advocate*, 1930 J.C. 68 (an indecent assault case); *H.M. Advocate* v. *A.E.*, 1937 J.C. 96 (an incest case) and *Ogg* v. *H.M. Advocate* 1938 J.C. 152 (a case of indecent conduct with male persons).

[In *Moorov* v. *H.M. Advocate*, 1930 J.C. 68, at pp. 73–4, Lord Clyde, L.J.-G. said:] "Before the evidence of single credible witnesses to separate acts can provide material for mutual corroboration, the connection between the separate acts (indicated by their external relation in time, character, or circumstance) must be such as to exhibit them as subordinates in some particular and ascertained unity of intent, project, campaign, or adventure, which lies beyond or behind—but is related to—the separate acts. The existence of such an underlying unity, comprehending and governing the separate acts, provides the necessary connecting link between them, and becomes a circumstance in which corroboration of the evidence of the single witnesses in support of the separate acts may be found—whether the existence of such underlying unity is established by independent evidence, or by necessary inference from the evidence of the single witnesses themselves, regarded as a whole."

[In *H.M. Advocate* v. *A.E.*, 1937 J.C. 96, at pp. 98–100, Lord Aitchison, L.J.-C. said:] "Now, it is a well-established rule in our criminal law that you do not prove one crime by proving another or by leading evidence tending to show that another crime has been committed. That is a good general rule. But then, when you are dealing with this class of crime there is some relaxation of the rule, otherwise you might never be able to bring the crime home at all. Let me give you an illustration that is not at all unfamiliar—there are many cases of it, especially in our large cities—you get a degraded man who finds some little girl in the street, and he gives her a penny, and gets her to go up a close, and there he does something immoral with her, and then he sends her away. Nobody sees what he has done; there is only the evidence of the child. And then the same thing happens with another child, and again nobody sees that; and then there is a third child, and the same thing happens again. Well, of course, if you had to have two witnesses to every one of these acts—they are all separate crimes—you would never prove anything at all. But that is not the law. The law is this, that, when you find a man doing the same kind of criminal thing in the same kind of way towards two or more people, you may be entitled to say that the man is pursuing a course of criminal conduct, and you may take the evidence on one charge as evidence on another. That is a very sound rule, because a great many scoundrels would get off altogether if we had not some such rule in our law. Now, I give you this direction in law. If the conduct which is the subject of these charges is similar in character and circumstances, and substantially coincident in time, and you believe the evidence of both of these girls, then the evidence of the one may be taken as corroboration of the evidence of the other. This is in substance what was laid down in the High Court in the case of *Moorov* v. *Lord Advocate,* 1930 J.C. 68."

In addition to the valuable direction to the jury, this summing-up appears to me to contain a proposition which is central to the nature of corroboration, but which does not appear to date to have been emphasized in any reported English decision until the opinion delivered in *R.* v. *Hester,* [1973] A.C. 296, H.L.; [1972] 3 All E.R. 1056, by Lord Morris of Borth-y-Gest although it is implicit in them all. Corroboration is only required or afforded if the witness requiring corroboration or giving it is otherwise credible. If his evidence is not credible, a witness's testimony should be rejected and the accused acquitted, even if there could be found evidence capable of being corroboration in other testimony. Corroboration can only be afforded to or by a witness who is otherwise to be believed. If a witness's testimony falls of its own inanition the question of his needing, or being capable of giving, corroboration does not arise. It is for this reason that evidence of complaint is acceptable in rape cases to defeat any presumption of consent and to establish consistency of conduct, but not as corroboration. The jury is entitled to examine any evidence of complaint, in order to consider the question whether the witness is credible at all. It is not entitled to treat that evidence as corroboration because a witness, though otherwise credible, "cannot corroborate himself", i.e., the evidence is not "independent testimony" to satisfy the requirements of corroboration in *R.* v. *Baskerville* [1916] 2 K.B. 658, at p. 667; [1916–17] All E.R. Rep. 38, at p. 43, C.C.A. Of course, the moment at which the jury must make up its mind is at the end of the case. They must look at the evidence as a whole before asking themselves whether the evidence of a given witness is credible in itself and whether, if otherwise credible, it is corroborated. Nevertheless, corroboration is a doctrine applying to otherwise credible testimony and not to testimony incredible in itself. In the present case Mark's evidence (count 3) was corroborated. But it was not credible and the conviction founded on it was rightly quashed.

It seems to me that the only way in which the doctrine upon which the decision of the Court of Appeal was founded can be supported, would be if there were some general rule of law to the effect that witnesses of a class requiring corroboration could not corroborate one another. For this rule of law counsel for the respondent expressly contended. I do not believe that such a rule of law exists. . . .

In *R.* v. *Hester,* [1973] A.C. 296; [1972] 3 All E.R. 1056, this House has stigmatized this argument as fallacious. With respect, I wholly agree, and I hope no more will be heard of it.

The other ground upon which the general proposition may be defended is the bald proposition that one accomplice cannot corroborate another. In support of this proposition were cited *R.* v. *Noakes* (1832) 5 C. & P. 326 *per* Littledale, J.; *R.* v. *Gay* (1909) 2 Cr. App. Rep. 327, C.C.A.; *R.* v. *Prater* [1960] 2 Q.B. 464, at p. 465; [1960] 1 All E.R. 298, at p. 299, C.C.A.; *per* Edmund Davies, J.; *R.* v. *Baskerville* [1916] 2 K.B. 658, at p. 664; [1916–17] All E.R. Rep. 38, at p. 42, C.C.A. citing *Noakes*; and *R.* v. *Cratchley* (1913) 9 Cr. App. Rep. 232, C.C.A.

I believe these citations have been misunderstood. They all refer to fellow accomplices: see *per* Lord Diplock in *R.* v. *Hester,* [1973] A.C. 296; [1972] 3 All E.R. 1056, H.L. Obviously where two or more fellow accomplices give evidence against an accused their evidence is equally tainted. The reason why accomplice evidence requires corroboration is the danger of a concocted story designed to throw the blame on the accused. The danger is not less, but may be greater, in the case of fellow accomplices. Their joint evidence is not "independent" . . . and a jury must be warned not to treat it as a corroboration. But this illustrates the danger of mistaking the shadow for the substance. I feel quite sure that, for instance, where an unpopular officer in the army or the unpopular headmaster of a school could have been the victim of a conspiracy to give false evidence of this kind as the suggestion was in R. v. *Bailey,* [1924] 2 K.B. 300, C.C.A., a similar warning should be given. As Lord Hewart, C.J. said in that case (which turned, however, on a wholly different point), at p. 305:

> "The risk, the danger, the logical fallacy is indeed quite manifest to those who are in the habit of thinking about such matters. It is so easy to derive from a series of unsatisfactory accusations, if there are enough of them, an accusation which at least appears satisfactory. It is so easy to collect from a mass of ingredients, not one of which is sufficient, a totality which will appear to contain what is missing."

On the other hand, where the so-called accomplices are of the third class listed by Lord Simonds, L.C. in *Davies* v. *Director of Public Prosecutions* [1954] A.C. 378, at p. 400; [1954] 1 All E.R. 507, at p. 513, H.L. the danger is or may be nugatory. The real need is to warn the jury of the danger of a conspiracy to commit perjury in these cases, and, where there is the possibility of this, it is right to direct them not to treat as corroborative of one witness the evidence of another witness who may be part of the same conspiracy, but who cannot be an accomplice because if the evidence is untrue there has been no crime committed. This prompts me to point out that although the warning must be given in every appropriate case, the dangers to be guarded against may be quite different. Thus the evidence of accomplices is dangerous because it may be perjured. The evidence of Lady Wishfort complaining of rape may be dangerous because she may be indulging in undiluted sexual fantasy. A Mrs. Frail making the same allegation may need corroboration because of the danger that she does not wish to admit the consensual intercourse of which she is ashamed. In another case the danger may be one of honestly mistaken identity as when the conviction of the accused depends on an identification by a single uncorroborated witness to whom he was previously unknown. These matters should, in suitable cases, be explored when the nature and degree of danger is being discussed, as suggested in R. v. *Price,* [1969] 1 Q.B. 541, at p. 546; [1968] 2 All E.R. 282, at p. 285, C.A. I do not, therefore, believe that there is a general rule that no persons who come within the definition of accomplice may be mutually corroborative. It applies to those in the first and second of Lord Simonds, L.C.'s categories and to many other cases where witnesses are not or may not be accomplices. It does not necessarily apply to all witnesses in the same case who may deserve to be categorized as "accomplice". In particular it does not necessarily apply to accomplices of Lord Simonds, L.C.'s third class, where they give independent evidence of separate incidents, and where the circumstances are such as to exclude the danger of a jointly fabricated story.

Whatever else it is, the rule about fellow accomplices is not authority for the proposition that no witness who may himself require corroboration may afford corroboration for another to whom the same consideration applies, and this alone is what would help the respondent. When a small boy relates a sexual incident implicating a given man he may be indulging in fantasy. If another small boy relates such an incident it may be a coincidence if the detail is insufficient. If a large number of small boys relate similar incidents in enough detail about the same person, if it is not conspiracy it may well be that the stories are true. Once there is a sufficient nexus it must be for the jury to say what weight is given to the combined testimony of a number of witnesses.

LORD REID: The main difficulty in the case is caused by observations in the case of R. v. *Manser* (1934) 25 Cr. App. Rep. 18, C.C.A. to the effect that the evidence of one witness which required corroboration cannot be used as corroboration of that of another witness which also requires corroboration. For some unexplained reason it was held that there can be no mutual corroboration in such a case.

I do not see why that should be so. There is nothing technical in the idea of corroboration. When in the ordinary affairs of life one is doubtful whether or not to believe a particular statement one naturally looks to see whether it fits in with other statements or circumstances relating to the particular matter; the better it fits in, the more one is inclined to believe it. The doubted statement is corroborated to a greater or lesser extent by the other statements or circumstances with which it fits in.

In ordinary life we should be, and in law we are required to be, careful in applying this idea. We must be astute to see that the apparently corroborative statement is truly independent of the doubted statement. If there is any real chance that there has been collusion between the makers of the two statements we should not accept them as corroborative. And the law says that a witness cannot corroborate himself. In ordinary affairs we are often influenced by the fact that the maker of the doubted statement has consistently said the same thing ever since the event described happened. But the justification for the legal view must, I think, be that generally it would be too dangerous to take this into account and therefore it is best to have a universal rule.

So when we are considering whether there can be mutual corroboration between witnesses each of whom requires corroboration, the question must or at least ought to be whether it would be too dangerous to allow this. It might often be dangerous if there were only two children. But here we are dealing with cases where there is a "system", and I do not think that only two instances would be enough to establish a "system". Where several children, between whom there can have been no collaboration in concocting a story, all tell similar stories it appears to me that the conclusion that each is telling the truth is likely to be inescapable and the corroboration is very strong. So I can see no ground at all for the law refusing to recognize the obvious. Once there are enough children to show a "system" I can see no ground for refusing to recognize that they can corroborate each other.

Many of the authorities cited deal with accomplices where the rule as to the need of warning that there should be corroboration is similar to the rule with regard to children. I do not think it useful to regard children as accomplices; the rule with regard to children applies whether or not they are accomplices.

In most of the authorities the accomplices were accomplices to a single crime so the danger that they collaborated in concocting their story is obvious, and it is therefore quite right that there should be a general rule that accomplices cannot corroborate each other. Whether that should be a universal rule I greatly doubt, but I need not pursue that matter in this case.

Then there are indications of a special rule for homosexual crimes. If there ever was a time for that, that time is past, and on the view which I take of the law any such special rule is quite unnecessary. . . .

I find this very difficult to understand. I do not see how evidence with regard to count B can help the jury to determine whether evidence with regard to count A is true unless it amounts to corroboration of that evidence. I can see no difference between saying that evidence corroborates other evidence, and saying that evidence helps one to determine the truth of the other evidence.

Any attempt to apply [the distinction stated in R. v. *Campbell*, [1956] 2 Q.B. 432, at pp. 438–9; [1956] 2 All E.R. 272, at p. 276, C.C.A.] in practice must, I think, lead to confusion. How is the jury to be directed? Counsel were unable to suggest and I cannot suggest any better way than this. The judge must tell the jury to consider each count separately. He must then warn them of the danger of accepting the evidence of the child to whom count 1 relates unless it is corroborated. Then he must tell them that the evidence of the other children is not corroboration. Then he must tell them that they can act on the uncorroborated evidence of the first child if they feel sure that it is true and that in considering that matter they can obtain help by taking into consideration the evidence of the other children. I should be surprised if any jury understood such a direction: it could only confuse them. . . .

The trouble has arisen from the rule that the Court of Appeal is not permitted to reconsider an earlier judgment of that court. So in order to do justice they may have to invent a distinction without a difference. For a long time the courts appear to have been reluctant to reach the logical result required by the *Manser* doctrine. In my judgment this House should now set the matter at rest.

LORD SIMON: . . . Corroboration is therefore nothing other than evidence which "confirms" or "supports" or "strengthens" other evidence. . . . It is, in short, evidence which renders other evidence more probable. If so, there is no essential difference between, on the one hand, corroboration and, on the other, "supporting evidence" or "evidence which helps to determine the truth of the matter". Each is evidence which makes other evidence more probable. Once it is accepted that the direct evidence on one count is relevant to another by way of circumstantial evidence, it follows that it is available as corroboration if corroboration is required. Whether it operates as such depends on what weight the jury attaches to it, and what inferences the jury draws as to whether the offences demonstrate an underlying unity. For that purpose the jury will be directed in appropriate terms to take into account the proximity in time of the offences, their multiplicity, their similarity in detail and circumstance, whether such similarity has any unusual feature, what, if any, risk there is of collaboration in presenting a false case, and any other matter which tends to suggest or rebut an underlying unity—a system—something which would cause common sense to revolt at a hypothesis of mere coincidence.

[LORDS MORRIS OF BORTH-Y-GEST and CROSS agreed.]

Hoffman: The South African Law of Evidence
2nd Edn. P. 421

Courts have sometimes found difficulty in holding that the evidence of witness A deposing to one offence could corroborate the evidence of witness B deposing to a different offence. On the other hand, the evidence of witness A will not be admissible under the similar fact rule unless it is sufficiently relevant to the question of whether the accused committed the other offence. If it is admissible at all, it must be on the ground that it confirms the evidence of witness B in a material particular affecting the accused. It should therefore be capable of corroborating his evidence.

Question

Do you find Lord Hailsham's view that "Corroboration is only required or afforded if the witness requiring corroboration or giving it is otherwise credible" helpful?

Comment

The fallacy attacked by the House of Lords in *Kilbourne* is a common one; e.g. *R. v. Witham*, [1962] Qd. R. 49, where Hanger, J. (dissenting) admitted similar fact evidence but held it to be incapable of being corroboration.

viii Mere opportunity

Mere opportunity is not corroboration without more. As one American judge rather gloomily remarked in a sex case, "If proof of opportunity to commit a crime were alone sufficient to sustain a conviction, no man would be safe" (*Power* v. *State* (1934), 30 P. 2d 1059, at p. 1060 *per* Lockwood, J.). Repeated opportunities have often been held corroboration of intercourse, however, as has a period of close association, particularly if the association is exclusive (*Moore* v. *Hewitt* [1947] K.B. 831; [1947] 2 All E.R. 270).

IV JURY DIRECTION

How should the judge direct the jury?

It seems they must be told what corroboration is (though the word itself need not actually be used) and what sorts of evidence are corroborative, though there is no need to do the latter if there is in fact no corroboration (*Director of Public Prosecutions* v. *Hester*, [1973] A.C. 296, at p. 328; [1972] 3 All E.R. 1056, at p. 1076, H.L.). They should be told if there is no corroboration. It is unnecessary for the judge to go through the evidence and indicate which particular items are capable of being corroborative, though this often happens. If the judge wrongly describes certain items of evidence as corroborative the conviction may be quashed (see *R.* v. *Goddard*, [1962] 3 All E.R. 582, C.C.A.; *R.* v. *O'Reilly*, [1967] 2 Q.B. 722; [1967] 2 All E.R. 766, C.A.). Where there is a danger that the jury will treat as corroboration something which is not corroboration, e.g. a complaint, the judge should say that it is not (*R.* v. *Goddard*).

Often there are several grounds for giving a warning. A witness might be a consensual child victim in a sex case testifying to her identification of the accused: each of the four grounds for the warning should be stated.

One common criticism of the standard form of summing up is that of Salmon, L.J. in *R.* v. *O'Reilly*, [1967] 2 Q.B. 722, at p. 727; [1967] 2 All E.R. 766, at p. 768, C.A.: "It may perhaps seem strange that where evidence is called which, if accepted, indisputably must amount to corroboration, it is, according to the present state of the law, always necessary to tell the jury how dangerous it would have been to convict if there had been no such evidence." This is open to question. Certainly if the corroborating evidence is believed, the warning is otiose. But how can the judge be sure the evidence will be believed? The reason he must warn the jury is that if they do not believe the corroboration, *then* it is dangerous to convict even though at first sight the complainant seems credible.

It has been suggested that an astute defendant, by admitting nearly all the elements of the crime with which he is charged, and limiting his defence to a very small area, may entitle himself to a direction that as to this small area there is no corroboration so that it is dangerous to convict him (see *Forgie* v. *Police*, [1969] N.Z.L.R. 101 and R.J.S., [1968] N.Z.L.J. 465). For example, on a charge of rape, if the accused admits everything but says the victim consented at the last moment, all the evidence which would be corroboration if the accused raised an alibi, or denied sexual intercourse, or violence, or the initial objections of the victim, becomes useless to corroborate the victim in her denials of last-minute consent. The answer to such an attempt to reduce the corroboration rule to absurdity is that in this instance the jury does not need actual corroboration, only a corroboration warning, and the more the accused admits, the safer it becomes to convict without corroboration. Only where corroboration is mandatory will this succeed, and this is a diminishing area.

The premise of the foregoing paragraph was apparently contradicted by Curran, L.J. in the Northern Ireland Court of Criminal Appeal when he said that the character of the *Baskerville* test did "not depend on which part of the accomplice's evidence is corroborated so long as its materiality and implicative nature are clear, and we know of no authority for restricting the requisite corroboration to the part or parts of the accomplice's testimony that the accused chooses to put in issue. On the contrary, admissions have for long been held corroborative and it is hard to see how this could be so if the argument under consideration were sound" (*R. v. Hodgett*, [1957] N.I. 1, at p. 8). But not all admissions are corroborative: the example discussed above assumes that the admissions made are not probative of guilt.

It should be noted that even if no corroboration rule of any kind applies, the evidence of a single witness need not be acted upon even though it is uncontradicted. Stephen (*History of the Criminal Law of England*, Vol. I, pp. 400–1) noted disapprovingly that seventeenth century juries "seem to have thought (as they very often still think) that a direct unqualified oath by an eye- or ear-witness has, so to speak, a mechanical value, and must be believed unless it is distinctly contradicted. . . . [J]uries do attach extraordinary importance to the dead weight of an oath." This approach was also attacked by Wigmore as a "loose and futile but not uncommon heresy" (para. 2034, n. 3). The reasons why uncontradicted evidence should sometimes be ignored were stated thus by Stephen: "The circumstances may be such that there is no check on the witness and no power to obtain any further evidence on the subject. . . . [Juries] may very reasonably say we do not attach so much credit to the oath of a single person of whom we know nothing, as to be willing to destroy another person on the strength of it. This case arises where the fact deposed to is a passing occurrence—such as a verbal confession or a sexual crime— leaving no trace behind it, except in the memory of an eye- or ear-witness. . . . The justification for this is, that the power of lying is unlimited, the causes of lying and delusion are numerous, and many of them are unknown, and the means of detection are limited."

Further reading

Andrews, [1964] Crim. L.R. 769; Anon., (1972); 81 Yale L.J. 1365; Bates, (1973), 47 A.L.J. 178; (1974), 48 A.L.J. 85; Ludwig, (1970), 36 Brooklyn L.R. 378; Coscowe, (1960), 25 Law and Contemporary Problems 222; Williams, Chap. 6.

V   REFORM

The Criminal Law Revision Committee proposed fairly drastic changes in the law of corroboration.

Criminal Law Revision Committee (11th Report)
1972. Cmnd. 4991

180. The rules undoubtedly have the great disadvantage of being sometimes difficult to apply owing to technical distinctions, for example as to what kinds of evidence may be corroboration and as to whether a person is an accomplice. . . . One disadvantage in particular is that a conviction may have to be quashed if the judge directs the jury that a piece of evidence is capable of being corroboration but the Court of Appeal holds that it was not capable of being so . . . even if there is plenty of other evidence. . . . The strictness of the present law . . . has often caused judges, out of caution, to follow too closely in their summing up the wording of the enactment requiring corroboration or the words used in a judgment; and as a result the jury may be confused or even get the impression that they should not convict unless the evidence achieves moral certainty as distinct from proof beyond reasonable doubt.

181. The rules requiring the giving of a warning of the danger of convicting in the absence of corroboration have been the subject of special ciriticism. . . . [I]t is said that the direction is absurd in that the judge, having warned the jury that it is dangerous to convict, may go on to say that they may nevertheless convict. It is true that the direction, looked at carefully, implies that it is in general dangerous to convict on the evidence of the kind in question but that in the particular case there may be no danger; but the distinction is a subtle one. . . .

182. It seems to us that there is a great deal of substance in many of the criticisms levelled against the rules as to corroboration. Some members would have liked to abolish all or most of the requirements altogether and replace them with a general provision enjoining judges to give a direction as to the special need for care in deciding whether to act on any particular piece of evidence if the circumstances of the witness required this. But the majority came to the conclusion that in some cases corroboration or a warning (of a different kind from the present) was necessary. . . .

185. . . . The effect of [clause 20 (1)], so far as accomplices are concerned, will be that it will be for the judge to consider whether the circumstances are such that a special warning should be given. . . . There will be no need to consider whether the witness is or is not an accomplice, but only what may be his motives in giving the evidence that he does; and it will be as if the principle in *Prater* [[1960] 2 Q.B. 464; [1960] 1 All E.R. 298, C.C.A.] . . . was extended so as to swallow up the rule about accomplices. . . . [W]e hope that the inclusion of the provision will serve as a reminder of the need to consider the giving of a warning even in cases where a warning is not required under the present law. . . . [W]e are proposing that the rule that the evidence of one accomplice cannot corroborate that of another accomplice should be abolished by the general provision in clause 19 (1).

188. . . . We shall be recommending later that . . . children under [fourteen] should in all cases give their evidence unsworn and those over that age should give it sworn. Where the complainant [in a sex case] is fourteen or over, we recommend that the judge should warn the jury that, if they find that the complainant's evidence is not corroborated, there will be a "special need for caution" before convicting [clause 17 (1)]. . . . In the case of a sexual offence against a child under fourteen we think that there should still be a requirement of corroboration. . . . [W]e regard it as unnecessary to preserve the special provisions in the Sexual Offences Act 1956 requiring corroboration in the case of certain sexual offences. . . .

191. . . . [T]he requirement [of corroboration] in s. 13 of the Perjury Act should be confined to perjury in judicial proceedings. . . .

[**192.** The requirement that corroboration of perjury be found in a second witness, so far as it exists, should be abolished.

194. The rule against mutual corroboration, so far as it exists, should be abolished.]

196. . . . We regard mistaken identification as by far the greatest cause of actual or possible wrong convictions. . . .

199. The majority of the committee are in favour of a statutory requirement that the judge should give a warning of the special need for caution before convicting in reliance on the correctness of one or more identifications of the accused where the case depends wholly or substantially on this. . . . The provision is in clause 21. It will be noted that it avoids referring to corroboration at all and expressly provides for the giving of the direction even when there is more than one identification. The clause is not limited to cases where the accused was previously unknown to the witness, because even where they are known to each other there may be a danger that the identification is mistaken. . . .

200. It would also help . . . if the police made it a practice in all cases to supply the defence with copies of any descriptions of the offender which any likely witness has given them. This would assist the defence to challenge the value of the witness's identification of the accused. . . . It would also, we think, be desirable that, where the circumstances allow, the police should ask an informant to write down or dictate his description as soon as possible and *before* being shown a photograph of the suspect. . . .

201. . . . The majority of the committee, while agreeing strongly that in general it is right that a witness who is to identify the accused in court as the offender should be asked first to attend an identification parade, do not think that there should be a statutory requirement. . . .

202. We considered a dilemma which arises when the accused is first picked out by a witness from a photograph shown to him by the police. . . . It is argued that the fact that the witness first identified the accused in this way greatly weakens the value of his evidence in court that the accused is the offender, because there is the danger that the identification in court may be more from the photograph than from the witness's recollection of seeing the offender at the time of the offence. . . . On the other hand, for the defence to bring out the fact that the accused was first identified from a photograph reveals the fact that the police possessed the accused's photograph and this implies almost certainly that he has a criminal record. . . . [The majority of the committee oppose any statutory change because] they think that it must be left to the defence to estimate which is the greater danger.

Questions

1. How would you solve the problem discussed in the last paragraph quoted?

2. Which of the following do you favour:
a) a standard corroboration direction for particular cases;
b) a corroboration direction which varies with circumstances but is mandatory (as in England now for accomplices, sworn children and complainants);
c) a discretionary warning, recommended as the general rule by the Criminal Law Revision Committee;
d) no provision for a warning at all, so that the only safeguard is the Court of Appeal's right to interfere when the verdict is unsafe?

6

The Privilege against Self-Incrimination

I INTRODUCTION

A witness when testifying must answer all relevant questions unless he can invoke some privilege to remain silent. The privilege against self-incrimination was stated by Goddard, L.J. in this way: "no one is bound to answer any question if the answer thereto would, in the opinion of the judge, have a tendency to expose the deponent to any criminal charge, penalty or forfeiture which the judge regards as reasonably likely to be preferred or sued for" (*Blunt* v. *Park Lane Hotel Ltd.*, [1942] 2 K.B. 253, at p. 257; [1942] 2 All E.R. 187, C.A.). The privilege also extends to the production of incriminating documents. The privilege does not absolve a deponent from answers which tend to expose him to any other civil action; in particular, *Blunt's* case decided that it did not apply where the answer might tend to establish the deponent's adultery. The "penalty" referred to is a statutory penalty. The rarity of recovering penalties make this part of the privilege of narrow scope. Further, in civil cases s. 16 (1) (*a*) of the Civil Evidence Act 1968 omits from the scope of the privilege answers which would tend to expose the witness to a forfeiture, and a similar change for criminal proceedings can only be a matter of time. The same may be said of other parts of the Civil Evidence Act resolving doubts in the common law for civil cases. The effect of these is that the privilege only applies to criminal offences and penalties under United Kingdom law, not foreign law (s. 14 (1) (*a*)) but it extends not only to questions tending to expose the witness to prosecution or the recovery of a penalty, but also to questions which have this effect on the witness's spouse (s. 14 (1) (*b*)). However, the privilege remains the witness's, and he can waive it even if the spouse objects.

The privilege is in fact very personal. It is not analogous to Crown privilege, where the contents of a document are privileged in the sense that no-one can give evidence of them (Chap. 18, *post*). If one who possesses a privilege against self-incrimination chooses to waive it, no litigant adversely affected can object. Indeed, if a litigant's witness makes a claim for privilege which is wrongly rejected, this is not a ground of appeal. The witness can by waiving his privilege give the evidence voluntarily; "if instead of giving his evidence voluntarily he gives it under compulsion, what is the difference?" (*R.* v. *Kinglake* (1870), 22 L.T. 335, at p. 336 *per* Blackburn, J.). It is different if the court wrongly

123

allows a claim of privilege, for here one party is improperly deprived of favourable evidence, where if the privilege is wrongly disallowed it simply results in the admission of relevant evidence (*Cloyes* v. *Thayer* (1842), 3 Hill 564, at p. 566). No adverse inference should be drawn from the fact that the privilege is claimed since otherwise the privilege would be destroyed (*Wentworth* v. *Lloyd* (1864), 10 H.L.C. 589, at pp. 590–2, H.L.), though it may be difficult to prevent the trier of fact (if the witness is a party to the case) or the prosecuting authorities (if he is not) from drawing such an inference. In this connexion it is worth noting that the privilege only prevents answers being given, it does not prevent questions being asked, even though the mere asking of the question will sometimes cause as much damage as the answer. Of course, to claim the privilege does not necessarily indicate guilt. Pollock, C.B. once pointed out that "a man may be placed under such circumstances with respect to the commission of a crime, that if he disclosed them he might be fixed upon by his hearers as a guilty person, so that the rule is not always the shield of the guilty, it is sometimes the protector of the innocent" (*Adams* v. *Lloyd* (1858), 3 H. & N. 351, at p. 363). Irrelevant questions, as opposed to relevant though incriminating ones, may be objected to, but by the litigant affected rather than his witness.

II THE ROLE OF THE JUDGE

The privilege against self-incrimination applies not only to answers directly incriminating the witness but also to answers that tend to do so indirectly. A number of such answers taken together or taken with other evidence might incriminate the witness in such a way that if he is forced to answer the dangers avoided by the privilege will occur (*R.* v. *Slaney* (1832), 5 C. & P. 213). But the witness's own view is not necessarily to be accepted: the court can override it.

R. v. Boyes
(1861), 1 B. & S. 311; [1861–73] All E.R. Rep. 172

The witness invoking the privilege had been handed a pardon under the Great Seal. The effect of this was to prevent his prosecution for the offence, though not his impeachment, the latter being a very unlikely prospect. The Court of Queens Bench (Cockburn C.J., Crompton, Hill and Blackburn JJ.) denied his right to privilege.

[T]o entitle a party called as a witness to the privilege of silence, the Court must see, from the circumstances of the case and the nature of the evidence which the witness is called to give, that there is reasonable ground to apprehend danger to the witness from his being compelled to answer. We indeed quite agree that, if the fact of the witness being in danger be once made to appear, great latitude should be allowed to him in judging for himself of the effect of any particular question: there being no doubt . . . that a question which might appear at first sight a very innocent one, might, by affording a link in a chain of evidence, become the means of bringing home an offence to the party answering. Subject to this reservation, a Judge is in our opinion, bound to insist on a witness answering unless he is satisfied that the answer will tend to place the witness in peril.

Further than this, we are of opinion that the danger to be apprehended must be real and appreciable, with reference to the ordinary operation of law in the ordinary course of things—not a danger of an imaginary and unsubstantial character, having reference to some extraordinary and barely possible contingency, so improbable that no reasonable man would suffer it to influence his conduct. We think that a merely remote and naked possibility, out of the ordinary course of the law and such as no reasonable man would be affected by, should not be suffered to obstruct the administration of justice. The object of the law is to afford to a party, called upon to give evidence in a proceeding inter alios, protection against being brought by means of his own evidence within the penalties of the law. But it would be to convert a salutary protection into a means of abuse if it . . . were to be held that a mere imaginary possibility of danger, however remote and improbable, was sufficient to justify the withholding of evidence essential to the ends of justice.

Now, in the present case, no one seriously supposes that the witness runs the slightest risk of an impeachment by the House of Commons.

It appears to us, therefore, that the witness in this case was not, in a rational point of view, in any the slightest real danger from the evidence he was called upon to give when protected by the pardon from all ordinary legal proceedings; and that it was therefore the duty of the presiding Judge to compel him to answer.

Re Reynolds, *ex parte* Reynolds
(1882), 20 Ch.D. 294; [1881–5] All E.R. Rep. 997, C.A.

BACON, C.J.: What is the case before me? The witness is alleged to be a trustee of a settlement the validity of which the trustee in bankruptcy seeks to impeach. He is called as a witness, and the deed being produced, he is asked whether it is executed by him, and the answer is, "I decline to answer because it might criminate me." Am I not bound to exercise such portion of common sense as I possess, and to say whether an answer to that question can possibly criminate anybody? If a suit were instituted in the Court of Chancery against a trustee such a question would be beyond all doubt, whether under the old practice or under the modern practice of interrogatories (the object of the Court being that there should be no needless expense in proving the execution of the deed), be allowed, and it could not upon any conceivable ground have the effect of criminating the witness. It is the same, I think, with all the other questions. It is not suggested that the witness has done anything criminal. It could not be criminal to execute a deed. It could not be criminal to deal with the property comprised in the deed—if he did deal with it—I do not say that he did. It could not be criminal to charge him with having received a sum of £1000 and paid it unto his bankers. It cannot be said that any one of the questions put to the witness could ever form a link in any criminal action which might be brought against him. There is no doubt the principle is a very important one, I was going to say a sacred one, because the liberty of the subject is at all times a sacred matter, and if I saw there was any chance of the answer to the question whether he executed a deed or not forming a link in a chain, one end of which would be the accusation and the other the conviction of the witness, I should hesitate very much before I compelled him to answer; but as it stands no one who has listened to this examination can entertain any doubt that it comes clearly within the cases pointed out, where the Court has been satisfied that the witness is trifling with the Court, and is setting up excuses which have no kind of foundation. I do not hesitate to say that the witness is bound to answer the questions, and therefore he must submit to an examination before the Registrar. If he does not answer, I need not point out to him the consequence that would attend his refusal.

Court of Appeal

JESSEL, M.R.: There are two questions to be decided; one of general importance, the other confined to the circumstances of the particular case. The question of general importance is, whether, when a witness objects to answer a question put to him on the ground that the answer to it may tend to criminate him, the mere statement of his own belief that it will tend to criminate him is sufficient to excuse him from answering, or whether the Judge is entitled to decide, not merely accepting the witness's statement, whether the proposed question has really a tendency to criminate him, or may fairly be considered, under all the circumstances of the case, as having that tendency.

Now upon that, there are various *dicta* and one express decision in R. v. *Boyes*. I am quite aware that the decision of the Court of Queen's Bench in R. v. *Boyes* is not technically binding on this Court, but at the same time it is a decision of the full Court of Queen's Bench, composed at that time of very eminent Judges, and I need not say that I should differ from them with very great hesitation.

That decision, as it appears to me, states the law correctly, and if it were necessary for the Court of Appeal to affirm it, we should, I think, be doing well and wisely in saying that we do affirm it. It is unnecessary after it to refer to the prior authorities; they are all mere *dicta*. But, as regards the subsequent case of *Re Firth; Ex parte Schofield*, decided in 1877, I will say this, that I am not sure it is a mere *dictum*; I rather think it is a decision. There Lord Justice James said, with regard to an examination under this very 96th section ((1877), 6 Ch. D. 230, at p. 233): "Of course when a witness objects on this ground to answer a question, the Judge will satisfy himself whether the objection is a genuine one."

. . . [I]f you allowed the witness merely on his own statement of his belief that an answer to the question would tend to criminate him (for that is all, he is only bound to believe that) to refuse to answer, it would enable a friendly witness, who wished to assist one of the parties, to escape examination altogether, and to refuse to give his evidence. That would be an evil so great as far to overbear, as a question of public policy, the danger, if it is to be treated as a danger, of occasionally assisting to convict a guilty man out of his own mouth. Perhaps our law has gone even too far in the direction of protecting a witness from the chance of convicting himself. But without at all impugning the policy of the law, there must certainly be a larger policy which requires that a witness should answer when the Judge thinks that he is objecting to answer, not *bona fide* with the view of claiming privilege to protect himself, but in order to prevent other parties from getting that testimony which is necessary for the purposes of justice.

And even those Judges who have entertained the contrary opinion have made an exception in the case of *mala fides*. I need only refer for that to what was said by the late Lord Chief Baron Pollock in *Adams* v. *Lloyd*, where, having stated the rule in favour of the protection of a witness on his own oath, he added ((1858), 3 H. & N. at p. 362): "The only exception I know of is this,—where the Judge is perfectly certain that the witness is trifling with the authority of the Court, and availing himself of the rule of law to keep back the truth, having in reality no ground whatever for claiming the privilege, then the Judge is right in insisting on his answering the question."

Well now, this being so, the second question we have to consider is whether there is any reasonable ground for fearing that the questions, when answered, will tend to convict the witness of a criminal offence, or to criminate him in any way. Now, in order to decide that point the Court must consider what the nature of the case is, and what the witness has said. When we look at the questions which the witness has refused to answer, the conviction, I think, must force itself upon the mind of any one that he refused to answer because he did not want to give the information, and that he was trifling with the Court.

I do not for a moment think that the witness is under any *bona fide* belief that there will be any charge of conspiracy made against him, or that he had any idea of such a charge; in fact I think the notion of such an indictment could only present itself to the mind of some one who was very familiar indeed with the law of conspiracy. It appears to me that the witness did not wish to afford any assistance to the bankrupt's creditors in obtaining possession of the property which had been kept from them. I think that was the prevailing motive with him, and not any real fear of criminal proceedings.

[COTTON and LINDLEY, L.JJ. gave judgments to the same effect.]

Brebner v. Perry

[1961] S.A.S.R. 177

The witness Seeley invoked the privilege against self-incrimination in criminal proceedings against Perry. Seeley had already made admissions to the police implicating himself and Perry in the commission of the offence charged. The Supreme Court of South Australia disallowed the claim.

MAYO, J.: What is the general proposition in regard to the compulsion of a witness to answer where he objects? The matter was discussed and principles stated and elaborated in *J. H. Sherring & Co.* v. *Hinton*, [1932] S.A.S.R. 233, and in *Matthew* v. *Flood*, [1938] S.A.S.R. 312. Where a witness who is on oath objects that the answer to a question put to him may incriminate him, and there is good reason to accept the objection as wellfounded he will be excused. . . . Where the risk is removed by a pardon or by a lapse of time, certainly if there be a statutory limitation upon proceedings, the privilege of the witness no longer remains: *Roberts* v. *Allatt* (1828), Mood. & M. 192; *Dover* v. *Maestaer* (1803), 5 Esp. 92, at p. 93; *A.-G.* v. *Cunard Steamship Co.* (1887), 4 T.L.R. 177. The claim by the witness, although on oath, even if there be no doubt as to his credibility, is not sufficient. It must be shown to the Court, from the circumstances, and the nature of the testimony that is sought to be educed, that there is reasonable ground he may be implicated in some offence by his answer. The fact that an offence (if any) would be of a trifling nature might be treated by the Court as precluding reliance on privilege. On the other hand, the rarity of prosecutions of a nature that might be framed wil not be regarded as an answer to an objection by the witness: *Triplex Safety Glass Co., Ltd.* v. *Lancegaye Safety Glass (1934), Ltd.*, [1939] 2 K.B. 395; [1939] 2 All E.R. 613, C.A. [a case involving a risk of criminal prosecutions for libel].

A point that, at times, may have some importance is that any fact a witness is *wrongly* forced to disclose in answer to questions after he had objected to answer will be inadmissible if criminal proceedings are subsequently brought against him. . . .

. . . Where a question concerns conduct that is in itself innocent, and will only involve risk to a witness as a link in chain of proof, he must satisfy the Court by facts that will, in that event, be outside the terms of the question that the answer would, or might tend to, incriminate him, e.g. *R.* v. *Cox and Railton* (1884), 14 Q.B.D. 153, at p. 175; [1881–5] All E.R. Rep. 68, at p. 76. On the other hand questions can bear on their face sufficient indication of matter to which the witness will be exposed if he answer in a certain way: *Re Genese, ex parte Gilbert* (1886), 3 Morr. 223, at p. 226. . . .

Where an objection to answer is not *bona fide* for the protection of a witness himself, he will be compelled to answer. . . .

Apply that aspect to the present matter. The witness had already, so far as it had been shown to the Court, made himself liable to any prosecution that might have been laid. Can his objection to answer be treated as *bona fide*? I think not. He was not concerned with his own protection. His conduct was in the interest of the defendant.

The fact that an offence was committed many years ago may also cause the court to deny the claim to privilege. But the fact that a successful prosecution is unlikely through the soft-heartedness of prosecutor or jury does not destroy the privilege (*Triplex Safety Glass Co., Ltd.* v. *Lancegaye Safety Glass (1934), Ltd.*, [1939] 2 K.B. 395; [1939] 2 All E.R. 613, C.A.).

One problem that stems from the rule that the witness's word as to the incriminating nature of what he is about to say is not enough is that "The privilege must . . . be violated in order to ascertain whether it exists. The secret must be told in order to see whether it ought to be kept" (*R.* v. *Cox and Railton* (1884), 14 Q.B.D. 153, at p. 175; [1881–5] All E.R. Rep. 68, at p. 76, *per* Stephen, J.). Often it will not be necessary for the entire secret to be told before the court has before it sufficient material to grant the privilege.

But what if it is necessary to tell all, or even part of the secret is incriminating? Cross suggests (p. 247) that "If difficulties were to arise in this regard they could no doubt be surmounted by allowing the witness to make his submission wholly or partially *in camera*, or under the protection of an understanding that no use could be made of his statements outside the proceedings in which they were given." For examples of the practice, see Josling, [1954] Crim. L. Rev. 916, at p. 917, and Heydon, [1971] Crim. L. Rev. 13, at pp. 33–4. Such undertakings are not binding as the law stands.

If a claim to privilege is wrongly rejected, anything the witness says will be treated as involuntary and inadmissible in subsequent proceedings (*R. v. Garbett* (1847), 1 Den. 236).

The privilege must be expressly invoked by the witness (*Boyle* v. *Wiseman* (1855), 10 Ex. Ch. 647, at p. 653, *per* Pollock, C.B.). In this respect it contrasts with the accused's rights not to be cross-examined about certain matters under s. 1 (*f*) of the Criminal Evidence Act 1898. If the witness could have claimed the privilege but fails to do so, the evidence will be admissible in the instant and in later proceedings (*R. v. Sloggett* (1856), Dears. 656). It might be thought that the witness should be warned of his right and of how he can recognize it, but the judge is not required to give such a warning.

R. v. Coote
(1873), L.R. 4 P.C. 599

Sir Robert Collier: The Chief Justice indeed suggests, that Coote may have been ignorant of the law enabling him to decline to answer criminating questions, and that if he had been acquainted with it he might have withheld some of the answers which he gave. As a matter of fact, it would appear that Coote was acquainted with so much of the law; but be this as it may, it is obvious, that to institute an inquiry in each case as to the extent of the prisoner's knowledge of law, and to speculate whether, if he had known more, he would or would not have refused to answer certain questions, would be to involve a plain rule in endless confusion. Their Lordships see no reason to introduce, with reference to this subject, an exception to the rule, recognized as essential to the administration of the Criminal Law, "*Ignorantia juris non excusat.*" With respect to the objection, that Coote when a witness should have been cautioned in the manner in which it is directed by statute, that persons accused before magistrates are to be cautioned (a question said by Mr. Justice Badgley not to have been reserved, but which is treated as reserved by the Court), it is enough to say, that the caution is by the terms of the statutes applicable to accused persons only and has no application whatever to witnesses.

Wigmore: Treatise on the Anglo-American System of Evidence in Trials at Common Law
3rd Edn. Para. 2269

... [S]uch a warning would be an anomaly; it is not given for any other privilege; witnesses are in other respects supposed to know their rights; and why not here? ... [I]n practical convenience, there is no demand for such a rule; witnesses are usually well enough advised beforehand by counsel as to their rights when such issues impend, and judges are too much concerned with other responsibilities to be burdened with the prevision of individual witnesses' knowledge; the risk of their being in ignorance should fall rather upon the party summoning than the party opposing.

A different view was reached in South Africa, partly on the ground that whatever knowledge of the law might be presumed amongst other populations, knowledge of the privilege could not be presumed to exist in South Africa where "the masses still include humble Bantu bemusedly endeavouring to adjust an untutored outlook to the complexities of civilization". If the warning is not given there the evidence will ordinarily be inadmissible in the proceedings (*S. v. Lwane* 1966 (2) S.A. 433, at p. 444).

Lord Eldon, L.C. once said that giving such warnings was "that, which every judge in the country used to do, though it is not so much in practice now as it was at that time" (*Re Worrall, ex parte Cossens* (1820), 1 Buck. 531, at p. 544), and a warning is in fact still often given. The court probably has a discretion to exclude the evidence in a later trial if the privilege could have been but was not claimed (*Re Shanahan* (1912), 45 I.L.T.R. 254, at p. 258, *per* Holmes, L.J.).

It should be noted that a witness who fears he may be asked incriminating questions cannot refuse to be sworn at all. He must at least listen to each question and suffer any incriminating effect the question has by itself. If he wants to claim privilege he must do so in respect of each individual question. The old doctrine that once a witness chose to begin replying he had to answer every question relevant to the transaction in question was reversed in *R. v. Garbett* (1847), 1 Den. 236.

Modern statutes setting up administrative tribunals often expressly preserve the privilege against self-incrimination in proceedings before them, e.g. National Insurance Act 1946, s. 49 (4).

The Criminal Evidence Act 1898 enabled the accused to give evidence on his own behalf. But it was thought that if he retained the privilege against self-incrimination even in respect of the offence charged he would be too favourably placed, because he would be immune, if he so chose, from answering any questions in cross-examination. S. 1 (e) therefore provides:

"A person charged and being a witness in pursuance of this Act may be asked any question in cross-examination notwithstanding that it would tend to incriminate him as to the offence charged."

III THE IMPORTANCE OF THE PRIVILEGE

The privilege has often been praised or justified. English judges have called it "a most important right" (*Orme v. Crockford* (1824), 13 Price 376, at p. 388, *per* Alexander; L.C.B.); "most sacred" (*Re Worrall, ex parte Cossens* (1820), 1 Buck. 531, at p. 540, *per* Lord Eldon, L.C.); a "general rule established with great justice and tenderness" (*Harrison v. Southcote and Moreland* (1751), 2 Ves. Sen. 389, at p. 394, *per* Lord Hardwicke, L.C.); "a maxim of our law as settled, as important and as wise as almost any other in it" (*R. v. Scott* (1856), Dears. & B. 47, at p. 61, *per* Coleridge, J.). The American Founding Fathers inserted it into the Fifth Amendment to the Constitution as one of those "principles of natural justice which had become permanently fixed in the jurisprudence of the mother country" (*Brown v. Walker*, (1896), 161 U.S. 591, at p. 600). There it is regarded as "one of the great landmarks in man's struggle to make himself civilized . . . an expression of one of the fundamental decencies in this relation we have developed between government and man" (Erwin N. Griswold, *The Fifth Amendment Today* (Cambridge, Mass., 1955) pp. 7–8, partially quoted in *Ullmann v. U.S.*, (1955), 350 U.S. 422, at p. 426, *per* Frankfurter, J. See also *Murphy v. Waterfront Commission of New York Harbour*, (1964), 378 U.S. 52, at pp. 55–6, *per* Goldberg, J.).

The privilege against self-incrimination was worked out by the late Stuart judges (see Wigmore, para. 2250). By the time of Blackstone it was settled law that, in his words, "at the common law, *nemo tenebatur prodere seipsum*: and his fault was not to be wrung out of himself, but rather to be discovered by other means and other men" (*Commentaries* (12th Edn., London, 1795), IV, Chap. 22, p. 296). For this there were historical reasons. In the early seventeenth century some prerogative courts indulged in unrestrained and wanton interrogation of suspects, often using torture. Selden reported that "The rack is used nowhere as in England. In other countries 'tis used in judicature, when there is a *semi-plena probatio*, a half-proof against a man, then to see if they can make it full, they rack him to try if he will confess. But here in England they take a man and rack him, I do not know why, nor when, not in time of judicature, but when somebody bids" (*Table Talk* (ed. Pollock, London, 1927), p. 133). By the late seventeenth century there was a strong judicial revulsion against this and against every feature of the prerogative courts. As Bentham said, "what could be more natural than that, by a people infants as yet in reason, giants in passion, every distinguishable feature of a system of procedure directed to such ends should be condemned in the lump, should be involved in one undistinguishing mass of odium and abhorrence" (Bentham, IX, part IV, c. iii, p. 456). Bentham called this the "argument by reference to unpopular institutions" (*ibid.*, p. 455).

A similar argument is the argument that since the privilege appears in the same part of the American constitution as the freedom of religion, of speech, and of the press, and provisions against unreasonable searches and seizures of the home, it is necessarily as important as these. The privilege has acquired "a borrowed radiance from its close connection with these other rights which are genuine essentials of ordered liberty. It has gained a sort of sanctity by association" (McCormick, p. 290).

Bentham is the principal opponent of the privilege.

Bentham: A Rationale of Judicial Evidence
Book IX, Pt. 4, c. iii

(a) Pretences for exclusion [of the accused's testimony on compulsion]. . . .

2. The old woman's reason. The essence of this reason is contained in the word *hard*; 'tis hard upon a man to be obliged to criminate himself. Hard it is upon a man, it must be confessed, to be obliged to do anything that he does not like. That he should not much like to do what is meant by his criminating himself, is natural enough; for what it leads to, is, his being punished. What is no less hard upon him, is, that he should be punished: but did it ever yet occur to a man to propose a general abolition of all punishment, with this hardship for a reason for it? Whatever hardship there is in a man's being punished, that, and no more, is there in his thus being made to criminate himself. . . .

Nor yet is all this plea of tenderness,—this double-distilled and treble-refined sentimentality, anything better than a pretence. From his own mouth you will not receive the evidence of the culprit against him; but in his own hand, or from the mouth of another, you receive it without scruple: so that at bottom, all this sentimentality resolves itself into neither more nor less than a predilection—a confirmed and most extensive predilection, for bad evidence. . . .

3. The fox-hunter's reason. This consists in introducing upon the carpet of legal procedure the idea of *fairness,* in the sense in which the word is used by sportsmen. The fox is to have a fair chance for his life: he must have (so close is the analogy) what is

called *law*—leave to run a certain length of way for the express purpose of giving him a chance for escape. While under pursuit, he must not be shot: it would be as *unfair* as convicting him of burglary on a hen-roost in five minutes' time, in a court of conscience.

In the sporting code, these laws are rational, being obviously conducive to the professed end. Amusement is that end; a certain quantity of delay is essential to it: dispatch, a degree of dispatch reducing the quantity of delay below the allowed minimum, would be fatal to it. . . . To different persons, both a fox and a criminal have their use; the use of a fox is to be hunted; the use of a criminal is to be tried. . . .

Wigmore: Treatise on The Anglo-American System of Evidence in Trials at Common Law

3rd Edn. Para. 2251

The current judicial habit is . . . to laud it undiscriminatingly with false cant. A stranger from another legal sphere might imagine, in the perusal of our precedents, that the guilty criminal was the fond object of the Court's doting tenderness, guiding him at every step in the path of unrectitude, and lifting up his feet lest he fall into the pits digged for him by justice. The judicial practice, now too common, of treating with warm and fostering respect every appeal to this privilege, and of amicably feigning each guilty invocator to be an unsullied victim hounded by the persecutions of a tyrant, is a mark of traditional sentimentality. . . .

There ought to be an end of judicial cant towards crime. We have already had too much of what a wit has called "justice tampered with mercy".

. . . Courts should unite to keep the privilege strictly within the limits dictated by historic fact, cool reasoning, and sound policy.

The privilege admittedly has drawbacks. It generally favours the guilty. It may encourage authorities to use means of obtaining information more improper than questioning. It is less necessary in these days of a generally fair criminal procedure. But it will be suggested that it still serves some useful purposes. It ought not to be abolished or weakened merely because in particular cases its "restraints are inconvenient or because the supposed malefactor may be a subject of public execration or because the disclosures of his wrongdoing will promote the public weal" (*Doyle* v. *Hofstader* (1931), 177 N.E. 489, at p. 491, *per* Cardozo, C.J.). In Maguire's words, "Liberty never comes free of charge" (*Evidence of Guilt* (Boston, 1959), para. 2.02, n. 6). What are the useful purposes served by the privilege? First, if it did not exist, some witnesses would be faced with a painful trilemma. They would have a choice between punishment for silence when they have a duty to speak, punishment for perjury if they speak falsely, and punishment for their crimes if they speak the truth. This trilemma produces undesirable results. The privilege is thus said to protect the "conscience and dignity of man" (*Ullmann* v. *U.S.* (1950), 350 U.S. 422, at p. 446, *per* Black and Douglas, JJ.). Admittedly, as Bentham pointed out in the passage quoted above, such an argument is often said to be based on the sporting theory of justice: "the use of a fox is to be hunted; the use of a criminal is to be tried" (Bentham, *op. cit.*, p. 454). That is, just as it is poor fun if the fox has no chance to escape, so the criminal must not be unduly handicapped. Bentham also ridiculed it as "the old woman's reason", imbued with a feeble sentimentalism which ought not to be displayed towards criminals. The sporting theory of justice may be ludicrous, and the notion of tenderness to criminals can be carried too far, but the privilege against self-incrimination does seem to be based on a deeply-felt public need. Public confidence in the administration of the law is an important value. "Accustomed personal safeguards, fixed in men's minds by usage of decades and centuries, are not lightly to be destroyed" (Maguire, *Evidence of Guilt*, p. 14).

Secondly, the privilege against self-incrimination is merely one rule among many which depend on the view that at least in theory the accused's guilt must be proved by the prosecution at an English criminal trial. Some have thought that this principle goes too far. The Canadian judge, Riddell, J., once said: "We have not yet arrived at the point that one accused of crime has so many and so high rights that the people have none. The administration of our law is not a game in which the cleverer and more astute is to win, but a serious proceeding by a people in earnest to discover the actual facts for the sake of public safety, the interest of the public generally. It is the duty of every citizen to tell all he knows for the sake of the people at large, their interest and security" (*R. v. Barnes* (1921), 61 D.L.R. 623, at p. 638). There is of course no "duty" of the kind suggested except as provided by statute. More importantly, there is something to be said in favour of weighting the scales in favour of the subject and against the state. The state has much better machinery for protecting its interests than its subjects; it should be made to rely on it. In Wigmore's words:

. . . "*any system of administration which permits the prosecution to trust habitually to compulsory self-disclosure as a source of proof must itself suffer thereby*. The inclination develops to rely mainly upon such evidence, and to be satisfied with an incomplete investigation of the other sources. The exercise of the power to extract answers begets a forgetfulness of the just limitations of that power. . . . If there is a right to an answer, there soon seems to be a right to the expected answer" (para. 2251).

Stephen's information as to why Indian policemen indulged in torture was that "it is far pleasanter to sit comfortably in the shade rubbing red pepper into a poor devil's eyes than to go about in the sun hunting up evidence" (*History of the Criminal Law of England* (London, 1883), I, p. 442). This may be regarded as a very extreme form of the danger under consideration, but Parliament has often shared the view that there is a danger to be controlled. Thus in some cases where the privilege is completely abrogated by statute, safeguards are substituted. One is that only officials above a certain rank may extract answers under threat of lawful punishment. Another is that such a power should only be exercised with the approval of a high-ranking official. The Official Secrets Act 1920, s. 6 (substituted by Official Secrets Act 1939, s. 1) illustrates both methods: only policemen of the rank of at least *inspector*, acting with the consent of a chief officer of police and the Secretary of state can exercise powers of compulsory questioning. Thus sometimes when Parliament removes the privilege it feels the need of safeguards against the abuses that come from a lack of maturity, responsibility or sophistication. It is said that the argument cannot "sustain the constant recognition of this privilege in purely civil proceedings where the government is not a factor" (Maguire, *Evidence: Common Sense and Common Law* (Chicago, 1947), p. 106). But there too it would be undesirable to allow the government to rely on one civil litigant's power to force admissions of criminal conduct out of another.

Thirdly, the privilege removes one obstacle preventing witnesses coming forward. "The witness-stand is today sufficiently a place of annoyance and dread. The reluctance to enter it must not be increased. . . . To remove all limits of inquiry into the secrets of the persons who have no stake in the cause but can furnish help in its investigation, would be to add to the motives which now sufficiently dispose them to evade their duty" (Wigmore, para. 2251). Maguire considers that this only "affects an extremely small percentage of the total number of useful witnesses" (*Evidence of Guilt*, pp. 13–14). But it this so? Parties to civil suits may invoke the privilege, though perhaps their interests may be set aside as deserving little sympathy. In England, the accused may invoke it, for though he is compelled to be present, and though he has no privilege against incriminating himself with respect to the offence charged (Criminal Evidence Act 1898, s. 1 (e)), he may wish to enter the box and claim the privilege with respect to other matters. There remain a large number of possible witnesses in civil and criminal cases whose reluctance to come forward and assist the interests of justice will be reduced if they know they have the privilege against self-incrimination. It is said that the privilege is not a real inducement to come forward because it is embarrassing to invoke (the public assumes guilt), and because a claim of privilege will alert the police that the witness may have a criminal past (Meltzer, (1951), 18 Univ. of Ch.L.R. 687, at p. 699). But the risks of embarrassment and of alerting the police will vary in gravity enormously from case to case, and do not destroy the overall value of the privilege.

Fourthly, because of the general terrors of appearing in court, a witness, it has been cogently argued, is "under duress—his mind disturbed by the extraordinary situation in which he [finds] himself placed, and called on in the midst of these trying circumstances to weigh and consider the nature of each question, and the consequences of his answers; and if so, the law cannot estimate the exact degree of influence of the duress on the human mind" (*R. v. Wheater* (1838), 2 Mood. C.C. 45, at pp. 46–7, *per* Dundas *arguendo*). The point is that witnesses in a state of agitation are likely to perform poorly and possibly tell unconscious falsehoods; anything that reduces their fears makes their evidence more valuable.

Fifthly, the risk of perjury is reduced, because one important incentive to lie is absent if a claim to the privilege is upheld. The court can thus be more confident in the evidence it does hear from the witness. It has often been objected that the privilege involves an unacceptable sacrifice in the number of convictions. But it is questionable whether the problem is so serious. A successful claim of privilege does not completely absolve someone with a criminal past, for his objection will alert the investigating authorities to the fact that he has something to hide and they will thus increase their efforts to prove it by other evidence, if it exists. Another objection to the privilege is that it causes less evidence to be placed before the court, and this is unjust to those involved in the proceedings in that the truth is less likely to be discovered. However, if a witness's evidence really is important, it can be obtained by special devices such as a pardon, a promise by the authorities not to prosecute, or an immunity statute of the kind we shall consider below. It is of course difficult to balance the beneficial effects of removing a general reason for not testifying from all potential witnesses against the detrimental effect of losing particular pieces of evidence in consequence of successful privilege claims proceeding from a small proportion of the total class of witnesses.

Finally, if a witness, in an attempt at self-preservation, simply refuses to answer and there is no privilege against self-incrimination to permit this, the courts may not be able to enforce their demands. The remedy for contempt may disrupt the orderly flow of the trial; it may destroy the appearance of judicial impartiality. The privilege thus reflects the law's unwillingness to order the impossible.

One other commonly advanced argument should be noted. It is not in fact a sound one as a matter of principle, but it explains the popularity of the privilege to some extent. The argument is that the privilege helps to frustrate bad laws and bad procedures. Sometimes the laws in question are those persecuting the holders of certain political beliefs. Thus in the United States during the 1950s the Fifth Amendment was praised for protecting certain freedoms of thought which were not then adequately protected by the First Amendment. The laws in question may be those proscribing conduct popular among large sections of the population—particular forms of gambling, liquor consumption and sexual activity. The procedures which are felt to be bad are inquiries by administrative and legislative committees. The publicity they attract during and after their operation ''can have devastating effect upon people dragged into them. Their pronouncements or implications are not always controlled by practised habit of cautious and thorough inquiry'' (Maguire, *Evidence of Guilt*, p. 14). Here the privilege is praised because it helps to protect privacy.

Arguments of this last kind are commonly advanced against bad laws. But the problem is that if the privilege is too exclusive it tends to frustrate not only bad laws and improperly officious inquiries, but all laws and inquiries, good or bad. Further, the answer to bad laws is not to depend on other rules to frustrate them indirectly, but to repeal them directly. As Stephen said:

> "In the old Ecclesiastical Courts and in the Star Chamber [the 'ex officio' oath] was understood to be and was used as an oath to speak the truth on the matters objected against the defendant—an oath, in short, to accuse oneself. It was vehemently contended by those who found themselves pressed by this oath that it was against the law of God, and the law of nature, and that the maxim '*nemo tenetur prodere seipsum*' was agreeable to the law of God, and part of the law of nature. In this, I think, as in most other discussions of the kind, the real truth was that those who disliked the oath had usually done the things of which they were accused, and which they regarded as meritorious actions, though their judges regarded them as crimes. People always protest with passionate eagerness against being deprived of technical defences against what they regard as bad law, and such complaints often give a spurious value to technicalities when the cruelty of the laws against which they have afforded protection has come to be commonly admitted" (*History of the Criminal Law*, I, p. 342).

It is thought that the privilege against self-incrimination is adequately supported without reliance on the ''bad laws'' argument, however.

IV STATUTORY RESTRICTIONS ON THE PRIVILEGE

There are a large number of statutes which have removed the privilege against self-incrimination. They empower state officials to obtain information under the compulsion of punishment for failure to provide it satisfactorily. Sometimes these statutes make precise provision regarding the admissibility of the evidence in subsequent proceedings. Some statutes provide an "immunity bath", as the American phrase has it, in which the risk of conviction is washed away if full disclosure is made. Thus the Larceny Act 1916, s. 43 (2) (now repealed by the Theft Act 1968, Sched. 3, Pt. I) provides that the informant shall not be convicted of certain crimes in regard to any act done by him which he has first disclosed in a certain way. The Canada Evidence Act 1952, s. 5 (2) is even wider in granting immunity from prosecution for all crimes save perjury in respect of the evidence given. Another group of statutes provides that the information given shall not be admissible against the enforcement in "any proceedings, civil or criminal" (Representation of the People Act 1949, s. 123 (7) (*b*)) or in particular kinds of proceedings (Bankruptcy Act 1914, s. 166).

The real problem arises with statutes which make no provision for immunity or continued privilege but simply state that the information may be "used in evidence against" the informant (Companies Act 1948, s. 270 (7)), or say nothing at all (Purchase Tax Act 1963, s. 24 (6)). It is a problem of some practical importance. These statutes relate to company officials in winding-up proceedings, officials investigating liability to taxation (*supra*), the public examination of bankrupts (Bankruptcy Act 1914, s. 15 (8)), inquiries into election offences (Representation of the People Act 1949, s. 123 (7)); police questioning with regard to certain offences (Road Traffic Act 1960, s. 232; Official Secrets Act 1920, s. 6, substituted by Official Secrets Act 1939, s. I); and many other areas.

The rule is that if the information has been lawfully obtained and the statute does not restrict the use to be made of it, it is admissible in subsequent proceedings. *Pro tanto*, then, the statutes in question have abolished the privilege against self-incrimination.

R. v. Scott
(1856), Dears. & B. 47

LORD CAMPBELL, C.J.: The judgment which I will now read is concurred in by my Brothers Alderson, Willes, and Bramwell; my Brother Coleridge differs. We are of opinion that the defendant's examination before the Court of Bankruptcy was properly admitted in evidence by my Brother Willes, and that the conviction ought to be confirmed. This examination was taken in strict conformity with section 117 of 12 & 13 Vict. c. 106, which enacts that the bankrupt may be examined by the Court "touching all matters relating to his trade, dealings, or estate, or which may tend to disclose any secret grant, conveyance or concealment of his lands, tenements, goods, money or debts". . . . In R. v. *Garbett* (1 Den. C. C. 236), and in other cases, it has been held that where the defendant has been improperly compelled to answer questions tending to criminate himself, his answers cannot be given in evidence against him; but as the report of R. v. *Merceron* (1818), 2 Stark. 366 was said by Lord Tenterden not to be correct, we have no decision to guide us as to the admissibility of this examination which was perfectly lawful. Being a genuine document signed by the defendant, *prima facie* it is admissible against him; and we will consider the several grounds on which the defendant's counsel has argued that it is not admissible. . . . [One is that] the examination was compulsory. It is a trite maxim that the confession of a crime, to be admissible against the party confessing, must be voluntary; but this only means that it shall not be induced by improper threats or promises, because, under such circumstances, the party may have been influenced to say what is not true, and the supposed confession cannot be safely acted upon. Such an objection cannot apply to a lawful examination in the course of a judicial proceeding. Then the defendant's counsel objects that, in the course of this examination, threats were used; the alleged threats, however, were merely an explanation of the enactment of the Legislature upon the subject, and a warning to the defendant of the consequences which, in point of law, would arise from his refusing to give a true answer to the questions put to him. Finally, the defendant's counsel relies upon the great maxim of English law *"nemo tenetur se ipsum accusare"*. So undoubtedly says the common law of England. But Parliament may take away this privilege, and enact that a party may be bound to accuse himself; that is, that he must answer questions by answering which he may be criminated. This Act of Parliament, 12 & 13 Vict. c. 106, creates felonies and misdemeanors, and compels the bankrupt to answer questions which may shew that he has been guilty of some of those felonies or misdemeanors. The maxim of the common law therefore has been overruled by the Legislature, and the defendant has been actually compelled to give and has given answers, shewing that he is guilty of the misdemeanor with which he is charged. The accusation of himself was an accomplished fact, and at the trial he was not called upon to accuse himself. The maxim relied upon applies to the time when the question is put, not to the use which the prosecutor seeks to make of the answer when the answer has been given. If the party has been unlawfully compelled to answer the question, he shall be protected against any prejudice from the answer thus illegally extorted; but a similar protection cannot be demanded where the question was lawful and the party examined was bound by law to answer it. At the trial the defendant's written examination, signed by himself, was in Court, and the reading of it as evidence against him could be no violation of the maxim relied upon. The only argument, as we conceive, that can plausibly be put for the defendant is, that there is an implied proviso to be subjoined to the 117th section, *viz.* "that the examination shall not be used as evidence against the bankrupt on any criminal charge". To make it evidence there could be no necessity for any express enactment for that purpose, and an implied proviso appears all that can be contended for. But by this interpolation we may be more likely to defeat than to further the intention of the Legislature. Considering the enormous frauds practised by bankrupts upon their creditors, the object may have been, in an exceptional instance, to allow a procedure in England universally allowed in many highly civilized countries. Suppose section 117 had begun with a preamble reciting the frauds of bankrupts, and the importance of having these frauds detected and punished, it would be difficult to say that the Legislature intended that no use should be made of the examination except for civil purposes. When the Legislature compels parties to give evidence accusing themselves, and means to protect them from the consequences of giving such evidence, the course of legislation has been to do so by express enactment, as in 6 Geo. IV. c. 129, s. 6, and the five other instances adduced in the argument on behalf of the prosecution. We therefore think we are bound to suppose that in this instance, in which no such protection is provided, it was the intention of the Legislature to compel the bankrupt to answer interrogatories respecting his dealings and conduct as a trader, although he might thereby accuse himself and to permit his answers to be used against him for criminal as well as civil purposes.

COLERIDGE, J.: I have the misfortune in this case to differ from the rest of the Court; and entertaining unfeignedly a great distrust of my own opinion I should gladly surrender it to theirs, if I could divest myself of the belief that the judgment, which I venture to think erroneous, goes also to impair a maxim of our law as settled, as important and as wise as almost any other in it; and, consequently, that it is a duty to enter my protest, however ineffectually, against it. The maxim to which I allude will, of course, be understood to be that which is familiar to all lawyers,—that no person can be compelled to criminate himself. It would be a wasting of time to support this maxim by authorities or to dwell upon its importance. The judgment from which I differ does not proceed upon a denial or disparagement of it; but on some such argument as this— every lawful examination of a party charged, conducted according to law, is admissible evidence against him; this examination was lawful by statute and has been lawfully conducted; therefore this examination is admissible evidence against the prisoner. Now I deny the major premise of this syllogism. I say that it is not true in the general and unqualified way in which it is stated. I say that an examination may be lawful for certain purposes and be lawfully conducted with these purposes in view; and yet not be admissible in evidence against the party charged when upon his trial on a criminal charge, even if that charge be founded on the matters before lawfully inquired into. We have here on the one hand an undisputed and indisputable maxim of the common law that no man shall be bound to accuse himself; on the other we have a statute not in terms professing to abrogate this maxim, but authorizing commissioners of bankrupts to examine a bankrupt "touching all matters relating to concealment of his lands, tenements, goods, money or debts"; and subjecting him to imprisonment indefinitely, without bail, if he refuse to answer. The same statute makes it a felony, punishable with transportation for life, for a bankrupt to conceal any part of his real or personal estate to the value of £10, with intent to defraud his creditors. How, then, upon general principles, are we to proceed in a seeming conflict between the common law and these provisions of the statute? Not, I apprehend, by assuming at once that there is a real conflict, and sacrificing the common law; but by carefully examining whether the two may not be reconciled, and full effect be given to both; and for this purpose it is most material to ascertain with what intent, and for what object, the bankrupt is compellable to undergo this examination, and to answer the questions put. If, for example, it should appear that he was to be examined with a view of procuring evidence against him on a criminal charge, instituted, or to be instituted, whatever one might think of the justice of such an enactment it would be idle to contend that it had not abrogated *pro tanto* the common law. If, on the other hand, it should be clear that the examination was authorized solely for the better discovery of the bankrupt's estate, and the bringing it into distribution amongst his creditors—that it would be unlawful to examine him for any other purpose—that he might lawfully refuse to answer any question put merely for the purpose of extracting evidence against him on a criminal charge, then I conceive that you would be far advanced on your way to a conclusion which will prevent the statute from breaking in upon the common law.

ALDERSON, B.: I have nothing to say to what has fallen from my Brother Coleridge but this—that my judgment proceeds upon the ground, that if you make a thing lawful to be done, it is lawful in all its consequences; and one of its consequences is, that what may be stated by a person in a lawful examination, may be received in evidence against him. That is quite settled and conformable to a most important maxim of English law.

This decision has been approved by the Privy Council (*R. v. Coote* (1873), L.R. 4 P.C. 599); the Court of Crown Cases Reserved (*R. v. Erdheim*, [1896] 2 Q.B. 260; [1895–9] All E.R. Rep. 610); the Court of Appeal (*Commissioners of Customs and Excise v. Ingram*, [1948] 1 All E.R. 927, C.A.) and by *dicta* in the House of Lords in *Harz's Case*.

Commissioners of Customs and Excise v. Harz
[1967] 1 A.C. 760; [1967] 1 All E.R. 177, H.L.

The defendants were accused of defrauding the Revenue of purchase tax; the main evidence against them consisted of statements obtained under threat of prosecution for infringing s. 24 (6) of the Purchase Tax Act 1963. The House of Lords stated that these statements would have been admissible if obtained in accordance with the statute.

LORD REID: On February 27, 1963, customs officers took possession of a number of Lee's books and began to question Harz and others. Harz said: "We are not talking," but the officers told him that he would be prosecuted if he did not answer. He gave certain answers on that occasion. On subsequent occasions, the last being in August, he and his solicitor, who was present, continued to believe that there was power to prosecute if he did not answer and in the course of long interrogations, one of which lasted more than three hours, he made certain incriminating admissions. I am of opinion that it must be held that this threat of prosecution was intended by the customs officers to apply and was thought by Harz to apply on all these occasions, and that this is a typical case of a suspected person being induced by a threat to make incriminating admissions. I think that it is clear that Harz would not have made these admissions if he had not been told that he must answer the officers' questions there and then and that if he refused he would be prosecuted.

In my opinion, the officers had no right to require Harz to submit to this prolonged interrogation and he could not have been prosecuted if he had refused to answer. The officers' power to interrogate was said to be derived from section 20 (3) of the Finance Act, 1946 (now replaced by section 24 (6) of the Purchase Tax Act, 1963), which provides as follows:

"Every person concerned with the purchase or importation of goods, or with the application to goods of any process of manufacture, or with dealings with imported goods, shall furnish to the commissioners, within such time and in such form as they may require, information relating to the goods, or to the purchase or importation of them or to the application of any process of manufacture to them, or to dealings with them as they may specify, and shall, upon demand made by any officer or other person authorized in that behalf by the commissioners, produce any books or accounts or other documents of whatever nature relating thereto for inspection by that officer or person at such time and place as that officer or person may require."

There is here a clear distinction between the right of an officer to demand production of documents and the right of the commissioners to require information to be furnished at such time and in such manner as they may require. The right of the officer is to require immediate production of documents and if the trader fails to produce documents in his possession of the kinds demanded he can be prosecuted. No doubt the officer can ask questions relating to documents of the kinds which he has demanded and the trader's answer or refusal to answer may be admissible in evidence. But the prosecution will not be for refusal to answer questions; it will be for refusal to produce documents, and I can see nothing to require the trader to give answers which may incriminate him.

The right of the commissioners to require information is quite different. If a demand for information is made in the proper manner, the trader is bound to answer the demand within the time and in the form required, whether or not the answer may tend to incriminate him, and, if he fails to comply with the demand, he can be prosecuted. If he answers falsely he can be prosecuted for that and if he answers in such a manner as to incriminate himself I can see no reason why his answer should not be used against him. Some statutes expressly provide that incriminating answers may be used against the person who gives them and some statutes expressly provide that they may not. Where, as here, there is no such express provision the question whether such answers are admissible evidence must depend on the proper construction of the particular statute. Although I need not decide the point, it seems to me to be reasonably clear that incriminating answers to a proper demand under this section must be admissible if the statutory provision is to achieve its obvious purpose.

If the admissions with which the appeal is concerned had been obtained by a proper exercise of this power of the commissioners they might well have been admissible in evidence in this prosecution. It was argued in the first place that the officers who conducted the interrogation had not been properly authorized by the commissioners to exercise their powers. Probably they had not, but I need not pursue that because I think that the respondents succeed in their second argument. The trader is only bound to furnish information within such time and in such form as the commissioners require.

The information will often be complicated and the commissioners can be relied on to fix a reasonable time. If the information required is simple and easily provided, the time required may be short. But I do not think that this entitles the commissioners to send a representative to confront the trader, put questions to him orally and demand oral answers on the spot. And I am certainly of opinion that it does not entitle them to send their representative to subject the trader to a prolonged interrogation in the nature of a cross-examination. This provision is in sharp contrast with provisions which expressly entitle officers to question persons with regard to particular matters, for example, to question passengers entering the country with regard to their luggage. When it is intended that officers shall obtain information by asking oral questions that is made plain in the statute. The Solicitor-General was asked whether he was aware of any other case in which a government department claimed the right to send a representative to interrogate a person for hours on end under the sanction that he would be prosecuted if he failed to answer any question and that any incriminating answer which he might give under threat of prosecution for failing to answer could be used in evidence against him. But he was unable to cite any parallel case. I am not to be taken as saying that every inquisitorial procedure is inherently objectionable: this case may indicate the contrary. But if any such procedure were introduced it would certainly contain safeguards which are absent from the procedure which the appellants support in this case.

[Lords Morris of Borth-Y-Gest, Hodson, Pearce and Wilberforce agreed.]

There are several arguments against the *Scott* doctrine, some of which are very ably put by Coleridge, J. in his dissenting judgment. See also Heydon (1971), 87 L.Q.R. 214 and [1971] Crim. L. Rev. 13, at pp. 24–34. The principal objections are these.

A court's attempt to give effect to as many of a statute's possible aims as it can is foolish and self-stultifying, because these aims often conflict among themselves. If the purposes of questioning a taxpayer are to recover the taxes due, investigate tax evasion with a view to future prevention, discover leads to other criminals and punish the taxpayer's dishonesty, they cannot all be achieved by direct questioning. The fear of criminal prosecution for the evasion will induce a man to stay silent or to lie, and if he is successful, none of the aims of the investigation will be carried out. It is true that there are punishments for silence, but these will usually be less than for the crime of tax evasion which is concealed. Indeed the twin dangers of punishment for silence and punishment for tax evasion will force the taxpayer to lie (*R. v. Pike* [1902] 1 K.B. 552). He still runs a risk of punishment for lying, but it will often be a remote risk because *ex hypothesi* the Commissioners do not yet have enough independently acquired evidence to make a successful prosecution for tax evasion likely, and therefore will not have enough to prove that the taxpayer is lying.

The following general approach for the interpretation of statutes which provide for compulsory questioning is suggested. A statute will often have several possible purposes to be collected from a reading of it as a whole. Thus the information obtained by the Commissioners under the Purchase Tax Act 1963, s. 24 (6) could be used to claim the full tax owed by the individual questioned; it could be used to help the authorities understand the processes of tax evasion with a view to prevention of this by future legislation; it could be used to prosecute accomplices of the informant; and it could be used to prosecute the informant himself. Clearly the first three possible aims can only be carried out by forcing the taxpayer to answer all the questions, and to that extent the privilege against self-incrimination is abrogated, both because of the express words of s. 24 (6) ("shall furnish") and because any other conclusion would nullify those aims. But are his answers admissible at his later criminal trial? If so, the privilege against self-incrimination is completely destroyed. So severe a result can be avoided by regarding the aim of recovering tax as the statute's major purpose; the minor and obscure aim of helping to convict the taxpayer clashes with the clear purposes of the privilege against self-incrimination, and cannot in the absence of clear words be allowed to take effect. The other minor aims of preventing future tax evasion and prosecuting accomplices can take effect, because they do not conflict with the privilege. So although the taxpayer may have had to confess crimes at his interrogation, no purpose served by the privilege has been thwarted. Any later criminal prosecution will be based on independently obtained evidence. The state will not be tempted to relax in its efforts to obtain such evidence. The taxpayer's tendency to tell unconscious falsehoods through fear will be lessened because he knows no harm will come of the examination, and there will be no inducement to commit perjury out of fear of later criminal punishment. Of course, if the statutory aim is clearly to prevail over the purposes of the privilege it must be given full effect. What is suggested is that the privilege should not be held to be discarded lightly in a given case.

Questions

1. Is the limitation of the privilege in civil cases to crimes under United Kingdom law only sound? Would not any abuse of the privilege by appeal to possible incrimination under foreign systems be controlled by using the *Boyes* test of whether the danger is "imaginary and unsubstantial"?

2. Should corporations be able to claim the privilege?

3. Should the privilege extend to a refusal to reveal one's facial or other bodily features?

4. What are the similarities and differences between the privilege and the confession rule? (See Chap. 8, *post*, and Wigmore, para. 2266.)

5. Should witnesses be warned of the fact that they have the privilege? If so, what consequences should follow a failure to give the warning?

6. What inferences against the witness can be legitimately drawn from a claim of privilege? How can the trier of fact be prevented from drawing others?

7. Does the law satisfactorily control inferences against a party by reason of the privilege being claimed by a non-party witness? Would you permit cross-examination attempting to show why the witness is silent and whether it reflects on either party?

8. Would an answer not in itself incriminatory but which enables the police to derive evidence of the witness's guilt from other sources fall within the privilege?

9. Should a witness be entitled to answer questions in chief respecting a particular matter but claim the privilege as to other questions in cross-examination on that matter?

10. How convincing are the justifications offered for the privilege?

11. Was *R. v. Scott* rightly decided? Should the principle of the decision be followed in future?

7

The Right to Silence

I INTRODUCTION

Except as provided by certain statutes, there is no duty in English law to answer the out-of-court questions of the police or anyone else. Silence is not punishable: in this sense there is a right to silence. But silence may form the basis of certain common sense inferences against a party. Three kinds of reasoning may be involved.

First, his silence may be taken as consent to whatever has been said to him; as an implied admission. This inference arises where a denial would be expected if the statement was false. Here silence operates rather like a nod; it is as if the party did not think it worth while wasting words in assenting to what he and the speaker know is obvious.

Secondly, silence may be taken, by itself or with other evidence, as a sign that the party is conscious of guilt or liability which he may be trying to hide. In this sense silence is a piece of conduct, like a lie or other interference with the course of justice, which operates as an implied admission that the party's case is bad. This is often confused with the first kind of implied admission but it is clearly different from it. The first kind of admission amounts to agreement with what is said; whereas the latter need not entail agreement with what is said, because the guilt evidenced may relate to some other crime. By the first kind of silence the party intends to convey agreement with what is said; by the second, he does not intend to convey agreement but shows a consciousness of guilt despite himself. Further, in the second case the statement made to the party may in fact not be strictly or even substantially true, but may remind the party of his guilt so that he then displays it. Hence the statement would not logically (as in the first case) be evidence of its truth, but would simply tend to prove that the party was guilty of some misconduct. If a man is accused of killing A and B and is silent, and in fact there is evidence that he killed A and C, his silence may amount to an assent to killing A and a sign that he is conscious of his guilt of killing C.

A slightly different form of this "consciousness of guilt" reasoning may be used when the accused is silent in the face of an accusation but advances a defence at his trial. An inference is drawn from the belatedness of the defence to a consciousness at the time of the accusation that he has no true defence. In other words, though normally one may infer silence from guilt at the very moment of silence, sometimes the occurrence of later events permits the inference because they change the character of the silence.

The third common-sense inference takes a number of forms, but essentially it is that silence makes any defence advanced difficult to believe, so that the opposing case, being uncontradicted, becomes stronger. The difficulty of believing the defence may exist because the failure to disclose it until trial prevents any checking of it, or because it has the appearance of being an afterthought, or because it is unsupported by the sworn evidence, tested in cross-examination, of one who is best able to support it. Plainly the distinction between this third inference and the first two, between using silence to weaken the defence case and *thus* strengthen the prosecution's, and using it directly to strengthen the prosecution's, is subtle, though real, and not easy to understand.

Sometimes the three inferences may all be drawn from a given set of facts; sometimes none can. Let us assume that a parent accuses a teacher of stealing money from a pupil's wallet at 6 p.m. on Monday, and that the teacher says nothing but bursts into tears. At the trial six weeks later he alleges for the first time that on Monday at 6 p.m. he was in a pub with friends. It may be possible legitimately to make the following common-sense inferences. The teacher admits guilt by not denying the outrageous charge at once as an innocent man would; the teacher's silent and ashamed demeanour indicates a consciousness of guilt of this and similar crimes; the alibi is unsupported because the friends cannot now remember whether on that day the accused drank with them as he sometimes did, and so the inferences from the prosecution's evidence become stronger. Changes in the facts will entail changes in the possible inferences.

The problem is that it is often dangerous to draw these common-sense inferences. Silence is quite unlike an express admission or even such an implied admission as a lie, or flight, or interference with the course of justice by destruction of evidence; silence is so equivocal. A man may be silent in the face of an accusation for many reasons other than guilt. He may not have heard or understood what was said; he may not consider the charge to have been addressed to him; he may be silent because he is attempting to work out the meaning of an ambiguous statement. The accusation may be so sudden as to make him silent through confusion, as where he has just woken up. He may fear misreporting of any reply he makes; he may be shocked into silence by a false but serious charge; he may indignantly and contemptuously consider it beneath his dignity to begin a debate about baseless and dishonourable accusations. He may not answer because he lacks knowledge of the matter in question. He may fear that to protest too much will be taken as a sign of guilt. He may believe he has a right of silence of which he wishes to avail himself, perhaps because he thinks an early disclosure of his defence will enable the other side to interfere with his witnesses. He may be silent because he wishes to protect others or to avoid disclosing discreditable but irrelevant facts about himself or others. Further, human reactions vary so much; the guilty may deny guilt strongly while the innocent stay silent. Shaw, C.J. once told a Massachusetts jury: "Have you any experience that an innocent man, stunned under the mere imputation of such a charge though conscious of innocence, will always appear calm and collected? Or that a guilty man who, by knowledge of his danger, might be somewhat braced up for the consequences, would always appear agitated? Or the reverse? Judge you concerning it." (*Webster's Trial*, Bemis' Rep. 486; quoted by Wigmore, para. 273.)

Another difficulty is determining how much of a statement a man approves by being silent—all or only part? If a man charged with murder pleads self-defence, and also denies that he has the *mens rea* for murder, what follows from his silence? Do we infer that he had *mens rea* and justification, or one, or the other? Common sense will often suggest inferences from silence, but will more often require extreme caution.

Does the law allow triers of fact to draw such inferences as common sense suggests? This is one of the most difficult questions in the law of evidence. Let us first consider the situation where a defendant's counsel raises a defence at the trial (which may or may not be supported by his sworn testimony) not mentioned by the defendant earlier, and then consider the inferences to be drawn from silence at the trial (whether or not the defendant was silent before the trial).

II OUT OF COURT SILENCE

R. v. Christie
[1914] A.C. 545; [1914–15] All E.R. Rep. 63, H.L.

A small boy said in the presence of the accused that the latter had indecently assaulted him. The accused said, "I am innocent."

The trial judge admitted this evidence and the House of Lords reversed the Court of Criminal Appeal's decision to quash the conviction.

LORD ATKINSON: [T]he rule of law undoubtedly is that a statement made in the presence of an accused person, even upon an occasion which should be expected reasonably to call for some explanation or denial from him, is not evidence against him of the facts stated save so far as he accepts the statement, so as to make it, in effect, his own. If he accepts the statement in part only, then to that extent alone does it become his statement. He may accept the statement by word or conduct, action or demeanour, and it is the function of the jury which tries the case to determine whether his words, action, conduct, or demeanour at the time when a statement was made amounts to an acceptance of it in whole or in part. It by no means follows, I think, that a mere denial by the accused of the facts mentioned in the statement necessarily renders the statement inadmissible, because he may deny the statement in such a manner and under such circumstances as may lead a jury to disbelieve him, and constitute evidence from which an acknowledgment may be inferred by them.

Of course, if at the end of the case the presiding judge should be of opinion that no evidence has been given upon which the jury could reasonably find that the accused had accepted the statement so as to make it in whole or in part his own, the judge can instruct the jury to disregard the statement entirely. It is said that, despite this direction, grave injustice might be done to the accused, inasmuch as the jury, having once heard the statement, could not, or would not, rid their mind of it. It is, therefore, in the application of the rule that the difficulty arises. The question then is this: Is it to be taken as a rule of law that such a statement is not to be admitted in evidence until a foundation has been laid for its admission by proof of facts from which, in the opinion of the presiding judge, a jury might reasonably draw the inference that the accused had so accepted the statement as to make it in whole or in part his own, or is it to be laid down that the prosecutor is entitled to give the statement in evidence in the first instance, leaving it to the presiding judge, in case no such evidence as the above mentioned should be ultimately produced, to tell the jury to disregard the statement altogether?

In my view the former is not a rule of law, but it is, I think, a rule which, in the interest of justice, it might be most prudent and proper to follow as a rule of practice.

LORD MOULTON: . . . [T]he deciding question is whether the evidence of the whole occurrence is relevant or not. If the prisoner admits the charge the evidence is obviously relevant. If he denies it, it may or may not be relevant. For instance, if he is charged with a violent assault and denies that he committed it, that fact might be distinctly relevant if at the trial his defence was that he did commit the act, but that it was in self-defence. The evidential value of the occurrence depends entirely on the behaviour of the prisoner, for the fact that some one makes a statement to him subsequently to the commission of the crime cannot in itself have any value as evidence for or against him. The only evidence for or against him is his behaviour in response to the charge, but I can see no justification for laying down as a rule of law that any particular form of response, whether of a positive or negative character, is such that it cannot in some circumstances have an evidential value. I am, therefore, of opinion that there is no rule of law that evidence cannot be given of the accused being charged with the offence and of his behaviour on hearing such charge where that behaviour amounts to a denial of his guilt. . . .

But while I am of opinion that there is no such rule of law, I am of opinion that the evidential value of the behaviour of the accused where he denies the charge is very small either for or against him, whereas the effect on the minds of the jury of his being publicly or repeatedly charged to his face with the crime might seriously prejudice the fairness of his trial.

LORD READING: A statement made in the presence of one of the parties to a civil action may be given in evidence against him if it is relevant to any of the matters in issue. And equally such a statement made in the presence of the accused may be given in evidence against him at his trial.

In general, such evidence can have little or no value in its direct bearing on the case unless the accused, upon hearing the statement, by conduct and demeanour, or by the answer made by him, or in certain circumstances by the refraining from an answer, acknowledged the truth of the statement either in whole or in part, or did or said something from which the jury could infer such an acknowledgment, for if he acknowledged its truth, he accepted it as his own statement of the facts. . . .

It might well be that the prosecution wished to give evidence of such a statement in order to prove the conduct and demeanour of the accused when hearing the statement as a relevant fact in the particular case, notwithstanding that it did not amount either to an acknowledgment or some evidence of an acknowledgment of any part of the truth of the statement. I think it impossible to lay down any general rule to be applied to all such cases, save the principle of strict law to which I have referred.

VISCOUNT HALDANE, L.C. and LORDS DUNEDIN and PARKER OF WADDINGTON concurred.

R. v. Grills
(1910), 11 C.L.R. 400

ISAACS, J. [in the High Court of Australia]: It is an elementary rule of law, going to the very foundation of justice, that no man shall be adjudged to be guilty of a crime upon evidence of another person's previous assertion. It matters not whether the assertion was made in the absence or the presence of the accused, as a mere assertion it cannot be regarded as any proof of the culpability of the accused or any confirmation of his accusers. But it is evident that upon such an assertion being made, and equally whether in the accused's absence or presence, he may admit its truth, and if he does, then it becomes evidence against him of his guilt, not because another has said it, but because of the admission. It is then equivalent to his own statement, and is receivable in that character. And it is further manifest that the acknowledgment of its correctness may be made in an infinite variety of ways. There may be an express and unqualified admission, or there may be a guarded admission, or there may be no direct but merely an implied acknowledgment, or there may be conduct, active or passive, positive or negative, from which, having regard to the ordinary workings of human nature, a total denial may be considered by reasonable men to be precluded, because, if innocence existed, an unequivocal or a qualified denial would in such a situation be expected.

R. v. Leckey
[1944] K.B. 80; [1943] 2 All E.R. 665, C.C.A.

VISCOUNT CALDECOTE, C.J.: In the course of his summing-up to the jury Singleton, J. thrice commented on the silence of the appellant after he had been cautioned by a police officer, and it is argued that those comments amounted to such misdirection as should lead this court to quash the conviction.

This subject has been dealt with more than once by this court. In R. v. *Whitehead* (1928), 21 Cr. App. Rep. 23, at pp. 24–25, C.C.A., Lord Hewart, C.J. in dealing with a case of a conviction for unlawful carnal knowledge of a girl under the age of sixteen, said: "When the police officer served the summons, he cautioned the appellant in the usual way, and the appellant said: 'I do not want to say anything about it now,' and the jury were directed that it was for them to decide whether there was corroboration or not according as they thought whether a respectable man would or would not deny such a charge; if they thought the failure on appellant's part to make a denial when the charge was sprung upon him by the police officer corroborated the girl's evidence then they would probably accept more readily that evidence as being corroborated to that extent. This is a misdirection," and he then went on to say the conviction must be quashed. In R. v. *Charavanmuttu* (1930), 22 Cr. App. Rep. 1, at p. 4, a case of a conviction for indecent conduct towards two boys, Lord Hewart, C.J. in dealing with what had been treated at the trial as evidence of corroboration, said: "It is quite clear that three matters were treated, if not indeed, as being evidence of corroboration, as being matters which tended to support the evidence of the boys. One was the silence of the accused at the time when the charge was made—silence amounting to this, at any rate, that at the stage then reached he said he reserved what he had to say. It is true that this remark was not treated as corroboration under the name of corroboration, but at the close of the summing-up the incident was brought prominently to the attention of the jury as something which might help them on the main question. It would be unfortunate if the jury thought that mere silence of the accused might amount to corroboration, for it is well settled since the decision in R. v. *Whitehead*, [1928] 1 K.B. 99, C.C.A., that it could not be." Those two cases, I observe, were dealing with the question of corroboration, corroboration being needed, or, at any rate, desirable in such cases.

In R. v. *Naylor*, [1933] 1 K.B. 685; [1932] All E.R. Rep. 152, C.C.A., the appellant had been cautioned in these words at the police court: "Do you wish to say anything in answer to the charge? You are not obliged to say anything unless you desire to do so, but whatever you say will be taken down in writing and may be given in evidence upon your trial." In reply to that caution the appellant said: "I do not wish to say anything except that I am innocent." The recorder, in his summing-up, said: "Imagine a purely innocent man accused of housebreaking and having these words put to him—'Do you wish to say anything in answer to the charge?' Surely, if he is innocent, one would think he would give some explanation of where he was and what he was doing at the particular time, and would make his defence then and there. . . . Of course, what lurks in the background of this sort of hanging back and not disclosing his defence is that he gives the prosecution and the police no time to inquire into any statement he may make, so that it might be possible to show that these statements are not true." Lord Hewart, C.J. said, "We do not think that the words of the caution can properly be construed in the sense that the prisoner remains silent after being cautioned at his peril and may find his silence made a strong point against him at his trial. In our view, the words mean what they say, and a prisoner is entitled to reply to the caution that he does not wish to say anything." Lastly, in R. v. *Littleboy*, [1934] 2 K.B. 408, at pp. 412–13; [1934] All

E.R. Rep. 434, C.C.A., Lord Hewart, C.J. made these observations: "The real point urged on behalf of the appellant is that the judge was wrong in making observations upon the fact that the defence of alibi had not been disclosed before the magistrates, and our attention has been directed to R. v. *Naylor*, [1933] 1 K.B. 685; [1932] All E.R. Rep. 152, C.C.A. It is important to observe that in that case the fact that the appellant had not disclosed his defence at an earlier date was employed as being evidence against him in corroboration of an alleged accomplice, who had given evidence for the prosecution. It is important to remember that the judgment in that case was given with reference to those facts. It is quite true that there are sentences to be found in the report of that judgment which appear to be of universal application. We do not think, however, that it was ever intended to lay down the proposition that a judge may not in a proper case comment on the fact that the defence has not been disclosed on an earlier occasion. It is one thing to make an observation with regard to the force of an alibi, and to say that it is unfortunate that the defence was not set up at an earlier date so as to afford the opportunity of its being tested; it is another thing to employ that non-disclosure as evidence against an accused person and as corroborating the evidence of an accomplice."

Having considered those cases, and, in particular, the clear and emphatic language used in R. v. *Naylor*, [1933] 1 K.B. 685; [1932] All E.R. Rep. 152, C.C.A., I turn to the question whether or not the passages which I have read from the summing-up of Singleton, J. in the present case amount to a misdirection justifying the quashing of the conviction. On three occasions the judge seems to suggest to the jury that they might infer the appellant's guilt by considering the fact of his silence after being cautioned. In our view, that amounted to a misdirection, and it is proper ground on which this conviction should be quashed. If it were not so, a caution might obviously be a trap instead of the means for finding out the truth in the interests of justice. An innocent person might well, either from excessive caution or for some other reason, decline to say anything when charged and cautioned, and, if that could be held out to a jury as ground on which they might find him guilty, he might obviously be in great peril.

R. v. Sullivan
(1966), 51 Cr. App. Rep. 102, C.A. (C.D.)

SALMON, L.J.: [T]he learned judge said in the course of his summing-up: "Sullivan refused to answer any questions. Of course bear in mind that he was fully entitled to refuse to answer questions, he has an absolute right to refuse to do just that, and it is not to be held against him that he did that. But you might well think that if a man is innocent he would be anxious to answer questions. . . ." It seems pretty plain that all the members of the jury, if they had any common sense at all, must have been saying to themselves precisely what the learned judge said to them. . . . The difficulty, however, lies in this . . . . [A] judge is not entitled in any circumstances to suggest to a jury, when a man refuses to answer any questions after having been cautioned, that, if he were innocent, it is likely that he would have answered the questions. What a judge may say to a jury when a man refuses to answer is, perhaps, not so plain. There are cases in which the comment in the summing-up upon an accused's silence is clearly unfair [e.g. R. v. *Leckey*, [1944] K.B. 80; [1943] 2 All E.R. 665, C.C.A., and R. v. *Naylor*, [1933] 1 K.B. 685; [1932] All E.R. Rep. 152, C.C.A.]. There are other cases, however, and this is one of them, in which the circumstances are such that it does not appear that there is any unfairness involved in the comment. The line dividing what may be said and what may not be said is a very fine one, and it is perhaps doubtful whether in a case like the present it would be even perceptible to the members of any ordinary jury. But there can be no doubt . . . that . . . what was said . . . amounted to a misdirection.

Notes

1. Since "fairness" does not assist a comment otherwise objectionable, it might be better not to use the idea.

2. Compare Salmon, L.J.'s implicit criticism of the current law here with his attack on clause I of the Criminal Evidence Bill proposed by the 11th Report of the Criminal Law Revision: 388 H.L. Deb. 1603–10.

Hall v. R.
[1971] 1 All E.R. 322, P.C.

The accused was convicted of unlawful possession of ganja. A policeman told him after the search of his home which discovered the ganja that a co-accused had said the ganja belonged to him. He remained silent. He appealed to the Privy Council.

LORD DIPLOCK: It is a clear and widely-known principle of the common law in Jamaica, as in England, that a person is entitled to refrain from answering a question put to him for the purpose of discovering whether he has committed a criminal offence. *A fortiori* he is under no obligation to comment when he is informed that someone else has accused him of an offence. It may be that in very exceptional circumstances an inference may be drawn from a failure to give an explanation or a disclaimer, but in their Lordships' view silence alone on being informed by a police officer that someone else has made an accusation against him cannot give rise to an inference that the person to whom this information is communicated accepts the truth of the accusation. This is well established by many authorities such as R. v. *Whitehead* [1929] 1 K.B. 99; [1928] All E.R. Rep. 86, C.C.A. and R. v. *Keeling*, [1942] 1 All E.R. 507, C.C.A. Counsel has sought to distinguish these cases on the ground that in them the accused had already been cautioned and told in terms that he was not obliged to reply. Reliance was placed on the earlier case of R. v. *Feigenbaum* [1919] 1 K.B. 431; [1918–19] All E.R. Rep. 489, C.C.A., where the accused's silence when told of the accusation made against him by some children was held to be capable of amounting to corroboration of their evidence. It was submitted that the distinction between R. v. *Feigenbaum* and the later cases was that no caution had been administered at the time at which the accused was informed of the accusation. The correctness of the decision in R. v. *Feigenbaum* was doubted in R. v. *Keeling*. In their Lordships' view the distinction sought to be made is not a valid one and R. v. *Feigenbaum* ought not to be followed. The caution merely serves to remind the accused of a right which he already possesses at common law. The fact that in a particular case he has not been reminded of it is no ground for inferring that his silence was not in exercise of that right, but was an acknowledgment of the truth of the accusation.

i Silence as consent

Normally the trier of fact may draw the inference that the silence of the party in the face of the accusation is consent to it if this is open as a matter of common sense, and the judge may give a direction to this effect. The exception to the rule is where the accusation is made in the presence of a policeman to an accused person; the Privy Council held in *Hall v. R. (supra)* that a blanket rule of prudence prevents the inference being drawn, whether or not the policeman cautioned the accused that he had a right to stay silent. Its justification is that in many cases innocent accused persons may fear the consequences of speaking and do not feel psychologically at liberty to do so.

In cases where the inference may be drawn, the test is whether a denial could reasonably be expected in the circumstances. The circumstances of a business relationship commonly permit the inference to be drawn; a defendant's silence in the face of correspondence becomes much more relevant in business cases than in affiliation cases. But in affiliation cases, in the absence of such special circumstances as a threat of legal action if there is no reply, or where the girl's father and the putative father are related, it is most unlikely that silence will prove paternity (*Thomas* v. *Jones*, [1921] 1 K.B. 22; [1920] All E.R. Rep. 462, C.A.). It is much more natural to reply to accusations made publicly to one's face than to those in letters. There are many more reasons for not replying to letters than for silence—laziness, the time and money used, a dislike for or lack of facility in writing, the urgency of other affairs, a desire to discourage importunity. And there are reasons of policy against allowing evidence to be acquired in this way just as there are against "inertia sellers". Holmes, J. once said that a man can in this way "no more impose a duty to answer a charge than he can impose a duty to pay by selling goods" (*A. B. Leach & Co.* v. *Peirson* (1927), 275 U.S. 120, at p. 128).

Regard must be paid to the status of the accuser. It is futile to argue with a madman, a drunk, a baby, or an hysterical mother whose child has just been run over (*Thatcher* v. *Charles* (1961), 104 C.L.R. 57). Where the accuser was on her death bed the accused's silence was not evidence, partly because it was inappropriate to contradict her in such circumstances and partly because the accused was relying on the presence of his solicitor for protection (*R.* v. *Mitchell* (1892), 17 Cox C.C. 503). Accusations among relatives are often held to call for an answer because there are less likely to be inhibitions against speaking. If the party is in some respect superior to his accuser, silence may be due to contempt rather than consent, and officious busybodies who have little to do with the relevant events need not be answered.

Another factor is the situation of the party charged and the circumstances surrounding the charging. A man is not expected to speak after an accident if he is physically injured or shocked (*Thatcher* v. *Charles* (1961), 104 C.L.R. 57). Silence on being identified as a criminal is not an admisson if the accused does not know what crime he is supposed to have committed, or the accusation does not relate to the appropriate issue. Windeyer, J. once said: "A failure to answer an accusation 'You drive too fast round here' could hardly be an admission by the appellant that he ought not to have backed his car where and when he did" (*Thatcher* v. *Charles* (1961), 104 C.L.R. 57, at p. 70). If the party's attempts to deny accusations are inhibited by the efforts of others present or by the need for decorum and orderly procedure in formal inquiries, silence is of no weight. A husband's failure to deny his wife's claim that marital relations had ceased would not be an admission; it is reasonable not to discuss intimate problems in public.

When will an indignant reply be expected? One test is the seriousness of an accusation, e.g. a charge of incest by a daughter to her father (*R.* v. *Power*, [1940] Q.S.R. 111), or a breach of promise of marriage (*Bessela* v. *Stern* (1877), 2 C.P.D. 265, C.A.). Another is where there is more than a mere charge of crime, as in *R.* v. *Cramp*, where a father said to the accused: "I have here those things which you gave my daughter to produce abortion" ((1880), 14 Cox C.C. 390). Another is the solemnity of the form of the accusation; so an executor's failure to dispute an affidavit alleging that he owes the estate money may be an admission (*Freeman* v. *Cox* (1878), 8 Ch.D. 148).

It is easier to infer an admission from silence to particular questions out of a large number than it is from a general refusal to answer any questions at all (*Paterson* v. *Martin* (1966), 40 A.L.J.R. 312, at p. 314).

It might be noted that implied admissions by silence often merge into implied admissions by vague and equivocal answers. An example is *Mars* v. *McMahon*, [1929] S.A.S.R. 179 where the respondent in an affiliation case was addressed as follows: "I understand that you do not deny having had connection with the girl [ten seconds' silence], but that others have also had connection with her." The respondent replied: "It's pretty rotten when she picks on me when I know that others have also been out with her."

ii Silence evidencing a consciousness of guilt

In *R. v. Christie*, [1914] A.C. 545, at pp. 565–6; [1914–15] All E.R. Rep. 63, at pp. 71–2, H.L. Lord Reading said that a statement made in the accused's presence was sometimes admissible "in order to prove the conduct and demeanour of the accused when hearing the statment as a relevant fact in the particular case, notwithstanding that it did not amount . . . to an acknowledgment . . . of the truth of the statement". The Criminal Law Revision Committee is technically correct in saying that this doctrine is not affected by the decision in *Hall* that silence in the presence of a policeman cannot be an admission of guilt, but it may be doubted whether the spirit of *Hall* is compatible with the application of the *Christie* doctrine to cases where a policeman is present. An inference that silence shows a consciousness of guilt is as dangerous as an inference that it shows an admission when a policeman is present.

The principle here is that normally the urge of self-preservation will induce a man to speak if charged with unlawful conduct; so silence shows that he is conscious of guilt.

Where silence is consent, a statement made to the party is admitted to prove the truth of its contents; the party has in effect adopted it. But the question may be whether "the reaction of an accused person to the making of a statement in his presence may afford evidence of something other than the facts suggested in the statement". This means that it may be difficult to discover what the party is impliedly admitting. If other evidence suggests the accused committed the crime charged, "any conduct . . . demonstrative of guilt may go far to support a conclusion that the accused committed the very crime charged. But when there is no other evidence implicating the accused, an attitude of guilt, without more, may mean only that the accused was a participant in some wrongdoing, not that he committed the crime alleged, in manner and form alleged" (*Woon v. R.* (1964), 109 C.L.R. 529, at pp. 536, 542).

The inference of consciousness of guilt may be made from silence alone, but it is more commonly made from silence coupled with other conduct. The Supreme Court of Canada once drew the inference from silence followed by contradictory explanations (*Hubin v. R.* (1927), 48 C.C.C. 172). Where the accused's reply was "What I have to say I will say to the Court", the judge legitimately remarked that the reply was an odd one when court proceedings had not yet been mentioned (*R. v. Gerard*, [1948] 1 All E.R. 205, C.C.A.).

There are many examples where a consciousness of guilt has been detected in silence. The failure of a victim of crime to complain speedily, e.g. the victim of rape, may be evidence of consent, unless there is some good reason for this such as fear of vengeance by the criminals (*R. v. Gandfield* (1846), 2 Cox C.C. 43). As with the case of silence as consent to a statement, a selective refusal to answer questions is more suspicious than a general refusal (*Woon v. R.* (1964), 109 C.L.R. 529).

In *R. v. Christie*, [1914] A.C. 545; [1914–15] All E.R. Rep. 63, H.L., the House of Lords decided that statements made in the presence of a party could be put to the jury before there was evidence of any admission from his conduct, though the contrary procedure was desirable. If there is no evidence of admission, injustice may be caused because the jury become so prejudiced by hearing the statements that they ignore any warning to put them aside. For this reason it is often necessary either to prevent the statement going before the jury or having a new trial. Rule 5 of the Judges' Rules ameliorates the position slightly by forbidding the police to tell the accused of a co-accused's statement, but permitting them to hand the accused a copy. Breach of the rule may, but will not necessarily, result in the exclusion of any admission made.

iii Silence as strengthening inferences from the opposing case

The judge may warn the jury that they may give greater weight to the case against a silent party because of the absence of any credible defence; and this is so even if a warning of the right to silence has been given. A defence may not be credible because it was raised late (*R. v. Ryan* (1966), 50 Cr. App. Rep. 144, C.C.A.), or because its lateness prevented the police checking it (*R. v. Parker*, [1933] 1 K.B. 850; [1932] All E.R. Rep. 718, C.C.A.; *R. v. Littleboy*, [1934] 2 K.B. 408; [1934] All E.R. Rep. 434, C.C.A.). In Napier, J.'s phrase, "a fishy story is all the worse for being stale" (*Hinton v. Trotter*, [1931] S.A.S.R. 123, at p. 127).

Various examples of this reasoning may be noted. Silence strengthens the inference that a possessor of stolen goods is the thief or receiver of them (e.g. *R. v. Seymour*, [1954] 1 All E.R. 1006, C.C.A.). The inference arises because theft or receiving is by far the commonest way of obtaining property unlawfully; so it is not open where the property was unlawfully obtained in some other way unless there are special circumstances, such as an association between the possessor and the person who originally obtained the goods (*Director of Public Prosecutions v. Nieser*, [1959] 1 Q.B. 254, D.C., at pp. 266–7; [1958] 3 All E.R. 662, at p. 669). Silence strengthens the inference of breaking and entering with intent which can be drawn from illegal presence in another's house (*R. v. Wood* (1911), 7 Cr. App. Rep. 56, C.C.A.). Silence strengthens the inferences in favour of the plaintiff who proves facts to which the maxim *res ipsa loquitur* applies.

Though comment which does more than suggest that silence strengthens the inferences from other evidence is not permissible if a policeman is present during questioning it may be permitted if it is based not on silence alone but on the adequacy of an explanation which the accused had chosen to give for his silence. Thus in *R. v. Tune* (1944), 29 Cr. App. Rep. 162, C.C.A., where the accused said he would prefer to have advice before explaining the matter in writing, the Court of Criminal Appeal upheld the judge's comment on the defence advanced: "could not that have been said without legal advice?"

III   INFERENCES FROM SILENCE IN COURT

R. v. Burdett
(1820), 4 B. & Ald. 95, at pp. 161–2

ABBOTT, C.J.: No person is to be required to explain or contradict, until enough has been proved to warrant a reasonable and just conclusion against him, in the absence of explanation or contradiction; but when such proof has been given, and the nature of the case is such as to admit of explanation or contradiction, if the conclusion to which the proof tends to be untrue, and the accused offers no explanation or contradiction, can human reason do otherwise than adopt the conclusion to which the proof tends? [See also BEST, J. and HOLROYD, J. to the same effect at pp. 121–2 and 140.]

McQueen v. Great Western Rail. Co.
(1875), L.R. 10 Q.B. 569, at p. 574

COCKBURN, C.J.: If a *prima facie* case is made out, capable of being displaced, and if the party against whom it is established might by calling particular witnesses and producing particular evidence displace that *prima facie* case, and he omits to adduce that evidence, then the inference fairly arises, as a matter of inference for the jury and not as a matter of legal presumption, that the absence of that evidence is to be accounted for by the fact that even if it were adduced it would not disprove the *prima facie* case. But that always presupposes that a *prima facie* case has been established; and unless we can see our way clearly to the conclusion that a *prima facie* case has been established, the omission to call witnesses who might have been called on the part of the defendants amounts to nothing.

R. v. Adams
(1957) (Sybille Bedford, *The Best We Can Do* (Collins, 1958) p. 249)

DEVLIN, J. (summing up): You sit to answer one limited question: Has the prosecution satisfied you beyond reasonable doubt that the Doctor murdered Mrs. Morell? On that question the Doctor stood on his rights and did not speak. I have made it quite clear that I am not criticizing that. I do not criticize it at all. [With a measure of fervour] I hope that the day will never come when that right is denied to any Englishman. It is not a refuge of technicality: the law on this matter reflects the natural thought of England. So great is our horror at the idea that a man might be questioned, forced to speak and perhaps to condemn himself out of his own mouth [for the first time without detachment], that we afford to everyone suspected or accused of a crime, at every stage, and to the very end, the right to say: "Ask me no questions, I shall answer none. Prove your case."

Williams: The Proof of Guilt
3rd Edn. P. 61

[In *Adams*] the case for the prosecution had already been undermined by cross-examination of the prosecution's witnesses, as well as evidence for the defence. Where a case of strong suspicion has been built up, the judge's comment upon the defendant's failure to testify is unlikely to be so lenient.

Note

The fact remains that Devlin, J.'s remarks were perfectly general. It is probable that judges differ on the propriety and form of any judicial comment, as the judicial response to the 11th Report of the Criminal Law Revision Committee shows.

R. v. Bathurst
[1968] 2 Q.B. 99; [1968] 1 All E.R. 1175, C.A.

The accused at his trial for murder pleaded diminished responsibility. The defence called two psychiatrists, but the accused did not testify and the judge commented on this. The Court of Appeal criticized his comment.

LORD PARKER, C.J.: [T]his court feels strongly that while it may be that there are cases in which a defendant ought to go into the witness box, albeit his plea is one of diminished responsibility, yet the cases when comment on his failure to do so can properly be made must be very rare. . . . [I]n almost every case counsel defending a prisoner raising this defence would prevent him going if he could into the witness box. He may well be suffering from delusions, he may be on the border of insanity. . . .

[However] there might be a case where the prosecution, by cross-examining the psychiatrist called for the defence, indicated that they were challenging some particular point, and a point which could only be spoken to by the defendant as opposed to some relations, friends, or the like, and in such a case, probably a very rare case, some comment might be justified. . . .

[Here comment was improper because] there was no real challenge of the truthfulness of [the accused in] answering questions, and giving information to the medical experts.

. . . [T]he form of the comment, if comment is justified in any particular case on a plea of diminished responsibility, is a comment which is undoubtedly different from the comment which is justified when the burden is on the prosecution. Then, as is well known, the accepted form of comment is to inform the jury that, of course, he is not bound to give evidence, that he can sit back and see if the prosecution have proved their case, and that while the jury have been deprived of the opportunity of hearing his story tested in cross-examination the one thing they must not do is to assume that he is guilty because he has not gone into the witness box.

When one comes to this sort of case, the case where the burden is on the defence and the defendant does not go into the witness box, the comment is directed to something quite different; it would more likely take this form, that he is not bound to go into the witness box, nobody can force him to go into the witness box, but the burden is upon him, and if he does not, he runs the risk of not being able to prove his case.

R. v. Sparrow
[1973] 2 All E.R. 129, C.A.

In the course of a car theft by two accused a policeman was shot. Sparrow's defence was that the gun used was only intended to frighten policemen. The judge said that if Sparrow "never contemplated . . . that any shooting was going to take place, is it not essential that he should go into the witness box and tell you that himself and be subject to cross-examination about it?" The Court of Appeal criticized this direction.

LAWTON, L.J.: Counsel for the appellant submitted with his usual incisiveness that this comment would have been understood by the jury as a direction that they should assume that there was nothing in the appellant's defence and that he was guilty because he had not given evidence. In our judgment this is how the trial judge's comment would have been understood; but we think that this is how the jury would have assessed the situation if the judge's comment had not been made. In our experience of trials, juries seldom acquit persons who do not give evidence when there is a clear case for them to answer and they do not answer it. Lord Goddard, C.J., recognized this, as one would have expected him to do, in his judgment in R. v. *Jackson* (1953), 37 **Cr.** App. Rep. 43, at p. 50:

"... whatever may have been the position very soon after the Criminal Evidence Act 1898, came into operation . . . everybody now knows that absence from the witness-box requires a very considerable amount of explanation..."

The reason lies in common sense. An innocent man who is charged with a crime, or with any conduct reflecting on his reputation, can be expected to refute the allegation as soon as he can by giving his own version of what happened. Juries know this; and they must often be perplexed why they should be told by judges, as they often have been since the passing of the Criminal Evidence Act 1898, that when considering their verdict they should not take into account the fact that the accused has said not a word in his own defence even though the case against him is a strong one. The law, however, has set limits on what judges may say about an accused's election not to give evidence. Our task is to adjudge whether the trial judge went too far in this case.

The limits have been set by the judges; and the experience of this court is that in recent years many judges at first instance have come to think that their right to comment on the absence of the accused from the witness box has been restricted by the decision of the Judicial Committee of the Privy Council in *Waugh* v. R., [1950] A.C. 203, P.C., and the judgment of this court in R. v. *Bathurst*, [1968] 2 Q.B. 99, C.A.; [1968] 1 All E.R. 1175, to which I have referred above. Sometimes judges stress the right of the accused not to give evidence, as Devlin J. did in R. v. *Adams* (p. 151 *supra*); and what he said in that case, taken out of context, is often used by defending counsel as an excuse for not calling the accused.

Two propositions founded on *Waugh* v. R. and R. v. *Bathurst* are argued from time to time: first, that if a judge does decide to comment he should do so once only and that if he makes any more comments he is acting unfairly; and secondly, that any substantial variation from the form of comment suggested by Lord Parker, C.J. in R. v. *Bathurst* is unfair. Present-day doubts about what a judge can and cannot say by way of comment have led us to examine what principles, if any, apply.

Before the passing of the Criminal Evidence Act 1898 there was no problem of this kind because the accused had no right to give evidence. As soon as that Act came into operation, the question arose whether a judge had any right to comment on the election of the accused not to give evidence on his own behalf. It was answered in R. v. *Rhodes*, [1899] 1 Q.B. 77, at pp. 83–4 by Lord Russell of Killowen, C.J. in these words:

> "There is nothing in the Act that takes away or even purports to take away the right of the Court to comment on the evidence in the case, and the manner in which the case has been conducted. The nature and degree of such comment must rest entirely in the discretion of the judge who tries the case; and it is impossible to lay down any rule as to the cases in which he ought or ought not to comment on the failure of the prisoner to give evidence, or as to what those comments should be. There are some cases in which it would be unwise to make any such comment at all; there are others in which it would be absolutely necessary in the interests of justice that such comments should be made. That is a question entirely for the discretion of the judge; and it is only necessary now to say that that discretion is in no way affected by the provisions of the Criminal Evidence Act 1898."

That clear statement of the law has never been questioned; it is the law. From 1899 until *Waugh*'s case, [1950] A.C. 203, P.C., in 1950, it was the practice of judges when justice required them to do so to comment in robust terms on an accused's absence from the witness box. An example of such comments which has been remembered at the Bar is provided by R. v. *Nodder* (1937), unreported, which was tried in 1937. The accused had been indicted for the murder of a small girl. Swift, J. began his summing-up by reminding the jury that they had heard evidence from several witnesses as to where the murdered girl had been up to a certain time when the accused was with her but none from the accused himself, although he alone could have given evidence of where she was afterwards. The justice of that case called for that comment; and at the time it was made, informed opinion at the Bar did not question the propriety of it. But it would be questioned today. Why?

Many would say that the change in judicial practice resulted from *Waugh* v. R., [1950] A.C. 203, P.C. There the appellant had been convicted of murder. The case against him was weak, so weak indeed that the police authorities, after they had completed their investigations, accepted his explanation as to what had happened and decided not to prosecute him. A coroner, however, ordered his prosecution. The only evidence of any strength against him was provided by a statement which the deceased had made shortly before his death. At the trial the appellant did not give evidence. In the summing-up the trial judge had commented nine times on this fact and on two of them he had made comments in much the same terms as Swift, J. had done in *Nodder's* case. The Judicial Committee of the Privy Council disapproved of these comments. Lord Oaksey delivered the reasons for the Board's report. He said ([1950] A.C. 203, at p. 211):

> "Whilst much of the summing-up is unexceptionable there are certain parts of it which, in their Lordships' view, do constitute a grave departure from the rules that justice requires, and they are therefore of opinion that the conviction must be quashed. It is true that it is a matter for the judge's discretion whether he shall comment on the fact that a prisoner has not given evidence; but the very fact that the prosecution are not permitted to comment on that fact shows how careful a judge should be in making such comment."

He went on to point out how weak the prosecution's case had been and continued (*ibid.*, at p. 212):

> "*In such a state of the evidence* [the italics are ours] the judge's repeated comments on the appellant's failure to give evidence may well have led the jury to think that no innocent man could have taken such a course . . . in the present case their Lordships think that the prisoner's counsel was fully justified in not calling the prisoner, and that the judge, if he made any comment on the matter at all, ought at least to have pointed out to the jury that the prisoner was not bound to give evidence and that it was for the prosecution to make out the case beyond reasonable doubt."

Lord Oaksey went on to find that the dying declaration had been wrongly admitted and inaccurately commented on. In our judgment *Waugh* v. R. establishes nothing more than this: it is a wrongful exercise of judicial discretion for a judge to bolster up a weak prosecution case by making comments about the accused's failure to give evidence; and implicit in the report is the concept that failure to give evidence has no evidential value. We can find nothing in it which qualifies the statement of principle in R. v. *Rhodes*, [1899] 1 Q.B. 77. Our view of *Waugh* v. R., [1950] A.C. 203, seems to have been that of Lord Goddard, C.J. in R. v. *Jackson* when he said (1953), 37 Cr. App. Rep. 43, at p. 50:

> "I do not want in the least to be whittling down what their Lordships in the Judicial Committee said on this matter, but, of course, each case on such a point as this must depend on its own facts . . . It has to be remembered, among other things, in this case that the charge against the appellant was receiving stolen property, and if ever there is a case in which a prisoner might be expected to give evidence offering an explanation with regard to the offence of which he is alleged to be guilty, that is the case."

In the present case, the charge was murder, and the evidence went to establish that when the detective sergeant was shot by Skingle, the appellant was standing close by and after the shooting, the pair of them drove off together and one of them within a short time in the presence of the other reloaded the pistol; and there has to be added to this submission of the appellant's counsel that the prosecution's evidence was consistent with the possibility that the joint enterprise between Skingle and the appellant was merely to frighten the police officer with a pistol (which the appellant knew was loaded) and that Skingle departed from it by pressing the trigger a number of times.

In the judgment of this court, if the trial judge had not commented in strong terms on the appellant's absence from the witness box, he would have been failing in his duty. The object of a summing-up is to help the jury and in our experience a jury is not helped by a colourless reading out of the evidence as recorded by the judge in his notebook. The judge is more than a mere referee who takes no part in the trial save to intervene when a rule of procedure or evidence is broken. He and the jury try the case together and it is his duty to give them the benefit of his knowledge of the law and to advise them in the light of his experience as to the significance of the evidence; and when an accused person elects not to give evidence, in most cases but not all, the judge should explain to the jury what the consequences of his absence from the witness box are and if, in his discretion, he thinks that he should do so more than once, he may; but he must keep in mind always his duty to be fair. A. T. Lawrence, J. pointed out in R. v. *Voisin*, [1918] 1 K.B. 531, C.C.A., at p. 536; [1918–19] All E.R. Rep. 491, at p. 492: "Comments on the evidence which are not misdirections do not by being added together constitute a misdirection."

How should this be done? In R. v. *Bathurst*, [1968] 2 Q.B. 99; [1968] 1 All E.R. 1175, C.A., Lord Parker, C.J. gave judges some guidance but what he said was an *obiter dictum,* as he appreciated it was. . . .

In many cases, a direction in some such terms as these will be all that is required; but we are sure that Lord Parker, C.J. never intended his words of guidance to be regarded as a judicial directive to be recited to juries in every case in which an accused elects not to give evidence. What is said must depend on the facts of each case and in some cases the interests of justice call for a stronger comment. The trial judge, who has the feel of the case, is the person who must exercise his discretion in this matter to ensure that a trial is fair. A discretion is not to be fettered by laying down rules and regulations for its exercise. . . . What, however, is of the greatest importance in Lord Parker, C.J.'s advice to judges is his reference to the need to avoid telling juries that absence from the witness box is to be equated with guilt.

How should these principles be applied in this case? In our judgment there is nothing in the complaint about the cumulative effects of the comments, particularly as the trial judge at the beginning of his summing-up explained accurately and clearly that the appellant had a right to remain silent and to rest his defence on the presumption that he was innocent until proved guilty. The interests of justice required that the trial judge should get the jury to understand that an exculpatory statement, unverified on oath, such as the appellant had made after arrest, was not evidence save in so far as it contained admissions; and his task was not made easier by the present state of the law which required the Attorney-General to say nothing about the appellant's silence but allowed counsel for Skingle to say what he liked and, had he been so minded, to put into words what it is almost certain the majority of the jurors were thinking, i.e. that, having regard to the strength of the evidence, if the appellant was innocent why had he not gone into the witness box to say so. Our law, however, does not require an accused to give evidence and a judge must not either by express words or impliedly give jurors to understand that a defence cannot succeed unless the accused gives evidence. Unfortunately, probably by a slip of the tongue, that is what the trial judge did when he said to the jury:

"Is it not essential that he should go into the witness box and tell you that himself and be subject to cross-examination about it? Well he did not do so and there it is."

He did overstep the limits of justifiable comment; he should not have said what he did.

i Silence as amounting to consent

It is not possible for silence to be taken as consent to the other side's case where the defendant contests all the issues of fact or pleads not guilty (*Tumahole Bereng v. R.,* [1949] A.C. 253, at p. 270, P.C.); the expressed intention will exclude any implied admission. However, where not every issue of fact is contested in a civil case silence may be an admission. Failure to deny a charge of adultery is not always or by itself evidence of adultery, because there are many reasons for taking this course other than actually having committed adultery; e.g. the supposed adulterer may simply wish to end proceedings quickly and cheaply (*Inglis* v. *Inglis and Baxter* (1965) [1968] P. 639, at p. 646; [1967] 2 All E.R. 71, at p. 76). But failure to deny adultery may be evidence of it if damages are claimed against the co-respondent, since in such circumstances there is more incentive for an innocent man to deny the charge (*Pidduck* v. *Pidduck*, [1961] 3 All E.R. 481).

ii Silence evidencing consciousness of guilt

It is clear that the silence of an accused at the trial is not evidence of a consciousness of guilt (*Waugh* v. *R.*, [1950] A.C. 203, P.C.). However, the silence of a party in a civil case may be (*Cracknell* v. *Smith*, [1960] 3 All E.R. 569). The reasons for the distinction probably turn on the importance of a finding of criminal guilt, the high criminal standard of proof, the risk of the accused convicting himself by a bad performance in the box, and the dangers of the accused exposing himself to cross-examination on his record. These points either do not apply in civil cases or are less important.

Silence may evidence guilt in this way: in *Mash* v. *Darley*, [1914] 3 K.B. 1226, C.A., a putative father did not testify at the assizes that the mother was "fast", though he had done so in earlier proceedings before the magistrates. From this it could be inferred that the statement was a lie and that it proceeded from a consciousness of guilt.

iii Silence strengthening inferences from opposing evidence

A party's failure to testify or to produce evidence in a civil case "gives colour to the evidence against him" (*Boyle* v. *Wiseman* (1855), 10 Exch. 647, at p. 651, *per* Alderson, B.). The same is true in criminal cases.

Three conditions must be satisfied before silence in court can be used to strengthen inferences from opposing evidence. First, there must be a case to answer. The trial may be stopped at the close of the proponent's case if it is too weak, and even if it continues on other issues a non-existent case cannot be strengthened by failure to answer it. The second condition is that the silent party must have been capable of answering the case against him. "All evidence is to be weighed according to the proof which it was in the power of one side to have produced, and in the power of the other to have contradicted" (*Blatch* v. *Archer* (1774), 1 Cowp. 64, at p. 65, *per* Lord Mansfield, C.J.). Thirdly, there must be no apparent reason for silence other than inability to answer truthfully the case made. Such reasons include insanity, protection of others, and fear of disclosure of an accused's record.

A comment is unlikely if the prosecution case has been damaged by cross-examination or the defence story has been adequately put through other witnesses. It is likely to be made if the facts in issue are peculiarly within the accused's knowledge, e.g. issues of intent, or if the accused advances an innocent explanation of incriminating facts rather than denying the facts themselves (*R.* v. *Mutch*, [1973] 1 All E.R. 178, C.A.).

The Criminal Law Revision Committee says (para. 109) that the present law entitles the judge to make a much stronger comment on the accused's silence in court than his silence out of court. Certainly there are many more reported comments on in court silence, and a stronger comment would be justified by the fact that there is less excuse for silence. First, the chance of being misunderstood or misreported is less; counsel and the judge are there to protect the accused against improper cross-examination; there is less likelihood of panic, confusion and inadequate preparation. Secondly, when the time comes for the accused to testify there is *ex hypothesi* a *prima facie* case against him, for he has either not submitted or unsuccessfully submitted that there is no case to answer, and so he runs a serious risk in not testifying.

The English Criminal Evidence Act 1898 s. 1 (*b*) forbids prosecution comment on the accused's silence but says nothing about comment of counsel for a co-accused. It has been held that he has a right to comment on the other co-accused's failure to testify and the judge has no discretion to prevent this (*R.* v. *Wickham* (1971)), 55 Cr. App. Rep. 199, C.A.). The decision seems justified by analogy with the position under s. 1 (*f*) (iii) of the English Act and its equivalents, by which a co-accused has an absolute right, unfettered by any discretion in the court, to cross-examine a co-accused on his record once he gives evidence against the first co-accused (*Murdoch* v. *Taylor*, [1965] A.C. 574; [1965] 1 All E.R. 406, H.L.).

It is often thought that jurymen know an accused has a right to testify, and individual jurymen sometimes show such knowledge. If the judge comments, the jury will be guided as to which inferences are possible and which are inappropriate. If the judge does not comment, the jury may draw all the common-sense inferences, some of which, as we have seen, are impermissible. There is very little evidence of any requirement that the jury be warned of the dangers of inferring too much, except where the case involves a corroboration rule. Here the judge should say, where appropriate, that certain items of evidence which the jury thinks might be corroboration are in law incapable of being corroboration. In the light of the recent ending of distinctions between corroborative and other evidence (*Director of Public Prosecutions* v. *Kilbourne*, [1973] A.C. 729; [1973] 1 All E.R. 440, H.L.), does this suggest that the judge should warn the jury in all cases where they might draw an impermissible inference from silence? So long as no direct inference of guilt from the silence of an accused in court or out is permissible, the author favours an increased judicial use of such warnings in appropriate cases. The main danger in their use is that they will stress the fact of the accused's silence too strongly to the jury, which will then draw the wrong inferences anyway; but if doubts of this kind are really well-founded, it may be time to devise a better tribunal of fact.

Secondly, the wording of the caution is not apt to indicate the true effect of silence. It says that if the suspect speaks, the answers may be used in evidence. It does not say that his silence may strengthen the inferences to be drawn from the prosecution case. The difficulty is that the point is too subtle to be easily understood by a suspect.

IV REFORM

The most controversial of the Criminal Law Revision Committee's proposed reforms concerned the right to silence. The Report argues that trials should be less of a game and more of an inquiry into truth. They are hemmed about with extensive safeguards to deal with dangers that no longer exist. Trials are now more carefully and less hastily conducted. There has been a great increase in legal representation for the accused. Since 1898 the accused can give evidence and he has much greater rights of appeal. Juries are better educated, magistrates are now trained and assisted by legally qualified clerks.

Further, "there is now a large and increasing class of sophisticated professional criminals who are not only highly skilful in organizing their crimes and in the steps they take to avoid detection but are well aware of their legal rights and use every possible means to avoid conviction if caught. These include refusal to answer questions by the police and the elaborate manufacture of false evidence" (para. 21). There is a "notably high proportion of acquittals in contested trials on indictment" (para. 22).

Accordingly they recommended that the accused's out-of-court silence as to a fact subsequently relied on in his defence, which it would have been reasonable for him to mention in pre-trial questioning, should be left to the trier of fact to draw whatever inferences as to guilt as appeared proper. This may be relied on in committal proceedings, and also in the trial (by the court in deciding whether there is a case to answer, and by the jury or the magistrates in deciding whether the accused is guilty). Inferences from silence may also be used as corroboration. The current system of cautions will be replaced by a single caution in writing stating:

> "You have been charged with . . . If there is any fact on which you intend to rely in your defence in court, you are advised to mention it now. If you hold it back till you go to court, your evidence may be less likely to be believed and this may have a bad effect on your case in general. If you wish to mention any fact now, and you would like it written down, this will be done" (para. 44).

The Committee did not favour compulsory interrogation before a magistrate as either the sole or an auxiliary permissible method of questioning. By a majority they recommended that tape recorders should be used as an experiment. (A minority favoured suspending cl. I of the draft Bill, abolishing the right to silence, until there was compulsory use of tape recorders widely and regularly in police stations; their reasons are given Chap. 8, *post*.

These proposals were the most controversial in the entire report. The right of silence has been the subject of sharp divisions since at least Bentham's time. Much of the criticism has been intemperate and unthinking, but the author does support substantial parts of it. What is wrong with abolishing the right to silence?

Cross: The Right to Silence and the Presumption of Innocence— Sacred Cows or Safeguards of Liberty?
(1970), 11 J.S.P.T.L. 66

[T]he right to silence has come to be regarded in England as a fundamental right, like those of freedom of speech and freedom of worship, without which democracy simply will not work. I think this is utterly wrong, that insistence upon it has produced rules of criminal procedure which are offensive to common sense and that the accused is adequately protected from oppressive behaviour by the prosecution by the presumption of innocence.

Subject to this point, the only practical objection which has been raised against the suggestions I have made is that they fail to make allowance for the innocent man who has good reason for not wanting to give evidence. He may think, or have been told, that he will be a poor witness, or there may be something sinister which will inevitably be revealed in the course of his evidence. Whatever the cause of his reluctance to testify may be, it would be shocking, so the argument runs, not to allow the accused to make an unsworn statement or to permit adverse comment to be made by the prosecution on his failure to testify, or to treat such failure as an item of evidence against him. I can only say that I would not be shocked. The generalizations upon which the various major premises governing every item of circumstantial evidence are based are subject to rare exceptions, but this does not prevent Courts from acting on circumstantial evidence. . . . [B]arrels sometimes fall out of windows without anyone having been negligent, but this does not prevent the fall from being treated as *prima facie* evidence of negligence because barrels do not normally fall out of windows. Innocent men do not normally keep out of the witness box, so the risk that one such man will occasionally court conviction by doing so is one which may legitimately be taken; we can console ourselves with the reflection that such a man would to a large extent be the architect of his own misfortunes.

. . . You will have observed that my approach to the right not to testify comes to this: "the accused is not obliged to testify, but it should be made plain that he fails to do so at the risk of adverse inferences being drawn against him". How would a similar approach fare in the case of police questioning? Why should the law not be that a suspect's refusal to answer questions by the police may, in appropriate cases, count as an item of evidence against him? Once again it is important to bear in mind the existence of a saving clause constituted by those words "in appropriate cases". You will observe that I do not suggest that there should be a general offence of refusing to answer police questions for there are all manner of different situations in which the failure to answer would either have no evidential significance or else be made to lose its evidential significance very easily. A police officer asked me what the time was when I had dinner in my house a month ago last Tuesday; my reply is either "I can't answer" or "I won't answer" and, unless there is something very unusual in the circumstances, I will not have provided evidence against myself because people do not ordinarily remember these things. A police officer asked me where I slept last night, I refuse to answer; assuming that the question is relevant, I have provided evidence against myself, although, were I subsequently to go into the witness box and give an explanation of my refusal to answer, the significance of that particular item of evidence might be made to disappear.

. . . What, apart from talk about a fundamental right to silence, could be urged against the utilization, on appropriate facts, of the suspect's refusal to answer police questions as evidence against him at his trial? I can only think of two points; the first relates to police methods, the second to privacy.

As to police methods, I concede that the possibility of a suspect's refusal to answer questions becoming evidence against him at his trial might enhance the chances of an improper browbeating of a lonely suspect in a protracted interrogation at a police station; but surely the answer is, "Tape record all interrogations and give the accused every opportunity to consult his legal adviser." I am aware of the fact that the answer gives rise to possible practical difficulties, but an academic address on the right to silence is no place for a discussion of them, although I entertain no doubt with regard to their superability.

As to privacy, if a police officer were to knock on the door of my house and tell me that he wanted to ask me questions about my movements yesterday, I hope I would say "Why?" rather than "That would be a gross infringement of my right of privacy". If to my "Why?" he were to reply "I am not telling you", I would certainly feel justified in slamming the door in his face. If, on the other hand, he were to reply "Because I am told you spent most of yesterday with Smith, and Smith's body was found riddled with bullets in his office two minutes after you left the place", I hope I would recognize that my social duty to assist the police with their reasonable enquiries had priority over my right of privacy. You will notice I spoke of my social duty to answer "reasonable" police enquiries. I see the danger of harassment by unreasonable enquiries, but this would seem to me to be a poor ground for the total exclusion of unreasonable refusals to answer reasonable questions. It has always seemed to me to be one of the fantasies of modern thought on the whole subject of the control of police questioning to suppose that the law of evidence can render any really effective assistance.

. . . I have said enough to show why I think that the right to silence is a sacred cow obstructing the operation of common sense; but I would like to add a little more to combat the thesis that it is a fundamental tenet of the democratic state to be ranked on a par with freedom of speech and freedom of worship. I know of no more eloquent exposition of this thesis than that part of the opinion of Goldberg, J. in *Murphy* v. *Waterfront Commission of New York Harbour* (1964), 378 U.S. 52, at p. 55 in which he speaks of the privilege against self-incrimination, and I therefore propose to take you through it clause by clause.

> "It reflects many of our fundamental values and most noble aspirations: our unwillingness to subject those suspected of crime to the cruel trilemma of self-accusation, perjury or contempt; . . ."

If my suggestions were adopted, the trilemma would be different because there would be no liability for contempt, even by refusing to answer questions in the witness box. It would be self-accusation, perjury or, on appropriate facts, the risk of adverse inferences. If that is thought cruel, and I can't see why it should be, then abolish the accused's largely theoretical liability to be prosecuted for perjury in giving false evidence. Most continentals consider it to be an Anglo-American absurdity anyway.

> "Our preference for an accusatorial rather than an inquisitorial system of criminal justice; . . ."

What is there that is particularly inquisitorial in saying to a man, "You need not go into the witness box, but, if you don't, the jury will be told that they may use their common sense." Again, what is there that is particularly inquisitorial in a police officer's saying to someone he suspects of murder by shooting, "We can't compel you to answer, but, if you decline to say whether you have got a gun, the Court may draw adverse inferences about your ownership of any guns found in the lodging house to which you returned shortly after the murder had been committed by someone."

> "Our fear that incriminating statements will be elicited by inhumane treatment and abuses; . . ."

What possible danger of inhumanity would be involved in allowing counsel for the prosecution to comment either on the accused's failure to testify or on his refusal to answer police questions?

> "Our sense of fair play which dictates a fair state-individual balance by requiring the Government to leave the individual alone until good cause is shown for disturbing him and by requiring the Government in its contest with the individual to shoulder the entire load; . . ."

The trouble about the privilege against self-incrimination is that those who rely on it wish that it should continue long after the accused has, by refusing to answer questions or to testify, shown good cause why he should be disturbed. As to the State's bearing the entire load, I agree that it should, but I also concede, in deference to common sense, that in any system which enables the accused to testify, adverse inferences will be drawn if he does not do so.

> "Our respect for the inviolability of the human personality and of the right of each individual to a private enclave; . . ."

Once there are reasonable grounds for setting the criminal process in motion, these legitimate objects of respect must yield to the individual's duty to assist in the enquiry.

"Our distrust of self-depreciatory statements and our realization that the privilege, while sometimes a shield to the guilty, is often a protection to the innocent."

I don't share either the distrust or the realization.

After Goldberg, J.'s rhetoric I cannot resist a further quotation from Bentham on the right to silence:

"If all criminals of every class had assembled, and framed a system after their own wishes, is not this rule the very first which they would have established for their security?" (*Treatise on Evidence,* p. 241).

I hope I shall not be thought guilty of insularity if I say that I prefer Bentham to Goldberg, J.

I have already gone a long way towards committing myself to not regarding the presumption of innocence as a sacred cow, and I am relieved to find two compelling reasons for disregarding the dictates of common sense concerning the burden of proof which I have already mentioned. After all, my argument was rather crude; it was that, as most of the people put up for trial are guilty, the jury should be told that any doubts they entertain on the subject of guilt should be resolved in favour of the prosecution. One of the objections to this argument may be described as "constitutional", the other as "moral".

The constitutional objection is related to the separation of powers. We simply can't have judges instructing juries or themselves that the police are usually right, however much that may be the case. The mind boggles at the thought of the corrupting effect that such a practice would have on the behaviour of the police. For how long would the ordinary run of police officers resist the temptation of telling a recalcitrant suspect that he had better confess because the judges always support the police? The mind boggles even more at the thought of the disastrous effect of such a practice on the public image of the judge.

I approach the moral point with the assumption that the conviction and punishment of someone known to be innocent of the offence with which he is charged is absolutely unacceptable. The problem then becomes one of the extent to which it is proper to take the risk of the conviction and punishment of an innocent man. The function of the presumption of innocence is to minimize that risk. The risk obviously cannot be eliminated. In spite of the occasional extraordinary assertion to the contrary, we all know that it is possible for an innocent person to be convicted under our system. I have already mentioned the case of the innocent man who is convicted because he stayed out of the witness box through fear of being a bad witness, and there is of course the converse case in which an innocent man is convicted because he makes such a poor witness. Would anyone be prepared to maximize the risk by eliminating the presumption of innocence altogether and placing the burden of establishing his innocence beyond reasonable doubt or on balance of probability on the accused in every criminal case? Speaking for myself I would need to have a far greater faith in the "police always get the right man" theory than I have in order to obviate what I can only describe as my moral scruples at what would amount to the reckless disregard of the possibility of the conviction and punishment of an innocent man.

Field: The Right to Silence—a Rejoinder to Professor Cross
(1970), 11 J.S.P.T.L. 76

In this discussion of police questioning, Professor Cross puts himself in the role of the man being questioned, I suggest, with respect, that this puts the problem in a thoroughly misleading context. I am not concerned about Professor Cross's ability to cope with an inquiry about where he slept last night. He cannot escape being accompanied by a first-class lawyer, and the advice he gives himself will be sound advice. My worry is over the people actually being charged today with crimes of violence. Not the Rupert Crosses of the world, but the ignorant, suspicious, frightened, highly suggestible people who are simply not able to face up to police questioning even if that questioning is scrupulously fair—an ideal often not attained.

Twining: The Way of the Baffled Medic: Prescribe First, Diagnose Later—If at All
(1973), 12 J.S.P.T.L. 348, at p. 353

. . . [H]ow without facts and figures can the Felicific Calculus operate? . . .

Come to our legislators in 1972—ask them how many sophisticated criminals? Chuck. How many cases contested by sophisticated criminals? Chuck. How many ignorant, feckless, cowed or slow-witted accused are unrepresented? How many cases of improper methods of interrogation? How many cases of hardened criminals refusing to answer questions at all? What are the effects of the disciplinary principle? On every factual assumption, on every item of information relevant to diagnosis of the problem, *chuck, chuck, chuck* is still the answer.

Cross: A Very Wicked Animal Defends the 11th Report of the Criminal Law Revision Committee
[1973] Crim. L.R. 329

I recognize that the Report contains some unsupported statements about the doings of sophisticated professional criminals and the extent to which the present rules of evidence lead to wrongful acquittals. I do not wish to decry this possibility, but I would now wish to stress the need for rationalizing the law of evidence. I think most of the provisions of the Bill can be justified on this ground. . . . It follows that I attach little, if any, importance to the charge that the Committee neither did nor commissioned any empirical research. Even if it were the case that the present rule of evidence produced no wrongful acquittals, I would still be in favour of most if not all of the Committee's recommendations for the simple reason that their adoption would spare the judge from talking gibberish to the jury, the conscientious magistrate from directing himself in imbecile terms and the writer on the law of evidence from drawing distinctions absurd enough to bring a blush to the most hardened academic face.

Question

How far could the Committee's investigations have been entirely or more empirically based?

C. H. Rolph: Personal Identity
(London, 1957). Pp. 120–2

Now the judges in the superior courts are always saying that if your defence amounts to a complete alibi you should disclose it at the earliest possible moment in the Magistrate's Court.

. . . [W]hatever the judges say, the general practice in most Magistrate's Courts is for the prisoner to hold his fire, *especially if he has a criminal record*. There are two good reasons why he should do this, even where he has a genuine alibi. One is that his own solicitor probably won't believe him and will advise him to drop it; and therefore to produce the alibi too soon is to put a needless strain on solicitor-and-client relationships. The other is that when, as a long-established criminal you find yourself wrongly accused, you often take that to be part of an unending contest in which you must "box clever"; and it is not boxing clever to blurt out all the names and addresses of the witnesses who can prove your alibi. There may be a long interval between the magistrate's hearing and the trial by judge and jury, and during that time those witnesses of yours may retain their value the more surely for being *incognito*. An official system that can produce this tissue of false accusations against you is capable (you may genuinely believe) of getting at your witnesses if it knows who they are; and some of them are perhaps criminals enjoying a precarious liberty that the police are in a position to terminate at any moment.

[Rolph was once a policeman.]

Wigmore: Treatise on the Anglo-American System of Evidence in Trials at Common Law
3rd Edn. Para. 2251

[I]*t is the innocent that need protection.* Under any system which permits John Doe to be forced to answer on the mere suspicion of an officer of the law, or on public rumour, or on secret betrayal, two abuses have always prevailed and inevitably will prevail; first, the petty judicial officer becomes a local tyrant and misuses his discretion for political or mercenary or malicious ends; secondly, a blackmail is practised by those unscrupulous members of the community who through threats of inspiring a prosecution are able to prey upon the fears of the weak or the timid. . . .

When we come to the case of an *accused duly charged* by indictment and *now placed on trial,* we reach a somewhat different set of considerations. Here the question is merely whether he shall be required to disclose all that he knows of the crime charged against him. None of the considerations applicable to the foregoing situations have here any bearing. What is there to exempt the accused from simple and straightforward answers of denial, confession, or explanation?

Are there fair criticisms to be made of the Committee's views?

First, although the Committee mentions many changes favouring the accused, some changes have hurt him in the last century and a half. One is the formation of the police as an organized force possessing much greater power than the accused. This has meant that the criminal trial must in some sense be a game rather than a proper inquiry into truth. Of the two parties to the inquiry, the police have greater means for discovering the truth, but there is a risk that they may not seek it, preferring a conviction secured without regard for the precise facts. No doubt the accused even more commonly has motives for obscuring the truth, but if he is innocent he lacks the means to inquire into truth, to track down and question witnesses. Most criminal defences have to depend on a technicality or on an appeal to the heaviness of the burden of proof resting on the prosecution because the accused has no more straightforward way of having his innocence declared. The Mafia and their ilk in turn are even stronger than the police; should the problems of dealing with a minute proportion of suspects be used as a ground for seriously disadvantaging the vast bulk of suspects, some of whom are innocent? Another change which has hurt the accused is that now 98 per cent of all crimes are tried before magistrates where the chances of acquittal are much worse than before a jury. This proportion has been steadily rising. Further, statute has often made it easier for the prosecution to prove its case by putting the onus of proof on the accused or undermining the requirement of *mens rea*: offences of strict liability are much more common. Further, though lawyers are much more available than formerly in superior courts, this is much less true of magistrate's courts, and not true at all as regards out-of-court interrogation.

Secondly, it is misleading to rely on the fact that about half those tried on indictment are acquitted. Most of those tried before magistrates are convicted. McCabe and Purvis show in *The Jury at Work* (Oxford, 1971) that the acquittals include those directed by the judge for want of evidence, cases withdrawn by the prosecution and cases where some technical error in procedure has occurred. Abolition of the right to silence might enable more convictions to be got in these cases, but so serious a lack of evidence can surely not be fully met by inferences from silence. And the right of silence is quite irrelevant to many of the reasons for acquittal. These include the odd perverse verdict, inevitable under any system, and cases where the prosecution witnesses have performed poorly. They include prosecutions not wholeheartedly supported by the police but brought to satisfy a particular complainant. They include other cases where the police believe strongly in a man's guilt (perhaps because of a record), know success is unlikely, but hope the jury will share their own belief in guilt, particularly if the accused's defence is mishandled. Finally, there are prosecutions undertaken not to secure convictions but to appease local pressure and deter future crimes by the fear of the trial itself even without punishment on conviction. The high acquittal rate, it is thought, is adequately explained by these facts of life and these police practices. It is not likely to be reduced much by drawing inferences from silence. High acquittal rates are more likely to be due to shortages of police officers and equipment than to the rules of evidence. It might also be noted that the McCabe–Purvis figures are confirmed by the views of judges and practitioners that those acquitted are almost all in fact innocent (Lord Salmon, 388 H.L. Deb. cols. 1603–10).

Thirdly, abolition of the right to silence by permitting inferences to be drawn will force suspects to speak; and there is a real danger of the innocent convicting themselves in the process. Most suspects are not strong-willed, intelligent, alert or articulate. They are weak, frightened and suggestible. They may fail to understand the true significance of questions. In a complicated factual situation they will almost always be incapable of putting their views adequately and convincingly. They may contradict themselves and strengthen the case against themselves because of incompetence rather than guilt. It is a common experience that most people are unable to sort out the factual aspects of their problems even after time for studied reflection in discussions with friendly legal advisers. How much worse off would they be answering questions without prior thought in a hostile atmosphere and in the absence of advice?

Fourthly, as Lord Devlin has said, to abolish the pre-trial right to silence would be "as startling as if, under our civil procedure, the defendant on receipt of a writ was required to call at the office of the plaintiff's solicitor to tell him what his defence was going to be to an undisclosed statement of claim, and to submit to questioning upon it" (quoted in Bar Council's Memorandum on the 11th Report, para. 22). Indeed, the proposed reform would look odd in a civil case even though there are civil safeguards absent from criminal procedure. In civil cases there is pre-trial discovery of documents; there is pleading which gives notice of the case each side hopes to make and defines the issues. In criminal cases, though the accused gets good notice of the charge, the police do not tell the accused which facts they hope to prove beyond what appears in the Particulars of Offence, which witnesses may be relevant and so on. Nor do the police hand over the proofs of witnesses, whether or not those witnesses are going to be relied on at the trial. Cross's response to this reasoning is: "I understand that a much favoured assertion amongst a certain class of suspects is 'I don't know what you are talking about', but are there really many suspects who are unaware of the case against them by the time they are charged?' " ([1973] Crim. L.R. 329, at p. 335).

Fifthly, it seems undesirable to permit police fishing expeditions. A suspect could be asked many questions, without being informed what charge the police had in mind. He would think his failure to answer could count as evidence against him on some charge or other.

Sixthly, compulsion to answer police questions is one thing, for which there are strong though not in the writer's view wholly persuasive arguments. It is another to introduce compulsion to answer the questions of non-public officials like shop detectives—uncontrolled by Parliament, public opinion or a sound tradition.

Seventhly, the Committee grants that there may be reasons for silence consistent with innocence—the accusation may shock the suspect into silence or forgetfulness; the exculpatory fact may harm the accused's reputation or his family. But they say that the jury can judge whether there was a reason sufficient to account for the accused's silence and to prevent adverse inferences being drawn. This is unclear; in any event there are other reasons for silence. The events may have happened a long time ago; the accused may have forgotten when questioned but remembered by the time of the trial. The accused may regard an imputation against him as not worth answering (admittedly this is more true of sudden accusations than prolonged detailed interrogation). A grave charge may make some people eager to deny it, but others will wish to reserve their defence.

Finally, it is common for perfectly innocent people to lie when questioned by the police. They think it better to invent an alibi in an attempt to terminate questioning. The lie tells against them when it is subsequently discovered. This undesirable tendency would probably be accentuated if cl. 1 were enacted, for if it looks bad to say nothing or to say "I don't remember", suspects will be tempted to lie.

In brief, the proposed position would be virtually opposite to the American position. The *Escobedo–Miranda* doctrine requires that the accused be told of his right to silence and to counsel at the public expense (Chap. 8, *post*). Cl. 1 provides that silence may count against a suspect; and nothing is done to strengthen the rather inchoate right to a lawyer.

It might be noted that Bentham's famous remarks, quoted by the Committee (para. 31), in favour of abolishing the right to silence were directed not to out-of-court silence but to silence before the judge, and it is thought the former is much more defensible. Bentham was in fact suspicious of information devised from out-of-court questioning, which he termed "necessarily incomplete and fallacious; for how much of what the accused may have said extra-judicially reaches the judge? Only so much as the deposing witness is able and willing to recollect; and even in this what security is there for the accuracy of his memory and the veracity of his character?"

It might also be noted that though the Committee's Report does little to strengthen any right to a lawyer that may exist, at least one of the Committee's members supports this. If a lawyer *were* present throughout interrogation, cl. 1 would be much less dangerous. (See Cross, [1973] Crim. L.R. 329.)

The Criminal Law Revision Committee's proposals regarding silence in court are contained in cl. 5. It provides that if the court considers there is a case for the accused to answer, it shall call on him to give evidence, and if he refuses to do so or refuses to answer any question without good cause, the trier of fact may draw any appropriate inferences against the accused and these may count as corroboration. The court must warn the accused of the position. The prosecution is to be entitled to comment on the accused's silence, so that s. I (*b*) will be repealed. "A few suggestions have been put to us that only the judge should be able to comment because the prosecution may not use enough discretion in doing so; but we do not think that this is a strong enough argument, especially when both the defence and the court will be able to put the matter into perspective. . . . We would stress that our proposals depend on there being a *prima facie* case against the accused. Failure to give evidence may be of little or no significance if there is no case against him or only a weak one. But the stronger the case is, the more significant will be his failure to give evidence. The procedure will not apply if "it appears to the court that the physical or mental condition of the accused makes it undesirable for him" to testify (cl. 5 (I) (*c*)). The "good cause" for refusing to answer particular questions would be that it would disclose his record in an impermissible way; that it would infringe his privilege against incriminating himself or his wife of other offences, or legal professional privilege; or that the question is oppressive and the court in its discretion excuses him.

In the writer's view this reform of the right to silence is far more defensible than the proposals for out-of-court silence. Many of the *bona fide* reasons for silence—insanity, oppressiveness, or some privilege—are taken account of. Since there must be a case against the accused, it is wrong to say, as the Criminal Bar Association does, that the change would "force a person into the witness box on the flimsiest and most unsatisfactory allegation of crime" (Bar Council Memorandum, para. 29). Are there other reasons for silence not met by cl. 5? One is said to be that uneducated or inarticulate persons need a right to silence, as do foolish persons who do their cause harm by lying on immaterial points. But though silence out of court may be needed as a right for such people, there is much less need for silence in court. They will often be represented, the court has a duty to protect them from oppressive questioning, they will have had a chance to think out their story carefully and in detail. Another reason offered for the right to silence is that it prevents the accused being forced to disclose conduct on his or another's part which though non-criminal is highly embarrassing. But cl. 5 (5) (*b*) meets this by giving the court a general discretion to excuse the prisoner from answering particular questions.

Another reason for silence is said to be to reduce the chance of the accused's record being disclosed. The argument is that though it will only be revealed if the accused gives evidence of his own good character or attacks either the prosecution or his co-accused, the precise circumstances in which these events will be held to have occurred are sometimes obscure, and it is safer to avoid the problem by silence. Kalven and Zeisel, *The American Jury* (Boston 1966), pp. 143–8 show that this is probably the real reason for silence in America (where the record of one who testifies is more likely to be admitted than in England). 18 per cent of their accused stayed silent. Of those with a record, 26 per cent did not testify. Of those with a record where the case was strongly in their favour, 47 per cent did not testify. In English conditions there is probably a little in this argument, because there have been odd decisions on s. I (*f*) of the Criminal Evidence Act 1898, which controls the admissibility of the record (Chap. 10, *post*).

A different justification for the right to silence runs thus. It is possible for a submission of no case to answer to fail and yet for the accused to be acquitted; for apart from the fact that the judge will generally be less defence-minded than the jury, there is a considerable difference in the quantum of evidence required to prove a *prima facie* case and that to prove a case beyond reasonable doubt. The accused's counsel can sometimes estimate this difference accurately and therefore confidently advise his client not to testify. Hence some of those who believe the fact that the burden of proof rests on the prosecution is a real safeguard of innocence believe that the accused should be entitled to rely on it by not giving evidence.

The reply usually made to these points is a simple and unconvincing one. Since innocent men are normally eager to tell their story, at least in the safe atmosphere of a court, the cases when they do not are special ones, and the cases where they have a legitimate reason for not testifying are rare. It is rare for a sane man to do himself an injustice in the box and for the accused to throw away his shield against cross-examination on his record involuntarily. If a rule will operate satisfactorily in most cases and badly only in a few it should be adopted.

It might be noted that the proposed changes do not do more than permit common-sense inferences to be drawn, they do not make silence presumptive of guilt or equivalent to guilt. The dangers of using silence as evidence of guilt and the possible reasons for silence discussed above (pp. 142–3, *ante*) will have to be considered by the trier of fact. The changes are theoretically large, but not revolutionary. In practice the effect of the changes might well be fairly slight because there is no practice of warning a jury of the limited value of silence. If a critical comment is made, then the jury are properly guided; but often a benevolent judge will make no comment, and the jury are free to make inferences which are both impermissible in law and dangerous as a matter of common sense. There are a number of quite strong arguments against cl. I and 5 but they can only be advanced without inconsistency if one is willing to support a much wider warning to the jury on the status of silence than is commonly now given.

8

Confessions

A confession is a statement by the accused in which he admits committing an offence, or admits some fact that goes to show he committed an offence. In some jurisdictions a distinction is drawn between inculpatory and exculpatory statements, with the special rules of admissibility we are about to discuss applying only to the former; the distinction was suggested by Wigmore (para. 821). But it is not part of English law (*Customs and Excise Commissioners v. Harz*, [1967] 1 A.C. 760, at pp. 817–18; [1967] 1 All E.R. 177, at p. 182, H.L.) and its popularity is waning (e.g. Canada has now adopted the English position: *Piche* v. *R.* (1970), 11 D.L.R. (3d) 700).

There are three rules to bear in mind when considering the admissibility of confessions. If the confession is "involuntary", it is *strictly inadmissible as a matter of law*. If it infringes the Judges' Rules, a code of procedure drafted by the judges to guide the police while they question suspects, it *may be excluded in the discretion of the court*. The third rule is that if admission of an otherwise admissible confession would operate against the accused unfairly, again it *may be excluded in the discretion of the court*.

I THE INVOLUNTARINESS RULES

A. Nature of the inducement

A confession is inadmissible against the accused unless it is not obtained by inducement; that is, unless it is "voluntary in the sense that it has not been obtained from him by fear of prejudice or hope of advantage, exercised or held out by a person in authority, or by oppression". This question of admissibility is decided by the judge on a "*voir dire*", i.e. in the absence of the jury, and the judge must be satisfied of voluntariness even though the accused does not raise the point. This "voluntariness" rule was authoritatively so stated as principle (e) in the introduction to the Judges' Rules.

An inducement depends on a "fear of prejudice or hope of advantage", which suggests an inquiry into the actual state of the accused's mind. But in fact no such inquiry is made; the test is quite technical, external and objective. The law of confessions for the most part rests on the probable effect of inducements rather than their actual effect. However, subjective considerations are relevant in connection with the oppression rule, which will be considered later (p. 183, *post*). They are also relevant where the inducement proceeds from a person who is not in authority.

R. v. Richards
[1967] 1 All E.R. 829, C.A.

WINN, L.J.: . . . Whatever be the nature of the inducement so made and however trivial it may seem to the average man to have been, such an inducement will be at least capable of rendering the statement then made inadmissible; it will have that effect unless in a given case it becomes plain beyond a reasonable doubt that it did not operate at all on the mind of the person to whom it was made. . . .

Here, a police officer said to the appellant at a time when already a number of questions had been asked and he had been pressed somewhat about his movements during the material afternoon and had made lying replies, "I think it would be better if you made a statement and told me exactly what happened", and a statement was then made. Clearly that was something coming from a person in authority, capable of constituting an inducement. It does not matter how mild may be the inducement so made, as is illustrated by R. v. *Smith*, [1959] 2 Q.B. 35; [1959] 2 All E.R. 193, where a sergeant-major addressed troops on parade about a theft which had been discovered and, if my memory serves me correctly, said, "None of you will go off parade until I know the truth about this." This sphere of inducement is quite separate from the sphere in which persons not in authority make promises or threats which are alleged subsequently to have induced a statement or confession. In that latter sphere the essential question is always what was in fact the effect of the inducement? Did it go so far as to deprive the person to whom it was made of free will and choice whether he would or would not make a statement as he did?

"Inducement" is usually defined in the double form given above: "fear of prejudice or hope of advantage". Though occasional remarks are made to the contrary (*R. v. Williams* (1968), 52 Cr. App. Rep. 439), nothing ought to turn on this dichotomy between threats and promises. The two limbs are really the same because in any given case the inducement can be regarded either way. A prisoner always has two alternatives, pleasant if he confesses, painful if he does not. Sometimes the carrying out of the threat or promise involves a change in the *status quo* (e.g. the commencement of a beating), sometimes not (e.g. the continuation of a beating). But there are not really two distinct kinds of inducement. This further indicates that the word "voluntary" is a misnomer. The accused in confessing has made a choice. He has consciously uttered certain words and his conduct is voluntary (in a sense in which the conduct of one suffering from epilepsy is not). The real question is whether one factor in his choice has been unduly strong. The foundation of the confession rule at this point depends on what one conceives to be its purpose. If the purpose is to avoid the risk of untrue confessions, more will be admitted perhaps than if it is to control police misconduct.

In the earlier nineteenth century the rules as to what could constitute an inducement became wider and wider. This trend of "liberalism run wild" was consciously stopped by the Court for Crown Cases Reserved in *R. v. Baldry* (see Baker, *The Hearsay Rule* (London, 1950), p. 54).

R. v. Baldry
(1852), 2 Den. 430

A constable said to the prisoner that he need not say anything to incriminate himself, but what he did say would be taken down and used as evidence against him. He was convicted on the basis of his confession. His appeal to the Court for Crown Cases Reserved failed.

POLLOCK, C.B.: I am of opinion that the conviction is right—that the evidence was properly received. I consider that the grounds for not receiving such evidence, are not those stated by the learned Counsel in his elaborate and able argument from a review of all the cases, that there is a presumption of law one way or other. The ground for not receiving such evidence is, that it would not be safe to receive a statement made under any influence or fear. There is no presumption of law that it is false or that the law considers such statement cannot be relied upon; but such confessions are rejected because it is supposed that it would be dangerous to leave such evidence to the jury.

PARKE, B.: By the law of England, in order to render a confession admissible in evidence it must be perfectly voluntary; and there is no doubt that any inducement in the nature of a promise or of a threat held out by a person in authority, vitiates a confession. The decisions to that effect have gone a long way; whether it would not have been better to have allowed the whole to go to the jury, it is now too late to inquire, but I think there has been too much tenderness towards prisoners in this matter. I confess that I cannot look at the decisions without some shame when I consider what objections have prevailed to prevent the reception of confessions in evidence; . . . the rule has been extended quite too far, and justice and common sense have, too frequently, been sacrificed at the shrine of mercy. We all know how it occurred. Every Judge decided by himself upon the admissibility of the confession, and he did not like to press against the prisoner, and took the merciful view of it.

ERLE, J.: . . . I am of opinion that when a confession is well proved it is the best evidence that can be produced; and that unless it be clear that there was either a threat, or a promise to induce it, it ought not to be excluded. . . . [I]n many cases where confessions have been excluded, justice and common sense have been sacrificed, not at the shrine of mercy, but at the shrine of guilt.

[WILLIAMS, J. and LORD CAMPBELL, C.J. agreed.]

Cf. *R.* v. *Moore* (1852), 2 Den. 522, decided at the same time, where Parke, B. said that if an inducement were held out the confession must be excluded "however slight the threat or inducement".

There were a number of reasons why the trend of decision towards a wide definition of "inducement" was so strong before *Baldry*. First, prisoners generally came from the poorer classes during a time of considerable social dislocation. They rarely knew their rights to remain silent. Judges accordingly felt a need to protect them and regarded statements made by them with great suspicion. Secondly, the judges tended to distrust the early police as novelties; indeed they continued to do so throughout the nineteenth century. Cave, J. said in *R.* v. *Thompson*, [1893] 2 Q.B. 12, at p. 18; [1891–4] All E.R. Rep. 376: "I always suspect these confessions, which are supposed to be the off-spring of penitence and remorse, and which nevertheless are repudiated by the prioner at the trial. It is remarkable that it is of very rare occurrence for evidence of a confession to be given when the proof of the prisoner's guilt is otherwise clear and satisfactory; but, when it is not clear and satisfactory, the prisoner is not unfrequently alleged to have been seized with the desire born of penitence and remorse to supplement it with a confession;—a desire which vanishes as soon as he appears in a court of justice."

Thirdly, criminal punishments were savage and the sentencing of prisoners to death, if not their execution, was common. As a matter of mercy the judges tried to exclude confessions which inevitably led to convictions.

Fourthly, there was little possibility of appeal. The only practical method was for the judge to reserve a point of law for the Court of Crown Cases

Reserved. Rather than delay the trial by doing this the judge would tend to decide the point in favour of the prisoner, particularly if he could safely be convicted on other evidence. Thus a mass of *nisi prius* decisions in favour of the accused was built up, constituting collectively a strong body of authority.

Fifthly, the accused's incompetence as a witness, which lasted until 1898, meant that if a confession by him was admitted he had no opportunity of going into the box and explaining it away. (Indeed prisoners did not even have any general right to counsel until 1836.) It may be for this reason that the Court of Criminal Appeal said in *R. v. Priestly* (1966), 50 Cr. App. Rep. 183, that pre-1898 cases on the meaning of inducement had no validity in modern practice. In any event, this *dictum* was questioned in *R. v. Richards*, [1967] 1 All E.R. 829; [1967] 1 W.L.R. 653, C.A., and it is out of line with several modern decisions (e.g. *R. v. Cleary* (1963), 48 Cr. App. Rep. 116, C.C.A.; *R. v. Smith*, [1959] 2 Q.B. 35; [1959] 2 All E.R. 193, and *Customs and Excise Commissioners v. Harz and Power*, [1967] 1 A.C. 760; [1967] 1 All E.R. 177, H.L. A final suggestion is that the judges were influenced by "lack of means on the part of the prisoner which, in some cases, prevented him from calling witnesses. In such a position any gamble upon a promise or half-promise of tolerance or mercy was not an unreasonable choice" (Kaufman, *Admissibility of Confessions* (Toronto, 2nd Edn., 1974, at pp. 16–17).

To a large extent these conditions have changed. Prisoners are better educated; the police are more trustworthy; punishments are less brutal; appeal on points of law has been available since the creation of the Court of Criminal Appeal in 1907; and the prisoner is a competent witness, often entitled to legally aided counsel. But pre-1898 cases are still followed; and since *Baldry* stopped but did not reverse a trend, the law on inducements is very unrealistic and technical. In *R. v. Jarvis* (1867), L.R. 1 C.C.R. 96, "you had better tell the truth" was said to have acquired a technical meaning as an inducement. This has often been followed, e.g. *R. v. Richards*, [1967] 1 All E.R. 829; [1967] 1 W.L.R. 653, C.A. It is probably as far as the courts will go. In *R. v. Reeve* (1872), L.R. 1 C.C.R. 362, the words "You had better, as good boys, tell the truth" were held permissible, but perhaps as a moral rather than temporal promise. In this case Willes, J. remarked that the rules on inducement had gone so far at one time that "Tell the truth" apparently meant "Tell a lie". "It will be the right thing . . . to make a clean breast of it" was held to be an inducement in *R. v. Thompson*, [1893] 2 Q.B. 12; [1891–4] All E.R. Rep. 376.

R. v. Smith
[1959] 2 Q.B. 35; [1959] 2 All E.R. 193

A regimental sergeant-major investigating fighting which resulted in a murder told a company of troops he would keep them on parade until he learnt who had been involved in the fighting. Shortly afterwards the accused confessed. The Courts-Martial Appeals Court held that the confession was induced.

LORD PARKER, C.J.: The court is quite clear that while there was nothing improper in the action taken by the regimental sergeant-major, the evidence of what took place was clearly inadmissible at the prisoner's trial. What the sergeant-major did might well have been a very useful course of action in order to enable further inquiries to be made, but the court is satisfied that if the only evidence against the prisoner was a confession obtained in those circumstances, it would be quite inadmissible at his trial. It has always been a fundamental principle of the courts, and something quite apart from the Judges' Rules of Practice, that a prisoner's confession outside the court is only admissible if it is voluntary. In deciding whether an admission is voluntary the court has been at pains to hold that even the most gentle, if I may put it in that way, threats or slight inducements will taint a confession. To say to all those on parade, "You are staying here and are not going to bed until one of you owns up" is in the view of this court clearly a threat. It might also, I suppose, be looked upon as an inducement in that the converse is true, "If one of you will come forward and own up, the rest of you can go to bed"; but whichever way one looks at it, the court is of opinion that while the action was perfectly proper and a useful start no doubt to inquiries, evidence in regard thereto was clearly inadmissible.

The Court stated the R.S.M.'s conduct was "a very useful course of action" and that there was "nothing improper" in it. Nor would the threat to keep soldiers on parade be likely to intimidate them much. Yet it led to the confession being excluded. There is force in Lord Reid's view in *Customs and Excise Commissioners* v. *Harz*, [1967] A.C. 760, at p. 820; [1967] I All E.R. 177, at p. 184, H.L. that "many of the so-called inducements have been so vague that no reasonable man would have been influenced by them, but one must remember that not all accused are reasonable men and women: they may be very ignorant and terrified by the predicament in which they find themselves. So it may have been right to err on the safe side." A slightly different point made by Maguire is that "the inducements are not directed to average persons picked at random, but to persons actively suspected of crime, usually under arrest, and not infrequently aware of the availability of evidence tending to incriminate them. Hence suggested alleviations which would not greatly tempt the average individual to self-accusing falsehood may have substantial persuasive power" (*Evidence of Guilt* (Boston, 1959), para. 3. 062, n. 9). Further, sometimes the statement "it is better to tell the truth" may be genuinely coercive, for "what is *truth*? Not infrequently, for prosecutor or policeman, the conviction to which his mind has come. Where that definition of the word is apparent, forceful assertion that it is 'better to tell the truth' may indeed elicit a lie" (*ibid.*, n. 11).

But despite these points some of the cases go too far. The inducement rule sometimes operates quite arbitrarily and technically, without any reference to any purpose it might legitimately fulfil.

In general, the phrase "inducement" covers two main threats: first, threats of bodily harm to the accused (or presumably one he loves), e.g. continued detention or violence, or absence from his family; secondly, threats of non-physical harm to the accused or those he loves, e.g. public rather than secret trial (*Sparks* v. *R.*, [1964] A.C. 964, [1964] I All E.R. 727 P.C.;), prosecution rather than non-prosecution, lenient rather than harsh treatment.

However, the inducement must not be too vague; it must point to some consequence. This may be the explanation for holding that the following remarks did not vitiate a confession: "Be sure to tell the truth" (*R.* v. *Court* (1836), 7 C. & P. 486); "I need to take a statement" (*R.* v. *Joyce*, [1957] 3 All E.R. 623; [1958] I W.L.R. 140).

However, very weak inducements have sufficed. "Tell me where the things are and I will be favourable to you" (*R.* v. *Thompson* (1783), I Leach 291); "If you don't tell me you may get yourself into trouble and it will be worse for you" (*R.* v. *Coley* (1868), 10 Cox C.C. 536); "I only want my money, if you give me that you may go to the devil'' (R. v. *Jones* (1809), Russ & Ry. 152); ''Put your cards on the table and tell them the lot'' (R. v. *Cleary* (1963), 48 Cr. App. Rep. 116, C.C.A.). The last is so weak that it may be authority for a rule that some vague inducements are dangerous in giving the suspect's terrors greater scope. It may be compared with R. v. *Bentley*, [1963] Q.W.N 10 (''If you do not tell the truth you will get yourself into a tangle''—confession admitted).

There must be some limitation of the weakness of an inducement which will render a confession inadmissible, if only because the formulation of the rule seems to require that the statement be *obtained from* the accused by it. If it is so weak as to have no causative effect it cannot be an inducement.

Further, as the New South Wales Court of Criminal Appeal said in R. v. *Bodsworth*, [1968] 2 N.S.W.R. 132, at p. 139, it is desirable ''to avoid putting ingenious constructions on colourless words so as to detect a hint of improper inducement, as was at one time the case, but rather to construe the words only according to their natural, obvious and commonsense meaning''.

One consequence of the inducement requirement is that unprovoked hopes by the accused that he will be better off for confessing do not invalidate the confession (R. v. *Godinho* (1911), 7 Cr. App. Rep. 12, C.C.A.).

The use of a trick to obtain a confession—e.g. telling the accused that the murder victim is alive and has identified him—does not render it inadmissible; nor *a fortiori* does a confession based on a mistake. Tricks and mistakes would only be relevant if they were likely to induce an untrue confession; a confession so obtained might be excluded as unreliable or left to the jury with a warning about weight. Thus ''if an incarcerated suspect is hoaxed into the belief that he can go free by paying a bribe and making a confession to the prosecutor, a real incentive to falsehood is brought into play'' (Maguire, *Evidence of Guilt* (Boston, 1959), para. 3. 062).

Tricks and mistakes might be relevant in some circumstances with regard to any discretion the court has to exclude a confession on grounds of unfairness (see p. 208, *post*).

The inducement must relate only to temporal rather than spiritual or moral consequences (R. v. *Gilham* (1828), 1 Mood. C.C. 186). Hence the following inducements have not rendered confessions inadmissible: ''I hope you will tell me the truth, in the presence of the Almighty'' (R. v. *Wild* (1835), 1 Mood. C.C. 452); ''Don't run your soul into more sin, but tell the truth'' (R. v. *Sleeman* (1853), Dears. 249); ''Be a good girl and tell the truth'' (R. v. *Stanton* (1911), 6 Cr. App. Rep. 198, C.C.A.). This particular limitation on the rule may be thought odd, for spiritual inducements will often be far more powerful to religious persons than temporal ones. Further, in other areas the law assumes that spiritual beliefs have coercive force, e.g. the importance of the oath, the fact that the test for giving sworn evidence is understanding the religious nature of an oath, and the fact that hearsay evidence admitted from a declarant under a settled hopeless expectation of death is made sufficiently reliable by the fact that the declarant knows he is about to account for his life before his Maker. It is true, however, that these latter areas of the law are quite commonly attacked. Joy's defence of the rule (supported by Wigmore, para. 840) does not seem wholly sound. He wrote: ''It seems difficult to imagine that a man under spiritual convictions and the influence of religious impressions would therefore confess himself guilty of a crime of which he was *not* guilty. . . . Such spiritual convictions or spiritual exhortations seem, from the nature of religion, the most likely of all motives to produce truth. . . . If temporal hopes exist, they may lead to falsehood. Spiritual hopes can lead to nothing but truth" (*Confessions*, p. 51). But if the inducement is "Tell the truth or you will go to Hell", a credulous accused will translate this as "Confess (truthfully or not) or you will go to Hell". This is only likely to be a practical problem in a simpler and more pious age; but such a remark from a priest to a simple parishioner in the presence of a policeman might be calculated to lead to an untruth, however sound the rule is in the generality of cases.

There is no doubt that an accused who makes one confession is likely to make others. As Jackson J. said in one American case, "after an accused has once let the cat out of the bag by confessing, no matter what the inducement, he is never thereafter free of the psychological and practical disadvantages of having confessed. He can never get the cat back in the bag" (*U.S.* v. *Bayer* (1947), 331 U.S. 532). Confessions subsequent to an involuntary one may be admissible if the improper inducement has become ineffective due to some intervening cause.

One such intervening cause is lapse of time.

R. v. Smith
[1959] 2 Q.B. 35; [1959] 2 All E.R. 193

After making an inadmissible confession (see p. 161, *ante*), the accused confessed again nine hours later and after being cautioned.

LORD PARKER, C.J.: The court thinks that the principle to be deduced from the cases is really this: that if the threat or promise under which the first statement was made still persists when the second statement is made, then it is inadmissible. Only if the time-limit between the two statements, the circumstances existing at the time and the caution are such that it can be said that the original threat or inducement has been dissipated can the second statement be admitted as a voluntary statement.

. . . This court, however, is of the clear opinion that the second statement was admissible. No doubt the opening reference to what it was said he had said to the regimental sergeant-major put the appellant in a difficulty. No doubt it was introduced by Sergeant Ellis in the hope that thereby he might get a continued confession; but it is clear that the effect of any original inducement or threat under which the first statement was made had been dissipated. Quite apart from the fact that the caution was given and given twice, some nine hours had elapsed and the whole circumstances had changed. The parade had ended. The rest of the company had gone to bed. The effect of the threat or the inducement was spent. On those grounds this court has come to the conclusion that the oral and written statements made to Sergeant Ellis were clearly admissible.

Another intervening cause making an inducement ineffective may be a caution, particularly if administered by one of superior rank to the original person in authority (*R.* v. *Bate* (1871), 11 Cox 686). But this is not always so (*Sparks* v. *R.*, [1964] A.C. 964, [1964] 1 All E.R. 727 P.C.;).

The inducement must be held out to the accused. It is not enough that he overhears an inducement offered to a fellow prisoner (*R.* v. *Jacobs* (1849), 4 Cox C.C. 54). This may be thought anomalous in the sense that if the inducement is likely to produce an untrue confession the confession should be excluded; but any risk of untruth can be dealt with under the *Richards* rule

(p. 169, *ante*) or by a direction as to weight. The real dangers of untruth only arise where the confession stems from an inducement offered directly to a particular accused.

The inducement need not relate to the prosecution, as was formerly thought.

Customs and Excise Commissioners v. Harz
[1967] 1 A.C. 760; [1967] 1 All E.R. 177, H.L.

The accused made a confession after customs officers unlawfully threatened to prosecute them for breach of a supposed statutory obligation to speak. The House of Lords held the confession inadmissible.

Lord Reid: [I]t was argued that there is a difference between confessions and admissions which fall short of a full confession. A difference of that kind appears to be recognized in some other countries. In India and Ceylon legislative enactments severely limit the admissibility of confessions, and the courts have construed these enactments as not preventing the admission in evidence of other incriminating statements obtained by fair means though not in the manner required for confessions. And for some reason not made clear in argument some such distinction appears to be recognized at least in some states in the United States. But there appears to be no English case for more than a century in which an admission induced by a threat or promise has been admitted in evidence where a full confession would have been excluded. If such a case had occurred since appeal to the Court of Criminal Appeal became possible I find it very difficult to believe that there would not have been an appeal. I can see no justification in principle for the distinction. In similar circumstances one man induced by a threat makes a full confession and another induced by the same threat makes one or more incriminating admissions. Unless the law is to be reduced to a mere collection of unrelated rules, I see no distinction between these cases. And it is noteworthy that the new Judges' Rules published in 1964 (Home Office Circular No. 31/1964, p. 5) make no such distinction. They are clear and emphatic:

> "... (*e*) That it is a fundamental condition of the admissibility in evidence against any person, equally of any oral answer given by that person to a question put by a police officer, or of *any statement*" (my italics) "made by that person that it shall have been voluntary in the sense that it has not been obtained from him by fear of prejudice or hope of advantage exercised or held out by a person in authority or by oppression. The principle set out in paragraph (*e*) above is overriding and applicable in all cases."

I must now deal a little more fully with the next argument because it was accepted by Thesiger, J. and forms the basis of his dissent. It is said that if the threat or promise which induced the statement related to the charge or contemplated charge against the accused, the statement is not admissible; but that if it related to something else, the statement is admissible. This distinction does appear in some, but by no means all, modern textbooks and it has a very curious history. There is no mention of it in the earlier works of authority—Hale, *Pleas of the Crown*, Chap. 38; Hawkins, *Pleas of the Crown*, Chap. 46; East, *Pleas of the Crown*, Chap. 16. Apparently it first appears in the 1840s. Joy states (*Confessions* (1842), p. 13):

> "But the threat or inducement held out must have reference *to the prisoner's escape from the charge*, and be such as would lead him to suppose, it will be better for him to admit himself to be guilty of an offence, which he never committed."

And Taylor, *Evidence* (1st Edn.) 1848), p. 592) says:

> "We come now to the nature of the inducement: and here it may be laid down as a general rule that in order to exclude a confession, the inducement whether it be in the

shape of a promise, a threat, or mere advice must have reference to the prisoner's escape from the criminal charge against him."

This is merely an inference which those learned writers draw from a few cases, none of which appears to me to warrant it. The most striking is R. v. *Lloyd* (1834), 6 C. & P. 393. There the inducement was that the gaoler would let the prisoner see his wife, and Patteson, J., without giving any reason, held that that did not make the confession inadmissible. The report is short and we do not know all the circumstances. He may well have thought the inducement too small to matter. But suppose the wife had been at death's door: I can imagine no inducement more likely to lead to a false confession, and I cannot believe that in such a case Patteson J. would have held it to be admissible. Yet the rule invented by these learned authors would mean that the confession would have been admissible. . . .

The "rule" was not adopted by Archbold or Starkie but it has been adopted by some later writers. Roscoe, *Law of Evidence in Criminal Cases* (6th Edn. (1862), p. 41) rightly says: "Upon this point there are but few authorities," and he does not seem enthusiastic for the rule. Sir James Stephen, in his *Digest of the Law of Evidence* (1st Edn. (1876), p. 28), simply says that the inducement must have reference to the charge against the accused person. Phipson, writing in 1892, *Evidence* (1st Edn., p. 156) simply cites Taylor, Stephen and Russell as his authorities. I get little from Russell. And later authors do no more than copy those who preceded them.

There appears to have been no judicial consideration of this "rule" for more than a century after it was first formulated. But in R. v. *Joyce*, [1957] 3 All E.R. 623; [1958] 1 W.L.R. 140, Slade, J. based his judgment on the rule as stated in Kenny (see Kenny's *Criminal Law* 19th Edn. (1966), p. 531). I doubt whether he need have done. The constable had only said: "I need to take a statement from you." Unless he misled the man into thinking that he was bound to make a statement and would suffer in some way if he refused, I would not regard that as involving any threat or inducement at all. The only case in the Court of Criminal Appeal brought to our notice was R. v. *Shuter* (1965), *Times*, 27 November. There Fenton Atkinson, J. said: "In our view inducement will not vitiate a confession when the proffered benefit has no bearing on the course of the prosecution and on this point the textbook writers speak with one voice." Research in preparing the present case shows that there are notable exceptions. . . . And then he said: "That principle must have been acted upon times without number for very many years past." I would venture to doubt that. Appeal has been easy for nearly 60 years, and, unless counsel have been very much less astute than I would suppose, I can scarcely think that many opportunities to appeal on this matter can have been missed.

One suggested justification of this rule appears to be that the tendency to exclude confessions which followed on some vague threat or inducement had been carried much too far and that the formula set out in many textbooks affords a useful and time-honoured way of limiting this tendency. But the common law should proceed by the rational development of principles and not by the elaboration of rules or formulae. I do not think that it is possible to reconcile all the very numerous judicial statements on rejection of confessions but two lines of thought appear to underlie them: first, that a statement made in response to a threat or promise may be untrue or at least untrustworthy: and, secondly, that nemo tenetur seipsum prodere. . . . But if the tendency to reject confessions is thought to have been carried too far, it cannot be proper to try to redress the balance by engrafting on the general principle an illogical exception, which at best can only operate sporadically, leaving the mischief untouched in the great majority of cases.

That the alleged rule or formula is illogical and unreasonable I have no doubt. Suppose that a daughter is accused of shop-lifting and later her mother is detected in a similar offence, perhaps at a different branch, where the mother is brought before the manager of the shop. He might induce her to confess by telling her that she must tell him the truth and it will be worse for her if she does not: or the inducement might be that if she will tell the truth he will drop proceedings against the daughter. Obviously the latter would in most cases be far the more powerful inducement and far the more likely to lead to an untrue confession. But if this rule were right the former inducement would make the confession inadmissible but the latter would not. The law of England cannot be so ridiculous as that.

In R. v. *Smith*, [1959] 2 Q.B. 35; [1959] 2 All E.R. 193, [t]he . . . inducement clearly was that, if the culprit confessed, his comrades would be released. It had nothing to do with any impending charge. But it was held sufficient to make the confession inadmissible. . . . This case must have been wrongly decided if the alleged rule exists.

In the well-known statement of the general principle by Lord Sumner in *Ibrahim* v. R., [1914] A.C. 599; [1914–15] All E.R. Rep. 874, P.C., this rule is omitted. And, perhaps more important, it is omitted from the passage from the Judges' Rules which I have already quoted. I do not think that these omissions are likely to have been due to mere oversight. So I come without hesitation to the conclusion that this alleged rule should not be adopted; indeed that it never has been part of the law of England.

[Lords Morris of Borth-y-Gest, Hodson, Pearce and Wilberforce agreed.]

B. Person in authority

The inducement must proceed from a person in authority. After *Harz's* case some thought that since it decided that the inducement need not relate to the prosecution, and since the definition of person in authority depends on his ability to influence the prosecution, the requirement that an inducement should proceed from a person in authority should be abandoned.

Deokinanan v. R.
[1969] 1 A.C. 20; [1968] 2 All E.R. 346, P.C.

The accused confessed to Balchand, a "trusted friend", while in police custody, in response to Balchand's promise to help him recover certain money he was alleged to have stolen. The Privy Council held the confession admissible.

Viscount Dilhorne: In R. v. *Wilson*; R. v. *Marshall-Graham*, Lord Parker, C.J. said ([1967] 2 Q.B. 406, at p. 415; [1967] 1 All E.R. 797, at p. 801, C.A.):

> "The first question that rises is whether Captain Birkbeck was a person in authority. There is no authority so far as this court knows which clearly defines who does and who does not come within that category. It is unnecessary to go through all the cases; it is clear, however, in R. v. *Thompson*, [1893] 2 Q.B. 12; [1891–4] All E.R. Rep. 367, that the chairman of a company whose money was said to have been embezzled by the prisoner was held to be a person in authority. It is also clear that in some cases it has been held that the prosecutor's wife is a person in authority, and in one case that the mother-in-law of a person whose house had been destroyed by arson was said to be a person in authority vis-à-vis a young girl employed by the owner of the house, in other words she was looked upon as a person in authority in relation to that girl.
>
> Mr. Hawser in the course of the argument sought to put forward the principle that a person in authority is anyone who can reasonably be considered to be concerned or connected with the prosecution, whether as initiator, conductor or witness. The court find it unnecessary to accept or reject the definition, save to say that they think that the extension to a witness is going very much too far."

In this case at the time of the confession Balchand was no more than a possible witness for the prosecution and their Lordships agree that the mere fact that a person may be a witness for the prosecution does not make him a person in authority.

Sir Kenneth Stoby, Chancellor, based his judgment in the Court of Appeal primarily upon the ground that Balchand was not and could not have appeared to the appellant to be a person in authority. Cummings, J.A. in his dissenting judgment, said that Balchand must have appeared to the appellant from the part he played in the search to have been "close to the police" and "someone who perhaps in the mind of the accused could influence the course of investigation by virtue of his position". He thought that Balchand "could reasonably in the mind of the accused have been regarded as a person in authority".

Their Lordships do not agree. In their opinion the evidence shows clearly that the appellant did not so regard him. He thought that Balchand was his friend. If he had not thought that and had thought that Balchand was "close to the police", it is not likely that he would have asked Balchand to become in effect an accessory after the fact. He cannot have thought Balchand when he met him in the lockup at Whim a person in authority.

Mr. Kellock argued that a person in authority meant a person who could fulfil the promise made and that as Balchand could have done what he promised, he was a person in authority. He contended that in the cases where confessions induced by promises made by persons in authority had been excluded, the promisor always had power to fulfil the promise.

If this be the case, it does not follow that that is the meaning to be given to the words "person in authority". The fact that a person could have kept his promise may show the reality of the promise and that it was a real inducement, but it is not a definition of those words. Mr. Kellock was unable to cite any case in support of his contention. In their Lordships' opinion his contention cannot be sustained.

Mr. Kellock also argued that it was to be inferred from the decision in *Customs and Excise Commissioners* v. *Harz*, R. v. *Power*, [1967] 1 A.C. 760; [1967] 1 All E.R. 177, H.L., that it was no longer necessary and part of the law that to be inadmissible a confession has to be induced by a person in authority. He submitted that it is illogical that a confession should not be regarded as inadmissible if the inducement came from someone without authority and yet a confession brought about by the same inducement is inadmissible if induced by a person in authority. Although the inducement is the same, in one case the confession is regarded as free and voluntary and in the other it is not.

This question was not considered in *Customs and Excise Commissioners* v. *Harz*, R. v. *Power* and it cannot be concluded that the decision in that case inferentially declared that what has long been regarded as part of the law was not the law.

In R. v. *Todd* the accused was induced to confess by two detectives who were not peace officers, representing that they were members of an organized gang of criminals and that to gain admission to the gang he had to satisfy them that he had committed a crime of a serious nature. Dubuc, J. held that the promise was not made by a person in authority and consequently the confession was admissible. Bain, J., who was of the same opinion, said ((1901), 13 Man. L.R. 364, at p. 376):

"A person in authority means, generally speaking, anyone who has authority or control over the accused or over the proceedings or the prosecution against him. And the reason that it is a rule of law that confessions made as the result of inducements held out by persons in authority are inadmissible is clearly this, that the authority that the accused knows such persons to possess may well be supposed in the majority of instances both to animate his hopes of favour on the one hand and on the other to inspire him with awe. . . ."

The fact that an inducement is made by a person in authority may make it more likely to operate on the accused's mind and lead him to confess. If the ground on which confessions induced by promises held out by persons in authority are held to be inadmissible is that they may not be true, then it may be that there is a similar risk that in some circumstances the confession may not be true if induced by a promise held out by a person not in authority, for instance if such a person offers a bribe in return for a confession.

There is, however, in their Lordships' opinion, no doubt that the law as it is at present only excludes confessions induced by promises when those promises are made by persons in authority.

Question

Do you agree with the Criminal Law Revision Committee that "the Privy Council clearly doubted the justification for the [person in authority] rule as a matter of principle" (11th Report, para. 58)?

The result of *Deokinanan*, and the retention of the "person in authority" requirement, may be justified by the fact that if an inducement proceeds from a person in authority it is more likely to operate on the accused's mind and make him confess. That is, whether an inducement relates to the prosecution or not does not affect its coercive force. But its coercive force may well be affected, or is more likely to be affected, by whether it comes from a person in authority. *Some* inducements from persons not in authority are coercive, and these are governed by the *Richards* doctrine (p. 169, *ante*).

Who is a person in authority? Traditionally the answer was "a person who has influence over the prosecution". In fact, the actual course of decision seems to give the answer "anyone whom the prisoner might reasonably suppose to have influence over the prosecution". Examples include policemen, magistrates, prosecutors, prosecutor's wives (*R. v. Upchurch* (1836), 1 Mood. C.C. 465), prosecutor's solicitors, gaolers. There are early nineteenth-century cases holding that an employer is one in authority. These may have been justified by contemporary social conditions, in that employers may in fact have had control over prosecutions in a way they do not now, or at any rate employees may have thought this. But in *R. v. Moore* (1852), 2 Den. 522 Parke, B. made it clear that an employer or his wife could only be a person in authority if they were also prosecutors. This decision was probably motivated by a similar spirit to that of *Baldry*—to curb the confession rule. As Parke, B. said, "The cases on this subject have gone quite far enough, and ought not to be extended" (*ibid.*, p. 526).

In *R. v. Wilson*, [1967] 2 Q.B. 406; [1967] 1 All E.R. 797, C.A. (see p. 177, *ante*) the court held that the victim of the crime was a person in authority because he was technically the prosecutor though in fact it would almost certainly be impossible for him to prevent the charge being brought.

A higher-ranking officer is a person in authority, like the sergeant in *R. v. Smith*, [1959] 2 Q.B. 35; [1959] 2 All E.R. 193. A headmistress is in authority over schoolgirls (*R. v. McLintock*, [1962] Crim. L.R. 549, C.C.A.). Though these persons could not in fact influence the prosecution, the prisoner may well think differently. In modern conditions, of course, only the police can generally prevent prosecutions.

Wives of policemen, prison chaplains, doctors (*R. v. Gibbons* (1823), 1 C. & P. 97), insurance adjusters (*R. v. Eftoda* (1963), 37 D.L.R. (2d) 269) and fellow servants (*Keefe v. R.* (1919), 21 W.A.R. 88) are not in authority.

Deokinanan decided that a "trusted friend" is not a person in authority, nor is a potential prosecution witness. It seems, however, that one known by the accused to be "close to the police" may be a person in authority because he would reasonably be regarded by the accused as capable of influencing the prosecution. The friend in *Deokinanan*, however, was not regarded by the accused in this light, but simply as a trusted friend.

Sometimes persons may be constructively in authority. If an improper inducement is held out by someone not in authority in the presence of someone who is, the confession will be inadmissible unless the person in actual authority disassociates himself from the inducements (*R.* v. *Cleary* (1963), 48 Cr. App. Rep. 116, C.C.A.).

Such decisions are defensible because if questioning by a person in authority is intimidating the same is likely to be true of his mere presence. But they pose a great difficulty for the person in authority. If the third party says "Tell them the truth and they won't oppose bail," what is the person in authority to do? If he says nothing, the confession is inadmissible. If he denies what is said—"Even if you tell us the truth we will oppose bail"—there will be no confession.

The confession rule applies with equal force when the inducement appears not as an offer from the police to the accused but as a suggestion from him to them (*R.* v. *Northam* (1967), 52 Cr. App. Rep. 97, C.A.; *R.* v. *Zaveckas*, [1970] 1 All E.R. 413, [1970] 1 W.L.R. 516, C.A.). Again, the police are in an impossible position. If they assent to the proposed inducement, the confession is inadmissible; if they refuse to assent, they may be lying and they also probably lose the confession.

If one person in authority makes an inducement and a confession is then made, but to a different person in authority, it is capable of being excluded (e.g. *R.* v. *Cooper* (1833), 5 C. & P. 535); the result is different if the inducement proceeds from one not in authority and the confession is made to one in authority (*R.* v. *Tyler and Finch* (1823), 1 C. & P. 129; *Deokinanan* v. *R.*, [1969] 1 A.C. 20; [1968] 2 All E.R. 346, P.C.).

C. The roles of the judge and jury

If defence counsel wishes to object to the admissibility of a confession, he should inform the prosecution before the trial begins and counsel for the prosecution should not refer to that evidence in opening. At the time when the prosecution wishes to produce the confession, a procedure called the "trial within the trial", or *voir dire* begins. The jury is sent from the court, and the judge hears evidence of the circumstances in which the confession was obtained, since the issue of voluntariness is a question of law to be decided by him, and to be decided by him even if the accused does not raise the matter. Voluntariness is the only issue at this stage; the truth of the confession is irrelevant. However, the method by which the confession was obtained has a bearing on its truth, since if it was obtained by violence, for example, it is less likely to be true than if given freely. So if the judge decides the confession is voluntary, any witness who gave evidence in the *voir dire* may be called to give evidence again before the jury in an attempt to convince them it is untrue. If the judge decides on the *voir dire* that the confession is voluntary, but later evidence in the main trial causes him to change his mind, he may direct the jury to disregard the confession; or direct the jury to acquit if there is no other substantial evidence against the accused; or direct a new trial.

An orthodox approach to the separation of judge-jury functions would require first that questions of truth should not be raised on the *voir dire* and secondly that a confession which the jury thinks to be true and which the judge has held to be voluntary should be acted on by them even if they do not think it voluntary. The first view is contradicted by *R. v. Hammond*, and the second by some English cases of the 1950s which are now of little authority.

R. v. Hammond
[1941] 3 All E.R. 318, C.C.A.

On the *voir dire* the accused testified that his confession had been extracted by police violence, and in answer to a question "Is it true?" said "Yes". The Court of Criminal Appeal held the question and answer admissible.

HUMPHREYS, J.: This appeal is brought on the sole ground that the question which was put by counsel for the prosecution in cross-examination of the accused was inadmissible. In our view, it clearly was not inadmissible. It was a perfectly natural question to put to a person, and was relevant to the issue of whether the story which he was then telling of being attacked and ill-used by the police was true or false. It may be put as it was put by Viscount Caldecote, L.C.J., in the early part of the argument of counsel for the appellant, that it surely must be admissible, and in our view is admissible, because it went to the credit of the person who was giving evidence. If a man says, "I was forced to tell the story. I was made to say this, that and the other," it must be relevant to know whether he was made to tell the truth, or whether he was made to say a number of things which were untrue. In other words, in our view, the contents of the statement which he admittedly made and signed were relevant to the question of how he came to make and sign that statement, and, therefore, the questions which were put were properly put.

This is a strange case. The accused's answer was as a matter of fact extraordinary and unexpected. The Court's reasoning that the truth of the confession is relevant to the question whether the accused can be believed in saying it was extracted by violence is odd. If the confession is true this presumably shows that the accused tends to tell the truth, which suggests that he is telling the truth in saying the police were violent. Yet the Court apparently thinks it tends to show him a liar on the basis that confessed criminals are likely to be liars, but if so his confession should be false. As a matter of policy, questions as to truth should not be permitted on the *voir dire* because they operate as an incitement to perjury and because the subsequent attitude of judge and counsel cannot remain unaffected by the accused's admission of guilt on the *voir dire*. Further, there is Queensland authority (*R. v. Gray*, [1965] Qd. R. 373; *R. v. Toner*, [1966] Q.W.N. 44) for the view that the privilege against self-incrimination can be claimed by the accused on the *voir dire*, even though it cannot during the main trial (Criminal Evidence Act 1898, s. 1 (e)). There is South Australian authority for the view that the judge has a discretion to exclude the accused's admissions on the *voir dire* from the jury's consideration when the main trial resumes (*R. v. Wright*, [1969] S.A.S.R. 256). For these reasons there has been a division of opinion among Commonwealth courts as to whether *Hammond* should be followed (it was criticized in *R. v. Weighill* (1945), 2 D.L.R. 471 and *R. v. Hnedish* (1959), 29 C.R. 347) and future English courts are unlikely to respect it. However, the Supreme Court of Canada has (*De Clerq v. R.* (1969), 70 D.L.R. (2d) 530). See Neasey (1960), 34 A.L.J. 110.

D. Burden and standard of proof

Confessions are admitted as an exception to the rule against hearsay, and the burden of proving them voluntary falls on the prosecution in accordance with the general rule as to establishing facts making hearsay admissible (*R. v. Thompson*, [1893] 2 Q.B. 12, [1891–4] All E.R. Rep. 376; see also dying declarations: *R. v. Jenkins* (1869), L.R. 1 C.C.R. 187). This involves the prosecution in the difficulty of proving a negative. There is probably an exception where involuntariness through oppression is alleged, where at least an evidential burden rests on the accused (*Sinclair v. R.* (1947), 73 C.L.R. 316, at p. 340). What is the standard of proof? On this a difference of view exists between England and Australia. England favours proof beyond a reasonable doubt (*R. v. Sartori*, [1961] Crim. L.R. 397), Australia favours proof on a balance of probabilities (*Wendo v. R.* (1963), 109 C.L.R. 559). In the 1950s the English position could be justified by the fact that according to *R. v. Bass*, [1953] 1 Q.B. 680; [1953] 1 All E.R. 1064, C.C.A. voluntariness was a matter for the jury as well as the judge so that the ordinary criminal standard of proof on jury questions should apply; but *Bass* is no longer good law. The merit of the English position is that since admission of a confession usually ensures the accused's conviction, great care should be taken before putting it to the jury. The merit of the Australian position is that it falls in line with the general rule that when the judge decides collateral facts (i.e. those relevant to admissibility), he decides on the balance of probabilities. The Criminal Law Revision Committee recommend no change in the English position. In practice the question of which test to apply probably makes no difference, at least in this area, since normally it will be a question simply of whether the judge believes the police or believes the accused.

Sometimes it is said that defence counsel should not allege involuntariness unless the accused is prepared to testify to that effect on oath (*R. v. O'Neill* (1950), 34 Cr. App. Rep. 108). This, which is probably merely an example of a general rule about alleging improbable facts, is in practice unimportant since even though the burden of proof is on the prosecution, the accused's story is unlikely to be accepted in circumstances where the prosecution have made out some kind of case of voluntariness unless he testifies.

The orthodox view that the jury has no right to exclude confessions which they consider involuntary was contradicted by certain English cases of the 1950s, (e.g. *R. v. Bass*, [1953] 1 Q.B. 680; [1953] 1 All E.R. 1064, C.C.A.). The High Court of Australia attacked these in *Basto v. R.* (1954), 91 C.L.R. 628, and the Privy Council and recent English courts have returned to orthodoxy. In *Chan Wei Keung v. R.*, [1967] 2 A.C. 160; [1967] 1 All E.R. 948, P.C., the Privy Council held it was not an error to fail to tell the jury that they must be satisfied of the voluntariness of a confession, and the Court of Appeal reached the same result in *R. v. Burgess*, [1968] 2 Q.B. 112; [1968] 2 All E.R. 54., C.A. The Court of Appeal has now held positively that it is wrong to tell the jury to disregard a confession if they think it involuntary: *R. v. Ovenell*, [1969] 1 Q.B. 17; [1968] 1 All E.R. 933, C.A. The current English position seems better than that of the 1950s for several reasons. A jury is likely to regard it as absurd if they are told that even though they think a statement true they should not act on it if they think it involuntary. The legal test for voluntariness may be hard for a jury to understand, particularly since parts of it have ceased to be based on common sense. If the confession rule is based on the need to control the police this is better done by an experienced judge than a jury perhaps sitting for the first and last time. The 1950s rule was called in America the "humane" rule because it gave the accused a double chance of having the confession excluded (*Commonwealth* v. *Preece*, (1885), 5 N.E. 494). But is it humane? Some judges may be reluctant to call the police liars and may resolve any doubt in favour of admissibility, relying on the jury's right of exclusion; that is, the second safeguard may make the judge lax, even though his experience and skill should make him the main safeguard. It is difficult to see any reason for departing from the orthodox division of functions by which admissibility is for the judge and weight for the jury. (See McKenna, [1967] Crim. L.R. 336.)

E. The limits of the rule

Normally the whole confession should be put in evidence, both the parts that tell against an accused and those in his favour. However, sometimes it is appropriate to put before the jury an edited version omitting matters prejudicial to the defendant (*R.* v. *Weaver*, [1968] 1 Q.B. 353; [1967] 1 All E.R. 277).

A confession is admissible only against its maker, not other accused, save in the case of conspiracy before the common enterprise is at an end. But where two accused are tried together, a confession by one implicating the other may be read out, it being the judge's duty to warn the jury that it is evidence only against its maker.

The confession rules do not apply to co-ordination tests performed by motorists (*Benney* v. *Dowling*, [1959] V.R. 237; *Walker* v. *Viney*, [1965] Tas. S.R. 96). Nor do they apply to real evidence obtained from the accused e.g. blood samples.

Such matters are governed in England by the rules relating to illegally obtained evidence. Further, the confession rules do not apply to the accused's non-testimonial conduct, i.e. to "non-assertive" evidence.

In *R.* v. *Voisin*, [1918] 1 K.B. 531, [1918–19] All E.R. Rep. 491, C.C.A., the police were investigating the murder of a woman whose body was found in a parcel with a piece of paper containing the words "Bladie Belgium". The accused was asked by them to write "Bloody Belgian", and wrote "Bladie Belgium". This evidence was held admissible because the accused's conduct was voluntary, but the question of voluntariness was really irrelevant since conduct is not confessional. A similar piece of evidence was important in the Lindbergh kidnapping case in America. The kidnap notes always put the dollar sign after the number (e.g. 5$), and always transposed "gh" to "hg" (e.g. "ouhgt"). Bruno Richard Hauptmann, who was executed for the crime, was given a test in which he made these errors (G. Walker, *Kidnap* (Hamish Hamilton, London, 1961), p. 237). There is obviously little danger of such non-testimonial "confessions" being false, and it would seem that they are not in fact confessions but acts which identify the accused as much his face or his other physical features like fingerprints.

F. Oppression

The Court has a duty to exclude as "involuntary" confessions obtained in oppressive circumstances. This duty is often confused with its discretion to exclude voluntary confessions obtained in breach of the Judges' Rules or otherwise unfairly. The duty is an example of the general involuntariness rule, though admittedly a much purer version of it than is presented by the rules on inducements; the question is, was the accused's free will so sapped as to make him speak where otherwise he would have remained silent? The exercise of the discretion, on the other hand, depends on a number of factors of which reliability is probably the most important (p. 208, *post*).

R. v. Prager
[1972] 1 All E.R. 1114, C.A.

The accused was questioned for ten hours out of seventeen, the last seven of which were consecutive. The Court of Appeal held that the trial judge had not erred in admitting the confession.

EDMUND DAVIES, L.J.: . . . [W]as the voluntary nature of the alleged oral and written confessions established? In *Customs and Excise Commissioners* v. *Harz*, [1967] 1 A.C. 760; [1967] 1 All E.R. 177, H.L., Lord Reid, in a speech with which all the other Law Lords agreed, treated the test laid down in principle (*e*) in the introduction to the Judges' Rules as a correct statement of the law. As we have already indicated, the criticism directed in the present case against the police is that their interrogation constituted "oppression". This word appeared for the first time in the Judges' Rules 1964, and it closely followed the observation of Lord Parker, C.J. in *Callis* v. *Gunn*, [1964] 1 Q.B. 495; [1963] 3 All E.R. 677, D.C., condemning confessions "obtained in an oppressive manner".

The only reported judicial consideration of "oppression" in the Judges' Rules of which we are aware is that of Sachs, J. in R. v. *Priestley* (1965), 51 Cr. App. Rep. 1, at pp. 1–2 where he said:

> " . . . to my mind, this word in the context of the principles under consideration imports something which tends to sap, and has sapped, that free will which must exist before a confession is voluntary . . . Whether or not there is oppression in an individual case depends upon many elements. I am not going into all of them. They include such things as the length of time of any individual period of questioning, the length of time intervening between periods of questioning, whether the accused person has been given proper refreshment or not, and the characteristics of the person who makes the statement. What may be oppressive as regards a child, an invalid or an old man or somebody inexperienced in the ways of this world may turn out not to be oppressive when one finds that the accused person is of a tough character and an experienced man of the world."

In an address to the Bentham Club in 1968 ((1968), 21 C.L.P. 10), Lord MacDermott described "oppressive questioning" as—

> "questioning which by its nature, duration or other attendant circumstances (including the fact of custody) excites hopes (such as the hope of release) or fears, or so affects the mind of the suspect that his will crumbles and he speaks when otherwise he would have stayed silent."

We adopt these definitions or descriptions and apply them to the present case.

Cornelius v. R.
(1936), 55 C.L.R. 235

The accused was subjected to "very drastic and far-reaching" questioning but his confession was held on appeal to the High Court of Australia to have been properly admitted.

Dixon, Evatt and McTiernan, JJ.: [Confessions are involuntary if obtained by] prolonged and sustained pressure by police officers upon a prisoner in their hands, until, through mental and physical exhaustion to which want of sleep and food sometimes contributes, he consents, in order to obtain relief, to make a confession of the crime. If it is alleged that the confession is the outcome of pressure, the question whether by persistent interrogation, or by other means, a prisoner has been constrained to confess so that his statement cannot be regarded as voluntary must sometimes be decided as a matter of degree.

McDermott v. R.
(1948), 76 C.L.R. 501

Dixon, J. (in the High Court of Australia): At common law a confessional statement made out of court by an accused person may not be admitted in evidence against him upon his trial for the crime to which it relates unless it is shown to have been voluntarily made. This means substantially that it has been made in the exercise of his free choice. If he speaks because he is overborne, his confessional statement cannot be received in evidence and it does not matter by what means he has been overborne. If his statement is the result of duress, intimidation, persistent importunity, or sustained or undue insistence or pressure, it cannot be voluntary. But it is also a definite rule of the common law that a confessional statement cannot be voluntary if it is preceded by an inducement held out by a person in authority and the inducement has not been removed before the statement is made. . . . The extreme applications which were made at one time of the principle that confessions obtained by the use by persons in authority of hope or fear were inadmissible gave this head of inducement an importance which has tended to obscure other forms of inducement. It is perhaps doubtful whether, particularly in this country, a sufficiently wide operation has been given to the basal principle that to be admissible a confession must be voluntary, a principle the application of which is flexible and is not limited by any category of inducements that may prevail over a man's will.

But, as the prisoner's counsel conceded, it is plain that the present case cannot be brought within the operation of the imperative rules of exclusion, common law and statutory. Certainly the fact that the prisoner was questioned by the police is not enough, even if he were in custody. The warning was given, there was no importunity, no pressure, nothing to overbear the accused man's will.

R. v. Buchanan
[1966] V.R. 9

An issue arose as to the admissibility of a statement made by the accused while he was suffering from a head injury.

Sholl, J. (in the Victorian Full Court): . . . [W]hen a question is raised, when a person had a head injury, whether statements made by him ought to be admitted in evidence or not . . ., there may well be two separate questions for decision, one of voluntariness and the other of reliability. Here, I think the evidence raised no real question as to reliability at all. . . . [As to voluntariness it was argued] that he had not sufficient intellectual capacity at that time to determine whether he would or would not exercise his right to refuse to answer.

. . . [T]here is no suggestion in the evidence that there was a suspension of the faculty of judgment, and the mere reduction of that faculty by head injury or drink could not be held to be sufficient to render a confession or admission involuntary. . . . I would not be prepared to exclude such a statement as involuntary unless the evidence showed that . . . the accused was incapable of appreciating that he had a choice to remain silent, or incapable of exercising sufficient volition to give effect to what he knew was such a right of choice.

In *R. v. Phillips*, [1949] N.Z.L.R. 316, at p. 322, Gresson, J. said: "The question is in large measure a psychological one, and the age, condition, temperament and intelligence of an accused are relevant considerations." Though there seems to be no modern English case excluding a confession on grounds of oppression, there is substantial Commonwealth authority for this. Examples include cases where the accused was physically (*R. v. Sykes and Campi (No.* 1), [1969] V.R. 631), or mentally ill (*Jackson v. R.* (1962), 36 A.L.J.R. 198), when he has recently fainted (*R. v. Burnett*, [1944] V.L.R. 115), or is under hypnosis (*R. v. Booker*, [1928] 4 D.L.R. 795), or is suffering the effects of first attempted suicide by poison and drowning and then consequential vomiting and stomach pumping (*R. v. Williams*, [1959] N.Z.L.R. 502 and see *R. v. Treacey*, [1944] 2 All E.R. 229). Recent New Zealand authority has qualified this by suggesting that mere fatigue does not make a confession inadmissible unless caused by another person who overbears the accused's will (*Naniseni v. R.* [1971] N.Z.L.R. 269), but this may be doubted. (Even that case permits factors such as fatigue, lack of sleep, strain and drunkenness to be taken into account by the court in deciding whether to exclude the confession in its discretion: p. 208, *post*). As the extracts quoted above indicate, prolonged questioning may also constitute oppression. The police conduct permitted will vary depending on the weakness, general health and degree of education of the suspect, and in this respect the oppression doctrine is like parts of the modern American law of confessions (p. 210, *post*).

R. v. Jeffries
(1946), 47 S.R.N.S.W. 284

STREET, J.: It is the mental condition of the accused, when answering, that is the determining factor in deciding upon the admissibiity of such evidence. Even without threats or promises on the part of police, if by his confinement or from other circumstances, for example, exhaustion or lack of comprehension, it appears to the presiding Judge that he has been subjected to such a degree of moral suasion on the part of the police in whose power he then was that his answers could not fairly be regarded as reliable, then the Judge should exclude the evidence. But the mere fact that in answer to questions he makes admissions that operate to his own prejudice does not make such answers inadmissible.

G. The purposes of the confession rule

Why are involuntary confessions inadmissible? A number of reasons have been advanced over the last two hundred years from the earliest appearance of the doctrine.

R. v. Warickshall
(1783), 1 Leach 263

NARES, J. and EYRE, B.: It is a mistaken notion that the evidence of confessions and facts which have been obtained from prisoners by promises or threats is to be rejected from a regard to public faith: no such rule ever prevailed. . . . Confessions are received in evidence or rejected as inadmissible under a consideration whether they are or are not intitled to credit. A free and voluntary confession is deserving of the highest credit, because it is presumed to flow from the strongest sense of guilt, and therefore it is admitted as proof of the crime to which it refers; but a confession forced from the mind by the flattery of hope or the torture of fear comes in so questionable a shape when it is to be considered as evidence of guilt that no credit ought to be given to it, and therefore it is rejected.

Wigmore: Treatise on the American System of Evidence in Trials at Common Law
3rd Edn. Paras. 822, 823, 851, 866, 867

The law cannot attempt to weigh testimony before even listening to it. But it can take note of certain objective circumstances as leading with high probability to falsities. The circumstances which thus call for the rejection of a confession are usually described as involving either a *promise* or a *threat*. Thus a promise of certain pardon, when attached to a confession, may conceivably make a confession, irrespective of its truth, seem more desirable than silence with its contingencies; or a threat of instant hanging by a mob, unless a confession is forthcoming, may conceivably make the contingencies of a confession more desirable than the certain consequences of silence. . . .

. . . A confession is not excluded because of any *breach of confidence* or of good faith which may thereby be involved. . . . Thus, so far as a promise, whether of secrecy, of favour, or of other action, or a misrepresentation of facts, has been the means of obtaining the confession, the exclusion that might ensue would in no way rest on the mere fact that a promise has been broken, a confidence violated, or a deception deliberately planned and carried out.

. . . A confession is not excluded because of any *illegality* in the method of obtaining it or in the speaker's situation at the time of making it. The general principle—that the illegality of the source of evidence is no bar to its reception—is well established. . . .

. . . [A] confession is not rejected because of any connection with the *privilege against self-incrimination*. . . . Thus, where a compulsory disclosure is offered, it may be admissible so far as the privilege against self-incrimination is concerned, and yet the question of its propriety as a confession may be raised. . . . The sum and substance of the difference is that the confession-rule aims to exclude self-criminating statements which are *false*, while the privilege-rule gives the option of excluding those which are *true*. . . .

. . . [E]very guilty person is almost always ready and desirous to confess, as soon as he is detected and arrested. This psychological truth, well known to all criminal trial judges, seems to be ignored by some Supreme Courts. The nervous pressure of guilt is enormous; the load of the deed done is heavy; the fear of detection fills the consciousness; and when detection comes the pressure is relieved; and the deep sense of relief makes confession a satisfaction. At that moment, he will tell all, and tell it truly. To forbid soliciting him, to seek to prevent this relief, is to fly in the face of human nature. It is natural and should be lawful, to take his confession at that moment—the best one. And this expedient, if sanctioned, saves the State a delay and expense in convicting him after he has reacted from his first sensations, has yielded to his friends' solicitations, and comes under the sway of the natural human instinct to struggle to save himself by the aid of all technicalities.

[Why do opinions differ sharply on the value of confessions?] We must separate (1) the confession as a proved fact, from (2) the process of proving an alleged confession.

(1) Now, assuming the making of a confession to be a completely proved fact—its authenticity beyond question and conceded—then it is certainly true that we have before us the highest sort of evidence. The confession of a crime is usually as much against a man's permanent interests as anything well can be. . . . [I]t carries a persuasion which nothing else does, because a fundamental instinct of human nature teaches each one of us its significance.

(2) But how do we get to believe in the fact of a confession having been made? Always and necessarily by somebody's testimony. And what is our experience of that sort of testimony on which we are asked to believe that a confession was made? A varying and sometimes discouraging experience. Paid informers, treacherous associates,

angry victims, and over-zealous officers of the law—these are the persons through whom an alleged confession is oftenest presented; and it is at this stage that our suspicions are aroused and our caution stimulated. . . . [S]uppose the accused denies absolutely the fact of confession; suppose the judge now to think to himself, "Here is a confession which, if authentic, would make this man's guilt clear beyond doubt. But do you expect us to take it as authentic, against his denial, on the word of this man alone, who has such and such strong motives for inventing it or for misinterpreting what was said? Must we not listen to him with the greatest doubt and suspicion?"

. . . [T]he only real danger and weakness in a confession—the danger of a false statement—is of a slender character, and the cases of that sort are of the rarest occurrence. . . .

. . . [T]he notion that confessions should be guarded against and discouraged is not a benefit to the innocent, but a detriment. A full statement of the accused person's explanations, made at the earliest moment, is often the best means for him of securing a speedy vindication. The circumstances of suspicion may often be disposed of by a simple explanation, so clear and convincing that immediate release follows as a matter of course; while the clues which the innocent accused may be able to furnish will be equally serviceable in securing that evidence against the real culprit which a delay may frequently render unavailable. . . .

The policy of the future, then, should be to receive all well-proved confessions in evidence, and to leave them to the jury, subject to all discrediting circumstances, to receive such weight as may seem proper.

Foster: High Treason
C. III, s. 8

Hasty confessions, made to persons having no authority to examine, are the weakest and most suspicious of all evidence. Proof may be too easily procured; words are often misreported—whether through ignorance, inattention, or malice, it mattereth not to the defendant, he is equally affected in either case; and they are extremely liable to misconstruction; and withal, this evidence is not in the ordinary course of things to be disproved by that sort of negative evidence by which the proof of plain facts may be and often is confronted.

Bram v. U.S.
(1897), 168 U.S. 532

WHITE, J.: A brief consideration of the reasons which gave rise to the adoption of the Fifth Amendment, of the wrongs which it was intended to prevent, and of the safeguards which it was its purpose unalterably to secure, will make it clear that the generic language of the amendment was but a crystallization of the doctrine as to confessions, well-settled when the amendment was adopted.

[Wigmore's comment is (para. 823, n. 5): "no assertions could be more unfounded."]

R. v. Johnston
(1864), Ir.C.L. 60

HAYES, J.: [A] confession will be rejected if it appear to have been extracted by the presumed pressure and obligation of an oath, or by pestering interrogatories, or if it have been made by the party to rid himself of importunity, or if, by subtle and ensnaring questions, as those which are framed so as to conceal their drift and object, he has been taken at a disadvantage and thus entrapped into a statement which, if left to himself, and in the full freedom of volition, he would not have made. . . . [I]t is manifest to everyone's experience that, from the moment a person feels himself in custody on a criminal charge, his mental condition undergoes a very remarkable change, and he naturally becomes much more accessible to every influence that addresses itself either to his hopes or fears.

H. R. Trevor-Roper: The European Witch Craze of the Sixteenth and Seventeenth Centuries
Penguin, 1969, pp. 44–5

... [T]he Dark Ages knew no witch mania because they lacked judicial torture ... the decline and disappearance of witch-beliefs in the eighteenth century is due to the discredit and gradual abolition of torture in Europe. . . .

. . . [W]itches' confessions became more detailed with the intensification of inquisitorial procedure; . . . the identity of such confessions is more often to be explained by the identity of procedure than by any identity of experience. . . . Accused witches often admitted to their confessors that they had wrongly accused both themselves and others. . . . Some judges refused to allow testimony because they knew that it had been obtained by torture and was therefore unreliable. . . .

Spano v. New York
(1959), 360 U.S. 315

WARREN, C.J.: The abhorrence of society to the use of involuntary confessions does not turn alone on their inherent untrustworthiness. It also turns on the deep-rooted feeling that the police must obey the law while enforcing the law; that in the end life and liberty can be as much endangered from illegal methods used to convict those thought to be criminals as from the actual criminals themselves.

McCormick: Handbook of the Law of Evidence
(1954). Paras. 109, 110

The possibility that the declarant's statement may be the product of an abnormal mind is an infirmity to which all testimony is susceptible. Is there a substantial *special* danger here in respect to confessions? Possibly there may be. No adequate scientific study of the question seems to have been made, but the literature on psychiatry at the lawyer's level indicates that persons suffering with melancholia have a recognizable tendency toward self-accusation, which conceivably might be so exaggerated as to lead to a false confession of crime. Terror and excitement over an accusation may be so shocking as to cause a state of abnormal suggestibility and a delusion of guilt. . . . [A] brutal and notorious crime often brings an aftermath of false confessions by half-wits. . . . [But] these cases are much more often encountered by the doctors than by the police; and that when they do come before the police, they are usually, though not always, recognizable as abnormal by experienced officers. On the whole they can hardly be said to present a substantial special danger of untrustworthiness peculiar to confessions.

. . . [T]he subtlest and most laborious form of indirect pressure is the cumulative suggestive force of mere protracted questioning alone. Practically always the interrogation is conducted by a battery of questioners operating in relays, and usually the questioning is continuous, or nearly so, for such time as to deprive the victim of normal sleep. . . . Prolonged and insistent questioning alone seems effective to shatter the resistance of at least the average casual suspect who is not a professional criminal. Obviously this form of pressure can usually only be carried out by denying the prisoner his right to communicate with friends and counsel.

Best: Principles of the Law of Evidence
11th Edn. P. 539

By artful questioning and working on their feelings, weak-minded individuals can be made to confess or impliedly admit almost anything; and to resist continued importunities to acknowledge even falsehood requires a mind of more than average firmness.

The common law of England . . . has . . . taken great care, perhaps too great care, to prevent suspected persons from being terrified, coaxed, cajoled, or entrapped into criminative statements, and it . . . prohibits judicial interrogation. . . .

. . . It is sometimes impossible to ascertain the motive which has led to a confession indisputably false. In November, 1580, a man was convicted and executed, on his own confession, for the murder, near Paris of a widow who was missing at the time but who two years afterwards returned to her home. And the celebrated case of *Joan Parry* and her two sons—who were executed in this country in the seventeenth century, for the murder of a man named Harrison who reappeared some years afterwards—affords another instance. . . .

. . . Weak and timorous persons, confounded at finding themselves in the power of the law, or alarmed at the testimony of false witnesses, or the circumstantial evidence against them, or distrustful of the honesty or capacity of their judges, hope by an avowal of guilt to obtain leniency at their hands.

Moreover, an innocent man, accused or suspected of a crime, may deem himself exposed to annoyance at the hands of some person, to whom his suffering as for that crime would be acceptable . . . [as] where the evidence necessary to establish the innocence of the confessionalist would be the means of disclosing transactions which it was the interest of many to conceal; or would bring before the world in the character of a criminal, some eminent individual, whose reward for a false acknowledgment of guilt would be great and whose vengeance for exposure might be terrible. Under circumstances like these, the accused is induced by threats or bribes to suppress the defence, and own himself the author of the crime imputed to him.

. . . [A] false confession of an offence may be made with the view of stifling inquiry into other matters; as for instance, some more serious offence of which the confessionalist is as yet unsuspected.

The most fantastic shape of this anomaly springs from the state of mental unsoundness which is known by the name of *taedium vitae*. Several instances are to be found where persons tired of life have falsely accused themselves of *capital* crimes, which were either purely fictitious, or were committed by others.

. . . [Vanity may produce a confession.] False statements of this kind are sometimes the offspring of a morbid love of notoriety at any price. The motive that induces the adventurous youth to burn the temple of Ephesus would surely have been strong enough to induce him to declare himself, however innocent, the author of the mischief had it occurred accidentally.

Instances may be found of false confessions made with a view to some specific collateral end. . . . Soldiers engaged on foreign service not unfrequently declare themselves guilty of having committed crimes at home, in order that . . . they may escape from military duty. . . . And whether from such morbid love of notoriety, or mere weak-mindedness or a love of mischief, it is almost invariably the case that murders of a specially horrible kind—as for instance, the Whitechapel murders of prostitutes in 1888 and 1889—are followed by a series of false confessions.

. . . [There are cases] where the person who makes the false confession is desirous of benefiting others; as, for instance, to save the life, fortune or reputation of, or to avert suffering from, a party whose interests are dearer to him than his own. . . .

The desire of *injuring* others has occasionally led to the like consequence. Persons reckless of their own fate have sought to work the ruin of their enemies by including false confessions of crimes and describing them as participators. We shall feel little surprise at this when we recollect how often persons have inflicted grievous wounds on themselves, and even in some instances, it is said, committed suicide, in order to bring down suspicion of intended or actual murder on detested individuals.

. . . [E]*xtrajudicial*, confessorial statements . . . are subject to additional infirmative hypotheses, which are sometimes overlooked in practice. These are *mendacity* in the report, *misinterpretation* of the language used, and *incompleteness* of the statement.

1. "*Mendacity*". . . . [O]f all sorts of evidence, that which we are now considering is

the most easy to fabricate, and however false the most difficult to confront and expose by any sort of counter-evidence. . . .

2. *"Misinterpretation"*. . . . [E]ntirely fallacious conclusions may be drawn from language uttered in jest, or by way of bravado. . . . [E]qually unfounded inferences are sometimes drawn from words . . . used with reference to an act not identical with the subject of accusation or suspicion; as where a man who has robbed or beaten another, learning that he has since died, utters an exclamation of regret for having ill-treated him. . . . [The greatest dangers arise from] the haste and eagerness of witnesses, and the love of the marvellous, so natural to the human mind, by which people are frequently prompted to mistake expressions, as well as to imagine or exaggerate facts, especially where the crime is either very atrocious or very peculiar.

3. The remaining cause of error in confessorial evidence . . . is "incompleteness"; i.e. where words, though not misunderstood in themselves, convey a false impression for want of some explanation which the speaker either neglected to give, or was prevented by interruption from giving, or which has been lost in consequence of the deafness or inattention of the hearers. "Ill hearing makes ill rehearsing," said our ancestors. Experience may have been forgotten or unheeded in consequence of witnesses not being aware of their importance, e.g. a man suspected of larceny acknowledges that he took the goods against the will of the owner, adding that he did so because he thought they were his own. Many a bystander, ignorant that this latter circumstance constitutes a legal defence, would remember only the first part of the statement.

. . . [I]t must never be forgotten that, in general, . . . confessions constitute proof of a very satisfactory . . . character. Reason and the universal voice of mankind alike attest this, and the legitimate use of the unhappy cases above recorded . . . is to put tribunals on their guard against attaching undue weight to this sort of evidence. The employing them as bugbears to terrify, or the converting them into excuses for indiscriminate scepticism or incredulity, is a perversion, if not a prostitution, of the human understanding.

Macaulay: History of England
(Everyman Edn.), Vol. I, Chap. 5, p. 437

Words may easily be misunderstood by an honest man. They may easily be misconstrued by a knave. What was spoken metaphorically may be apprehended literally. What was spoken ludicrously may be apprehended seriously. A particle, a tense, a mood, an emphasis, may make the whole difference between guilt and innocence.

Hans Gross: Criminal Psychology
(Trans. Kallen, 1911) Para. 8, p. 31 (quoted by Wigmore, *Principles of Judicial Proof* (Boston, 1913), No. 277)

The confession is a very extraordinary psychological problem. In many cases the reasons for confession are very obvious. The criminal sees that the evidence is so complete that he is soon to be convicted and seeks a mitigation of the sentence by confession, or he hopes through a more honest narration of the crime to throw a great degree of the guilt on another. In addition there is a thread of vanity in confession—as among young peasants who confess to a greater share in a burglary than they actually had (easily discoverable by the magniloquent manner of describing their actual crime). Then there are confessions made for the sake of care and winter lodgings: the confession arising from "firm conviction" (as among political criminals and others). There are even confessions arising from nobility, from the wish to save an intimate, and confessions intended to deceive, and such as occur especially in conspiracy and are made to gain time (either for the flight of the real criminal or for the destruction of compromising objects). Generally, in the latter case, guilt is admitted only until the plan for which it was made has succeeded; then the judge is surprised with a well-founded, regular, and successful establishment of an alibi. Not infrequently confession of small crimes is made to establish an alibi for a greater one. . . .

Although this list of explicable confession types is long, it is in no way exhaustive. It is only a small portion of all the confessions that we receive; of these the greater part remain more or less unexplained. . . . A number of cases may perhaps be explained through pressure of conscience, especially where there are involved hysterical or nervous persons who are plagued with vengeful images in which the ghost of their victim would appear, or in whose ear the unendurable clang of the stolen money never ceases, etc.

One justification for the confession rule suggested by Wigmore and by the judges in the influential early case of R. v. *Warickshall*, is that while voluntary confessions are very likely to be true because they proceed from the promptings of remorse and the strain of continuously lying, and because of the unlikelihood of an innocent man acting so strongly against his self-interest as to falsely confess himself guilty, involuntary confessions may well be false. In an ideal world this basis for excluding confessions would demand an investigation of the accused's mind: was his motive for confessing such as to make it untrue? But motives being hard to investigate, the law has developed the objective and sometimes extreme rules of inducement to exclude confessions. There are several possible sources of unreliability. One is the risk that the confession is fabricated, or misheard, or misreported. Another is that the innocent may confess out of a desire for notoriety, or from shock, or suggestion, or hallucination. Another is that the confessor may wish to protect another, or confess to a minor crime in order to avoid conviction for a major one, or obtain some other advantage from detention, e.g. protection or shelter. Thus the categories of voluntariness and truth are obviously not coincident; as the High Court of Australia remarked in Basto v. R. (1954), 91 C.L.R. 628, at p. 640: "A confessional statement may be voluntary and yet to act upon it might be quite unsafe; it may have no probative value. Or such a statement may be involuntary and yet carry with it the greatest assurance of its reliability or truth." However, the vast bulk of confessions held involuntary under the current rules are probably true, so that the reliability justification cannot support the width of the current law. Hence those who base the confession rule solely on reliability, like Wigmore, are strong critics of the current law.

But the reliability criterion supports the current law to a greater extent than is commonly realized (see Customs and Excise Commissioners v. Harz, [1967] 1 A.C. 760, at p. 820; [1967] 1 All E.R. 177, at p. 184, H.L., per Lord Reid).

It is difficult to estimate the effect of inducements on particular suspects; it is difficult to calculate an individual's strengths and weaknesses, experience of the law and knowledge of his rights. So a wide rule excluding all confessions with an objective risk of untrustworthiness is defensible. However, there are some cases that are insupportable even on this basis.

There is much authority for the view that reliability is not the sole criterion. Thus in R. v. *Baldry* (1852), 2 Den. 430, at p. 442, Pollock, C.B. said: "There is no presumption of law that it is false or that the law considers such statement cannot be relied upon" (followed in Ibrahim v. R., [1914] A.C. 599; [1914–15] All E.R. Rep. 874, P.C. and Sparks v. R., [1964] A.C. 964, [1964] 1 All E.R. 727, P.C.). In R. v. *Thompson*, [1893] 2 Q.B. 12; [1891–4] All E.R. Rep. 376,

Cave, J. said that a finding that statements made to the accused were calculated to elicit the truth was quite immaterial.

A second reason for the confession rule is that it is "dangerous to leave such evidence to the jury" (*R.* v. *Baldry* (1852), 2 Den. 430, at p. 442, *per* Pollock, C.B.). A jury will too easily think a confession is decisive of guilt without paying attention to the other evidence. Confession evidence, which is so likely to result in a conviction if it is admitted, should be very carefully scrutinized.

Thirdly, as Lord Reid suggests in *Customs and Excise Commissioners* v. *Harz*, [1967] 1 A.C. 760, at p. 820; [1967] 1 All E.R. 177, at p. 184, H.L., there is a popular feeling that when a man is convicted solely on the basis of his own confession, the duty of the prosecution to prove him guilty has not been discharged. The prosecution should prove its own case, before a judge and jury in open court; it should not rely on men condemning themselves secretly under pressure in police stations, for there is a risk of agitated and frightened men lying even though innocent. This justification for the rule is like part of the rationale for the privilege against self-incrimination: the state should be made to rely on its powers of independent detection, not on confessions (see *McDermott* v. *R.* (1948), 76 C.L.R. 501, at p. 513, *per* Dixon, J.). This is so even though Wigmore may be correct in asserting that there is no historical connexion between the two rules.

Fourthly, the exclusive of involuntary confessions tends to discourage undesirable police practices. The improprieties in question are of two kinds. One is a true prediction of an unlawful consequence ("Tell us the truth or we'll hit you"). The other is an untrue statement of law coupled with threats of criminal prosecution which, as the police know, will fail, e.g. the facts of *Harz*'s case, involving threats to prosecute for failing to give information the police were not entitled to demand. This method of controlling impropriety is said to be indirect and clumsy—police misconduct should be controlled by disciplining the police. But at the moment the police discipline themselves. It is also said that the exclusion of confessions obtained by mild pressure, a very necessary form of evidence, may anger and frustrate the police so much that they become determined to use serious illegalities to bring the guilty to justice or at any rate destruction. Further, a confession may be used to obtain leads to other evidence even if not itself used in court. The issues here are similar to those respecting the exclusion of illegally obtained evidence. There is no doubt that the confession rule does tend to exclude confessions which result from police misconduct though not in a very precise way.

H. Reform

The Criminal Law Revision Committee wish the law to be based solely on the reliability criterion. However, they recommend a change which would preserve the bulk of the current law while removing only its more extreme aberrations. A confession, under cl. 2 (2), would be excluded if there were "oppressive treatment of the accused" or a "threat or inducement of a sort likely, in the circumstances existing at the time, to render unreliable any confession which might be made by the accused in consequence thereof". The question under this test is not whether the *actual* confession is unreliable

CME—G

but whether the circumstances were *likely* to produce an unreliable confession. This makes the test objective and not very radical; indeed, the effect will be directed partly to controlling police misconduct, not merely to guaranteeing reliability. This is the effect of this formulation of the confession rule as it operates in Victorian and New Zealand statutes.

The Committee also recommend the abolition of the person in authority rule on the ground that effective inducements are just as likely to proceed from persons not in authority.

One change which would seem desirable as part of a more general scheme of pre-trial discovery would be the introduction of legislation providing for pre-trial discovery by the prosecution of any confessions they propose to introduce. The accused would thus be helped to prepare a defence.

II   THE JUDGES' RULES

The subject matter of both this and the following section is closely related, for as Lord Devlin has said, the Judges' Rules "are an expression of the judge's discretionary power to exclude evidence unfairly or oppressively obtained" (*The Criminal Prosecution in England* (London, 1960), p. 38). However, it is convenient to consider them separately.

During the nineteenth century the judges began developing ideas independently of the confession rule on how police interrogation should be conducted. As has been noted earlier, there was substantial judicial suspicion of the police. Some judges thought the police should ask no questions of a man in custody, because the accused was incompetent and could not explain away admissions. In *R. v. Male* (1893), 17 Cox C.C. 689, at p. 690, Cave, J. said: "The law does not allow the judge or the jury to put questions in open court to prisoners; and it would be monstrous if the law permitted a police officer to go, without anyone being present to see how the matter was conducted, and put a prisoner through an examination, and then produce the effects of that examination against him." More succinctly, "a policeman should keep his mouth shut and his ears open". Others thought that questioning was permissible, provided the suspect was cautioned—told he was not obliged to say anything. The purpose of the caution was to remove any thought in the accused's mind that he *must* talk. Some judges thought it to be necessary in all cases, others thought its absence was merely *prima facie* evidence of involuntariness. To clear up doubts the police requested assistance: thus Hawkins, J. in 1882 wrote a foreword to the Police Code containing many points similar to the later Judges' Rules. But doubts persisted. In 1906, at the Birmingham Assizes, one policeman was judicially criticized for using the caution, and another for not using it. In 1912 a code called the Judges' Rules was issued; over the years it has been revised and the current Rules were issued in 1964. Their spirit is that police questioning must be permitted but controlled.

R. v. Cook
(1918), 34 T.L.R. 515, C.C.A.

DARLING, J.: It would be a lamentable thing if the police were not allowed to make enquiries, and if statements made by prisoners were excluded because of a shadowy notion that if the prisoners were left to themselves they would not have made them.

Practice Note (Judges' Rules)
[1964] 1 All E.R. 327; [1964] 1 W.L.R. 152, C.C.A.

LORD PARKER, C.J. The origin of the Judges' Rules is probably to be found in a letter dated October 26, 1906, which the then Lord Chief Justice, Lord Alverstone, wrote to the Chief Constable of Birmingham in answer to a request for advice in consequence of the fact that on the same circuit one judge had censured a member of his force for having cautioned a prisoner, whilst another judge had censured a constable for having omitted to do so. The first four of the present rules were formulated and approved by the judges of the King's Bench Division in 1912; the remaining five in 1918. They have been much criticized, *inter alia,* for alleged lack of clarity and of efficacy for the protection of persons who are questioned by police officers; on the other hand it has been maintained that their application unduly hampers the detection and punishment of crime. A committee of judges has devoted considerable time and attention to producing, after consideration of representative views, a new set of rules which has been approved by a meeting of all the Queen's Bench Judges.

The judges control the conduct of trials and the admission of evidence against persons on trial before them: they do not control or in any way initiate or supervise police activities or conduct. As stated in paragraph (*c*) of the introduction to the new rules, it is the law that answers and statements made are only admissible in evidence if they have been voluntary in the sense that they have not been obtained by fear of prejudice or hope of advantage, exercised or held out by a person in authority, or by oppression. The new rules do not purport, any more than the old rules, to envisage or deal with the many varieties of conduct which might render answers and statements involuntary and therefore inadmissible. The rules merely deal with particular aspects of the matter. Other matters such as affording reasonably comfortable conditions, adequate breaks for rest and refreshment, special procedures in the case of persons unfamiliar with the English language or of immature age or feeble understanding, are proper subjects for administrative directions to the police.

These rules do not affect the principles:

(*a*) That citizens have a duty to help a police officer to discover and apprehend offenders;

(*b*) That police officers, otherwise than by arrest, cannot compel any person against his will to come to or remain in any police station;

(*c*) That every person at any stage of an investigation should be able to communicate and to consult privately with a solicitor. This is so even if he is in custody provided that in such a case no unreasonable delay or hindrance is caused to the processes of investigation or the administration of justice by his doing so;

(*d*) That when a police officer who is making inquiries of any person about an offence has enough evidence to prefer a charge against that person for the offence, he should without delay cause that person to be charged or informed that he may be prosecuted for the offence;

(*e*) That it is a fundamental condition of the admissibility in evidence against any person, equally of any oral answer given by that person to a question put by a police officer and of any statement made by that person, that it shall have been voluntary, in the sense that it has not been obtained from him by fear of prejudice or hope of advantage, exercised or held out by a person in authority, or by oppression.

The principle set out in paragraph (*e*) above is overriding and applicable in all cases. Within that principle the following rules are put forward as a guide to police officers conducting investigations. Non-conformity with these rules may render answers and statements liable to be excluded from evidence in subsequent criminal proceedings.

RULES

I. When a police officer is trying to discover whether, or by whom, an offence has been committed he is entitled to question any person, whether suspected or not, from whom he thinks that useful information may be obtained. This is so whether or not the person in question has been taken into custody so long as he has not been charged with the offence or informed that he may be prosecuted for it.

II. As soon as a police officer has evidence which would afford reasonable grounds for suspecting that a person has committed an offence, he shall caution that person or cause him to be cautioned before putting to him any questions, or further questions, relating to that offence.

The caution shall be in the following terms:

"You are not obliged to say anything unless you wish to do so but what you say may be put into writing and given in evidence."

When after being cautioned a person is being questioned, or elects to make a statement, a record shall be kept of the time and place at which any such questioning or statement began and ended and of the persons present.

III.—(*a*) Where a person is charged with or informed that he may be prosecuted for an offence he shall be cautioned in the following terms:

"Do you wish to say anything? You are not obliged to say anything unless you wish to do so but whatever you say will be taken down in writing and may be given in evidence."

(*b*) It is only in exceptional cases that questions relating to the offence should be put to the accused person after he has been charged or informed that he may be prosecuted. Such questions may be put where they are necessary for the purpose of preventing or minimizing harm or loss to some other person or to the public or for clearing up an ambiguity in a previous answer or statement.

Before any such questions are put the accused should be cautioned in these terms:

"I wish to put some questions to you about the offence with which you have been charged (*or* about the offence for which you may be prosecuted). You are not obliged to answer any of these questions, but if you do the questions and answers will be taken down in writing and may be given in evidence."

Any questions put and answers given relating to the offence must be contemporaneously recorded in full and the record signed by that person or if he refuses by the interrogating officer.

(*c*) When such a person is being questioned, or elects to make a statement, a record shall be kept of the time and place at which any questioning or statement began and ended and of the persons present.

IV. All written statements made after caution shall be taken in the following manner:

(*a*) If a person says that he wants to make a statement he shall be told that it is intended to make a written record of what he says. He shall always be asked whether he wishes to write down himself what he wants to say; if he says that he cannot write or that he would like someone to write it for him, a police officer may offer to write the statement for him. If he accepts the offer the police officer shall, before starting, ask the person making the statement to sign, or make his mark to, the following:

"I, ..., wish to make a statement. I want someone to write down what I say. I have been told that I need not say anything unless I wish to do so and that whatever I say may be given in evidence."

(*b*) Any person writing his own statement shall be allowed to do so without any prompting as distinct from indicating to him what matters are material.

c) The person making the statement, if he is going to write it himself, shall be asked to write out and sign before writing what he wants to say, the following:

> "I make this statement of my own free will. I have been told that I need not say anything unless I wish to do so and that whatever I say may be given in evidence."

(*d*) Whenever a police officer writes the statement, he shall take down the exact words spoken by the person making the statement, without putting any questions other than such as may be needed to make the statement coherent, intelligible and relevant to the material matters: he shall not prompt him.

(*e*) When the writing of a statement by a police officer is finished the person making it shall be asked to read it and to make any corrections, alterations or additions he wishes. When he has finished reading it he shall be asked to write and sign or make his mark on the following certificate at the end of the statement:

> "I have read the above statement and I have been told that I can correct, alter or add anything I wish. This statement is true. I have made it of my own free will."

(*f*) If the person who has made a statement refuses to read it or to write the above mentioned certificate at the end of it or to sign it, the senior police officer present shall record on the statement itself and in the presence of the person making it, what has happened. If the person making the statement cannot read, or refuses to read it, the officer who has taken it down shall read it over to him and ask him whether he would like to correct, alter or add anything and to put his signature or make his mark at the end. The police officer shall then certify on the statement itself what he has done.

V. If at any time after a person has been charged with, or has been informed that he may be prosecuted for an offence a police officer wishes to bring to the notice of that person any written statement made by another person who in respect of the same offence has also been charged or informed that he may be prosecuted, he shall hand to that person a true copy of such written statement, but nothing shall be said or done to invite any reply or comment. If that person says that he would like to make a statement in reply, or starts to say something, he shall at once be cautioned or further cautioned as prescribed by rule III (*a*).

VI. Persons other than police officers charged with the duty of investigating offences or charging offenders shall, so far as may be practicable, comply with these rules.

Ibrahim v. R.
[1914] A.C. 599; [1914–15] All E.R. Rep. 874, P.C.

LORD SUMNER: The appellant's objection was rested on the two bare facts that the statement was preceded by and made in answer to a question, and that the question was put by a person in authority and the answer given by a man in his custody. This ground, in so far as it is a ground at all, is a more modern one. With the growth of a police force of the modern type, the point has frequently arisen, whether, if a policeman questions a prisoner in his custody at all, the prisoner's answers are evidence against him, apart altogether from fear of prejudice or hope of advantage inspired by a person in authority.

It is to be observed that logically these objections all go to the weight and not to the admissibility of the evidence. What a person having knowledge about the matter in issue says of it is itself relevant to the issue as evidence against him. That he made the statement under circumstances of hope, fear, interest or otherwise strictly goes only to its weight. In an action of tort evidence of this kind could not be excluded when tendered against a tortfeasor, though a jury might well be told as prudent men to think little of it.

R. v. Voisin
[1918] 1 K.B. 531; [1918–19] All E.R. Rep. 491, C.C.A.

A. T. LAWRENCE, J.: In 1912 the judges, at the request of the Home Secretary, drew up some rules as guides for police officers. These rules have not the force of law; they are administrative directions the observance of which the police authorities should enforce upon their subordinates as tending to the fair administration of justice. It is important that they should do so, for statements obtained from prisoners, contrary to the spirit of these rules, may be rejected as evidence by the judge presiding at the trial.

R. v. Ovenell
[1969] 1 Q.B. 17; [1968] 1 All E.R. 933, C.A.

Three things require to be said about the Judges' Rules. First, they are not mandatory upon or even directed to the court at all. They are rules of conduct directed to the police and no more—indeed, to no one but the police, although it is understandable that investigating officers of other services might be thought to be comparably placed with police officers. Secondly, where a statement has been made without caution in circumstances where compliance with the rules would have necessitated a caution, it is a matter for the trial judge to exercise his own discretion as to whether the statement should be admitted or not. No doubt in exercising that discretion, so long as the statement is not inadmissible, he will apply his mind, *inter alia*, to such factors and principles as the balance between probative value and potential prejudice.

McDermott v. R.
(1948), 76 C.L.R. 501

The accused made a confession while under arrest and after being cautioned but before being charged. He had been questioned for one hour, and the trial judge found that there had been no insistence or pressure by the police. An appeal to the High Court of Australia failed.

DIXON, J.: The application for special leave is based upon the view that the learned judge possessed a discretion to exclude the statements and that he erroneously exercised this discretion in deciding to admit them. The view that a judge presiding at a criminal trial possesses a discretion to exclude evidence of confessional statements is of comparatively recent growth. To some extent the course of its development is traced by Lord Sumner in *Ibrahim's Case*, [1914] A.C. 599, at pp. 611–14; [1914–15] All E.R. Rep. 874, P.C. In part perhaps it may be a consequence of a failure to perceive how far the settled rule of the common law goes in excluding statements that are not the outcome of an accused person's free choice to speak. In part the development may be due to the fact that the judges in 1912 framed or approved of rules for the guidance of the police in their inquiries . . . and not unnaturally have sought to insist on their observance. In part too it may be due to the existence of the jurisdiction of the Court of Criminal Appeal to quash a conviction if the court is of opinion that on any ground whatsoever there was a miscarriage of justice. But whatever may be the cause, there has arisen almost in our own time a practice in England of excluding confessional statements made to officers of police if it is considered upon a review of all the circumstances that they have been obtained in an improper manner. The abuse of the power of arrest by using the detention of an accused person as an occasion for securing from him evidence by admission is treated as an impropriety justifying the exclusion of the evidence. So is insistence upon questions or an attempt to break down or qualify the effect of an accused person's statement so far as it may be exculpatory. The practice of excluding statements so obtained is supported by the Court of Criminal Appeal in England, which will quash convictions where evidence has been received which in the opinion of that Court has been obtained improperly, that is, in some such manner.

It is acknowledged that the rules drawn up by the judges at the request of the Home Secretary as guides for police officers have no binding force upon the courts. . . . Nevertheless the tendency among English judges appears to be strong to treat them as standards of propriety for the purpose of deciding whether confessional statements should be received.

It is apparent that a rule of practice has arisen, deriving almost certainly from the strong feeling for the wisdom and justice of the traditional English principle expressed in the precept *nemo tenetur se ipsum accusare*. It may be regarded as an extension of the common law rule excluding voluntary statements. In referring the decision of the question whether a confessional statement should be rejected to the discretion of the judge, all that seems to be intended is that he should form a judgment upon the propriety of the means by which the statement was obtained by reviewing all the circumstances and considering the fairness of the use made by the police of their position in relation to the accused. The growth of rules of practice and their hardening so that they look like rules of law is a process that is not unfamiliar. . . .

. . . Here as well as in England the law may now be taken to be, apart from the effect of such special statutory provisions as s. 141 of the *Evidence Act* 1928 (Vict.), that a judge at the trial should exclude confessional statements if in all the circumstances he thinks that they have been improperly procured by officers of police, even although he does not consider that the strict rules of law, common law and statutory, require the rejection of the evidence. The Court of Criminal Appeal may review his decision and if it considers that a miscarriage has occurred it will allow an appeal from the conviction.

But the facts of the present case do not bring it within any rule established in Australia which requires the rejection of the confessional statements complained of. The fact that the police intended to arrest the prisoner, that they virtually held him in custody and delayed for an hour making the charge, and that they asked him questions are not in themselves enough to require that the statements the prisoner made to them should be excluded. The character of the questions, the absence of any insistence or pressure in putting them, the fact that no questions were put directed to breaking down or destroying the prisoner's answers or statements and the fact that there was no attempt to entrap, mislead or persuade him into answering the questions, still less into answering them in any particular way, these are all matters which negative such a degree of impropriety as to require the exclusion of the testimony as to the prisoner's admissions.

[LATHAM, C.J. and WILLIAMS, J. agreed.]

R. *v.* Lee
(1950), 82 C.L.R. 133

After three hours' questioning one accused confessed and on being confronted with the confession the other two did so as well. Their appeals to the High Court of Australia against admitting the evidence failed.

LATHAM, C.J., McTIERNAN, WEBB, FULLAGAR and KITTO, JJ.: There seems to be really one rule, the rule that a statement must be voluntary in order to be admissible. Any one of a variety of elements, including a threat or promise by a person in authority, will suffice to deprive it of a voluntary character. It is implicit in the statement of the rule, and it is now well settled, that the Crown has the burden of satisfying the trial judge in every case as to the voluntary character of a statement before it becomes admissible. . . .

No question of discretion can arise unless the statement in question is a voluntary statement in the common law sense. If it is non-voluntary it is . . . legally inadmissible. If it is voluntary, circumstances may be proved which call for an exercise of discretion. The only circumstance which has been suggested as calling for an exercise of the discretion is the use of "improper" or "unfair" methods by police officers in interrogating suspected persons or persons in custody (*McDermott* v. R. (1948), 76 C.L.R. 501, at pp. 507-7 and 513). What is impropriety in police methods and what would be unfairness in admitting in evidence against an accused person a statement obtained by improper methods must depend upon the circumstances of each particular case, and no attempt should be made to define and thereby to limit the extent or the application of these conceptions. . . .

. . . The placing of an onus on the Crown in connexion with the exercise of a discretion to reject evidence of the kind in question represents in our opinion a new departure, and we do not think that there is any justification for it. The discretion rule represents an exception to a rule of law, and we think that it is for the accused to bring himself within the exception. We have called attention to the great breadth of the common law rule that a statement is not admissible unless it is proved to be voluntary. If it is proved to be voluntary then it is *prima facie* admissible. It is admissible as a matter of law unless reason is shown for rejecting it in the exercise of discretion.

. . . Surely, if the judge thought that the "impropriety" was calculated to cause an untrue admission to be made, that would be a very strong reason for exercising his discretion against admitting the statement in question. If, on the other hand, he thought that it was not likely to result in an untrue admission being made, that would be a good reason, though not a conclusive reason, for allowing the evidence to be given. . . .

With regard to the Chief Commissioner's Standing Orders, which correspond in Victoria to the Judges' Rules in England, they are not rules of law, and the mere fact that one or more of them have been broken does not of itself mean that the accused has been so treated that it would be unfair to admit his statement. Nor does proof of a breach throw any burden on the Crown of showing some affirmative reason why the statement in question should be admitted. As has already been pointed out, the protection afforded by the rule that a statement must be voluntary goes so far that it is only reasonable to require that some substantial reason should be shown to justify a discretionary rejection of a voluntary admission. The rules may be regarded in a general way as prescribing a standard of propriety, and it is in this sense that what may be called the spirit of the rules should be regarded. But it cannot be denied that they do not in every respect afford a very satisfactory standard. Their language is in some cases imperative and in others merely advisory: sometimes the word "must" is used: sometimes the word "should", and the tendency to take them as a standard can easily develop into a tendency to apply rejection of evidence as in some sort of sanction for a failure by a police officer to obey the rules of his own organization, a matter which is of course entirely for the executive. It is indeed, we think, a mistake to approach the matter by asking as separate questions, first, whether the police officer concerned has acted improperly, and if he has, then whether it would be unfair to reject the accused's statement. It is better to ask whether, having regard to the conduct of the police and all the circumstances of the case, it would be unfair to use his own statement against the accused. We know of no better exposition of the whole matter than that which is to be found in the two passages from the judgment of Street, J.—in R. v. *Jeffries* (1947), 47 S.R. N.S.W. 284, at p. 312, His Honour said:

"It is a question of degree in each case, and it is for the presiding Judge to determine, in the light of all the circumstances, whether the statements or admissions of the accused have been extracted from him under conditions which render it unjust to allow his own words to be given in evidence against him."

His Honour then proceeded to refer to the account of the trial of Jones and Hulton published in the *Old Bailey Trial Series*. "It was conceded," he said, that in that case "the examination demonstrably transgressed the limits permitted under the Judges' Rules". It appeared, however, that the accused was a condition properly to answer to the "gruelling questioning" which had been administered to him, and the learned trial judge admitted the evidence. An appeal was dismissed by the Court of Criminal Appeal. His Honour then concludes:

> The obligation resting upon police officers is to put all questions fairly and to refrain from anything in the nature of a threat, or any attempt to extort an admission. But it is in the interests of the community that all crimes should be fully investigated with the object of bringing malefactors to justice, and such investigations must not be unduly hampered. Their object is to clear the innocent as well as establish the guilt of the offender. They must be aimed at the ascertainment of the truth, and must not be carried out with the idea of manufacturing evidence or extorting some admission and thereby securing a conviction. Upon the particular circumstances of each case depends the answer to the question as to the admissibility of such evidence."

... But in any case an invitation to explain established facts can hardly be called cross-examination in any relevant sense. It is cross-examination in the sense of breaking down the will and extorting admissions by persons who are being questioned by the police that is to be reprehended. Rule 8 was not applicable at any material time.

... It is, of course, of the most vital importance that detectives should be scrupulously careful and fair. The uneducated—perhaps semi-illiterate—man who has a "record" and is suspected of some offence may be practically helpless in the hands of an over-zealous police officer. The latter may be honest and sincere, but his position of superiority is so great and so over-powering that a "statement" may be "taken" which seems very damning but which is really very unreliable. The case against an accused person in such a case sometimes depends entirely on the "statement" made to the police. In such a case it may well be that his statement, if admitted, would prejudice him very unfairly. Such persons stand often in grave need of that protection which only an extremely vigilant court can give them. They provide the real justification for the Judges' Rules in England and the Chief Commissioner's Standing Orders in Victoria, and they provide (if we are to assume that the requirement of voluntariness is not enough to ensure justice) a justification for the existence of an ultimate discretion as to the admission of confessional evidence. The duty of police officers to be scrupulously careful and fair is not, of course, confined to such cases. But, where intelligent persons are being questioned with regard to a murder, the position cannot properly be approached from quite the same point of view. A minuteness of scrutiny, which in the one case may be entirely appropriate, may in the other be entirely misplaced and tend only to a perversion of justice. Each case must, of course, depend upon its own circumstances considered in their entirety. No better guidance is, we think, to be found than in the passages from the judgment of Street, J. in R. v. *Jeffries* which we have quoted above.

Lord Devlin: The Criminal Prosecution in England
(O.U.P., London, 1960). P. 30

The form of caution expresses two things. First, there is the reminder that the accused is not obliged to talk: secondly, there is the warning that, if he does talk, what he says will be taken down in writing and given in evidence. From the lawyer's point of view both are statements of the obvious. Just as an accused or suspect is never obliged to talk, so the police are always at liberty to take down what an accused or suspect says and give it in evidence. The real significance of the caution is that it is, so to speak, a declaration of war. By it the police announce that they are no longer representing themselves to the man they are questioning as the neutral inquirer whom the good citizen ought to assist; they are the prosecution and are without right, legal or moral, to further help from the accused; no man, innocent or guilty, need thereafter reproach himself for keeping silent, for that is what they have just told him he may do. The caution, the charge, the arrest—any of these three things show that hostilities have begun and that the suspect has formally become the accused.

This, then, is how the dividing line is drawn and how the point is defined when the Judges' Rules begin to operate. But before I describe how they operate there remains one preliminary to be dealt with, and that is the ordinary rule about the admissibility of confessions. The common law has always accepted the principle that any confession made by an accused must be made voluntarily—that is, it must not be induced by any promise of favour or by any menace. This was laid down by the judges many years ago and might itself, I suppose, be regarded as an exercise of judicial control over the inquiry into crime. But it is not what I have had in mind in talking of judicial control. It can be justified simply as a rule of evidence; an induced confession is not admissible because if it is made under threat or under promise of favour, there is no sufficient guarantee that it will contain the truth, and there is reason to suppose it may not. No doubt there is also an element of public policy in the rule. The use of violence or the threat of it are not in any civilized country recognized as legitimate aids to interrogation; the holding out of hope is equally poisonous, for it is easy for an innocent man awaiting trial to be reduced to despair, and a despairing man may confess to anything. . . .

. . . The Rules apply expressly only to prisoners and persons in custody and were no doubt intended for the protection of such persons who are particularly at a disadvantage. But if a prisoner were to be released on bail and a police officer were then to go and interview him at his home and obtain from him by means of cross-examination a statement about a crime, it is inconceivable (and almost inconceivable that the attempt should be made) that such a statement should be admitted in evidence. Yet, if excluded, it would have to be rejected as an exercise of ordinary judicial power and not by virtue of any specific rule. The essence of the thing is that a judge must be satisfied that some unfair or oppressive use has been made of police power. If he is so satisfied, he will reject the evidence notwithstanding that there is no rule which specifically prohibits it: if he is not so satisfied, he will admit the evidence even though there may have been some technical breach of one of the Rules. It must never be forgotten that the Judges' Rules were made for the guidance of the police and not for the circumscription of the judicial power.

Lawyer-like tendencies flourish to an even greater extent among the police than they do at the Bar or on the Bench. The police have sometimes seemed to treat the Judges' Rules as if they were a drill manual and to be unwilling to admit to the slightest deviation from the text. Rather than become engaged in a discussion about whether a question was or was not necessary to remove an ambiguity, some police witnesses seem to have preferred stoutly to deny that they asked any questions at all and even to maintain that they hardly opened their mouths. Consequently, statements have sometimes been put in evidence which have been said to be the prisoner's own unaided work as taken down by the police officer and in which the prisoner has recounted in the stately language of the police station (where, for example, people never eat but partake of refreshment and never quarrel but indulge in altercations) the tale of his misdeeds. The fact that it took two hours or so to fill a page of foolscap could presumably only be explained on the basis that the prisoner was carefully picking his words. The rule that I have referred to as requiring that a record should be kept of the time at which the taking of the statement started and finished was contained in the circular of 1947 and was doubtless intended to deal with this. So also, I daresay, was the rule that the statement should be written down as nearly as possible in the actual words used and should not be translated into "official" vocabulary, which as the circular says "may create a misleading impression as to the genuineness of the statement".

The Rules undoubtedly require the observance of a very high standard and it may be of a higher standard than the average policeman was in the first instance naturally inclined to adopt. It is difficult to say to what extent the spirit of the Rules is infringed because, as I have said, it is the general habit of the police never to admit to the slightest departure from correctness. This is a habit which must be noted in any study of police methods of inquiry. There are, I think, three factors contributing to it. The first is that the police are necessarily a tightly disciplined body; and where there is strict discipline, a little breach is often considered as grave a matter as a big breach. The second is that policemen cannot afford to make too many mistakes. They have to be sure of themselves and of what they have seen and done. If they are not, they are of no use to the prosecution, for the prosecution have to present a case that makes the jury feel sure of the prisoner's guilt, and they will not do that if their main witnesses do not feel sure about their own evidence. As a corollary to this, it is a habit—and this is the third factor—of counsel for the defence to make the most of minor uncertainties or discrepancies and to deal with a police officer in cross-examination as if any venial sin to which he might admit justified his professional damnation. The result of this is that police witnesses allow themselves sometimes to be almost bullied into a complete denial.

Let me illustrate the sort of thing I am talking about, in a way that will also give some information about the practice of the police in making notes of what a suspect or accused says before the stage is reached when he makes a formal statement. When the police first interview a man whom they subsequently accuse, a great deal that is important may be said before the time has come to charge him. The evidence of what the man then says depends upon the police officers' memory supplemented by notes that they made at the time. Unless it is in the nature of a formal interview, the police do not attempt to make notes as the accused is actually speaking; if they have visited the accused unexpectedly and are looking for evidence of his complicity, they will have much else to do besides noting down what he says; moreover, they may have to be prepared to make an arrest which might be resisted. Again, the accused man may, in spite of the caution, talk on his way to the police station in circumstances where what he says cannot be written down at the very moment of speech. It is therefore the custom of police officers to write down anything which the accused says and which they believe to be of importance at the police station as soon as they are at liberty to do so— generally within at most an hour of the occurrence. Almost invariably there are two or more police officers engaged in such an operation. When giving evidence at the trial, the police officer is entitled to use his notebook; and whether he does so or not, the defence is entitled to call for it in order to compare his oral evidence with the entries which he may have made. The question which always seems to worry such a pair of police officers unduly is whether their notes agree. If they are not precisely the same, counsel for the defence will seize upon small differences and suggest that one or other of the officers must be at fault. If on the other hand they resemble each other closely, counsel for the defence will stress every similarity so as to suggest to the jury that the police officers must have put their heads together in order to produce an agreed version. The police always seem to think it necessary to impale themselves on one horn or the other of this artificial dilemma; the two officers are often, if their evidence is to be believed, led by heavenly inspiration to arrive at just the same words, sentences, and phrases used by the accused as deserving of perpetuation. In 1953 Mr. Justice Byrne, a judge of great experience in criminal matters who had for many years been one of the Treasury Counsel at the Old Bailey, made this comment (R. v. *Bass* (1953), 37 Cr. App. Rep. 51, at p. 59):

> "This Court has observed that police officers nearly always deny that they have collaborated in the making of notes and we cannot help wondering why they are the only class of society who do not collaborate in such a matter. It seems to us that nothing could be more natural or proper when two persons have been present at an interview with a third person than that they should afterwards make sure that they have a correct version of what was said. Collaboration would appear to be a better explanation of almost identical notes than the possession of a superhuman memory."

Dicta like this help the police to take a more realistic view of the effect of the evidence which they give. They are learning how to live in the world of fantasy that is often created by a defence counsel at a loss for anything better to do on behalf of his client. Recently, an enterprising detective superintendent decided that, since police officers were now judicially permitted to collaborate in note-taking, there was no particular merit in their each copying down the joint version in their notebooks; accordingly after collaboration the joint version was put down in only one notebook, which each officer used when in the box. This happened in a case in 1957 and the departure from precedent shocked defence counsel; the judge, in summing up, told the jury that he could see nothing wrong in it R. v. *Adams,* [1957] Crim. L.R. 773.

Police officers now no longer maintain the same stubborn refusal to admit that during the taking of a statement the talking was not all on one side. Questions that are intended to elicit the facts are always permissible; and it is obvious that in the case of an uneducated or loquacious man a great deal of editing is sometimes necessary before the statement can be made intelligible at all. Whether the questioning goes beyond the permissible limits, and whether, if it does, the extent to which it does is sufficiently grave to justify the exclusion of the evidence, are matters about which judges and juries wish to judge for themselves and about which a defending counsel naturally wants the true facts in order that he may make his submission. The Bench and the Bar do not like it if this legitimate avenue of inquiry is closed by a blanket, and sometimes incredible, refusal to admit that any question was ever asked at all. Often in the past, when the prisoner has gone into the witness box and the jury has had an opportunity of contrasting the voluble incoherences which every question—even the kindest from his own counsel—touched off, with the lucid and well-punctuated flow of statement taken at the police station, they must have known that the police account of the way in which the interview was carried on was nonsense. They were then left bewildered, unwilling to accept the police evidence at its face value but also quite unwilling to believe that the whole thing was a concoction; it is out of bewilderment of this sort that errors of justice—mistaken acquittals as well as mistaken convictions—often arise. I believe that in the past a professional criticism of police evidence—that is, criticism by the legal practitioner—has concerned itself much more with police pretensions to infallibility and perfection than it has with the very occasional cases of deliberate malpractice. A jury has frequently to be asked by the defence to accept explanations of a prisoner's conduct which are so ridiculous that the mere asking must seem to them to involve an estimate of their intelligence insultingly low; but there are times when police evidence has sounded just as silly.

Police evidence of this sort may be the policeman's equivalent of the lawyer's conclusive presumption. The drill manual says that the thing is to be done in such-and-such a way; therefore it must be conclusively presumed to have been done in that way and no one is entitled to go behind the presumption. A number of what the police officer regards as ritualistic questions will be asked by counsel for the defence which call only for the appropriate ritualistic responses. It is a form of equivocation rather than perjury: it is as if the police officer by his denial were saying: "You know as well as I do that you have no business to be asking me questions of this sort; you know that I cannot possibly admit to even the slightest deviation from the prescription of the drill manual." The real danger of this attitude is that it harms the prosecution so much more than it does the defence. It produces the wrong acquittal much more often than the wrong conviction, since if the confidence of the jury in the reliability of police evidence is shaken, they are likely to acquit. This seems to me to be natural. Just as what is said by the accused is heard by police hearers, so what they observe is seen through police eyes. In both cases they have to select what is relevant. The judge and every intelligent juryman knows that; and what they are looking for are signs that the selection has been done fairly and impartially or otherwise. If lack of candour on the policeman's part means that the jury feels it is unsafe to rely on his sense of fairness, the prosecution's case may be irreparably harmed.

. . . The fault to be looked for to-day . . . is not the frame-up but the tendency to press interrogation too hard against a man believed to be guilty. It is a very understandable fault. The police come into much closer contact with criminals than the lawyer does, and no doubt they find some of them quite despicable and revolted by the prospect that they may be left at large to hurt others. Take, for example, the case of a man accused of offences against small girls or boys. The policeman may sincerely believe that the complaint is true; it is possible that he may be in a better position to judge of that than the jury will be; he may know more about the background, whether the child is reliable and so on, than will ever emerge in court; he has perhaps a better chance of weighing the truth of the child's story as it is told to him quietly and informally at school or in the parent's house than the jury will have when the child gets up into the box and has to tell it all in public and be subjected to cross-examination. The police officer may know what the jury generally will not know, that the man has been convicted before of similar offences. But the officer also knows that the jury will be warned that without corroboration it will be dangerous to convict; and he may not be able to find in the surrounding circumstances any corroboration. He knows then that the only chance of corroboration lies in some admission or some unguarded statement made by the accused. It is often in circumstances of that sort that a police officer will be found to have pressed questioning too hard. It is understandable that in those circumstances he should be very reluctant for the prosecution to fail. It is easy for the lawyers to say that it is better for ninety-nine guilty men to be acquitted than for one innocent to be convicted; but to those in daily contact with the ninety-nine and who see at close quarters the harm that they do the maxim has less appeal. It is not corruption or the desire to pervert justice, nor is it always the natural ardour of the chase (though this no doubt plays its part) that makes the police less fair and dispassionate than they should be. It is often just honest indignation, such as the ordinary citizen himself experiences if he is suddenly brought into contact with some pestilential crime in which the innocent child or the poor man has been maltreated or defrauded. . . .

I have said that the accused's statement to the police often plays a great part in the prosecution's case. There can be no doubt of that, and it is as well that I should emphasize it. In any study of the inquiry into crime, it would be far less important than it is to examine police methods of interrogation if it were not true to say that the evidence which such interrogation produces is often decisive. The high degree of proof which the English law requires—proof beyond reasonable doubt—often could not be achieved by the prosecution without the assistance of the accused's own statement. I do not mean by this that prosecutions are frequently launched with the accused's confession as the only evidence against him. If it is the sole evidence, although it is open to the jury to convict, I believe that unless they found the confession to be of a character that was quite convincing, they would be disinclined to convict. . . .

When I say that the statement plays a decisive part, I do not mean that it is necessarily a complete confession. It may even be an emphatic denial. The danger to the accused is that so often it turns out that he has said things to the police which it is difficult or impossible to fit in with the line of defence that is advanced at the trial.

Letter from English Policeman on use of Judges' Rules

(Quoted in W. T. Fryer (Ed.), *Selected Writings on the Law of Evidence and Trial* (St. Paul, Minn., 1957), p. 846)

. . . the more serious the offence the more formally are the Rules kept to because the greater is going to be the light of publicity, cross-examination, etc., at the subsequent trial. On odd occasions a type of third degree is used, but the detective using it would not even let his companions know that he had done so unless they were also involved with him because he has as much to fear from his superiors in the Police Force, who would sack him immediately to cover themselves, as from the judge. It is hard to explain but though the judges fondly imagine that their Rules are carried out to the letter they in fact very rarely are. All sorts of avoiding actions are taken or otherwise the percentage of detections would be more than halved. You may have gathered that the said avoidance causes policemen to commit no little perjury in the box, and that would be a true assessment. . . .

. . . Everything is done to help the criminal. We have to break the law to enforce it— I cannot even fingerprint or photograph a person who has admitted the offence unless he consents or the magistrates make an order. When I said to you that prisoners always opened their mouths too much, I meant it, but what they usually do is to make a statement which they think, in their ignorance of the law, excuses them, e.g., they will frequently say something to this effect: "I didn't break into the house. It was Smith that did it. I only went with him." Or: "I didn't steal the money. Smith took it and gave me some of it." Frequently they will apologize thinking that then we will let them go, e.g. "I'm sorry I did it. I don't know what made me, and I won't do it again." This may all sound fantastic to you, but it is literally true. The ignorance of the Great British Public neutralizes the Judges' Rules. When we deal with an educated man who knows his rights, we have had it, unless we have outside evidence enough.

Note

1. Technical breaches of the Judges' Rules do not affect admissibility: the judge has a discretion, usually exercised in favour of admission. As we shall see, this makes English law in practice substantially different from American.

2. Arresting persons on one charge and questioning them on another is permitted. There should be no cross-examination after the accused is charged respecting the offence charged, but this may occur respecting other offences (*R. v. Buchan*, [1964] 1 All E.R. 502; [1964] 1 W.L.R. 365.

3. The "evidence" mentioned in Rule II must be evidence admissible in court; so the police can question a man without cautioning him on the basis of a hearsay underworld tip-off (*R. v. White*, [1964] Crim. L.R. 720, C.C.A.; *R. v. Osborne*, [1973] 1 Q.B. 678; [1973] 1 All E.R. 649, C.A.).

4. For the purposes of Rule III, "charged" means that the accused must be formally charged at a police station, not merely be told why he is being arrested. "Informed that he may be prosecuted" covers cases where the suspect has not been arrested but where in the course of questioning a time comes when the police contemplate that a summons may be issued (*R. v. Collier*, [1965] 3 All E.R. 136; [1965] 1 W.L.R. 1470, C.C.A.). The implication is that since more evidence is needed to support a charge than to support an arrest, it is possible to question persons in custody.

5. Even if the exact words are taken down in accordance with Rule IV, there are dangers where a statement obtained by question and answer is reduced to a continuous narrative. The qualifying context of what is said will be changed by the omission of the questions and by the juxtaposition of answers that may not have originally appeared together. The reproduction of the exact form of interviews extending over hours may of course be prohibitively expensive. The fact that times of questioning must be noted is designed to help determine whether a neat and well-constructed statement in fact corresponds with what occurred. If two hundred words took five hours to obtain, this suggests that the statement should be carefully scrutinized.

6. In *R. v. Nichols* (1967), 51 Cr. App. Rep. 233 the Court of Appeal said that Rule VI extends beyond the police to professional investigators who are likely to know the caution and not ordinary citizens who by chance find themselves in a position where they happen to be interrogating suspects. Thus the Rules apply to shop detectives but not a shop manager questioning a suspect shop lifter. They do not apply to foreign detectives seeking extradition of a

suspect: *Beese* v. *Governor* of *Ashford Remand Centre*, [1973] 3 All E.R. 689, at p. 693, H.L.

7. The caution is usually attacked on two grounds. It is said to hamper the police in that it might cause the accused to say nothing. But the accused has a right to silence; he must be told of it, otherwise the law will only be protecting hardened criminals who know their rights. Secondly, it is said to silence innocent men who if they spoke might clear themselves. To meet this objection in part, the words "against you" were dropped from older forms of caution.

8. Principle (c), preceding the Rules, raises these problems: what if a man is not warned of his right to a lawyer? What if he asks for one and the police refuse him one? It is not the practice to warn suspects of their "right", and in England, unlike America, this has no consequences for admissibility. If his request for a lawyer is refused, and a statement is then made, this may be evidence that improper pressure has been put on an accused to make him change his earlier resolve not to talk without legal advice.

9. The Criminal Law Revision Committee's 11th Report asserts that "in practice it seems that nowadays, before the prosecution can adduce evidence of a statement obtained in breach of the rules, there must be a positive decision by the court to exercise its discretion in favour of admitting the statement" (para. 45). There is some evidence for this as a legal rule (e.g. *R.* v. *Collier*, [1965] 3 All E.R. 136, at p. 138, C.C.A., but in practice most breaches of the Judges' Rules do *not* lead to exclusion.

10. The burden of proving that a breach of the Rules should lead to exclusion rests on the accused (*R.* v. *Batty*, [1963] V.R. 451).

Criminal Law Revision Committee: 11th Report
1972, Cmnd. 4991. Paras. 43, 52

It is of no help to an innocent person to caution him to the effect that he is not obliged to make a statement. Indeed, it might deter him from saying something which might serve to exculpate him. On the other hand the caution often assists the guilty by providing an excuse for keeping back a false story until it becomes difficult to expose its falsity. . . . In any event practised criminals have little respect for the caution.

. . .[T]he first caution . . . has been objected to on the ground that it interrupts the natural course of interrogation and unduly hampers the police, as there may be a good deal more information which they wish to get, perhaps involving other offences and persons, after the stage when they have "evidence which would afford reasonable grounds for suspecting that [the person being questioned] has committed an offence".

. . .

[A minority] consider that statutory provision should be made for the compulsory use of tape recorders at police stations in the larger centres of population. . . . Their reasons are given below.

(i) . . . Perhaps a provision for the electronic recording of interrogations would not always eliminate the use of "third degree" methods . . ., but the knowledge that a recorder is running during an interview would surely exercise a deterrent effect. . . .

(ii) . . . [T]he use of tape recorders may help to reduce the occasions on which the police are tempted to fabricate confessions. . . . [T]here is a widespread impression, not only among criminals, that in tough areas a police officer who is certain that he has got the right man will invent some oral admission (colloquially known as a "verbal") to clinch the case. . . . If the accused alleges that the evidence against him is perjured, he is not likely to be believed, and the mere making of the allegation . . . in . . . evidence enables the prosecution . . . to elicit . . . his previous record.

(iii) Short of using violence or perjury, the police may get confessions by the use of various kinds of persuasion, which is all the more effective when the suspect is isolated from his friends. The present position is that the courts do not exclude evidence of confessions merely because they were obtained by questioning at night or in the small hours [though they probably may do so]. It is demonstrated from time to time that even ordinary questioning can produce false confessions, but the risk is greatly increased if oppressive methods are used.

(iv) . . . [T]he police officer may write a narrative which is in part a blend of question and answer. . . . Since the statement does not distinguish between question and answer, one cannot tell from the statement what facts were suggested to the suspect by the way in which the question was worded. And the written word does not produce the inflection of the voice on which meaning may depend. One may not even be sure that the officer understood what the suspect said, or that the suspect understood the written statement when he read it through or had it read to him. His signature is not a guarantee that the written statement exactly reproduces what he said.

(v) The possibilities of error are multiplied if, as often happens, the statement is not reduced to writing at the time and signed by the suspect. The investigating officer may simply embody what he regards as the kernel of the suspect's statement in his notebook. . . . If there are two or more investigating officers, they are allowed to agree their evidence together before writing up their notes [R. v. *Bass*, [1953] 1 Q.B. 680; [1953] 1 All E.R. 1064, C.C.A.]. The officers may even prepare a joint note. If they are inclined to stretch the case a bit against the accused, perhaps because he has a "record" and appears to them to be guilty, they know that they will be able to back each other up at the trial and will be virtually impregnable from attack. . . .

III   UNFAIRNESS

The Judges' Rules are only an example of the way in which confessions may be excluded in the court's discretion notwithstanding their voluntariness. This is usually known as the "unfairness" jurisdiction, though this is a misnomer. The jurisdiction depends not on fairness but on such issues as reliability and police standards. There is little authority because in practice the Judges' Rules tend to cover most of the field. One reason for excluding evidence is where its probative value is small in relation to its prejudicial effect on the accused. This reason is acted on throughout the law of evidence in criminal cases (e.g. illegally obtained evidence, cross-examination on the accused's record, similar fact evidence), but it has been applied here so as to exclude the confession of an adult whose mental age did not exceed five and one half years in R. v. *Stewart* (1972), 56 Cr. App. Rep. 272. The judge, relying on *Sinclair* v. *R.* (1946), 73 C.L.R. 316, said that "the circumstances must be very special to warrant exclusion" but that they existed in the case before him. (See also R. v. *Phillips*, [1949] N.Z.L.R. 316, at p. 347 and cf. R. v. *Wray* (1970), 11 D.L.R. (3d) 673 (p. 242, *post*), adopting a narrow view of the doctrine.)

However, the discretion to exclude on grounds of unfairness extends beyond unreliability. For example, it would apply to serious police misconduct falling outside the Judges' Rules. The discretion is controversial and to a large extent obscure, but the Criminal Law Revision Committee recommend its retention (para. 278).

Sinclair v. R.

(1946), 73 C.L.R. 316

An argument that the accused's confession should have been excluded because he was at that time mentally unsound was rejected by the High Court of Australia.

DIXON, J.: The tendency in more recent times has been against the exclusion of relevant evidence for reasons founded on the supposition that the medium of proof is untrustworthy, in the case of a witness, because of his situation and, in the case of evidentiary material, because of its source. The days are gone when witnesses were incompetent to testify because they were parties or married to a party, because of interest, because of their religious beliefs or want of them or because of crime or infamy. We now call the evidence and treat the factors which formerly excluded it as matters for comment to the tribunal of fact, whose duty it is to weigh the evidence. It must be remembered that the rules relating to the presumptive involuntariness of confessions were developed at a time when the incompetency of witnesses on such grounds was a matter of daily inquiry and, moreover, when the prisoner could not testify. These are all considerations against extending the principle upon which confessions resulting from intimidation or from a threat made or promise given in reference to the charge by a person in authority are excluded as involuntary to cases of insanity where the will may be affected or there may be a liability to confuse the data of experience with those of imagination, so that such factors without more would be enough to exclude a confession.

It is hardly necessary to say that, where there has been pressure or other inducement, the mental condition of a person purporting to confess invalidates his confession as evidence. That objection, in my opinion, cannot be sustained unless a description or degree of derangement is shown much more destructive of the possibility of safely using the confession as a circumstance tending to prove the criminal acts.

Boyd Sinclair's mental state did not disable him from observing, appreciating, re-collecting and recounting real occurrences, events or experiences. The fact that his mind, in its schizophrenic state, may have been stored with imaginary episodes and with the memory of unreal dramatic situations would, of course, make it impossible to place reliance upon his confessional statements as intrinsically likely to be true. The tendency of his mental disorder to dramatic and histrionic assertion formed another difficulty in attaching an inherent value to what he said. But it is to be noticed that his condition did no more than make it possible that the source of any confessional statement made, lay in these tendencies. His was not a case in which it could be said that the higher probability was in favour of his confession of such a crime being the product of imagination. Reason suggests that in such circumstances it is for the tribunal of fact to ascertain or verify the factual basis of the statements of a man in such a mental condition by comparing their contents with the independent proofs of the circumstances and occurrences to which they relate. It happens that external facts independently proved do supply many reasons for supposing that the confessional statements made by Boyd Sinclair were substantially correct. Though this consideration is not relevant to the question of the legal admissibility of such statements, it provides an example of the inconvenience or undesirability of a rule of rigid exclusion.

It may be conceded that a confession may in fact be made by a person whose un-soundness of mind is such that no account ought to be taken of his self-incriminating statements for any evidentiary purpose as proof of the criminal acts alleged against him. In such a case it might properly be rejected. It is enough in the present case to say that I do not think that Boyd Sinclair's derangement was such as to place his confessional statements in that category. His mental condition was not shown to be inconsistent with any standard or criterion we should adopt as the test of admissibility in evidence of confessional statements. A confession is not necessarily inadmissible as evidence upon a criminal trial because it appears that the prisoner making it was at the time of unsound mind and, by reason of his mental condition, exposed to the liability of confusing the products of his disordered imagination or fancy with fact.

[LATHAM, C.J. and RICH, STARKE and McTIERNAN, JJ. agreed.]

IV AMERICAN LAW

The relevant American law can be divided into three groups: the *McNabb–Mallory* rule, the due process requirement, and the *Escobedo–Miranda* doctrine.

The *McNabb–Mallory* rule requires federal courts to exclude even voluntary confessions obtained during a period of illegal detention, i.e. during a period when the accused should have been brought before a committing magistrate. The rule is not binding on state courts because it does not proceed from the Bill of Rights but rather the U.S. Supreme Court's supervisory powers over inferior federal courts (*McNabb* v. *U.S.*, (1943), 318 U.S. 332; *Mallory* v. *U.S.* (1957), 354 U.S. 449). Most of the states have declined to follow it.

The rules worked out by the Supreme Court regarding breach of the due process clauses of the Bill of Rights do bind the states. It is clear that due process is infringed by a confession extorted by physical torture (*Brown* v. *Mississippi* (1936), 297 U.S. 278). What of interrogation? It is not "inherently coercive, as is physical violence. Interrogation does have social value in solving a crime, as physical force does not. . . . The limits in any case depend upon a weighing of the circumstances of pressure against the power of resistance of the person confessing" (*Stein* v. *New York* (1953), 346 U.S. 156, at pp. 184–5. Confessions have been excluded on grounds of frightening interrogation practices such as moving prisoners from jail to jail; questioning unclothed, standing, sleepless or very hungry prisoners; very long relay questioning; questioning during lengthy incommunicado detention; the excessive use of pretended sympathy with the prisoner; particularly when these methods are used against very young, or ignorant, or timid, or mentally or physically ill prisoners, or prisoners whose race puts them at a social disadvantage. The balancing process used means that a strong-minded man can suffer a lot of unpleasantness and his confession will not be excluded (e.g. *Lisenba* v. *California* (1941), 314 U.S. 219). The due process requirement has thus led to an expansion of the voluntariness requirement. Further, a confession obtained as the result of an illegal search and seizure is inadmissible (*Wong Sun* v. *U.S.* (1963), 83 S. Ct. 407; *People* v. *Rodriguez* (1962), 183 N.E. 2d 651).

Finally, there is the *Escobedo–Miranda* doctrine. Defendants have a right to be warned of their right to silence and of their right to counsel (*Escobedo* v. *Illinois*, (1964), 378 U.S. 478) at public expense (*Gideon* v. *Wainwright* (1963), 372 U.S. 335). A long interrogation will be treated as evidence of the accused not having waived these rights even if the police testify that he has. This case law is based on the Fifth Amendment ("No person shall be compelled in any criminal case to be a witness against himself") and the Sixth ("the accused shall . . . have the Assistance of Counsel"). The doctrine was most fully formulated in *Miranda*.

Miranda v. Arizona
(1966), 384 U.S. 436

The accused made a confession of kidnapping and rape after two hours' questioning. He had not been warned of his right to have a lawyer present during the interrogation. The U.S. Supreme Court held the confession inadmissible.

WARREN, C.J.: Our holding will be spelled out with some specificity in the pages which follow but briefly stated it is this: the prosecution may not use statements, whether exculpatory or inculpatory, stemming from custodial interrogation of the defendant unless it demonstrates the use of procedural safeguards effective to secure the privilege against self-incrimination. By custodial interrogation, we mean questioning initiated by law enforcement officers after a person has been taken into custody or otherwise deprived of his freedom of action in any significant way. As for the procedural safeguards to be employed, unless other fully effective means are devised to inform accused persons of their right of silence and to assure a continuous opportunity to exercise it, the following measures are required. Prior to any questioning, the person must be warned that he has a right to remain silent, that any statement he does make may be used as evidence against him, and that he has a right to the presence of an attorney, either retained or appointed. The defendant may waive effectuation of these rights, provided the waiver is made voluntarily, knowingly and intelligently. If, however, he indicates in any manner and at any stage of the process that he wishes to consult with an attorney before speaking there can be no questioning. Likewise, if the individual is alone and indicates in any manner that he does not wish to be interrogated, the police may not question him. The mere fact that he may have answered some questions or volunteered some statements on his own does not deprive him of the right to refrain from answering any further inquiries until he has consulted with an attorney and thereafter consents to be questioned. . . .

[These cases] share salient features—incommunicado interrogation of individuals in a police-dominated atmosphere, resulting in self-incriminating statements without full warnings of constitutional rights. . . .

Again we stress that the modern practice of in-custody interrogation is psychologically rather than physically oriented. . . . Interrogation still takes place in privacy. Privacy results in secrecy and this in turn results in a gap in our knowledge as to what in fact goes on in the interrogation rooms. A valuable source of information about present police practices, however, may be found in various police manuals and texts which document procedures employed with success in the past, and which recommend various other effective tactics. . . .

. . . The current practice of incommunicado interrogation is at odds with one of our Nation's most cherished principles—that the individual may not be compelled to incriminate himself. Unless adequate protective devices are employed to dispel the compulsion inherent in custodial surroundings, no statement obtained from the defendant can truly be the product of his free choice.

The question in these cases is whether the privilege [against self-incrimination] is fully applicable during a period of custodial interrogation. . . . We are satisfied that all the principles embodied in the privilege apply to informal compulsion exerted by law-enforcement officers during in-custody questioning. An individual swept from familiar surroundings into police custody, surrounded by antagonistic forces, and subjected to the techniques of persuasion described above cannot be otherwise than under compulsion to speak. As a practical matter, the compulsion to speak in the isolated setting of the police station may well be greater than in courts or other official investigations, where there are often impartial observers to guard against intimidation or trickery. . . .

. . . The entire thrust of police interrogation . . . in all the cases today, was to put the defendant in such an emotional state as to impair his capacity for rational judgment. The abdication of the constitutional privilege—the choice on his part to speak to the police—was not made knowingly or competently because of the failure to apprise him of his rights; the compelling atmosphere of the in-custody interrogation, and not an independent decision on his part, caused the defendant to speak.

The Fifth Amendment privilege is so fundamental to our system of constitutional rule and the expedient of giving an adequate warning as to the availability of the privilege so simple, we will not pause to inquire in individual cases whether the defendant was aware of his rights without a warning being given. Assessments of the knowledge the defendant possessed, based on information as to age, education, intelligence, or prior contact with authorities, can never be more than speculation; a warning is a clearcut fact. More important, whatever the background of the person interrogated, a warning at the time of the interrogation is indispensable to overcome its pressures and to insure that the individual knows he is free to exercise the privilege at that point in time.

The warning of the right to remain silent must be accompanied by the explanation that anything said can and will be used against the individual in court. This warning is needed in order to make him aware not only of the privilege, but also of the consequences of forgoing it. It is only through an awareness of these consequences that there can be any assurance of real understanding and intelligent exercise of the privilege. Moreover, this warning may serve to make the individual more acutely aware that he is faced with a phase of the adversary system—that he is not in the presence of persons acting solely in his interest.

The circumstances surrounding in-custody interrogation can operate very quickly to overbear the will of one merely made aware of his privilege by his interrogators. Therefore, the right to have counsel present at the interrogation is indispensable to the protection of the Fifth Amendment privilege under the system we delineate today. Our aim is to assure that the individual's right to choose between silence and speech remains unfettered throughout the interrogation process.

The presence of counsel at the interrogation may serve several significant subsidiary functions as well. If the accused decides to talk to his interrogators, the assistance of counsel can mitigate the dangers of untrustworthiness. With a lawyer present the likelihood that the police will practice coercion is reduced, and if coercion is nevertheless exercised the lawyer can testify to it in court. The presence of a lawyer can also help to guarantee that the accused gives a fully accurate statement to the police and that the statement is rightly reported by the prosecution at trial.

If an individual indicates that he wishes the assistance of counsel before any interrogation occurs, the authorities cannot rationally ignore or deny his request on the basis that the individual does not have or cannot afford a retained attorney. The financial ability of the individual has no relationship to the scope of the rights involved here. The privilege against self-incrimination secured by the Constitution applies to all individuals. The need for counsel in order to protect the privilege exists for the indigent as well as the affluent. In fact, were we to limit these constitutional rights to those who can retain an attorney, our decisions today would be of little significance. The cases before us as well as the vast majority of confession cases with which we have dealt in the past involve those unable to retain counsel. While authorities are not required to relieve the accused of his poverty, they have the obligation not to take advantage of indigence in the administration of justice.

The Court's new rules aim to offset these minor pressures and disadvantages intrinsic to any kind of police interrogation. The rules do not serve due process interests in preventing blatant coercion since, as I noted earlier, they do nothing to contain the policeman who is prepared to lie from the start. The rules work for reliability in confessions almost only in the Pickwickian sense that they can prevent some from being given at all. . . .

HARLAN, J. (whom STEWART and WHITE, JJ. joined) dissenting: What the Court largely ignores is that its rules impair, if they will not eventually serve wholly to frustrate, an instrument of law enforcement that has long and quite reasonably been thought worth the price paid for it. There can be little doubt that the Court's new code would markedly decrease the number of confessions. To warn the suspect that he may remain silent and remind him that his confession may be used in court are minor obstructions. To require also an express waiver by the suspect and an end to questioning whenever he demurs must heavily handicap questioning. And to suggest or provide counsel for the suspect simply invites the end of the interrogation. . . .

How much harm this decision will inflict on law enforcement cannot fairly be predicted with accuracy. . . . We do know that some crimes cannot be solved without confessions that ample expert testimony attests to their importance in crime control and that the Court is taking a real risk with society's welfare in imposing its new regime on the country. The social costs of crime are too great to call the new rules anything but a hazardous experimentation.

While passing over the costs and risks of its experiment, the Court portrays the evils of normal police questioning in terms which I think are exaggerated. Albeit stringently confined by the due process standards interrogation is no doubt often inconvenient and unpleasant for the suspect. However, it is no less so for a man to be arrested and jailed, to have his house searched, or to stand trial in court, yet all this may properly happen to the most innocent given probable cause, a warrant, or an indictment. Society has always paid a stiff price for law and order, and peaceful interrogation is not one of the dark moments of the law.

CLARK, J. dissented.

The debate on the American position is represented by the following. Inbau and Reid's *Criminal Interrogation and Confessions* (Baltimore, 1967, 2nd Edn.) is one of a group of interrogation manuals widely used among the American police. The practices described in its 1st edition were one factor in the Supreme Court's decision in cases like *Miranda* to extend its protection of suspects, and in that sense it defeated its own ends. Its fascinating mixture of commonsense and oppressive methods, presented with a solemnity at times hilarious, is adequately represented by part of its contents pages.

J. Have the Subject Place Himself at the Scene of the Crime or in Some Sort of Contact with the Victim or the Occurrence..............................

K. Seek an Admission of Lying about Some Incidental Aspect of the Occurrence ....

L. Appeal to the Subject's Pride by Well-Selected Flattery or by a Challenge to His Honor...

M. Point out the Futility of Resistance to Telling the Truth....................

N. Point out to the Subject the Grave Consequences and Futility of a Continuation of His Criminal Behavior..

O. Rather Than Seek a General Admission of Guilt, First Ask the Subject a Question as to Some Detail of the Offense, or Inquire as to the Reason for Its Commission..

P. When Co-Offenders Are Being Interrogated and the Previously Described Techniques Have Been Ineffective, "Play One Against the Other"..........

Tactics and Techniques for the Interrogation of Suspects Whose Guilt is Uncertain

Q. Ask the Subject if He Knows Why He is Being Questioned ....

R. Ask the Subject to Relate All He Knows about the Occurrence, the Victim, and Possible Suspects..

S. Obtain from the Subject Detailed Information about His Activities before, at the Time of, and after the Occurrence in Question.........................

T. Where Certain Facts Suggestive of the Subject's Guilt are Known, Ask Him about Them Rather Casually and as Though the Real Facts Were Not Already Known..

U. At Various Intervals Ask the Subject Certain Pertinent Questions in a Manner which Implies that the Correct Answers Are Already Known............

V. Refer to Some Non-Existing Incriminating Evidence to Determine whether the Subject Will Attempt to Explain It Away; if He Does, That Fact Is Suggestive of His Guilt...

W. Ask the Subject whether He Ever "Thought" about Committing the Offense in Question or One Similar to It..

X. In Theft Cases, if a Suspect Offers to Make Restitution, That Fact Is Indicative of Guilt..

Y. Ask the Subject whether He Is Willing to Take a Lie-Detector Test. The Innocent Person Will Almost Always Steadfastly Agree to Take Practically Any Test to Prove His Innocence, whereas the Guilty Person Is More Prone to Refuse to Take the Test or to Find Excuses for not Taking It, or for Backing Out of His Commitment to Take It....................................

Z. A Subject Who Tells the Interrogator, "All Right, I'll Tell You What You Want, but I Didn't Do It," Is, in All Probability, Guilty................

GENERAL SUGGESTIONS REGARDING THE INTERROGATION OF CRIMINAL SUSPECTS....

1. Interview the Victim, the Accuser, or the Discoverer of the Crime Before Interrogating the Suspect Himself..

2. Be Patient ....

3. Make No Promises When Asked, "What Will Happen to Me if I Tell the Truth?" ....

4. View with Skepticism the So-called "Conscience-Stricken" Confession........

5. When a Subject Has Made Repeated Denials of Guilt to Previous Interrogators, First Question Him, Whenever Circumstances Permit, about Some Other, Unrelated Offense of a Similar Nature of Which He Is Also Considered to be Guilty..

6. An Unintelligent, Uneducated Criminal Suspect, with a Low Cultural Background, Should Be Interrogated on a Psychological Level Comparable to That Usually Employed in the Questioning of a Child Respecting an Act of Wrongdoing ....

Criminal offenders whose guilt is unknown to the police will rarely surrender themselves and confess their guilt. The instinct for self-preservation stands in the way. Consequently, an interrogator should view with considerable scepticism any conscience-stricken confession. Such a confession is very likely to be false. It may be the product of a mentally ill person, or it may stem from an otherwise normal person's effort to incur a temporary police detention in order to gain some other deliberately conceived objective. Among the latter possibilities are instances where an individual may merely be seeking free transportation back to the state or community where the crime was committed. In other instances the purpose may be that of being incarcerated, either for a brief or even a relatively long period, in order to evade police consideration of him as a suspect for a much more serious crime. Then, too, there are times when the only motive of a conscience-stricken confession is the publicity the confessor seeks to achieve.

One completely false assumption accounts for most of the legal restrictions on police interrogations. It is this, and the fallacy is certainly perpetuated to a very considerable extent by mystery writers, the movies, and TV: whenever a crime is committed, if the police will only look carefully at the crime scene they will almost always find some clue that will lead them to the offender and at the same time establish his guilt; and once the offender is located, he will readily confess or disclose his guilt by trying to shoot his way out of the trap. But this is pure fiction; in actuality the situation is quite different....

  1. Many Criminal Cases, Even When Investigated by the Best Qualified Police Departments, Are Capable of Solution Only by Means of an Admission or Confession from the Guilty Individual or upon the Basis of Information Obtained from the Questioning of Other Criminal Suspects....

  2. Criminal Offenders, Except, of Course, Those Caught in the Commission of Their Crimes, Ordinarily Will Not Admit Their Guilt unless Questioned under Conditions of Privacy, and for a Period of Perhaps Several Hours.

This point is one which should be readily apparent not only to any person with the least amount of criminal investigative experience, but also to anyone who will reflect momentarily upon the behaviour of ordinary law-abiding persons when suspected or accused of nothing more than simple social indiscretions. Self-condemnation and self-destruction not being normal behaviour characteristics, human beings ordinarily do not utter unsolicited, spontaneous confessions. They must first be questioned regarding the offence. In some instances, a little bit of information inadvertently given to a competent interrogator by the suspect may suffice to start a line of investigation which might ultimately establish guilt. On other occasions, a full confession, with a revelation of details regarding a body, the loot, or the instruments used in the crime, may be required to prove the case; but whatever the possible consequences may be, it is impractical to expect any but a very few confessions to result from a guilty conscience unprovoked by an interrogation. It is also impractical to expect admissions or confessions to be obtained under circumstances other than privacy. Here again recourse to our everyday experience will support the basic validity of this requirement. For instance, in asking a personal friend to divulge a secret, or embarrassing information, we carefully avoid making the request in the presence of other persons, and seek a time and place when the matter can be discussed in private. The very same psychological factors are involved in a criminal interrogation, and even to a greater extent. For related psychological considerations, if an interrogation is to be had at all, it must be one based upon an unhurried interview, the necessary length of which will in many instances extend to several hours, depending upon various factors, such as the nature of the case situation and the personality of the suspect.

3. In Dealing with Criminal Offenders, and Consequently Also with Criminal Suspects Who May Actually Be Innocent, the Interrogator Must of Necessity Employ Less Refined Methods Than Are Considered Appropriate for the Transaction of Ordinary, Everday Affairs by and between Law-Abiding Citizens.

From the criminal's point of view, *any* interrogation of him is objectionable. To *him* it may be a "dirty trick" to be talked into a confession, for surely it was not done for his benefit. Consequently, any interrogation of him might be labelled as deceitful or unethical.

Of necessity, criminal interrogators must deal with criminal offenders on a somewhat lower moral plane than that upon which ethical, law-abiding citizens are expected to conduct their everyday affairs. That plane, in the interest of innocent suspects, need only be subject to the following restriction: Although both "fair" and "unfair" interrogation practices are permissible, nothing shall be done or said to the subject that will be apt to make an innocent person confess.

Note

Many of these techniques are calculated to produce an untrue confession in that they entail asking for the accused's assent to a relatively innocuous version of what he has done. In court this may deliberately or by a misunderstanding be presented as a confession to a much more serious crime. The oppressive and fatiguing nature of the above kind of questioning may have the same tendency.

Watts v. Indiana
(1949), 338 U.S. 49

JACKSON, J. (in the U.S. Supreme Court): . . . The suspect neither had nor was advised of his right to get counsel. This presents a real dilemma in a free society. To subject one without counsel to questioning which may and is intended to convict him, is a real peril to individual freedom. To bring in a lawyer means a real peril to solution of the crime because, under our adversary system, he deems that his sole duty is to protect his client—guilty or innocent—and that in such a capacity he owes no duty whatever to help society solve its crime problem. Under this conception of criminal procedure, any lawyer worth his salt will tell the suspect in no uncertain terms to make no statement to police under any circumstances.

Culombe v. Connecticut
(1961), 367 U.S. 568

FRANKFURTER, J. (U.S. Supreme Court majority opinion): Despite modern advances in the technology of crime detection, offences frequently occur about which things cannot be made to speak. And where there cannot be found innocent human witnesses to such offences, nothing remains—if police investigation is not to be balked before it has fairly begun—but to seek out possibly guilty witnesses and ask them questions, witnesses, that is, who are suspected of knowing something about the offence precisely because they are suspected of implication in it. . . .

But persons who are suspected of crime will not always be unreluctant to answer questions put by the police. Since under the procedures of Anglo-American criminal justice they cannot be constrained by legal process to give answers which incriminate them, the police have resorted to other means to unbend their reluctance, lest criminal investigation founder. Kindness, cajolery, entreaty, deception, persistent cross-questioning, even physical brutality have been used to this end. In the United States, "interrogation" has become a police technique, and detention for purposes of inter-rogation a common, although generally unlawful practice. Crime detection officials, finding that if their suspects are kept under tight police control during questioning they are less likely to be distracted, less likely to be recalcitrant and, of course, less likely to make off and escape entirely, not infrequently take such suspects into custody for "investigation".

This practice has its manifest evils and dangers. Persons subjected to it are torn from the reliances of their daily existence and held at the mercy of those whose job it is—if such persons have committed crimes, as it is supposed they have—to convict them for it. They are deprived of freedom without a proper judicial tribunal having found them guilty, without a proper judicial tribunal having found even that there is probable cause to believe that they may be guilty. What actually happens to them behind the closed door of the interrogation room is difficult if not impossible to ascertain. Certainly, if through excess of zeal or aggressive impatience or flaring up of temper in the face of obstinate silence, a prisoner is abused, he is faced with the task of overcoming, by his lone testimony, solemn official denials. The prisoner knows this—knows that no friendly or disinterested witness is present—and the knowledge may itself induce fear. But, in any case, the risk is great that the police will accomplish behind their closed door precisely what the demands of our legal order forbid: make a suspect the unwilling collaborator in establishing his guilt. This they may accomplish not only with ropes and a rubber hose, not only by relay questioning persistently, insistently subjugating a tired mind, but by subtler devices.

In the police station a prisoner is surrounded by known hostile forces. He is dis-oriented from the world he knows and in which he finds support. He is subject to coercing impingements, undermining even if not obvious pressures of every variety. In such an atmosphere, questioning that is long continued—even if it is only repeated at intervals, never protracted to the point of physical exhaustion—inevitably suggests that the questioner has a right to, and expects, an answer. This is so, certainly, when the prisoner has never been told that he need not answer and when, because his commit-ment to custody seems to be at the will of his questioners, he has every reason to believe that he will be held and interrogated until he speaks.

. . . But if it is once admitted that questioning of suspects is permissible, whatever reasonable means are needed to make the questioning effective must also be conceded to the police. Often prolongation of the interrogation period will be essential, so that a suspect's story can be checked and, if it proves untrue, he can be confronted with the lie; if true, released without charge. Often the place of questioning will have to be a police interrogation room, both because it is important to assure the proper atmosphere of privacy and non-distraction if questioning is to be made productive, and because, where a suspect is questioned but not taken into custody, he—and in some cases his associates—may take prompt warning and flee the premises. Legal counsel for the suspect will generally prove a thorough obstruction to the investigation. Indeed, even to inform the suspect of his legal right to keep silent will prove an obstruction. What-ever fortifies the suspect or seconds him in his capacity to keep his mouth closed is a potential obstacle to the solution of crime.

Arthur E. Sutherland, Jr.
(1965), 79 Harv. L.R. 21

Suppose a well-to-do testatrix says she intends to will her property to Elizabeth. John and James want her to bequeath it to them instead. They capture the testatrix, put her in a carefully designed room, out of touch with everyone but themselves and their convenient "witnesses", keep her secluded there for hours while they make insistent demands, weary her with contradictions of her assertions that she wants to leave her money to Elizabeth, and finally induce her to execute the will in their favour. Assume that John and James are deeply and correctly convinced that Elizabeth is unworthy and will make base use of the property if she gets her hands on it, whereas John and James have the noblest and most righteous intentions. . . .

At once one will hear the response that the testatrix is not a criminal; that obtaining a surrender of rights from a criminal is different; that the interest of the state demands that criminals should not be coddled. That is to say we are told that a man with his life at stake should be able to surrender an ancient constitutional right to remain silent, under compulsions which in a surrender of a little property would obviously make the transaction void.

Reardon, J.:
(1969), 43 A.L.J. 508

The broad discretion to exclude evidence improperly obtained is perhaps best employed by the judge who is a true professional judge, who is appointed for life, and who is removed from all extrinsic pressures. This can be said of but a few of the judges in [the United States]. We have . . . some 3,500 *nisi prius* jury trial judges in the fifty states and only a very small percentage of those are appointed for life as are the members of our Federal judiciary. . . . [T]hey may serve as judges for six years, sometimes be defeated, return to practice and then run again, the net effect being that . . . continuity of service . . . is too seldom found. . . . This has something to do with the endeavours which Chief Justice Warren made in the *Miranda* case to set down in precise terms the tests for admission or non-admission of confessions.

Wigmore: Treatise on the Anglo-American System of Evidence in Trials at Common Law
3rd Edn. Para. 851

A thorough questionig of the first suspected person who is caught makes possible the pursuit of the right trail for the others. To forbid this is to tie the hands of the police. The attitude of some judges towards these necessary police methods is lamentable; one would think that the police, not the criminals, were the enemies of society. . . .

But, it is argued, there are abuses by the police. Very true, here and there, at least. It does not follow, however, that a strict rule of exclusion for confessions is the proper remedy. . . . The first remedy is to improve police personnel. The second one is to provide a means of speedy confession which shall be less susceptible to abuses, while still taking advantage of the inherent psychological situation. In short, let an *authorized skilled magistrate* take the confession. . . .

To keep Law abreast of Science let a sound film be made and let no confession be received that is not so recorded.

Sir Reginald Sholl:
(1968), Aust. & N.Z. Journal of Criminology 137

It is no good telling me, after many years' experience as a trial lawyer and a judge, that the *Miranda* decision has not affected the proof of crime. Some academics have attempted, by exercises conducted at police stations, to suggest this.

. . . [I]n your enthusiasm for liberalism at all costs, you have developed . . . a hyperlegalism which is impeding legal administration.

Jerome H. Skolnick: Justice without Trial
New York, 1966. P. 219

Arguments about legal standards are usually unrealistic, whether they come from civil liberties advocates or law enforcement spokesmen. Each group assumes the

behavioural efficacy of legally formulated restraints. The civil libertarian typically feels
that tighter strictures ought to be placed on police, and that if they were, police would
feel obliged to conform. The law enforcement spokesman makes a matching behavioural
assumption when he argues that restraints on police behaviour are already too severe.
My observations suggest, in contrast to both these positions, that norms located within
police organization are more powerful than court decisions in shaping police behaviour,
and that actually the process of interaction between the two accounts ultimately for
how police behave.

Omnibus Crime Control and Safe Streets Act of 1968
82 Stat. 210 (1968)

SEC. 701. (a) Chapter 223, title 18, United States Code (relating to witnesses and
evidence) is amended by adding at the end thereof the following new sections:

"§ 3501. Admissibility of confessions

(*a*) In any criminal prosecution brought by the United States or by the District of
Columbia, a confession, as defined in subsection (*e*) hereof, shall be admissible in evidence if it is voluntarily given. Before such confession is received in evidence, the trial
judge shall, out of the presence of the jury, determine any issue as to voluntariness. If
the trial judge determines that the confession was voluntarily made it shall be admitted
in evidence and the trial judge shall permit the jury to hear relevant evidence on the
issue of voluntariness and shall instruct the jury to give such weight to the confession
as the jury feels it deserves under all the circumstances.

(*b*) The trial judge in determining the issue of voluntariness shall take into consideration all the circumstances surrounding the giving of the confession, including
(1) the time elapsing between arrest and arraignment of the defendant making the confession, if it was made after arrest and before arraignment, (2) whether such defendant
knew the nature of the offense with which he was charged or of which he was suspected
at the time of making the confession, (3) whether or not such defendant was advised or
knew that he was not required to make any statement and that any such statement
could be used against him, (4) whether or not such defendant had been advised prior to
questioning of his right to the assistance of counsel; and (5) whether or not such
defendant was without the assistance of counsel when questioned and when giving such
confession.

The presence or absence of any of the above-mentioned factors to be taken into consideration by the judge need not be conclusive on the issue of voluntariness of the
confession.

(*c*) In any criminal prosecution by the United States or by the District of Columbia, a
confession made or given by a person who is a defendant therein, while such person
was under arrest or other detention in the custody of any law-enforcement officer or
law-enforcement agency, shall not be inadmissible solely because of delay in bringing
such person before a commissioner or other officer empowered to commit persons
charged with offenses against the laws of the United States or of the District of Columbia
if such confession is found by the trial judge to have been made voluntarily and if the
weight to be given the confession is left to the jury and if such confession was made or
given by such person within six hours immediately following his arrest or other
detention."

Note

1. *Orozco v. Texas* (1969), 394 U.S. 324 holds that *Miranda* applies when a
suspect is questioned *in his own home* at 4 a.m., not merely in a police station.
The case illustrates the harshness of the doctrine, as is revealed by White,
J.'s dissent. The suspect was awake when police entered. They asked his name,
whether he had been at a certain restaurant that night, whether he owned a

pistol and where it was. He answered the first three questions quickly, and the fourth was then repeated. He then showed them the pistol hidden in a nearby washing machine. This was not the long-drawn-out psychological questioning aimed at by *Miranda*. Had he stayed in bed he could have been arrested, his house searched and his gun found, quite legally.

A rather questionable limitation of the *Miranda* doctrine was devised in *Harris* v. *N.Y.*, 401 U.S. 222 (1971). The Supreme Court there held that a confession inadmissible in the prosecution's case in chief for violating *Miranda* could be used to impeach the credibility of the defendant's testimony at the trial if its trustworthiness were adequate. Cross's comment is "could any decision make the law look more of a hypocrite?" ([1973] Crim. L.R. 329, at p. 330.)

The Court purported to follow *Walder* v. *U.S.*, (1954), 347 U.S. 62, but there illegally obtained real evidence was used to impeach the accused's testimony not on matters directly related to the case against him but on matters collateral to the crime charged. The accused not only denied the charges but said he never dealt in or possessed drugs, and the evidence was to rebut the latter claim and to challenge credibility.

As Brennan, J. said, dissenting in *Harris*, "The Court today tells the police that they may freely interrogate an accused incommunicado and without counsel and know that although any statement they obtain in violation of *Miranda* cannot be used on the State's direct case, it may be introduced if the defendant has the temerity to testify in his own defence" (401 U.S. 222, at p. 232).

2. American judge-made confessions law has changed, first from sole reliance on the common law to the common law rule combined with an investigation of the particular circumstances of a defendant to see if he could stand up to the treatment given him (the due process requirement).

There has been superadded a stricter and more objective test of whether certain warnings have been given *(Miranda)*. The legislature has dictated a return to the second position in the Omnibus Crime Control and Safe Streets Act 1968, s. 701.

3. The differences between English and American law on police procedure is sometimes attributed to differences in social composition, public trust for the police and for the judges who administer the very discretionary English rules, and public respect for the criminal law generally. See *infra*, p. 251.

4. Kalven and Zeisel (*op. cit.*, p. 142) present some evidence of the importance of confessions to the prosecution. A confession was offered in 19 per cent of cases investigated overall; 43 per cent of homicides, 16 per cent assaults, 27 per cent rape, 30 per cent burglary, 1 per cent drunken driving and 3 per cent narcotics offences. It must be remembered that confessions are often very useful to the police even if they are not introduced at the trial because they provide leads to other evidences or incriminating real evidence; or because they cause the accused to plead guilty. (See (1966), 79 Harv. L.R. 935, at pp. 942–3).

5. A study of the operation of the confession rule in New Haven, Connecticut ((1967), 76 Yale L.J., 1519) suggests there have been more confessions since *Miranda*, not less. Though about one quarter of suspects were not warned of their rights at all, and a majority were not given the full *Miranda* warnings,

more of those who were warned confessed than those who were not warned. This may be because detectives always warned those they thought were on the point of confessing, to ensure the admissibility of the confession. The full *Miranda* warnings tended to be given in cases where the police had enough evidence to go to trial, but not enough for a conviction. If there was a lot of evidence against the accused they did not bother. A further reason for the fact that warnings did not reduce the likelihood of a confession was that "on several occasions we noted that a suspect seemed to be thrown off guard by the warnings. He apparently thought that if the police could give these warnings they must have him." (p. 1573). The study also casts light on a number of the issues in the *Miranda* debate. The decision was bad for police morale, since they regarded it as insulting. Suspects often failed to understand or grasp the significance of the warnings, perhaps because of the bored police manner of giving them. The study shows that interrogation is less necessary than is sometimes thought, because in most cases where it was used the police had enough evidence to convict the suspect without interrogation. Interrogation was used simply to confirm the case or discover accomplices. Indeed, "unless the criminal is caught red-handed or unless witnesses are available, the police with their limited resources for scientific investigation cannot amass even enough evidence to arrest a suspect. And since such evidence when available is all but conclusive, by the time the police have a suspect . . . interrogation is unnecessary" (p. 1613). Finally, the study indicated that police methods are less harsh than Inbau and Reid suggest.

Let us look briefly at the position in other jurisdictions.

In Scotland, confessions proceeding from threats, promises or undue influence on the part of persons in authority are inadmissible. Further, statements made to the police after arrest and even when the accused has become a suspect are almost always excluded, unless completely spontaneous (*Chalmers* v. *H.M. Advocate*, 1954 J.C. 66; *Manuel* v. *H.M. Advocate*, 1958 J.C. 41). Before a person is under suspicion he may be freely questioned; the principal difficulty is thus to determine when the accused ceased to be an ordinary member of the public helping the police and became a suspect. The accused should be cautioned at the stage when he becomes a suspect. The police may and do ask the accused further questions about matters irrelevant to the actual charge (e.g. the whereabouts of stolen property or the accused's accomplices), but these matters are not intended to be put in the evidence, nor could they be. The position is thus much more pro-accused than in England, when the practical effect of the Judges' Rules is weaker. Corroboration of the accused's implication in the crime (not merely that the crime was committed) is necessary.

It is sometimes suggested that the Indian Evidence Act system (drafted by Sir James Fitzjames Stephen and in force in India and parts of Africa) be enforced generally. It provides for confessions only being admissible if made in the presence of a magistrate. But it would not necessarily restrict coercion, which could equally occur before the accused is brought before the magistrate. Secondly, the public reputation for impartiality of the judiciary might suffer were they brought into the investigatory process.

In France the accused may not be interrogated by the police, but he may be questioned by the examining magistrate (*juge d'instruction*), who can depute a policeman to make inquiries.

What possibilities are there for confessions other than the current English position? The American Supreme Court operates an expanded doctrine of voluntariness, a requirement of certain technical warnings and an exclusion of statements made by unlawfully detained persons. The Criminal Law Revision Committee favours the abolition of cautions and a basing of confessions on reliability alone. Another possibility is to put all confessions to the jury, leaving it to them to discard the unreliable. Questioning after suspicion has fallen on the accused might be substantially forbidden, as in Scotland. Police interrogation might be forbidden except before a magistrate (India) or by his direction (France). An expensive and not wholly reliable supplement to several of the above methods would be to tape record or film interrogation: this would no doubt increase the length of trials. This variety of practices and panaceas shows the difficulty of the problem.

Further reading

Anon., (1966), 79 Harv. L.R., 935; Andrews, [1963] Crim. L.R. 15, 77; Baker, *The Hearsay Rule* (London, 1950), pp. 53–63; Brownlie, [1960] Crim. L.R. 298 and [1967] Crim. L.R. 75; Burtt, *Legal Psychology* (New York, 1931), 173–5; Kaufman, *The Admissibility of Confessions in Criminal Matters* (Toronto, 2nd Edn., 1974); Lord MacDermott (1968), 21 C.L.P. 1; Neasey, 43 (1969), A.L.J. 482; Smith, [1964] Crim. L.R. 176; Sutherland, (1965), 79 Harv. L.R. 21; Williams, [1960] Crim. L.R. 325.

9

Improperly Obtained Evidence

I CONFESSIONS CONFIRMED BY SUBSEQUENTLY DISCOVERED FACTS

If the accused has made a confession which is inadmissible because of an inducement, two problems, usually discussed together, arise. To what extent is any evidence discovered in consequence of the confession admissible? To what extent is the confession itself admissible in whole or in part? It should be noted that the latter problem can only arise when the confession is in some way confirmed by the subsequently discovered evidence, since only then can it be said that the risk of the confession being unreliable is lessened. The point is illustrated by R. v. *Jenkins* (1822), Russ. & Ry. 492, where the accused was induced to confess that he had stolen some gowns and he pointed out to a constable the place where and the individual to whom he had transferred them. The judges held that the admission of evidence of these latter facts at the trial had been wrong. "The confession was excluded, because being made under the influence of a promise it could not be relied upon, and the acts of the prisoner, under the same influence, not being confirmed by the finding of the property, were open to the same objection. The influence which might produce a groundless confession might also produce groundless conduct."

The law on this subject is difficult to discover and state. Most of the authorities are ill-reported and ill-reasoned; until recently there were very few of the leading cases characteristic of a well-settled legal point. There are five possible positions and for each there is some authority.

A. Admission of the fact discovered but nothing else

R. v. Warickshall
(1783), 1 Leach 263

The accused was charged with receiving stolen property. It was found hidden in her bed in consequence of her improperly induced confession. The evidence of the finding was admitted.

NARES, B. (with whom EYRE, B. agreed): Confessions are received in evidence, or rejected as inadmissible, under a consideration whether they are or are not intitled to credit. . . . This principle respecting confessions has no application whatever as to admission or rejection of facts . . . for a fact, if it exist at all, must exist invariably in the same manner, whether the confession from which it is derived be in other respects true or false. Facts thus obtained, however, must be fully and satisfactorily proved, without

223

calling in the aid of any part of the confession from which they may have been derived. . . . [T]he fact may be admitted on other evidence; for as no part of an improper confession can be heard, it can never be legally known whether the fact was derived through the means of such confession or not. . . . [A]nd the consequences to public justice would be dangerous indeed; for if men were enabled to regain stolen property, and the evidence of attendant facts were to be suppressed, because they had regained it by means of an improper confession, it would be holding out an opportunity to compound felonies. . . . It is true, that many able judges have conceived, that it would be an exceedingly hard case, that a man whose life is at stake, having been lulled into a notion of security by promises of favour, and in consequence of those promises has been induced to make a confession by the means of which the property is found, should afterwards find that the confession with regard to the property found is to operate against him. But this subject has more than once undergone the solemn consideration of the Twelve Judges; and a majority of them were clearly of opinion, that although confessions improperly obtained cannot be received in evidence, yet that any acts done afterwards might be given in evidence, notwithstanding that they were done in consequence of such confession.

Note

R. v. *Mosey* (1784), 1 Leach 265, n., and R. v. *Harvey* (1800), 2 East P.C. 658 (1803) are to the same effect, and R. v. *Lockhart* (1785), 1 Leach 386 extended the doctrine to permit the reception of the evidence whose identity had been discovered through the confession.

R. v. Berriman
(1854), 6 Cox C.C. 388

The accused was charged with concealment of the birth of her child. Erle, J. refused to admit a confession made to a magistrate. The report continues:

"Locke . . . [counsel for the prosecution] then proposed to put to a witness a question, whether in consequence of the answer she had given to the magistrate, he had made a search in a particular spot, and had found a certain thing.

"ERLE, J.: No! *Not in consequence of what she said.* You may ask him what search was made, and what things were found, but under the circumstances, I cannot allow that proceeding to be connected with the prisoner."

The prisoner was acquitted.

Chalmers v. H.M. Advocate
1954 J.C. 66

The accused made a confession which was inadmissible and then took police officers to a cornfield where he pointed out the purse of a murder victim. The High Court of Judiciary held that evidence of the pointing out had been wrongly admitted.

LORD COOPER, L.J.-G.: I take next the episode of the cornfield. This is related to the interrogation in two ways. In point of time the visit to the cornfield followed immediately after the further interrogation which followed the taking of the "statement". Moreover it is admitted that during the further interrogation the appellant was asked what happened to the purse, and that it was "in consequence of" his answer to that question that he was taken to the cornfield "to facilitate any search". I therefore regard the visit to the cornfield under the surveillance of the police as part and parcel of the same transaction as the interrogation, and, if the interrogation and the "statement" which emerged from it are inadmissible as "unfair", the same criticism must attach to the conducted visit to the cornfield. Next, I feel unable to accept the distinction drawn by the presiding Judge between statements and "actings", and I suspect that a fallacy lurks in the word "actings". The actings of an accused, if unattended by such circumstances as are here presented, are normally competent evidence against him. For instance, if the police had kept watch on the accused and had seen him go to the cornfield to retrieve the purse, such evidence would have been perfectly competent. Again "actings", in the sense of conduct, may be perfectly neutral as a communication of specific information; but "actings", in the sense of a gesture or sign, may be indistinguishable from a communication by word of mouth or by writing. The question here was—Where exactly is the purse? and this question might have been answered by an oral description of the place where it was, or by going to the place and silently pointing to that place. It seems to me to make no difference for present purposes which method of answering the question was adopted; from which it follows that, if, in the circumstances of this case, the "statement" was inadmissible, the episode of the cornfield was equally inadmissible. The significance of the episode is plain, for it showed that the appellant knew where the purse was. If the police had simply produced, and proved the finding of, the purse, that evidence would have carried them little or no distance in this case towards implicating the appellant. It was essential that the appellant should be linked up with the purse, either by oral confession or by its equivalent—tacit admission of knowledge of its whereabouts obtained as a sequel to the interrogation

LORD THOMSON, L.J.-C. and LORDS CARMONT, PATRICK and MACKINTOSH concurred.]

See also *People* v. *O'Brien,* [1965] I.R. 142, at p. 166, *per* WALSH, J., p. 238, *post.*

The English Criminal Law Revision Committee have proposed the following clause in their draft Criminal Evidence Bill: 2 (5) "The fact that a confession is wholly or partly excluded . . . shall not affect the admissibility in evidence:
  (*a*) of any facts discovered as a result of the confession. . . ."

Comment

Chalmers is the strongest authority in favour of the view that the subsequent fact, but no more, is admissible. This is so partly because of its modernity and partly because the activities of the Scottish courts in the general area of illegally and unfairly obtained evidence have produced more satisfactory results than those of the English and other common law courts. It was followed by the Supreme Court of Queensland (Gibbs, J.) in *R.* v. *Beere,* [1965] Qd. R. 370.

As Lord Cooper, L.J.-G. points out, the admission of the subsequent fact and nothing more will sometimes incriminate the accused and sometimes not. It did not in *Chalmers,* because there was no connexion between the accused and the place where the purse was discovered; similarly *Berriman.* It did in *Warickshall;* the discovery of stolen property concealed in the accused's bed calls for an explanation. The fortuitous operation of the doctrine does not make it very useful for the prosecution.

Question

Is the *Warickshall* doctrine compatible with the rationale of the modern confession rule?

B. Admission of the fact discovered, and that its discovery was a consequence of something the accused said

Nares, J. indicated in *Warickshall* that not all contemporary judges agreed with the doctrine there stated. In 1803 East was accordingly able to cite two

CME—H

unreported cases, *R. v. Grant* (1801) and *R. v. Hodge* (1794), for his view that it was "proper" to leave to the jury "the fact of the witness having been directed by the prisoner where to find the goods, and his having found them accordingly; but not the acknowledgment of the prisoner's having stolen or put them there, which is to be collected or not from all the circumstances of the case; and this is now the more common practice" (2 *Pleas of the Crown* 658).

Criminal Law Revision Committee: 11th Report
1972 Cmnd. 4991. Para. 69

We are opposed to any general provision for admissibility of evidence of statements contained in a confession on the ground that the truth of the statement is confirmed by the discovery of facts as a result of it. For this would mean that the judge, for the purpose of ruling on admissibility, would have to decide whether the confession, or the part in question, seemed to him likely to be true; and even though the judge's opinion would be provisional and would not be binding on the jury, it would probably be difficult for the jury not to be impressed by it. . . . [H]owever . . . [t]he majority would allow evidence to be given that the discovery of the fact in question was made "as a result of" a statement made by the accused, even though this statement was inadmissible. Whether this is allowed at present is not clear. The cases are in conflict. . . . [W]e believe that in practice it is common for the witness reporting the discovery to say that he made it "as a result of" something which the accused said. The majority think it reasonable to allow this. A minority dissent on the ground that it is wrong that the jury should be informed indirectly of something which it is thought that the interests of justice require that they should not be informed directly.

Wigmore: Treatise on the Anglo-American System of Evidence in Trials at Common Law
3rd Edn. Para. 858

No principle appears ever to have been offered to justify or explain this [position]. . . . There is, however, apparently an explanation for it. In the case of a confession of stealing goods and their subsequent discovery as described (almost the only situation over which this question arises), there is just one hypothesis on which the jury may stop short of believing the confession after this confirmation, namely, the accused may know of the stealing and of the place of hiding, but he may still *not* be the thief. Now we may determine to ignore the improbability of the latter consequence, but we cannot ignore the former. That his confession of stealing is true may be hard to avoid, but that he knew where the stolen goods were . . . is impossible to avoid. We shall admit, then, what as rational beings we are obliged to admit, but we shall stubbornly draw the line there; that seems to be the rationale of the above distinction. The result is, that so far as the discovery shows that the person knew where the stolen goods were, we are to hear about it, but we are to hear nothing more.

Now, in thus accepting whatever bears on his knowledge, the line becomes hard to draw. There may be several places to draw it. (1) The law may admit merely the fact that the discovery was made, and that it was made in consequence of a statement by that person. Or (2) it may go further and admit the details of the accused's conduct in that he went to the place and pointed out the goods, etc. Or (3) it may go still further and admit the words of his statement describing the property and the place, exhibiting as they do a detailed knowledge on his part, and yet falling short of a confession of the stealing. All these show knowledge and only knowledge.

The distinction, then, while it is artificial and against common sense, has at least a certain intelligibility beneath it.

[But Wigmore had earlier (para. 857) stated his view that it was false.] [A] confirmation on material points produces ample persuasion of the trustworthiness of the whole. It can hardly be supposed that at certain parts the possible fiction stopped and the truth began, and that by a marvellous coincidence the truthful parts are exactly those which a subsequent search (more or less controlled by chance) happened to confirm. . . . If we are to cease distrusting any part, we should cease distrusting all.

Comment

The acceptance of this position by the English Criminal Law Revision Committee means that future English courts are likely to adopt it in spite of a paucity of authority. Its drawbacks are that it undercuts the confession rule so far as that rule seeks to control police misconduct, and, as Wigmore points out, that problems may arise in determining how much should be admitted apart from the consequential fact.

C. Admission of the fact discovered together with as much of the confession as relates strictly to it

The basis for this position is said to be that "the reason of rejecting extorted confessions is the apprehension that the prisoner may have been thereby induced to say what is false; but the fact discovered shows that so much of the confession as immediately relates to it is true" (R. v. *Butcher* (1798, 1 Leach 265, n.).

R. v. Gould

(1840), 9 C. & P. 364

The accused was charged with burglary. He was improperly induced to confess and as a result a lantern was found by a policeman in a certain pond. "Tindal, C.J. and Parke, B. were both of the opinion that the words used by the prisoner, with reference to the thing found, might be given in evidence, and the policeman accordingly stated that the prisoner told him that he had thrown a lantern into a pond in Pocock's Fields. The other parts of the statement were not given in evidence."

Comment

There is little English authority for this position, which is sometimes understandably confused with the second possible position and probably has the same effect in practice. It has been adopted in Canada: R. v. St. *Lawrence*, [1949] O.R. 215, approved by the Supreme Court of Canada in R. v. *Wray* (1970), 11 D.L.R. (3d) 673. There are also doubts as to the correct formulation; sometimes the question is said to be whether those parts of the confession confirmed by the subsequent facts are admissible. But the admission of Gould's statement that he had thrown the lantern into the pond cannot be justified on the ground that the finding of the lantern there verified it. If the test depends on what "strictly relates" to the fact discovered, there will be serious problems of degree in interpreting the quoted words.

Question

In R. v. *Griffin* (1809), Russ. & Ry. 151 the accused was improperly induced to confess and handed over a £5 Reading bank note, saying that it was one of the notes stolen from the prosecutor. The prosecutor could not identify the note except that its sum and drawee corresponded with those of one of the stolen notes. A majority of the judges held that it was right to admit the prisoner's description of the note as well as the fact of delivery. In *R. v. Jones* (1809), Russ. & Ry. 152 the accused gave the prosecutor 11s. 6½d., saying that it was all he had left of the stolen money. Neither the surrender of the money nor the accompanying statement was admitted. Can you reconcile these decisions, which were reached almost simultaneously by the same judges?

D. Admission of the fact discovered and the entire confession

R. v. Garbett
(1847), 2 Car. & Kir. 474

Martin [counsel for the prosecution]: I submit that a statement made by a person is always evidence against him, except in two cases, [the second being that of a] statement made by a person under a charge of crime, where an inducement is held out to him by some person in authority; and the latter is rejected on the ground that it may not be founded in truth. . . . And even in those cases the confession of a theft is received if the property can be found in consequence.

LORD DENMAN, C.J.: Because it leads to the inference that the party was not accusing himself falsely.

Comment

The English authority for this view is not strong, consisting as it does of Lord Denman, C.J.'s *sub silentio* approval in argument of a suggestion by counsel in a case not concerned with confessions but with the privilege against self-incrimination. The argument in favour of admission is that stated by Lord Denman, C.J. (and see the passage from Wigmore, para. 857, quoted p. 227, *ante*). The argument against is that an induced confession may contain both true and false statements, and the confirmation of the true does not confirm the false.

E. Exclusion of the whole confession and of all facts discovered in consequence of it

R. v. Barker
[1941] 2 K.B. 381; [1941] 3 All E.R. 33, C.C.A.

The accused was charged with taxation offences. A Ministerial statement from Hansard was read to him and as a result he was in effect promised that if he made full disclosure of past frauds no criminal proceedings would be instituted. The accused then produced fraudulent documents on the basis of which he was convicted. The Court of Criminal Appeal allowed his appeal.

TUCKER, J.: Mr. Burt has referred the court to *R. v. Cason* (1935), 14 A.T.C. 471 in which Judge Dodson, when sitting at the Central Criminal Court as commissioner, ruled that a document which had been brought into existence as the result of the reading to the defendant of this extract from Hansard was not admissible in evidence on the ground that it was a confession or a statement which had been made as the result of an inducement. In the present case Mr. Byrne, on behalf of the Crown, says that the ledgers and working papers produced by Robinson and the appellant should be distinguished from the document which Judge Dodson decided was not admissible because they were not brought into existence as the result of a promise or a threat, if there be a promise or threat contained in this extract from Hansard, but at all times had been in existence and were part and parcel of the method whereby the fraud had been committed. He contended that they could be given in evidence although they were produced by the appellant and Robinson as the result of having the extract from Hansard read to them. He cited a passage setting out what he submitted was the law on this matter as summarized in Archbold's *Criminal Pleading, Evidence and Practice,* 30th Edn., p. 402: "Although a confession for the above or any other reasons may not be receivable in evidence, yet any discovery that takes place in consequence of such confession, or any act done by the defendant, if it is confirmed by the finding of the property, will be admitted." The court accepts that statement of the law and does not desire to question that there may be cases in which evidence can be given of facts the existence of which have come to the knowledge of the police as the result of an inadmissible confession. But in the present case the promise or inducement which was implied in this extract from Hansard expressly related to the production of business books and records, and the court is of opinion that if, as a result of a promise, inducement or threat, such books and documents are produced by the person or persons to whom the promise or inducement is held out, or the threat made, those documents stand on precisely the same footing as an oral or a written confession which is brought into existence as the result of such a promise, inducement or threat.

R. v. Leatham
(1861), 8 Cox C.C. 498

The Court of Queen's Bench held that a document referred to by the defendant in an enquiry by Commissioners under the Corrupt Practices Act was admissible in evidence against him even though the Act provided that testimony before the Commissioners should not be admissible.

CROMPTON, J.: Suppose by threats and promises a confession of murder obtained, which would not be admissible, but you also obtain a clue to a place where a written confession may be found, or where the body of a person murdered is secreted; could not that latter evidence be made use of because the first clue to it came from the murderer? It matters not how you get it; if you steal it even, it would be admissible in evidence.

I do not at all see why we should suppose that the Legislature, when they could so easily have said that no documents shall be used against him, as to which any clue has arisen on examination before the Commissioners, would not have said that. It would have been a most inconvenient thing if the Legislature had said so, because . . . you would have to enquire in every case, was this clue furnished by something the defendant said in his examination. He perhaps dropped some observation which led the Commissioners to institute another inquiry; and by sending officers to this place or that, something then comes out which is evidence against him; it would, in short, be the widest inquiry at *nisi prius* that could be conceived.

Gotlieb: Confirmation by Subsequent Facts
72 L.Q.R. 209, at pp. 222-3

[I]t may be argued that where a confession is improperly obtained, it would always be unfair to allow in evidence matters discovered in consequence, but in *Barker's* case, it may be that in view of the fact that the inducement was made specifically to get the evidence, and in view of the breach of faith involved in later using that evidence, the unfairness to the accused would have been especially great if the evidence were admitted. Thus there is in the case the clear implication that confessions are not excluded exclusively on grounds of credibility, and it is possible that the importance of the decision is not limited to the facts of the case alone. It appears to involve an application of a special principle of non-admissibility of evidence where the facts of the case are such that it would be specially unfair to receive the evidence. It was not so much that the documents in *Barker's* case were inadmissible, as that they ought not, on the facts of the case, to have been admitted.

Comment

Barker is the only English authority for this position, though it is probably coming to be the law in America by analogy with the exclusion of evidence illegally obtained in violation of the Fourth Amendment (search and seizure): see, e.g., *People v. Ditson* (1962), 369 P. 2d 714. Few cases in the English law of evidence are so generally disapproved. It is odd to treat existing documents as equivalent to confessions, for there can be no question of their falsity. The discussion of earlier authority, all of which is against the decision, is quite inadequate; in *Leathem* a written statement of guilt made before the confession and discovered through it was said to be admissible. *Cason*, apparently relied on by the Court, did not concern documents predating the inducement, but documents brought into existence as a result of it. Gotlieb's approach probably represents the only way the decision can be defended within the current legal framework. As a matter of policy, the decision does avoid any conflict with the confession rule, and its merits essentially depend on how important it is thought controlling the police by the law of evidence is: this matter is more fully discussed below. It should be remembered, however, that the more widely the idea of "*consequential* evidence" is treated, the worse off the police will be. As the Criminal Law Revision Committee remark, "[i]t would be too great an interference with justice to prevent the police from using any 'leads' obtained from an inadmissible confession. For example, this would mean that, if the police have been led to arrest other persons involved in the crime who were named in the confession, no evidence could be given against these other persons, even though perhaps the police would eventually have discovered their guilt by other means" (para. 68).

Further reading

Cowen and Carter, Chap. 2; Gotlieb, 72 L.Q.R. 209.

II IMPROPERLY OBTAINED EVIDENCE IN GENERAL

So much for evidence obtained by an induced confession. What about other kinds of improperly obtained evidence? Is evidence obtained by a crime, tort, breach of contract or confidence, invasion of privacy, trick or agent provocateur admissible? The answer of the common law courts outside America is that such evidence is admissible but may be excluded in the discretion of the Court. The law is theoretically very similar in Scotland, but in practice the Scottish courts, whose decisions have been very influential, are more ready to exercise their discretion in favour of exclusion and to some extent they have worked out consistent principles to govern the discretion. As the following cases illustrate, the same cannot be said of other jurisdictions.

A. The Commonwealth

Lawrie v. Muir
1950 S.L.T. 37

The defendant was convicted of using milk bottles without the consent of the true owners. The Scottish Milk Bottle Exchange Ltd. carried on the business of collecting and restoring bottles to their true owners. It was approved by the Scottish Milk Marketing Board; all contracts between the Board and producers and distributors of milk provided that the company's inspectors might inspect the premises of any producer or distributor in contractual relations with the Board to examine bottles in their possession. Two inspectors displayed their warrant cards to the defendant who was entitled to refuse them permission to inspect because she was not in contractual relations with the Board. But she did not do so and the inspectors found the bottles. The High Court of Justiciary held that the evidence had been wrongly admitted.

Lord Cooper, L.J.-G.: From the standpoint of principle it seems to me that the law must strive to reconcile two highly important interests which are liable to come into conflict—(*a*) the interest of the citizen to be protected from illegal or irregular invasions of his liberties by the authorities, and (*b*) the interest of the State to secure that evidence bearing upon the commission of crime and necessary to enable justice to be done shall not be withheld from courts of law on any merely formal or technical ground. Neither of these objects can be insisted upon to the uttermost. The protection of the citizen is primarily protection for the innocent citizen against unwarranted, wrongful and perhaps high-handed interference, and the common sanction is an action of damages. The protection is not intended as a protection for the guilty citizen against the efforts of the public prosecutor to vindicate the law. On the other hand, the interest of the State cannot be magnified to the point of causing all the safeguards for the protection of the citizen to vanish, and of offering a positive inducement to the authorities to proceed by irregular methods. It is obvious that excessively rigid rules as to the exclusion of evidence bearing upon the commission of a crime might conceivably operate to the detriment and not the advantage of the accused, and might even lead to the conviction of the innocent; and extreme cases can easily be figured in which the exclusion of a vital piece of evidence from the knowledge of a jury because of some technical flaw in the conduct of the police would be an outrage upon common sense and a defiance of elementary justice. For these reasons . . . I adopt as a first approximation to the true rule the statement of Lord Justice Clerk Aitchison [in *H.M. Advocate* v. *M'Guigan* 1936 J.C. 16] that "an irregularity in the obtaining of evidence does not *necessarily* make that evidence inadmissible".

. . . Lord Aitchison seems to me to have indicated that there was in his view no absolute rule and that the question was one of circumstances. I respectfully agree. It would greatly facilitate the task of judges were it possible to imprison the principle within the framework of a simple and unqualified maxim, but I do not think that it is feasible to do so. . . . Irregularities require to be excused, and infringements of the formalities of the law in relation to these matters are not lightly to be condoned. Whether any given irregularity ought to be excused depends upon the nature of the irregularity and the circumstances under which it was committed. In particular, the case may bring into play the discretionary principle of fairness to the accused which has been developed so fully in our law in relation to the admission in evidence of confessions or admissions by a person suspected or charged with a crime. That principle would obviously require consideration in any case in which the departure from the strict procedure had been adopted deliberately with a view to securing the admission of evidence obtained by an unfair trick. Again, there are many statutory offences in relation to which Parliament has prescribed in detail in the interests of fairness a special procedure to be followed in obtaining evidence; and in such cases . . . it is very easy to see why a departure from the strict rules has often been held to be fatal to the prosecution's case. On the other hand, to take an extreme instance figured in argument, it would usually be wrong to exclude some highly incriminating production in a murder trial merely because it was found by a police officer in the course of a search authorized for a different purpose or before a proper warrant had been obtained.

. . . I am unable to accept the suggestion that a distinction should be drawn between the statutory offence, the *malum prohibitum,* and the common law crime, the *malum in se,* for the interests of the State are as much involved in offences against penal statutes as in offences against the common law, and the former category has greatly expanded in recent times. . . . It is specially to be noted that the two inspectors who in this instance exceeded their authority were not police officers enjoying a large residuum of common law discretionary powers, but the employees of a limited company acting in association with the Milk Marketing Board, whose only powers are derived from contracts between the Board and certain milk producers and distributors, of whom the appellant is not one. Though the matter is narrow I am inclined to regard this last point as sufficient to tilt the balance against the prosecution, upon the view that persons in the special position of these inspectors ought to know the precise limits of their authority and should be held to exceed these limits at their peril. It is found that the inspectors acted in good faith, but it is incontrovertible that they obtained the assent of the appellant to the search of her shop by means of a positive misrepresentation made to her.

[Cf. R. v. *Matthews and Ford*, [1972] V.R. 3.]

M'Govern v. H.M. Advocate
1950 S.L.T. 133

The accused was suspected of blowing open a safe with explosives. Before arresting and charging him the police scraped his fingernails for traces of explosives, which chemical analysis subsequently revealed to be present. This conduct amounted to assault, since there was no right to search without warrant before arrest. The High Court of Justiciary held that the evidence had been wrongly admitted.

LORD COOPER, L.J.-G.: [I]rregularities of this kind always require to be "excused" or condoned, if they can be excused or condoned, whether by the existence of urgency, the relative triviality of the irregularity or other circumstances. This is not a case where I feel disposed to "excuse" the conduct of the police. The proper procedure for search of the appellant's house by obtaining a search warrant was duly followed out, and it would have been very simple for the police to have adopted the appropriate procedure in relation to a search of his person. Why they did not do so, we do not yet know. Exactly the same information was available to them when they scraped the appellant's fingernails as when they charged and apprehended him shortly afterwards; and, if the charge and apprehension were justified, these should have preceded and not followed the examination of his person.

. . . [T]here is no option but to quash this conviction because, unless the principles under which police investigations are carried out are adhered to with reasonable strictness, the anchor of the entire system for the protection of the public will very soon begin to drag.

Fairley v. Fishmongers of London
1951 S.L.T. 54

An inspector employed by the respondents reported his opinion that the appellant was in unlawful possession of salmon in breach of the Salmon Fisheries (Scotland) Act 1868 to the Ministry of Food, who had a duty to investigate breaches of the salmon laws. A Ministry of Food official with an official warrant helped the respondent's inspector to search local cold stores, from one of which salmon owned by the appellant was removed by the respondent's inspector, who had no search warrant under the 1868 Act. The evidence was held by the High Court of Justiciary to have been rightly admitted.

LORD COOPER, L.J.-G.: The respondent's inspector could have applied for a search warrant . . . and I have little doubt that, if he had, he would have got one. He did not. Moreover, while the Ministry enforcement officer was, I think, entitled to enter the store in search of evidence bearing upon any contravention of the food regulations or of the Order dealing with salmon, he had no concern with infringements of the Salmon Fisheries (Scotland) Acts though it would have been quite in order for him to have reported to the proper authorities any evidence incidentally obtained by him and bearing upon such an infringement. It follows that the procedure whereby the incriminating evidence was obtained was not strictly in accordance with any statutory or other authority. On the other hand, . . .[i]n the words of finding, "The said inspectors acted in good faith, in a mistaken belief as to their powers and in an endeavour in the public interest to vindicate the law in relation to an offence which constituted a considerable evil and was difficult to detect". The approach to the Ministry of Food was not improper in view of their possible interest in the matter. I can find nothing to suggest that any departure from the strict procedure was deliberately adopted with a view to securing the admission of evidence obtained by an unfair trick. . . . [I]n the present instance the irregularity ought to be "excused". . . .

[Lords Carmont and Keith agreed.]

H.M. Advocate v. Turnbull
1951 S.L.T. 409

A warrant was granted to search for documents in the possession of the accused, an accountant. It was limited to documents relating to a particular client of the accused, but other documents were seized, and it was held that the latter were not admissible in evidence because they had been obtained by an illegal search or seizure. Lord Guthrie in the High Court of Justiciary excluded the evidence.

Lord Guthrie: In the present case there were, first, no circumstances of urgency. Second, the retention and use over a period of six months of the documents bearing to relate [sic] to other matters than that mentioned in the petition show that the actions complained of were deliberate. The police officers did not accidentally stumble upon evidence of a plainly incriminating character in the course of a search for a different purpose. If the documents are incriminating, their incriminating character is only exposed by careful consideration of their contents. Third, if information was in the hands of the criminal authorities implicating the accused in other crimes, these could have been mentioned in the petition containing the warrant under which the search was authorized. If they had no such information, the examination of private papers in the hope of finding incriminating material was interference with the rights of a citizen. Therefore to hold that evidence so obtained was admissible would, as I have said, tend to nullify the protection afforded to a citizen by the requirements of a magistrate's warrant, and would offer a positive inducement to the authorities to proceed by irregular methods. Fourth, when I consider the matter in the light of the principle of fairness to the accused, it appears to me that the evidence so irregularly and deliberately obtained is intended to be the basis of a comparison between the figures actually submitted to the Inspector of Taxes and the information in the possession of the accused. If such important evidence upon a number of charges is tainted by the method by which it was deliberately secured, I am of opinion that a fair trial upon these charges is rendered impossible.

Note

A striking feature of this case was that it could be seen at once that the retention of the documents was not justified by the warrant, but it required six months' examination to discover fraudulent matter in them. The illegality on the officers' part was thus deliberate.

Kuruma, Son of Kaniu v. R.

[1955] A.C. 197; [1955] 1 All E.R. 236, P.C.

The accused, a Kenyan African, while travelling to his reserve, passed along a road on which he knew there would be a road block. He could have gone by another route on which there was no road block. He was stopped and searched illegally in that the searchers were not of the rank of assistant inspector or above. The police alleged that they found two rounds of ammunition and a pocket knife. The accused was convicted of unlawful possession of ammunition, and appealed to the Privy Council, who held the evidence admissible.

LORD GODDARD: It is only right to say that the two rounds of ammunition differed from those which the police officers then had as part of their equipment. The prisoner all along denied that he was carrying these rounds, and at the trial also denied that he had a pocket knife on him. The police said they had returned the knife to him after he was in custody. No explanation was given of this remarkable action on their part, nor was the knife produced at the trial nor any reason given for its absence. It is also to be observed that three other persons, two police officers and one civilian, were said to have been present when the prisoner was searched, one of them indeed was said to have actually picked up the two rounds after they had fallen from the prisoner's shorts. Their Lordships think it was most unfortunate, considering the grave character of the offence charged, which carries a capital penalty, that these important witnesses were not called by the prosecution: it was not suggested that they were not available. The assessors were all in favour of an acquittal, but the magistrate overruled them and convicted the appellant. . . .

In their Lordships' opinion the test to be applied in considering whether evidence is admissible is whether it is relevant to the matters in issue. If it is, it is admissible and the court is not concerned with how the evidence was obtained. While this proposition may not have been stated in so many words in any English case there are decisions which support it, and in their Lordships' opinion it is plainly right in principle. In R. v. *Leatham* (1861), 8 Cox C.C. 498, an information for penalties under the Corrupt Practices Act, objection was taken to the production of a letter written by the defendant because its existence only became known by answers he had given to the commissioners who held the inquiry under the Act, which provided that answers before that tribunal should not be admissible in evidence against him. The Court of Queen's Bench held that though his answers could not be used against the defendant, yet if a clue was thereby given to other evidence, in that case the letter, which would prove the case it was admissible. Crompton, J. said: [at p. 501] "It matters not how you get it; if you steal it even, it would be admissible." *Lloyd* v. *Mostyn* (1842), 10 M. & W. 478 was an action on a bond. The person in whose possession it was objected to produce it on the ground of privilege. The plaintiff's attorney, however, had got a copy of it and notice to produce the original being proved the court admitted the copy as secondary evidence. To the same effect was *Calcraft* v. *Guest*, [1898] 1 Q.B. 759; [1895–9] All E.R. Rep. 346. There can be no difference in principle for this purpose between a civil and a criminal case. No doubt in a criminal case the judge always has a discretion to disallow evidence if the strict rules of admissibility would operate unfairly against an accused. This was emphasized in the case before this Board of *Noor Mohamed* v. R. [1949] A.C. 182; [1949] 1 All E.R. 365, P.C. and in the recent case in the House of Lords, *Harris* v. *Director of Public Prosecutions*, [1952] A.C. 694, H.L.; [1952] 1 All E.R. 1044. If, for instance, some admission of some piece of evidence, e.g., a document, had been obtained from a defendant by a trick, no doubt the judge might properly rule it out. It was this discretion that lay at the root of the ruling of Lord Guthrie in *H.M. Advocate* v. *Turnbull* 1951 J.C. 96. The other cases from Scotland to which their Lordships' attention was drawn, *Rattray* v. *Rattray* (1897), 25 R. (Ct. of Sess.) 315, *Lawrie* v. *Muir* 1950 J.C. 19 and *Fairley* v. *Fishmongers of London* 1951 J.C. 14, all support the view that if the evidence is relevant it is admissible and the court is not concerned with how it is obtained. No doubt their Lordships in the Court of Justiciary appear at least to some extent to consider the question from the point of view whether the alleged illegality in the obtaining of the evidence could properly be excused, and it is true that Horridge, J. in *Elias* v. *Pasmore*, [1934] 2 K.B. 164; [1934] All E.R. Rep. 380; used that expression. It is to be observed, however, that what the judge was there concerned with was an action of trespass, and he held that the trespass was excused. In their Lordships' opinion, when it is a question of the admission of evidence strictly it is not whether the method by which it was obtained is tortious but excusable but whether what has been obtained is relevant to the issue being tried. Their Lordships are not now concerned with whether an action for assault would lie against the police officers and express no opinion on that point. Certain decisions of the Supreme Court of the United States of America were also cited in argument. Their Lordships do not think it necessary to examine them in detail. Suffice it to say that there appears to be considerable difference of opinion among the judges both in the State and Federal courts as to whether or not the rejection of evidence obtained by illegal means depends on certain articles in the American Constitution. At any rate, in *Olmstead* v. *United States* (1928), 277 U.S. 438 the majority of the Supreme Court were clearly of the opinion that the common law did not reject relevant evidence on that ground. It is right, however, that it should be stated that the rule with regard to the admission of confessions, whether it be regarded as an exception to the general rule or not, is a rule of law which their Lordships are not qualifying in any degree whatsoever. The rule is that a confession can only be admitted if it is voluntary, and therefore one obtained by threats or promises held out by a person in authority is not to be admitted. It is only necessary to refer to *R.* v. *Thompson*, [1893] 2 Q.B. 12; [1891–4] All E.R. Rep. 376 where the law was fully reviewed by the Court for Crown Cases Reserved.

As they announced at the conclusion of the arguments, their Lordships have no doubt that the evidence to which objection has been taken was properly admitted.

Question

Dixon, C.J. once uttered the following dictum on the admissibility of improperly obtained evidence: "I do not think that in this or any other jurisdiction the question has been put at rest by *Kuruma*" (*Wendo* v. *R.* (1963), 109 C.L.R. 559, at p. 562). Do you agree?

H.M. Advocate v. Hepper
1958 J.C. 39

Police officers investigating a particular offence called at the accused's house and were given permission by him to search it. They removed an attaché case unconnected with the matter being investigated but relevant to a later charge of theft. Lord Guthrie in the High Court of Justiciary held the evidence admissible.

LORD GUTHRIE: [T]he problem is always to reconcile the interest of society in the detection of crime with the requirement of fairness to an accused person. . . . In *Turnbull* [p. 233, *ante*] at p. 103, I distinguished that case, in which I excluded evidence as to documents taken possession of by police officers searching the accused's premises under a search warrant which clearly did not cover these documents, from a case in which police officers accidentally stumbled upon evidence of a plainly incriminating character in the course of a search for a different purpose. . . . It may be that the article which the police officers stumbled upon in their search of the accused's house was not an article of a plainly incriminating character, but it was at least an article of a very suspicious character, since it was an attaché case which contained within it the name and address of another person. In the circumstances, I do not think that the police officers acted in any way improperly in taking away that article in order to make further inquiries about it. If they had not done so, it might have disappeared. . . . But even if it cannot be put so highly, and if it be thought that their action was irregular, I am still of opinion that the evidence, even if irregularly obtained, is admissible in view of the interest of society in the detection of crime.

H.M. Advocate v. M'Kay
1961 J.C. 47

An objection was made to the admission at a trial in Scotland of documents seized during a search of the accused's house in Dublin by the Dublin police under an Eire warrant; the documents seized were not in the accused's name. Lord Wheatley in the High Court of Justiciary admitted the evidence.

LORD WHEATLEY: [E]ven if . . . there was irregularity here, the two tests of fairness and urgency fall to be applied. It is suggested that, since the warrant to search merely referred to authority to search for cash to the amount of £35,000, it would be unfair to the accused to allow evidence of other documents recovered to be admitted on the authority of such a warrant, because, while the accused and his wife had taken no objection to a search for money under that warrant, that did not mean that they might not have taken objection to a search for other documents. . . . [B]ut it would seem reasonable to suppose that they accepted [the warrant] as authority to search the house for money or for some trace of it.

[The court therefore held that there was no unfairness. The matter was urgent since the documents might be lost or deliberately destroyed, the accused had escaped from Scottish prison custody pending the charge and had been living under a false name in Eire. The documents were accordingly admitted.]

R. v. Payne
[1963] 1 All E.R. 848, C.C.A.

LORD PARKER, C.J.: This appellant was convicted on 27 July 1962, at London Sessions of driving a car whilst unfit through drink and of being in charge of a car while unfit. . . . It is against those two convictions that he now appeals. . . .

The short point here is almost identical with the point which was taken in the case of R. v. *Court*, [1962] Crim. L.R. 697, C.C.A. which came before this court on the very day when London Sessions were dealing with the present appellant, namely, 27 July 1962. In both R. v. *Court* and this case the appellants were asked when they went to the police station whether they were willing to be examined by a doctor, and it was made clear to them in each case that the purpose of that was that the doctor should see whether the appellant was suffering from any illness or disability. In each case the respective appellant was told that it was no part of the doctor's duty to examine him in order to give an opinion as to his unfitness to drive. Those statements to the appellants were made at that time pursuant to a definite policy, which was that the doctor called would not examine a defendant in order to ascertain whether he was unfit to drive, but would examine him merely in order to see whether he was suffering from any other illness or physical disability and in particular whether he was fit to leave the police station.

In the present case the doctor was a Dr. Henry. He was in fact called as a witness for the prosecution and, having been called he proceeded to give evidence and strong evidence, in regard to the extent to which the appellant was under the influence of drink. The chairman said in his summing-up:

"At the end the doctor came to the conclusion, having examined him very thoroughly, you may think—he did not complete it for about half an hour—that the accused was under the influence of drink to such an extent as to be unfit to have proper control of a car."

In R. v. *Court*, this court pointed out that while such evidence from the doctor in circumstances such as these was clearly admissible, nevertheless the chairman in the exercise of his discretion ought to have refused to allow that evidence to be given on the basis that if the accused realized that the doctor would give evidence on that matter he might refuse to subject himself to examination.

The present case is, in the opinion of this court, on all fours with R. v. *Court*, and in those circumstances the court is constrained to quash the convictions on counts one and three, and the order for disqualification.

R. v. Murphy
[1965] N.I. 138

Certain police officers acted as agents provocateurs in posing as I.R.A. agents and thus induced the accused to disclose information useful to an enemy, contrary to s. 60 (1) of the Army Act 1955. The Court-Martial Appeal Court held the evidence admissible.

LORD MACDERMOTT, L.C.J.: In English law the general rule seems to be that evidence induced by a trick or procured by some wrongful or illegal course of conduct is not, if relevant, inadmissible in point of law. . . . [T]he proposition that . . . [i]n a criminal trial the court has a discretion to reject admissible evidence which might operate unfairly against the accused . . . also is established law. . . . Is the discretion spent once it has been exercised against the accused and the evidence has been admitted? We are not aware of any authority on the question, but on general principles we are of opinion that the court's discretionary powers are not necessarily at an end when the relevant evidence has been admitted. Sometimes the true bearing of evidence said to operate unfairly against an accused person may only appear clearly to do so when seen in the light of evidence adduced at a later stage of the trial and after the material objected to has become part of the record. To say that it is then too late to reconsider the objection would, we think, be to run the risk of letting the technicalities of the situation prevail over the requirements of justice. . . . We are, therefore, of opinion that the discretion under discussion may, in certain circumstances, properly be the subject of reconsideration.

. . . [W]hat Lord Goddard said in *Brannan* v. *Peek*, [1948] 1 K.B. 68; [1947] 2 All E.R. 572 [criticising police use of agents provocateurs] does not mean, and was not intended to mean, that evidence produced by police participation in an offence must, because of its nature, be ruled out of account. Accordingly, even if the police witnesses in this case could be considered as participating in the offence charged, so as to be guilty of it, we would not regard Lord Goddard's observations as determining how the court-martial should have acted in the exercise of its discretion.

. . . [There is] no ground for saying that any evidence obtained by any false representation or trick is to be regarded as oppressive and left out of consideration. Detection by deception is a form of police procedure to be directed and used sparingly and with circumspection; but as a method it is as old as the constable in plain clothes and, regrettable though the fact may be, the day has not yet come when it would be safe to say that law and order could always be enforced and the public safety protected without occasional resort to it. We find that conclusion hard to avoid on any survey of the preventive and enforcement functions of the police but it is enough to point to the salient facts of the present appeal. The appellant was beyond all doubt a serious security risk; this was revealed by the trick or misrepresentation practised by the police as already described; and no other way of obtaining this revelation has been demonstrated or suggested. . . .

. . . Unfairness in this context cannot be closely defined. But it must be judged of in the light of all the material facts and findings and all the surrounding circumstances. The position of the accused, the nature of the investigation, and the gravity or otherwise of the suspected offence, may all be relevant. That is not to say that the standard of fairness must bear some sort of inverse proportion to the extent to which the public interest may be involved, but different offences may pose different problems for the police and justify different methods. . . . We think . . . that with no element of duress or bribery or other form of temptation present (as was the case) it would have been difficult for the court-martial to decide otherwise than it did.

Comment

The police conduct in this case is known as entrapment: see Heydon, [1973] Cambridge L.J. 268. Similar conduct led to evidence being excluded in *R. v. Foulder*, [1973] Crim. L.R. 45 and *R. v. Burnett and Lee* [1973] Crim. L.R. 748; cf. *Sneddon v. Stevenson;* [1967] 2 All E.R. 1277; [1967] 1 W.L.R. 1051; *R. v. McEvilly*, [1974] Crim. L.R. 239, C.A.

People v. O'Brien
[1965] I.R. 142

Premises to be searched were inadvertently misdescribed in the warrant as "118 Cashel Road, Crumlin" instead of "118 Captain's Road, Crumlin". The search led to the discovery of stolen goods which were the subject of the charge, but it was technically a trespass in consequence of the misaddressing. The evidence was held by the Eire Supreme Court to have been correctly admitted.

KINGSMILL MOORE, J. (with whom LAVERY and BUDD, JJ. agreed): Three answers are possible. First, that if evidence is relevant it cannot be excluded on the ground that it was obtained as a result of illegal action: second, that if it was obtained as a result of illegal action it is never admissible: third, that where it was obtained by illegal action it is a matter for the trial judge to decide, in his discretion, whether to admit it or not, subject, in cases where the evidence has been admitted, to review by an appellate court.

It seems to me that neither the first nor the second answer is sustainable. The first answer represents the earlier portion of Lord Goddard's judgment in *Kuruma's Case*, [1955] A.C. 197; [1955] 1 All E.R. 236, P.C. but even Lord Goddard found it necessary to allow exceptions to the rule, namely where the strict rules of admissibility would operate unfairly against the accused, instancing the obtaining of a document by a trick. Courts in both England and Ireland have frequently refused to admit evidence which was undoubtedly relevant where the probative value of the evidence would be slight and its prejudicial effect would be great. . . . Moreover, the Attorney-General has refused to argue for this rule in its unqualified form, conceding that evidence obtained by methods of gross personal violence or other methods offending against the essential dignity of the human person should not be received. . . .

The second answer would open up equal difficulties. The excusionary rule laid down in *Weeks* v. *U.S.*, (1914), 232 U.S. 383 was not accepted in many of the State courts. An absolute exclusionary rule prevents the admission of relevant and vital facts where unintentional or trivial illegalities have been committed in the course of ascertaining them. Fairness does not require such a rule and common sense rejects it.

Some intermediate solution must be found. . . . [I]n every case a determination has to be made by the trial judge as to whether the public interest is best served by the admission or by the exclusion of evidence of facts ascertained as a result of, and by means of, illegal actions, and that the answer to the question depends on a consideration of all the circumstances. On the one hand, the nature and extent of the illegality have to be taken into account. Was the illegal action intentional or unintentional, and, if intentional, was it the result of an *ad hoc* decision or does it represent a settled or deliberate policy? Was the illegality one of a trivial or technical nature or was it a serious invasion of important rights the recurrence of which would involve a real danger to necessary freedoms? Were there circumstances of urgency or emergency which provide some excuse for the action? Lord Goddard in *Kuruma's Case*, [1955] A.C. 197; [1955] 1 All E.R. 236, P.C. mentions as a ground for excluding relevant evidence that it had been obtained by a 'trick' and the Lord Justice-General in *Lawrie's Case* 1950 S.L.T. 37 refers to an 'unfair trick'. These seem to me to be more dubious grounds for exclusion. The police in the investigation of crime are not bound to show their hand too openly, provided they act legally. I am disposed to lay emphasis not so much on alleged fairness to the accused as on the public interest that the law should be observed even in the investigation of crime. The nature of the crime which is being investigated may also have to be taken into account. . . .

. . . [Here] the mistake was a pure oversight and it has not been shown that the oversight was noticed by anyone before the premises were searched. I can find no evidence of deliberate treachery, imposition, deceit or illegality; no policy to disregard the provisions of the Constitution or to conduct searches without a warrant; nothing except the existence of an unintentional and accidental illegality to set against the public interest of having crime detected and punished.

. . . I do not think that the necessity of a collateral inquiry is an adequate reason for establishing a general rule that all relevant evidence is admissible notwithstanding the illegality of the means used to prove it.

WALSH, J. (with whom O'DALAIGH, C.J. agreed): [I]n this country the practice in modern times has been to exclude every part of a confession which had been improperly obtained or induced irrespective of whether part of it at least could be shown by subsequent facts to have been true. It is also true to say that the practice has always been to admit in evidence facts, if they were relevant, which had been derived from the inadmissible statement or confession. . . . Every Judge in our Courts is bound to uphold the laws and while he cannot condone or even ignore illegalities which come to his notice, his first duty is to determine the issue before him in accordance with law and not to be diverted from it or permit it to be wrongly decided for the sake of frustrating a police illegality, or drawing public attention to it. . . .

In my judgment the law in this country has been that the evidence in this particular case is not rendered inadmissible and that there is no discretion to rule it out by reason only of the fact that it was obtained by means of an illegal as distinct from an unconstitutional seizure. . . . If a stage should be reached where this court was compelled to come to the conclusion that the ordinary law and police disciplinary measures have failed to secure compliance by the police with the law, then it would be preferable that a rule of absolute exclusion should be formulated rather than that every trial judge, when the occasion arises, should also be asked to adjudicate upon the question of whether the public good requires the accused should go free without full trial rather than that the police should be permitted the fruits of the success of their lawless ventures. Apart from the anomalies which might be produced by the many varying ways in which that discretion could be exercised by individual judges, the lamentable state of affairs which would call for such a change in the existing law of evidence would certainly justify absolute exclusion rather than a rule which might appear to lend itself to expediency rather than to principle.

[Art. 40, para. 5 of the Constitution provides: "The dwelling of every citizen is inviolable and shall not be forcibly entered save in accordance with law."] The courts in exercising the judicial powers of government of the state must recognize the paramount position of constitutional rights and must uphold the objection of an accused person to the admissibility at his trial of evidence obtained or procured by the state or its servants or agents as a result of a deliberate and conscious violation of the constitutional rights of the accused person where no extraordinary excusing circumstances exist, such as the imminent destruction of vital evidence or the need to rescue a victim in peril. A suspect has no constitutional right to destroy or dispose of evidence or to imperil the victim. I would also place in the excusable category evidence obtained by a search incidental to and contemporaneous with a lawful arrest although made without a valid search warrant. [Here the violation was not deliberate and hence the evidence was admissible.]

Hay *v*. H.M. Advocate
1968 S.L.T. 334

A warrant was granted to two police doctors to examine the accused's teeth to see if they corresponded with marks on the body of a murdered girl. The High Court of Justiciary held that even if the warrant was not legal, the medical evidence had been properly admitted because "there was in this case an element of urgency, since a visit to the dentist or an injury to the accused's teeth could have destroyed the evidence".

King *v*. R.
[1969] I A.C. 304; [1968] 2 All E.R. 610, P.C.

LORD HODSON: On January 11, Sergeant Isaacs, Acting Corporal Gayle, Acting Corporal Linton and other police went to 20 Ladd Lane to search for ganja under the Dangerous Drugs Law. The warrant was read by Sergeant Isaacs on the premises. It was read to a woman on the premises and not apparently directly to the appellant but the appellant and another man, who was also searched, were told that the police were there to carry out a search for ganja. Corporal Gayle searched the appellant and found the ganja in one of his trouser pockets and arrested him. The ganja was subsequently analysed by the government analyst and a certificate obtained on analysis put in evidence.

Although the search was not authorized by the Dangerous Drugs Law or the Constabulary Force Law there was no evidence that the appellant was wilfully misled by the police officers or any of them into thinking that there was such authorization.

Corporal Gayle admitted at the trial that he knew the warrant was to search the premises of Joyce Cohen and that it referred to the search of no-one else. He suspected that the appellant might have had ganja on him and did not offer him the opportunity of being searched in front of a justice of the peace although he knew of that right of a citizen.

It can therefore be said that he should have had the advantage of a search before a magistrate and the choice of this was never offered to him.

The substantial argument on behalf of the appellant was that, in the discretion of the court, the evidence produced as a result of the search, which was the whole of the evidence against him, ought, though admissible, to have been excluded as unfair to him.

Before referring to *Kuruma, Son of Kaniu* v. R., [1955] A.C. 197; [1955] I All E.R. 236, P.C. it is convenient to refer to some earlier decisions. *Jones* v. *Owens*, (1870) 34 J.P. 759 was a decision of the Divisional Court of the King's Bench Division. There a constable who had no right to search the person of the appellant did so and finding 25 young salmon in his pocket summoned him under the Salmon Fishery Acts for illegally having these in his possession. The appellant was convicted by the justices and on appeal it was said by Mellor, J. (at p. 760) (Lush, J. concurring):

"I think it would be a dangerous obstacle to the administration of justice if we were to hold, because evidence was obtained by illegal means it could not be used against a party charged with an offence. The justices rightly convicted the appellant."

This matter has been discussed in a number of Scottish cases which were reviewed in *Kuruma, Son of Kaniu* v. R., [1955] A.C. 197; [1955] I All E.R. 236, P.C.

It should be prefaced that in the Scottish cases to which reference will be made the court is directing its mind to the admissibility of evidence and in this connexion to a discretion to be exercised whether or not to admit evidence in cases where it could be said to be unfair to the accused to do so.

In the English cases the evidence under consideration is admissible in law (whether illegally obtained or not) and the exercise of discretion is called for in order to decide whether, even though admissible, it should be excluded in fairness to the accused. The same end is reached in both jurisdictions though by a slightly different route. . . .

The discretion in criminal cases to disallow evidence if the strict rules of admissibility would operate unfairly against an accused has been emphasized before this Board in *Noor Mohamed* v. R., [1949] A.C. 182; [1949] 1 All E.R. 365, P.C., and in the House of Lords in *Harris* v. *Director of Public Prosecutions*, [1952] A.C. 694; [1952] 1 All E.R. 1044, H.L. as was pointed out by Lord Goddard in *Kuruma, Son of Kaniu* v. R., [1955] A.C. 197; [1955] 1 All E.R. 236, P.C. . . .

Callis v. *Gunn*, [1964] 1 Q.B. 495; [1963] 3 All E.R. 677, D.C. is another case where *Kuruma, Son of Kaniu* v. R. was considered. It was held that evidence of finger prints was relevant and admissible. It had been excluded by magistrates and on appeal by the prosecutor, which was allowed, it was held by the Divisional Court that, while the court had an overriding discretion to disallow evidence if its admission would operate unfairly against a defendant, there were no representations by the police officer who took the finger prints and nothing to justify the justices in excluding the evidence.

Lord Parker, C.J. in referring to the discretion said (p. 502) that as he understood it,

". . . it would certainly be exercised by excluding the evidence if there was any suggestion of it having been obtained oppressively, by false representations, by a trick, by threats, by bribes, anything of that sort". . .

The appellant relied in support of his submission that the evidence illegally obtained against him should be excluded on the argument that it was obtained in violation of his constitutional rights, and reference was made to an Irish case of *The People* v. *O'Brien*, [1965] I.R. 142 where the point was discussed by the Supreme Court of Eire. The provision of the Jamaican Constitution scheduled to the Jamaica Order in Council, No. 1550 of 1962 (para. 19) gives protection to persons against search of persons or property without consent.

This constitutional right may or may not be enshrined in a written constitution, but it seems to their Lordships that it matters not whether it depends on such enshrinement or simply upon the common law as it would do in this country. In either event the discretion of the court must be exercised and has not been taken away by the declaration of the right in written form.

Having considered the evidence and the submissions advanced, their Lordships hold that there is no ground for interfering with the way in which the discretion has been exercised in this case.

This is not in their opinion a case in which evidence has been obtained by conduct of which the Crown ought not to take advantage. If they had thought otherwise they would have excluded the evidence even though tendered for the suppression of crime.

R. v. Ireland (No. I)
[1970] S.A.S.R. 416; [1970] A.L.R. 727

At the trial a photograph of the accused which a policeman had wrongly told him he had to have taken was admitted, as was evidence of a medical examination for which there was no statutory warrant. The full Court of the Supreme Court of South Australia held the photograph inadmissible.

BRAY, C.J. (holding that the photograph was inadmissible): I do not suggest that Detective Bator acted otherwise than in good faith; but in my view if the police not only make on an accused person a demand with which he is not bound to comply, but in addition give him to understand that compliance is legally necessary, and he complies believing that he has to comply, then this Court should discourage such conduct in the most effective way, namely, by rejecting the evidence.

ZELLING, J. (holding that both pieces of evidence were inadmissible): [I]n my respectful opinion not sufficient attention has been paid to the distinction between rules of the common law and rules laid down by statute. Where the rule said to be infringed is a rule of the common law or one arising out of case law (or in States and countries which have the Judges Rules out of the Judges Rules) then it seems to me that it is reasonable for the judges to mould their own law and their own rules in the light of public policy. Where a power to interfere with a man's civil rights and to obtain evidence thereby is specifically given by statute exercisable only on the performance of certain conditions precedent then to rule that that evidence may be obtained by methods other than those sanctioned by the statute and then successfully used in court is not simply to declare the law but to amend the law and this no judge has any right to do. In traditional language, it is *jus dare* and not *jus dicere*.

The other matter to which I wish to refer is the pious reference to the fact that the accused has after all an action for damages. Much good it would do him. As far as ordinary damages are concerned, he would be met immediately by the defence that he has suffered no damage because he was found guilty by the jury. It is true that he could ask for exemplary damages for a high-handed invasion of his rights but exemplary damages do not find much favour these days and in any case would not compensate the accused for the period he spends in prison.

[WALTERS, J. dissented on the ground that the evidence was highly relevant and the accused had not proved any oppression.]

The High Court of Australia held both items of evidence inadmissible.

BARWICK, C.J.: Evidence of relevant facts or things ascertained or procured by means of unlawful or unfair acts is not, for that reason alone, inadmissible. This is so, in my opinion, whether the unlawfulness derives from the common law or from statute. But it may be that acts in breach of a statute would more readily warrant the rejection of the evidence as a matter of discretion: or the statute may on its proper construction itself impliedly forbid the use of facts or things obtained or procured in breach of its terms. On the other hand . . . [w]henever such unlawfulness or unfairness appears, the judge has a discretion to reject the evidence. He must consider its exercise.

. . . I am far from satisfied that the [trial judge] exercised any such discretion. . . . In my opinion, as the evidence stands before us, the photographs and the testimony of the medical practitioner ought to have been excluded in the proper exercise of discretion.

[McTIERNAN, WINDEYER, OWEN and WALSH, JJ. agreed.]

R. v. Wray
(1970), 11 D.L.R. (3d) 673

The accused told the police in an induced confession that he had thrown the murder weapon into a swamp, to which he directed them and in which it was found next day. The trial judge refused to allow the introduction of evidence as to the accused's part in finding the weapon, and the accused was acquitted. The Crown unsuccessfully appealed to the Ontario Court of Appeal, but the majority of the Supreme Court of Canada allowed a further appeal by the Crown and ordered a new trial.

MARTLAND, J. (with whom FAUTEUX, ABBOTT, RITCHIE and PIGEON, JJ. concurred): [The strict rule of admissibility is that so much of the confession as is confirmed by the discovery of the subsequent fact, and the fact itself, is admissible.] The issue of law before this Court is as to validity of the principle stated in the reasons of the Court of Appeal of Ontario ([1970] 2 O.R. 3) that a trial Judge in a criminal case has a discretion to reject evidence, even of substantial weight, if he considers that its admission would be unjust or unfair to the accused or calculated to bring the administration of justice into disrepute.

I will deal with the latter part of this proposition first. I am not aware of any judicial authority in this country or in England which supports the proposition that a trial judge has a discretion to exclude admissible evidence because, in his opinion, its admission would be calculated to bring the administration of justice into disrepute. . . .

The extent to which a discretion exists to disallow evidence if the strict rules of admissibility would operate unfairly against an accused . . . will be considered later in these reasons. The exercise of a discretion of that kind is a part of the function of the Court to ensure that the accused has a fair trial. But other than that, in my opinion, under our law, the function of the Court is to determine the issue before it, on the evidence admissible in law, and it does not extend to the exclusion of admissible evidence for any other reason.

I turn next to the statement that a trial Judge in a criminal case has a discretion to reject evidence, even of substantial weight, if its admission would be unjust or unfair to the accused. . . .

[Lord Goddard in *Kuruma,* [1955] A.C. 197; [1955] 1 All E.R. 236, P.C.] supported his statement [to that effect] by reference to . . . *Noor Mohamed* v. R., [1949] A.C. 182; [1949] 1 All E.R. 365, P.C. and . . . *Harris* v. *Director of Public Prosecutions*, [1952] A.C. 694; [1952] 1 All E.R. 1044, H.L. In both these cases the matter in issue was as to the admissibility of evidence of other prior offences, and it was in relation to the use of that kind of evidence that the frequently quoted *dictum* of Lord du Parcq in the *Noor Mohamed* case . . . was stated. . . .

. . .[T]he authorities . . . indicate that the proposition of law as to judicial discretion which, at the outset, was stated, in very limited terms, as to evidence of similar facts, by Lord du Parcq in [*Noor Mohamed*] . . . has emerged full blown into a statement, such as that made by Ashworth, J. in *Rumping* v. *Director of Public Prosecutions*, [1962] A.C. 814, C.C.A., at p. 820; [1962] 2 All E.R. 233, at p. 236:

"There is, of course, ample authority for the proposition that a judge has an overriding discretion to exclude evidence even if such evidence is in law admissible." . . .

This development of the idea of a general discretion to exclude admissible evidence is not warranted by the authority on which it purports to be based. The *dictum* of Lord Goddard, in the *Kuruma* case, appears to be founded on *Noor Mohamed,* and it has, I think, been unduly extended in some of the subsequent cases. It recognized a discretion to disallow evidence if the strict rules of admissibility would operate unfairly against the accused. Even if this statement be accepted, in the way in which it is phrased, the exercise of a discretion by the trial Judge arises only if the admission of the evidence would operate unfairly. The allowance of admissible evidence relevant to the issue before the Court and of substantial probative value may operate unfortunately for the accused, but not unfairly. It is only the allowance of evidence gravely prejudicial to the accused, the admissibility of which is tenuous, and whose probative force in relation to the main issue before the Court is trifling, which can be said to operate unfairly. . . .

Lord Goddard's own view as to the scope of the proposition which he was stating can be determined, to some extent, by his failure to apply it to the rather unusual facts of the *Kuruma* case. . . .

The pocket knife was never presented in evidence. The police claimed that it was returned to the accused after his arrest. The constables also contended that the search and discovery of the ammunition on the person of the accused were witnessed by three other persons. Yet no such witnesses were called by the Crown and the conviction was obtained on the sole testimony of the constables. The accused was not entitled under Kenya law to a jury trial. . . . Instead, his case was heard by a Magistrate and three assessors. The Magistrate, in reaching his decision, ignored the unanimous advice of the assessors.

If Lord Goddard intended that the discretion which he defined was applicable if the trial Judge felt that the proposed evidence had been obtained in an unfair manner, it is difficult to see how he could avoid saying that the discretion should have been exercised in Kuruma's favour. If, however, he meant that the discretion arose where the admission of evidence, though legally admissible, would operate unfairly, because, as stated in *Noor Mohamed,* it had trivial probative value but was highly prejudicial then the course followed in the disposition of the *Kuruma* case is quite understandable.

In such cases as R. v. *Court,* [1962] Crim. L.R. 697, C.C.A. and R. v. *Payne,* [1963] 1 All E.R. 848; [1963] 1 W.L.R. 637, C.C.A. I think confusion has arisen between "unfairness" in the method of obtaining evidence, and "unfairness" in the actual trial of the accused by reason of its admission. The result of those two cases was, in effect, to render inadmissible evidence which the *ratio decidendi* of the *Kuruma* case had held to be admissible. The view which they express would replace the *Noor Mohamed* test, based on the duty of a trial Judge to ensure that the minds of the jury be not prejudiced by evidence of little probative value, but of great prejudicial effect, by the test as to whether evidence, the probative value of which is unimpeachable was obtained by methods which the trial Judge, in his discretion, considers to be unfair. Exclusion of evidence on this ground has nothing whatever to do with the duty of a trial Judge to secure a fair trial for the accused.

The difficulty of achieving any sort of uniformity in the application of the law if a broad discretion of this kind is recognized is clearly illustrated in the cases which I have considered. What is the standard of "unfairness" which excludes the medical opinions in the cases of *Court* and *Payne,* in which the accused had been misled as to the purpose of the medical examinations, and yet permits the admission of evidence obtained by an illegal search of the person in the *Kuruma* case and in the *King* case, and evidence obtained through deception by agents provocateurs in the *Murphy* case, [1965] N.I. 138?

Judson, J. (Fauteux and Abbott, JJ. concurring): If this law is to be changed, a simple amendment to the Canada Evidence Act, R.S.C. 1952, c. 307, would be sufficient. . . . Such a change should not be effected by turning to a theory of judicial discretion to admit or reject relevant evidence based upon . . . unsubstantial *dicta.* . . . Judicial discretion in this field is a concept which involves great uncertainty of application.

Cartwright, C.J.C. (dissenting): [The trial Judge had a discretion to exclude evidence obtained by such means as to bring the administration of justice into disrepute if it were admitted.] [T]he nature of the investigation as a result of which the respondent disclosed the whereabouts of the murder weapon was such as to reflect no credit on the authorities concerned. The Court of Appeal were not guilty of overstatement when they said ([1970] 3 C.C.C. 122, at p. 123): "Admittedly, the confession or statement by the accused was procured by trickery, duress and improper inducements and it was clearly inadmissible."

Added to this was the circumstance that the police failed to let the lawyer retained by the respondent's family get in touch with him and did so for the stated reason that this might prevent the accused taking the police to the place where the murder weapon was located.

[Hall and Spence, JJ. also dissented.]

Question

Martland, J. implies that *Kuruma* was not a case where the evidence was of suspect probative value. In the light of the features of the case stressed by him, do you agree?

Notes

1. The discretion to exclude improperly obtained evidence is often stated but rarely acted on outside Scotland and Eire; apart from R. v. *Court,* [1962] Crim. L.R. 697, C.C.A., R. v. *Payne,* [1963] I All E.R. 848; [1973] I W.L.R. 637, C.C.A. and R. v. *Ireland* (No. I), [1970] A.L.R. 727, reference should be made

to *Scott* v. *Baker*, [1969] 1 Q.B. 659; [1968] 2 All E.R. 993, D.C. and *R.* v. *Demicoli*, [1971] Qd. R. 358 (cf. *R.* v. *Barnsley*, [1972] 2 N.S.W.L.R. 220); *R.* v. *Foulder*, [1973] Crim. L.R. 45 and *R.* v. *Burnett*, [1973] Crim. L.R. 748 (cf. *R.* v. *McEvilly*, [1974] Crim. L.R. 239, C.A.).

2. Compare the quite detailed range of factors isolated by the Scots and Eire courts as being relevant to the discretion with the very vague position in the rest of the Commonwealth. The difficulty of codifying the relevant factors may be one reason why the Criminal Law Revision Committee recommended no change in the law (para. 68).

B. America

The current American rules have only been arrived at after fifty years' controversy, and are quite likely to change, perhaps substantially, as a result of recent changes in the membership of the Supreme Court.

Before 1914 the position was that improperly obtained evidence was always admissible (*Adams* v. *N.Y.* (1904), 192 U.S. 585). Since then the law has changed through judicial construction of two amendments to the Constitution, the Fourth and Fourteenth. The Fourth provides: "The right of the people to be secure in their persons, houses, papers, and effects, against unreasonable searches and seizures, shall not be violated, and no warrants shall issue but upon probable cause, supported by oath or affirmation, and particularly describing the place to be searched, and the persons or things to be seized." In 1914 the Supreme Court decided in *Weeks* v. *U.S.* that evidence obtained in violation of the Fourth Amendment was inadmissible in Federal criminal trials, because if it could be used, "the protection of the Fourth Amendment . . . [would be] of no value and . . . might as well be stricken from the Constitution" ((1914), 232 U.S. 383, at p. 393, *per* Day, J.). This exclusionary doctrine was extended to "the fruit of the poisonous tree"—evidence indirectly derived from a breach of the Fourth Amendment, such as leads suggested by the results of the search and seizure (*Silverthorne Lumber Co.* v. *U.S.* (1920), 251 U.S. 385). The doctrine applies not only to real evidence, but oral evidence, e.g. statements overheard by driving a spike mike into the wall of a house (*Silverman* v. *U.S.* (1961), 365 U.S. 505), or statements made to police during an unlawful search of the accused's house (*Wong Sun* v. *U.S.* (1963), 371 U.S. 471).

The issue raised by the Fourteenth Amendment is whether the "liberties" guaranteed by the first eight amendments are liberties within the Fourteenth Amendment's guarantee that a State shall not "deprive any person of life, liberty or property, without due process of law". In 1937 the Supreme Court decided that only rights "implicit in the concept of ordered liberty" fell within the Fourteenth Amendment (*Palko* v. *Connecticut* (1937), 302 U.S. 319, at p. 325, *per* Cardozo, J.). In 1949, in *Wolf* v. *Colorado*, the whole Fourth Amendment was held to guarantee such rights, and was therefore binding on the States as well as the Federal Government. But the Supreme Court refused to hold that the exclusionary doctrine by which Federal courts were bound also applied to State courts, because the States were entitled to rely on other effective methods of enforcing the Fourth Amendment if they wished, and many of them did not operate the exclusionary rule ((1949), 338 U.S. 25). In *Rochin* v. *California* another aspect of the due process requirements of the Fourteenth Amendment was revealed when it was held that the forcible stomach pumping of the accused, which showed that he had swallowed drugs, infringed this Amendment because it shocked the conscience ((1952), 342 U.S. 165). The next step was *Elkins* v. *U.S.* (1960), 364 U.S. 206, where the Supreme Court abandoned the "silver platter" doctrine which had permitted the admission of evidence in Federal courts if unconstitutionally obtained by a State officer and handed over to the Federal prosecutor. This foreshadowed the decision in *Mapp* v. *Ohio* (1961), 367 U.S. 643, that the exclusionary doctrine should be applied to State courts as well as Federal: *Wolf* was reversed, it was said, because the majority of the States now favoured the exclusionary rule, and alternative methods of vindicating the Fourth Amendment had proved their inadequacy. Three limitations on the exclusionary rule should be noted. An accused has no standing to invoke the rule if the evidence was obtained through an invasion of *another's* rights (*Alderman* v. *U.S.* (1969), 394 U.S. 165; cf. *People* v. *Martin* (1955), 290 P. 2d 855, where the Californian Supreme Court in bank took the opposite view). Secondly, the rule does not apply if the evidence was obtained by a private individual other than a state official (*Burdeau* v. *McDowell* (1921), 256 U.S. 465). Thirdly, the rule does not apply where the evidence is admitted not on the issue of the accused's guilt but on some collateral issue (*Walder* v. *U.S.* (1954), 347 U.S. 62); *Harris* v. *N.Y.* (1971), 401 U.S. 222).

The related issues of eavesdropping and wire tapping have been treated as follows. In *Olmstead* v. *U.S.* wiretapping from outside the accused's premises was held not to be a search and seizure and therefore not to infringe the Fourth Amendment; the fact that it infringed state legislation did not make it inadmissible ((1928), 277 U.S. 438). The Fourth Amendment was for many years held only to apply to evidence obtained by electronic devices which penetrated into premises (*Silverman* v. *U.S.* (1961), 365 U.S. 505) though section 605 of the Federal Communications Act 1934 provided that "no person not being authorised by the sender shall intercept any communication and divulge or publish the existence, contents, substance, purport, effect or meaning of such intercepted communication to any person". This was held to prohibit the use of evidence thus obtained by a federal officer in court (*Nardone* v. *U.S.* (No. 1) (1937), 302 U.S. 379) or to obtain leads to other evidence used in court (*Nardone* v. *U.S.* (No. 2) (1939), 308 U.S. 338). Now, however, it has been held that *Olmstead* is wrong and that the Fourth Amendment applies to wiretapping and eavesdropping, the test being whether the Government's activities "violated the privacy upon which [the accused] justifiably relied" (*Katz* v. *U.S.* (1967), 389 U.S. 347; *U.S.* v. *White* (1971), 401 U.S. 745). State courts will be bound in accordance with the *Mapp* doctrine. (Thus the effect of *Schwartz* v. *Texas* (1952), 344 U.S. 199, holding that the rule excluding evidence obtained in violation of s. 605 did not apply to state courts, is reversed). Finally, the Omnibus Crime Control and Safe Streets Act 1968 prohibits any person from intercepting or attempting to intercept by the use of any electronic, mechanical or other device any wire or oral communication without a court order.

These developments are controversial. What follows is a small sample of the immensely detailed and passionate American debate over the last sixty years.

People v. Defore
150 N.E. 585 (1926)

The New York Court of Appeals refused to exclude illegally obtained evidence.

CARDOZO, J.: We are confirmed in this conclusion when we reflect how far-reaching in its effect upon society the new consequences would be. The pettiest peace officer would have it in his power, through overzeal or indiscretion, to confer immunity upon an offender for crimes the most flagitious. A room is searched against the law, and the body of a murdered man is found. If the place of discovery may not be proved, the other circumstances may be insufficient to connect the defendant with the crime. The privacy of the home has been infringed, and the murderer goes free. . . . We may not subject society to these dangers until the Legislature has spoken with a clearer voice.

Olmstead v. U.S.
277 U.S. 438 (1928)

The majority of the United States Supreme Court held that the use in evidence of private telephone conversations obtained by wiretapping did not infringe the Fourth and Fifth Amendments.

HOLMES, J. (dissenting): I think, as Mr. Justice Brandeis says, that apart from the Constitution the Government ought not to use evidence obtained and only obtainable by a criminal act. There is no body of precedents by which we are bound, and which confines us to logical deduction from established rules. Therefore we must consider the two objects of desire, both of which we cannot have, and make up our minds which to choose. It is desirable that criminals should be detected, and to that end that all available evidence should be used. It also is desirable that the Government should not itself foster and pay for other crimes, when they are the means by which the evidence is to be obtained. If it pays its officers for having got evidence by crime I do not see why it may not as well pay them for getting it in the same way, and I can attach no importance to protestations of disapproval if it knowingly accepts and pays and announces that in the future it will pay for the fruits. We have to choose, and for my part I think it a less evil that some criminals should escape than that the Government should play an ignoble part.

For those who agree with me, no distinction can be taken between the Government as prosecutor and the Government as judge. If the existing code does not permit district attorneys to have a hand in such dirty business it does not permit the judge to allow such iniquities to succeed.

BRANDEIS, J. (dissenting): The defendants were convicted of conspiring to violate the National Prohibition Act. Before any of the persons now charged had been arrested or indicted, the telephone by means of which they habitually communicated with one another and with others had been tapped by federal officers. To this end, a lineman of long experience in wire-tapping was employed, on behalf of the Government and at its expense. He tapped eight telephones, some in the homes of the persons charged, some in their offices. Acting on behalf of the Government and in their official capacity, at least six other prohibition agents listened over the tapped wires and reported the messages taken. Their operations extended over a period of nearly five months. The typewritten record of the notes of conversations overheard occupies 775 typewritten pages. . . .

The Government makes no attempt to defend the methods employed by its officers. Indeed, it concedes that if wire-tapping can be deemed a search and seizure within the Fourth Amendment, such wire-tapping as was practised in the case at bar was an unreasonable search and seizure, and that the evidence thus obtained was inadmissible. But it relies on the language of the Amendment; and it claims that the protection given thereby cannot properly be held to include a telephone conversation.

"We must never forget", said Mr. Chief Justice Marshall in *McCulloch* v. *Maryland*, 4 Wheat. 316, at p. 407, "that it is a constitution we are expounding." Since then, this Court has repeatedly sustained the exercise of power by Congress, under various clauses of that instrument, over objects of which the Fathers could not have dreamed. . . .

When the Fourth and Fifth Amendments were adopted, "the form that evil had theretofore taken", had been necessarily simple. Force and violence were then the only means known to man by which a Government could directly effect self-incrimination. It could compel the individual to testify—a compulsion effected, if need be, by torture. It could secure possession of his papers and other articles incident to his private life—a seizure effected, if need be, by breaking and entry. Protection against such invasion of "the sanctities of a man's home and the privacies of life" was provided in the Fourth and Fifth Amendments by specific language. *Boyd* v. *United States*, 116 U.S. 616, at p. 630. But "time works changes, brings into existence new conditions and purposes". Subtler and more far-reaching means of invading privacy have become available to the Government. Discovery and invention have made it possible for the Government, by means far more effective than stretching upon the rack, to obtain disclosure in court of what is whispered in the closet.

Moreover, "in the application of a constitution, our contemplation cannot be only of what has been but of what may be". The progress of science in furnishing the Government with means of espionage is not likely to stop with wire-tapping. Ways may some day be developed by which the Government, without removing papers from secret drawers, can reproduce them in court, and by which it will be enabled to expose to a jury the most intimate occurrences of the home. Advances in the psychic and related sciences may bring means of exploring unexpressed beliefs, thoughts and emotions. "That places the liberty of every man in the hands of every petty officer" was said by James Otis of much lesser intrusions than these. To Lord Camden, a far slighter intrusion seemed "subversive of all the comforts of society". Can it be that the Constitution affords no protection against such invasions of individual security? . . .

The protection guaranteed by the Amendments is much broader in scope. The makers of our Constitution undertook to secure conditions favourable to the pursuit of happiness. They recognized the significance of man's spiritual nature, of his feelings and of his intellect. They knew that only a part of the pain, pleasure and satisfactions of life are to be found in material things. They sought to protect Americans in their beliefs, their thoughts, their emotions and their sensations. They conferred, as against the Government, the right to be let alone—the most comprehensive of rights and the right most valued by civilized men. To protect that right, every unjustifiable intrusion by the Government upon the privacy of the individual, whatever the means employed, must be deemed a violation of the Fourth Amendment. And the use, as evidence in a criminal proceeding, of facts ascertained by such intrusion must be deemed a violation of the Fifth.

Applying to the Fourth and Fifth Amendments the established rule of construction, the defendants' objections to the evidence obtained by wire-tapping must, in my opinion, be sustained. It is, of course, immaterial where the physical connection with the telephone wires leading into the defendants' premises was made. And it is also immaterial that the intrusion was in aid of law enforcement. Experience should teach us to be most on our guard to protect liberty when the Government's purposes are beneficent. Men born to freedom are naturally alert to repel invasion of their liberty by evil-minded rulers. The greatest dangers to liberty lurk in insidious encroachment by men of zeal, well-meaning but without understanding.

Independently of the constitutional question, I am of opinion that the judgment should be reversed. By the laws of Washington, wire-tapping is a crime.

[Stone, J. concurred with Holmes and Brandeis, JJ.]

Brinegar *v.* U.S.
338 U.S. 160 (1949)

JACKSON, J. (dissenting in the U.S. Supreme Court): Uncontrolled search and seizure is one of the first and most effective weapons in the arsenal of every arbitrary government. And one need only briefly to have dwelt and worked among a people possessed of many admirable qualities but deprived of these rights to know that the human personality deteriorates and dignity and self-reliance disappear where homes, persons and possessions are subject at any hour to unheralded search and seizure by the police.

But the right to be secure against searches and seizures is one of the most difficult to protect. Since the officers are themselves the chief invaders, there is no enforcement outside of court.

Only occasional and more flagrant abuses come to the attention of the courts, and then only those where the search and seizure yields incriminating evidence and the defendant is at least sufficiently compromised to be indicted. . . . There may be, and I am convinced that there are, many unlawful searches of homes and automobiles of innocent people which turn up nothing incriminating, in which no arrest is made, about which courts do nothing, and about which we never hear.

Courts can protect the innocent against such invasion only indirectly and through the medium of excluding evidence obtained against those who frequently are guilty. . . .

We must remember that the extent of any privilege of search and seizure without warrant which we sustain, the officers interpret and apply themselves and will push to the limit. We must remember, too, that freedom from unreasonable search differs from some of the other rights of the Constitution in that there is no way in which the innocent citizen can invoke advance protection. For example, any effective interference with freedom of the press, or free speech, or religion, usually requires a course of suppressions against which the citizen can and often does go to the court and obtain an injunction. Other rights, such as that to an impartial jury or the aid of counsel, are within the supervisory power of the courts themselves. Such a right as just compensation for the taking of private property may be vindicated after the act in terms of money.

But an illegal search and seizure usually is a single incident, perpetrated by surprise, conducted in haste, kept purposely beyond the court's supervision and limited only by the judgment and moderation of officers whose own interests and records are often at stake in the search. There is no opportunity for injunction or appeal to disinterested intervention. The citizen's choice is quietly to submit to whatever the officers undertake or to resist at risk of arrest or immediate violence.

And we must remember that the authority which we concede to conduct searches and seizures without warrant may be exercised by the most unfit and ruthless officers as well as by the fit and responsible, and resorted to in case of petty misdemeanors as well as in the case of the gravest felonies.

Wigmore: Treatise on the Anglo-American System of Evidence in Trials at Common Law
3rd Edn. Paras. 2183–4

Necessity does not require, and the spirit of our law does forbid, the attempt to do justice incidentally and to enforce penalties by indirect methods. An employer may perhaps suitably interrupt the course of his business to deliver a homily to his office-boy on the evils of gambling or the rewards of industry. But a judge does not hold court in a street-car to do summary justice upon a fellow-passenger who fraudulently evades payment of his fare; and, upon the same principle, he does not attempt, in the course of a specific litigation, to investigate and punish all offences which incidentally cross the path of that litigation. Such a practice might be consistent with the primitive system of justice under an Arabian sheikh; but it does not comport with our own system of law. It offends, in the first place, by trying a violation of law without that due complaint and process which are indispensable for its correct investigation. It offends, in the next place, by interrupting, delaying, and confusing the investigation in hand, for the sake of a matter which is not a part of it. It offends further, in that it does this unnecessarily and gratuitously; for since the persons injured by the supposed offence have not chosen to seek redress or punishment directly and immediately, at the right time and by the proper process, there is clearly no call to attend to their complaints in this indirect and tardy manner. The judicial rules of Evidence were never meant to be an indirect process of punishment. It is not only anomalous to distort them to that end, but it is improper (in the absence of express statute) to enlarge the fixed penalty of the law, that of fine or imprisonment, by adding to it the forfeiture of some civil right through loss of the means of proving it. The illegality is by no means condoned; it is merely ignored. . . .

[The spread of the *Weeks* doctrine is due] to the temporary recrudescence of individualistic sentimentality for freedom of speech and conscience, stimulated by the stern repressive war-measures against treason, disloyalty and sedition, in the years 1917–1919. In a certain type of mind, it was impossible to realize the vital necessity of temporarily subordinating the exercise of ordinary civic freedom during a bloody struggle for national safety and existence. In resistance to these war-measures, it was natural for the misguided pacifistic or semi-pro-German interests to invoke the protection of the Fourth Amendment. Thus invoked and made prominent, all its ancient prestige was revived and sentimentally misapplied. In such a situation, the always watchful forces of criminality, fraud, anarchy and law-evasion perceived the advantage and made vigorous use of it. After the enactment of the Eighteenth Amendment and its auxiliary legislation, prohibiting the sale of intoxicating liquors, a new and popular occasion was afforded for the misplaced invocation of this principle; and the judicial excesses of many Courts in sanctioning its use give an impression of easy complaisance which would be ludicrous if it were not so dangerous to the general respect for law and order in the community. . . .

. . . For the sake of indirectly and contingently protecting the Fourth Amendment, this view appears indifferent to the direct and immediate result, *viz.*, of making Justice inefficient, and of coddling the law-evading classes of the population. It puts Supreme Courts in the position of assisting to undermine the foundations of the very institutions they are set there to protect. It regards the over-zealous officer of the law as a greater danger to the community than the unpunished murderer or embezzler or panderer. . . .

The doctrine of *Weeks* v. *U.S.* also exemplifies a trait of our Anglo-American judiciary peculiar to the mechanical and unnatural type of justice. The natural way to do justice here would be to enforce the healthy principle of the Fourth Amendment directly, i.e. by sending for the high-handed, over-zealous marshal who had searched without a warrant, imposing a thirty-day imprisonment for his contempt of the Constitution, and then proceeding to affirm the sentence of the convicted criminal. But the proposed indirect and unnatural method is as follows:

> "Titus, you have been found guilty of conducting a lottery; Flavius, you have confessedly violated the Constitution. Titus ought to suffer imprisonment for crime, and Flavius for contempt. But no! We shall let you *both* go free. We shall not punish Flavius directly, but shall do so by reversing Titus' conviction. . . . Our way of upholding the Constitution is not to strike at the man who breaks it, but to let off somebody else who broke something else."

C. Conclusion

Let us examine the debate on the merits of a rule of general inclusion as opposed to one of general exclusion. It turns on the following principal points.

(i) The first point is based on certain supposed differences between the societies and legal systems of England and America. It is said that though the American rule may be necessary there, it serves no useful purpose in English conditions. No strict exclusionary rule is needed to deter British police from excesses, for they are trustworthy, their methods are basically proper, and they face much less serious problems than American police forces. Hence "England, with a generally homogeneous society, has been able to afford the luxury of thinking that civil liberties somehow take care of themselves" (Karlen, *Anglo-American Criminal Justice* (London, 1967), p. 98). Another point is that most conduct branded as criminal in England is popularly felt to be rightly so stigmatized and to merit punishment, so that trivial police illegalities can be tolerated in the prosecution of what are felt to be serious crimes. Search and seizure problems in England mainly concern the recovery of stolen goods and the obtaining of breath and blood samples in connexion with drunken driving charges. But most American cases concern gambling and the illicit possession of liquor and drugs. These are popularly felt not to be blameworthy. A seizure of real evidence is usually necessary for their successful prosecution. At common law searches must be incidental to a lawful arrest, or they require the obtaining of consent or a warrant; these powers are inadequate because they allow time for the destruction of evidence. In other words, illegal means are inevitable if these unpopular victimless crimes are to be prosecuted; a strict exclusionary rule is needed to control the resulting widespread lawlessness in law enforcement, and this is feasible since the powers of American courts to order a retrial are much wider than those of English. In America, unlike England, the disproportion between a trivial unpopular crime and a serious police illegality can be stark. Finally, since the English judiciary is much smaller and more homogeneous than the American, it is said to be safer to leave a discretion to admit illegally obtained evidence in their hands, since it is much more likely to be uniformly exercised.

These arguments are less convincing than they were twenty years ago. Whether justifiably or not, the public reputation of the police has declined; and some British cities are moving towards the American mixture of minorities, unemployment and poverty which is said to make the crime problem so intractable. An increasing part of the public takes the same attitude today to drug offences as in America. And there are now a very large number of High Court and Crown Court judges exercising the *Kuruma* discretion, not to mention twenty thousand magistrates; it is too much to hope for a uniformly administered discretion in these circumstances.

(ii) Another argument for the English position is that the American law involves the sacrifice of reliable evidence for the sake of deterring the police from misconduct, thus favouring only the guilty and causing two wrongs to occur instead of only one.

Pursuit of this collateral enquiry delays and confuses the accused's trial. The sole purpose of such a trial is to discover the truth and make a correct finding as to the accused's guilt or innocence. It is not a game in which the prosecution's hands are to be tied so that it can only act "fairly". The impropriety of the police conduct in no way disables the court from giving a fair and impartial judgment. The wrong-doing policeman should not be punished by exclusion of the evidence, which injures only the public at large and not the policeman, but by the pursuit of other remedies. The accused might launch a private prosecution, or sue in tort. The policeman's superiors may criticize or discipline him, or prevent his promotion, or even prosecute him. Well-publicized judicial criticism and the consequential arousing of public opinion will deter the police better than the exclusion of the evidence; and if it does not, there is probably something wrong with the police too deep-rooted to be cured by the law of evidence. In any event, the exclusionary rule is not an effective deterrent for several reasons. Most illegal conduct is designed not to obtain evidence in court but to harass criminals unpunishable in other ways, and the exclusionary rule accentuates these police tendencies. It is difficult for the police to understand technically worded, often unreasoned rulings which may appear inconsistent with each other and which may change in future. Finally, reliance on the exclusionary rule may sap the eagerness of officials to pursue alternative ways of controlling the police.

These arguments are vulnerable at a number of points. It is not necessarily true that the exclusionary rule protects only the guilty: its deterrent effect ensures that in future both guilty *and innocent* persons will be protected from illegal investigation. Nor is it necessarily true that illegally obtained real evidence is reliable: for as *Kuruma* shows, there will sometimes be a doubt whether the evidence is in fact connected with the accused.

It is true that the exclusionary rule involves a collateral inquiry in a criminal trial, but it does at least vindicate the accused's rights at once; he need not start new proceedings in another court to obtain redress, thus incurring more expense. Further, the English rule involves even more of a collateral inquiry, for not only must there be an investigation of whether illegality has occurred, but also an inquiry into whether fairness demands exclusion. Then the remedies other than exclusion, more direct though they may be, are unsatisfactory. Criminal prosecutions may fail because of the sympathy of jury and magistrates for the accused. Police solidarity means that the state is unlikely to undertake them. As an American judge put it, "Self-scrutiny is a lofty ideal, but its exaltation reaches new heights if we expect a District Attorney to prosecute himself or his associates for well-meaning violations of the search and seizure clause during a raid the District Attorney or his associates have ordered" (*Wolf* v. *Colorado,* (1949), 338 U.S. 25, at p. 42, *per* Murphy, J. dissenting). Police leaders will be sympathetic to the illegal conduct of their inferiors as long as the latter remain within the unwritten traditions, codes and norms of the force as opposed to the law of the land. There is no independent civilian body to prosecute or investigate the police. The poor and uneducated who comprise the bulk of criminals and the bulk of innocent police victims are unlikely to know how to prosecute the police, or to be able to do so, particularly if they are in prison as a result of the admission of the evidence illegally obtained. Even the innocent victim of criminal police conduct may be reluctant to prosecute because he will not wish it to be known he was under suspicion.

Civil actions for trespass, assault, false arrest and damage to property may be unsatisfactory in several ways. The individual policeman may not be thought to be worth suing. In any event he will not be deterred by the fear of such actions because of the convention that the local police authority indemnifies him. Section 48 of the Police Act 1964 provides that Chief Constables are vicariously liable for torts committed by constables under their direction, and a successful claim may lead to better internal discipline; but damages and costs are payable out of the police fund and not by the Chief Constable personally. The victim may fear the further loss of privacy entailed in a suit, or subsequent police victimization. Substantial damages are only recoverable in the event of actual loss or malice; they may be mitigated by the plaintiff's bad reputation, which will also affect his credibility and increase the chance of a finding of reasonable cause for arrest. Aggravated damages may be awarded in respect of oppressive, arbitrary or unconstitutional conduct by State servants, but juries are unlikely so to punish an officer whose efforts, albeit illegal, uncovered crime. In *Elias* v. *Pasmore,* [1934] 2 K.B. 164, at p. 173; [1934] All E.R. Rep. 380, at p. 384, Horridge, J. held that no action would lie if the evidence seized is subsequently used in a criminal prosecution; this doctrine was cut down in *Ghani* v. *Jones,* [1970] 1 Q.B. 693; [1969] 3 All E.R. 700, C.A., by the Court of Appeal so as to permit seizure only where the police have reasonable grounds for believing that a serious offence has been committed, that the evidence is material, and that the person in possession of it is party to the crime. Despite this narrowing, there remains a substantial area of immunity which will tempt the police to act even when the conditions in which it arises do not exist. Often there will be no remedy either because the police conduct has not been unlawful at all (e.g. nontrespassory invasions of privacy) or because even though their conduct is criminal no civil action lies.

As for the deterrent effect of the exclusionary rule, though this will operate more respecting police conduct designed to produce evidence in court than other conduct, American research indicates that the rule has some effect in improving police training in civil liberties matters. It has also led to more compliance with the law in relation to searches for gambling apparatus and stolen goods, though not drugs and weapon offences (Oaks, (1970) 37 U. of Chi. L.R. 665). Accordingly, though the exclusion of illegally obtained evidence would be unnecessary if there were a well-established statutory civil action against the state coupled with the establishment of an independent authority to prosecute the individuals responsible for illegality, at the moment there seems to be some case for the exclusion of illegally obtained evidence.

(iii) The exclusionary rule is said to place too big a burden on the police in an age of rising crime rates in that some crimes can only be prosecuted by relying on illegally obtained real evidence. Criminals are not restricted in their choice of weapons; nor should the police be. An exclusionary rule will injure police morale; it will cause them to perjure themselves about such matters as whether the requirements for lawful arrest were satisfied; it will cause them in their search for evidence, to commit serious illegalities which they hope will not be discovered, on the principle that they may as well run the risk of being hung for a sheep as for a lamb; and will lead them to harass those they cannot convict. Trivial police blunders should not lead to the exclusion of evidence, for this destroys respect for the law by letting the guilty go free on what the police and the public think are mere technicalities. Further, the rule gives corrupt policemen the power to immunize criminals from conviction by collusively making what appear to be illegal searches, thus satisfying, in a sham way, public pressure for law enforcement.

Answers can be found to these points. It is not so much the exclusionary rule of evidence which hampers the police, but the substantive rules governing warrants, arrest, search and so forth. It may be that these rules, largely formed before the appearance of modern police forces and modern crimes and criminals, require modification, but this should be done directly, not by admitting evidence obtained in breach of them. It may be easier to convict criminals by admitting such evidence; it does not follow that it is impossible to convict them without it. To permit its use on any large scale encourages laziness and inefficiency, for the police may come to rely on improperly obtained evidence instead of more normal detective methods. In so far as some crimes are very difficult to prosecute without real evidence, the burden should be borne by the prosecution as is normal, not the defence. The causes of the modern crime wave are various, but exclusionary rules of evidence are unlikely to be among them to any significant degree. Respect for the law may be weakened by the spectacle of criminals escaping conviction on technicalities; it will be even more weakened if the police get convictions from serious misconduct. It is wrong for the state to participate in and condone illegal conduct by individual policemen, and thus profit from its own wrong; the judicial process must not be contaminated.

The government's behaviour should be a model for that of private citizens. Though perhaps blunders should be condoned, persistent and deliberate misconduct should not be. Finally, the immunizing of the guilty by corrupt policemen does not seem a grave danger. If a policeman is corrupt, he has many other methods of helping criminals without going to these lengths. In any case, if other police misconduct is controlled by internal police discipline, why not this form of it?

Questions

1. How satisfactory do you find the Privy Council's handling of American law in *Kuruma, Son of Kaniu* v. *R.* [1955] A.C. 197; [1955] 1 All E.R. 236, P.C.? How satisfactory was its handling of Scots law?

2. Ought distinctions to be drawn between evidence obtained by illegal means depending on whether the illegality arises by a rule of the common law, or a statutory rule, or a constitutional rule, or a rule entrenched in a written constitution?

3. Should a distinction be drawn between illegally and unfairly obtained evidence?

4. It has been suggested that illegally obtained evidence should be excluded

more readily than unfairly obtained evidence, because illegal acts usually effect both guilty and innocent adversely, but tricks do not. For example, if a car driver is persuaded by the police to take a medical examination after an accident, supposedly to see if he has concussion but in fact to see if he is drunk enough to be prosecuted, this will benefit the innocent and injure only the guilty (see J.T.C., [1969] Jur. Rev. 55, at p. 69). Do you agree?

5. Why are involuntary confessions excluded and not illegally obtained evidence?

6. Which do you favour: the *Kuruma* rule, the *Wray* rule, the Scottish rule or the American position? Why?

Reading

Andrews, [1963] Crim. L.R. 15; J.T.C., [1969] Jur. Rev. 55; Cowen and Carter, Chap. 3; Gray, [1966] Jur. Rev. 89; Heydon, [1973] Crim. L.R. 603; Weinberg, (1975) 21 McGill L.J.; Williams, [1955] Crim. L.R. 339.

10

The Accused's Character: Part 1

I SIMILAR FACT EVIDENCE

A. The Common Law Rule

1 *General*

Introduction. Three rules govern the admissibility of past bad behaviour offered as evidence that a particular act was done. First, the bad behaviour must be relevant to the alleged act: it must tend to prove it. Evidence that a boy stole apples in 1913 is not relevant to whether in 1943 he robbed a bank. Evidence of consensual intercourse is irrelevant to an earlier charge of rape (*R. v. Rodley*, [1913] 3 K.B. 468; [1911–13] All E.R. Rep. 688, C.C.A.).

Secondly, even if it is relevant, the past bad behaviour is inadmissible if its only relevance is to show that the actor has a bad disposition, and his disposition is not highly relevant to some issue at the trial. Evidence of a man's convictions for robbing banks would be admissible if his explanation for possessing money stolen from a bank in 1943 was that he found it in the street: for his disposition would be highly relevant to his supposedly innocent state of mind. But such evidence would be inadmissible if he said that at the time of the robbery he was in another country robbing a bank: his disposition would not then be relevant to any issue at the trial. However, evidence that he broke into a bank on Tuesday and was found removing clothing discovered by bank officials after a robbery on Monday would be admissible because it has a relevance other than proving bad disposition: it shows actual participation in the Monday crime.

Thirdly, in criminal cases, even though evidence of bad behaviour is technically admissible under the first two rules, it may be excluded because its prejudicial effect exceeds its probative value. Thus if evidence of a man's prior bank robberies proceeded only from a paid police informer known to have a grudge against the accused, the evidence might well be excluded.

The first rule is largely a matter of common sense. Because relevance is an issue of degree on which minds can differ, some cases cited under the second rule may be examples of the first, and vice versa (e.g. *Harris v. Director of Public Prosecutions*, [1952] A.C. 694; [1952] 1 All E.R. 1044, H.L.). A fairly clear example of the first rule is *H. R. Lancey Shipping Co., Pty., Ltd. v. Robson*, [1938] A.L.R. 429. There a man was injured by the breaking of a ship's block shackle; evidence of a later fall of the mast was excluded because there was no proof of any common cause. Another is *Cooper v. R.* (1961), 105 C.L.R. 177: the fact the accused was a Communist atheist hostile to missionaries was irrelevant to whether he was likely to publish seditious words. There is little authority on the third rule, for it is of recent origin and depends very much on a discretion governed only by the particular facts. Matters such as unreliability or staleness (*R. v. Cole* (1941), 165 L.T. 125) would be relevant to the discretion; also the fact that it is unclear whether the conduct is criminal (*R. v. Doughty*, [1965] 1 All E.R. 560; [1965] 1 W.L.R. 331, C.C.A.). There is a doubt as to whether the discretion applies in civil cases: *Manenti* v. *Melbourne and Metropolitan Tramways Board*, [1954] V.L.R. 115; *Gosschalk* v. *Rossouw*, [1966] 2 S.A. 476.

This chapter is mainly concerned with the second rule, but let us first briefly look at a case which shows how hard it sometimes is to distinguish the first two rules.

Harris v. Director of Public Prosecutions
[1952] A.C. 694; [1952] 1 All E.R. 1044, H.L.

The accused was charged with eight larcenies of money committed in May, June and July 1951 from a certain office in an enclosed market at times when most of the gates were shut and the accused, a police officer, might have been on solitary duty there. In each case the same means of access were used and only part of the amount which might have been taken was taken. No thefts occurred while the accused was on leave. The accused was found by two detectives in the immediate vicinity of the office at the time of the last larceny. Though they were well-known to him he avoided them for a period sufficient to hide marked money taken from the office till and found in a coal bin near where he was first seen. The accused was convicted on only the eighth count. He appealed against conviction to the Court of Criminal Appeal unsuccessfully and to the House of Lords successfully on the ground that evidence of the first seven thefts was irrelevant to the eighth.

VISCOUNT SIMON: In my opinion, the principle laid down by Lord Herschell, L.C. in *Makin* v. *A.-G. for New South Wales* [1894] A.C. 57; [1891–4] All E.R. Rep. 24, P.C. remains the proper principle to apply, and I see no reason for modifying it. *Makin's* case was a decision of the Judicial Committee of the Privy Council, but it was unanimously approved by the House of Lords in *R. v. Ball*, [1911] A.C. 47, H.L.; and has been constantly relied on ever since. It is, I think, an error to attempt to draw up a closed list of the sort of cases in which the principle operates: such a list only provides instances of its general application, whereas what really matters is the principle itself and its proper application to the particular circumstances of the charge that is being tried. It is the application that may sometimes be difficult, and the particular case now before the House illustrates that difficulty.

The principle as laid down by the then Lord Chancellor is as follows [1894] A.C. 57, at p. 65; [1891–4] All E.R. Rep. 24, at pp. 25–6, P.C.:

> "It is undoubtedly not competent for the prosecution to adduce evidence tending to show that the accused has been guilty of criminal acts other than those covered by the indictment, for the purpose of leading to the conclusion that the accused is a person likely from his criminal conduct or character to have committed the offence for which he is being tried. On the other hand, the mere fact that the evidence adduced tends to show the commission of other crimes does not render it inadmissible if it be relevant to an issue before the jury, and it may be so relevant if it bears upon the question whether the acts alleged to constitute the crime charged in the indictment were designed or accidental, or to rebut a defence which would otherwise be open to the accused." . . .

There is a second proposition which ought to be added under this head. It is not a rule of law governing the admissibility of evidence, but a rule of judicial practice followed by a judge who is trying a charge of crime when he thinks that the application of the practice is called for. Lord du Parcq referred to it in *Noor Mohamed* v. R., [1949] A.C. 182, at p. 192; [1949] 1 All E.R. 365, at p. 370, P.C. immediately after the passage above quoted, when he said that

> "in all such cases the judge ought to consider whether the evidence which it is pro-
> posed to adduce is sufficiently substantial, having regard to the purpose to which it is
> professedly directed, to make it desirable in the interest of justice that it should be
> admitted. If, so far as that purpose is concerned, it can in the circumstances of the
> case have only trifling weight, the judge will be right to exclude it. To say this is not
> to confuse weight with admissibility. The distinction is plain, but cases must occur in
> which it would be unjust to admit evidence of a character gravely prejudicial to the
> accused even though there may be some tenuous ground for holding it technically
> admissible. The decision must then be left to the discretion and the sense of fairness
> of the judge."

This second proposition flows from the duty of the judge when trying a charge of crime to set the essentials of justice above the technical rule if the strict application of the latter would operate unfairly against the accused. If such a case arose, the judge may intimate to the prosecution that evidence of "similar facts" affecting the accused, though admissible, should not be pressed because its probable effect "would be out of proportion to its true evidential value" (*per* Lord Moulton in R. v. *Christie* [1914] A.C. 545, at pp. 559; [1914–15] All E.R. Rep. 63, at p. 69, H.L.). Such an intimation rests entirely within the discretion of the judge.

It is, of course, clear that evidence of "similar facts" cannot in any case be admissible to support an accusation against the accused unless they are connected in some relevant way with the accused and with his participation in the crime. . . . But evidence of other occurrences which merely tend to deepen suspicion does not go to prove guilt. This is the ground, as it seems to me, on which the Judicial Committee of the Privy Council allowed the appeal in *Noor Mohamed* v. R. [1949] A.C. 182; [1949] 1 All E.R. 365, P.C. The Board there took the view that the evidence as to the previous death of the accused's wife was not relevant to prove the charge against him of murdering another woman, and if it was not relevant it was at the same time highly prejudicial. . . .

It remains to examine certain reported cases dealing with admissibility of evidence of "similar facts" decided since *Makin's* case, [1894] A.C. 57, P.C. to which the Attorney-General referred us. Rightly understood, these cases do not seem to me to involve any enlargement of the area within which evidence of "similar facts" might be admitted.

In R. v. *Smith* (1915), 84 L.J. K.B. 2153; [1914–15] All E.R. Rep. 262, C.C.A. the accused was charged with murdering a woman, immediately after going through a form of marriage with her, by drowning her in a bath in the lodging where they were staying. Evidence was held to be rightly admitted of very similar circumstances which connected the accused with the deaths at a later date of two other women who were drowned in their baths after the accused had gone through a form of marriage with each of them in turn. In all three cases it was shown that the accused benefited by the death. In all three cases the prisoner urged the woman to take a bath and was on the premises when she prepared to do so. The ground on which the evidence of the two later occurrences was admissible was that the occurrences were so alike and the part taken by the accused in arranging what the woman would do was so similar in each case as to get rid of any suggestion of accident. The decision . . . therefore involved no extension of the principle laid down in *Makin's* case. The challenged evidence was admissible both to show that what happened in the case of the first woman was not an accident and also to show what was the intention with which the accused did what he did.

In R. v. *Armstrong*, [1922] 2 K.B. 555, C.C.A., at p. 566; [1922] All E.R. Rep. 153, at p. 155, the accused was indicted for the murder of his wife by administering arsenic to her. The wife was shown to have died from arsenical poisoning, but the defence urged that it was not shown that the husband had administered the poison to her, but that she had committed suicide. The accused had purchased a quantity of arsenic and made it up into a number of small packets, each containing what would constitute a fatal dose, but offered the explanation that he had purchased the poison merely to use it as a weed-killer in his garden. The prosecution called evidence to show that, eight months after the death of his wife, he secretly administered arsenic to another person. The Court of Criminal Appeal held that this evidence was admissible because it went to disprove the suggestion that he had purchased and kept arsenic for an innocent purpose. The decision . . . appears to me to involve no enlargement of the principle in *Makin's* case. Lord Hewart, C.J. rightly observed, [1922] 2 K.B. 555, C.C.A., at p. 566; [1922] All E.R. Rep. 153, at p. 155:

> "The fact that he was subsequently found not merely in possession of but actually using for a similar deadly purpose the very kind of poison that caused the death of his wife was evidence from which the jury might infer that that poison was not in his possession at the earlier date for an innocent purpose." . . .

In R. v. *Sims*, [1946] K.B. 531; at p. 539; [1946] 1 All E.R. 697, at p. 701, C.C.A., there is a passage in the judgment of Lord Goddard, C.J. which appears to have raised doubts in some quarters as to whether the principle in *Makin's* case was being extended. The Lord Chief Justice there observed that one method of approaching the relevant problem is to start with the general proposition that all evidence that is "logically probative" is admissible unless excluded by established rules, and that it would follow that evidence for the prosecution "is admissible irrespective of the issues raised by the defence". It is the words "logically probative" which have raised doubts in some minds. Such a phrase may seem to invite philosophic discussion which would be ill-suited to the practical business of applying the criminal law with justice to all concerned. But I do not understand the Lord Chief Justice by the use of such a phrase to be enlarging the ambit of the principle in *Makin's* case at all or to be disregarding the restrictions which Lord Herschell indicated. In one sense, evidence of previous bad conduct or hearsay evidence, might be regarded as having, logically, a probative value, but, of course, the judgment in *Sims'* case is not opening the door to that. I understand the passage quoted to mean no more than what I have already formulated, *viz.*, that the prosecution may advance proper evidence to prove its case without waiting to ascertain what is the line adopted by the defence. Lord du Parcq, in *Noor Mohamed* v. R., [1949] A.C. 182, at pp. 194–6; [1949] 1 All E.R. 365, at pp. 371–2, P.C. points out the possibility of misunderstanding the Lord Chief Justice's words and proceeds to put his own construction upon them. In substance, I agree with his interpretation. There is, however, this to be added. The proper working of the criminal law in this connexion depends on the due observance of both the propositions which I have endeavoured to expound in this judgment. . . . A criminal trial in this country is conducted for the purpose of deciding whether the prosecution has proved that the accused is guilty of the particular crime charged, and evidence of "similar facts" should be excluded unless such evidence has a really material bearing on the issues to be decided. . . . With this explanation, I see no reason to differ from the conclusion in R. v. *Sims*.

[Lords Porter, Morton of Henryton and Tucker agreed.]

Lord Oaksey (dissenting): I do not understand your Lordships to hold that the evidence of what happened in July was inadmissible or should have been excluded on any of the counts 1 to 7 and, if that is so, it could, in my opinion, only be because of the same similarities in the evidence, from which it might be inferred that the accused stole the money on the first seven occasions although there was no direct evidence that he was in fact present when the money was stolen on any one of those occasions. The question may be tested in this way: can it be said that no jury could reasonably find that one person committed all eight thefts? In my opinion, the same similarity must be equally relevant whether it is adduced on one count or on the others.

Rationale

The law is wary of admitting similar fact evidence for the following reasons.

First, the effect of this evidence may be unduly prejudicial even on a trained tribunal; before a completely untrained jury it may have an effect entirely disproportionate to its actual probative value. Sometimes its probative value is great; sometimes it is small because it is stale, or not similar enough, or of infrequent occurrence. The jury may too easily hang a dog because he has a bad name. They may be unwilling to entertain the possibility that a bad man has reformed. "The more revolting the suggestion, the more a jury may be likely to lose sight of the fact that it may not be true" (Cowen and Carter, p. 146). And even if they are not fully convinced he is guilty of this charge, they may feel compelled to punish him for this past behaviour. Secondly, similar fact evidence raises many collateral issues which it may be too distracting, expensive and time consuming to investigate in the light of the main issues of the case. Thirdly, it may take the person against whom it is tendered by surprise unless he is prepared to defend himself with respect to all the bad acts of his life. Fourthly, if similar fact evidence is too freely admissible it may encourage the police not to search for the real criminal but instead to discover someone with a possible opportunity and a record. In the same way it may be possible for the criminal to cover his tracks by committing the crime in circumstances where another man with a record may be suspected.

Limits

Similar fact evidence is usually introduced by the prosecution against the accused; but it could be introduced by the accused against the prosecution, e.g. to show that certain policemen habitually induce involuntary confessions (*S.* v. *Letsoko*, [1964] 4 S.A. 768). Evidence of prior intercourse between the accused and a woman complaining of rape is admissible as relevant to consent (*R.* v. *Riley* (1887), 18 Q.B.D. 481). Similar fact evidence is also introduced in civil cases (e.g. *Hales* v. *Kerr*, [1908] 2 K.B. 601, D.C.; cf. *Manenti* v. *Melbourne and Metropolitan Tramways Board*, [1954] V.L.R. 115). In civil cases the special need to avoid prejudicing the accused is absent, and trial is not usually by jury. There seems no reason why a party should not introduce relevant evidence of his own bad character provided he understands what he is doing.

Evidence of prior good conduct is often rejected for want of relevance or weight, or because it would raise too many collateral issues (*Holcombe* v. *Hewson* (1810), 2 Camp. 391; *Hollingham* v. *Head* (1858), 4 C.B.N.S. 388). However, the accused may raise his good character as evidence of innocence.

Conduct in respect of which the accused was acquitted cannot normally be relied on as similar fact evidence (*Kemp* v. *R.* (1951), 83 C.L.R. 341; *G.* v. *Coltart*, [1967] 1 Q.B. 432; [1967] 2 All E.R. 271 D.C.; cf. *R.* v. *Miles* (1943), 44 S.R.N.S.W. 198).

The defence which similar fact evidence rebuts must be "raised in substance if not in so many words. . . . The mere theory that a plea of not guilty puts everything material in issue is not enough for this purpose. The prosecution cannot credit the accused with fancy defences in order to rebut them at the outset with some damning piece of prejudice" (*Thompson* v. *R.*, [1918] A.C.

221, at p. 232; [1918–19] All E.R. Rep. 521, at p. 526, H.L., *per* Lord Sumner). Of course, if the prosecution had always to wait for a defence to be raised expressly, the accused might often succeed unfairly in a submission that there is no case to answer despite the availability of admissible and weighty similar fact evidence: so the prosecution may rebut defences reasonably likely to be run by the accused on the facts (*Harris* v. *Director of Public Prosecutions*, [1952] A.C. 694, at pp. 706–7; [1952] 1 All E.R. 1044, at p. 1047, H.L.). An admission of the fact which the prejudicial evidence is meant to prove will prevent it being admitted (*R.* v. *Rogan* (1916), 35 N.Z.L.R. 265, at p. 304). But a mere plea of not guilty is not enough to prevent similar fact evidence being admitted, for defences fairly attributable to the accused can be rebutted. (See Gooderson, [1959] C.L.J. 210, at pp. 224–8).

Basis of admission

The admissibility of similar fact evidence depends on its relevance in the light of an appeal to the unlikelihood of coincidence.

In particular, admissibility depends not only on strong similarity between the similar fact evidence and the main evidence, but on an appeal to a strong dissimilarity between all the events and what might ordinarily be expected to happen. In *Thompson* v. *R.*, [1918] A.C. 221; [1918–19] All E.R. Rep. 521, H.L. the appeal is "Wouldn't it be odd if two boys wrongly identified as a man who interfered with them an innocent man who was in fact a practising homosexual?" In *R.* v. *Ball*, [1911] A.C. 47, H.L., it is: "Wouldn't it be odd if a brother and sister who had committed incest frequently in the past now lived together as man and wife, sleeping in the same bed, without committing incest?" A simple example is *R.* v. *Smith* (1915), 84 L.J.K.B. 2153; [1914–15] All E.R. Rep. 262, C.C.A. Smith was charged with murdering his wife in her bath by drowning. There was no direct evidence of this other than opportunity. But two other wives had been drowned in the same way. "No reasonable man would believe it possible that Smith had successively married three women, persuaded them to make wills in his favour, bought three suitable baths, placed them in rooms which could not be locked, taken each wife to a doctor and suggested to him that she suffered from epileptic fits, and then had been so unlucky that each of the three had had some kind of fit in the bath and been drowned" (*per* Lord Maugham, quoted by Williams, p. 230). It follows that attention must be paid both to the issues in the case and the facts as a whole.

The precise issues must be identified because, for example, the disposition of the accused will make his innocence a much stranger coincidence if he admits the *actus reus* but denies some part of the *mens rea* than if he denies the *actus reus* (see *R.* v. *Flack*, [1969] 2 All E.R. 784, C.A.). The *actus reus* may nevertheless be proved by sufficiently strong similar fact evidence: *Makin* v. *A.-G.* for *New South Wales*, [1894] A.C. 57; [1891–4] All E.R. Rep. 24, P.C.; *R.* v. *Ball*, [1911] A.C. 47, H.L. Probably the similarities in the evidence must be greater when the *actus reus* is in question.

The evidence as a whole must be borne in mind, because a very clearly proved disposition to commit a particular crime may be inadmissible if there is nothing to connect the accused with the crime charged. A very slight connexion, such as possible opportunity, may suffice, however (*R.* v. *Straffen* [1952] 2 Q.B. 911; [1952] 2 All E.R. 657, C.C.A.). And the accused may even be convicted though there is no directly proved connexion other than possible opportunity between him and the similar facts, e.g. cases of poisoning in a household (*R. v. Geering* (1849), 18 L.J.M.C. 215; *R. v. Grills* (1954), 73 W.N.N.S.W. 303; and see *R. v. Chandler* (1956), 56 S.R.N.S.W. 335). This is why *Harris v. Director of Public Prosecutions*, [1952] A.C. 694, H.L.; [1952] 1 All E.R. 1044 is so controversial. Further, relatively weak evidence of disposition may be admissible if the other evidence is very strong (e.g. *R. v. Ball*, [1911] A.C. 47, H.L.).

But the difficulties of this reasoning should be remembered. In Lord Hewart, C.J.'s words: "The risk, the danger, the logical fallacy is indeed quite manifest to those who are in the habit of thinking about such matters. It is so easy to derive from a series of unsatisfactory accusations, if there are enough of them, an accusation which at least appears satisfactory. It is so easy to collect from a mass of ingredients, not one of which is sufficient, a totality which will appear to contain what is missing" (*R. v. Bailey*, [1924] 2 K.B. 300, at p. 305; [1924] All E.R. Rep. 466, at p. 467).

It is just because admissibility depends on the evidence as a whole that the following procedure is standard. Before the case begins defence counsel should object to the admissibility of any evidence he thinks fit; but the argument about admissibility should not take place until the evidence is tendered. Only then will the full relevance of the evidence objected to be seen because its relevance will be affected by the other evidence (*R. v. Patel*, [1951] 2 All E.R. 29, C.C.A.).

The strength of the appeal to the unlikelihood of coincidence often depends on the high degree of similarity of similar fact evidence. It tends to limit the number of persons likely to commit the crime. Sometimes so much similarity has been demanded that the court has placed "too high a premium on versatility and too heavy a penalty on dullness" (D.W.L., 54 L.Q.R. 335 at p. 336 (1938)). But in general it is right that where the means of committing a crime "might have been adopted in either case by anyone of an indefinite number of persons and where no other connexion . . . is shown to have existed" the evidence is inadmissible (*R. v. Aiken*, [1952] V.L.R. 265, at p. 268). Similarly, the possession of material suitable for safebreaking is inadmissible on a charge of housebreaking: *Thompson v. R.* (1968), 42 A.L.J.R. 16. Similarity narrows the gap between proving the accused was a wrongdoer in general and proving he did this particular wrong. The similarity must often be so marked as to suggest a special system or technique identifying the accused as the criminal; but the use of terms like "system" or "technique" obscures the fact that the basic test is a high degree of relevance, and this depends on all the evidence. The need for some special connexion proved through similarity used as the basis for an appeal to coincidence means that similar fact evidence is more readily admitted in unusual crimes than common ones: e.g. poisoning, incest, unnatural sexual cases, perverted murders. If crimes are common others may have done them. If crimes are rare, most people are inhibited from committing them, and proof of lack of inhibition is very relevant.

Further, the amount of proximity in time to be looked for depends partly on the crimes involved. "A man whose course of conduct is to buy houses, insure them, and burn them down, or to acquire ships, insure them, and scuttle them, or to purport to marry women, defraud and desert them, cannot repeat the offence every month, or even perhaps every six months" (*Moorov v. H.M. Advocate*, 1930 J.C. 68, at p. 89 *per* Lord Sands).

The similarity of admissible similar facts may vary; so may their number. One previous abortion was enough in *R. v. Bond*, [1906] 2 K.B. 389; [1904–7] All E.R. Rep. 24; many previous burglaries might not be enough. If a man has aborted one servant girl pregnant by him, he would do well not to conduct a medical examination of another one: the suggestion of systematic misconduct is strong. But a convicted burglar cannot help walking near houses. If he were found in a house, or some marked similarity of method were proved, fewer similar facts would need to be proved (Williams, p. 232).

The similar fact rules offer a clear example of judicial power to control jury verdicts. If the judge admits the evidence, a conviction is made virtually certain. Since the basic test for admission is the judge's view of the overall strength of the evidence, he is able to prevent perverse jury verdicts.

Reported similar fact cases, of which there are vast numbers, are notorious for disputes and doubts about rules of law, though most of them are probably rightly decided. Opinions differ as to which are rightly decided largely because the question is one of relevance and therefore of degree. Not too much weight should be placed on seemingly identical prior authorities: like modern negligence cases, these are decisions of fact dressed up as decisions of law. They have very little binding effect on later courts. *Dicta* or even decisions in one case may be inapplicable to later cases because they are based on unexplained assumptions about which issues are relevant and how striking similarities are (e.g. this is especially so when indecent photographs are inspected: see *R. v. Morris* (1969) 54 Cr. App. Rep. 69, C.A.; Eggleston in Glass (Ed.) p. 87).

The main principles can be observed in the following cases.

Thompson v. R.
[1918] A.C. 221; [1918–19] All E.R. Rep. 521, H.L.

The accused was charged with committing acts of gross indecency on two boys on March 16. They said that on that day he arranged to meet them again on March 19 near a public toilet. On that date he told them to go away, gave them money and said that the tall man nearby was a policeman. He was then arrested. The accused's defence was an alibi. He said that he had never seen the boys before March 19, and only gave the boys money to buy soap to get their faces washed, to make them stop staring at him and to go away. Two powder puffs found on the accused when arrested and several photographs of naked boys discovered at his lodgings were admitted. The accused's appeals against conviction to the Court of Criminal Appeal and House of Lords failed.

LORD ATKINSON: . . . It would be strange, indeed, if one man should commit with the boys the offence charged on the 16th, and make an assignation with them to commit it again upon the 19th, that another man should, with an intent to do the same, take up and fulfil the first man's engagement, personate him as it were, and keep the appointment the first had made. It would appear to me that evidence which goes to prove that the prisoner had in his transactions with these boys on the 19th an intent or desire to commit an indecent offence with them, if circumstances should permit, becomes evidence to identify him as the person who actually committed on the 16th the offence for which he was indicted. . . . For what purpose could the prisoner carry upon him on this day the powder puffs? He could not, by them, promote the cause of charity or cleanliness. He could not have carried them for such a purpose—the time had not arrived for their use; but can it be reasonably doubted that they were carried to be used when needed? The possession of them is in my opinion admissible in evidence to show, when taken in connexion with the facts proved, that the prisoner harboured on that day an intent to commit an act of indecency with these boys should occasion offer. Well, if these photographs of naked boys, some when apparently approaching adolescence, all I think indecent in their attitude, and some apparently depraved in suggestion, had been found on the person of the accused I do not see how any distinction could well have been drawn between them and the powder puffs. They too are, it is stated, implements for carrying out the same design. I do not know, and it is not stated, whether they are used to stimulate the depraved lusts of those given to such practices, or to corrupt the mind of those whose assistance or sufferance such people seek; but this I think is clear, that they could not be needed for the work of a hygienic enthusiast to devote to youthful cleanliness that he gave to two boys he had never met before; and who had teased him by staring at him, two shillings to get their dirty faces washed. The fact that they were found in the prisoner's drawer and not on his person may make them less cogent evidence of a criminal intent towards these boys than if they had been found upon his person; but still, in my view, the possession of them is some evidence of the existence of a criminal intent towards these boys on March 19, and, if so, some evidence of the identity of the person harbouring that intent with the person who had committed the crime charged upon March 16.

LORD SUMNER: . . . The actual criminal made an appointment to meet the same boys at the same time and place three days later and presumably for the same purpose. This tends to show that his act was not an isolated act, but was an incident in the habitual gratification of a particular propensity. The appellant, as his possession of the photographs tends to show, is a person with the same propensity. Indeed, he went to the place of the appointment with some of the outfit, and he had the rest of it at home. The evidence tends to attach to the accused a peculiarity which, though not purely physical, I think may be recognized as properly bearing that name. Experience tends to show that these offences against nature connote an inversion of normal characteristics which, while demanding punishment as offending against social morality, also partake of the nature of an abnormal physical property. A thief, a cheat, a coiner, or a house-breaker is only a particular specimen of the genus rogue, and, though no doubt each tends to keep to his own line of business, they all alike possess the by no means extraordinary mental characteristic that they propose somehow to get their livings dishonestly. So common a characteristic is not a recognizable mark of the individual. Persons, however, who commit the offences now under consideration seek the habitual gratification of a particular perverted lust, which not only takes them out of the class of ordinary men gone wrong, but stamps them with the hall-mark of a specialized and extraordinary class as much as if they carried on their bodies some physical peculiarity. . . . [T]he photographs, found as they were and after a short interval of time, tend to show that the accused had this recognizable propensity, which it was shown was also the propensity of the criminal of March 16. It was accordingly admissible evidence of his identity with that criminal. Its weight was for the jury. No doubt it required considerable discretion in introducing it at all and a careful direction from the learned judge, but it is admitted that this was given in unexceptionable terms.

. . . If a man could be convicted of a particular burglary, in which it was clear that no tools had been used at all, merely because at another place and time burglar's implements were found on his premises, it is difficult to see what limit could be put to the admissibility of general evidence of bad character, and the fact that evidence of articles found on the premises of accused persons is constantly given without much question, though I doubt not in the vast majority of cases quite rightly, is really only misleading, unless at the same time we ask the question what exactly does this purport to prove and by what probative nexus does it seek to prove it.

[LORDS FINLAY, L.C., PARKER OF WADDINGTON and PARMOOR agreed.]

Notes

1. The case depends on an appeal to the unlikelihood of an innocent man identified on the 19th having the same characteristic as the guilty man of the

16th—homosexuality. "That common characteristic might have been a cauliflower ear or an Old Etonian tie: it happened to be a propensity" (Cowen and Carter, p. 119). The appeal weakens as the characteristic becomes more common, and the likelihood of homosexuals assembling near public toilets must be considered. If the place was not a frequent resort of homosexuals, or not at that time, the appeal grows stronger. It weakens, however, as the strength of the evidence of practising homosexuality declines. This evidence, based on the powder puffs, was strong in *Thompson*. This case was subsequently misinterpreted to permit evidence of homosexual tendencies in all homosexual cases; *R. v. Horwood*, [1970] 1 Q.B. 133; [1969] 3 All E.R. 1156, C.A. stopped this trend. General homosexual tendencies will only be admissible in exceptional circumstances; prior homosexual conduct is much more likely to be admissible to prove its repetition with the same person. The same is true of other sexual relations (e.g. *R. v. Ball*, [1911] A.C. 47, H.L., and see the lengthy review of the case law in *R. v. Allen*, [1937] St. R. Qd. 32).

2. Lord Sumner's analogy with a physical defect is misleading: that is usually permanent, but homosexual lust and the power of self-control comes and goes.

3. The courts have since become more alert to the dangers of both children's evidence and identification evidence. Despite this and the foregoing points, it is not suggested that *Thompson* is wrong as a decision on the identity issue on its own facts, however much it was later misunderstood.

R. v. Horwood
[1970] 1 Q.B. 133; [1969] 3 All E.R. 1156, C.A.

The accused was convicted of attempting to procure the commission with himself of an act of gross indecency by a fourteen year old boy. The accused gave the boy a lift along a country road. The boy said they got out to look for rabbits when the accused made the proposal and he ran away. The accused said he got out to urinate and on returning to the car found the boy had gone. At a police interview the accused was asked: "Are you a homosexual?" He replied, "I used to be: I'm cured now. The doctor's given me some pills to take when the urge comes on. I go out with girls now like anyone else." The question and answer were admitted. The Court of Appeal held this to be wrong.

O'CONNOR, J.: In R. v. *King*, [1967] 2 C.A. Q.B. 338; [1967] 1 All E.R. 379, two boys alleged that the defendant met them in a public lavatory in the afternoon and committed acts of indecency; and that by arrangement he met them again in the evening, took them to his flat for the night and committed acts of indecency. The defendant denied the afternoon meeting, admitted the evening meeting, admitted that he took the boys home, admitted that he slept in the same bed as one of the boys but denied any act of indecency. In cross-examination he was asked: "Are you a homosexual." He answered: "Yes." This court held that the question and answer were properly admitted.

[Lord Parker, C.J. said:] "It is no different to put to a man the question, 'Are you a homosexual?', than to put to him certain indecent photographs of a homosexual nature found in his possession and say to him: 'Are these yours?' In the judgment of the court, following the case of *Thompson*, [1918] A.C. 221, [1918–19] All E.R. Rep. 521, H.L., that question was *prima facie* perfectly legitimate. In passing, it is to be observed that the principle laid down by Lord Sumner is not one of completely general application, but must be limited to certain particular crimes, and the common one to which it has been applied is sexual cases."

In *Thompson* v. R., the only issue was the identity of the accused, and it is clear that, in that case, evidence of the possession of the photographs was admitted in proof of identity and for no other purpose. In R. v. *King*, there was an issue of identity as to the afternoon incidents spoken to by the boys, the subject of counts in the indictment. No doubt that fact was in this court's mind when applying *Thompson* v. R. Having said that, we are satisfied that the real ground for admitting the evidence in that case was to rebut the defence of innocent association. . . .

Assuming that the expression "I am a homosexual" does not necessarily convey that the accused has committed homosexual offences, it must be only in very exceptional circumstances that evidence of this nature can be admitted to rebut innocent association. R. v. *King* was an exceptional case; the admitted facts were such that the admission that the accused was a homosexual could properly be said to be relevant to the issue before the jury. In our judgment, that decision cannot be taken as authority for the proposition that in all cases where a man is charged with a homosexual offence he may be asked either by the police or in the witness box the question: "Are you a homosexual?" In cases where identity is not in issue, the occasions on which such evidence can properly be admitted must be very rare. In the present case, the nature of the admitted association, namely, the appellant taking the boy for a drive in his motor car in broad daylight, can be contrasted with that in R. v. *King*, taking the boy home and getting into bed with him. In the present case, the real dispute was whether the opportunity for comitting the offence had ever arisen, for there was no suggestion of indecency in the motor car.

Note

This affirms the so-called "narrow view" of R. v. *Sims*, [1946] K.B. 531; [1946] 1 All E.R. 697, to the effect that evidence of homosexual disposition is only admissible where, as in that case, there was a strikingly similar technique or where as in *Thompson* v. R., [1918] A.C. 221, H.L.; [1918–19] All E.R. Rep. 521 the appeal to the unlikelihood of coincidence on the facts is very strong for some other reason. It rejected the "broad view" that evidence of homosexuality is always admissible on homosexual charges. On principle the broad view seems wrong. It would be a wide exception to the general rule against similar fact evidence; it assumes too readily that homosexuals may not change their habits; it increases the power of policemen and blackmailers unduly; and in any event, a tendency to homosexuality does not necessarily entail promiscuity. See now *Boardman* v. *Director of Public Prosecutions*, [1974] 3 All E.R. 887, [1974] 3 W.L.R. 673, H.L.

R. v. Flack

[1969] 2 All E.R. 784, C.A.

The accused was charged with committing incest with his three sisters. The trial judge stated that the evidence on any one count was admissible against the accused on the others. The Court of Appeal held this to be wrong.

SALMON L.J.: The passage in R. v. *Sims*, [1946] K.B. 531, at p. 540; [1946] 1 All E.R. 697, at p. 701, C.C.A. relied on by the Crown read as follows:

"The probative force of all the acts together is much greater than one alone; for, whereas the jury might think one man might be telling an untruth, three or four are hardly likely to tell the same untruth unless they were conspiring together. If there is nothing to suggest a conspiracy their evidence would seem to be overwhelming. Whilst it would no doubt be in the interests of the prisoner that each case should be considered separately without the evidence on the others, we think that the interests of justice require that on each case the evidence of the others should be considered, and that even apart from the defence raised by him, the evidence would be admissible."

The passage in R. v. *Campbell*, [1956] 2 Q.B. 432, p. 439; [1956] 2 All E.R. 272, at p. 276, C.C.A. relied on by the Crown is shorter, but to much the same effect, and reads as follows:

"At the same time we think a jury may be told that a succession of these cases may help them to determine the truth of the matter provided they are satisfied that there is no collaboration between the children to put up a false story".

These passages seem to suggest that, whenever a man is charged with a sexual offence against A, evidence may always be adduced by the Crown in support of that charge of similar alleged offences by the accused against B, C and D. This court does not think that those passages were ever intended to be so understood. If, however, this is their true meaning, they go much further than was necessary for the purpose of the decisions, and cannot, in the view of this court, be accepted as correctly stating the law.

In R. v. *Sims*, the accused had admitted that he invited each of the men to his house. He said he had done so solely for the purpose of conversation and playing cards. Each man said he had been invited to the house for the purpose of buggery. The question was whether this was a guilty or an innocent association. As Lord Goddard, C.J., said ([1946] K.B. 531, at p. 540; [1946] 1 All E.R. 697, at p. 701) C.C.A.:

". . . the visits of the men to the prisoner's house were either for a guilty or innocent purpose; that they all speak to the commission of the same class of acts upon them tends to show that in each case the visits were for the former and not the latter purpose."

This was plainly right, and the correctness of the decision in R. v. *Sims* has never been doubted. The evidence of B, C and D was clearly admissible, against A to negative the defence of innocent association.

In R. v. *Campbell*, the passage to which reference has been made was unnecessary for the decision which turned on the extent to which the evidence of one child could amount to corroboration of another. The correctness of the decision itself in R. v. *Campbell* has never been questioned. It is only the passage to which reference has already been made about which any criticism is possible. In R. v. *Chandor* Lord Parker, C.J., referring to the passage from R. v. *Campbell* which has been read, said ([1959] 1 Q.B. 545, at pp. 549–50; [1959] 1 All E.R. 702, at p. 704, C.C.A.):

"Unqualified it would appear to cover a case where the accused was saying that the incident in question never took place at all. To take an incident in the present case, the accused said that in respect of an alleged offence with a boy . . . at View Point—he . . . had never met the boy at View Point at all. Yet, if this passage in R. v. *Campbell* is unqualified it would apply to just such a case. We do not think that the passage in R. v. *Campbell* was ever intended to cover that. Indeed, so far as we know the authorities have never gone so far as that, nor do we see how they could . . . There are, of course, many cases in which evidence of a succession of incidents may properly be admissible to help to determine the truth of any one incident, for instance, to provide identity, intent, guilty knowledge or to rebut a defence of innocent association. On such issues evidence of a succession of incidents may be very relevant, but we cannot say that they have any relevance to determine whether a particular incident ever occurred at all."

This court respectfully agrees with every word of Lord Parker, C.J.'s judgment in R. v. *Chandor*.

In the present case, the defence consisted of a complete denial that any such incident as that to which the appellant's sisters spoke had ever occurred. No question of identity, intent, system, guilty knowledge, or of rebutting a defence of innocent association ever arose. That was plain at any rate at the conclusion of the evidence, whatever may have been the position when the application for separate trials was originally made. Accordingly, the evidence of an alleged offence against one sister could not be evidence of the alleged offences against the others.

R. v. Ball
[1911] A.C. 47, C.C.A. and H.L.

The accused, a brother and sister, were convicted of incest committed during certain periods in 1910. The main prosecution evidence was that the accused, who held themselves out as married, were seen together at night in a house which had only one furnished bedroom, containing a double bed showing signs of occupation by two persons. The brother had been seen coming from the bedroom in a half-dressed state while the woman was in nightdress. The similar fact evidence admitted by Scrutton, J. was that three years earlier, before incest was made criminal, the accused had lived together as man and wife sharing a bed, and that a baby had been born, the accused being registered as its parents.

SCRUTTON, J.: I am of opinion that evidence of previous acts would be admissible to explain the relation in which two parties are found which has to be interpreted by the jury. I do not like to use the word "scheme", although that word is used; but I think relation is the word which best expresses the principle which I wish to convey.

I only wish further to say that as I understand the case of *Makin* v. *A.-G. for New South Wales*, [1894] A.C. 57, [1891–4] All E.R. Rep. 24, P.C. it does involve very much the same principle. In that case the prisoner was being tried for the murder of a child, and what was proved was that he had received the child from the mother for a very small sum, and that its skeleton was found in his back garden. Now those facts in themselves are consistent with death by an ordinary disease and irregular burial, or they are consistent with murder to get rid of the child and to take advantage of the sum received for its maintenance. It was proposed to tender evidence that a number of other skeletons had been found in the back garden of a previous residence of the prisoners, and that a number of other children had been entrusted to the prisoner also for inadequate sums, and that all those children had disappeared. I do not think that that evidence was given to show intent, because the first thing to show was not intent, but that the prisoners had done the act at all, that they had actually killed the child; it was not till they killed the child that the question of the intent with which they did it arose, and I think that that evidence must have been given to enable the jury to draw the proper inference as to the sort of business or transaction that the prisoners were carrying on, of which the disappearance of this particular child was one incident. From proving the sort of business carried on to proving the relation of the parties seems to me a very small step.

[The accused's appeal to the Court of Criminal Appeal succeeded.]

DARLING, J.: If on the facts of this case an act of intercourse was proved, no question could arise as to the *mens rea* with which the act was done, for the statute forbids the act as in itself criminal. If without the admission of the disputed evidence the fact of the two accused persons occupying the same bed on the date or dates charged was insufficient proof that intercourse took place between them on that date or those dates, then the fact that intercourse took place between them on former occasions could only be tendered to show that they were persons likely to have intercourse on the particular dates—a ground on which evidence is not receivable.

[The prosecutor's appeal to the House of Lords succeeded.]

LORD ATKINSON (in argument): . . . Surely in an ordinary prosecution for murder you can prove previous acts or words of the accused to show he entertained feelings of enmity towards the deceased, and that is evidence not merely of the malicious mind with which he killed the deceased, but of the fact that he killed him. You can give in evidence the enmity of the accused towards the deceased to prove that the accused took the deceased's life. Evidence of motive neessarily goes to prove the fact of the homicide by the accused, as well as his "malice aforethought", inasmuch as it is more probable that men are killed by those who have some motive for killing them than by those who have not.

Lord Loreburn, L.C.: . . . I consider that this evidence was clearly admissible on the issue that this crime was committed—not to prove the *mens rea*, as Darling, J. considered, but to establish the guilty relations between the parties and the existence of a sexual passion between them as elements in proving that they had illicit connexion in fact on or between the dates charged. Their passion for each other was as much evidence as was their presence together in bed of the fact that when there they had guilty relations with each other.

My Lords, I agree that Courts ought to be very careful to preserve the time-honoured law of England, that you cannot convict a man of one crime by proving that he had committed some other crime; that, and all other safeguards of our criminal law, will be jealously guarded; but here I think the evidence went directly to prove the actual crime for which these parties were indicted.

[The Earl of Halsbury and Lords Ashbourne, Alverstone, C.J., Atkinson, Gorell, Shaw of Dunfermline, Mersey and Robson agreed.]

Question

Would the similar fact evidence have been admissible if the accused had shared a house but slept in different bedrooms?

Notes

1. The case shows that the previous misconduct need not be a criminal or civil wrong. See also *R. v. Shellaker*, [1914] 1 K.B. 414, C.C.A. and *Griffith v. R.* (1937), 58 C.L.R. 185.

2. The similar fact evidence might be thought weak in two respects: the events were not very recent, and the statute making incest a crime would be a new deterrent to its commission. But this was compensated for by the strength of the other evidence.

R. v. Straffen
[1952] 2 Q.B. 911; [1952] 2 All E.R. 657, C.C.A.

The accused was charged with strangling a young girl, Linda Bowyer. The death occurred in a quiet country area at a time when the accused was in the area having escaped for a short time from Broadmoor, an institution for the criminally insane. The accused said to the police: 'I did not kill her" at a time when neither the police nor the newspapers had referred to the death of a girl. Cassels, J. admitted evidence of two previous murders of young girls committed by the accused. The Court of Criminal Appeal upheld his decision.

Slade, J.: . . . The grounds on which the admissibility of the evidence was urged by the Solicitor-General in the court below was the similarity of the deaths and of the circumstances surrounding them in the case of the two murders at Bath, on the one hand, with the circumstances of the murder at Little Farley, on the other. He stated the similarities to be, first, that each of the victims was a young girl; secondly, that each of the young girls was killed by manual strangulation; thirdly, that in each case there was no attempt at sexual interference or any apparent motive for the crime; fourthly, that in none of the three cases was there any evidence of a struggle; and, fifthly, that in none of the three cases was any attempt made to conceal the body although the body could have been easily concealed. Those similarities were fortified by the medical evidence....

... In the opinion of the court, [the] evidence was rightly admitted, not to show, to use the words of counsel for the appellant, that the appellant was a professional strangler but to show that he strangled Linda Bowyer—in other words, to identify the murderer of Linda Bowyer as being the same person as the person who had murdered the other two little girls in precisely the same way. I see no distinction in principle between this case and *Thompson* v. *R.*, [1918] A.C. 221; [1918–19] All E.R. Rep. 521, H.L. and, indeed, I think one cannot distinguish abnormal propensities from identification. Abnormal propensity is a means of identification.

... [There it was] the abnormal propensity of homosexuality. In the present case it is an abnormal propensity to strangle young girls without any apparent motive, without any attempt at sexual interference, and to leave their dead bodies where they can be seen and where presumably their deaths would be rapidly detected.

Question

Would the similar fact evidence had been admitted if (*a*) Straffen had not shown knowledge of the death of a girl in his statement to the police; or (*b*) someone else who had a record of murdering old women had escaped from Broadmoor about the same time; or (*c*) the murder was committed in central London?

ii Formulation

The formulation of the similar fact rule has sometimes caused controversy. The most commonly cited is Lord Herschell's in *Makin* v. *A.-G. for New South Wales*, [1894] A.C. 57, at p. 65; [1891–4] All E.R. Rep. 24, at pp. 25–26 (p. 256, *ante*); but others should be noted.

Cross on Evidence
4th Edn. P. 310

Evidence of the misconduct of a party on other occasions (including his possession of incriminating material) must not be given if the only reason why it is substantially relevant is that it shows a disposition towards wrongdoing in general, or the commission of the particular crime or civil wrong with which such party is charged.... [But] if the argument can be rendered more specific, and made to support a suggestion that the accused is disposed towards a particular method, as opposed to a particular kind, of wrongdoing, evidence of his misconduct on other occasions may become admissible.

Hoffmann: The South African Law of Evidence
2nd Edn. Pp. 34 and 38–39

The prosecution may not adduce evidence of improper conduct by the accused on other occasions if its only relevance is to show that the accused is a person of bad disposition, and his disposition is not highly relevant to an issue raised at the trial.... [S]imilar fact evidence will be admissible *either* (i) if it has a relevance in addition to showing the accused's disposition *or* (ii) if it shows only the accused's disposition but this is highly relevant to the issue of guilt. Under the first head, similar fact evidence may be technically admissible even though its relevance is very slight. The courts have therefore emphasized the judge's discretion to exclude such evidence in cases where its prejudicial content is so out of proportion to its true evidential value that it would be unfair to the accused to admit it. Under the second head, this problem cannot arise.

There has been a sterile debate about whether Lord Herschell was stating a general exclusionary rule subject to a list of specific exceptions, or whether he was stating a general rule excluding evidence for some purposes and a general rule including the same evidence for others. For what it is worth, the latter view is now generally thought to be the sounder (*Harris* v. *Director of Public Prosecutions*, [1952] A.C. 694, at p. 705; [1952] 1 All E.R. 1044, at p. 1046, H.L.), though as a matter of convenience lists of exceptional areas where similar fact evidence is likely to be admitted are made.

Lord Herschell suggests that the similar fact evidence to be admitted must be relevant in some way different in kind from proof of disposition. But this is not always so. In *R. v. Straffen*, [1952] 2 Q.B. 911; [1952] 2 All E.R. 657, C.C.A. the only relevance of the similar fact evidence was to prove Straffen's disposition; given his disposition, the killing must have been done by him. In *R. v. Ball*, [1911] A.C. 47, H.L. the only relevance of the prior incest was to prove a disposition to commit incest; it supported an inference that the accused took advantage of the many opportunities to commit incest afforded by sharing a bed. (See also *Thompson v. R.*, [1918] A.C. 221; [1918–19] All E.R. Rep. 521 H.L.) On the other hand, the evidence in *Makin* was introduced to show all the babies had been murdered: it was unlikely that so many would die of natural causes. That conclusion achieved, it followed that the accused had murdered them because they had the best opportunities and motives. The relevance of the evidence was to prove the fact of the crime, not the disposition of the accused.

In substance the views of Cross and Hoffmann are the same, but Hoffmann's formulation is perhaps to be preferred. The difference is that the former suggests evidence proving a particular method of acting on a disposition is admissible, while the latter says that evidence of disposition is admissible if highly relevant to any issue. Similar fact evidence is often thought of as rebutting particular defences associated with want of *mens rea*, but it can also rebut denials by the accused that he had anything to do with the *actus reus* and that there was any *actus reus* at all.

Similar fact evidence is also thought of as requiring a high degree of similarity with the crime charged, and Cross's definition expresses this. This overlooks the fact that the admissibility of similar fact evidence must always be considered in the light of the main evidence in the case.

Cl. 3 (2) of the Criminal Law Revision Committee's draft Criminal Evidence Bill followed the Hoffmann view.

iii Examples of similar fact evidence
Facts which are part of the same transaction.—Two groups of cases which are often said to illustrate similar fact evidence are those concerning offences of a continuing nature and those involving proof of discreditable incidents as part of the particular crime charged. These are only examples in a limited sense because they do not involve the use of past misconduct to prove a present crime; they simply involve proof of particular matters all of which are part of one crime. Further, they are not true examples because often the misconduct proved is not similar to that charged.

Offences of a continuing nature render admissible past misconduct by virtue of the definition of the offence. Committing a public nuisance by making a highway dangerous, or permitting premises to be used as a brothel are not crimes which depend on certain single acts at a particular moment; a single crime is committed over a period, and particular incidents during it may be proved.

If a crime occurs at a particular time but events before or after are so closely connected with it in time, place or other circumstance as properly to be part of the same transaction, then evidence of those events is admissible.

O'Leary v. R.
(1946), 73 C.L.R. 566

The employees of a timber camp went on a drunken orgy lasting several hours. One was found near death next morning, having been struck eight or nine times on the head with a bottle; kerosene had been poured on him and his clothes ignited. Several circumstances connected the accused with the crime. The High Court of Australia held that evidence of violent assaults by the accused on other employees, including the deceased, during the orgy, all of which were brutal blows to the head, was admissible, not as similar fact evidence but because it disclosed a connected series of events to be considered as one transaction.

DIXON, J.: The evidence disclosed that, under the influence of the beer and wine he had drunk and continued to drink, he engaged in repeated acts of violence which might be regarded as amounting to a connected course of conduct. Without evidence of what, during that time, was done by those men who took any significant part in the matter and especially evidence of the behaviour of the prisoner, the transaction of which the alleged murder formed an integral part could not be truly understood and, isolated from it, could only be presented as an unreal and not very intelligible event. The prisoner's generally violent and hostile conduct might well serve to explain his mind and attitude and, therefore, to implicate him in the resulting homicide. . . . In my opinion, for the reasons given, evidence of his conduct was admissible for the purpose stated.

In the charge to the jury the evidence was not presented exactly in this way. It was put rather that the crime, in its circumstances, was of a description which showed that it must have been committed by a man of a particular disposition, that such a disposition amounted to a specific means of connecting or identifying the culprit and that the prisoner's conduct earlier in the period might be considered to show that, for the time being, he possessed that disposition. I do not think that this is an accurate way of treating the purpose for which the conduct of the prisoner was admissible. I am unable to see in the mere brutality of the crime or the fact that the assailant concentrated his attack on the head of the deceased any such specific connexion with the prior acts of the prisoner as to afford, so to speak, an identifying mark of the sort referred to in the decisions which appear to have been in the learned judge's contemplation.

[LATHAM, C.J., RICH, J. and WILLIAMS, J. agreed. STARKE, J. held the evidence admissible as similar fact evidence but not on the majority ground. McTIERNAN, J. dissented.]

Other examples of this doctrine include: a series of events showing a background of hostility between the parties (*R. v. Garner*, [1964] N.S.W.R. 1131); a series of crimes committed under the influence of a continuing threat (*R. v. Rearden* (1864), 4 F. & F. 76); other crimes confessed by the accused to his victim as part of his criminal plan (e.g. *R. v. Chitson*, [1909] 2 K.B. 945, C.C.A.), other crimes which confirm the stories of accomplices of the accused (*R. v.*

Kennaway, [1917] I K.B. 25; [1916–17] All E.R. Rep. 651, C.C.A.); other crimes which explain the conduct of the victim of the main crime (*R. v. Lovegrove*, [1920] 3 K.B. 643, C.C.A.); crimes which confirm parts of a confession to other crimes (*R. v. Evans*, [1950] I All E.R. 610, C.C.A.); and where the accused commits three burglaries in one night, stealing a shirt at one place and leaving it at another: *R. v. Wylie* (1804), I B. & P. (N.R.) 92, at p. 94; *R. v. O'Meally (No. 2)*, [1953] V.L.R. 30.

Rebutting defences.—The usual way of setting out the law of similar fact evidence is to list defences which are rebuttable by such evidence. This is convenient and not harmful as long as it is remembered that the list is not closed and that the overriding questions are those of relevance and weight. Many of the cases cited above involve the use of similar fact evidence to rebut denial of the *actus reus*, or denial that it was caused voluntarily (cf. *R. v. Harrison-Owen*, [1951] 2 All E.R. 726, C.C.A.) or intentionally (*R. v. Mortimer* (1935), 25 Cr. App. Rep. 150, C.C.A.). "That the same accident should repeatedly occur to the same person is unusual, especially so when it confers a benefit on him" (*R. v. Bond*, [1906] 2 K.B. 389, at pp. 420–1; [1904–7] All E.R. Rep. 24, at p. 41, *per* A. T. Lawrence, J.).

Other defences rebuttable by similar fact evidence are mistake (e.g. *R. v. Francis* (1874), L.R. 2 C.C.R. 128); innocent motive (e.g. the use of instruments for a medical examination rather than to procure abortion: *R. v. Bond*, [1906] 2 K.B. 389; [1904–7] All E.R. Rep. 24, at p. 41, or possessing arsenic to kill weeds rather than unwanted wives and professional rivals: *R. v. Armstrong*, [1922] 2 K.B. 555; [1922] All E.R. Rep. 153, C.C.A.); and innocent association (*R. v. Hall*, [1952] I K.B. 302; [1952] I All E.R. 66, C.C.A.). The defence of mistaken identity may be rebutted by appealing to the unlikelihood of a mistakenly identified innocent man having the accused's disposition, the latter being proved either by past bad acts (*R. v. Straffen*, [1952] 2 Q.B. 911; [1952] 2 All E.R. 657, C.C.A.) or possession of the instruments of the crime charged (*Thompson v. R.* [1918] A.C. 221; [1918–19] All E.R. Rep. 521, H.L.; *R. v. Twiss*, [1918] 2 K.B. 853, C.C.A.). Many frauds would be incapable of proof without similar fact evidence (*Blake v. Albion Life Assurance Society* (1878), 4 C.P.D. 94, at p. 101).

Reading

Brett, 6 Res Judicatae 471 (1954); Cowen and Carter, Chap. 4; Cross, 75 L.Q.R. 333 (1959); [1973] Crim. L.R. 400; Eggleston in Glass, pp. 53–89; Gooderson, [1959] C. L.J. 210; Hoffmann, pp. 34–58; Stone, 46 Harv. L.R. 954 (1933); Tapper, 36 M.L.R. 56 (1973); Williams, pp. 229–38.

B. Statutory rules

A number of statutes permit the introduction of the accused's record. For example, the Theft Act 1968, s. 27 (3) provides that on a charge of handling stolen goods, evidence of handling goods stolen within the previous twelve months, or of convictions for theft or handling within the previous five years shall be admissible to prove the accused's knowledge or belief that the goods were stolen. This and similar provisions exist because of the frequent difficulty of proving *mens rea*. (See Cross, pp. 341–3; Phipson, paras. 491–4.)

C. Reform

The Criminal Law Revision Committee recommended a slight increase in admissibility. They said that in cases where the defence admitted the conduct in respect of which the accused was charged, but denied that he was guilty of an offence in respect of it, then evidence of other conduct showing a disposition to commit the kind of offence charged should be admitted to show *mens rea* notwithstanding the lack of sufficient similarity to have the evidence admitted under the current law. Where evidence is admitted in this way, they recommend that prior convictions be admissible by themselves without the need to adduce evidence of the facts on which the convictions were based. In other cases of admissible similar fact evidence, evidence of convictions should be admitted in conjunction with the facts on which they are based (paras. 92–9). They propose repeal of the Theft Act 1968, s. 27 (3).

The proposed changes in the common law rule are slight. In view of the notorious difficulty of codifying basic common law rules, it is not surprising to learn of the drafting difficulties experienced by the Committee (Cross, [1973] Crim. L.R. 400).

II OTHER ASPECTS OF THE ACCUSED'S CHARACTER

Evidence of the accused's good character may be introduced by his own testimony, examination of defence witnesses, or cross-examination of prosecution witnesses. The evidence is admissible to show the unlikelihood of him committing the offence charged and to enhance his credibility. This can be regarded as a generous exception to the rule prohibiting evidence of disposition so far as the first purpose is concerned, and a generous exception to the normal rule against accrediting witnesses so far as the second is concerned. If the evidence is introduced for the first purpose it must be relevant to the crime charged. "[S]uppose a man charged with an unnatural crime; would it be any evidence at all to that man's character that he paid his bills regularly . . .?" (Erskine, *arguendo*, R. v. *Hardy* (1794), 24 State Tr. 1076). The position is less clear if character evidence is introduced solely to enhance credibility. The normal rule is that the credibility of witnesses may be impeached by any conviction: is any evidence of good character admissible to prove the likelihood of truth-telling? Character here strictly means "reputation" (R. v. *Rowton* (1865), Le. & Ca. 520; [1861–73] All E.R. Rep. 549). It does not include a witness's opinions of the accused's disposition, though in practice the accused's past good acts are often referred to. This is certainly so when the accused himself is testifying to his good character: one can hardly testify to one's own reputation with any confidence, for a man's reputation is what people say about him when he is not there (Hoffmann, p. 32). This development does something to temper a rather irrational rule (see Wigmore para. 1986).

If the accused testifies to his good character, he may be cross-examined as to his record under the Criminal Evidence Act 1898 s. 1 (*f*) (ii) (p. 289, *post*). If the accused's witnesses testify to his good character, the prosecution may cross-examine them about their credibility, and about their knowledge of the accused's reputation; his convictions are admissible to rebut his good character

(*R. v. Redd*, [1923] 1 K.B. 104, at p. 107; [1922] All E.R. Rep. 435, at p. 436, C.C.A.; *R. v. Winfield*, [1939] 4 All E.R. 164, C.C.A.); and the prosecution may call witnesses to the accused's bad character. If prosection witnesses under cross-examination admit that the accused has a good character, the prosecution may contradict it by evidence of his bad reputation and convictions. It seems that the proof of the accused's bad character by means of his convictions is permissible despite their irrelevance either to his guilt of the crime charged or his credibility (*R. v. Winfield*, [1939] 4 All E.R. 164, C.C.A.; cf. *R. v. Shrimpton* (1851), 2 Den. 319, at p. 322). If the accused has testified, this follows from the general rule that any witness's credit may be destroyed by proving his convictions; if the accused has not testified, the anomaly has an independent existence (Gooderson, 11 C.L.J. 377).

Apart from the above instances and the law of similar fact evidence, the accused's bad character is inadmissible unless it is a fact in issue (*R. v. Butterwasser* [1948] 1 K.B. 4; [1947] 2 All E.R. 415, C.C.A.).

But in fact one of the above instances—cross-examination as to character of an accused who puts his good character in issue—is common in practice. It is part of the general question, one of the most difficult in the law of Evidence, of cross-examining the accused on his record. This is the subject of the next chapter.

11

The Accused's Character: Part II

The Criminal Evidence Act 1898, s. 1 (e) and (f) provides:

(e) A person charged and being a witness in pursuance of this Act may be asked any question in cross-examination notwithstanding that it would tend to criminate him as to the offence charged:

(f) A person charged and called as a witness in pursuance of this Act shall not be asked, and if asked shall not be required to answer, any question tending to show that he has committed or been convicted of or been charged with any offence other than that wherewith he is then charged, or is of bad character, unless—

(i) the proof that he has committed or been convicted of such other offence is admissible evidence to show that he is guilty of the offence wherewith he is then charged; or

(ii) he has personally or by his advocate asked questions of the witnesses for the prosecution with a view to establish his own good character, or has given evidence of his good character, or the nature or conduct of the defence is such as to involve imputations on the character of the prosecutor or the witnesses for the prosecution; or

(iii) he has given evidence against any other person charged with the same offence.

Section 1 (f) of the Criminal Evidence Act 1898 was enacted to make special provision for the accused when his common law incapacity to testify was abolished. Had he been given complete immunity from cross-examination as to character, he would have been much better off than other witnesses. He would have had a licence to smear his accusers without any sanction other than punishment for perjury, which is little feared by one already being tried for another and perhaps more serious crime. He would have been free to attack his co-accused, which might have resulted in his own unjust acquittal or the co-accused's unjust conviction. He would have been free to allege his own good character without the risk of embarrassing cross-examination. And admissible similar fact evidence could not have been put to him. On the other hand, had he been treated as an ordinary witness, he would have been liable to cross-examination on all past convictions to show his lack of *credibility*; and these might have been misused by the jury to prove his *guilt* of the crime charged. In this way a possibly innocent man with a record would have been deterred from doing his case justice by telling his story on oath; the great gift of the right to testify would have been denied to the bulk of accused.

The legislation is thus a compromise. The accused is shielded from disclosure of his record until he "throws away his shield" either by raising his own good character or by casting imputations on the prosecution, or by

275

casting imputations on his co-accused. He can be cross-examined on admissible similar fact evidence under s. 1 (*f*) (i) independently of the way he conducts his case. This compromise has often been admired and it is perhaps better than either of the extremes it seeks to avoid. But there are numerous problems on s. 1 (*f*) and the decisions on it are in certain respects in a state of hopeless conflict.

I   THE PROHIBITIONS

A. General

S. 1 (*f*) applies to questions not only by prosecution counsel, but the judge (*R. v. Ratcliffe* (1919), 89 L.J.K.B. 135, C.C.A.) and counsel for a co-accused (*R. v. Roberts*, [1936] 1 All E.R. 23, C.C.A.). But the accused can voluntarily tender his own record (*Jones* v. *Director of Public Prosecutions*, [1962] A.C. 635, H.L., at p. 663; [1962] 1 All E.R. 569, at p. 575 *per* Lord Reid).

S. 1 ((*f*) depends on the effect, not the motive, of the questioning: the Act does not say "with a view to show" but "tending to show" (*R. v. Ellis*, [1910] 2 K.B. 746, C.C.A., at p. 757; [1908–10] All E.R. Rep. 488, at p. 491). The judge's approval should be obtained before questions infringing s. 1 (*f*) are asked: as much harm could be caused by the question as by the answer (R. v. *McLean* (1926), 134 L.T. 640 C.C.A.). Counsel must not drive or trap the accused into throwing away his shield (*R. v. Baldwin;* [1925] All E.R. Rep. 402, C.C.A.; *R. v. Eidenow* (1932), 23 Cr. App. Rep. 145, C.C.A.). Further, questions falling within the prohibition may not be put unless the exceptions apply even though on other grounds they would be permissible (*Jones* v. *Director of Public Prosecutions*, [1962] A.C. 635; [1962] 1 All E.R. 569, H.L.).

B. The relation between s. 1 (e) and s. 1 (f)

On one view s. 1 (e) permits questions directly criminating the accused as to the offence charged, while s. 1 (*f*) prohibits questions indirectly criminating the accused by eliciting and suggesting inferences from his record or which impugn his credibility (*Maxwell* v. *Director of Public Prosecutions*, [1935] A.C. 309, at p. 318; [1934] All E.R. Rep. 168, at pp. 172–3, H.L., *per* Viscount Sankey, L.C.; *R. v. Cokar*, [1960] 2 Q.B. 207; [1960] 2 All E.R. 175, C.C.A.). The other view is that s. 1 (e) permits questions which tend to criminate the accused as to the offence charged directly or indirectly, while s. 1 (*f*) merely prohibits cross-examination as to credit (see *R. v. Chitson*, [1909] 2 K.B. 945, C.C.A.; *R. v. Kurasch*, [1915] 2 K.B. 749, C.C.A.; *R. v. Kennaway*, [1917] 1 K.B. 25; [1916–17] All E.R. Rep. 671, C.C.A.; *R. v. Miller*, [1952] 2 All E.R. 667; and the obscure *dicta* of the High Court of Australia in *Attwood* v. *R.* (1960), 102 C.L.R. 353, at pp. 361–2). This is the South African view (Hoffman, p. 62). It would seem, however, to make s. 1 (*f*) (i) otiose (cf. *Attwood* v. *R.* (1960), 102 C.L.R. 353, at pp. 361–2).

In *Jones* v. *Director of Public Prosecutions*, [1962] A.C. 635; [1962] 1 All E.R. 569, H.L., the majority of the House of Lords upheld the first view, and the cases supporting the second can only be regarded as correct on some other ground. The first view has a tendency to give the prohibition on cross-examination of the accused in s. 1 (*f*) a wide operation, but this tendency is limited by the majority's decision in *Jones* that the prohibition on questions "tending to show'' a bad record refers to questions ''tending to reveal for the first time to the jury'' rather than ''tending to support or prove''.

Jones v. Director of Public Prosecutions
[1962] A.C. 635; [1962] 1 All E.R. 569, H.L.

The accused was charged with murdering a girl guide. Before the trial the accused set up a false alibi; in his evidence he alleged instead that he had spent the night in question with a prostitute and testified to his wife's angry reaction to his late return. This testimony was strikingly similar to that given by him at an earlier trial during which he was convicted of raping a girl guide. The prosecution obtained leave to cross-examine the accused to show that the similarities were so close as to make the defence incredible, and did so in a way which, though vague, "must have created the impression in the minds of the jury that the appellant had shortly before the murder of [the girl guide] either committed or been charged with some offence on a Friday night which was reported in a newspaper on the following Sunday" ([1962] A.C. 635 at p. 643; [1961] 3 All E.R. 668, at pp. 672–3, C.C.A.). In his own evidence in chief the accused admitted having been "in trouble" with the police before, and his counsel had put before the jury a similar admission contained in a statement of the accused's to the police.

The Court of Criminal Appeal and the House of Lords (by a 3–2 majority) discussed appeals against conviction on the ground that the cross-examination did not "tend to show" the accused's bad record or character: "tend to show" meant "tend to reveal to the jury for the first time" rather than "tend to prove".

LORD REID (with whom VISCOUNT SIMONDS agreed): It is well established that the 1898 Act has no application to evidence given by any person other than the accused: where it was competent before that Act for a witness to prove or refer to a previous conviction of the accused, that is still competent. What the Act does is to alter the old rules as regards the accused. It might merely have provided that the accused should be a competent witness; then the ordinary rules would have applied to him. But it goes on to afford to him protection which the ordinary rules would not give him: it expressly prohibits certain kinds of question being put to him. That must mean questions which would be competent and relevant under the ordinary rules, because there was no need to prohibit any question which would in any event have been excluded by the ordinary rules. So what must now be considered is what kinds of question, which would have been competent and relevant under the ordinary rules of evidence, does the Act prohibit. . . .

This raises at once the question what is the proper construction of the words in proviso (*e*), "tend to criminate him as to the offence charged". Those words could mean "tend to convince or persuade the jury that he is guilty", or they could have the narrower meaning—"tend to connect him with the commission of the offence charged". If they have the former meaning, there is at once an insoluble conflict between provisos (*e*) and (*f*). No line of questioning could be relevant unless it (or the answers to it) might tend to persuade the jury of the guilt of the accused. It is only permissible to bring in previous convictions or bad character if they are so relevant, so, unless proviso (*f*) is to be deprived of all content, it must prohibit some questions which would tend to criminate the accused of the offence charged if those words are used in the wider sense. But if they have the narrower meaning, there is no such conflict. So the structure of the Act shows that they must have the narrower meaning.

So I turn to consider proviso (*f*). It is an absolute prohibition of certain questions unless one or other of three conditions is satisfied. It says the accused "shall not be asked, and if asked shall not be required to answer", certain questions. It was suggested that this applies to examination in chief as well as to cross-examination. I do not think so. The words "shall not be required to answer" are quite inappropriate for examination in chief. The proviso is obviously intended to protect the accused. It does not prevent him from volunteering evidence, and does not in my view prevent his counsel from asking questions leading to disclosure of a previous conviction or bad character if such disclosure is thought to assist in his defence.

The questions prohibited are those which "tend to show" certain things. Does this mean tend to prove or tend to suggest? Here I cannot accept the argument of the Attorney-General. What matters is the effect of the questions on the jury. A veiled suggestion of a previous offence may be just as damaging as a definite statement. In my judgment, "tends to show" means tends to suggest to the jury. But the crucial point in the present case is whether the questions are to be considered in isolation or whether they are to be considered in the light of all that had gone before them at the trial. If the questions or line of questioning has to be considered in isolation I think that the questions with which this appeal is concerned would tend to show at least that the accused had previously been charged with an offence. The jury would be likely to jump to that conclusion, if this was the first they had heard of this matter. But I do not think that the questions ought to be considered in isolation. If the test is the effect the questions would be likely to have on the minds of the jury that necessarily implies that one must have regard to what the jury had already heard. If the jury already knew that the accused had been charged with an offence, a question inferring that he had been charged would add nothing and it would be absurd to prohibit it. If the obvious purpose of this proviso is to protect the accused from possible prejudice, as I think it is, then "show" must mean "reveal", because it is only a revelation of something new which could cause such prejudice.

I shall not detain your Lordships by analysing the questions to which objection is taken to see whether they contained any material revelation of anything which the jury were unlikely to infer from the evidence already given by the accused in chief. I need only refer to the speech about to be delivered by my noble and learned friend, Lord Morris of Borth-y-Gest, and to the judgment of the Court of Criminal Appeal. For the reasons which they give, I am of opinion that this appeal should be dismissed on the ground that these questions were not prohibited because they did not "tend to show" any of the matters specified in proviso (*f*).

But, in case it should be thought that some of the views which I have expressed are not in accord with what was said by Lord Simon in *Stirland* v. *Director of Public Prosecutions*, [1944] A.C. 315; [1944] 2 All E.R. 13, H.L. I must say something about that case. That was a case where the accused had put his character in issue and the questions which it was held ought not to have been put to him in cross-examination dealt with an occasion when a former employer had questioned him about a suspected forgery. But the case did not turn on proviso (*f*) because the second exception in the proviso was satisfied by the accused having given evidence of his good character and therefore the proviso was excluded.

Lord Simon did, however, state six rules which should govern cross-examination to credit of an accused person. First he set out proviso (*f*). Then comes the rule which gives rise to the difficulty ([1944] A.C. 315, at p. 326; [1944] 2 All E.R. 13, at p. 18, H.L.):

"2. He may, however, be cross-examined as to any of the evidence he has given in chief, including statements concerning his good record, with a view to testing his veracity or accuracy or to showing that he is not to be believed on his oath."

Applied to a case where the accused has put his character in issue I think that is correct, because then proviso (*f*) does not apply. But I do not think that Lord Simon can have meant it to apply in its general form to a case where proviso (*f*) does operate, because earlier in his speech he said ([1944] A.C. 315, H.L., at p. 322; [1944] 2 All E.R. 13, at p. 16):

"This House has laid it down in *Maxwell* v. *Director of Public Prosecutions* [1935] A.C. 309; [1934] All E.R. Rep. 168, H.L. that, while paragraph (*f*) of this section absolutely prohibits any question of the kind there indicated being put to the accused in the witness box unless one or other of the conditions (i), (ii) or (iii) is satisfied, it does not follow that such questions are in all circumstances justified whenever one or other of the conditions is fulfilled."

Thus he recognized the absolute character of the prohibition except where one or other of the conditions is satisfied, so he cannot have intended to say that there is another case, not covered by the conditions, where the proviso also does not apply, namely, where questions are put with a view to testing the veracity of the accused's evidence in chief. But if he did mean that it was certainly *obiter* and I would not agree with it. It would in effect be legislating by adding a fourth condition to proviso (*f*). The Attorney-General refused to take this point and I think he was perfectly right.

It is said that the views which I have expressed involve overruling two decisions of the Court of Criminal Appeal, R. v. *Chitson*, [1909] 2 K.B. 945, C.C.A. and R. v. *Kennaway*, [1917] 1 K.B. 25, C.C.A.; [1916–17] All E.R. Rep. 651. I do not think so. I think the decisions were right but the reasons given for them were not. In the former case the accused was charged with having had carnal knowledge of a girl aged 14. Giving evidence, she said that the accused told her that he had previously done the same thing to another girl, who, she said, was under 16. No objection was taken to this evidence, I assume rightly. So before the accused gave evidence the jury already knew that he was alleged to have committed another offence. If the views which I have already expressed are right, cross-examining the accused about this matter disclosed nothing new to them and therefore did not offend against the prohibition in proviso (*f*). But the judgment of the court was not based on that ground: it was said that although the questions tended to prove that the accused was of bad character they also tended to show that he was guilty of the offence with which he was charged. For the reasons which I have given I do not think that that is sufficient to avoid the prohibition in proviso (*f*).

R. v. *Kennaway*, [1917] 1 K.B. 25, C.C.A; [1916–17] All E.R. Rep. 651 was a prosecution for forgery. Accomplices giving evidence for the prosecution described the fraudulent scheme of which the forgery was a part and related a conversation with the accused in which he stated to them that some years earlier he had forged another will in pursuance of a similar scheme. Then in cross-examination the accused was asked a number of questions about this other forgery. Those questions were held to have been properly put to him. Here, again, these questions disclosed nothing new to the jury and I can see no valid objection to them. But again that was not the ground of the court's decision. Their ground of decision was similar to that in *Chitson's* case [1909] 2 K.B. 945, C.C.A., and I need not repeat what I have said about that case.

LORD DENNING: My Lords, much of the discussion before your Lordships was directed to the effect of section 1 (*f*) of the Criminal Evidence Act 1898: and, if that were the sole paragraph for consideration, I should have thought that counsel for the Crown ought not to have asked the questions he did. My reasons are these:

First: The questions *tended* to show that Jones had previously been charged in a court of law with another offence. True it is that they did not point definitely to that conclusion, but they conveyed that impression, and that is enough. Counsel may not have intended it, but that does not matter. What matters is the impression the questions would have on the jury. The Attorney-General said that, if the questions left the matter evenly balanced, so that there was some other conclusion that could equally well be drawn, as, for instance, that Jones had not been "charged" in a court of law but had only been interrogated in a police station, there was no bar to the questions being asked. I cannot agree. If the questions asked by the Crown are capable of conveying two impressions—one objectionable and the other not—then they "tend to show" each of them: and the questions must be excluded, lest the jury adopt the worse of the two impressions. I do not think that it is open to the prosecution to throw out prejudicial hints and insinuations—from which a jury might infer that the man had been charged before—and then escape censure under the cloak of ambiguity.

Second: I think that the questions tended to *show* that Jones had been charged with an offence, even though he had himself brought out the fact that he had been "in trouble" before. It is one thing to confess to having been in trouble before. It is quite another to have it emphasized against you with devastating detail. Before these questions were asked by the Crown, all that the jury knew was that at some unspecified time in the near or distant past, this man had been in trouble with the police. After the questions were asked, the jury knew, in addition, that he had been very recently in trouble for an offence on a Friday night which was of so sensational a character that it featured in a newspaper on the following Sunday—in these respects closely similar to the present offence—and that he had been charged in a court of law with that very offence. It seems to me that questions which tend to reveal an offence, thus particularized, are directly within the prohibition in section 1 (*f*) and are not rendered admissible by his own vague disclosure of some other offence. I do not believe that the mere fact that he said he had been in trouble before with the police—referring as he did to an entirely different matter many years past—let in this very damaging cross-examination as to recent events.

Third: The questions do not come within the exception (i) to section 1 (*f*). There was no evidence before the court of any "other offence" which would be admissible evidence to show that he had been guilty of this murder. If the prosecution had given evidence of the previous rape with its attendant circumstances, there might have been such similarities as to render the proof of that offence admissible to prove identity, see *R. v. Straffen*, [1952] 2 Q.B. 911; [1952] 2 All E.R. 657, C.C.A.: but in the absence of such evidence, I do not see how these questions could be justified in cross-examination under exception (i). Before any cross-examination is permissible under exception (i), the prosecution must lay a proper foundation for it by showing some "other offence which is admissible evidence to show that he is guilty". The prosecution should normally do it by giving evidence in the course of their case; though there may be cases in which they might, with the leave of the judge, do it for the first time in cross-examination. No such foundation was laid here.

If the case rested solely on section 1 (*f*), I would therefore have held that these questions were inadmissible. But I do not think it rests on section 1 (*f*). In my judgment, the questions were admissible under section 1 (*e*), which says that a person charged

"may be asked any question in cross-examination notwithstanding that it would tend to criminate him as to the offence charged."

As to this subsection, Viscount Sankey, L.C., speaking for all in this House in *Maxwell's* case, [1935] A.C. 309, at p. 318; [1934] All E.R. Rep. 168, at pp. 172–3, H.L. said that under section 1 (*e*)

"a witness may be cross-examined in respect of the offence charged, and cannot refuse to answer questions directly relevant to the offence on the ground that they tend to incriminate him: thus if he denies the offence, he may be cross-examined to refute the denial."

I would add that, if he gives an explanation in an attempt to exculpate himself he may be cross-examined to refute his explanation. And none the less so because it tends incidentally to show that he had previously been charged with another offence.

Let me first say why I think in this case the questions were directly relevant to the offence charged. They were directly relevant because they tended to refute an explanation which the accused man had given. He had given a detailed explanation of his movements on the crucial weekend, and so forth, all in an attempt to exculpate himself. The prosecution sought to show that this explanation was false: and I think it was of direct relevance for them to do so. From the very earliest times, long before an accused man could give evidence on his own behalf, the law has recognized that, in considering whether a man is guilty of the crime charged against him, one of the most relevant matters is this: What explanation did he give when he was asked about it? Was that explanation true or not? If he gives a true explanation, it tells in his favour. If he gives a false explanation, it tells against him. The prosecution have, therefore, always been entitled, as part of their own case, to give evidence of any explanation given by the accused and of its truth or falsity. Thus if a man, who is found in possession of a stolen watch, tells a policeman that he bought it for £5 from a tradesman, whom he names, the prosecution can call that tradesman, as part of their case, to say whether that was true or not. If true, it is an end of the case against the accused. If false, it goes a long way to prove his guilt, see R. v. *Crowhurst* (1844), 1 Car. & Kir. 370 by Alderson, B., R. v. *Smith* (1845), 2 Car. & Kir. 207 by Lord Denman, C.J. So also if a man, who is charged with murder at a specified time and place, tells a policeman that he was at the house of his sister-in-law at the time, as Jones did here, the prosecution can call the sister-in-law, as part of their case, to say it was false and that he was not at her house at all. So also if he tries, as Jones did, to get his sister-in-law to say that he was at her house at that time, contrary to the fact, the prosecution can call the sister-in-law to say that he tried to suborn her to give false testimony: for the simple reason that "the recourse to falsehood leads fairly to an inference of guilt", see *Moriarty* v. *London, Chatham and Dover Rail Co.* (1870), L.R. 5 Q.B. 314, at p. 319, by Cockburn, C.J. In this very case Jones's sister-in-law, Mrs. Eldridge, gave such evidence for the prosecution without any objection being taken to it, even though it tended to show that he was guilty of another offence, namely, the offence of attempting to pervert the course of justice.

Now, suppose the man does this further thing which Jones did here. He discards the story that he went to his sister-in-law's house and puts forward a different story. He says that he went up to London and was with a prostitute, but he does not identify her. So the prostitute cannot be called to falsify his story. Nevertheless the prosecution can falsify it by other evidence, if they have it available. They can call such evidence as part of their own case, even though it tends incidentally to show that he was guilty of another offence. For instance, they could prove that his finger-prints were on the window of a house that was broken into at Yateley that night. ". . . the mere fact that the evidence adduced tends to show the commission of other crimes does not render it inadmissible if it be relevant to an issue before the jury," see *Makin* v. *A.-G. of New South Wales* [1894] A.C. 57, at p. 65; [1891–4] All E.R. Rep. 24, at p. 26, P.C. Evidence that he had committed burglary would not be admissible to prove that he had committed murder: but evidence that he was at Yateley would be admissible to prove that he was in the vicinity and had recourse to falsehood to explain his whereabouts. The prosecution would be entitled to call this evidence, even though it tended to show that he was guilty of burglary.

Such is the law as it is, and always has been, as to the evidence which can be called for the prosecution. They can, in the first place, give evidence of any explanation given by the accused of his movements and they can, in the second place, give evidence that his explanation is false, even though it tends incidentally to show the commission by him of some other offence. Now, when Parliament in 1898 enabled an accused man to give evidence on his own behalf, they did not cut down evidence of this kind for the prosecution. And when the prosecution gives such evidence, it must be open to the accused man himself to answer it. He must be able to give evidence about it and to be cross-examined upon it. He can be cross-examined as to any explanation he has given and as to its truth or falsity: and he can be cross-examined upon it none the less because incidentally it may tend to show that he has been guilty of some other offence.

No one, surely, can doubt the validity of R. v. *Chitson*, [1909] 2 K.B. 945, C.C.A., and R. v. *Kennaway* [1917] 1 K.B. 25, C.C.A.; [1916–17] All E.R. Rep. 651 at least to this extent, that when the prosecution have legitimately given in evidence any explanation or statement made by the accused relative to the offence charged, he can be cross-examined as to the truth or falsity of it, even though incidentally it may tend to show that he has been guilty of some other offence or is of bad character.

Now, the only difference is that, whereas in those cases the accused man made his explanation or statement *before* the trial, in the present case he made his explanation (about his conversations with his wife, and so forth) for the first time *at* the trial when he went into the witness box to give evidence on his own behalf. But this cannot give him any protection from a cross-examination to which he would otherwise be exposed. His explanation is not made sacrosanct, it is not made incapable of challenge, simply because he gives it at the trial instead of at an earlier stage. The prosecution are entitled to expose its falsity, no matter whether he gives it at the trial or beforehand. And they are not precluded from doing so merely because the exposure of it tends to show that he has been guilty of some other offence or is of bad character. The situation is precisely covered by the second proposition in *Stirland's* case, [1944] A.C. 315, at p. 326; [1944] 2 All E.R. 13, at p. 18, H.L. where Viscount Simon, L.C. in this House, with the assent of all present, said that, notwithstanding the prohibition in section 1 (*f*), the accused man

"may, however, be cross-examined as to any of the evidence he has given in-chief, including statements concerning his good record,"

and including, I would add, any explanation offered by him "with a view to testing his veracity or accuracy or to showing that he is not to be believed on his oath".

It is noteworthy that everyone at the trial of Jones acted on this view of the law. No one suggested that the questions were absolutely prohibited. All that was suggested was that it was a matter of discretion. And that is, I think, the true position. The judge was entitled in his discretion to exclude them if he thought they were so prejudicial as to outweigh their probative value. It was his discretion, not that of the prosecution. He did not exclude them but permitted them to be asked. They were, therefore, properly put.

In conclusion I would say that I view with concern the suggestion that the reasoning in *R. v. Chitson* [1909] 2 K.B. 945, C.C.A. and *R. v. Kennaway* [1917] 1 K.B. 25; [1916–17] All E.R. Rep. 651, C.C.A. was wrong and that what Viscount Simon, L.C. said in *Stirland's* case [1944] A.C. 315, [1944] 2 All E.R. 13, H.L. is no longer a safe guide. Those cases have governed the practice in our criminal courts for years: and the result has been wholly beneficial. It is not, in my opinion, right to resort now to a literal reading of the Act so as to displace them.

LORD MORRIS OF BORTH-Y-GEST: . . . My Lords, it seems to me that the clearest guidance as to provisos (*e*) and (*f*) was given in *Maxwell's* case. In his speech, [1935] A.C. 309, at pp. 318–19; [1934] All E.R. Rep. 168, at pp. 172–3, H.L. Viscount Sankey, L.C. said:

"In section 1, proviso (*e*), it has been enacted that a witness may be cross-examined in respect of the offence charged, and cannot refuse to answer questions directly relevant to the offence on the ground that they tend to incriminate him: thus if he denies the offence, he may be cross-examined to refute the denial. These are matters directly relevant to the charge on which he is being tried. Proviso (*f*), however, is dealing with matters outside, and not directly relevant to, the particular offence charged; such matters, to be admissible at all, must in general fall under two main classes: one is the class of evidence which goes to show not that the prisoner did the acts charged, but that, if he did these acts, he did them as part of a system or intentionally, so as to refute a defence that if he did them he did them innocently or inadvertently. . . .

The other main class is where it is sought to show that the prisoner is not a person to be believed on his oath, which is generally attempted by what is called cross-examination to credit. Closely allied with this latter type of question is the rule that, if the prisoner by himself or his witnesses seeks to give evidence of his own good character, for the purpose of showing that it is unlikely that he committed the offence charged, he raises by way of defence an issue as to his good character, so that he may fairly be cross-examined on that issue, just as any witness called by him to prove his good character may be cross-examined to show the contrary. All these matters are dealt with in proviso(*f*). . . ."

In his speech in *Stirland* v. *Director of Public Prosecutions*, [1944] A.C. 315, at p. 324; [1944] 2 All E.R. 13, at p. 17, H.L. Viscount Simon, L.C. said that he was disposed to think that in(*f*), where the word "character" occurs four times, there is a combination of the conceptions of general reputation and of actual moral disposition.

Having regard to what has been laid down in *Maxwell's* case and in *Stirland's* case, I do not find it necessary to embark upon "a close study and comparison" of earlier cases such as R. v. *Chitson*, [1909] 2 K.B. 945, C.C.A. and R. v. *Kennaway*, [1917] 1 K.B. 28; [1916–17] All E.R. Rep. 651, C.C.A. If the results reached in those cases can be supported it must not be on any line of reasoning that runs counter to what has been laid down in *Maxwell's* case and in *Stirland's* case.

LORD DEVLIN: My Lords, I would dismiss this appeal on the short ground that the questions objected to were relevant to an issue in the case upon which the appellant had testified in chief. It is not disputed that the issue to which the questions related was a relevant one. It concerned the identification of the appellant as being at the material time at the scene of the crime. He testified that at the material time he was with a prostitute in the West End and he supported this alibi by giving evidence of a conversation which he had with his wife about it a day or two later. The purpose of the questions objected to was to obtain from the appellant an admission (which was given) that when he was being questioned about his movements in relation to another incident some weeks earlier he had set up the same alibi and had supported it with an account of a conversation with his wife in almost identical terms; the prosecution suggested that these similarities showed the whole story of the alibi to be an invented one. In order to make good his point by means of cross-examination it was necessary for Mr. Griffith-Jones for the prosecution to identify to some extent the occasion on which the previous questioning had taken place and to refer to a newspaper report which had entered into the conversation between the appellant and his wife. On this the Court of Criminal Appeal has said:

"In our view this part of the cross-examination of the appellant, taken as a whole, must have created the impression in the minds of the jury that the appellant had shortly before the murder of Brenda Nash either committed or been charged with some offence on a Friday night which was reported in a newspaper on the following Sunday."

The Attorney-General has argued that the questions do not go as far as the Court of Criminal Appeal thought. This is a difficult point, but I do not think it has to be considered in the bare form in which it was put. If the questions are relevant to an issue, they are, in my view, admissible, notwithstanding that incidentally they suggest that the appellant has committed an offence. If they are not relevant to an issue, the prosecution had no business to introduce the matter at all. They were suggestive and damaging questions and objectionable as such; and it is unnecessary to determine whether the objection is more securely based on the terms of the Act of 1898 or upon the ground that it was irrelevant matter "tending to lead the minds of the jury astray into false issues"; *Maxwell* v. *Director of Public Prosecutions* [1935] A.C. 309; [1934] All E.R. Rep. 168, H.L. But the concession of relevance supplies in my opinion the short and simple answer to the whole case. . . .

I turn now to consider an alternative construction of the Act that avoids these difficulties. Hitherto, I have been using the word "character" in the sense in which it was used in the argument, that is, as meaning the quality or disposition of the man. But in the law of evidence "character" normally means "reputation". Strictly speaking, it is not permissible to give evidence of particular acts done by the prisoner, unconnected with the offence charged, in order to show his disposition, whether his general character is in issue or not; for a man's character in the eyes of the law depends not on his disposition but on his reputation. This interpretation explains a feature of the proviso that puzzled the Court of Criminal Appeal in this case, namely, why a distinction is drawn in it between evidence showing previous offences and evidence showing bad character; the two overlap unless the latter is construed, as the court thought it ought to be, as evidence showing "that the accused is otherwise (that is, apart from any offence within the first part) of bad character". The true answer, I think, is that the Act is dealing with two entirely different categories of evidence. Evidence of previous offences would not strictly under the old rule have been allowed as evidence of bad character; that must be spoken to by persons who know of the reputation which the prisoner actually enjoyed, whether deserved or not. Evidence of bad reputation would, of course, have been inadmissible to prove the commission of a specific offence. This interpretation of "character" explains also why evidence of discreditable acts falling short of an offence is not, where relevant, exempted from the prohibition, while evidence showing a previous offence is, where relevant, so exempted. Discreditable acts falling short of an offence are not within the terms of the prohibition at all. That does not mean that such evidence, because not specifically prohibited, is admissible; under the ordinary law of evidence it is excluded unless it is relevant to an issue. All reference to bad character is therefore naturally excluded from the first exception; there are no circumstances in which reputation can be admissible on the issue; evidence of reputation is admissible only if the accused introduces character under the second and third exceptions.

My Lords, I find it impossible to believe that the framers of the Act of 1898 did not intend "character" to have the meaning of "reputation". Although the merits of the rule had frequently been questioned, it was firmly settled in the eighteenth century. A vigorous attempt to dislodge it was made in 1865 and was unsuccessful. In R. v. *Rowton* (1865), Le. & Ca. 520; [1861–73] All E.R. Rep. 549 it was authoritatively laid down by eleven out of the thirteen judges sitting in the Court of Crown Cases Reserved that evidence of the prisoner's character must not be evidence of particular facts but evidence of general reputation only. Even the two dissenting judges, though they were prepared to interpret character as including actual moral disposition, did not consider that evidence could be given of concrete examples of conduct. Not all the judges liked the rule. But Cockburn, C.J. said (1865), Le. & Ca. 520, at p. 532; [1861–1873] All E.R. Rep. 549, at p. 552:

"I take my stand on this: I find it uniformly laid down in the books of authority that the evidence to character must be evidence of general character in the sense of reputation. . . ."

On the first proposition I have already referred to R. v. *Rowton* (1865), Le. & Ca. 520; [1861–73] All E.R. Rep. 549 and have indicated that the rule which that case laid down was never popular with practitioners. As early as 1809 Lord Ellenborough, C.J. said in R. v. *Jones* (1809), 31 St. Tr. 251, at p. 310:

". . . it is very remarkable, but there is no branch of evidence so little attended to."

It appears that under the Act of 1898 character was almost invariably treated as including moral disposition. In R. v. *Dunkley*, [1927] 1 K.B. 323, C.C.A.; [1926] All E.R. Rep. 187 counsel for the defence cross-examined the principal witness for the prosecution and suggested that her story was fabricated because she thought she had a grievance against the prisoner; and the prisoner in his evidence in chief said that the witness's story was untrue and was due to malice. On this the prisoner was cross-examined about his own character. In the Court of Criminal Appeal one of the arguments advanced for the appellant was that the reputation of the witness had not been attacked. On this argument Lord Hewart, C.J. after reciting the proviso, spoke as follows, [1927] 1 K.B. 323, C.C.A., at p. 329; [1926] All E.R. Rep. 187, at p. 190:

"It is apparent that within the space of a very few lines the word "character" is used in this part of this section no fewer than four times. It is also apparent that the imputations which are spoken of in the closing words of the passage I have read are described, not as imputations on the prosecutor or the witnesses for the prosecution, but as imputations on the character of the prosecutor or the witnesses for the prosecution. In those circumstances it is not difficult to suppose that a formidable argument might have been raised on the phrasing of this statute, that the character which is spoken of is the character which is so well known in the vocabulary of the criminal law—namely, the general reputation of the person referred to; in other words, that "character" in that context and in every part of it, in the last part no less than in the first, in the third part no less than in the second, bears the meaning which the term "character" was held to bear, for example, in the case of R. v. *Rowton* [1865], Le. & Ca. 520; [1861–73] All E.R. Rep. 549. . . . Nevertheless, when one looks at the long line of cases beginning very shortly after the passing of the Criminal Evidence Act 1898, it does not appear that that argument has ever been so much as formulated. It was formulated yesterday. One can only say that it is now much too late in the day even to consider that argument, because that argument could not now prevail without the revision, and indeed to a great extent the overthrow, of a very long series of decisions."

In *Stirland* v. *Director of Public Prosecutions*, [1944] A.C. 315, H.L., at p. 326; [1944] 2 All E.R. 13, at p. 17 Lord Simon, L.C. referred to this case and said that he was disposed to think that in the word "character" in proviso (*f*) both conceptions were combined. . . .

If R. v. *Dunkley*, [1927] 1 K.B. 323; [1926] All E.R. Rep. 187, C.C.A. is not to be upheld and character means "reputation", it follows, for the reasons I have already given, that the prohibition in proviso (*f*) was not infringed by the questioning objected to in this case. Undoubtedly the questions tended to show that the accused had done something discreditable which had brought him into trouble with the police, but they did not present him as a man of generally bad reputation. If, as may well be argued, they went further than that and tended to show that he had committed some offence, nevertheless they were not prohibited because the evidence about that offence was an essential part of an incident that was admissible to show that the accused was guilty of the offence for which he was being tried.

If R. v. *Dunkley*, [1927] 1 K.B. 323; [1926] All E.R. Rep. 187, C.C.A. is to be upheld, it can in my opinion be upheld only on the reasoning on which the judgment is itself based, namely, that it is too late to argue—at any rate in relation to the Act of 1898—that "character" should bear the meaning of reputation only. Indeed, I cannot see any other ground on which the decision could be defended. To take only one point, is it possible to argue that when Parliament in proviso (*f*) (ii) referred to the accused as giving "evidence of his good character", it contemplated that he might give evidence to show that he was a man of good moral disposition when 30 years before the court which was then of final appeal had in one of the most fully considered judgments in its history decided that that was precisely what he could not do? . . .

The difficulty and danger inherent in the approach adopted by the Court of Criminal Appeal is that it sets no clear limits to the extent of the cross-examination. If cross-examination is permitted because it goes to an issue raised by the defence, the judge knows where he is; he will permit cross-examination that is relevant to that issue and no more. Thus, in the present case counsel could have asked about the nature of the "trouble" because, if it were shown to be quite trivial, it would be an inadequate excuse for manufacturing a false alibi. If the issue were different, it might be relevant to show the gravity of the trouble instead of its triviality. In other cases, it might be improper to go into the nature of the trouble at all. Relevance affords a clear guide as to what the limit should be; revelation does not. If it means no more than that the accused can be asked to repeat himself, it is at best otiose and at worst objectionable. It would, for example, be objectionable if it were done merely for the purpose of "rubbing it in". If the accused can be asked to do more than repeat himself, how much more? When the accused puts his whole character in issue, the door is thrown wide open; but when he puts only a part of it in issue, I can see no satisfactory way of defining a limit except by the test of relevance. I do not think that some vague rule which enables the prosecution to ask what it likes so long as it does not make out the accused's character to be substantially worse than he himself had suggested would be at all a safe guide. If, for instance, in this case the questions had not been relevant to the second alibi, I think it would have been quite wrong, just because the prisoner had mentioned a previous record and trouble with the police, to refer to an incident in the newspaper, thus running the risk that the jury might feel that they ought to pay attention to the newspaper publicity in connexion with the earlier offence.

Comments

1. Although in *Jones* the prior evidence showing bad character was put in by the defence, it may be given by prosecution witnesses provided it is validly admitted. The evidence of the prosecutrix in *R. v. Chitson*, [1909] 2 K.B. 945, C.C.A., and of the accomplices testifying for the prosecution in *R. v. Kennaway*, [1917] 1 K.B. 25; [1916–17] All E.R. Rep. 671, C.C.A. was held to permit cross-examination on the accused's bad character thus revealed, because it tended to reveal nothing new. It is this inclusion of prior *prosecution* evidence which really minimizes the impact of the majority's narrow interpretation of s. 1 (*e*) and broad interpretation of s. 1 (*f*). The Criminal Law Revision Committee recommended that the doubt about the meaning of "tending to show" be resolved by a statutory amendment adopting the majority view; but they recommended that the minority view of the relation between (e) and (f) be adopted (para. 117).

2. The Privy Council in *Malindi* v. *R.*, [1967] 1 A.C. 439; [1966] 3 All E.R. 285, P.C. supported the view that "character" included "disposition". It was held that where the accused was charged with conspiring for political ends to commit arson, cross-examination on passages in his notebooks stating that violence was politically necessary infringed s. 1 (f) because it suggested bad character in the sense of a disposition to resort to violence.

3. In *Attwood* v. *R.* (1960), 102 C.L.R. 353, at pp. 361–2 the High Court of Australia appeared to adopt the view of the minority in *Jones*. They said:

"One argument against that interpretation is to be found in sub-para. (i) of para. (*e*) of s. 399 [of the Victorian Crimes Act, 1958]. Why, it is naturally asked, should the express provision be made in favour of allowing questions as to the commission of offences and convictions of offences where relevant if without any provision expressly permitting it the accused as a witness may be asked questions simply because they are relevant to proof of the ingredients of the crime, notwithstanding that they do affect his character? The reason is, one may reasonably suppose, that the draftsman saw the two things in different lights. When he expressly prohibited proof of the commission of an offence or of a conviction of an offence the draftsman saw that he was expressly prohibiting proof of a fact he definitely identified independently of its operation or of the ground of introducing it in evidence. On the other hand, in the case of 'questions tending to show that he (the accused) is of bad character' the draftsman was dealing with a description of cross-examination going to credit which he thought of as, *ex hypothesi*, outside the field of relevancy altogether. In other words, in the case of strictly relevant facts he was regarding them as open to proof as part of the Crown case and as necessarily, or at least as naturally, the subject of evidence by the accused if he were called as a witness on his trial and he regarded them as not matter going to the bad character of the accused but as matter going to proof of his guilt. The words describe questions as to that kind of evidence excluded at common law upon the trial of criminal issues as a matter of policy but allowable in the cross-examination to credit of an ordinary witness. It follows that in so far as the questions excepted to in the case of the present applicant were relevant to the issues they were not excluded by the operation of s. 399 (*e*)."

What does this passage mean? Even if it explains the omission of "character" from s. 1 (*f*) (i), does it explain the omission of questions about being "charged"? These will only rarely be relevant on cross-examination as to credit.

Question

Evaluate the arguments for the views of the majority and of the minority in *Jones* on the relation between s. 1 (e) and s. 1 (f) and on the meaning of "tending to show" in s. 1 (f).

C. Charges and acquittals

Maxwell *v.* Director of Public Prosecutions
[1935] A.C. 309; [1934] All E.R. Rep. 168, H.L.

The accused was charged with manslaughter of a woman in the course of procuring an abortion. He gave evidence of his good character and was asked in cross-examination about a previous acquittal on the same charge. The House of Lords quashed his conviction.

VISCOUNT SANKEY, L.C.: The substantive part of that proviso is negative in form and as such is universal and is absolute unless the exceptions come into play. Then come the three exceptions: but it does not follow that when the absolute prohibition is superseded by a permission, that the permission is as absolute as the prohibition. When it is sought to justify a question it must not only be brought within the terms of the permission, but also must be capable of justification according to the general rules of evidence and in particular must satisfy the test of relevance. Exception (i) deals with the former of the two main classes of evidence referred to above, that is, evidence falling within the rule that where issues of intention or design are involved in the charge or defence, the prisoner may be asked questions relevant to these matters, even though he has himself raised no question of his good character. Exceptions (ii) and (iii) come into play where the prisoner by himself or his witnesses has put his character in issue, or has attacked the character of others. Dealing with exceptions (i) and (ii), it is clear that the test of relevance is wider in (ii) than in (i); in the latter, proof that the prisoner has committed or been convicted of some other offence, can only be admitted if it goes to show that he was guilty of the offence charged. In the former (exception (ii)), the questions permissible must be relevant to the issue of his own good character and if not so relevant cannot be admissible. But it seems clear that the mere fact of a charge cannot in general be evidence of bad character or be regarded otherwise than as a misfortune. It seemed to be contended on behalf of the respondent that a charge was *per se* such evidence that the man charged, even though acquitted, must thereafter remain under a cloud, however innocent. I find it impossible to accept any such view. The mere fact that a man has been charged with an offence is no proof that he committed the offence. Such a fact is, therefore, irrelevant; it neither goes to show that the prisoner did the acts for which he is actually being tried nor does it go to his credibility as a witness. Such questions must, therefore, be excluded on the principle which is fundamental in the law of evidence as conceived in this country, especially in criminal cases, because, if allowed, they are likely to lead the minds of the jury astray into false issues; not merely do they tend to introduce suspicion as if it were evidence, but they tend to distract the jury from the true issue—namely, whether the prisoner in fact committed the offence on which he is actually standing his trial. It is of the utmost importance for a fair trial that the evidence should be *prima facie* limited to matters relating to the transaction which forms the subject of the indictment and that any departure from these matters should be strictly confined.

It does not result from this conclusion that the word "charged" in proviso (*f*) is otiose: it is clearly not so as regards the prohibition; and when the exceptions come into play there may still be cases in which a prisoner may be asked about a charge as a step in cross-examination leading to a question whether he was convicted on the charge, or in order to elicit some evidence as to statements made or evidence given by the prisoner in the course of the trial on a charge which failed, which tend to throw doubt on the evidence which he is actually giving, though cases of this last class must be rare and the cross-examination permissible only with great safeguards.

Again, a man charged with an offence against the person may perhaps be asked whether he had uttered threats against the person attacked because he was angry with him for bringing a charge which turned out to be unfounded. Other probabilities may be imagined. Thus, if a prisoner has been acquitted on the plea of *autrefois* convict such an acquittal might be relevant to his credit, though it would seem that what was in truth relevant to his credit was the previous conviction and not the fact that he was erroneously again charged with the same offence; again, it may be, though it is perhaps a remote supposition, that an acquittal of a prisoner charged with rape on the plea of consent may possibly be relevant to a prisoner's credit.

But these instances all involve the crucial test of relevance. And in general no question whether a prisoner has been convicted or charged or acquitted should be asked or, if asked, allowed by the judge, who has a discretion under proviso (*f*), unless it helps to elucidate the particular issue which the jury is investigating, or goes to credibility, that is, tends to show that he is not to be believed on his oath; indeed the question whether a man has been convicted, charged or acquitted ought not to be admitted, even if it goes to credibility, if there is any risk of the jury being misled into thinking that it goes not to credibility but to the probability of his having committed the offence of which he is charged. I think that it is impossible in the present case to say that the fact that the prisoner had been acquitted on a previous charge of murder or man-slaughter, was relevant, or that it tended in the present case to destroy his credibility as a witness.

[Lords BLANESBURGH, ATKIN, THANKERTON and WRIGHT concurred.]

Comments

1. In *Stirland* v. *Director of Public Prosecutions*, [1944] A.C. 315, H.L.; [1944] 2 All E.R. 13 Lord Simon said that despite the prohibition on questions about charges, the accused may be asked about them if he has denied them under oath, for he may be asked about any of his statements to test veracity. But the House of Lords held that the word "charged" meant "charged in court" so that an accused who had been taxed by his employer with some criminal act was not lying in saying that he had never been charged.

2. The prohibition on questions about irrelevant charges entails a prohibition on questions about acquittals, save in exceptional cases of which Lord Sankey gives examples in *Maxwell* (see the rather obscure case of *R*. v. *Waldman* (1934), 24 Cr. App. Rep. 204, C.C.A., and *R*. v. *Deighton*, (1954] Crim. L.R. 208, C.C.A., where a previous acquittal was admitted as being relevant to the defence of mistake on a charge of obtaining money by false pretences).

II SECTION 1 (*f*) (i)

Cross-examination under s. 1 (*f*) (i) is permissible whether or not the Crown has first adduced evidence in chief to prove that the accused committed the other crime. S. 1 (*f*) (i) requires only that the evidence be "admissible", not that it "has been admitted" (*Jones* v. *Director of Public Prosecutions*, [1962] A.C. 635, at p. 685; [1962] 1 All E.R. 569, at p. 589, H.L.). "Nevertheless we think it might in general be undesirable that such matter should be first adduced in cross-examination; in a case, unlike the present, in which the accused desired to dispute or explain the alleged similarity of circumstances or pattern of the two offences he would thereby both be deprived of any opportunity to cross-examine prosecution witnesses and be exposed to the gravely prejudicial effect of suggestive questions to which his negative answers might be of no avail" (*Jones* v. *Director of Public Prosecutions*, [1962] A.C. 635, at p. 646; [1961] 3 All E.R. 668, at p. 675, C.C.A.; see also Lord Denning at pp. 668 and [1962] 1 All E.R. 569, at p. 578, and Lord Morris at pp. 685 and [1962] 1 All E.R. 569, at p. 589).

The paragraph principally covers cross-examination on admissible similar fact evidence but also convictions proved in chief under special statutory exceptions (p. 272, *ante*). Had it not been enacted the similar fact rule, so far as it is a rule of inclusion, would have been abolished by the main part of s. 1 (*f*).

III THE FIRST LIMB OF SECTION 1 (*f*) (ii)

What is usually called "the first limb of s. 1 (*f*) (ii)" permits cross-examination on the accused's record if he seeks to establish "his good character". "Character" means both "reputation" and "disposition" throughout s. 1 (*f*) (*Selvey* v. *Director of Public Prosecutions*, [1970] A.C. 304; [1968] 2 All E.R. 497, H.L.). The accused is usually seeking to assert that his reputation or past good acts or statements by himself or a witness of his disposition make it unlikely that he had the disposition to commit the crime. The paragraph does not apply when a defence witness praises the accused's character without being asked to (*R.* v. *Redd*, [1923] 1 K.B. 104; [1922] All E.R. Rep. 435, C.C.A.), nor when the accused asserts that the circumstances surrounding the crime show him to be innocent (*R.* v. *Ellis*, [1910] 2 K.B. 746; [1908–10] All E.R. Rep. 488, C.C.A.; *Malindi* v. *R.*, [1967] 1 A.C. 439, at p. 543; [1966] 3 All E.R. 285, at p. 293, P.C.). It was held not to apply when the accused said he had once been fined in order to show that he feared being arrested for not paying the fine and had therefore run away from a policeman: he did not mean to suggest that this was his only conviction (*R.* v. *Thompson*, [1966] 1 All E.R. 505, C.C.A.; and see *R.* v. *Wattam* (1952), 36 Cr. App. Rep. 72, C.C.A., at p. 78). The purpose of the cross-examination when the paragraph is infringed is to prove the accused's guilt and challenge his credibility (*R.* v. *Samuel* (1956), 40 Cr. App. Rep. 8, C.C.A.; cf. *Donnini* v. *R.* (1973), 47 A.L.J.R. 69, at p. 73, *per* Barwick, C.J.).

The modern authorities on balance favour the view that the accused's character is "indivisible": if he throws away his shield, his entire record can be admitted, whether or not his past crimes suggest defective credibility or suggest by their similarity to the crime charged that he is likely to have committed it (*R. v. Winfield*, [1939] 4 All E.R. 164, C.C.A.; *Stirland* v. *Director of Public Prosecutions*, [1944] A.C. 315, at p. 324; [1944] 2 All E.R. 13, at p. 18, H.L.; cf. *R. v. Shrimpton* (1851), 2 Den. 319, at p. 322). So far as the record is introduced to shake credibility, this strange result follows not from any fault in s. 1 (*f*) (ii) but from the general rule that any conviction of a witness can be put to him to shake his credibility under the Criminal Procedure Act 1865, s. 6.

IV THE SECOND LIMB OF SECTION 1 (*f*) (ii)

Selvey v. Director of Public Prosecutions
[1970] A.C. 304; [1968] 2 All E.R. 497, H.L.

The accused was charged with committing buggery on a young man. The prosecution evidence included, apart from the complainant's testimony, medical evidence that the complainant had been sexually interfered with and indecent photographs found in the accused's room. The accused denied the charge; denied knowledge of the photographs and alleged that they had been planted; and said that the complainant had told him in the accused's room on the afternoon of the relevant day that he was "prepared to go on the bed" and that already that day he had permitted an act of buggery on himself for £1 and would do the same again for money. Stable, J. asked the accused whether he was inviting the jury to disbelieve the complainant because he was "that sort of young man"; the accused said: "Yes." Stable, J. then permitted cross-examination on the accused's prior homosexual offences but not on his convictions for dishonesty; he warned the jury that the only relevance of the record was to prove lack of credibility. The accused's appeals against conviction failed before the Court of Criminal Appeal and the House of Lords.

VISCOUNT DILHORNE: The cases to which I have referred, some of which it is not possible to reconcile, in my opinion finally establish the following propositions:

(1) The words of the statute must be given their ordinary natural meaning (*R. v. Hudson*, [1912] 2 K.B. 464, C.C.A.; *R. v. Jenkins*, 114 L.J.K.B. 425, C.C.A.; *R. v. Cook*, [1959] 2 Q.B. 340; [1959] 2 All E.R. 97, C.C.A.).

(2) The section permits cross-examination of the accused as to character both when imputations on the character of the prosecutor and his witness are cast to show their unreliability as witnesses independently of the evidence given by them and also when the casting of such imputations is necessary to enable the accused to establish his defence (*R. v. Hudson*; *R. v. Jenkins*; *R. v. Cook*).

(3) In rape cases the accused can allege consent without placing himself in peril of such cross-examination (*R. v. Sheean*, 21 Cox C.C. 561; *R. v. Turner*, [1944] K.B. 463; [1944] 1 All E.R. 599, C.C.A.). This may be because such cases are *sui generis* (*per* Devlin, J. in *R. v. Cook*, [1959] 2 Q.B. 340, at p. 347; [1959] 2 All E.R. 97, at p. 101), or on the ground that the issue is one raised by the prosecution.

(4) If what is said amounts in reality to no more than a denial of the charge, expressed, it may be, in emphatic language, it should not be regarded as coming within the section (*Rouse*, [1904] 1 K.B. 184; *R. v. Grout* (1909) 74 J.P. 30, C.C.A.; *R. v. Jones*, 87 J.P. 147, C.C.A.; *Clark*, [1955] 2 Q.B. 469, C.C.A.; [1955] 3 All E.R. 29, C.C.A.).

Applying these propositions to this case, it is in my opinion clear beyond all doubt that the cross-examination of the accused was permissible under the statute.

I now turn to the question whether a judge has discretion to refuse to permit such cross-examination of the accused even when it is permissible under the section. Mr. Caulfield submitted that there was no such discretion and contended that a judge at a criminal trial had no power to exclude evidence which was admissible. He submitted that the position was correctly stated by Bankes, J. in *R. v. Fletcher* (1913), 9 Cr. App. Rep. 53, at p. 56, when he said:

"Where the judge entertains a doubt as to the admissibility of evidence, he may suggest to the prosecution that they should not press it, but he cannot exclude evidence which he holds to be admissible."

Since that case it has been said in many cases that a judge has such a discretion. In R. v. *Christie,* [1914] A.C. 545; [1914–15] All E.R. Rep. 63, H.L. where the question was as to the admissibility of a statement made in the presence and hearing of the accused, Lord Moulton said, at pp. 559 and 69:

"Now, in a civil action evidence may always be given of any statement or communication made to the opposite party, provided it is relevant to the issues. The same is true of any act or behaviour of the party. The sole limitation is that the matter thus given in evidence must be relevant. I am of opinion that, as a strict matter of law, there is no difference in this respect between the rules of evidence in our civil and in our criminal procedure. But there is a great difference in the practice. The law is so much on its guard against the accused being prejudiced by evidence which, though admissible, would probably have a prejudicial influence on the minds of the jury which would be out of proportion to its true evidential value, that there has grown up a practice of a very salutary nature, under which the judge intimates to the counsel for the prosecution that he should not press for the admission of evidence which would be open to this objection, and such an intimation from the tribunal trying the case is usually sufficient to prevent the evidence being pressed in all cases where the scruples of the tribunal in this respect are reasonable. Under the influence of this practice, which is based on an anxiety to secure for everyone a fair trial, there has grown up a custom of not admitting certain kinds of evidence which is so constantly followed that it almost amounts to a rule of procedure."

In R. v. *Watson,* 8 Cr. App. Rep. 249, C.C.A., at p. 254, the first case when the exercise of discretion in relation to cases coming within the section was mentioned, Pickford, J. said:

"It has been pointed out that to apply the rule" [in R. v. *Hudson,* [1912] 2 K.B. 464, C.C.A.] "strictly is to put a hardship on a prisoner with a bad character. That may be so, but it does not follow that a judge necessarily allows the prisoner to be cross-examined to character; he has a discretion not to allow it, and the prisoner has that protection."

In *Maxwell* v. *Director of Public Prosecutions,* [1935] A.C. 309; [1934] All E.R. Rep. 168, H.L. and in *Stirland* v. *Director of Public Prosecutions,* [1944] A.C. 315; [1944] 2 All E.R. 13, H.L. it was said in this House that a judge has that discretion. In R. v. *Jenkins,* 31 Cr. App. Rep. 1, at p. 15, C.C.A., Singleton, J. said:

"If and when such a situation arises" [the question whether the accused should be cross-examined as to character] "it is open to counsel to apply to the presiding judge that he may be allowed to take the course indicated. . . . Such an application will not always be granted, for the judge has a discretion in the matter. He may feel that even though the position is established in law, still the putting of such questions as to the character of the accused person may be fraught with results which immeasurably outweigh the result of questions put by the defence and which make a fair trial of the accused person almost impossible. On the other hand, in the ordinary and normal case he may feel that if the credit of the prosecutor or his witnesses has been attacked, it is only fair that the jury should have before them material on which they can form their judgment whether the accused person is any more worthy to be believed than those he has attacked. It is obviously unfair that the jury should be left in the dark about an accused person's character if the conduct of his defence has attacked the character of the prosecutor or the witnesses for the prosecution within the meaning of the section. The essential thing is a fair trial and that the legislature sought to ensure by section 1, subsection (*f*)."

Similar views were expressed in *Noor Mohamed* v. R., [1949] A.C. 182; [1949] 1 All E.R. 365, P.C. by Lord du Parcq, in *Harris* v. *Director of Public Prosecutions*, [1952] A.C. 694; [1952] 1 All E.R. 1044, H.L., in *Cook*, [1959] 2 Q.B. 340, C.C.A.; [1959] 2 All E.R. 97, in *Jones* v. *Director of Public Prosecutions*, [1962] A.C. 635; [1962] 1 All E.R. 569, H.L., and in other cases.

In the light of what was said in all these cases by judges of great eminence, one is tempted to say, as Lord Hewart said in *Dunkley*, [1927] 1 K.B. 323; [1926] All E.R. Rep. 187, C.C.A. that it is far too late in the day even to consider the argument that a judge has no such discretion. Let it suffice for me to say that in my opinion the existence of such a discretion is now clearly established.

Mr. Caulfield posed the question, on what principles should such a discretion be exercised. In R. v. *Flynn*, [1963] 1 Q.B. 729, at p. 737; [1961] 3 All E.R. 58, at p. 63, C.C.A. the court said:

". . . where . . . the very nature of the defence necessarily involves an imputation, against a prosecution witness or witnesses, the discretion should, in the opinion of this court, be as a general rule exercised in favour of the accused, that is to say, evidence as to his bad character or criminal record should be excluded. If it were otherwise, it comes to this, that the Act of 1898, the very Act which gave the charter, so to speak, to an accused person to give evidence on oath in the witness box, would be a mere trap because he would be unable to put forward any defence, no matter how true, which involved an imputation on the character of the prosecutor or any of his witnesses, without running the risk, if he had the misfortune to have a record, of his previous convictions being brought up in court while being tried on a wholly different matter."

No authority is given for this supposed general rule. In my opinion, the court was wrong in thinking that there was any such rule. If there was any such general rule, it would amount under the guise of the exercise of discretion, to the insertion of a proviso to the statute of the very kind that was said in R. v. *Hudson*, [1912] 2 K.B. 464, C.C.A., not to be legitimate.

I do not think it possible to improve upon the guidance given by Singleton, J. in the passage quoted above from R. v. *Jenkins* (1945), 31 Cr. App. Rep. 1, at p. 15, C.C.A. by Lord du Parcq in *Noor Mohamed* v. R., [1949] A.C. 182; [1959] 2 All E.R. 297, P.C. or by Devlin, J., in R. v. *Cook*, [1959] 2 Q.B. 340; [1949] 1 All E.R. 365, C.C.A. as to the matters which should be borne in mind in relation to the exercise of the discretion. It is now so well established that on a charge of rape the allegation that the woman consented, although involving an imputation on her character, should not expose an accused to cross-examination as to character, that it is possible to say, if the refusal to allow it is a matter of discretion, that there is a general rule that the discretion should be so exercised. Apart from this, there is not, I think, any general rule as to the exercise of discretion. It must depend on the circumstances of each case and the overriding duty of the judge to ensure that a trial is fair.

It is desirable that a warning should be given when it becomes apparent that the defence is taking a course which may expose the accused to such cross-examination. That was not given in this case but the failure to give such a warning would not, in my opinion, justify in this case the allowing of the appeal.

LORD GUEST (agreed and said): If I had thought that there was no discretion in English law for a judge to disallow admissible evidence, as counsel for the Crown argued, I should have striven hard and long to give a benevolent construction to section 1 (*f*) (ii), which would exclude such cases as R. v. *Rouse*, [1904] 1 K.B. 184, "liar", R. v. *Rappolt* (1911), 6 Cr. App. Rep. 156, C.C.A., "horrible liar", R. v. *Jones* (1923), 17 Cr. App. Rep. 117, C.C.A., "fabricated evidence", R. v. *Turner*, [1944] K.B. 463; [1944] 1 All E.R. 599, C.C.A., rape and other sexual offences, R. v. *Brown* (1960), 44 Cr. App. Rep. 181, C.C.A., "self-defence". I cannot believe that Parliament can have intended that in such cases an accused could only put forward such a defence at peril of having his character put before the jury. This would be to defeat the benevolent purposes of the 1898 Act which was for the first time to allow the accused to give evidence on his own behalf in all criminal cases. This would deprive the accused of the advantage of the Act. But I am not persuaded by the Crown's argument and I am satisfied upon a review of all the authorities that in English law such a discretion does exist. . . .

I find it unnecessary to say much more on the principles upon which discretion should be exercised. The guiding star should be fairness to the accused. This idea is best expressed by Devlin, J. in R. v. *Cook*, [1959] 2 Q.B. 340; [1959] 2 All E.R. 97, C.C.A. In following this star the fact that the imputation was a necessary part of the accused's defence is a consideration which will no doubt be taken into account by the trial judge. If, however, the accused or his counsel goes beyond developing his defence in order to blacken the character of a prosecution witness, this no doubt will be another factor to be taken into account. If it is suggested that the exercise of this discretion may be whimsical and depend on the individual idiosyncrasies of the judge, this is inevitable where it is a question of discretion; but I am satisfied that this is a lesser risk than attempting to shackle the judge's power within a straitjacket.

LORD PEARCE (agreed and said): My Lords, ever since the Criminal Evidence Act 1898, came into force there has been difficulty and argument about the application of the words in section 1 (*f*) (ii) "the nature or conduct of the defence is such as to involve imputations on the character of the prosecutor or the witnesses for the prosecution."

Two main views have been put forward. One view adopts the literal meaning of the words. The prosecutor is cross-examined to show that he has fabricated the charge for improper reasons. That involves imputations on his character. Therefore, it lets in the previous convictions of the accused. The practical justification for this view is the "tit for tat" argument. If the accused is seeking to cast discredit on the prosecution, then the prosecution should be allowed to do likewise. If the accused is seeking to persuade the jury that the prosecutor behaved like a knave, then the jury should know the character of the man who makes these accusations, so that it may judge fairly between them instead of being in the dark as to one of them.

The other view would limit the literal meaning of the words. For it cannot, it is said, have been intended by Parliament to make a man liable to have his previous convictions revealed whenever the essence of his defence necessitates imputations on the character of the prosecutor. This revelation is always damaging and often fatal to a defence. The high-water mark of this argument is the ordinary case of rape. In this the vital issue (as a rule) is whether the woman consented. Consent (as a rule) involves imputations on her character. Therefore, in the ordinary case of rape, the accused cannot defend himself without letting in his previous convictions. The same argument extends in varying lesser degrees to many cases.

The argument in favour of a construction more liberal to the accused is supported in two ways.

First, it is said that character is used in the sense in which it was used in R. v. *Rowton* (1865), Le. & Ca. 520, where the full court ruled that evidence of good character must be limited solely to general reputation and not to a man's actual disposition. . . .

. . . [I]t might be justifiable to consider whether "character" means in the context solely general reputation, if a reassessment could lead to any clarification of the problem. But in my opinion it leads nowhere. For I cannot accept the proposition that to accuse a person of a particular knavery does not involve imputations on his general reputation. The words "involve" and "imputations" are wide. It would be playing with words to say that the allegation of really discreditable matters does not involve imputations on his general reputation, if only as showing how erroneous that reputation must be. The argument is, however, a valuable reminder that the Act is intending serious and not trivial imputations.

The second part of the argument in favour of a construction more liberal to the accused is concerned with the words "the conduct or nature of the defence". One should, it can be argued, read conduct or nature as something superimposed on the essence of the defence itself. In *O'Hara* v. *H.M. Advocate* 1948 J.C. 90, at p. 98, the learned Lord Justice-Clerk (Lord Thomson), after a careful review of the English cases, construed "conduct" as meaning the actual handling of the case by the accused or his advocate. He found difficulty with "nature" but said:

> "But the more general considerations which I have mentioned persuade me to the view that 'nature' is to be read, not as meaning something which is inherent in the defence, but as referable to the mechanism of the defence; nature being the strategy of the defence and conduct the tactics."

This argument has obvious force, particularly in a case of rape, where the allegation of consent is in truth no more than a mere traverse of the essential ingredient which the Crown have to prove, namely, want of consent. But the argument does not, and I think cannot, fairly stop short of contending that *all* matters which are relevant to the crime, that is, of which rebutting evidence could be proved, are excluded from the words "conduct or nature of the defence".

To take the present case as an example, the evidence having established physical signs on the victim of the alleged offence, his admission that he had previously committed it with somebody else was relevant. So, too, was his admission that he had been paid £1 for it, since, when the conversation was relevant, it could not be right to bowdlerize it. And, therefore, it is said, the putting of the allegation in cross-examination and the evidence given by the accused was an essentially relevant part of the defence and therefore was not within the words "the nature or conduct of the defence". If Mr. Jeremy Hutchison's forceful argument on the proper construction of the subsection is right, the story told by the accused did not let in the convictions.

So large a gloss upon the words is not easy to justify, even if one were convinced that it necessarily produced a fair and proper result which Parliament intended. But there are two sides to the matter. So liberal a shield for an accused is in many cases unfair to a prosecution.

[LORD HODSON gave reasons for agreeing and LORD WILBERFORCE agreed.]

Comments

1. The construction of the second limb of s. I (*f*) (ii) approved in *Selvey*'s case was classically stated in *R.* v. *Hudson*, [1912] 2 K.B. 464, at pp. 470–1, C.C.A. by Lord Alverstone, C.J. speaking for a five-man Court of Criminal Appeal. "We think that the words . . . must receive their ordinary and natural interpretation, and that it is not legitimate to qualify them by adding or inserting the words 'unnecessary', or 'unjustifiably', or 'for purposes other than that of developing the defence' or other similar words." The harshness of this orthodox doctrine is qualified in three main respects: (*a*) the *Turner* rule; (*b*) the *Rouse* rule; and (*c*) the 'incidental' doctrine.

(*a*) In *R.* v. *Turner* a full Court of Criminal Appeal held that for the accused in a rape case to allege consent on the part of a complainant was not an imputation despite the suggestion that the complainant was a dangerous liar and possibly promiscuous. The Court said, in defiance of *Hudson*, that "some limitation must be placed on the words of the section, since to decide otherwise would be to do grave injustice never intended by Parliament". Indeed the case was a strong one, involving an allegation not only that the victim consented but that she initiated intercourse by an act of gross indecency on the accused ([1944] K.B. 463; [1944] I All E.R. 599, C.C.A.). The merit of the *Turner* doctrine is thus that the accused can advance his entire defence—his view of all the events—with impunity. It was approved in *Selvey*. Three possible bases of the doctrine have been advanced. One is that it is an exception to the *Hudson* doctrine which is *sui generis* because of the peculiar harshness of applying *Hudson* to rape. But if the basis of *Hudson* is that the courts must obey the clearly expressed rule of Parliament, despite any hardships this causes, the same should apply to rape; and if it is legitimate to temper the statutory words in rape cases it must be legitimate to do so elsewhere. The injustice of not being able to run a proper defence to rape is no greater than not being able to run a proper defence to any other crime. A second basis of *Turner* is that since in rape the prosecution must prove non-consent, the accused in alleging consent is doing no more than denying the charge. But why should the accused's right to conduct his defence properly depend on whether his defence raises an issue on which the prosecution bears some burden of proof rather than he? The third basis of *Turner* is that rape is an area where the court's discretion to prevent cross-examination on the record will always be exercised in the accused's favour; but a discretion always exercised the same way can scarcely be called a discretion. Despite these problems, the existence of the *Turner* qualification is now beyond doubt.

(b) The other major limitation on the *Hudson* doctrine was first clearly stated in *R. v. Rouse*. The accused said of the Chief Prosecution witness' evidence: "It is a lie and he is a liar." This was held not to be an imputation because it was "a plea of not guilty put in forcible language such as would not be unnatural in a person in the defendant's rank in life" ([1904] 1 K.B. 184, at p. 186). It is thus possible to plead not guilty, and to deny particular facts alleged by the prosecution. It is even possible to make express attacks on the prosecution that do not elaborate too greatly the inferences often to be drawn from contradicting the prosecution, mainly that their witnesses are lying. To suggest a reason for a prosecution witness's lie is not an imputation unless the reason itself imputes bad character: to say that a witness lied because he wanted his wife to be out of contact with the accused is not an imputation because to be unhappily married is not a sign of bad character (*R. v. Manley* (1962), 126 J.P. 316, C.C.A.). The more elaborate and explicit the attack, the more likely it is that an imputation has been made. It is not an imputation to call a man a liar, but it is to say "his brother won't speak to him because he is a horrible liar" (*R. v. Rappolt* (1911), 6 Cr. App. Rep. 156, C.C.A.). Examples of imputations include statements that a prosecution witness is promiscuous (e.g. *R. v. Jenkins* (1945), 114 L.J.K.B. 425, C.C.A.); in charge of a disorderly house (*R. v. Morrison* (1911), 6 Cr. App. Rep. 159, C.C.A.); a thief (*R. v. Morris* (1959), 43 Cr. App. Rep. 206, C.C.A.); a police agent (and hence biased) (*R. v. Fisher*, [1964] N.Z.L.R. 1063); motivated by spite, revenge or self-interest (e.g. *R. v. McLean* (1926), 19 Cr. App. Rep. 104); and party to the offence (*R. v. Hudson*, [1912] 2 K.B. 464, C.C.A.). To deny making a confession is one thing, because it may simply imply that the police mistook what was said; but it is an imputation to say that the police induced confessions (e.g. *R. v. Cook*, [1959] 2 Q.B. 340, [1959] 2 All E.R. 97, C.C.A.); or fabricated them by dictating them and making the accused sign (*R. v. Clark*, [1955] 2 Q.B. 469; [1955] 3 All E.R. 29, C.C.A.); or obtained remands in order to fabricate evidence (*R. v. Jones* (1923), 87 J.P. 147, C.C.A.); or suppressed evidence favouring the defence (*R. v. Billings*, [1961] V.R. 127); or conspired in advance to concoct a story (*R. v. Davies*, [1963] Crim. L.R. 192, C.C.A.); or to plant evidence on the accused (*R.* v. *Curbishley*, [1963] Crim. L.R. 778, C.C.A.). The attribution to the prosecutor of drunken and incompetent driving and the abuse of other drivers is an imputation (*R.* v. *Brown* (1960), 124 J.P. 391, C.C.A.). So though the *Rouse* doctrine permits one to deny allegations, it does not permit the raising of the details which might make that denial credible. In particular, as Latham, C.J. has pointed out, it must tempt the police to extract confessions by violence from persons of bad character who cannot set up the violence at their trial for fear of exposing their records (*Curwood* v. *R.* (1944), 69 C.L.R. 561, at p. 577).

(c) Many courts have acted on the view that the words "nature or conduct of the defence" require them not to act on remarks of the accused which are "incidental" to the defence. In a way this is the reverse of the doctrine denied in *Hudson*. The pre-*Hudson* doctrine was that a remark necessary to the defence was not an imputation; this doctrine is that a remark *unnecessary* to the defence is not an imputation. A rem ark may be incidental for one of several reasons. First, it may be a remark which is not relevant to any issue in the case, as where the accused attacked the conduct of an identification parade which was unsuccessful and on which neither side relied (*R.* v. *Preston*, [1909] 1 K.B. 568, C.C.A.). Secondly, it may be spontaneous, "a mere unconsidered remark made by the prisoner without giving any serious attention to it" (*R.* v. *Preston*, [1909] 1 K.B. 568, C.C.A., at p. 576, *per* Channell, J.). Thirdly, "*prima facie*, answers in cross-examination are part of the case for the prosecution, and do not shew the nature or conduct of the defence" (*R.* v. *Jones* (1909), 3 Cr. App. Rep. 67, at p. 69 C.C.A.). So the shield will not be lost where prosecution counsel has deliberately tried to trap the accused (*R.* v. *Grout* (1909), 3 Cr. App. Rep. 64, C.C.A.), or asked leading questions, or the accused has responded reluctantly to repeated questions (e.g. *R.* v. *Eidinow* (1932), 23 Cr. App. Rep. 145, C.C.A.). But if the accused under cross-examination where these features are absent deliberately, repeatedly and clearly attacks the prosecution, he will have thrown away his shield; e.g. if under cross-examination he states specifically an allegation which in his evidence in chief was ambiguous or general (*R.* v. *Billings*, [1961] V.R. 127, at p. 134); *a fortiori* if the accused has simply been cross-examined in detail about a precise imputation made in chief. Thus in *Selvey* questions to the accused under cross-examination about the appellant's claim in chief that the complainant was a male prostitute "did no more than remove all possible doubt as to whether the appellant was seeking to discredit [the victim] on the ground that he was 'that sort of young man' " ([1970] A.C. 304, at p. 333; [1968] 2 All E.R. 497, at p. 503, H.L., *per* Viscount Dilhorne). Apart from this, it does not matter whether the attack proceeds from defence counsel in his speeches or his questions, or from the accused in answers in examination in chief or cross-examination.

The *Hudson* doctrine, even as qualified by the *Turner*, *Rouse* and "incidental" rules, is generally thought to be unduly narrow, because it makes it very difficult for the accused to raise a defence in any detail where he contradicts the prosecution rather than merely explaining away facts which the prosecution allege against him. The two main rivals to the *Hudson* doctrine might be called the *Dawson* doctrine and the pre-*Hudson* doctrine.

The *Dawson* doctrine is often called the *Curwood* doctrine—misleadingly, for what was in fact said by the High Court of Australia in *Curwood*'s case, (1944), 69 C.L.R. 561 was no different from the *Hudson* and *Rouse* doctrines,

and *Dawson* v. *R.* contradicts some of what was said in *Curwood*. The doctrine
was first stated in *Dawson's* case and has never been repeated. The essence of
it is that no imputation exists where the accused states expressly what would
follow implicitly from his evidence denying the Crown case and the evidence
supporting it. "The question is not one depending on forms of expression,
the use of phrases, the stating explicitly what is implicit." An imputation
depends on "the use of matter which will have a particular or specific tendency
to destroy, impair or reflect upon the character of the prosecutor or witnesses
called for the prosecution, quite independently of the possibility that such
matter, were it true, would in itself provide a defence" ((1961), 106 C.L.R. 1,
at pp. 9–10 and 13–14, *per* Dixon, C.J.). The last words indicate that this is
not what we will call the "pre-*Hudson* doctrine", which depends on attacks
necessary to the defence not being regarded as imputations. The merit of these
views is that they advance to the full logical extent of the position taken up
in *Rouse*. They deny the relevance of any distinction between inferring fabrication or lying and expressly stating it. *Rouse* represents a practical watering
down of the strictest *Hudson* position but involves an illogical distinction
between inferences from denials and (except in the case of assertions about
lies) express statements of impropriety. *Dawson* destroys that illogicality.
Thus in *Dawson* itself the accused denied guilt, denied confessing to the police
and alleged that the police had invented most of the questions and answers
in his record of interview. Dixon, C.J. considered the latter remark not to be
an imputation because it said no more than could be inferred from the accused's
other denials. The majority of the High Court of Australia disagreed.

The pre-*Hudson* position is that any attack on the prosecution which the
accused has to make in putting up his defence is permissible. A number of
different avenues have been used to reach this destination, and the precise
destination sometimes varies accordingly.

One avenue is frankly expediency. The section would be entirely harsh
and unworkable unless something is done to moderate the strictness of the
words. The Parliamentary legislation will cause injustice unless it is amended
by judicial legislation. It is unwise to rely solely on the use of the judge's
discretion for this will vary in its operation from judge to judge. In any event
there was no general discretion to exclude evidence in 1898, so that Parliament
must have intended the Act to be made workable in some other way.

A second avenue turns on the view that "character" means "general
reputation" rather than disposition or conduct. To say a policeman induced a
confession is not an attack on his reputation—on what the world thinks of
him—it merely asserts bad behaviour. In 1898 it was very likely that this was
the meaning of "character" because the Court for Crown Cases Reserved,
with thirteen judges sitting and two dissenting, had decided in *R.* v. *Rowton*
that evidence of the accused's "character" must be confined to evidence of
reputation ((1865) Le. & Ca. 520; [1861–73] All E.R. Rep. 549). Parliament
must have thought that the prosecutor's "character" would have the same
meaning; a legislator of 1898 would have seen no point in being more precise.
This argument is historically strong, but though it has some followers still
(notably Lord Devlin in *Jones* v. *Director of Public Prosecutions*, [1962] A.C. 635;
at pp. 710–11; [1962] 1 All E.R. 569, at p. 605, H.L.) and has been considered
intrinsically "formidable", it has been ignored by too large a mass of inconsistent authority since *R.* v. *Dunkley*, [1927] 1 K.B. 323, at p. 329; [1926] All

E.R. Rep. 187, at p. 190). A third avenue has been relied on in Scotland. Just as the accused cannot raise his own good character independently of the issues in the case without throwing away his shield under the first limb of s. 1 (*f*) (ii), so he cannot make a general attack on a prosecution witness's good character under the second limb. "But it is one thing to attack the character of a witness generally and another to do so inferentially by asking questions which are relevant to the defence and, indeed, without which the true facts cannot be ascertained" (*O'Hara* v. *H.M. Advocate* 1948 J.C. 90, at p. 98). This is essentially the distinction between cross-examining to the issue and cross-examining to credit.

A fourth avenue depends on the argument that the "nature or conduct of the defence" must refer to "something superimposed on the essence of the defence itself" (*Selvey* v. *Director of Public Prosecutions*, [1970] A.C. 304, at p. 354; [1968] 2 All E.R. 497, at p. 522, H.L., *per* Lord Pearce). Fifthly, Lanham has pointed out ((1972) 5 N.Z.U.L.R. 21, at p. 34) that under the first limb of s. 1 (*f*) (ii), the shield is not lost if the accused gives evidence of good character relevant to his defence. In *Malindi* v. *R.*, [1967] 1 A.C. 439; [1966] 3 All E.R. 285, P.C. the accused, charged with conspiracy to commit arson, was held by the Privy Council not to have thrown away his shield by giving evidence that at certain meetings he disagreed with and disapproved of violence. If evidence of the accused's good character necessary for the development of his defence can be admitted without loss of the shield under the first limb of s. 1 (*f*) (ii), why cannot evidence of a prosecution witness's bad character be admitted under the second?

The final test of which little has been made is one of proportionality. An attack will not be an imputation unless it is serious enough to justify the accused being subjected to the dangerous consequences of losing his shield (*R.* v. *Westfall* (1912), 7 Cr. App. Rep. 176, at p. 179). This approach has sometimes been used in connexion with the court's exercise of its discretion to prevent cross-examination after the shield has been thrown away. But it seems too uncertain to use as a rule of construction; and it is hard to see why the admissibility of the record should be controlled by what the defence is. "[I]f the conduct of the interviewer was criminal, the defendant must impute criminality. . . . [T]he defendant does not choose what conduct he will have the police officer adopt in questioning him" (Lanham (1972) 5 N.Z.U.L.R. 21, at p. 35).

However, whatever the drawbacks of *Hudson* or the merits of rival views, it is undoubtedly the law since the decision in *Selvey*.

2. The strictness of the *Hudson* doctrine is partly mitigated by the existence of the judicial discretion to prevent cross-examination. The recognition of this discretion is relatively recent in this as in other areas of the law of evidence. But the use of judicial discretion to overcome the problems of the section should be regarded as at most an ancillary aid for the following reasons. It leads to uncertainty in practice and differences from judge to judge: the accused's counsel will therefore never know how far the defence can safely go. Reliance on discretion to solve evidentiary problems tends to confuse settled rules of law and to cause loss of contact with fundamental principle; and it tends towards the reversal of established rules without express recognition of or adequate reason for the change. (See Livesey, [1968] C.L.J. 290, at pp. 302–9.)

In *R. v. Flynn*, [1963] 1 Q.B. 729, [1961] 3 All E.R. 58, C.C.A. it was said that the court should refuse to admit the record if the imputation is a necessary part of the defence. But in *Selvey*, the House of Lords said that this could only be regarded as one factor in the exercise of the discretion, not an overriding one. It was also said in *Flynn* that if there was nothing exceptional in the case the discretion should be exercised in the accused's favour. Though this was not disapproved in *Selvey* it seems to be little acted on. It seems to be agreed that the discretion should be exercised in the accused's favour in the following circumstances. One is where the damage caused by the defence attack is trivial and the accused's record is bad (*R. v. Turner*, [1944] K.B. 463, at pp. 470–1; [1944] 1 All E.R. 599, at p. 602, C.C.A.), particularly if the record contains convictions of crimes similar to that now charged, since the jury may wrongly use them as evidence of guilt; for this reason the judge ought to inform himself of the extent and gravity of the record before it is admitted (*R. v. Crawford*, [1965] V.R. 586). The thinness of the main case should be remembered, as well as the weakness of the evidence contradicting the accused's attack (*Dawson v. R.* (1961), 106 C.L.R. 1, at p. 16). In *R. v. Cook*, [1959] 2 Q.B. 340; [1959] 2 All E.R. 97, C.C.A. it was said that a discretion should be exercised in the accused's favour if he is not represented, or if the attack is not directly on the witness but on the police generally or the charge is not deliberate or elaborated, or if no warning to the accused or his counsel has been given by judge or prosecution counsel, or if a mere mistake rather than serious impropriety is alleged against the prosecution witnesses. Obviously the warning to the accused should not be given in open court (*R. v. Weston-Super-Mare Justices, ex parte Townsend*, [1968] 3 All E.R. 225). If the accused is charged on several counts and he makes an imputation against a witness on one count only, the record should not be admitted because it would prejudice him on all counts (*R. v. Curbishley*, [1963] Crim. L.R. 778, C.C.A.). On the other hand, ''if there is a real issue about the conduct of an important witness which the jury will inevitably have to settle in order to arrive at their verdict, then . . . the jury is entitled to know the credit of the man on whose word the witness's character is being impugned'' (*R. v. Cook*, [1959] 2 Q.B. 340, at p. 348; [1959] 2 All E.R. 97 at p. 101, C.C.A.). The discretion should also be exercised against the accused if he alleges that a prosecution witness is an accomplice in an attempt to gain the advantage of the rule requiring that the jury be warned of the danger of convicting on accomplice evidence without corroboration (*R. v. Manley* (1962), 126 J.P. 316, C.C.A.). It has been said that the record is more likely to be admitted the more it consists of crimes of dishonesty rather than violence, because the former are more relevant to credibility (*R. v. Heydon*, [1966] 1 N.S.W.R. 708, at pp. 733 and 735). This partial divisibility of the accused's character will be a welcome tendency.

3. What should be done about the second limb of s. 1 (*f*) (ii)? The *Hudson* doctrine tends to prevent an accused with a record proving misconduct in the prosecutor or impropriety in the making of a confession which is necessary to the accused's defence. It shares with the pre-*Hudson* doctrine the difficulty that the accused is deterred from attacking the prosecution's general credibility when this is, because of an undoubtedly bad record, highly suspect, particularly since the judge has no duty to acquaint the jury with a prosecution witness's record if defence counsel has chosen not to (*R. v. Carey* (1968), 52 Cr. App.

Rep. 305, C.A.). There is no equivalent rule deterring the prosecution from attacking defence witnesses. The *Hudson* rule is also unworkable: the decisions of several full English Courts of Criminal Appeal and one of the House of Lords have not sufficed to make it easy for trial judges to apply. It depends on a distinction between using the record to attack credibility and prove guilt which is unlikely to be grasped by juries. "The jury must not infer that the accused is guilty because he is the kind of man who would do the kind of thing charged, but they may disregard his protestations of innocence because he is the kind of man who would make false imputations against others" (Cross (1969), 6 Syd. L.R. 173, at p. 182; and see *R. v. Vickers*, [1972] Crim. L.R. 101, C.A.). It is strange that the law's decision about which evidence should be excluded because it is too dangerous for a jury should be reversed merely because the accused attacks the prosecution. The *Hudson* rule is an exception, against the accused, to the normal rules encouraging full freedom of speech in court. It is anomalous in being limited by the *Turner* doctrine and in not applying to attacks on dead victims of crime (*R. v. Biggin*, [1920] 1 K.B. 213; [1918–19] All E.R. Rep. 501, C.C.A.). The prosecution may reveal the bad character of their own witness to the jury, but the accused ought not to have to rely on the prosecution's discretion (Humphreys, [1955] Crim. L.R. 739, at p. 742). Admittedly one effect of the rule is to ensure fairness to the impugned witness. "A respectable man who was obliged to give evidence against his assailant or traducer may well feel a deep sense of injustice if he is subjected to a series of unfounded accusations by someone whom practically everyone except the jury before whom the farce is enacted knows to be a man with a criminal record" (Cross, *op. cit.*, p. 181). This may make respectable people unwilling to complain of crime and act as witnesses. But this problem is probably better handled in some other way. The judge has power to stop defence counsel offending in this way (*R. v. Billings*, [1961] V.R. 127, at pp. 136–7). Cross suggests that it might be desirable for the jury which tried the case to be reconvened to decide the further question of whether the accused committed perjury, or for the court to take irresponsibility in conducting the defence into account in determining the sentence (*op. cit.*, p. 181). But to rely on loss of the shield as a disincentive to perjury is unsatisfactory.

Some members of the English Criminal Law Revision Committee which considered these arguments recently were not persuaded by them and indeed would have preferred the accused to be treated in every respect as an ordinary witness. The majority were against this for the above reasons and on the additional ground that such a change would, as in Canada and the United States, induce the accused with a record not to testify and thus reduce the value of the trial as a means of determining the truth. Another minority favoured the complete repeal of the second limb of s. 1 (f) (ii). But the majority favoured amendment so that the accused would only throw away his shield by asking questions of which "the main purpose . . . was to raise an issue as to the witness's credibility." If the shield is thrown away, the cross-examination of the accused must be relevant only to his *credibility*, which may be intended to suggest that for this purpose his character is to be divisible, so that only lying or dishonest conduct can be put to him. The final suggested change is that imputations on the *prosecutor*, as opposed to a prosecution witness, should no longer throw away the shield (11th Report, para. 128).

These changes were in substance enacted in New South Wales in 1974: see Crimes Act, 1900–74, ss. 413A and 413B.

Questions

1. If the only relevance of the record under the second limb of s. 1 (*f*) (ii) is to credibility, as Stable, J. told the jury in *Selvey*, why were sexual convictions put to them and not convictions of dishonesty?

2. X, an accused person, (*a*) denies on oath making and signing a long detailed confession of assault; (*b*) says it was fabricated by the police; and (*c*) says that his defence is that he had to resist violently the victim's improper advances. Would (*a*), (*b*) or (*c*) have the effect of the accused's shield being lost under (i) the law stated in *Selvey*; (ii) the law stated by Dixon, C.J. in *Dawson*; (iii) the pre-*Hudson* doctrine?

3. Would it be desirable to allow the accused to indulge in normal cross-examination of prosecution witnesses as to credit?

V SECTION 1 (*f*) (iii)

Murdoch v. Taylor

[1965] A.C. 574; [1965] 1 All E.R. 406, H.L.

Murdoch, who had a criminal record, was jointly tried with Lynch, who did not, for receiving stolen cameras. Lynch gave evidence implicating Murdoch; Murdoch gave evidence alleging that Lynch alone had control and possession of a box containing the stolen cameras. He was then cross-examined on his record by Lynch's counsel. The Court of Criminal Appeal and the House of Lords discussed Murdoch's appeal.

LORD DONOVAN: It is now contended on behalf of Murdoch, first, that he had given no evidence against Lynch within the meaning of proviso (*f*) (iii). That expression in its context connotes, it is said, only evidence given in examination in chief and not evidence given in cross-examination. Alternatively, it refers only to evidence given with a hostile intent against a co-accused so that the test to be applied is subjective and not objective. In the further alternative, it is argued that, whatever be the true meaning of the expression, a trial judge has in all cases a discretion whether or not to allow questions to be put pursuant to proviso (*f*) (iii) just as he has in relation to proviso (*f*) (ii) of the section.

Prior to the Act of 1898 coming into force an accused person could not (speaking generally) give evidence in his own defence. The Act begins by enacting by section 1 that: "Every person charged with an offence . . . shall be a competent witness for the defence at every stage of the proceedings. . . ." Then follow a number of provisos, the first of which is: "(*a*) A person so charged shall not be called as a witness in pursuance of this Act except upon his own application." An accused person was thus given a new right of defending himself, if he wished, by his own sworn testimony. There is thus some initial impetus, at least, towards the view that when the legislature contemplated that he might give evidence against a co-accused, it was thinking of evidence produced directly by the testimony which the accused chose to give and not testimony which he might have preferred not to give but which was extracted from him under the pressure of cross-examination. Be that as it may, the words of the proviso are, in my opinion, too clear to admit of any such distinction. The object of proviso (*f*) (iii) is clearly to confer a benefit upon a co-accused. If evidence is given against him by another accused he may show, if he can, by reference to the latter's previous offences that his testimony is not worthy of belief. It is the effect of the evidence upon the jury which is material and which may be lessened or dissipated by invoking the proviso. The effect upon the jury is the same whether the evidence be given in examination in chief or in cross-examination; and the desirability of the co-accused being able to meet it by cross-examination as to credit is of the same importance, however the evidence is given. I feel no difficulty in holding that the first of the appellant's contentions must be rejected.

The like considerations also lead me to reject the argument that proviso (*f*) (iii) refers only to evidence given by one accused against the other with hostile intent. Again, it is the effect of the evidence upon the minds of the jury which matters, not the state of mind of the person who gives it. Were that the test, there would have to be something of the nature of a trial within a trial in order to determine the state of mind of the accused who gave the evidence, as was pointed out by the Court of Criminal Appeal in the case of *Stannard*, [1965] 2 Q.B. 1; [1964] 1 All E.R. 34, C.C.A. The language of the Act gives no support for the view that this was the intention. In my opinion, the test to be applied in order to determine whether one accused has given evidence against his co-accused is objective and not subjective.

What kind of evidence is contemplated by proviso (*f*) (iii), that is, what *is* "evidence against" a co-accused is perhaps the most difficult part of the case. At one end of the scale is evidence which does no more than contradict something which a co-accused has said without further advancing the prosecution's case in any significant degree. I agree with the view expressed by Winn, J. in giving judgment in *Stannard* that this is not the kind of evidence contemplated by proviso (*f*) (iii). At the other end of the scale is evidence which, if the jury believes it, would establish the co-accused's guilt, for example, in a case of theft: "I saw him steal the purse," or in a case of assault, "I saw him strike the blow." It is this kind of evidence which alone, so the appellant contends, will satisfy the words "has given evidence against". Again, I regret I cannot share that view. There may well be evidence which regarded in isolation would be quite innocuous from the co-acccused's point of view and, so regarded, could not be regarded as evidence "against" him. For example, what would be proved if one co-accused said of his co-accused: "He told me he knew of an easy job and persuaded me to help him"? If such evidence is kept unrelated to anything else it proves nothing criminal. But juries hear the whole of the evidence and they will consider particular parts of it, not in isolation but in conjunction with all the other evidence, and part of that other evidence may establish that "job" meant a housebreaking job. Then the item of evidence I have taken as an example obviously becomes evidence "against" the accused. If, therefore, the effect of the evidence upon the minds of the jury is to be taken as the test, it cannot be right to regard it in isolation in order to decide whether it is evidence against the co-accused. If Parliament had meant by proviso (*f*) (iii) to refer to evidence which was by itself conclusive against the co-accused it would have been easy to say so.

The test prescribed by the Court of Criminal Appeal in *Stannard*, [1965] 2 Q.B. 1; [1964] 1 All E.R. 34, C.C.A. was whether the evidence in question tended to support the prosecution's case in a material respect or to undermine the defence. I have no substantial quarrel with this definition. I would, however, observe that some danger may lurk in the use of the expression "tended to". There will probably be occasions when it could be said that evidence given by one accused "tended to" support the prosecution's case simply because it differed from the evidence of his co-accused; and the addition of the words "in a material respect" might not wholly remove the danger. The difficulty is not really one of conception but of expression. I myself would omit the words "tended to" and simply say that "evidence against" means evidence which supports the prosecution's case in a material respect or which undermines the defence of the co-accused.

The evidence in the present case was clearly against Lynch in that sense. It was evidence which, if the jury accepted it, put Lynch in sole control and possession of property which according to the rest of the evidence had been stolen the day before, and which Lynch had tried to sell for a price which was a fraction of its real value. Murdoch's evidence thus supported the case of the prosecution in a material respect and none the less so because Coles had already given evidence to a somewhat similar effect.

On the question of discretion, I agree with the Court of Criminal Appeal that a trial judge has no discretion whether to allow an accused person to be cross-examined as to his past criminal offences once he has given evidence against his co-accused. Proviso (f) (iii) in terms confers no such discretion and, in my opinion, none can be implied. It is true that in relation to proviso (f) (ii) such a discretion does exist; that is to say, in the cases where the accused has attempted to establish his own good character or where the nature and conduct of the defence is such as to involve imputations on the character of the prosecutor or of a witness for the prosecution.

But in these cases it will normally, if not invariably, be the prosecution which will want to bring out the accused's bad character—not some co-accused; and in such cases it seems to me quite proper that the court should retain some control of the matter. For its duty is to secure a fair trial and the prejudicial value of evidence establishing the accused's bad character may at times wholly outweigh the value of such evidence as tending to show that he was guilty of the crime alleged.

These considerations lead me to the view that if, in any given case (which I think would be rare), the prosecution sought to avail itself of the provisions of proviso (f) (iii) then here, again, the court should keep control of the matter in the like way. Otherwise, if two accused gave evidence one against the other, but neither wished to cross-examine as to character, the prosecution could step in as of right and reveal the criminal records of both, if both possessed them. I cannot think that Parliament in the Act of 1898 ever intended such an unfair procedure. So far as concerns the prosecution, therefore, the matter should be one for the exercise of the judge's discretion, as it is in the case of proviso (f) (ii). But when it is the co-accused who seeks to exercise the right conferred by proviso (f) (iii) different considerations come into play. He seeks to defend himself; to say to the jury that the man who is giving evidence against him is unworthy of belief; and to support that assertion by proof of bad character. The right to do this cannot, in my opinion, be fettered in any way.

Finally, it is said that the decision in *Stannard*, [1965] 2 Q.B. 1; [1964] 1 All E.R. 34, C.C.A., if upheld, will make it impossible for a person to defend himself at all effectively if he has a criminal record and is charged jointly with some other person. If he knows that the other person is guilty, and if in the witness box he speaks the truth, then he is liable to have his criminal past disclosed with fatal results.

This would, indeed, be a melancholy result, but I do not think the prospect is so gloomy. To test the matter, let me assume the case of two accused each charged with the same offence—No. 1 in fact being guilty but having no criminal record, No. 2 being in fact innocent but having such a record. No. 1 has nothing to lose by going into the witness box and accusing No. 2 of the crime; No. 2 quite truthfully in his evidence accuses No. 1, whereupon the past criminal record of No. 2 is disclosed to the jury by or on behalf of No. 1. It is said that No. 2 would have practically no hope of avoiding a conviction—hence the argument for an over-riding discretion in the judge, although this would not necessarily cure the situation.

But in the case supposed, what would be the position in practice? In the first place, if No. 2 were in fact innocent, it would be in the highest degree unlikely that he would be found relying simply on his own denial. There would almost invariably be some evidence to support his defence. In the second place, his counsel or the judge or both would explain to the jury just how it was that accused No. 1 was able to force the revelation of No. 2's record. The judge would probably go on to exhort the jury not to let that revelation sway their minds and to consider the case against No. 2 primarily on the basis of the other evidence. The assistant recorder in the present case indeed went further and told the jury to ignore Murdoch's past altogether. It would be a very un-usual jury which, in these circumstances, did not require cogent proof of guilt before convicting. Indeed, the effect of the disclosure of No. 2's past might have the result of causing the jury to give consideration to the case surpassing in carefulness even their usual high standard.

LORD REID (in the course of a judgment concurring with LORD DONOVAN): On the question of the discretion of the court I entirely agree with the view expressed by my noble and learned friend, Lord Donovan. But on the other question I find great difficulty in agreeing with what I understand to be the unanimous view of your Lordships. The words which we have to construe are those of section 1 (*f*) (iii) of the Criminal Evidence Act 1898—"he has given evidence against any other person charged with the same offence". In proviso (*e*) of the same section there is reference to any question which "would tend to criminate", and I have difficulty in believing that the word "against" in proviso (*f*) (iii) could have been used if the intention had been that this proviso should apply to all evidence which would tend to criminate the co-accused. If that had been the intention the obvious course would have been to say "tending to criminate" instead of "against". And there are other reasons which tend to strengthen my doubts. If this provision has this wide meaning, an accused person with previous convictions, whose story contradicts in any material respect the story of a co-accused who has not yet been convicted, will find it almost impossible to defend himself, and if he elects not to give evidence his plight will be just as bad. But I have been unable to find any satisfactory solution for the problem set by this proviso and therefore I shall not dissent.

[LORD EVERSHED agreed with LORD DONOVAN.]

LORD MORRIS OF BORTH-Y-GEST (in the course of a judgment concurring with LORD DONOVAN): If an accused person becomes a witness his sworn testimony, if admissible, becomes a part of the evidence in the case. What he says in cross-examination is just as much a part of that evidence as is what he says in examination in chief. The word "against" is one that is well understood. It is a clear and robust word. It has more decisiveness than is possessed by such phrases as "tending to show" or "such as to involve". It is a word that needs neither explanation nor translation. It calls for no synonym.

The Act does not call for any investigation as to the motives or wishes which may have prompted the giving of evidence against another person charged with the same offence. It is the nature of the evidence that must be considered. Its character does not change according as to whether it is the product of pained reluctance or of malevolent eagerness. If, while ignoring anything trivial or casual, the positive evidence given by the witness would rationally have to be included in any survey or summary of the evidence in the case which, if accepted, would warrant the conviction of the "other person charged with the same offence", then the witness would have given evidence against such other person. Such other person would then have that additional testimony against him. From his point of view that testimony would be just as damaging whether given with regret or whether given with relish.

LORD PEARCE (dissenting): It is common ground that, until the case of R. v. *Ellis*, [1961] 2 All E.R. 928, C.C.A. decided briefly to the contrary, the practice and the general view of bench and bar alike was that a judge had a discretion whether to give leave to cross-examine under section 1 (*f*) (iii). Moreover, it has long been established practice and law that the right to cross-examine under section 1 (*f*) (ii) is subject to the judge's discretion (see the cases of R. v. *Jenkins* (1945), 114 L.J.K.B. 425, C.C.A. and R. v. *Cook*, [1959] 2 K.B. 340; [1959] 2 All E.R. 97, C.C.A.). Therefore, the right under section 1 (*f*) (iii) would also seem, *prima facie* at least, to be subject to the judge's discretion. For there is nothing in the words of the Act which justifies any discrimination between the two subsections on the point in issue.

Admittedly the situation arising under section 1 (*f*) (ii) differs from that arising under section 1 (*f*) (iii). Under the former, an exercise of discretion could only deprive the prosecution of a right which they would otherwise have had; and the courts have always been ready to do that when fairness seemed to demand it. Under section 1 (*f*) (iii), however, the judge, in using a discretion to refuse the introduction of a defendant's bad record, could only do so at the expense of a co-defendant. And how, it is argued, can he properly do this?

It is certainly not an easy problem. But the difficult burden of holding the scales fairly, not only as between the prosecution and defendants, but also as between the defendants themselves, and of doing his best thereby to secure a fair trial for all concerned, falls inevitably on the trial judge and is generally achieved in practice with considerable success. The use of a judicial discretion under section 1 (*f*) (iii) as between co-defendants would be but an addition to the judge's existing burden.

The exercise of such a discretion would be within fairly narrow limits and the *prima facie* right could only be withheld for good judicial reasons. Two obvious examples occur to one of situations in which the judge ought to use a discretion to refuse a defendant's request to introduce a co-defendant's bad character. The first is where that defendant's counsel has deliberately led a co-defendant into the trap, or has, for the purpose of bringing in his bad record, put questions to him in cross-examination which will compel him, for the sake of his own innocence, to give answers that will clash with the story of the other defendant, or compel him to bring to the forefront implications which would otherwise have been unnoticed or immaterial. The second type of situation is where the clash between the two stories is both inevitable and trivial, and yet the damage by the introduction of a bad record (perhaps many years previous) will in the circumstances be unfairly prejudicial. Any attempt to deal with such a situation by means of the maxim *de minimis* is really to import some sort of discretion in disguise. For if a defendant is entitled to an absolute right, he can claim it on any technical ground that exists, whether it be large or small, fair or unfair: and however unfair or technical the ground may be, the right will be equally valuable to a defendant who can make his escape over the (perhaps innocent) body of a co-defendant.

In such a difficult matter which may not infrequently arise in borderline cases, the judge, who sees the general run of the case as it unfolds before him, can produce a fairer result by the exercise of a judicial discretion than by the strict and fettered application of an arbitrary rule of law.

In *Hill* v. R., [1953] Tas. S.R. 54 the Court of Criminal Appeal in Tasmania . . . made it clear that in their opinion a discretion existed. . . .

In my view, there should not be denied to the judges the discretion which in practice they exercised for so many years before the decision in the case of *Ellis*, [1961] 2 All E.R. 928, C.C.A. took it out of their capable hands.

Comments

1. The Criminal Law Revision Committee did not recommend any change in the rule that the Court has no discretion to prevent the co-accused cross-examining under s. 1 (*f*) (iii). It said: "there might be a case for giving a discretion to the court in order to enable it to do justice, as far as possible, in a case where A has, say, only one relevant conviction and B has twenty. Suppose A has given evidence that B committed the offence. B cross-examines A in order to show that A committed the offence and puts A's single conviction to him. B may then refuse to give evidence himself . . . but may call witnesses to say that A committed the offence. A cannot put B's record to him, and it might be thought fairer that the court should be able to redress the balance by forbidding B to question A about his conviction. But the majority think that the present rule should be preserved as the lesser of two evils. . . . In particular, . . . [there might be] too much difference in the way in which [any] discretion was exercised. For different judges might take different views on

the general question which of the two evils mentioned was the lesser one"
(11th Report, para. 132). Do you agree?

2. The court can refuse leave to the prosecution to cross-examine under
s. 1 (f) (iii) but cannot refuse it to a co-accused; however, it can refuse leave
to a co-accused under s. 1 (f) (ii). See *R. v. Lovett*, [1973] 1 All E.R. 744, at
p. 749, where the Court of Appeal said: "A and B are jointly charged with the
same offence; A (who has a criminal record) gives no evidence against B, but
he does make imputations against a Crown witness. On the other hand B
(with a clean record) has it in mind to throw all the blame upon A and, for
this purpose, it would obviously be helpful to him if he could discredit A by
cross-examining him on his bad record. In such circumstances, the Crown
themselves may or may not have it in mind to cross-examine A on these lines,
but in either case they unquestionably must first seek and obtain the court's
permission. Then ought B, against whom A has alleged nothing, to be in a
position to cross-examine A *as of right* on these matters? We think that justice
demands a negative answer. . . ."

3. The requirement that the accused be "charged with the same offence"
is interpreted literally. Fraudulent conversion is not the same offence as
using false pretences to procure the payment to the accused of the money
fraudulently converted (*R. v. Roberts*, [1936] 1 All E.R. 23). Theft of property is
not the same offence as dishonestly assisting in its disposal (*R. v. Lovett*,
[1973] 1 All E.R. 744, C.A.). But to be in possession of certain forged notes is
the same offence as being in possession of them at another time (*R. v. Russell*,
[1971] 1 Q.B. 151; [1970] 3 All E.R. 924). The Criminal Law Revision Committee sensibly recommends that s. 1 (f) (iii) be extended to cover all cases
where the accused are jointly tried.

4. Probably a co-accused may cross-examine his co-accused as of right on
matters other than his record (*Murdoch v. Taylor*, [1965] A.C. 574, at p. 584;
[1965] 1 All E.R. 406, at p. 409, H.L.; see Carvell, [1965] Crim. L.R. 419);
and also on his convictions and prior offences under s. 1 (f) (i) (*R. v. Miller*,
[1952] 2 All E.R. 667).

5. Evidence by an accused which if believed would lead to the acquittal of
the co-accused is not evidence "against" the latter (*R. v. Zangoullas*, [1962]
Crim. L.R. 544, C.C.A.).

VI MISCELLANEOUS

If the accused attacks the prosecution's witnesses without himself testifying
his record cannot be admitted under s. 1 (f), which refers only to questions
asked in cross-examination (*R. v. Butterwasser*, [1948] 1 K.B. 4; [1947] 2 All
E.R. 415, C.C.A.). But if he calls witnesses who testify to his good character,
his record can be put to them in rebuttal.

When inadmissible evidence accidentally gets before the jury the judge
has three choices. He can discharge the jury and recommence the trial; he
can direct the jury to take no account of the evidence; or, if he thinks the
first course too drastic and the second too likely to concentrate the jury's
mind on the evidence which they may have forgotten, he can say nothing.
(See *R. v. Weaver*, [1968] 1 Q.B. 353; [1967] 1 All E.R. 277, C.A.).

Further reading

C.L.R.C., 11th Report, paras. 114–32; Carvell, [1965] Crim. L.R. 419; Cross, 6 Syd. L.R. 173 (1969); Gooderson, 11 C.L.J. 377 (1953); Griew, [1961] Crim. L.R. 142, 213; Heydon, 7 Syd. L.R. 166 (1974); Lanham, 5 N.Z.U.L.R. 21 (1972); Livesey, [1968] C.L.J. 291; Stone, 51 L.Q.R. 443 (1935) and 58 L.Q.R. 369 (1942); Tapper, 36 M.L.R. 167 (1973).

PART FOUR

Hearsay

12

Hearsay: The Exclusionary Rule

There are many formulations of the rule against hearsay which vary slightly in detail. It could be put thus: "express or implied assertions which are not made at the trial by the witness who is testifying, and assertions in documents produced to the court when no witness is testifying, are inadmissible as evidence of the truth of that which was asserted" (see Cross, 3rd Edn., p. 387; Cowen and Carter, p. 1). In essence, witnesses must only be allowed to testify from personal knowledge. The only really controversial aspect of this definition is the inclusion of implied assertions (see p. 317, *post*). The prior consistent or inconsistent statements of witnesses do not generally fall within the hearsay ban at common law because such statements are not evidence of the truth of what they assert but merely go to credibility (pp. 431 and 433, *post*).

The rule against hearsay is applied against the accused as well as in his favour (*Sparks* v. *R.*, [1964] A.C. 964, P.C.; [1964] 1 All E.R. 727). In practice in civil cases it is often waived by the agreement of the parties.

There is a difficulty—perhaps only a temporary one—in discussing the rule against hearsay. In criminal cases, the common law rule with its many common law and statutory exceptions holds sway. In civil cases, the Civil Evidence Act 1968 has enacted a new regime. We will discuss certain general problems which are either common to both systems or a necessary preliminary to understanding both. A discussion of the rule in criminal cases in its main aspects and a separate discussion of the civil rule will follow in Chapters 13 and 14.

I RATIONALE

Several reasons are commonly given to justify the rule. First, hearsay statements when related to the court emanate originally from persons not under oath nor subject to cross-examination, "the greatest legal engine ever invented for the discovery of truth" (Wigmore, para. 1367). Hence they are unreliable. The maker's lack of veracity, or his defective powers of memory, perception and narration, cannot be tested by detailed questions; his demeanour cannot be observed. "Whoever has attended to the examination, the cross-examination, and the re-examination of witnesses . . . has observed what a very different shape their story appears to take in each of these stages. . . ." (*Berkeley Peerage Case* (1811), 4 Camp. 401, at p. 405, *per* Bayley, J.). There are certainly dangers springing from from the absence of cross-examination, but perhaps the unreliability is not so great as to justify an all-embracing exclusionary rule. The lack of an oath is not so important; for it is now regarded as less of a guarantee of truth than formerly, and statements on oath not made in the instant proceedings are hearsay: *R. v. Eriswell (Inhabitants)* (1790), 3 Term Rep. 707.

Secondly, it is said to be desirable that the best evidence be given: direct evidence should be given in preference to hearsay. But if the maker of the statement is dead or unobtainable, a hearsay report of the statement is the best evidence and should, on this reasoning, be admitted. Further, an out-of-court statement made soon after an event may be much more valuable than one made in court years later: it is less stale and may be unaffected by interest and the heat of litigation.

Thirdly, there is a danger of inaccuracy through repetition. If A tells the court what B told him C said, or did, there are two sources of possible error: B may have misheard C or misunderstood what he was doing, and A may have misheard B. As Baker says (p. 19): "Everyone is familiar with the ease and rapidity with which a story grows. As it is passed from mouth to mouth some additional fact is added; perhaps, too, a little colour to make it a better tale. With each handing on of the story, the further away from the truth it becomes; detail is added to detail as the story grows and in the end the accumulated mass swamps the core of truth at its centre. Misunderstanding, faulty memory, and misreporting make the story increasingly inaccurate and unreliable." This is a sound argument in the case of oral hearsay, but not written. And the danger is ignored or the risk is run in connexion with statements introduced to prove that they were made rather than to prove the truth of what they assert, for these fall outside the hearsay ban (p. 313, *post*).

Fourthly, it is said that if the rule were relaxed the courts would be swamped with a proliferation of evidence (some of it raising collateral issues which might protract the trial) directed to establishing a particular fact, i.e., both direct evidence and hearsay. This seems to be an unreal danger; expense and commonsense will ensure that the parties will in fact only put forward their strongest evidence. And though hearsay may raise collateral issues which lengthen the trial, it may equally be so convincing as to shorten it.

Fifthly, there is a fear that juries will attach undue weight to hearsay evidence without realizing its weaknesses: "no man can tell what effect it may have upon their minds" (*Berkeley Peerage Case* (1811), 4 Camp. 401, at p. 415, *per* Mansfield, C.J.). But some (though not all) think that the weaknesses of hearsay evidence are normally obvious as a matter of common sense to the better-educated modern jury and that any difficult cases can be dealt with by explicit judicial directions.

Whatever the strength of the arguments against admitting hearsay, there is no doubt that the present law in criminal cases has many disadvantages. The rule is unjust where it excludes hearsay evidence of a person who is dead, or unavailable, or unidentifiable. It means that a case will be decided without taking into account all the available evidence, imperfect though some of it may be. The need to call direct rather than hearsay evidence adds to the cost of proving facts which are not really in dispute. The rule tends to confuse witnesses by preventing them from telling their story in a natural way. The present law is very complicated; the many exceptions to the main exclusionary rule require much space to state. Finally, the evidence excluded is often highly reliable and would be thought convincing by ordinary men in their everyday affairs: see *Myers v. Director of Public Prosecutions*, [1965] A.C. 1001; [1964] 2

All E.R. 881, H.L. The rule may operate harshly in preventing the accused from clearing himself in reliance on hearsay (*Sparks* v. *R.*, [1964] A.C. 964; [1964] 1 All E.R. 727, P.C.).

II THE LIMITS OF THE RULE

A. Original evidence

Subramaniam v. Public Prosecutor
[1956] 1 W.L.R. 965, P.C.

The accused was charged with unlawful possession of ammunition. His defence was that he had been captured by terrorists and was acting under duress. The trial judge held that evidence of his conversations with terrorists were inadmissible unless the terrorists testified. The Privy Council allowed the appeal.

L. M. D. DE SILVA: In ruling out peremptorily the evidence of conversation between the terrorists and the appellant the trial judge was in error. Evidence of a statement made to a witness by a person who is not himself called as a witness may or may not be hearsay. It is hearsay and inadmissible when the object of the evidence is to establish the truth of what is contained in the statement. It is not hearsay and is admissible when it is proposed to establish by the evidence, not the truth of the statement, but the fact that it was made. The fact that the statement was made, quite apart from its truth, is frequently relevant in considering the mental state and conduct thereafter of the witness or of some other person in whose presence the statement was made. In the case before their Lordships statements could have been made to the appellant by the terrorists, which, whether true or not, if they had been believed by the appellant, might reasonably have induced in him an apprehension of instant death if he failed to conform to their wishes.

In the rest of the evidence given by the appellant statements made to him by the terrorists appear now and and again to have been permitted, probably inadvertently, to go in. But, a complete, or substantially complete, version according to the appellant of what was said to him by the terrorists and by him to them has been shut out. This version, if believed, could and might have afforded cogent evidence of duress brought to bear upon the appellant. Its admission would also have meant that the complete story of the appellant would have been before the trial judge and assessors and enabled them more effectively to have come to a correct conclusion as to the truth or otherwise of the appellant's story.

Charles Dickens: Pickwick Papers
Chapter 34

"I believe you are in the service of Mr. Pickwick, the defendant in this case. Speak up, if you please, Mr. Weller."

"I mean to speak up, sir," replied Sam. "I am in the service o' that 'ere gen'l'man, and a wery good service it is."

"Little to do, and plenty to get, I suppose?" said Sergeant Buzfuz, with jocularity.

"Oh, quite enough to get, sir, as the soldier said ven they ordered him three hundred lashes," replied Sam.

"You must not tell us what the soldier, or any other man, said, sir," interposed the judge, "it's not evidence."

"Wery good, my lord", replied Sam.

Subramaniam reveals the fallacy in what the judge said to Sam Weller. The evidence held admissible in *Subramaniam* is often called ''original'' evidence as opposed to "hearsay". The actual facts of the case concern proof of statements made to a person, not to show the truth of what was said in them, but to show the hearer's state of mind (see also *R.* v. *Willis*, [1960] 1 All E.R. 331; [1960] 1 W.L.R. 55). There are numerous other illustrations of it. Statements constituting defamation, injurious falsehood, passing off, or intimidation are admitted simply to prove that they were made. So too words of discharge to an employee. Statements to an accused are admissible to prove motive even though their truth is not in issue (*R.* v. *Edmunds* (1833), 6 C. & P. 164). The shouts of a mob are admissible to prove that the mob was likely to frighten bystanders (*R.* v. *Lord Gordon* (1781), 21 State Tr. 485). Where a road accident victim had to prove that she had made due inquiry and search for the identity of the car that struck her, her report that the police told her they could not find it was admissible: the issue was not the truth of the police statements but the fact that they were made (*Cavanagh* v. *Nominal Defendant*, (1959), 100 C.L.R. 375); see also *Perkins* v. *Vaughan* (1842), 4 Man. & G. 988; *The Douglas* (1882), 7 P.D. 151). Statements by a person may be relevant independently of their truth in several ways. Ludicrous statements may prove insanity. False statements may prove a consciousness of guilt (*A.-G.* v. *Good* (1825), M'Cle & Y. 286; *Mawaz Khan* v. *R.*, [1967] 1 A.C. 454; [1967] 1 All E.R. 80, P.C.). Demands for money by the complainant of rape may prove consent (*R.* v. *Guttridge* (1840), 9 C. & P. 471). Proof of failure of a doctor to object to a breath test being given to a driver is not hearsay if the only issue is whether he objected rather than whether a lack of objection was well founded (*R.* v. *Chapman*, [1969] 2 Q.B. 436, C.A.; [1969] 2 All E.R. 321).

One group of illustrations of original evidence are "operative words". "Operative words" are words which, under the substantive law, will render the speaker bound in some way because a reasonable man in the position of the hearer will believe the speaker to be bound. Words can only have such an effect if the substantive law has an objective test of the speaker's intention, as with words of gift or words of contractual offer. If the test is subjective, the question is not what the reasonable hearer would think to have been intended, but what was actually intended; the words are thus tendered as evidence of their truth and can only be admitted under an exception to the hearsay rule. (See *Walters* v. *Lewis* (1836), 7 C. & P. 344; *Lister* v. *Smith* (1863), 3 Sw. & Tr. 282.) Assertive statements may also be admitted without infringing the hearsay rule if they are put forward to qualify some act done, e.g. statements that money being handed to an executor was given to the declarant by the deceased. The statement is not evidence of the gift but it does prevent an inference that the declarant, by handing the money over, admits having no right to it: *Hayslep* v. *Gymer* (1834), 1 Ad. & El. 162.

B. The exclusion of reliable evidence

We might now consider evidence which, though plainly reliable, is excluded under the hearsay rule. The rule is based on the need to avoid unreliability, but in its operation it is a technical rule, independent of any reliability or unreliability existing on the particular facts. For English courts this was finally settled by *Myers* v. *Director of Public Prosecutions*, [1965] A.C. 1001, H.L.; [1964] 2 All E.R. 881.

The accused were charged with conspiracy. They bought wrecked cars with their logbooks. They stole other cars and disguised them so as to make them conform to the wrecked cars' logbooks. The stolen cars were then sold as renovated wrecks. To prove that the cars sold were stolen, the prosecution called an officer in charge of the records made by the manufacturers of the stolen cars. He produced microfilms of the cards filled in by workmen showing the numbers moulded into secret parts of the stolen cars' cylinder blocks. These numbers coincided with the cylinder block numbers of the cars sold. In effect this was evidence of what the officer had said the workmen had written. The trial judge admitted it. The Court of Criminal Appeal upheld his decision; they said the evidence was not hearsay because ''its probative value does not depend on the credit of an unidentified person but rather on the cirsumstances in which the record is maintained and the inherent probability that it will be correct rather than incorrect'' ([1965] A.C. 1001, at p. 1008; [1965] 1 All E.R. 881, at pp. 886–7, following *R. v. Rice* [1963] 1 Q.B. 857; [1963] 1 All E.R. 832, C.C.A.). The House of Lords allowed the appeal by a bare majority, holding that it was hearsay, that no existing hearsay exception applied, and that in the interests of certainty the creation of new hearsay exceptions was for Parliament, not the courts. It was hearsay because the officer was reporting the workmen's account of the numbers as evidence of the truth of what they said. It was true that the evidence was highly reliable, but the admissibility of evidence depended not on reliability but on technical satisfaction of the above test. There was no discretion to admit reliable evidence which infringed an exclusionary rule. The judicial refusal to change the law despite its faults has some force, but so has Lord Pearce's dissenting judgment. He said that the anonymity and reliability of modern records of mass production was a new social fact and the law should change to take account of it. Such evidence might be vital to an accused's defence, and it would be strange if so irrational and technical a rule could be permitted to lead to a wrong conviction. There was no reason to suppose that the courts had lost their nineteenth century power to create new exceptions; the law was already so untidy that it could hardly be made worse by new exceptions (and see *Potts v. Miller* (1940), 64 C.L.R. 282, at pp. 292, 302–4; see also *R. v. Seifert* (1956), 73 W.N.N.S.W. 358).

The actual result of *Myers* has been reversed by legislation (Criminal Evidence Act 1965, p. 330, *post*), but its reasoning has been relied on by other courts. We shall see that some courts have used specious reasoning to evade the consequences of the *Myers* approach; it would seem desirable to apply *Myers*, or to recognize frankly some new hearsay exception, but not to misapply the technical definition of hearsay mentioned in *Myers*. One sound application of the *Myers* reasoning was *Jones v. Metcalfe*, [1967] 3 All E.R. 205; [1967] 1 W.L.R. 1286. A collision caused by a lorry occurred. A witness took the lorry's number and reported it to the police. At the trial the witness said he had forgotten the number but had given it to the policeman. The policeman's evidence as to the number was held to be inadmissible hearsay. Any attempt to justify admissibility by arguing that the policeman was not advancing what was told to him as evidence of its truth, but simply revealing the result of the instruction to him to write the number down, must founder on the fact that the court is asked to act on the statement not because it was made, but because what it contains is true. The technicality of the result is demonstrated by the fact that if the policeman has been seen recording the witness's statement of the number, the latter could have refreshed his memory from the record and the number would have been admitted. (See also *Grew* v. *Cubitt*, [1951] 2 T.L.R. 305; *R.* v. *McLean* (1967), 52 Cr. App. Rep. 80, C.A). A statement on goods that they were manufactured in a particular place is hearsay (*Patel* v. *Customs Comptroller*, [1966] A.C. 356, P.C.; [1965] 3 All E.R. 593). A car's logbook is inadmissible evidence of the engine number (*R.* v. *Sealby*, [1965] 1 All E.R. 701). If a policeman interrogates a suspect whose language he does not understand through an interpreter, then the suspect's translated answers cannot be admitted unless the interpreter is called as a witness and either states that he remembered the original answers and his translations, or refreshes his memory from notes. What the interpreter said to the policeman is proferred as evidence of its truth (*R.* v. *Wong Ah Wong*, [1957] S.R.N.S.W. 582; *R.* v. *Attard* (1959), 43 Cr. App. Rep. 90). The interpreter cannot be regarded as the suspect's agent to make any admission; nor can the interpreter merely be regarded as a telephone or conduit-pipe, for telephones merely transmit sounds, but interpreters can make mistakes. In South Africa and Australia it has been held that the evidence is admissible as not being hearsay (*R.* v. *Mutche*, 1946 A.D. 874; *Gaio* v. *R.* (1960), 104 C.L.R. 419). Since some interpreters in these jurisdictions may forget the conversation and may be too illiterate to take notes, this view ensures that the criminal justice system does not break down; but it would seem better in principle to erect a new exception to the hearsay rule rather than juggle with the definition of hearsay. The interpreter's statements of what the suspect said are hearsay because the policeman has no personal knowledge of their accuracy.

Let us now examine some erroneous decisions on the scope of hearsay. In *R.* v. *Rice*, [1963] 1 Q.B. 857, C.C.A.; [1963] 1 All E.R. 832, C.C.A. it was held that an air ticket made out in the name of Rice was admissible evidence that Rice had travelled on the appropriate flight. Yet this would seem to be hearsay. The ticket in effect contains the booking clerk's report of what someone else said to him when booking the ticket, and is designed to prove the truth of what is said. The result accords with commonsense, but is technically wrong (see *Re Gardner; Ex parte R. J. Gardner Pty., Ltd.* (1967), 13 F.L.R. 345; cf. Hoffmann, p. 92, n. 15). The same may be said of *Edwards* v. *Brookes* (*Milk*), *Ltd.*, [1963] 3 All E.R. 62; [1963] 1 W.L.R. 795, D.C., where statements made by persons not called as witnesses who said they were agents of the accused were admitted. The evidence that the "agents" were agents came from them only and was reported to the court by others.

There is a group of cases in which police who answer phone calls at premises suspected of being used for unlawful betting are allowed to tell the court what the callers said. When the caller makes a bet, he is impliedly asserting that the receiver of the call is helping to run a betting business; this, when repeated several times, is some evidence that a betting business was being run on the premises. The basis of admissibility has never been discussed, but there are three possibilities. One is that implied assertions fall outside the hearsay rule: this question will be discussed below (p. 317, *post*). Another is that implied assertions fall within the hearsay rule but an exception exists which permits the admission of this kind of evidence. This may be sound, subject to the view that modern courts may not create hearsay exceptions (see *State* v. *Di Vincenti* (1957), 93 S. (2d) 676, where the statements were admitted under the *res gestae* exception). A third possibility is that the statements fall outside the hearsay rule because they are "operative words" or "verbal acts" (*State* v. *Tolisano* (1949), 70 A. 2d 118; *McGregor* v. *Stokes*, [1952] V.L.R. 347). This last possibility cannot be correct, for the statements are admitted to prove that the premises are used for betting, and if many callers believe this, it tends to prove the premises are so used. But this argument depends on what the callers say being tendered as evidence of the truth of their underlying belief.

C. Implied assertions

i General

It is clear that the hearsay rule extends to express assertions. Express assertions are normally statements intended to be assertive. But the phrase also includes conduct intended to be assertive, e.g. nods, gestures and signs. (See *Chandra Sekara* v. *R.*, [1937] A.C. 220; [1936] 3 All E.R. 865, P.C.) It is also clear that the rule does not extend to non-assertive behaviour, e.g. the leaving of fingerprints or footprints. But does the rule extend to implied assertions—statements or conduct not intended to be assertive but which rest on some assumption of fact believed by the maker of the statement or the doer of the act which can be inferred by the court? This is a difficult question and, so far as it has been considered, a controversial one.

The problem arises in a number of areas where evidence is generally held admissible, but it is unclear whether in the courts' view such evidence is not assertive, or whether it is an implied assertion falling outside the hearsay rule, or an implied assertion admitted as an exception to the hearsay rule. A learned writer, who has analysed the problem with exemplary clarity, divides the cases into six groups (Weinberg, (1973), 9 Melb. U.L.R. 268). One is the illegal gambling situation, where a policeman picks up a ringing telephone at premises suspected of being used for illicit gambling, and hears a caller attempting to make a bet: he is impliedly asserting a belief that he is speaking to a betting house (cf. *McGregor* v. *Stokes*, [1952] V.L.R. 347, where the calls were said not to be assertive at all). A second is where one suspected of misconduct flees, for this indicates a consciousness of guilt: he is impliedly asserting a belief in his own guilt. (The problem of admissibility is rarely discussed here because even if the flight is an implied assertion subject to the hearsay rule it will usually be admissible within the admissions exception.) Into this category might also be placed lies, interference with witnesses, and destruction of real evidence. Thirdly, the problem arises where a doctor is seen to treat a patient in a particular way: this is an implied assertion that the patient is ill. Fourthly, treatment by one person of another in an affectionate, or violent, or jeering, or paternal way is an implied assertion that the first is married to, or hates, or regards as mad, or regards as his child, the second. Such treatment is admissible evidence of relationship, but the question whether this is non-hearsay or an exception to hearsay is rarely discussed. Fifthly, silence in the face of an accusation or after receiving goods is an implied assent to the accusation or approval of the goods. The inference of assent will often be a dangerous one, however, making cross-examination particularly desirable. Finally, a statement by one person identifying another—"Hello, X!"— is an implied assertion that the second person is X. To Weinberg's categories we might add these: if a man does an act, he is impliedly asserting that about that time he had an intention to do it; if a man is in possession of property, he is impliedly asserting a right of ownership; if a man acts as holder of an office, he is impliedly asserting entitlement to do so.

In these cases the usual hearsay dangers are less strongly present than normal: the maker of the assertion is less likely to be lying. "People do not say 'Hello X' in order to deceive passers-by into thinking that X is there, and doctors do not place bodies on mortuary vans unless they have good reason to believe the bodies to be corpses" (Cross, pp. 406 and 407). This would be an unnecessarily elaborate kind of lie.

Wright v. Doe D. Tatham
(1837), 7 Ad. & E. 313

The issue was whether John Marsden had sufficient mental capacity to make a valid will. The following evidence of incompetency was received without objection: treatment with disrespect by his steward; treatment as a child by his menial servants and residents of his village; the fact that he was called "Silly Jack" and "Silly Marsden" by local residents; the fact that boys shouted at him "There goes crazy Marsden", threw dirt at him and persuaded a passer by to see him home. As evidence of competency, three letters addressed to Marsden were proferred, but were held inadmissible by the Court of Exchequer Chamber and the House of Lords. Parke B. discussed the problem of implied assertions in detail, and some remarks of Bosanquet, J. should be noted.

PARKE, B.: . . . [You] have no right to use in evidence the fact of writing and sending a letter to a third person containing a statement of competence, on the ground that it affords an inference that such an act would not have been done unless the statement was true, or believed to be true, although such an inference no doubt would be raised in the conduct of the ordinary affairs of life, if the statement were made by a man of veracity. But it cannot be raised in a judicial inquiry; and, if such an argument were admissible, it would lead to the indiscriminate admission of hearsay evidence of all manner of facts.

Further, it is clear that an acting to a much greater extent and degree upon such statements to a third person would not make the statements admissible. For example, if a wager to a large amount had been made as to the matter in issue by two third persons, the payment of that wager, however large the sum, would not be admissible to prove the truth of the matter in issue. You would not have had any right to present it to the jury as raising an inference of the truth of the fact, on the ground that otherwise the bet would not have been paid. It is, after all, nothing but the mere statement of that fact, with strong evidence of the belief of it by the party making it. Could it make any difference that the wager was between the third person and one of the parties to the suit? Certainly not. The payment by other underwriters on the same policy to the plaintiff could not be given in evidence to prove that the subject insured had been lost. Yet there is an act done, a payment strongly attesting the truth of the statement, which it implies, that there had been a loss. To illustrate this point still further, let us suppose a third person had betted a wager with Mr. Marsden that he could not solve some mathematical problem, the solution of which required a high degree of capacity; would payment of that wager to Mr. Marsden's banker be admissible evidence that he possessed that capacity? The answer is certain; it would not. It would be evidence of the fact of competence given by a third party not upon oath.

Let us suppose the parties who wrote these letters to have stated the matter therein contained, that is, their knowledge of his personal qualities and capacity for business, on oath before a magistrate, or in some judicial proceeding to which the plaintiff and defendant were not parties. No one could contend that such statement would be admissible on this issue; and yet there would have been an act done on the faith of the statement being true, and a very solemn one, which would raise in the ordinary conduct of affairs a strong belief in the truth of the statement, if the writers were faith-worthy.

The acting in this case is of much less importance, and certainly is not equal to the sanction of an extra-judicial oath.

Many other instances of a similar nature, by way of illustration, were suggested by the learned counsel for the defendant in error, which, on the most cursory consideration, any one would at once declare to be inadmissible in evidence. Others were supposed on the part of the plaintiff in error, which, at first sight, have the appearance of being mere facts, and therefore admissible, though on further consideration they are open to precisely the same objection. Of the first description are the supposed cases of a letter by a third person to any one demanding a debt, which may be said to be a treatment of him as a debtor, being offered as proof that the debt was really due; a note, congratulating him on his high state of bodily vigour, being proposed as evidence of his being in good health; both of which are manifestly at first sight objectionable. To the latter class belong the supposed conduct of the family or relations of a testator, taking the same precautions in his absence as if he were a lunatic; his election, in his absence, to some high and responsible office; the conduct of a physician who permitted a will to be executed by a sick testator; the conduct of a deceased captain on a question of seaworthiness, who, after examining every part of the vessel, embarked in it with his family; all these, when deliberately considered, are, with reference to the matter in issue in each case, mere instances of hearsay evidence, mere statements, not on oath, but implied in or vouched by the actual conduct of persons by whose acts the litigant parties are not to be bound.

BOSANQUET, J.: . . . It is obvious that the contents of letters may be dictated by various motives, according to the dispositions and circumstances of the writers. Language of affection, of respect, of rational or amusing information, may be addressed from the best of motives to persons in a state of considerable imbecility, or labouring under the strangest delusions. The habitual treatment of deranged persons as rational is one mode of promoting their recovery. A tone of insult or derision may be employed in a moment of irritation in writing to a person in full possession of his reason; what judgment can be formed of the intention of the writers, without an endless examination into the circumstances which may have influenced them? And what opinion can be collected of the capacity of the receiver without ascertaining how he acted when he read the language addressed to him? To me it appears that the admission in proof of capacity of letters unaccompanied by other circumstances than such as are stated in this record would establish an entirely new precedent in a Court of Common Law, from which very great inconvenience might result upon trials of sanity, as well of the living as of the dead. . . .

Comment

In *Stobart* v. *Dryden* (1836), 1 M. & W. 615 Parke, B. said that the signature of the attesting witness on a deed was admissible evidence of its due execution; it was a fact showing that he did what in the ordinary course of business he would have done had he seen the deed executed (cf. *Whitelocke* v. *Musgrove* (1833), 1 Cr. & M. 511). Yet on his reasoning in *Wright* it would seem to be an implied assertion. Cross (p. 408) therefore suggests that Parke, B. was prepared to admit implied assertions which did not raise side issues. This does not correspond with Parke, B.'s language.

Questions

1. What view would Parke, B. take of the evidence of incompetency admitted without objection in *Wright*? (Cf. *In re Hine*, 37 A. 384 (1897).)

2. In *Backhouse* v. *Jones* (1839), 6 Bing. N.C. 65, the acts of creditors in returning goods to a bankrupt were held not to be admissible as evidence of

the creditors' belief as to their entitlement to keep possession, any more than their express declarations would be.

Lloyd v. Powell Duffryn Steam Coal Co., Ltd.
[1914] A.C. 733, H.L.

The issue was whether a child was the son of a man killed by an accident arising out of and in the course of his employment with the respondents. The deceased, knowing the child's mother was pregnant, had promised to marry her; he had also told his landlady and a friend that he was going to marry her because of the pregnancy. The Court of Appeal held that these statements were declarations against interest, and hence admissible as a hearsay exception. The House of Lords held the statements admissible but not as an exception to the hearsay rule.

LORD ATKINSON: . . . To treat the statements made by the deceased as statements made by a deceased person against his pecuniary interest, and therefore, though hearsay, proof of the facts stated, is wholly to mistake their true character and significance. This significance consists in the improbability that any man would make these statements, true or false, unless he believed himself to be the father of the child of whom Alice Lloyd was pregnant.

LORD MOULTON: It can scarcely be contested that the state of mind of the putative father and his intentions with regard to the child are matters relevant to the issue, whether there was a reasonable anticipation that he would support the child when born. It may be that an intention on his part so to do might be implied from the fact of his paternity and his recognition of it. But whether this be so or not, the attitude of mind of the putative father is that from which alone one can draw conclusions as to the greater or less probability of his supporting the child when born, and therefore evidence to prove that attitude of mind must be admissible if it be the proper evidence to establish such a fact. Now, it is well established in English jurisprudence, in accordance with the dictates of common sense, that the words and acts of a person are admissible as evidence of his state of mind. Indeed, they are the only possible evidence on such an issue. It was urged at the Bar that although the acts of the deceased might be put in evidence, his words might not. I fail to understand the distinction. Speaking is as much an act as doing.

It must be borne in mind that there is nothing in the admission of such evidence which clashes with the rooted objection in our jurisprudence to the admission of hearsay evidence. The testimony of the witnesses is to the act, i.e., to the deceased speaking these words, and it is the speaking of the words which is the matter that is put in evidence and which possesses evidential value. The evidence is, therefore, not in any respect open to the objection that it is secondary or hearsay evidence.

[EARL LOREBURN and LORD SHAW OF DUNFERMLINE gave concurring judgments.]

Note

This was followed in *Nash* v. *Railways Commissioner*, [1963] S.R.N.S.W. 357. Conduct as evidence of the badness of beer was admitted in *Manchester Brewery Co., Ltd.* v. *Coombs*, [1901] 2 Ch. 608.

Question

Do you agree with the House of Lords view in *Lloyd's* case?

Teper v. R.
[1952] A.C. 480; [1952] 2 All E.R. 447, P.C.

The accused was convicted of arson. A policeman named Cato testified that at 2 a.m., at least twenty-six minutes after the fire started and more than a furlong away from it, he heard a woman shouting, "Your place burning and you going away from the fire."

He then noticed a black car containing a fair man resembling the accused. The woman was not called. The Privy Council held that the evidence was inadmissible; it did not fall·within the *res gestae* exception to the hearsay rule.

LORD NORMAND: The rule against the admission of hearsay evidence is fundamental. It is not the best evidence and it is not delivered on oath. The truthfulness and accuracy of the person whose words are spoken to by another witness cannot be tested by cross-examination, and the light which his demeanour would throw on his testimony is lost. Nevertheless, the rule admits of certain carefully safeguarded and limited exceptions, one of which is that words may be proved when they form part of the *res gestae*. The rules controlling this exception are common to the jurisprudence of British Guiana, England and Scotland. It appears to rest ultimately on two propositions —that human utterance is both a fact and a means of communication, and that human action may be so interwoven with words that the significance of the action cannot be understood without the correlative words and the dissociation of the words from the action would impede the discovery of truth. But the judicial applications of these two propositions, which do not always combine harmoniously, have never been precisely formulated in a general principle. Their Lordships will not attempt to arrive at a general formula, nor is it necessary to review all of the considerable number of cases cited in the argument. This, at least, may be said, that it is essential that the words sought to be proved by hearsay should be, if not absolutely contemporaneous with the action or event, at least so clearly associated with it, in time, place and circumstance, that they are part of the thing being done, and so an item or part of real evidence and not merely a reported statement: R. v. *Bedingfield* (1879), 14 Cox C.C. 341; *O'Hara* v. *Central S.M.T. Co., Ltd.*, 1941 S.C. 363. How slight a separation of time and place may suffice to make hearsay evidence of the words spoken incompetent is well illustrated by the two cases cited. In *Bedingfield's* case a woman rushed with her throat cut out of a room in which the injury had been inflicted into another room where she said something to persons who saw her enter. Their evidence about what she said was ruled inadmissible by Cockburn, C.J. In *O'Hara's* case, a civil action, the event was an injury to a passenger brought about by the sudden swerve of the omnibus in which she was travelling. The driver of the omnibus said in his evidence that he was forced to swerve by a pedestrian who hurried across his path. Hearsay evidence of what was said by a man on the pavement at the scene of the accident as soon as the injured party had been attended to was held to be admissible in corroboration of the driver's evidence. But what was said twelve minutes later and away from the scene by the same man was held not part of the *res gestae*. In R. v. *Christie*, [1914] A.C. 545; [1914–15] All E.R. Rep. 63, H.L. the principle of the decision in *Bedingfield's* case was approved by Lord Reading with whom Lord Dunedin concurred, and no criticism of it is to be found in the speeches of the other noble and learned Lords who sat with them. In R. v. *Gibson* (1887), 18 Q.B.D. 537, the prosecutor gave evidence in a criminal trial that, immediately after he was struck by a stone, a woman going past, pointing to the prisoner's door, said: "The person who threw the stone went in there." This evidence was not objected to at the trial, but it was admitted by counsel for the prosecution in a Case Reserved that the evidence was incompetent. The conviction was quashed, and from their judgments it is clear that the learned judges who took part in the decision were far from questioning the correctness of counsel's admission. In *Gibson's* case the words were closely associated in time and place with the event, the assault. But they were not directly connected with that event itself. They were not words spontaneously forced from the woman by the sight of the assault, but were prompted by the sight of a man quitting the scene of the assault and they were spoken for the purpose of helping to bring him to justice.

The special danger of allowing hearsay evidence for the purpose of identification requires that it shall only be allowed if it satisfies the strictest test of close association with the event in time, place and circumstances. . . .

CME—L·

There is yet another proposition which can be affirmed, *viz.*, that for identification purposes in a criminal trial the event with which the words sought to be proved must be so connected as to form part of the *res gestae* is the commission of the crime itself— the throwing of the stone, the striking of the blow, the setting fire to the building, or whatever the criminal act may be. Counsel for the Crown submitted that any relevant event or action may be accompanied by words which may have to be proved in order to bring out its true significance. There is a limited sense in which this is true, but it is not always true, and much depends on the use to be made of the evidence. In *Christie's* case hearsay evidence of certain words uttered by a child, the victim of indecent assault, in the presence and hearing of the accused were held to be admissible in explanation of the demeanour of the accused in response to them. But the evidence was held inadmissible for the purpose of showing that the child identified the accused as his assailant. In the present case identification is the purpose for which the hearsay was introduced, and its admission goes far beyond anything that has been authorized by any reported case.

Note

The probative value of the evidence depended on two identifications—the woman's and Cato's—of a man of another race at night. It depended on Cato's attention being directed to a particular person in a crowd when any other member of the crowd might have been meant. The innuendo in the statement was not unambiguously clear: on one view the evidence was irrelevant to the issue of who caused the fire. There was thus ample reason for excluding the evidence apart from the Privy Council's assumption that it was hearsay and their decision that it fell outside the *res gestae* exception.

Holloway v. McFeeters
(1956), 94 C.L.R. 470

After a car struck a pedestrian the driver ran away. In the High Court of Australia Dixon, C.J. and Kitto, J. said that this fact was inadmissible evidence of his negligence as an admission, and hence they were prepared to assume it was hearsay.

DIXON, C.J.: [O'Brien J. in the court below said] that the jury might infer that the driver knew that he had run down the man and severely injured him and had yet left him where he lay. The jury might regard this behaviour as implying a consciousness of guilt and as being the nature of an admission. As to the view that it is tantamount to an admission by conduct, the difficulty is that the driver is not a party to the proceedings nor is the nominal defendant sued on his behalf. The admissions of the driver would not, as such, be receivable in evidence against the nominal defendant.

Ratten v. R.
[1972] A.C. 378; [1971] 3 All E.R. 801, P.C.

About the time the accused's wife was shot by the discharge of his gun, which he asserted to be accidental, the telephonist at the local exchange received a call from the accused's house. The voice, which was hysterical and sobbing, said "Get me the police please". The telephonist's testimony was admitted at the trial and appeals to the Victorian Full Court and the Privy Council failed. The latter held that if the words were hearsay they were admissible under the *res gestae* exception, but that they were not hearsay.

LORD WILBERFORCE: The next question related to the further facts sought to be proved concerning the telephone call. The objection taken against this evidence was that it was hearsay and that it did not come within any of the recognized exceptions to the rule against hearsay evidence. In their Lordships' opinion the evidence was not hearsay evidence and was admissible as evidence of fact relevant to an issue.

The mere fact that evidence of a witness includes evidence as to words spoken by another person who is not called is no objection to its admissibility. Words spoken are facts just as much as any other action by a human being. If the speaking of the words is a relevant fact, a witness may give evidence that they were spoken. A question of hearsay only arises when the words spoken are relied on 'testimonially', i.e. as establishing some fact narrated by the words. . . .

The evidence relating to the fact of telephoning by the deceased was, in their Lordships' view, factual and relevant. It can be analysed into the following elements. (1) At about 1.15 p.m. the number Echuca 1494 rang. I plugged into that number. (2) I opened the speak key and said number please. (3) A female voice answered. (4) That voice was hysterical and sobbed. (5) The voice said "Get me the police please".

The factual items numbered (1)–(3) were relevant in order to show that, contrary to the evidence of the appellant, a call was made, only some three to five minutes before the fatal shooting, by a woman. It not being suggested that there was anybody in the house other than the appellant, his wife and small children, this woman, the caller, could only have been the deceased. Items (4) and (5) were relevant as possibly showing (if the jury thought fit to draw the inference) that the deceased woman was at this time in a state of emotion or fear (cf. *Aveson* v. *Lord Kinnaird* (1805), 6 East 188, at, p. 193, *per* Lord Ellenborough, C.J.). They were relevant and necessary evidence in order to explain and complete the fact of the call being made. A telephone call is a composite act, made up of manual operations together with the utterance of words (cf. *McGregor* v. *Stokes* [1952] V.L.R. 347 and remarks of Salmond, J., therein quoted). To confine the evidence to the first would be to deprive the act of most of its significance. The act had content when it was known that the call was made in a state of emotion. The knowledge that the caller desired the police to be called, helped to indicate the nature of the emotion—anxiety or fear at an existing or impending emergency. It was a matter for the jury to decide what light (if any) this evidence, in the absence of any explanation from the appellant, who was in the house, threw on what situation was occurring, or developing at the time.

If, then, this evidence had been presented in this way, as evidence purely of relevant facts, its admissibility could hardly have been plausibly challenged. But the appellant submits that in fact this was not so. It is said that the evidence was tendered and admitted as evidence of an assertion by the deceased that she was being attacked by the appellant, and that it was, so far, hearsay evidence, being put forward as evidence of the truth of facts asserted by his statement. It is claimed that the learned chief justice so presented the evidence to the jury and that, therefore, its admissibility, as hearsay, may be challenged.

[We do not believe any such implied assertion was relied on.]

Note

Lord Wilberforce says the words are only facts showing the woman was in a state of fear. Now if words are admitted as original rather than hearsay evidence, they are admitted not as evidence of the truth of what was asserted but simply to show they were said. That is, it does not matter whether they are true or false. It did not matter whether the terrorists' threats of death would be carried out in *Subramaniam*; they may have been joking but the accused was not to know this, and the only relevance of the threats was to explain his conduct. But here it matters very much whether the wife is really afraid or not, for the evidence has no probative value if she is not. The evidence is relied on not simply to prove that signs of fear were present, but that these signs were justified. It would seem that there was an implied assertion even on the Privy Council's view. (See also *Charlesworth* v. *Police,* [1970] N.Z.L.R. 174.)

What position is desirable?

One view is that all implied assertions are hearsay and inadmissible unless they fall within an existing exception (e.g. Baker, p. 6; *Wright* v. *Doe d. Tatham* (1837), 7 Ad. & El. 313, at p. 388, *per* Parke, B.; *Thompson* v. *Manhattan Ry. Co.* (1896), 42 N.Y.S. 896; *People* v. *Bush* (1921), 133 N.E. 201; *Marshall* v. *Watt,* [1953] Tas. S.R. 1, at p. 7, *per* Gibson, J.; *State* v. *Di Vincenti* (1957), 93 S. 2d 676; *Ratten* v. *R.,* [1972] A.C. 378; [1971] 3 All E.R. 801, P.C.). Advocates of this extreme view, while admitting that implied assertions are usually free from the risk of manufacture, feel they may be unreliable because of defects in the powers of perception, memory, or expression of the maker of the assertion. It is not an easy view to defend in an age of lawyers who, if they agree on anything, agree on the need to admit more hearsay evidence.

Another is that all implied assertions are hearsay, but new exceptions should be created to take account of special guarantees of reliability associated with some of this kind of evidence. Thus if the matters to be inferred from the actor's conduct are within his knowledge and his conduct was detrimental to him, it should be admitted (Morgan, (1935), 48 Harv. L.R. 1138, at pp. 1158–60). An example might be Parke, B.'s losing gambler. Another test is to give the court a discretion to admit the evidence if on the facts it seemed reliable, e.g. because the actor has based important decisions on the belief which he is impliedly asserting. An example might be Parke, B.'s sea captain who after testing a vessel embarks on it with his family.

A third view is that non-assertive statements are hearsay but not non-assertive conduct. (See *Davidson* v. *Quirke,* [1923] N.Z.L.R. 552, where the acts of phoning a gaming house were admitted as not being hearsay, and details of what the callers said were admissible under the hearsay exception for statements explaining the purpose of acts (p. 340, *post*).) This is Cross's view. He draws the distinction for three main reasons. One is that deeds speak louder than words. Another is that if conduct were hearsay the scope of the rule would be tremendously extended. Thirdly, the real reason for excluding much impliedly assertive conduct is not unreliability but the risk of a multiplicity of side-issues. Where there are few side-issues the evidence is admissible (Cross, p. 408 and (1969), 7 U. of Melb. L.R. 1, at pp. 12–13).

If no hearsay reform were likely, there would be much to be said for this view. But ours is a reforming age, and new exceptions could be created if the hearsay rule were widened. Further, Cross's view is illogical. "What possible rationale can there be for treating 'Hello X' as hearsay, but not the non-assertive conduct of a soldier seen saluting another person as evidence that the person concerned was an officer?" (Weinberg, *op. cit.,* p. 285). It is not in fact clear that deeds always do speak louder than words. What speaks loudly is a deed or a statement based on serious motives.

A final view is that no implied assertion is hearsay (e.g. *American Law Institute Model Code* (1942), r. 501 (1) and perhaps *Lloyd* v. *Powell Duffryn Steam Coal Co., Ltd.,* [1914] A.C. 733). But it is irrational to distinguish express assertions from implied, particularly since the dangers of inaccurate observation, memory and narration exist just as strongly without the safeguard of cross-examination in both cases.

Some American writers have tried to solve the implied assertions problem by asking if cross-examination of the maker of the assertion would assist in judging his veracity, memory, observation or narrative powers.

Thus Maguire (p. 16) puts these examples. (*a*) The issue is A's deafness. As he read a book aloud a mechanical buzzer was operated at different levels. A's tone of voice never changed, and expert testimony is that this could not have been maintained if the buzzing had been audible to A. (*b*) The issue is B's deafness. B was blindfolded and a tuning fork was moved towards and away from him. He stated its movements accurately. (*c*) The issue is whether C's leg is paralysed. A doctor testifies that when he thrust a needle into the leg in different places, C gave no sign of pain. (*d*) A man is shot dead in the middle of a crowd. D, an enemy of the victim, runs away. Maguire says that (*a*) is a case where cross-examination of A could not destroy our belief in his deafness However, (*b*) involves B's manifestation of belief, and there may be something fraudulent about the test which could be exposed by cross-examining B. But only veracity arises, not powers of memory, observation or narrative. If it is thought the risk of fraud is slight enough, the evidence might be admitted as not being a case where cross-examination could make any difference. In (*c*) the risk of fraud is greater. In (*d*) problems about D's sincerity and motives arise— because he may wish to distract attention from the real killer. Problems akin to narration arise—what did D mean by running away? It may be due to a consciousness of guilt, or to a fear of becoming mixed up in a discreditable affair. Problems akin to observation arise—D may mistakenly think he killed the man. Maguire concludes: "the decisions have not made us sure whether the rule may be invoked when only testimonial qualities *other than sincerity* could be dissected by the cross-examiner. This uncertainty is very bad indeed for practical administration of the rule" (p. 23). His analysis does reveal a possible line of division between hearsay and non-hearsay which would coin-cide with Parke, B.'s if it is drawn at the point when cross-examination begins to have some value on any aspect of sincerity, observation, memory or narration. If the line is drawn in a less exclusionary place it would not.

ii Negative hearsay

Does the common law rule apply to "negative hearsay"? Assume the issue is whether the accused purported to make payments to employees of his firm who in fact did not exist, and that there is a practice in the firm of making out a file on each employee. Is an accountant's evidence that he searched for the files of the employees allegedly paid but did not find them admissible? Such evidence was admitted in *S. v. Becker*, 1968 I S.A. 18. Yet an out of court statement "The accused employs only A, B and C, but not D" would be hear-say with respect to D's non-employment. The same must be so of a statement "The accused employs only A, B and C". If the hearsay rule extends to implied assertions by conduct, proof of a practice of making files on all employees and only finding files on A, B and C must also be hearsay. The N.S.W. Law Reform Commission on Evidence (Business Records) (L.R.C. 17, 1973) recommended that negative hearsay be admissible, which suggests it is hearsay, not admissible at common law (and see *R. v. Hally*, [1962] Qd.R. 214).

Reading

Baker, *The Hearsay Rule* (London, 1950); Cross (1956), 72 L.Q.R. 91; 7 U. of Melb. L.R. 1 (1969); Finman, (1962), 14 Stanford L.R. 682; Harrison (1955),

7 Res Judicatae 58; McCormick (1930), 39 Yale L.J. 489; Maguire (1961), 14 Vanderbilt L.R. 741; Morgan (1935), 48 Harv. L.R. 1138; (1948), 62 Harv. L.R. 177; Tribe (1974), 87 Harv. L.R. 957; Weinberg (1973), 9 U. of Melb. L.R. 268.

Questions

1. Guy Burgess is being tried for espionage. Three issues in the case are: (i) did Burgess post a letter just outside the Russian Embassy on March 1; (ii) is Burgess a habitual drunkard; and (iii) what is the age of Burgess' chauffeur?

Is any of the following evidence admissible on issue (i): (a) the fact that the envelope of the letter allegedly posted near the Embassy is postmarked "March 1" by a post office near the Embassy; (b) the evidence of a passer-by that on March 1 he heard Kim Philby (who cannot be found to testify) say to someone outside the Embassy "Goodbye, Guy"; (c) on March 1 an Old Etonian tie marked "G.B." is found near the Embassy; (d) as in (c), but a witness testifies that earlier that day he saw Burgess wearing such a tie.

Is any of the following evidence admissible on issue (ii): (d) the evidence of Donald McLean's butler that he always found empty whisky bottles in Burgess's room after his visits; (e) the evidence of a passer-by that he heard McLean say to Burgess, "You've been shaking very badly lately, Guy"; (f) the evidence of a steward at the Reform Club, of which Burgess was a member, that the Secretary often told him to lock up the whisky if Burgess was left alone in the bar?

Is any of the following admissible on issue (iii): (g) testimony of Burgess' chauffeur that his own age was twenty-four; (h) Burgess' testimony that the chauffeur was thirty-four? Could the jury be told to form their own view of the chauffeur's age by drawing inferences from his appearance?

2. Leopold and Leob go into an isolated cottage with a small boy. The boy is killed shortly before the police arrive. Leopold runs away and cannot subsequently be found. Is Leopold's flight admissible evidence in favour of Loeb at Loeb's trial for murdering the boy?

13

Hearsay Exceptions: Criminal Cases

At common law the hearsay rule became riddled with exceptions. A major piece of reform was undertaken in civil cases in the Evidence Act 1938, and a still more fundamental reform in the Civil Evidence Act 1968. Similarly wide reforms were proposed by the 11th Report of the Criminal Law Revision Committee, but these have not been enacted. It is therefore difficult to state briefly the hearsay exceptions. We will not discuss them all. Instead we will concentrate on those which have one or more of the following qualities: a continued importance even after reforms similar to the Civil Evidence 1968; present practical importance in criminal cases; and intrinsic interest. It might be noted that fundamental reform of the hearsay rule will have one blessing if no other: a substantial shortening of books on Evidence.

I STATEMENTS OF DECEASED PERSONS

A. Declarations against interest

The oral or written statement by a deceased person of a fact which he knew to be against his pecuniary or proprietary interest at the time he made it is admissible as evidence of the fact and all collateral facts mentioned provided the declarant had personal knowledge of them. The basis of admissibility is that truth is guaranteed by the unlikelihood of a man lying against his own interests. This exception arose in civil cases involving contract, property or status much more than in criminal, because the declarations had to tend to impose pecuniary or proprietary, but not criminal, liabilities.

B. Declarations in the course of duty

The oral or written statement by a deceased person made under a duty to record or report his acts is admissible evidence of the truth of such parts of of the statement as it was his duty to record or report, provided the record or report was made roughly contemporaneously with the act done, and provided the declarant had no motive to lie. The reasons for the exception are, first, necessity: there might be no other evidence of what an employee did; and secondly, that the likelihood of dismissal for incompetent recording or reporting guarantees reliability. This exception too largely arose in civil cases.

C. Declarations as to public or general rights

An oral or written statement by a deceased person concerning the reputed existence of a public or general right is admissible as evidence of its existence provided the declaration was made before a dispute had arisen, and in the case of general rights, provided the declarant had competent knowledge. Public rights affect the entire population, general rights affect particular classes of person. The exception exists because other evidence is usually unavailable; and because most neighbours know about local matters affecting the community, and are likely to discuss them in public, so that false statements will be contradicted. The exception is an extreme example of the admission of multiple hearsay—hearsay on hearsay. It has little modern application, but was preserved for civil cases by the Civil Evidence Act 1968, s. 9 (4) (c). It has virtually no application in practice to criminal cases.

D. Pedigree declarations

Oral or written statements of a deceased person, or statements to be implied from family conduct, are admissible as evidence of pedigree provided the declarant was a blood relation or the spouse of a blood relation of the person whose pedigree is in issue, and provided the declaration was made before the dispute arose. The exception is based on necessity and on the fact that it is natural for people to talk of their family in a truthful way if there is no interest to be served. It can have scarcely any application to criminal cases, except possibly incest; it was preserved in civil cases by the Civil Evidence Act 1968, s. 9 (4) (b).

E. Testators' declarations about their wills

The oral or written statement of a deceased testator after the execution of his will is admissible evidence of the contents, but not the execution, of the will. The exception is based on the testator's unique means of knowledge and his general lack of reason to lie. It is noteworthy as the last hearsay exception explicitly created by the English courts (*Sugden* v. *Lord St. Leonards* (1876), 1 P.D. 154; [1874–80] All E.R. Rep. 21, C.A.). It can have virtually no practical application in criminal cases.

F. Dying declarations

The oral or written statement of a deceased person is admissible evidence of the cause of his death at a trial for his murder or manslaughter provided that when the statement was made the declarant would have been a competent witness and was under a settled hopeless expectation of death.

R. v. Woodcock
(1789), 1 Leach 500

The accused was charged with murdering his wife. She made a statement implicating him at a time when her death was inevitable as a result of eight head wounds. She died forty-eight hours later. She remained coherent until death but never expressed any realization of dying. Eyre, C.B. left the issue of whether she was under a settled hopeless expectation of death to the jury, who convicted the accused.

EYRE, C.B.: [T]he general principle on which this species of evidence is admitted is, that they are declarations made in extremity, when the party is at the point of death, and when every hope of this world is gone: when every motive to falsehood is silenced, and the mind is induced by the most powerful considerations to speak the truth; a situation so solemn, and so awful, is considered by the law as creating an obligation equal to that which is imposed by a positive oath administered in a Court of Justice. . . . [I]nasmuch as she was mortally wounded, and was in a condition which rendered almost immediate death inevitable; as she was thought by every person about her to be dying . . .; her declarations . . . ought to be considered by a jury as being made under the impression of her approaching dissolution; for, resigned as she appeared to be, she must have felt the hand of death, and must have considered herself as a dying woman.

Notes

1. The same point about the basis of admissibility is made in R. v. *Hope*, [1909] V.L.R. 149. Normally no inquiry into the declarant's religious beliefs is made; but a four year old's declaration was excluded in R. v. *Pike* (1829), 3 C. & P. 598 and that of a ten year old admitted after enquiry in R. v. *Perkins* (1840), 9 C. & P. 395. In R. v. *Madobi* (1963), 6 F.L.R. 1 the dying declaration exception was not applied to the statement of an indigenous Papuan, whose community believed that the future life would be spent pleasantly on a nearby island (cf. R. v. *Kipali-Ikarum*, [1967–8] P. & N.G.L.R. 119). In India and Pakistan dying declarations, though admissible, are treated with suspicion, because of a practice of a dying man revenging himself on all his enemies by blaming them for his death. But in R. v. *Kuruwaru* (1900), 10 Q.L.J. 139 the dying declaration of a Mohammedan was admitted; Griffith, C.J. seemed to consider that it was enough that the declarant had a religious belief. Nor is any special inquiry undertaken in South Africa (Hoffman, pp. 121–4). The exception now probably operates quite independently of Eyre C.B.'s rationale (47 A.L.J. 92). It should probably either be abolished or rationalized: see Brazil (1960), 34 A.L.J. 195 and R. v. *Peagui Ambimp* (1972), 47 A.L.J. 93.

2. The condition of extremity that on one view helps guarantee veracity on another is a possible source of errors of memory, and narration. (The danger of having to rely on leading questions, for example, is considerable: R. v. *Mitchell* (1892), 17 Cox C.C. 503; and incomplete dying declarations are inadmissible: *Waugh* v. R. [1950] A.C. 203, P.C.) The jury should be told that the declaration is not subject to cross-examination (*ibid.*).

3. There need not be a settled hopeless expectation of immediate death: R. v. *Perry*, [1909] 2 K.B. 697, C.C.A. Quite long periods have elapsed, e.g. eleven days (R. v. *Mosley* (1825), 1 Mood, C.C. 97); three weeks (R. v. *Bernadotti* (1869), 11 Cox C.C. 316).

4. Despite *Woodcock*, the courts have been reluctant to infer a settled hopeless expectation of death (e.g. R. v. *Jenkins* (1869), L.R. 1 C.C.R. 187), though subsequent hopes of recovery do not affect the admissibility of a declaration made under such expectation (R. v. *Austin* (1912), 8 Cr. App. Rep. 27, C.C.A.). In particular, there has been reluctance to make an inference from the severity of wounds (e.g. R. v. *Morgan* (1875), 14 Cox C.C. 341; cf. R. v. *Donohoe*, [1962] N.S.W.R. 1144).

5. The statement is admissible for the accused as well as against him (*R. v, Scaife* (1836), 2 Lew C.C. 150).

Question

Is there any reason for limiting admissibility to murder and manslaughter prosecutions, as settled in *R. v. Mead* (1824), 2 B. & C. 605?

II STATEMENTS IN PUBLIC DOCUMENTS

A public document coming from the proper place or a certified copy of it is evidence of every fact stated in it. A public document must be made under a strict duty to inquire into all the circumstances recorded, must be concerned with a public matter, must be intended to be retained, and must be meant for public inspection. Examples are registers of births, deaths and marriages, and public surveys, reports and returns. The exception is justified by necessity and by the reliability of public records. It usually arises in civil cases but has some application to criminal ones.

III STATUTORY EXCEPTIONS

A. Criminal Evidence Act 1965

1.—(1) In any criminal proceedings where direct oral evidence of a fact would be admissible, any statement contained in a document and tending to establish that fact shall, on production of the document, be admissible as evidence of that fact if—

(*a*) the document is, or forms part of, a record relating to any trade or business and compiled, in the course of that trade or business, from information supplied (whether directly or indirectly) by persons who have, or may reasonably be supposed to have, personal knowledge of the matters dealt with in the information they supply; and

(*b*) the person who supplied the information recorded in the statement in question is dead, or beyond the seas, or unfit by reason of his bodily or mental condition to attend as a witness, or cannot with reasonable diligence be identified or found, or cannot reasonably be expected (having regard to the time which has elapsed since he supplied the information and to all the circumstances) to have any recollection of the matters dealt with in the information he supplied.

(2) For the purpose of deciding whether or not a statement is admissible as evidence by virtue of this section, the court may draw any reasonable inference from the form or content of the document in which the statement is contained, and may, in deciding whether or not a person is fit to attend as a witness, act on a certificate purporting to be a certificate of a fully registered medical practitioner.

(3) In estimating the weight, if any, to be attached to a statement admissible as evidence by virtue of this section regard shall be had to all the circumstances from which any inference can reasonably be drawn as to the accuracy or otherwise of the statement, and, in particular, to the question whether or not the person who supplied the information recorded in the statement did so contemporaneously with the occurrence or existence of the facts stated, and to the question whether or not that person, or any person concerned with making or keeping the record containing the statement, had any incentive to conceal or misrepresent the facts.

(4) In this section "statement" includes any representation of fact, whether made in words or otherwise, "document" includes any device by means of which information

is recorded or stored and "business" includes any public transport, public utility or similar undertaking carried on by a local authority and the activities of the Post Office.

The Act was enacted to reverse the decision in *Myers* v. *Director of Public Prosecutions*, [1965] A.C. 1001, H.L.; [1964] 2 All E.R. 881, H.L. The principal respect in which it is too narrow is perhaps the limitation to "trade or business" records: see *R.* v. *Gwilliam*, [1968] 3 All E.R. 821, C.A. See also *R.* v. *van Vreden* (1973), 57 Cr. App. Rep. 818, C.A. The Criminal Law Revision Committee recommended much wider reforms in their 11th Report.

B. Other

The Criminal Justice Act 1967, s. 9 provides for agreed statements of facts to be admitted. There are numerous instances where depositions of an absent deponent may be proved in criminal cases. (See Cross and Wilkins, *Outline of the Law of Evidence* (3rd Edn, London, 1971), Art. 37.)

IV ADMISSIONS

Admissions are statements adverse to the case of a party to legal proceedings. In criminal cases they are called confessions if made to a person in authority, and are subject to the special rules of voluntariness, (Chap. 8, *ante*). If not made to a person in authority in criminal cases, and in all civil cases, they are called admissions and are admissible against the maker as evidence of their truth under an exception to the hearsay rule. They are often called "informal", as distinct from formal, admissions (p. 6, *ante*). They should also be distinguished from adverse statements made during the proceedings: such a statement is admissible simply as the evidence of a witness, not as a hearsay exception. They are usually made expressly or implicitly in words, but may be made by conduct such as flight or silence (Chap. 7, *ante*). Reliability is enhanced by the unlikelihood of anyone telling lies against his own interest. But the rule is wider; the party need not realize the statement is against his interest. The rule is that he cannot prevent anything he says being used against him. "A litigant can scarcely complain if the court refuses to take seriously his allegation that his extra-judicial statements are so little worthy of credence that the trier of fact should not even consider them. He can hardly be heard to object that he was not under oath or that he had no opportunity to cross-examine himself" (Morgan (1929), 42 Harv. L.R. 461). Admissions, apart from being evidence of their truth, also help destroy their maker's credibility if he testifies differently at the trial. However, admissions are not estoppels; they may be explained away, contradicted and disproved.

A. Direct admissions

Admissions made when acting in a representative capacity are admissible against their maker when he is sued in a personal capacity (*Stanton* v. *Percival* (1855), 5 H.L. C. 257). But admissions made in a personal capacity are inadmissible against those the maker is representing if he is sued in a representative capacity (*Legge* v. *Edmonds* (1855), 25 L.J. Ch. 125). Indeed, as a general rule persons other than the maker are not bound by his admissions (*Willey* v. *Synan* (1937), 57 C.L.R. 200).

If a party's statements are in part self-serving and in part damaging, and his opponent seeks to have the admissions proved, the whole statement may be admitted; the effect, so far as the self-serving parts are concerned, is that another hearsay exception of a parasitic kind exists (*Harrison* v. *Turner* (1847), 10 Q.B. 482). The weight of the different parts may vary, however (*R. v. McGregor*, [1968] 1 Q.B. 371; [1967] 2 All E.R. 267, C.A.; *Allied Interstate Qld. Pty., Ltd.* v. *Barnes* (1968), 42 A.L.J.R. 348).

In criminal cases admissions not made on personal knowledge appear to be inadmissible (*Surujpaul* v. *R.*, [1958] 3 All E.R. 300, P.C., at p. 304). In civil cases such admissions may be of no weight (*Customs Comptroller* v. *Western Electric Co., Ltd.*, [1966] A.C. 367; [1965] 3 All E.R. 599, P.C.), but they are admissible (*Lustre Hosiery, Ltd.* v. *York* (1936), 54 C.L.R. 134).

The contents of documents to which a party has access and over which he has control are admissible evidence against him of their truth (*Alderson* v. *Clay* (1816), 1 Stark. 405).

Testimony as a witness in one case is admissible against the speaker in subsequent proceedings.

B. Vicarious admissions

Admissions made to a third party by those in privity with a party to litigation are evidence against him. Though testimony in court of one co-party is evidence against another, his out-of-court admissions are not, unless the statement is put forward merely to show it was made rather than as evidence of its truth (*Mawaz Khan* v. *R.*, [1967] 1 A.C. 454; [1967] 1 All E.R. 80, P.C.). The unsworn statement in court of a co-accused, however, is not evidence against another co-accused (*R. v. Simpson*, [1956] V.L.R. 490). The oral evidence of witnesses called by a party in former proceedings is inadmissible against him: the witness is not an agent. The party may not have, and ought not to have any control over what he is going to say, and may not even know what he is going to say (*British Thomson-Houston Co., Ltd.* v. *British Insulated and Helsby Cables, Ltd.*, [1924] 2 Ch. 160, C.A.; [1924] All E.R. Rep. 446, C.A.). But third party affidavits used by a party in earlier proceedings are admissible (*Richards* v. *Morgan* (1863), 4 B. & S. 641).

Cases where there is privity are of two main kinds which may overlap, as in the case of partners. One is where the party and the maker of the statement had an identity of interest or obligation—e.g. landowner and his predecessor in title, partners, and joint tenants. The second is where the maker of the statement had express or implied authority to make it on behalf of the party, e.g. partners, referees and conspirators so far as the admission relates to an act done in furtherance of the conspiracy. But the main examples are the relations of agent–principal and servant–master.

An agent's statements within the scope of his authority made during the continuance of his agency to third persons are admissible in litigation against his principal. The "scope of his authority" raises difficult problems. He need not be authorized to make the admission, but he must be authorized to make a communication to a third party in the course of which the admission is made. Such authority will usually be narrower than his general authority; "it is important to distinguish between authority to do an act and authority to talk about it" (Morgan, 42 Harv. L.R. 461, at p. 464).

The effect of the rule about the scope of the agent's authority is that the agent must usually be senior.

Fraser Henleins Pty., Ltd. *v.* Cody
(1945), 70 C.L.R. 100

A managing director made admissions relevant to black marketing offences with which his company was charged. The High Court of Australia held them admissible.

LATHAM, C.J.: . . . The next objection on behalf of the appellant is that the statements made by Crowther, a director and the manager of the company, were not admissible in evidence as against the company. It was argued that his authority in relation to past transactions related only to the carrying out of those transactions, and not to making admissions in respect of them after they were completed. But Crowther, as the manager of the company, must be regarded as having authority to deal with any inquiry into the affairs of the company in relation to a possible breach of the law by the company. He was the person who would naturally represent the company if any inquiry were made into such matters. See *Kirkstall Brewery Co.* v. *Furness Rail. Co.* (1874), L.R. 9, Q.B. 468 where it was suspected that a railway porter had stolen a parcel which was in the custody of the railway company. The stationmaster who had the sole management of the station from which the parcel was stolen made statements to a police officer who was inquiring into the matter, and it was held that his authority extended to putting the police in motion in order to secure the stolen goods; and because he had this authority the statements made by him to the police were admissible in evidence against the company. In the present case, the authority of Crowther was more extensive than the authority of the stationmaster in relation to the company and was more extensive than that of a person who held only the position of director of a company. He was also the general manager of the business of the company. He was not an agent whose authority in relation to a past transaction was limited to the carrying out of that transaction; he had general authority to act in and in relation to the business of the company, and therefore to deal with investigating officers in any matter concerning that business. In *Ex parte Gerard & Co. Pty., Ltd.*; *Re Craig* (1944) 44 S.R.N.S.W. 370 upon which the appellant company relied, it was held that when a director was answering questions under compulsion he was not acting in the usual course of business of the company or in the course of a business transaction of the company. In the present case, the questions were not answered on compulsion and the director was also the manager of the whole business of the company. If he could not bind the company by an admission, no-one could do so. It has never been held that only a formal act by the board of a company can bind the company by way of admission. In my opinion, the objection to the admissibility of the evidence fails.

[STARKE, DIXON, McTIERNAN and WILLIAMS, JJ. agreed.]

Cf. *Great Western Rail. Co.* v. *Willis* (1865), 18 C.B.N.S. 748.

A servant may be an agent within the vicarious admissions rule, but making admissions is usually outside the scope of his authority.

Notes

1. In practice admissions are often proved which are statements of non-expert opinion or contain conclusions of law or are themselves based on hearsay: "I stole the car," "I was negligent," "My servant says he was negligent." This may be wrong in theory, but an exception to this effect now seems to have grown up.

2. There is doubt about whether admissions by a deceased bind claimants

under the Fatal Accidents Acts or the Law Reform (Miscellaneous Provisions) Act 1934: cf. *Marks* v. *Portsmouth Corporation* (1937), 157 L.T. 261 and *Evans* v. *Hartigan* (1941), 41 S.R.N.S.W. 179).

Questions

1. Analyse the relationship between admissions and declarations against interest.

2. A machine injures an employee. The employer has it fenced more securely. What evidential value does the employer's act have?

Reading

Phipson, Chs. 16–18.

V *RES GESTAE*

"*Res gestae*" means "the transaction". Evidence relevant to a "transaction" and arising contemporaneously with it may be admissible. The *res gestae* label has never been very popular.

"If you wish to tender inadmissible evidence, say it is part of the *res gestae*" (Lord Blackburn, quoted by Cross, p. 37, n. 2). The rules are "huddled confusedly with a lot of rag-tag-and-bobtail material under the damnably unhelpful label '*res gestae*' " (Maguire, p. 148). It is "a phrase adopted to provide a respectable legal cloak for a variety of cases to which no formula of precision can be applied" (*Homes* v. *Newman*, [1931] 2 Ch. 112, at p. 120, *per* Lord Tomlin). It is "the lurking place of a motley crowd of conceptions in mutual conflict and reciprocating chaos" (Stone (1939), 55 L.Q.R. 66, at p. 67). Pollock once wrote to Holmes that "I am reporting, with some reluctance, a case on the damnable pretended doctrine of *res gestae*, and wishing some high legal authority would prick that bubble of verbiage: the unmeaning term merely judges the truth that there is no universal formula for all the kinds of relevancy" (*Pollock–Holmes Letters*, 23 April, 1931 (Cambridge, 1942), Vol. 2, pp. 284–5). "[T]here are few problems in the law of evidence more unsolved than what things are to be embraced in those occurrences that are designated in the law as the '*res gestae*' " (*Hunter* v. *State*, 40 N.J.L. 536, quoted by Wigmore, para. 1745). "This . . . collection of fact situations . . . is so confusing in its scope as almost to demand that a reader cease thinking before he go mad" (Wright, 20 Can. B. Rev. 714, at p. 716). "The marvellous capacity of a Latin phrase to serve as a substitute for reasoning, and the confusion of thought inevitably accompanying the use of inaccurate terminology are nowhere better illustrated than in the decisions dealing with the admissibility of evidence as '*res gestae*'. It is probable that this troublesome expression owes its existence and persistence in our law of evidence to an inclination of judges and lawyers to avoid the toilsome exertion of exact analysis and precise thinking" (Morgan (1922), 31 Yale L.J. 229).

As usual, Wigmore's comments are the fullest and strongest.

> "There has been such a confounding of ideas, and such a profuse and indiscriminate use of the shibboleth '*res gestae*', that it is difficult to disentangle the real basis of principle involved. On the one hand, to repeat without comment the often meaningless and unhelpful language of the courts is to shirk the duty of the expositor of the

law as it is. On the other hand, to discriminate between the principles genuinely involved is to risk the reproach of representing as law that which the courts do not concede. . . .

"... It ought ... wholly to be repudiated, as a vicious element in our legal phraseology. . . . [A]ny name would be preferable to an empty phrase so encouraging to looseness of thinking and uncertainty of decision" (paras. 1745, 1767).

Let us first consider why the subject causes such abuse and raises so much difficulty, and then consider the main examples.

A. Preliminary problems

One problem can be briefly stated. The rules as to what *res gestae* evidence is admissible are extraordinarily hard to formulate with precision, because they essentially depend on a high degree of relevance.

Another problem is whether *res gestae* evidence is original or hearsay. Some have considered that such evidence can only be admitted as original evidence and not evidence of the truth of what it asserts under a hearsay exception (e.g. *R. v. Christie*, [1914] A.C. 545, at p. 553, *per* Lord Atkinson; [1914–15] All E.R. Rep. 63, at p. 66, H.L.; *Adelaide Chemical and Fertilizer Co., Ltd. v. Carlyle* (1940), 64 C.L.R. 514, at pp. 530–3, *per* Dixon, J.). But this is not the modern view (*Carlyle's* case, at p. 526, *per* Starke, J.; *Ratten v. R.*, [1972] A.C. 378, P.C.; [1971] 3 All E.R. 801, p. 336, *post*). Sometimes *res gestae* evidence is admitted as original evidence and sometimes under an exception to the hearsay rule.

A third problem is that there are two views of the basis of admissibility as a hearsay exception. The traditional view depends heavily on the notion that the statement is part of the event comprised by independently proved facts in issue. For this reason a principal requirement is contemporaneity between the statement and the fact in issue, for the lack of time to reflect will reduce the chance of invention. Another factor looked for is any difference in location between event and utterance. Some English cases and almost all decisions of the High Court of Australia have interpreted these requirements very strictly. In *R. v. Bedingfield* (1879), 14 Cox C.C. 341 the deceased whose throat had just been cut walked out of a room in which the accused was and said "Oh dear, Aunt, see what Bedingfield has done to me!" or something similar. This was excluded because it was said "after the act was completed". In *Brown v. R.* (1913), 17 C.L.R. 570 the deceased's statements were excluded because they were uttered while he was walking away from where he had been attacked: his motive was not to avoid another attack but to obtain medical aid. *Teper v. R.*, [1952] A.C. 480, P.C.; [1952] 2 All E.R. 447 (p. 320, *ante*) is a sound application of this rule; the statement charging the accused with flight and implicitly with arson was made twenty-five minutes after the fire, which was the relevant event, not his flight. (The general unreliability of the evidence is discussed, p. 322, *ante*.)

A liberal approach is seen in *O'Hara v. Central S.M.T. Co.*, 1941 S.C. 363, where a statement by a pedestrian some minutes after a motor accident was admitted because the "accident must still have left a vivid impression on the minds of all who took part in the incident. . . . [T]he incident was so clearly bound up with the happening of the accident that without it the history of the accident as offered to the Court in evidence would not be complete'' (at p. 382, *per* Lord Normand).

But this is rather exceptional. The narrowness with which the traditional rule is generally interpreted seems mistaken. Morgan has pointed out that the evidence is admissible because the shortness of time ensures that there can be no unreliability caused by the declarant's defective memory or carefully worked out lie; and the hearer of the declaration will have opportunities to check the truth of what is said ((1922), 31 Yale L.J. 229, at pp. 236–9). Attention should be paid to these issues rather than to mechanical tests of the identity of the transaction or whether narration is occurring or whether strict contemporaneity exists.

However, the Privy Council has recently advanced what seems to be a new view which depends on reliability. Sometimes the guarantee of reliability will be found in a spontaneous response to an unusual event; sometimes in involvement in an event. It is similar to one developed by Wigmore (para. 1747). It may offer the courts a chance to reduce the exclusionary effect of the hearsay rule.

Ratten v. R.

[1972] A.C. 378; [1971] 3 All E.R. 801, P.C.

For the facts see p. 322, *ante.*

LORD WILBERFORCE: Their Lordships, as already stated, do not consider that there is any hearsay element in the evidence, nor in their opinion was it so presented by the trial judge, but they think it right to deal with the appellant's submission on the assumption that there is, i.e. that the words said to have been used involve an assertion of the truth of some facts stated in them and that they may have been so understood by the jury. The Crown defended the admissibility of the words as part of the *res gestae* a contention which led to the citation of numerous authorities.

The expression *res gestae*, like many Latin phrases, is often used to cover situations insufficiently analysed in clear English terms. In the context of the law of evidence it may be used in at least three different ways:

1. When a situation of fact (e.g. a killing) is being considered, the question may arise when does the situation begin and when does it end. It may be arbitrary and artificial to confine the evidence to the firing of the gun or the insertion of the knife without knowing, in a broader sense, what was happening. Thus in *O'Leary* v. R. evidence was admitted of assaults, prior to a killing, committed by the accused during what was said to be a continuous orgy. As Dixon, J. said ((1946), 73 C.L.R. 566, at p. 577):

> 'Without evidence of what, during that time, was done by those men who took any significant part in the matter and specially evidence of the behaviour of the prisoner, the transaction of which the alleged murder formed an integral part could not be truly understood and, isolated from it, could only be presented as an unreal and not very intelligible event.'

2. The evidence may be concerned with spoken words as such (apart from the truth of what they convey). The words are then themselves the *res gestae* or part of the *res gestae*, i.e. are the relevant facts or part of them.

3. A hearsay statement is made either by the victim of an attack or by a bystander—indicating directly or indirectly the identity of the attacker. The admissibility of the statement is then said to depend on whether it was made as part of the *res gestae*. A classical instance of this is the much debated case of R. v. *Bedingfield* (1879), 14 Cox C.C. 341, and there are other instances of its application in reported cases. These tend to apply different standards, and some of them carry less than conviction. The reason why this is so is that concentration tends to be focused on the opaque or at least imprecise

Latin phrase rather than on the basic reason for excluding the type of evidence which this group of cases is concerned with. There is no doubt what this reason is: it is twofold. The first is that there may be uncertainty as to the exact words used because of their transmission through the evidence of another person than the speaker. The second is because of the risk of concoction of false evidence by persons who have been the victim of assault or accident.

The first matter goes to weight. The person testifying to the words used is liable to cross-examination: the accused person (as he could not at the time when earlier reported cases were decided) can given his own account if different. There is no such difference in kind or substance between evidence of what was said and evidence of what was done (for example between evidence of what the victim said as to an attack and evidence that he (or she) was seen in a terrified state or was heard to shriek) as to require a total rejection of one and admission of the other.

The possibility of concoction, or fabrication, where it exists, is on the other hand an entirely valid reason for exclusion, and is probably the real test which judges in fact apply. In their Lordships' opinion this should be recognized and applied directly as the relevant test: the test should be not the uncertain one whether the making of the statement was in some sense part of the event or transaction. This may often be difficult to establish: such external matters as the time which elapses between the events and the speaking of the words (or vice versa), and differences in location being relevant factors but not, taken by themselves, decisive criteria. As regards statements made after the event it must be for the judge, by preliminary ruling, to satisfy himself that the statement was so clearly made in circumstances of spontaneity or involvement in the event that the possibility of concoction can be disregarded. Conversely, if he considers that the statement was made by way of narrative of a detached prior event so that the speaker was so disengaged from it as to be able to construct or adapt his account, he should exclude it. And the same must in principle be true of statements made before the event. The test should be not the uncertain one, whether the making of the statement should be regarded as part of the event or transaction. This may often be difficult to show. But if the drama, leading up to the climax, has commenced and assumed such intensity and pressure that the utterance can safely be regarded as a true reflection of what was unrolling or actually happening, it ought to be received. The expression *res gestae* may conveniently sum up these criteria, but the reality of them must always be kept in mind: it is this that lies behind the best reasoned of the judges' rulings.

A few illustrations may be given. One of the earliest, and as often happens also the clearest, is that of Holt, C.J. at *nisi prius* in *Thompson* v. *Trevanion* (1693), Skin. 402. He allowed that "what the wife said immediate upon the hurt received, and before that she had time to devise or contrive anything for her own advantage" might be given in evidence, a statement often quoted and approved. *R.* v. *Bedingfield* (1879), 14 Cox C.C. 341 is more useful as a focus for discussion, than for the decision on the facts. Their Lordships understand later indications of approval (*R.* v. *Christie*, [1914] A.C. 545, H.L.; [1914–15] All E.R. Rep. 63 and *Teper* v. *R.*, [1952] A.C. 480, P.C.; [1952] 2 All E.R. 447), to relate to the principle established, for, although in a historical sense the emergence of the victim could be described as a different *res* from the cutting of her throat, there could hardly be a case where the words uttered carried more clearly the mark of spontaneity and intense involvement.

In a lower key the evidence of the words of the careless pedestrian in *O'Hara* v. *Central S.M.T. Co.* 1941 S.C. 363 was admitted on the principle of spontaneity). The Lord President (Lord Normand) said (at p. 381) that there must be close association: the words should be at least *de recenti* and not after an interval which would allow time for reflection and concocting a story. Lord Fleming said (at p. 386):

"Obviously statements made after there has been time for deliberation are not likely to be entirely spontaneous, and may, indeed, be made for the express purpose of concealing the truth", and Lord Moncrieff (at pp. 389–90) refers to the "share in the event" which is taken by the person reported to have made the statement. He contrasts an exclamation "forced out of a witness by the emotion generated by an event" with a subsequent narrative. The Lord President reaffirmed the principle stated in this case in an appeal to this Board in *Teper* v. R. [1952] A.C. 480, [1952] 2 All E.R. 447, P.C., stressing the necessity for close association in time, place and circumstances between the statement and the crucial events.

In Australia, a leading authority is *Adelaide Chemical and Fertiliser Co., Ltd.* v. *Carlyle* (1940), 64 C.L.R. 514 in which the High Court considered the admissibility of a statement made soon after the breaking of a sulphuric acid jar over his legs by the injured man. This question was not decisive to the decision, but was discussed by Starke and Dixon, JJ. with numerous citations. Both emphasize and illustrate the uncertainty of decided cases and legal writers on the question of admissibility of statements of this type and on the question what they may be admitted to prove. Dixon, J. with some caution reaches the conclusion that although English law, in the general view of lawyers, admits statements only as parts or details of a transaction not yet complete, while in America, greater recognition is given to the guarantee of truth provided by spontaneity and the lack of time to devise or contrive, yet English decisions do show some reliance on the greater trustworthiness of statements made at once without reflection. In an earlier case in the High Court (*Brown* v. R. (1913) 17 C.L.R. 570) where evidence was excluded, Isaacs and Powers, JJ. in their joint judgment (at p. 597) put the exclusion on the ground that it was a mere narration respecting a concluded event, a narration not naturally or spontaneously emanating from or growing out of the main narration but arising as an independent and additional transaction.

In *People* v. *De Simone* (1919), 121 N.E. 761, the Court of Appeals of New York admitted evidence that a pass-by immediately after a shooting had shouted "He ran over Houston Street". Collin, J. referred to deeds and acts which are—

"forced or brought into utterance or existence by and in the evolution of the transaction itself, and which stand in immediate causal relation to it."

The evidence was, expressly, not admitted as part of the *res gestae*, because it was not so interwoven or connected with the principal event (i.e. the shooting which the person did not see) as to be regarded as part of it.

These authorities show that there is ample support for the principle that hearsay evidence may be admitted if the statement providing it is made in such conditions (always being those of approximate but not exact contemporaneity) of involvement or pressure as to exclude the possibility of concoction or distortion to the advantage of the maker or the disadvantage of the accused.

Before applying it to the facts of the present case, there is one other matter to be considered, namely the nature of the proof required to establish the involvement of the speaker in the pressure of the drama, or the concatenation of events leading up to the crisis. On principle it would not appear right that the necessary association should be shown only by the statement itself, otherwise the statement would be lifting itself into the area of admissibility. There is little authority on this point. In R. v. *Taylor*, [1961] 3 S.A. 616 where witnesses said they had heard scuffles and thuds during which the deceased cried out "John, please don't hit me any more. You will kill me", Fannin, A.J. said that it would be unrealistic to require the examination of the question (*sc.* of close relationship) without reference to the terms of the statement sought to be proved (at p. 619).

"Often the only evidence as to how near in time the making of the statement was to the act it relates to, and the actual relationship between the two, will be contained in the statement itself."

Facts differ so greatly that it is impossible to lay down any precise general rule: it is difficult to imagine a case where there is no evidence at all of connexion between statement and principal event other than the statement itself, but whether this is sufficiently shown must be a matter for the trial judge. Their Lordships would be disposed to agree that, amongst other things, he may take the statement itself into account.

In the present case, in their Lordships' judgment, there was ample evidence of the close and intimate connexion between the statement ascribed to the deceased and the shooting which occurred very shortly afterwards. They were closely associated in place and in time. The way in which the statement came to be made (in a call for the police) and the tone of voice used, showed intrinsically that the statement was being forced from the deceased by an overwhelming pressure of contemporary event. It carried its own stamp of spontaneity and this was endorsed by the proved time sequence and the proved proximity of the deceased to the appellant with his gun. Even on the assumption that there was an element of hearsay in the words used, they were safely admitted. The jury was, additionally, directed with great care as to the use to which they might be put. On all counts, therefore, their Lordships can find no error in law in the admission of the evidence. They should add that they see no reason why the judge should have excluded it as prejudicial in the exercise of discretion.

Questions

1. Is Lord Wilberforce's test any more certain than the traditional one?

2. Much *res gestae* evidence has been admitted in the past without some exciting event occurring. Is Lord Wilberforce's view limited to such events? He says the statement must be made "in circumstances of spontaneity or *involvement in the event* [so] that the possibility of concoction can be disregarded". Do the italicized words meet the problem?

3. Is the absence of a possibility of concoction merely an assumed and hoped-for consequence of other requirements or an independent requirement of admissibility? Is its presence sufficient for admissibility?

4. It is worth noting that though the High Court of Australia is normally conservative on the *res gestae* question, in *Brown v. R.* (1913), 17 C.L.R. 570, at p. 597 a statement was excluded because it was "not naturally or spontaneously emanating from or growing out of the main transaction, but arising as an independent and additional transaction" (*per* Isaacs and Powers, JJ.). This has some similarity with the *Ratten* test. It may show, however, that that test can be interpreted just as narrowly as the traditional tests.

5. How would *R. v. Bedingfield* (1879), 14 Cox C.C. 341 be decided under the *Ratten* test?

6. McCormick says: "Psychologists would probably concede that excitement stills the voice of reflective self-interest but they might question whether this factor of reliability is not over-borne by the distorting effect which shock and excitement might have on observation and judgment. But they might well conclude that contemporaneous statements both excited and unexcited are so valuable for the accurate reconstruction of the facts that the need is not to narrow the use of excited statements but to widen the exception to embrace as well unexcited declarations of observers near the time of the happening" (p. 579). Do you agree?

Note

1. Lord Wilberforce lists the three main ways in which so-called *res gestae* evidence is used. The second—as original evidence—is discussed at p. 313, *ante*. The third—as a hearsay exception—is under discussion here. The first was considered at p. 271, *ante*, as a quasi-exception to the general ban on similar

fact evidence. To avoid confusion it might be best to confine the term *res gestae* to evidence admitted as an exception to the hearsay rule because of its high degree of relevance to a fact in issue in time, place or some other way.

Vocisano v. Vocisano
(1974), 3 A.L.R. 97

Shortly after an accident the defendant stated to two witnesses that the plaintiff had been driving the car in which they were travelling. The High Court of Australia held these statements inadmissible.

BARWICK, C.J.: The question of whether statements form part of a *res gestae* is fraught with difficulty at any time. In the present case, the learned trial judge relied upon the views expressed by the Privy Council when giving its advice in *Ratten* v. R. [1972] A.C. 378; [1971] 3 All E.R. 801. This is not an appropriate occasion, it seems to me, to discuss whether any change in the established law, and if so its precise extent, was intended by their Lordships in expressing their views in that case. A reason for the doctrine that statements made as part of the *res* are admissible as evidence is that, because of their contemporaneity and the circumstances of their making, they were unlikely to be concocted and therefore might well be reliable: but that does not mean that statements made on an occasion when they are unlikely to be concocted are for that reason admissible. It is the contemporaneous involvement of the speaker at the time the statement is made with the occurrence which is identified as the *res* which founds admissibility. In *Ratten's* case, Lord Wilberforce seems to have regarded the relevant occurrence as the "drama" which began when it may be supposed a threat to kill his wife was made by the appellant in that case, and which ended with her death. So regarded, the telephone call was necessarily involved in the ocurrence and the deceased's statement to the telephonist clearly contemporaneously identified with it. But, in the present case, there was, in my opinion, no sufficient contemporaneity of the statements made to either of the witnesses Smith to warrant the conclusion that the statements were made as part of the *res*. The occurrence was the accident, and although the statements by the respondent were made proximately to the occurrence of the accident, they were in the nature of an historical account rather than in the nature of a statement made as part and parcel of the occurrence. Although, as the trial judge said, the circumstances may satisfy some of the expressions used by the Privy Council in expressing their Lordships' view, the statements were not, in my opinion, admissible as part of the *res gestae*. Accordingly, the evidence of those witnesses was inadmissible either as prior inconsistent statements or as statements made as part of the *res gestae*.

[STEPHEN and JACOBS, JJ. agree.]

B. Examples

An American judge once said: "The difficulty of formulating a description of the *res gestae* which will serve for all cases seems insurmountable. To make the attempt is something like trying to execute a portrait which shall enable the possessor to recognize every member of a numerous family" (*Cox* v. *State* (1879), 64 Ga. 374, at p. 410, quoted by Wigmore, para. 1745).

However, Cross (pp. 502–18) has usefully divided the cases of admissible *res gestae* evidence into four partly overlapping and probably non-exhaustive categories. In traditional doctrine they all shared the requirement of contemporaneity, which turns on difficult questions of degree and which we will not pursue further.

i Statements accompanying and explaining relevant acts

The statement must be made by the actor and it must relate to the act it accompanies (*R. v. Bliss* (1837), 7 Ad. & El. 550; [1835–42] All E.R. Rep. 372). He knows more about his motives than anyone else; the requirement of contemporaneity to some extent helps guarantee sincerity. The evidence is admissible to prove the actor's intention in acting and his reason for acting, but not to prove the existence of any fact mentioned in his statement of reasons (*Skinner & Co. v. Shew & Co.*, [1894] 2 Ch. 581). Examples are: a bankrupt's statements as to his intentions in going or remaining abroad (*Rouch v. Great Western Rail. Co.* (1841), 1 Q.B. 51); a statement of intention to remain in a certain country or a statement of reasons for going there (*Bryce v. Bryce,* [1933] P. 83; [1932] All E.R. Rep. 788; *Scappaticci v. A.-G.,* [1955] P. 47; [1955] 1 All E.R. 193, n.); a wife's statement as to why she was leaving her husband (*The Aylesford Peerage* (1885), 11 App. Cas. 1, at p. 3, H.L., *per* Lord Blackburn); a testator's statements of a non-testamentary intention at the time of executing a codicil (*Lister v. Smith* (1863), 3 Sw. & Tr. 282).

ii Statements concerning an event in issue

The relation between statement and event must be direct, and care must be devoted to the definition of "event". If the accused is charged with assault, the relevant event is the accused's act of assault, not his subsequent flight, so that an exclamation provoked by his flight is not part of the *res gestae* (*Teper v. R.* [1952] A.C. 480, at p. 488; [1952] 2 All E.R. 447, at p. 450, P.C., discussing *R. v. Gibson* (1887), 18 Q.B.D. 537). The maker of the statement must usually have witnessed the event in issue (*Poriotis v. Australian Iron & Steel Ltd.* (1963) 63 S.R.N.S.W. 991). For examples, see *R. v. Foster* (1834), 6 C. & P. 325; *Milne v. Leisler* (1862), 7 H. & N. 786, at p. 796; *Davies v. Fortior, Ltd.,* [1952] 1 All E.R. 1359 n.

iii Statements about the maker's mental or emotional state

The evidence is only admissible to prove what the maker's mental or emotional state was, but not to prove the existence of any fact he said he knew or believed (*Thomas v. Connell* (1838), 4 M. & W. 267; *R. v. Gunnell* (1886), 16 Cox C.C. 154).

By this means may be proved such matters as political or religious opinion; anger; a person's belief that libellous remarks refer to the plaintiff (*Jozwiak v. Sadek,* [1954] 1 All E.R. 3); marital affection (*Willis v. Bernard* (1832), 8 Bing. 376); dislike of a child (*R. v. Hagan* (1873) 12 Cox C.C. 357); and fear (*R. v. Vincent, Frost and Edwards* (1840), 9 C. & P. 275; *R. v. Gandfield* (1846), 2 Cox C.C. 43).

If a man's intention is proved by his hearsay statements to exist at one time, the question then arises whether the continuance or prior existence of the intention can be inferred, and whether the doing of an act can be inferred from the statement of an intention to do it.

What is sometimes called the presumption of continuance will permit the first inference to be drawn provided there is, in the circumstances, not too long an interval between the time of the statement and the time at which the intention must be proved to exist (e.g. *Re Fletcher, Reading v. Fletcher,* [1917] 1 Ch. 339, at p. 342). However, the self-serving statements of a party will not support such an inference unless made at the same time as a relevant act (*R. v. Petcherini* (1855), 7 Cox C.C. 79; *Bryce v. Bryce,* [1933] P. 83; [1932] All E.R. Rep. 788).

The authorities conflict on whether the doing of an act can be inferred from a statement of an intention to do it (cf. *R. v. Buckley* (1873), 13 Cox C.C. 293; and *Marshall* v. *Wild Rose* (*Owners*), [1910] A.C. 486; H.L., with *R. v. Pook*, (1871), 13 Cox C.C. 172; *R. v. Wainright* (1875), 13 Cox C.C. 171 and *R. v. Thomson*, [1912] 3 K.B. 19, C.C.A.). A controversial decision of the United States Supreme Court held that a statement of intention to meet a man could be admitted to prove that its maker did meet the man (*Mutual Life Insurance Co.* v. *Hillmon* (1892), 145 U.S. 285). In this case the inference of the happening of a bilateral act such as a meeting is harder to draw than the inference of an act which the speaker could perform by himself, without the reciprocal action of another. But in suitable circumstances there would seem to be no danger of unreliability in drawing the inference.

iv Statements of physical sensation

A man's statements of his contemporaneous physical sensation, but not its possible causes, are admissible as evidence of that fact (*Gilbey* v. *Great Western Rail. Co.* (1910), 102 L.T. 202). But if a patient's beliefs as to his physical condition are in issue, a doctor's statements to him are admissible as evidence of that belief, though not as evidence of the truth of what the doctor said (*Tickle* v. *Tickle*, [1968] 2 All E.R. 154). Contemporaneity seems to be more laxly interpreted here than in other *res gestae* cases (*Aveson* v. *Lord Kinnaird* (1805), 6 East 188; *R. v. Black* (1922), 16 Cr. App. Rep. 118, at p. 119).

v Original evidence

It is perhaps worth noting again that all the above cases are instances of *res gestae* evidence admitted as an exception to the hearsay rule. Depending on the issues, *res gestae* evidence may be original evidence (e.g. as a prior consistent statement made at the same time as an event in issue to support the witness's consistency: *Milne* v. *Leisler* (1862), 7 H. & N. 786, p. 432, *post*).

Reading

Gooderson, [1956] C.L.J. 199; [1957] C.L.J. 55; Hutchins and Slesinger (1929), 38 Yale L.J. 283; Maguire (1925), 38 Harv. L.R. 709; Morgan (1922), 31 Yale L.J. 229; Nokes (1954), 70 L.Q.R. 370; Stone (1939), 55 L.Q.R. 66.

C. Reform

The Criminal Law Revision Committee has made proposals for the reform of the *res gestae* doctrine in the rare cases where it will still be relevant if their other proposals for wide admission of hearsay are enacted (p. 343, *post*). The 11th Report says (para. 261):

"The test we propose is similar to that laid down in *Ratten* v. R, [1972] A.C. 378, P.C.; [1971] 3 All E.R. 801, though somewhat narrower. It is that the statement should be admissible if 'it directly concerns an event in issue in [the] proceedings which took place in the presence, sight or hearing of [the maker] and it was made by him as an immediate reaction to that event'. Before *Ratten* v. R. the English decisions left it uncertain whether a statement admissible under the *res gestae* rule was admissible as evidence of the facts stated or only as explaining the events referred to; but the balance of authority seems to have been that it is admissible for the former purpose, and this is in accordance with the analysis in *Ratten*. In any event it seems to us clearly right that the statement should be admissible for this purpose, and the clause provides accordingly. As this is an independent ground of admissibility, the conditions and restrictions provided for in other clauses will not apply. The result will be that a statement, for example, made by a very young child, or an otherwise inadmissible statement made by the spouse of the accused, may be admissible under the clause if it was made as an immediate reaction to the event in question."

VI WITNESSES IN PREVIOUS CASES

R v. Hall
[1973] Q.B. 496; [1973] I All E.R. I, C.A.

FORBES, J.: [W]e think it plain that a deposition properly taken before a magistrate on oath in the presence of the accused and where the accused has had the opportunity of cross-examination was always admissible at common law in criminal cases if the deponent was dead, despite the absence of opportunity to observe the demeanour of the witness. The only difference between such a deposition and the transcript of evidence given at a previous trial is that the transcript is not signed by the witness. Provided it is authenticated in some appropriate way, as by calling the shorthand writer who took the original note, there seems no reason to think that such a transcript should not be equally receivable in evidence.

VII REFORM

Criminal Law Revision Committee, 11th Report
1972. Paras. 229, 230, 235–48

229. We recognize that there is a case for preserving the rule against hearsay evidence in criminal trials. The principal arguments are related closely to the essential features of criminal trials as compared with civil trials. These are (i) the fact that in a criminal trial the evidence is mostly given orally, (ii) the fact that trials on indictment at least, once begun, are ordinarily continued without adjournments for further inquiries and (iii) the fact that there is little by way of preliminary proceedings (apart from committal proceedings). As a result jurors and spectators can follow the course of the trial and understand the issues without previous knowledge of the case. The high standard of proof required for a conviction (proof beyond reasonable doubt) is also an important consideration. Another argument which has much concerned us is the danger of manufactured evidence. Although this danger is not limited to the manufacture of evidence by the defence, it is perhaps greatest in the kind of case where a witness for the defence might give evidence that he heard somebody who must have seen the offence being committed, but who is said to be unavailable to give evidence, say something about the offence inconsistent with the guilt of the accused. We have no doubt that this is a real danger, and much of our discussion has been about how to provide against it; and we hope that the safeguards which we propose will go a long way to meet this danger even though it cannot be prevented altogether.

230. Nevertheless the arguments against the present rule are in our opinion very strong.

[The hearsay rule excludes valuable evidence, it is difficult to apply, its exceptions are numerous and obscure, the courts will undertake no reform of it after *Myers* v. *Director of Public Prosecutions*, [1965] A.C. 1001, H.L.; [1964] 2 All E.R. 881, and the majority of lawyers favour substantial relaxation.]

235. The fact that hearsay evidence is now widely admissible in civil proceedings under the Civil Evidence Act 1968 seems to us a fresh argument in favour of allowing such evidence in criminal proceedings. This is not only because it seems desirable in general that the law of evidence in civil and criminal proceedings should be as nearly alike as possible (though there are bound to be substantial differences) but because it would be particularly unfortunate if differences in the law were to lead to different results in proceedings relating to the same facts. For example, it is possible, in theory at least, that a person might be sued for fraud and be found not liable on the strength of hearsay evidence admissible under the Act of 1968 and yet be convicted of a criminal offence owing to the inadmissibility of similar evidence in criminal proceedings.

236. The scheme which we propose, stated shortly, is as follows:

   (i) to make admissible any out-of-court statement if (*a*) the maker is called as a witness or (*b*) he cannot be called because he is dead or for one of the reasons mentioned later in this paragraph;

  (ii) to make admissible statements contained in certain kinds of records if the information in the statement was supplied by a person having personal knowledge of the matter in question and the supplier (*a*) is called as a witness, (*b*) cannot be called for one of the reasons referred to or (*c*) cannot be expected to remember the matters dealt with in the information;

 (iii) to make special provision for the admissibility of information derived from computers;

  (iv) to restate the rule as to admissibility of statements forming part of the *res gestae*;

   (v) to provide that, subject to certain safeguards, out-of-court statements shall be admissible if the parties so agree;

  (vi) to clarify the law by providing that hearsay evidence shall be admissible only under the provisions mentioned, under any other statutory provision or under the common law rules specifically preserved by the Bill.

The cases where an out-of-court statement is to be admissible on account of the impossibility of calling the maker as a witness are (*a*) where he is unavailable because he is dead, unfit to attend as a witness, abroad, impossible to identify or impossible to find and (*b*) where he is available but is either not compellable as a witness and refuses to give evidence or is compellable but refuses (in court) to be sworn. On the same principle, the prosecution will be able to give in evidence against one accused a statement made by another accused jointly tried with him, as the maker cannot be called for the prosecution.

237. Under our scheme admissibility of hearsay statements will be subject to a number of restrictions, of which the following are the most important:

   (i) in the case of oral statements only first-hand evidence of the making of the statement will be admissible (unless the statement was made in giving evidence in court);

  (ii) a statement contained in a proof of evidence (including a proof incorporated in a record) given by a person who is called as a witness in the proceedings in question will not be admissible unless the court gives leave for this on the ground that in the circumstances it is in the interests of justice that the witness's evidence should be supplemented by the proof;

 iii) at a trial on indictment a statement will not be admissible by reason of the impossibility of calling the maker unless the party seeking to give it in evidence has given notice of his intention to do so with particulars of the statement and of the reason why he cannot call the maker;

  (iv) a statement said to have been made, after the accused has been charged, by a person who is compellable as a witness but refuses to be sworn or by a person said to be abroad, impossible to identify or find, or to have refused to give evidence, will not be admissible at all (and there will be a similar restriction in the case of the supplier of information contained in a record);

   (v) a statement made by the wife or husband of the accused (not being tried jointly with the accused) will not be admissible on behalf of the prosecution unless the maker gives evidence for the prosecution or would have been a compellable witness for the prosecution.

238. The purposes which we hope to achieve by this scheme are the following:

(i) to admit all hearsay evidence likely to be valuable to the greatest extent possible without undue complication or delay to the proceedings;

(ii) to ensure that evidence should continue to be given for the most part orally by allowing hearsay evidence only if the maker of the statement cannot be called or it is desirable to supplement his oral evidence;

(iii) to include necessary safeguards against the danger of manufactured hearsay evidence;

(iv) to follow the scheme of the Civil Evidence Act 1968 as far as the differences between civil and criminal proceedings allow.

Further comment on the purposes mentioned in (ii), (iii) and (iv) is made in the six following paragraphs. After this the proposed restriction mentioned in paragraph 237 (v) as to a statement made by the spouse of the accused is discussed.

239. The preservation of the principle of orality in criminal trials seems to us particularly important. We are not concerned to argue that the English system is the best system; but since this system is clearly going to be preserved in its essentials, it would be wrong to disrupt it by giving the parties complete freedom to choose between proving their case by oral evidence given by witnesses of the events in question and proving it by second-hand evidence of these events. To do so would alter the character of trials and be likely to confuse juries. The essence of our proposed scheme is to supplement the oral evidence by hearsay evidence which is likely to be valuable for the ascertainment of the truth and cannot be given because of the restrictions in the present law. In the case of a previous statement by a person who is called as a witness there is a special reason for proposing to make the statement admissible. It might be argued that, since the maker is giving evidence, there is no need to allow evidence to be given of what he said on a previous occasion. But assuming, as one must, that a person called as a witness in criminal proceedings is more likely than not to intend to try to tell the truth, it follows that what he said soon after the events in question is likely to be at least as reliable as his evidence given at the trial and will probably be more so. This may not always be the case, because the earlier statement may have been made in haste and perhaps under the influence of shock caused by the events in question, and the evidence given at the trial may be more carefully thought over; but at any rate, if there is a discrepancy, it is likely to be helpful to the court or jury to have both statements. In a case where the trial takes place long after the events in question the earlier statement may be particularly valuable. Sometimes, for example, in a complicated fraud case the trial takes place years after the offence. But if the earlier statement is a proof of evidence, or a document of a similar nature, it seems desirable to make special provision in order to ensure that the proof or other document does not take the place of oral evidence. For even if the person taking the proof has not tried to get the witness to tell his story in the way most favourable to the party in whose interest it is taken, it is obviously likely that it will come out in this way; and therefore it would be wrong to enable the party calling the witness, say, simply to call him, show him the proof and put it in as his evidence. It is for this reason that we propose that the leave of the court should be necessary for the proof to be given in evidence. In the ordinary case the court would no doubt require the witness to give his evidence without the aid of any document (except such as may be used for refreshing memory); but if, for example, the witness is clearly unable to remember the events described in his proof, then the court will be likely to allow the proof to be referred to. Whether a document is in the nature of a proof of evidence will depend on the circumstances. Ordinarily, for example, a statement taken by the police for use as a written statement under s. 2 or s. 9 of the Criminal Justice Act 1967 will count as a proof for this purpose.

240. The need to provide for safeguards against the use of manufactured evidence caused us more difficulty than did any of the other questions relating to hearsay evidence. We have mentioned this danger as one of the arguments against admitting hearsay evidence. Many of those who replied to our original request for observations expressed anxiety about this, as did several members during our discussion. We mentioned in particular the danger that the defence may seek to produce a statement, said to have been made by a person whom they are unfortunately unable to call as a witness, which, if true, would exculpate the accused. Apart from false alibis, there are several possible kinds of hearsay evidence which might be manufactured for this purpose. For example, there might be a statement by a supposed eye-witness of the offence describing the offender in a way totally inconsistent with his being the accused. Again, the statement might be that the maker himself committed the offence or that he had heard somebody else say that he had comitted it or was about to do so. How far this danger exists is a matter of opinion. Some think that to admit hearsay evidence would not greatly increase the possibility of manufactured evidence which already exists with first-hand evidence: others think that the danger would be much greater. In our view it must be taken that the danger, although not great enough to require the rejection of any hearsay evidence exculpating the accused in a way such as suggested, or the rejection of hearsay evidence in general, is great enough to require and justify the imposition of the proposed restriction as to giving notice of intention to give the statement in evidence and that as to statements made after the accused was charged.

241. The proposed requirement to give notice will enable the other parties to make inquiries as to the identity of the person supposed to have made the statement, as to whether it is really impossible to call him and as to the contents of the statement. The purpose will be similar to that served by the requirement in s. 11 of the Criminal Justice Act 1967 (c. 80) to give notice of intention to adduce evidence of an alibi; and, as in the case of the notice last mentioned, the court will have a discretion to allow the statement to be given in evidence, if the interests of justice require this, even though notice has for some reason not been given. The proposed provision excluding altogether a statement supposed to have been made after the accused has been charged may seem drastic. But in our opinion it might well be too dangerous to allow such a statement to be given in evidence at all, even subject to the discretion of the court, because this might well encourage the defence to present such a statement in the hope that leave would be given. A further justification for these restrictions is the fact that at present, if a person makes a statement and then disappears, there is no power to allow the statement to be read out (save with consent under s. 9 of the Criminal Justice Act 1967). It is for the party who has obtained the statement to ensure that the maker is present to give evidence.

242. Some such safeguards as these seem to us particularly necessary in criminal proceedings because, owing to the rule that the accused cannot be convicted unless his guilt is proved beyond reasonable doubt, a false statement of a kind mentioned might be sufficient, if not to convince a jury, at least to raise a sufficient doubt in their minds as to the guilt of the accused. But with these safeguards we hope that the danger that tricks of the kind mentioned will succeed will be reduced to a point at which it can be accepted in the interests of allowing hearsay evidence which ought to be allowed. In the nature of things there can be no complete safeguard, just as there can be no complete safeguard against manufactured first-hand evidence. We considered going further and excluding altogether a statement made by an unidentified person or by a person who, though identified, could not be found. In the case of an unidentified person there would also be the argument that his credit as a witness could not be attacked. But although to make these further restrictions would decrease the danger of manufactured evidence, we do not think that they would be justified. For the case of an unidentified person does not seem to differ sufficiently for present purposes from the case, for example, of an identified person who has died. In the case of an identified person who cannot be found there may be a stronger argument because of the danger of his being kept out of the way. But we do not think it neessary to make even this restriction, especially as the person concerned might have given his statement to the prosecution and the defence might be keeping him out of the way.

243. We said that one of our objects was to follow the scheme of the Civil Evidence Act 1968 as far as the differences between civil and criminal proceedings allowed. The special restrictions just referred to naturally do not correspond to any provisions in the Act; but although the provisions in the draft Bill look very different from those of the Act, the scheme of both is in essence similar. For in both cases the object is that evidence as to facts in dispute should in principle be oral evidence, and it should be only where this is unavailable or there is useful hearsay evidence to supplement the oral evidence that hearsay evidence should be allowed. The scheme of the Civil Evidence Act is that the party seeking to give a statement in evidence should give notice to the other parties, and the latter may by counter-notice object to its being given. If another party objects, the statement will not be admissible in evidence unless the maker is unavailable or the court gives leave. The purpose of the requirement in civil proceedings is to discourage litigants from offering hearsay evidence of a fact when direct evidence of the fact can be adduced without serious inconvenience or expense. This is secured by the system of notice and counter-notice. The system of notice and counter-notice is unsuitable for criminal proceedings in general, especially in the absence of interlocutory proceedings; and we hope that a similar result will be achieved by the requirements as to unavailability of the maker.

244. There is one particular respect in which our recommendations follow the Civil Evidence Act. This is the exclusion, as mentioned, of second-hand hearsay evidence. There are undoubtedly arguments for allowing even this, as it is possible that this evidence will sometimes be helpful. For example, if A has made a mental note of the number of a car involved in an offence and told B, B will be able to give evidence of what A told him; but if B has died or is unavailable, there may be nobody else who is in a position to give the number. On the other hand, to allow second-hand or remoter evidence of the making of a statement in all cases might let in very unreliable evidence. There would also be a greater danger of manufactured evidence if this was allowed. The committee generally came to the conclusion that, on balance, it would be safer to follow the Civil Evidence Act in restricting oral evidence of the making of a statement to first-hand evidence. In any event we thought it would be anomalous to allow second-hand and remoter hearsay evidence in criminal proceedings when it is not allowed in civil proceedings.

245. The proposal to restrict the admissibility of a statement made by the husband or wife of the accused is a matter of policy comparable with the questions as to competence and compellability of the spouse discussed above. On this our views differ. The majority think that to allow the prosecution to give in evidence a statement made by the spouse of the accused, in a case where the spouse does not give evidence or would not be compellable to do so, would be inconsistent with the policy that the spouse should in general have the right not to give evidence for the prosecution. It is argued, for example, that, if the police question the accused's wife about the receipt by him of stolen goods, she may say something which might incriminate the accused, although she could not be compelled to give evidence about this in court, and which she might regret saying. The police might tell her, truly, that she could not be compelled to give evidence against her husband, but omit to tell her that her statement might be given in evidence. In this and similar cases the majority think it wrong that the statement should be admissible. But a substantial minority think that the statement should be admissible because the principle of non-compellability is only that the wife should not be compelled to testify against her husband and does not require that something which she may have said out of court should not be admissible. The case where the spouse is tried jointly with the accused is dealt with later.

246. We considered a suggestion which has been made several times by legal writers and was put forward in some of the replies to our request for observations. This is that the problem of allowing useful hearsay evidence while excluding evidence which it would be too dangerous to allow should be solved by giving the court a discretion to admit otherwise inadmissible hearsay evidence. This course has the obvious attraction that the provision would be of the simplest. But we do not think it should be adopted, because it seems to us to involve four serious difficulties. First, with the differences of opinion about the value of hearsay evidence there would be bound to be large differences in practice between different courts. Second, there would be an almost inevitable tendency to allow hearsay evidence freely for the defence while restricting it when offered on behalf of the prosecution, and the committee generally are opposed to making distinctions between the parties in this way. Third, it would make it much more difficult for the parties to prepare their case, because there would be no way of knowing in advance whether a court would allow a particular piece of hearsay evidence. Fourth, in summary trials the court would ordinarily have to hear the statement in order to decide whether to exercise the discretion to admit it. Nor do we think it right to confer any particular exclusionary discretion on courts in relation to hearsay evidence in addition to the general discretion which they enjoy at present to exclude evidence where, for example, they are of opinion that its prejudicial effect would outweigh its probative value. But there seems no objection to giving the limited discretion proposed above to admit a statement in particular circumstances in the case of a previous statement made by a witness and in the case of failure to give notice of intention to give in evidence a statement by a person unavailable to give evidence.

247. We concluded, after considerable discussion, that the proposals mentioned above would provide the best way of allowing hearsay evidence which would be valuable while avoiding most of the difficulties inseparable from any general widening of the present law. Admittedly our proposals involve a certain amount of risk that unreliable evidence will be admitted and acted on; but there is much evidence other than hearsay evidence which is unreliable, and in our opinion it is better to accept the risk mentioned while providing such safeguards as can be provided without unduly restricting admissibility or complicating the law. We disagree strongly with the argument that juries and lay magistrates will be over-impressed by hearsay evidence and too ready to convict or acquit on the strength of it. Anybody with common sense will understand that evidence which cannot be tested by cross-examination may well be less reliable than evidence which can. In any event judges will be in a position to remind juries that the former is the case with hearsay evidence, and sometimes the judge may think it advisable to mention this to the jury at the time when the statement is admitted. On the other hand there is some hearsay evidence which would rightly convince anybody. Moreover, juries may have to consider hearsay evidence which is admissible under the present law, and there are other kinds of evidence which they may find it more difficult to evaluate than hearsay evidence—for example, evidence of other misconduct. It may also be objected that the provisions about hearsay evidence in the draft Bill are complicated. Admittedly this is so, and they may seem unduly complicated at first sight; but we believe that, if the provisions are adopted, the procedure as to the admission of hearsay evidence will be much less complicated than the provisions themselves look, and in any event we do not think it can be disputed that the provisions are much less complicated than is the present law.

248. The provisions to give effect to our recommendations are in clauses 30–41. Under them there will be several different grounds for admissibility, and the restrictions which apply to admissibility on some of the grounds will not apply to admissibility on some others. Clause 30 provides that a hearsay statement, to be admissible, will have to come under one or other of the clauses, under some other statutory provision or under one of the common law rules specifically preserved by clause 40. Thus there will be no room for an argument, based on the existing case law, in favour of admissibility of any other kind of hearsay evidence. Most of the clauses correspond very broadly to sections in Part I of the Civil Evidence Act 1968 for admissibility of hearsay in civil proceedings.

These proposals have been less widely attacked than those concerning the "right to silence".

Bar Council Memorandum on the 11th Report
(1973). Paras. 176–7

[T]here are certain problems which are peculiar to the criminal process (not the least of which is the standard of proof) and which must be borne in mind when considering whether or to what extent the present rules should be relaxed. In particular,

> (*d*) *the tribunal of fact in the vast majority of criminal cases is a bench of Magistrates and, where they are not involved, it will be, substantially, a jury;*
> (*e*) *the stakes involved in criminal cases are higher than in civil, in that a person's reputation and frequently, his liberty are at risk;* and
> (*f*) *the atmosphere is more highly charged, particularly in "complainant-orientated" cases such as sexual offences or certain categories of assault.*

Because of factors (*e*) and (*f*), above, the motives for and the willingness of witnesses (on both sides) in criminal trials to give unreliable or perjured evidence is far greater than in civil proceedings and, because of factor (*d*), above, the effect of such evidence may be more far-reaching.

177. We do not consider that the Committee has given sufficient weight to these factors. In our opinion, if the draft Bill were to be implemented in its present form, it would provide an opportunity to the mendacious to give lying evidence which could not be tested satisfactorily. If such an opportunity were to be provided, we are sure that it would be taken and, if taken, that in a high proportion of cases it would succeed in its purpose. Earlier in the Report, much is said about the problems posed by the sophisticated professional criminal. *Not the least of the arguments against the Committee's proposals is the advantage that would be taken by such criminals of the opportunities afforded them by this part of the Bill.*

Williams: The Proposals for Hearsay Evidence
[1973] Crim. L.R. 76

The difficulties and absurdities of the hearsay rule are a matter of such common knowledge that they hardly need to be stated. The rule excludes evidence that is sometimes extremely convincing. It applies, in general, even though the maker of the statement is not available to give evidence: e.g. because he is dead, so that there is no question of putting pressure upon the proponent to get better evidence. It excludes not only evidence of oral statements but documentary evidence. It excludes not only statements by non-witnesses but even previous statements by witnesses. It operates even against the defence. It fragments the evidence given by a witness. And it is immensely involved, with many exceptions.

Although these constitute strong arguments against the present law, the Committee eventually found itself unwilling to recommend the abolition of the hearsay rule completely, for four reasons.

(1) The rule against hearsay has the effect of preserving the orality of the trial. Cases are tried, in general, by the spoken statements of witnesses, not by reading accounts of what witnesses wish to depose. The jury (or magistrates) can study the demeanour of the witness, and he can be cross-examined to expose any deficiencies of observation, memory or reasoning, or any dishonesty. It was thought important to preserve this.

(2) The objection to what may be called first-mouth hearsay becomes far stronger for second-mouth hearsay, third-mouth hearsay, and so on. No one would normally attach

weight to a statement that Mrs. Brown said that Mrs. Green said that Mrs. Black
said. . . .

(3) To allow the prosecution to prove its case by adducing witnesses' statements
without calling the witness would encourage the police to relax their efforts to produce
the best evidence.

(4) A special difficulty in criminal matters is that the defendant may be a professional criminal who has large funds, no scruples, and a great deal to lose by being convicted. Generally there are one or two "bent" solicitors who are ready to connive at
deceptions practised by such defendants. If hearsay were admitted without restriction,
it would be possible to give evidence that some third person (who has since conveniently disappeared) called at the defendant's solicitor's office and "confessed" to the
crime. Or it would be possible to put in a written statement by a third person (who has
since been "called abroad on pressing business") giving the defendant an alibi. The
witness could not be cross-examined; and if it were alleged that his identity was unknown, the prosecution could not investigate whether he had a criminal record. The
jury, pressed with the rule that they must be satisfied of guilt beyond reasonable doubt,
might be sufficiently impressed by such evidence to say that they had a doubt.

I do not myself regard these as sufficient reasons for retaining any law of hearsay.
On the Continent they get on very well without the rule, and still base their trials on
oral evidence. The French courts, for example, have no rule against hearsay, but they
nevertheless prefer to hear the witnesses. We were informed that in France, even if the
witness is required only to produce a document, he will often attend the trial in case
there should be a dispute about the document. An expert's report can be read in court,
by agreement, without calling the expert, but he is always present to give evidence if
necessary, and is in fact nearly always called even if his report is agreed. This French
experience shows it is not necessary to have a hearsay rule to secure the orality of the
trial in fact. As for the unreliability of hearsay evidence, this is dealt with in France by
the president advising the jury that any particular item has little or no weight, whether
because it is hearsay or for any other reason.

In England we are not ready for this rationality, but the draft Bill, if accepted, will at
least strike off some of the notorious shackles imposed by the present law. It is designed
to supersede most of the present exceptions to the hearsay rule (though not the hearsay
rule itself) and also the whole of the rule against "narrative" or previous consistent
statements by a witness. . . .

One effect of this proposal will be that, for example, evidence can be given that the
victim of an assault denounced the defendant as the aggressor shortly after the assault.
At present, evidence of such a complaint can be given only when the assault is of a
sexual nature.

One consequence of the abolition of the rule against narrative is that a suspect will be
able in a sense to "manufacture" (true) evidence in his own favour. Suppose that a man,
when arrested for assault, states that he was acting in self-defence, the victim of the
alleged assault having been the aggressor. His wife witnessed the incident, and, without
having had the opportunity to know what her husband said, precisely corroborated his
account of what occurred. Both these statements will be admissible in evidence, and
should furnish a strong argument in support of the defence. (Under the present law,
evidence of the wife's earlier statement could be given only if there were a suggestion
of recent fabrication of what she now says; and no evidence could be given of the
defendant's earlier statement to show how it was independent of the wife's statement.)
It will be seen that under the proposed rule it may be highly advantageous for innocent
persons to give an early account to the police of what happened, and from this point of
view the proposed abolition of the "caution" and the substitution of an invitation by
the police to the suspect to state any matter of defence is logical and desirable.

Again, the proposal will generally enable evidence of a conversation to be given in a
natural way, instead of the artificial way that may now be insisted upon. Whereas a witness may relate what he said to X he is not at present supposed to relate what X said in

reply, except in particular circumstances. The witness is interrupted with the words "We can't have what X told you". One side of the interchange must be left out, perhaps to be filled in later by X. The witness is confused, because he cannot tell his story in proper detail, and the jury may be baffled, at least for a time, because the fragmented evidence is unintelligible. Under the Bill, the witness will be allowed to give the whole conversation, provided that X is to be called or is unavailable as a witness in one of the specified ways. If hearsay evidence is given in anticipation of the witness being called, and he cannot afterwards be called, the judge will tell the jury to disregard the evidence.

Another important effect of the proposal is that if, for example, a Crown witness is "got at" before the trial, and when in the witness box contradicts his previous statement, the statement may be proved not merely for the purpose of discrediting what he now says but for the purpose of inviting the jury to believe the previous statement. . . .

One of the criticisms expressed of the report was that the proposal that a statement by an unidentifiable person may be given in evidence would allow the prosecution to give evidence of an anonymous letter accusing the defendant. But it is hard to imagine that a prosecutor would ever offer such evidence, and if he did the judge would have a discretion to exclude it on the ground that its prejudicial effect exceeded its probative value. The proposal is more likely to help the defence than the prosecution, because, owing to the difference in the burden of proof, a slight piece of evidence favourable to the defence may win an acquittal, whereas the same evidence offered for the prosecution will not convict the defendant unless it is solidly supported by other circumstances. But there are cases where a statement by an unidentifiable or unfindable person may have considerable weight, in the general context of the other evidence, and where it should clearly be considered by the jury.

. . . Co-defendants are generally incompetent witnesses for the Crown, the Crown not being allowed to put one defendant in the box to testify against the other. It can of course cross-examine him if he chooses to testify in his own defence, and what he says will be evidence not only against himself but against his companion. Also, a defendant can become a Crown witness against a co-defendant if the issue against himself has been settled by a plea of guilty or a verdict of the jury, or if a *nolle prosequi* is entered against him or if separate trials are ordered. The only problem relates to out-of-court statements. The rule at common law is a difficult one: evidence can be given of a confession by one defendant, but the jury must be told that it is evidence only against that defendant, and not against his companion (unless the confession was made in the latter's presence, in which case his reaction to it may be an implied admission). The rule has been much criticised, because the jury, being informed of the confession and its terms, will be prone to treat it as telling not only against the confessor but against his companion, if it gives circumstantial details implicating the companion—particularly if the companion is afraid to give evidence. If he does give evidence, the Crown can cross-examine him on the basis of the other's statement, and perhaps make him very uncomfortable. Also, the other defendant who made the statement can be cross-examined on it, if he gives evidence, and perhaps induced to incriminate his companion on oath, in which case what he says will be evidence against his companion. On the whole there seems to be little virtue in a rule denying technical admissibility to the out-of-court statement by one in relation to the other. The Committee now proposes to alter the rule and to make the confession evidence against both defendants, even though the defendant who made the confession does not give evidence at the trial. . . .

Some alarm has been expressed about this proposal, because of the danger that a criminal who realizes that he is "for it" may take the opportunity of making a statement incriminating an innocent acquaintance in order to get his own back on him for some reason. Or he may falsely try to throw the greater share of the blame on one who was in fact merely a minor participant. The first defendant may decline to give evidence in court, and the second defendant, whom he has incriminated, cannot compel him to do so; accordingly, the second defendant may be faced by the damning evidence against him of the out-of-court statement without being allowed to cross-examine the maker of the statement—when if he were allowed to cross-examine he could perhaps show that the statement was altogether false.

In reply to these fears, it may be said that a defendant who does not give evidence is not likely to have his out-of-court allegations against a co-defendant believed, particularly if the co-defendant gives evidence denying them. The question is whether one should have rules to make evidence inadmissible merely because the evidence may sometimes be false or misleading. There can be no question that the confession of one offender may occasionally be persuasive as to the guilt of another—where it supplies details that fit with other suspicious circumstances proved against the companion. It seems to me to be right that the jury should be trusted to consider the evidence.

The only doubt, I think, concerning the justice of the rule is where the defendants are not tried together. Suppose that A and B are jointly charged; A pleads guilty, or is convicted in a separate trial; A's out-of-court statement will be admissible against B. This application of the rule has been criticized, and on reflection I think rightly. Clause 31 (2) should be confined to joint trials. In the situation supposed, the Crown can subpoena A to give evidence at B's trial (clause 4 (5)), and, if A refuses to admit his previous statement, give evidence of that statement. B would then be able to cross-examine A.

If two defendants are charged separately, clause 31 (2) will not apply. But in such a case the Crown may call one at the trial of the other, and he will be, at least theoretically, a compellable witness, except to the extent that he sets up a privilege against self-incrimination if he has not already been convicted. If he does not repeat his previous accusation against the present defendant, it may be proved from his statement. So the effect of these proposals is that it will no longer make a great difference to persons accused of committing crimes in concert whether they are tried together or separately. . . .

Certain questions relating to incompetent and non-compellable witnesses gave the Committee some trouble. Under the Bill, a child under fourteen is not to be sworn, but may give evidence otherwise than on oath if he has sufficient intelligence and understands the importance of telling the truth (clauses 22 (2), 45 (1)). Even if a child lacks these qualities, what he says shortly after a crime may be very convincing. Perhaps an illustration is *Sparks* v. R., [1964] A.C. 964; [1964] 1 All E.R. 727, P.C., where a small child complaining of a sexual assault said that "it was a coloured boy that did it". The defendant who was convicted of the assault was a white man aged 27, and evidence for the defence of what the child said was held by the Privy Council to be inadmissible, the child being too young to testify. Such a decision naturally raises severe doubts about the justice of the law; but it is deliberately left untouched by the new proposals. The view taken by the majority of the Criminal Law Revision Committee was that nothing could be done, because such evidence could not be admitted for the defence without being admitted for the prosecution, and as evidence for the prosecution it would be too dangerous. But why should it be assumed that the law of evidence cannot differ as between the defence and the prosecution? It certainly does in one respect, namely the burden of proof. The child's statement in *Sparks* was just the sort of evidence that might raise a reasonable doubt in the jury's mind as to the guilt of the defendant, even though it was not the sort of evidence on which, in different circumstances, if tendered by the prosecution, a conviction could be based.

Two practical solutions of the difficulty present themselves. Both presuppose that the prosecution tell the defence of the child's statement, which one would expect them to do. The time-honoured way of getting round the hearsay rule would be for the defence to cross-examine a police officer testifying for the prosecution somewhat as follows. "Did the child describe the person who assaulted him?" "Yes." "In consequence of what the child said did you begin by looking for a coloured boy?" That is, of course, a barefaced dodge, and ought not properly to be allowed. The second solution would be for the prosecution to agree for the hearsay evidence to be given by the officer, under clause 38 (see later).

The Criminal Law Revision Committee was divided on the subject of hearsay evidence of a statement by the defendant's spouse. Under the rule proposed by the Committee, the defendant's spouse is competent to give evidence against him but is not generally compellable to do so. The rule applies to spouses of either sex, but it is convenient for the purpose of the following discussion to take the usual case of a male defendant whose wife refuses to testify against him. Although the prosecution cannot compel her to testify (generally speaking), the police may be in possession of a statement she has made which inculpates her husband. Should they be allowed to give this statement in evidence?

The fact that the wife is not a compellable witness is not in itself a reason for excluding the statement. A defendant is not a compellable witness against himself, but the prosecution may give evidence of an admission he has made. Why should they not give evidence of an admission by his wife?

The fact that the wife spoke in an unguarded moment is again not a reason for excluding the evidence. Defendants make admissions in unguarded moments, yet the admission is receivable in evidence.

Whether admitting the evidence would be inconsistent with the wife's privilege from giving evidence against her husband depends on the reason why that privilege is accorded. According to the minority of the Committee, who were in favour of allowing evidence to be given of the wife's statement, the privilege is based simply on the unwillingness of the law to condemn the wife to prison for refusing to give evidence against her husband. The wife of a criminal may be torn between the conflicting duties of good citizenship and of loyalty to her husband. Because the moral issue is very difficult, and because many women are likely to stand by their husbands and refuse to give evidence, it seems politic to exempt the wife from the legal duty to testify for the prosecution. But if the prosecution are in possession of her statement and merely wish to put it in evidence there is no question of compelling her to give evidence or of sending her to prison for refusing to do so. Consequently, it would not be a breach or circumvention of her privilege to allow the evidence to be given.

However, the view of a bare majority of the Committee was that the real basis of the privilege is wider than the one just stated. The real basis was thought to be the desire of the law to preserve the marriage bond, even between an alleged criminal and his or her spouse. Allowing the wife's unguarded admissions to be given in evidence against her husband might lead to the breakdown of the marriage.

This argument is difficult to reconcile with the fact that the Committee unanimously recommended that the wife should be a competent witness for the prosecution. Take two situations. (1) A wife goes over to the side of the prosecution, gives evidence against her husband and has him convicted. (2) A wife is loyal to her husband and refuses to give evidence; but the prosecution puts in an admission made by the wife in an unguarded moment and the husband is convicted. In which of these two cases is the marriage in greater peril? It is clear that the answer is, the first. If the object of the law is to preserve the marriage, even at the cost of criminals going free, then the wife ought not to be allowed to testify against her husband. But this would be carrying consideration for the criminal's marriage beyond all reason.

[See also Williams: The New Proposals in Relation to Double Hearsay and Records, [1973] Crim. L.R. 139.]

14

Hearsay Exceptions: Civil Cases

There are several broad possibilities for reforming the rule against hearsay. One is to adopt the technique of the Criminal Evidence Act 1965; that is, to enact statutes on a piecemeal basis to destroy particular anomalies forced on the courts by the common law rule (e.g. *Myers* v. *Director of Public Prosecutions*, [1965] A.C. 1001; [1964] 2 All E.R. 881, H.L.). Another is to enact a hearsay code containing a broad hearsay rule with numerous clearly stated exceptions. A third is to abolish the ban on hearsay completely; the judge would exclude evidence of too little weight to go to the jury, but apart from that the weight of hearsay evidence would be left to the jury in the same way as direct evidence is now.

The technique adopted in the Civil Evidence Act 1968 was to provide that in civil cases hearsay evidence could only be admissible under statute or by agreement of the parties; that certain common law exceptions should be preserved by statute; and that some broad new statutory exceptions be created. It is an amalgam of methods one and two above.

The Civil Evidence Act 1968 provides:

1.—(1) In any civil proceedings a statement other than one made by a person while giving oral evidence in those proceedings shall be admissible as evidence of any fact stated therein to the extent that it is so admissible by virtue of any provision of this Part of this Act or by virtue of any other statutory provision or by agreement of the parties, but not otherwise.

(2) In this section "statutory provision" means any provision contained in, or in an instrument made under, this or any other Act, including any Act passed after this Act.

2.—(1) In any civil proceedings a statement made, whether orally or in a document or otherwise, by any person, whether called as a witness in those proceedings or not, shall, subject to this section and to rules of court, be admissible as evidence of any fact stated therein of which direct oral evidence by him would be admissible.

(2) Where in any civil proceedings a party desiring to give a statement in evidence by virtue of this section has called or intends to call as a witness in the proceedings the person by whom the statement was made, the statement—

   (*a*) shall not be given in evidence by virtue of this section on behalf of the party without the leave of the court; and

   (*b*) without prejudice to paragraph (*a*) above, shall not be given in evidence by virtue of this section on behalf of that party before the conclusion of the examination-in-chief of the person by whom it was made, except—

      (i) where before that person is called the court allows evidence of the making of the statement to be given on behalf of that party by some other person; or

(ii) in so far as the court allows the person by whom the statement was made to narrate it in the course of his examination-in-chief on the ground that to prevent him from doing so would adversely affect the intelligibility of his evidence.

(3) Where in any civil proceedings a statement which was made otherwise than in a document is admissible by virtue of this section, no evidence other than direct oral evidence by the person who made the statement or any person who heard or otherwise perceived it being made shall be admissible for the purpose of proving it:

Provided that if the statement in question was made by a person while giving oral evidence in some other legal proceedings (whether civil or criminal), it may be proved in any manner authorized by the court.

3.—(1) Where in any civil proceedings—

(a) a previous inconsistent or contradictory statement made by a person called as a witness in those proceedings is proved by virtue of section 3, 4 or 5 of the Criminal Procedure Act, 1865; or

(b) a previous statement made by a person called as aforesaid is proved for the purpose of rebutting a suggestion that his evidence has been fabricated,

that statement shall by virtue of this subsection be admissible as evidence of any fact stated therein of which direct oral evidence by him would be admissible.

(2) Nothing in this Act shall affect any of the rules of law relating to the circumstances in which, where a person called as a witness in any civil proceedings is cross-examined on a document used by him to refresh his memory, that document may be made evidence in those proceedings; and where a document or any part of a document is received in evidence in any such proceedings by virtue of any such rule of law, any statement made in that document or part by the person using the document to refresh his memory shall by virtue of this subsection be admissible as evidence of any fact stated therein of which direct oral evidence by him would be admissible.

4.—(1) Without prejudice to section 5 of this Act, in any civil proceedings a statement contained in a document shall, subject to this section and to rules of court, be admissible as evidence of any fact stated therein of which direct oral evidence would be admissible, if the document is, or forms part of, a record compiled by a person acting under a duty from information which was supplied by a person (whether acting under a duty or not) who had, or may reasonably be supposed to have had, personal knowledge of the matters dealt with in that information and which, if not supplied by that person to the compiler of the record directly, was supplied by him to the compiler of the record indirectly through one or more intermediaries each acting under a duty.

(2) Where in any civil proceedings a party desiring to give a statement in evidence by virtue of this section has called or intends to call as a witness in the proceedings the person who originally supplied the information from which the record containing the statement was compiled, the statement—

(a) shall not be given in evidence by virtue of this section on behalf of that party without the leave of the court; and

(b) without prejudice to paragraph (a) above, shall not without the leave of the court be given in evidence by virtue of this section on behalf of that party before the conclusion of the examination in chief of the person who originally supplied the said information.

(3) Any reference in this section to a person acting under a duty includes a reference to a person acting in the course of any trade, business, profession or other occupation in which he is engaged or employed or for the purposes of any paid or unpaid office held by him.

5.—(1) In any civil proceedings a statement contained in a document produced by a computer shall, subject to rules of court, be admissible as evidence of any fact stated therein of which direct oral evidence would be admissible, if it is shown that the conditions mentioned in subsection (2) below are satisfied in relation to the statement and computer in question.

(2) The said conditions are—

(*a*) that the document containing the statement was produced by the computer during a period over which the computer was used regularly to store or process information for the purposes of any activities regularly carried on over that period, whether for profit or not, by any body, whether corporate or not, or by any individual;

(*b*) that over that period there was regularly supplied to the computer in the ordinary course of those activities information of the kind contained in the statement or of the kind from which the information so contained is derived;

(*c*) that throughout the material part of that period the computer was operating properly or, if not, that any respect in which it was not operating properly or was out of operation during that part of that period was not such as to affect the production of the document or the accuracy of its contents; and

(*d*) that the information contained in the statement reproduces or is derived from information supplied to the computer in the ordinary course of those activities.

(3) Where over a period the function of storing or processing information for the purposes of any activities regularly carried on over that period as mentioned in subsection (2) (*a*) above was regularly performed by computers, whether—

(*a*) by a combination of computers operating over that period; or

(*b*) by different computers operating in succession over that period; or

(*c*) by different combinations of computers operating in succession over that period; or

(*d*) in any other manner involving the successive operation over that period, in whatever order, of one or more computers and one or more combinations of computers,

all the computers used for that purpose during that period shall be treated for the purposes of this Part of this Act as constituting a single computer; and references in this Part of this Act to a computer shall be construed accordingly.

(4) In any civil proceedings where it is desired to give a statement in evidence by virtue of this section, a certificate doing any of the following things, that is to say—

(*a*) identifying the document containing the statement and describing the manner in which it was produced;

(*b*) giving such particulars of any device involved in the production of that document as may be appropriate for the purpose of showing that the document was produced by a computer;

(*c*) dealing with any of the matters to which the conditions mentioned in subsection (2) above relate,

and purporting to be signed by a person occupying a responsible position in relation to the operation of the relevant device or the management of the relevant activities (whichever is appropriate) shall be evidence of any matter stated in the certificate; and for the purposes of this subsection it shall be sufficient for a matter to be stated to the best of the knowledge and belief of the person stating it.

(5) For the purposes of this Part of this Act—

(*a*) information shall be taken to be supplied to a computer if it is supplied thereto in any appropriate form and whether it is so supplied directly or (with or without human intervention) by means of any appropriate equipment;

(*b*) where, in the course of activities carried on by any individual or body, information is supplied with a view to its being stored or processed for the purposes of those activities by a computer operated otherwise than in the course of those activities, that information, if duly supplied to that computer, shall be taken to be supplied to it in the course of those activities;

(*c*) a document shall be taken to have been produced by a computer whether it was produced by it directly or (with or without human intervention) by means of any appropriate equipment.

(6) Subject to subsection (3) above, in this Part of this Act "computer" means any device for storing and processing information, and any reference to information being derived from other information is a reference to its being derived therefrom by calculation, comparison or any other process.

6.—(1) Where in any civil proceedings a statement contained in a document is proposed to be given in evidence by virtue of section 2, 4 or 5 of this Act it may, subject to any rules of court, be proved by the production of that document or (whether or not that document is still in existence) by the production of a copy of that document, or of the material part thereof, authenticated in such manner as the court may approve.

(2) For the purpose of deciding whether or not a statement is admissible in evidence by virtue of section 2, 4 or 5 of this Act, the court may draw any reasonable inference from the circumstances in which the statement was made or otherwise came into being or from any other circumstances, including, in the case of a statement contained in a document, the form and contents of that document.

(3) In estimating the weight, if any, to be attached to a statement admissible in evidence by virtue of section 2, 3, 4 or 5 of this Act regard shall be had to all the circumstances from which any inference can reasonably be drawn as to the accuracy or otherwise of the statement and, in particular—

(*a*) in the case of a statement falling within section 2 (1) or 3 (1) or (2) of this Act, to the question whether or not the statement was made contemporaneously with the occurrence or existence of the facts stated, and to the question whether or not the maker of the statement had any incentive to conceal or misrepresent the facts;

(*b*) in the case of a statement falling within section 4 (1) of this Act, to the question whether or not the person who originally supplied the information from which the record containing the statement was compiled did so contemporaneously with the occurrence or existence of the facts dealt with in that information, and to the question whether or not that person, or any person concerned with compiling or keeping the record containing the statement, had any incentive to conceal or misrepresent the facts; and

(*c*) in the case of a statement falling within section 5 (1) of this Act, to the question whether or not the information which the information contained in the statement reproduces or is derived from was supplied to the relevant computer, or recorded for the purpose of being supplied thereto, contemporaneously with the occurrence or existence of the facts dealt with in that information, and to the question whether or not any person concerned with the supply of information to that computer or with the operation of that computer or any equipment by means of which the document containing the statement was produced by it, had any incentive to conceal or misrepresent the facts.

(4) For the purpose of any enactment or rule of law or practice requiring evidence to be corroborated or regulating the manner in which uncorroborated evidence is to be treated—

(*a*) a statement which is admissible in evidence by virtue of section 2 or 3 of this

Act shall not be capable of corroborating evidence given by the maker of the statement; and

(*b*) a statement which is admissible in evidence by virtue of section 4 of this Act shall not be capable of corroborating evidence given by the person who originally supplied the information from which the record containing the statement was compiled.

(5) If any person in a certificate tendered in evidence in civil proceedings by virtue of section 5 (4) of this Act wilfully makes a statement material in those proceedings which he knows to be false or does not believe to be true, he shall be liable on conviction on indictment to imprisonment for a term not exceeding two years or a fine or both.

7.—(1) Subject to rules of court, where in any civil proceedings a statement made by a person who is not called as a witness in those proceedings is given in evidence by virtue of section 2 of this Act—

(*a*) any evidence which, if that person had been so called would be admissible for the purpose of destroying or supporting his credibility as a witness shall be admissible for that purpose in those proceedings; and

(*b*) evidence tending to prove that, whether before or after he made that statement, that person made (whether orally or in a document or otherwise) another statement inconsistent therewith shall be admissible for the purpose of showing that that person has contradicted himself:

Provided that nothing in this subsection shall enable evidence to be given of any matter of which, if the person in question had been called as a witness and had denied that matter in cross-examination, evidence could not have been adduced by the cross-examining party.

(2) Subsection (1) above shall apply in relation to a statement given in evidence by virtue of section 4 of this Act as it applies in relation to a statement given in evidence by virtue of section 2 of this Act, except that references to the person who made the statement and to his making the statement shall be construed respectively as references to the person who originally supplied the information from which the record containing the statement was compiled and to his supplying that information.

(3) Section 3 (1) of this Act shall apply to any statement proved by virtue of subsection (1) (*b*) above as it applies to a previous inconsistent or contradictory statement made by a person called as a witness which is proved as mentioned in paragraph (*a*) of the said section 3 (1).

8.—(1) Provision shall be made by rules of court as to the procedure which, subject to any exceptions provided for in the rules, must be followed and the other conditions which, subject as aforesaid, must be fulfilled before a statement can be given in evidence in civil proceedings by virtue of section 2, 4 or 5 of this Act.

(2) Rules of court made in pursuance of subsection (1) above shall in particular, subject to such exceptions (if any) as may be provided for in the rules—

(*a*) require a party to any civil proceedings who desires to give in evidence any such statement as is mentioned in that subsection to give to every other party to the proceedings such notice of his desire to do so and such particulars of or relating to the statement as may be specified in the rules, including particulars of such one or more of the persons connected with the making or recording of the statement or, in the case of a statement falling within section 5 (1) of this Act, such one or more of the persons concerned as mentioned in section 6 (3) (*c*) of this Act as the rules may in any case require; and

(*b*) enable any party who receives such notice as aforesaid by counter-notice to require any person of whom particulars were given with the notice to be called as a witness in the proceedings unless that person is dead, or beyond the seas, or unfit by reason of his bodily or mental condition to attend as a witness, or cannot with reasonable diligence be identified or found, or cannot reasonably be expected (having regard to the time which has elapsed since he was connected or concerned as aforesaid and to all the circumstances) to have any recollection of matters relevant to the accuracy or otherwise of the statement.

(3) Rules of court made in pursuance of subsection (1) above—

(*a*) may confer on the court in any civil proceedings a discretion to allow a statement falling within section 2 (1), 4 (1) or 5 (1) of this Act to be given in evidence notwithstanding that any requirement of the rules affecting the admissibility of that statement has not been complied with, but except in pursuance of paragraph (*b*) below shall not confer on the court a discretion to exclude such a statement where the requirements of the rules affecting its admissibility have been complied with;

(*b*) may confer on the court power, where a party to any civil proceedings has given notice that he desires to give in evidence—

(i) a statement falling within section 2 (1) of this Act which was made by a person, whether orally or in a document, in the course of giving evidence in some other legal proceedings (whether civil or criminal); or

(ii) a statement falling within section 4 (1) of this Act which is contained in a record of any direct oral evidence given in some other legal proceedings (whether civil or criminal),

to give directions on the application of any party to the proceedings as to whether, and if so on what conditions, the party desiring to give the statement in evidence will be permitted to do so and (where applicable) as to the manner in which that statement and any other evidence given in those other proceedings is to be proved; and

(*c*) may make different provision for different circumstances, and in particular may make different provision with respect to statements falling within sections 2 (1), 4 (1) and 5 (1) of this Act respectively;

and any discretion conferred on the court by rules of court made as aforesaid may be either a general discretion or a discretion exercisable only in such circumstances as may be specified in the rules.

(4) Rules of court may make provision for preventing a party to any civil proceedings (subject to any exceptions provided for in the rules) from adducing in relation to a person who is not called as a witness in those proceedings any evidence which could otherwise be adduced by him by virtue of section 7 of this Act unless that party has in pursuance of the rules given in respect of that person such a counternotice as is mentioned in subsection (2) (*b*) above.

(5) In deciding for the purposes of any rules of court made in pursuance of this section whether or not a person is fit to attend as a witness, a court may act on a certificate purporting to be a certificate of a fully registered medical practitioner.

· · ·

9.—(1) In any civil proceedings a statement which, if this Part of this Act had not been passed, would by virtue of any rule of law mentioned in subsection (2) below have been admissible as evidence of any fact stated therein shall be admissible as evidence of that fact by virtue of this subsection.

(2) The rules of law referred to in subsection (1) above are the following, that is to say any rule of law—

(*a*) whereby in any civil proceedings an admission adverse to a party to the proceedings, whether made by that party or by another person, may be given in evidence against that party for the purpose of proving any fact stated in the admission;

(*b*) whereby in any civil proceedings published works dealing with matters of a public nature (for example, histories, scientific works, dictionaries and maps) are admissible as evidence of facts of a public nature stated therein;

(*c*) whereby in any civil proceedings public documents (for example, public registers, and returns made under public authority with respect to matters of public interest) are admissible as evidence of facts stated therein; or

(*d*) whereby in any civil proceedings records (for example, the records of certain courts, treaties, Crown grants, pardons and commissions) are admissible as evidence of facts stated therein.

In this subsection "admission" includes any representation of fact, whether made in words or otherwise.

(3) In any civil proceedings a statement which tends to establish reputation or family tradition with respect to any matter and which, if this Act had not been passed, would have been admissible in evidence by virtue of any rule of law mentioned in subsection (4) below—

(*a*) shall be admissible in evidence by virtue of this paragraph in so far as it is not capable of being rendered admissible under section 2 or 4 of this Act; and

(*b*) if given in evidence under this Part of this Act (whether by virtue of paragraph (*a*) above or otherwise) shall by virtue of this paragraph be admissible as evidence of the matter reputed or handed down;

and, without prejudice to paragraph (*b*) above, reputation shall for the purposes of this Part of this Act be treated as a fact and not as a statement or multiplicity of statements dealing with the matter reputed.

(4) The rules of law referred to in subsection (3) above are the following, that is to say any rule of law—

(*a*) whereby in any civil proceedings evidence of a person's reputation is admissible for the purpose of establishing his good or bad character;

(*b*) whereby in any civil proceedings involving a question of pedigree or in which the existence of a marriage is in issue evidence of reputation or family tradition is admissible for the purpose of proving or disproving pedigree or the existence of the marriage, as the case may be; or

(*c*) whereby in any civil proceedings evidence of reputation or family tradition is admissible for the purpose of proving or disproving the existence of any public or general right or of identifying any person or thing.

(5) It is hereby declared that in so far as any statement is admissible in any civil proceedings by virtue of subsection (1) or (3) (*a*) above, it may be given in evidence in those proceedings notwithstanding anything in sections 2 to 7 of this Act or in any rules of court made in pursuance of section 8 of this Act.

(6) The words in which any rule of law mentioned in subsection (2) or (4) above is there described are intended only to identify the rule in question and shall not be construed as altering that rule in any way.

10.—(1) In this Part of this Act—

"computer" has the meaning assigned by section 5 of this Act;

"document" includes, in addition to a document in writing—

(*a*) any map, plan, graph or drawing;

(*b*) any photograph;

(*c*) any disc, tape, sound track or other device in which sounds or other data (not being visual images) are embodied so as to be capable (with or without the aid of some other equipment) of being reproduced therefrom; and (*d*) any film, negative, tape or other device in which one or more visual images are embodied so as to be capable (as aforesaid) of being reproduced therefrom;

"film" includes a microfilm;

"statement" includes any representation of fact, whether made in words or otherwise.

(2) In this Part of this Act any reference to a copy of a document includes—

(*a*) in the case of a document falling within paragraph (*c*) but not (*d*) of the definition of "document" in the foregoing subsection, a transcript of the sounds or other data embodied therein;

(*b*) in the case of a document falling within paragraph (*d*) but not (*c*) of that definition, a reproduction or still reproduction of the image or images embodied therein, whether enlarged or not;

(*c*) in the case of a document falling within both those paragraphs, such a transcript together with such a still reproduction; and

(*d*) in the case of a document not falling within the said paragraph (*d*) of which a visual image is embodied in a document falling within that paragraph, a reproduction of that image, whether enlarged or not,

and any reference to a copy of the material part of a document shall be construed accordingly.

I STATEMENTS GOVERNED BY THE ACT

The importance of the Act's ambit is this. If the common law hearsay rule covers certain statements in practice admitted under ill-defined exceptions, and the Act applies only to a narrower version of hearsay, the effect will be to exclude evidence admissible before the Act, which would be a strange result for liberalizing legislation. This will occur because there will be classes of evidence once admissible at common law not falling under the wide new statutory exceptions because they are outside the Act's scope, and no longer admissible at common law because all common law exceptions have been abolished except as the Act specifies.

The general rule of the Act is s. 1 (1): statements made other than by a witness testifying are admissible only by statute or by agreement. Section 10 (1) provides that "statement" includes any representation of fact, whether made in words or otherwise. "Representation" suggests that its maker must have intended to make an assertion, so that implied assertions are outside the Act. To avoid this result, Cross argues that here, as at common law, the hearsay rule should apply to implied assertions by way of statement but not by way of conduct (p. 430). This is open to the same objections made earlier (p. 324, *ante*).

It is also doubtful how far the Act applies to negative hearsay but the status of such evidence is even more obscure at common law than that of implied assertions (p. 325, *ante*).

The definition of statement means that no greater admissibility exists for opinion evidence than at common law (cf. the Evidence Act 1938: *Dass* v. *Masih*, [1968] 2 All E.R. 226, C.A.). But the Civil Evidence Act 1972, s. 1 has extended the 1968 Act to statements of opinion.

It may be that some common law exceptions have, by an oversight, not been preserved. Though the notice procedure of the Act does not apply to statements by the deceased in a probate action (R.S.C. Ord. 38, r. 21 (3)), it is unclear how far a post-testamentary declaration of a testator about the contents of his will is admissible under s. 2 (1). The section makes a statement admissible as "evidence of any fact stated therein of which direct oral evidence by him would be admissible". But no-one can give direct oral evidence in a probate action about his estate; if he is alive, the action will not have been brought; if he is dead, he cannot testify. The same is true of pre-testamentary declarations admitted as proof of the testator's state of mind. One way of avoiding this minor disaster would be to construe "direct oral evidence" as evidence which could have been given had he been alive. Another is to construe "would be admissible" as "would not be inadmissible": direct oral evidence would not be inadmissible if it existed, but it simply does not exist. Another is to assume that somehow proceedings about the contents of the will were capable of arising during the testator's lifetime. Indeed, such proceedings may be possible. Suppose that a father leaves all his property to one son and none to another, and the disinherited son reads the will, burns it, and by accident ignites the whole house. In a tort action against that son the contents of the will might be relevant as proving a motive for the defendant's conduct. It is to be hoped one of these devices or something similar is used to preserve the common law admissibility of the declarations about wills. Some slight authority against this view, however, may be found in *Taylor* v. *Taylor*, [1970] 2 All E.R. 609, at p. 614, C.A. where Davies, L.J. said that the transcript of a judicial summing up in one case might not be admissible under s. 2 (1) in another case because the judge cannot give evidence. But the incapacity of a judge is absolute; the incapacity of the testator hinges on the contingency of his death.

It should be noted that s. 1 preserves existing and future statutory exceptions. There are many statutory exceptions, on the whole of a very specialized kind. For some examples see Phipson, Chap. 32.

II   THE EXTENT OF ADMISSIBILITY

The effect of s. 2 is to abolish the rule against first-hand hearsay in civil proceedings subject to two conditions. One is that the maker is dead, beyond the seas, unfit, unidentifiable, or undiscoverable, or he cannot reasonably be expected to remember the facts in issue. The other is that the prescribed pre-trial procedure for establishing the first condition or the other side's consent to admissibility is followed (s. 8 (2) (*b*)). Even if these two conditions are not satisfied, the court has a discretion to admit first-hand hearsay (s. 8 (3)).

The effect of s. 2 (3) is to ensure that in general oral second-hand hearsay is inadmissible unless it was made in prior legal proceedings. It usually has very little probative value. However, multiple hearsay in documents or produced by computers is admissible under ss. 4 and 5. An example of admissibility under s. 2 (1) is a shorthand writer's transcript of prior proceedings: it is first-hand hearsay (*Taylor* v. *Taylor*, [1970] 2 All E.R. 609; [1970] 1 W.L.R. 1148, C.A.).

At common law an out-of-court admission by a non-party was not evidence against a party (*Legge* v. *Edmonds* (1855), 25 L.J. Ch. 125; *Burr* v. *Ware Rural District Council*, [1939] 2 All E.R. 688, C.A.), and an admission by one party was not evidence against another (*Rutherford* v. *Richardson*, [1923] A.C. 1, [1922] All E.R. Rep. 13, H.L.). Such statements would now be admissible under

s. 2. It is open to the person making the admission to give direct oral evidence to that effect, which would be evidence against a party or co-party. Hence s. 2 (1) makes his out-of-court admissions admissible. This removes one absurdity of the former law.

Another consequence of s. 2 is the almost complete abolition of the *res gestae* doctrine: it has been swallowed up by the much wider admissibility under s. 2. It is not preserved by s. 9 and hence can only continue to exist in areas not covered by the Act, e.g. where it is original evidence (*Milne* v. *Leisler* (1862), 7 H. & N. 786).

B. Documentary hearsay

Section 4 (1) renders admissible documentary hearsay statements of which direct oral evidence would be admissible if the document is, or forms part of, a record compiled by a person acting under a duty from information supplied by a person who had or may reasonably be supposed to have had personal knowledge. If that person did not supply the information directly to the computer, intermediaries who supplied it must have been under a duty to do so. There is an obvious overlap with s. 2 (1).

There are some obscurities. "Record" is left undefined; so is "duty". Section 4 (3) provides that a duty to compile or duty to pass on the information recorded arising in any trade business, professional or other occupation, or any paid or unpaid office is included. This is much wider than the Criminal Evidence Act 1965. But are social duties, e.g. to help the police enforce the law, also within s. 4? (See Cross and Wilkins, *Outline of the Law of Evidence* (3rd Edn., London, 1971, p. 38.) If A tells a policeman that X was the driver of a car and the policeman writes this down, his note is admissible: he had a duty to record and A need have no duty to supply. But if A tells the information to B who tells it to the policeman, B must be under a duty if the statement is to be admitted.

The introduction of the duty requirement has been attacked. "The reliability of a record derives from the fact that it was made in the course of ordinary repetitive business practice, not from any duty": Newark and Samuels (1968), 31 M.L.R. 668, at p. 670. The duty requirement is absent from the Criminal Evidence Act 1965.

A transcript of prior legal proceedings is admissible under s. 4 (1) as a record compiled by a shorthand writer acting under a duty (*Taylor* v. *Taylor*, [1970] 2 All E.R. 609, C.A.).

In certain circumstances the court will assume that the supplier of the information had personal knowledge. Thus in *Knight* v. *David*, [1971] 3 All E.R. 1066; [1971] 1 W.L.R. 1671 in which the title to land was in dispute, Goulding, J. admitted a map made in pursuance of the Tithe Act 1836 notwithstanding a lack of proof that it had been compiled from information supplied by persons having personal knowledge. He said: "having regard to the nature of the document and the lapse of time, it is right for the court to infer that this condition is satisfied" (pp. 1070–1). An objection that direct oral evidence of title would be inadmissible, so that s. 4 (1) could not apply, failed; it was enough if a living person would have stated "that a certain person was, and another was not, entered as proprietor of certain land" for the purpose of carrying out the machinery of the Tithe Act 1836.

It is sometimes said that if s. 4 is directed mainly to business records, it is wrong to devote attention to the reliability of the supplier and compiler and to require that the compiler be under a duty. It is said that whether there is a duty or not, business records may be relied on as being in the ordinary course of events reliable; the reliability is enhanced by various cross-checking devices such as balance sheets. At least this is true of day-to-day routine business. But if on the other hand s. 4 is intended to apply more widely (as it is), more attention should have been devoted to issues such as the competence of the supplier and compiler, and the extent to which the accuracy of the documentary record can be checked in other ways. That is, it is wrong to apply the same rules to normally reliable business records and a much wider class of more doubtful records.

These criticisms seem unfair and pedantic. The spirit of the Act is a reliance on common sense. Hearsay conservatives may fairly say that the dangers of "common sense" are not appreciated; hearsay radicals may fairly say that the entire Act is far too elaborate and unnecessarily complex: that the draftsman's faith in common sense is too qualified. But the radical critics of the Act cannot have it both ways. They cannot say both that greater and procedurally simpler admissibility of hearsay should be accepted and that greater safeguards should exist. The fact is that all the fears of the radicals will be rendered groundless by a competent court and all the conservative fears made real by incompetent courts. A court proceeding in the light of common sense will understand that some records are intrinsically reliable, some need cross-checks, some compilers and recorders must be cross-examined as to their experience, competence, and responsibility.

C. Computerized records

The provisions for admissibility of such records under s. 5 are worthy of note. As with s. 4, multiple hearsay is admitted. The records may contain facts of which no one has personal knowledge. But s. 5 also illustrates one feature of the Civil Evidence Act which many regard as a defect, namely, its extreme complication.

Though s. 4 and R.S.C. Ord. 38, r. 23 direct the court's attention to the reliability of the individuals who supplied and compiled the information recorded, s. 5 (2) does not: it stresses rather the reliability of the computer. But this is probably in practice a false contrast, for R.S.C. Ord. 38, r. 24 requires that notices contain particulars of those who held responsible positions not only in the management of the activities for which the computer was used and in the supply of information to it, but also in the operation of the computer. The latter persons could be examined as to the competence of those actually operating the computer, and though their incompetence, lack of training or experience, and unreliability might not generally affect admissibility it would affect weight. (On the factors affecting the reliability of computers and their operators, see Harding (1971), 45 A.L.J. 531, at p. 552.)

There are some parts of s. 5 raising inevitable difficulties of fact for the courts. When is a computer used "regularly"? When are activities carried on "regularly"? What is the "ordinary course" of activities? When is a computer not "operating properly"? Is there any implicit limitation on the wide definition of "computer"? (On some of these questions, see *Standard Oil Company of California* v. *Moore* (1958), 251 F. 2d 188, at p. 215.)

D. Miscellaneous

Sections 2 (2), 3 and 4 (2) concern proof of prior consistent and inconsistent statements of witnesses and will be dealt with during our discussion of the course of the trial (p. 432, *post*).

Section 6 enacts a number of provisions which are either self-explanatory (s. 6 (1), (2) and (5)), obvious (s. 6 (3)) or re-enactments of common law rules (s. 6 (4)).

Section 7 provides that for evidence challenging the credibility of the maker of a statement (other than discrediting evidence his denial of which, were he called, could not be contradicted).

Section 8 indicates what content the rules of court which govern procedure should have (pp. 365–8, *post*).

Section 9 (1) and (2) preserves the law relating to admissions, published works of a public nature as judicially noticed evidence of public facts, public documents and records. Such evidence sometimes involves oral multiple hearsay which might otherwise be excluded by s. 2 (3). Such evidence is free of the notice procedure, because, for example, it would force the plaintiff attempting to prove an admission by the defendant to call that defendant as his own witness if the defendant issued a counter-notice, and thus the plaintiff would lose the advantages of cross-examining him. Section 9 (3) and (4) provides for the admission of reputation and family tradition, which often involves multiple hearsay. Since sometimes the notice procedure is appropriate, s. 9 (3) and (4) only apply where the evidence would be inadmissible under ss. 2 and 4.

III PROCEDURE

The procedure for admission of hearsay evidence made admissible by the Act has two objectives. One is to deal with all questions of hearsay before the trial so that its smooth course is not interrupted by objections to the admissibility of hearsay. The other is to avoid either party being surprised by hearsay evidence at the trial so that they are unable to counter it. The procedure departs from the usual rule that no party is required to disclose in advance the evidence he intends to adduce at the trial; it is the price to be paid for the admission of hearsay evidence not open to cross-examination.

A party who wishes to introduce hearsay evidence at the trial should serve notice of his intention to do so on every other party whether or not the evidence will be admissible against that party (R.S.C. Ord. 38, r. 21). Such notice must contain certain details depending on what type of hearsay it is sought to have admitted. Thus if it is an oral statement admissible under s. 2, particulars must be given of the time, place, and circumstances of its making, the maker and the person to whom it was made, and the substance of the statement, including the words used if material. In the case of documentary statements admissible under s. 2, a copy or transcript of the document must be annexed to the notice. If the giver of the notice alleges that any person particularized in it cannot or should not be called because of death or one of the other relevant reasons, the notice must state which reason is relied on (R.S.C. Ord. 38, r. 22). Similar provisions are made for s. 4 statements (R.S.C. Ord. 38, r. 23), and s. 5 statements (R.S.C. Ord. 38, r. 24). Any party who complies with this procedure will be able to admit the evidence at the trial unless counter-notice is served. If he fails to comply with the procedure, or a counter-notice is served, the evidence will only be admissible if the court exercises its discretion to admit the evidence or the party can prove the maker of the statement is unavailable. (The need to serve a notice does not apply to probate actions, because the deceased's death is incontestable, nor to undefended divorces, because there is no active opponent likely to object to the admission of a hearsay statement.)

Anyone on whom a notice has been served may serve on the giver of the notice a counter-notice requiring the giver to call as a witness any named person particularized in the notice. If the notice gave a reason why the witness should not be called, the counter-notice must assert that he should be (i.e. must deny the existence of the reason). The counter-notice procedure is not to apply to statements made in previous proceedings. If the recipient of the counter-notice fails to comply with it, the statement is inadmissible unless one of the reasons for not calling the witness in fact exists; this issue may be determined by a Master or Registrar before trial (R.S.C. Ord. 38, rr. 26, 27 and 28). The effect of the counter-notice procedure is to prevent hearsay evidence being admitted if direct evidence is available. The server of a counter-notice will have to pay the costs of doing so if it was unreasonable to require the witness to be called (R.S.C. Ord. 38, r. 32).

R.S.C. Ord. 38, r. 29 gives the court discretion to admit hearsay evidence despite failure to comply with the notice and counter-notice procedure, following s. 8 (3) (a) of the Act. One special factor is stated: hearsay evidence should be admissible if a party would otherwise be obliged to call as a witness at the trial his opponent or his opponent's servant or agent.

Tremelbye (Selangor) Rubber Co., Ltd. v. *Stekel*, [1971] 1 All E.R. 940; [1971] 1 W.L.R. 226 was a case involving this possibility. Pennycuick, V.-C. exercised his discretion in favour of admitting, on the plaintiff company's motion, a transcript of evidence in prior criminal proceedings, on condition that the defendants should be allowed to cross-examine the individuals concerned on matters contained in the transcript of their evidence. If this occurred, the plaintiff company would be entitled to re-examine as he thought fit, unhindered by restrictions on the questions counsel could ordinarily ask of his own witness.

Section 8 (4) of the Act and R.S.C. Ord. 38, r. 30 prevent attacks, except by leave of the Court, on the credibility of the maker of out-of-court statements unless he is called as a witness and is thus able to defend himself. If it is proposed to introduce the previous inconsistent statements of such a non-witness under s. 7 (1) (b), then notice must be given of this intention to the party proposing to introduce the non-witness's hearsay statement (R.S.C. Ord. 38, r. 31).

The judge's discretion to admit evidence despite failure to comply with the procedural requirements is an important aspect of the machinery. It is not a merely formal discretion and is reviewable on appeal. In *Ford* v. *Lewis*, [1971] 2 All E.R. 983; [1971] 1 W.L.R. 623 C.A., Veale, J. at first instance admitted a statement of the defendant about how a motor accident arose, under s. 2 (1) (the defendant having since become mentally ill), and also hospital notes indicating that the plaintiff's father was drunk, under s. 4 (1), despite want of the requisite notice. No clear reason seems to have existed for the lack of notice about the hospital records; but notice was not given regarding the defendant's statement because defence counsel took a deliberate decision to this effect. He feared that if the plaintiff and her parents learnt of the statement before trial, their evidence would be adjusted to destroy it in advance. This fact only emerged before the Court of Appeal. Edmund Davies, L.J. said: "Put in plain words, this means that the tactics adopted were precisely those which the statutory provisions as to notice and counter-notice were designed to prevent, namely, the taking of a party by surprise by suddenly and without warning producing at the trial an out-of-court statement of someone not proposed to be called as a witness" (at p. 991). By a majority the Court of Appeal held that in such circumstances—"a deliberate withholding from the court of the reason for non-compliance"—the discretion should not be exercised in the defendant's favour. "A suitor who deliberately flouts the rules has no right to ask the court to exercise in his favour a discretionary indulgence created by those very same rules. Furthermore, a judge who, to his knowledge, finds himself confronted by such a situation would not, as I think, be acting judicially if he nevertheless exercised his discretion in favour of the recalcitrant suitor. . . . Slackness is one thing; deliberate disobedience another. The former may be overlooked; the latter never, even though, as here, it derives from mistaken zeal on the client's behalf" (p. 991). This seems sound, though Lord Diplock has said: "the decision in *Ford* v. *Lewis* was certainly not one expected by the Law Reform Committee" (45 A.L.J. 569). *Morris* v. *Stratford-on-Avon R.D.C.*, [1973] 3 All E.R. 263; [1973] 1 W.L.R. 1059 C.A., provides a contrast. There the evidence was admitted. No notice had been given, not because of any attempt to hamper the other side, but because it had not been thought necessary to have the statement admitted since the maker of the statement was to testify. However, he performed so badly as a witness that counsel applied for and obtained leave to put the prior written statement in. The Court of Appeal held this to be proper since it did not prejudice the other side.

If the discretion were to be freely exercised in favour of admission, some very unusual things could be done: the trial could become a trial by written statements and proofs rather than by orally given evidence. But the discretion is not likely to be widely used except where witnesses are unavailable because of death or one of the other good reasons in s. 8 (2) (*b*). As Cross says, "it would be possible in theory, though most improbable in practice, for the Court to allow a solicitor who said that he had mislaid a particular witness's proof and that the witness was not present in court because he had other things to do to testify from his recollection of what the witness told him" (p. 424).

It should be noted that the notice procedure renders more difficult the admission of evidence admissible under the Evidence Act 1938. The procedure has been criticized on several grounds. First, it is cumbersome. Secondly, it robs parties of the advantage of surprise, and interferes with the traditional rule that evidence need not be disclosed before trial. Thirdly, a party wishing to issue a counter-notice has the difficult task of deciding whether to demand the presence of the maker of a hearsay statement without knowing what the other evidence in the case is to be. Fourthly, in McInerney, J.'s words, "In my experience most practitioners really get to the bones of a case the night before it begins, and it is then that they discover all the relevant evidence; it is then that the S.O.S.'s are sent out for the missing witnesses, and how you are going to accommodate the facts of juristic life . . . to the necessity of notice and counter-notice, I don't know'' ((1971), 45 A.L.J. 566). Finally, there is some dislike of the existence of the discretion.

Some, but not all of these points have force. The problem of evidence which is discovered or seen to be relevant at a late stage can be dealt with by use of the inclusionary discretion. The notice procedure was adopted, according to Lord Diplock (45 A.L.J. 569), because ''we thought it was important that there should be no discretion to exclude hearsay if certain safeguards were provided. When you are preparing a case you must know what evidence will be admitted when you come to trial, and that is why our approach was that we shall give a discretion to admit but give no discretion to exclude if the necessary conditions of ensuring, as far as one can, the reliability of the hearsay evidence produced are complied with.'' It is desirable for the parties, in the interests of certainty and possible avoidance of litigation, to know as far as possible what evidence is admissible and what is not before the trial. But apart from this kind of answer, it may be said that the Act is only a stage in a long journey from the piecemeal statutory reforms for special areas (e.g. the Banker's Books Evidence Act 1879), to the Evidence Act 1938, to the Criminal Evidence Act 1965, to some future simpler system of widely admissible hearsay. A radical may see the Act as a further step in the education of a cautious profession. A conservative may see it as embodying necessary safeguards. If the safeguards turn out in the light of experience to be unnecessary, they can be dropped.

Reading

13th Report of the Law Reform Committee on Hearsay Evidence in Civil Proceedings, 1966, Cmnd. 2964; Harding (1971), 45 A.L.J. 531; Kean, *The Civil Evidence Act 1968* (London, 1969); Tapper (1966), 29 M.L.R. 653 and *Computers and the Law* (London, 1973).

15

Opinion Evidence and Prior Proceedings

I OPINION EVIDENCE

The orthodox doctrine is that a witness may not give his opinion unless (*a*) he is an expert testifying on a matter calling for the expertise he possesses; or (*b*) it is extremely difficult to separate opinions from facts, and the witness's opinion will help the court. There is a further rule that as far as possible the witness should not give his opinion on the ultimate issue—the very issue the court has to decide.

An opinion is an inference from observed facts. Since most human discourse is largely made up of opinions, an insistence that no statements of opinion be made would be unworkable. Expert opinions are necessary to point out to laymen the inferences they cannot themselves draw, and non-expert opinions must be admitted where this is convenient in the interests of a reasonably normal prose during the giving of testimony. But in practice English courts have applied the rule even more loosely so that common sense has had some triumphs. This is partly because of the lack of theoretical attention devoted to the subject and the paucity of leading cases. It contrasts with the American and to a lesser extent the Australian position.

Non-expert opinion evidence on matters requiring expertise is excluded because it is irrelevant or insufficiently weighty; such evidence on matters not requiring expertise which would not assist the court is superfluous. The rule against evidence on the ultimate issue depends on a fear of a witness usurping jury functions. There is a general feeling also that expert witnesses are selected to prove a case and are often close to being professional liars: "it is often quite surprising to see with what facility, and to what an extent, their views can be made to correspond with the wishes or the interests of the parties who call them. They do not, indeed, wilfully misrepresent what they think, but their judgments become so warped by regarding the subject in one point of view, that, even when conscientiously disposed, they are incapable of forming an independent opinion. Being zealous partisans, their Belief becomes synonymous with faith as defined by the Apostle, and it too often is but 'the substance of things *hoped for*, the evidence of things *not* seen' " (Taylor, p. 59). Lord Campbell put it more harshly: "hardly any weight is to be given to the evidence of what are called scientific witnesses; they come with a bias on their minds to support the cause in which they are embarked" (*Tracy Peerage*

369

(1843), 10 Cl. & Fin. 154, at p. 191). And Best says: "there can be no doubt that testimony is daily received in our courts as 'scientific evidence' to which it is almost profanation to apply the term; as being revolting to common sense, and inconsistent with the commonest honesty on the part of those by whom it is given" (p. 491).

A. Non-expert opinion evidence at common law

A non-expert may give his opinion if the facts on which it was based were too fleeting to be noticed or remembered, or if it would disturb the flow of his narrative too much to state them. He may give a compendious account of what he observed by stating an opinion. Questions about identity are very clear illustrations of both points. When we recognize Mr. Harold Wilson we do not consciously notice his white hair, his shortness, his pipe and so on; even if we did, we may not remember all the features that helped us to recognize him; and even if we remembered, it would make the giving and hearing of testimony intolerable if witnesses identifying Mr. Wilson listed all his physical traits and left it to the court to draw an inference. Other examples apart from identity of persons, things and handwriting are age; speed; temperature; weather; light; the passing of time; sanity; the condition of objects—new, shabby, worn; emotional and bodily states; and intoxication. The law's hostility to opinion evidence is partly supported by the fact that these are all cases where it is very easy for witnesses to make mistakes.

There has been some tendency to expand the admissibility of non-expert opinion evidence of this kind.

It is often said that courts are hostile to non-experts expressing their opinions on the ultimate issue, but the rule is often evaded and sometimes broken, as in the cases of estimates of value (*R.* v. *Beckett* (1913), 8 Cr. App. Rep. 204, C.C.A.); opinions as to whether an act would have been done had some circumstance been different (*Mansell* v. *Clements* (1874), L.R. 9 C.P. 139).

The English and Irish courts differ on the question of unfitness to drive through drink, the Irish considering that a non-expert can testify to this (*A.-G. (Ruddy)* v. *Kenny* (1960), 94 I.L.T.R. 185), the English considering that the witness's opinion on drunkenness alone can be admitted (*R.* v. *Davies*, [1962] 3 All E.R. 97). This is perhaps open to criticism, for "as in the case of the inference that a person is under the influence of drink, the inference that the same person was incapable of having proper control may depend on the whole picture, on the conjoint effect of numerous facts and circumstances which lead to a sound conclusion but cannot be faithfully or completely reproduced in evidence" (*Sherrard* v. *Jacob*, [1965] N.I. 151, at p. 163, *per* Lord MacDermott).

B. Expert opinion evidence at common law

Before giving his opinion, the expert must show himself to be properly qualified in the matter he is about to give his opinion of. The expertise may be acquired by training or experience.

The matter must be one calling for expertise, and this varies from time to time as common knowledge changes. The usual examples include scientific, architectural, engineering and technical issues, problems of tool marks and ballistics, blood tests, the provisions of foreign law, the identity of handwriting and fingerprints, questions of artistic taste, economic comment and prediction in restrictive trade practices cases, and issues of business practice and market value. There is some overlap with matters on which non-expert evidence is given. Normally the facts in reference to which the opinion was given are not proved by the expert; they must be separately proved and he must give an opinion on them put to him in hypothetical questions. He may, however, testify to the facts if he observed them.

In strict orthodoxy, he must be careful not to mix up hearsay evidence with his opinion. Thus the High Court of Australia has held that a doctor may not say what a patient told him about his past symptoms as evidence of the existence of those symptoms; but he may say what the patient told him so as to explain the grounds for his opinion of the patient's condition (*Ramsay* v. *Watson* (1961), 108 C.L.R. 642). Yet this rule is often not observed, particularly in valuation cases.

A valuer will often base his estimate of value on what others have told him of comparable jobs. Indeed, the opinion evidence of a valuer sometimes conflicts with another orthodox rule—that experts should reveal the facts on which their opinion is based. "Thus a valuer may be unable to recall all the details of all the sales on which he bases his opinion, yet he may be closer to the mark than a less experienced practitioner who has made an exhaustive examination of comparable sales . . . [I]t is permissible to qualify a valuer, ask his opinion as to value, and leave the opposition to cross-examine as to the material on which the opinion is founded (Eggleston, in Glass (Ed.), p. 70). In *English Exporters (London), Ltd.* v. *Eldonwall*, [1973] Ch. 415; [1973] 1 All E.R. 726, Megarry, J. confirmed this view in holding that an expert valuer could express his opinion on values even though substantial contributions to the formation of those opinions were made by hearsay; but he could not give hearsay evidence as to the facts of transactions lying outside his personal knowledge.

Further, in the course of testifying experts have a "duty to furnish the judge or jury with the necessary scientific criteria for testing the accuracy of their conclusions, so as to enable the judge or jury to form their own independent judgment by the application of these criteria to the facts proved in evidence" (*Davie* v. *Edinburgh Magistrates*, 1953 S.C. 34, at p. 40). The aim is to avoid the court being led into accepting an opinion based on false premises. This aim may be more difficult to achieve the more technical the criteria involved.

If agreed evidence conflicts the court must choose between the experts. This difficult task is perhaps only to be accomplished by comparing their qualifications, their experience and their general credibility.

The orthodox view is that experts may not testify on the ultimate issue, particularly if this is an issue of law.

Haynes v. Doman
[1899] 2 Ch. 13, C.A.

The case concerned the validity of a covenant against competition contained in a contract for the employment of a hardware manufacturer's servant.

LINDLEY, M.R.: . . . [T]here are affidavits from persons in the trade, stating their views of the reasonableness of the restrictive clause on which this case turns. The introduction of this class of evidence is a novelty. In my opinion it is inadmissible, and ought not to be attended to. Evidence from persons in the trade is admissible to inform the Court of its nature, and of what is customary in it, and of anything requiring attention in the mode of conducting it, and of any particular dangers requiring precautions, and what precautions are required in order to protect a person carrying on the business from injury by a person leaving his service. But the reasonableness of a contract depends on its true construction and legal effect, and is consequently a question for the Court, and on such a question the opinion of witnesses is out of place.

But there is an interesting tendency to permit testimony on the ultimate issue (*R. v. Mason* (1911), 76 J.P. 184, C.C.A.; *R. v. Holmes*, [1953] 2 All E.R. 324; [1953] 1 W.L.R. 686). In *Director of Public Prosecutions* v. *A. and B.C. Chewing Gum, Ltd.*, [1968] 1 Q.B. 159, at p. 164, Lord Parker, C.J. said:

"I cannot help feeling that with the advance of science more and more inroads have been made into the old common law principles. Those who practice in the criminal courts see every day cases of experts being called on the question of diminished responsibility, and although technically the final question 'Do you think he was suffering from diminished responsibility?' is strictly inadmissible, it is allowed time and time again without any objection." (Cf. *R. v. Calder & Boyars Ltd*, [1969] 1 Q.B. 151; [1968] 3 All E.R. 644, C.A.; *R. v. Anderson*, [1972] 1 Q.B. 304; [1971] 3 All E.R. 1152, C.A.).

As the Criminal Law Revision Committee say (para. 268), "This is natural, because it would often be artificial for the witness to avoid, or pretend to avoid, giving his opinion on a matter merely because it is the ultimate issue in the case and because his opinion on the ultimate issue may be obvious from the opinions which he has already expressed." It may also be said that an expert is far more likely to be right on an ultimate issue requiring expertise to determine than a lay judge or jury. The same might be said of valuation cases. It is certainly true that opinion evidence on the ultimate issue is more freely allowed for experts than for non-experts, e.g. the issue of unfitness to drive through drink (*R. v. Davies*, [1962] 3 All E.R. 97; [1962] 1 W.L.R. 1111).

The law of expert opinion evidence involves a constant tension between orthodoxy and common sense in which the latter is beginning to triumph both at common law and by legislation. The process may be traced in the High Court of Australia in the retreat from *Clark v. Ryan* (1960), 103 C.L.R. 486. That case adopted strict tests of expertise, depending on qualifications rather than experience; of the division between fact and inferences; of the corresponding division between expert witness functions and jury functions. It may have been unduly influenced by the unsatisfactoriness of the "expert" testimony received. However that may be, later decisions have gone close to reversing it, though Menzies, J. remained an adherent. (See, e.g., *Weal v. Bottom* (1966), 40 A.L.J.R. 436.)

C. Statutory reform

The Civil Evidence Act 1972 amends the law in civil cases, and the Criminal Law Revision Committee in its 11th Report has made proposals to the same effect for criminal cases (paras. 266–71). Hearsay statements of opinion are admissible in the same way as hearsay elements of fact. A witness may give his opinion on the ultimate issue; but a non-expert may not be asked for his opinion on the ultimate issue, though he may give it in the form of a statement "made as a way of conveying relevant facts personally perceived by him".

A witness may give evidence of foreign law whether or not he is entitled to practise in the relevant jurisdiction. A finding by an English court on a question of foreign law shall be *prima facie* evidence of that law; this will avoid the need for the point to be proved in later proceedings. There is power for the judge to sit with assessors—experts appointed by the court other than the parties—in Admiralty actions, but no extension of this was recommended by the Law Reform Committee, Cmnd. 4889, paras. 14–16.

Reading

Law Reform Committee, 17th Report, Evidence of Opinion and Expert Evidence, 1970, Cmnd. 4489; Cowen and Carter, Chap. 5; Hammelmann (1947), 10 M.L.R. 32; Learned Hand, (1901), 15 Harv. L.Rev. 40; Maguire, pp. 23–31.

II EVIDENCE OF PRIOR FINDINGS IN LATER PROCEEDINGS

A. Persuasive presumptions

The rule stated in *Hollington* v. *Hewthorn & Co. Ltd.*, [1943] K.B. 587, [1943] 2 All E.R. 35, C.A. was that convictions and judgments are not evidence in later proceedings of the facts on which they were founded. The rule was based partly on the view that the later court should not be bound by the earlier's opinion. There were exceptions to the rule: the proof of convictions in cross-examination as to credit, judgments as evidence of public rights, judgments as facts in issue or relevant facts (*Ingram* v. *Ingram*, [1956] P. 390; [1956] 1 All E.R. 785). In certain respects it operated sensibly. Plainly acquittals in criminal cases should not be taken as evidence of innocence in later civil cases, because of the higher standards of proof in criminal cases. But for many reasons the rule was found unsatisfactory and has been much criticized (the most damaging salvoes were fired by the New Zealand Court of Appeal in *Jorgensen* v. *News Media (Auckland) Ltd.*, [1969] N.Z.L.R. 961 and by Cowen and Carter, Chap. 6).

The Civil Evidence Act 1968 provides:

11.—(1) In any civil proceedings the fact that a person has been convicted of an offence by or before any court in the United Kingdom or by a court-martial there or elsewhere shall (subject to subsection (3) below) be admissible in evidence for the purpose of proving, where to do so is relevant to any issue in those proceedings, that he committed that offence, whether he was so convicted upon a plea of guilty or otherwise and whether or not he is a party to the civil proceedings; but no conviction other than a subsisting one shall be admissible in evidence by virtue of this section.

(2) In any civil proceedings in which by virtue of this section a person is proved to have been convicted of an offence by or before any court in the United Kingdom or by a court-martial there or elsewhere—

(a) he shall be taken to have committed that offence unless the contrary is proved; and

(b) without prejudice to the reception of any other admissible evidence for the purpose of identifying the facts on which the conviction was based, the contents of any document which is admissible as evidence of the conviction, and the contents of the information, complaint, indictment or charge-sheet on which the person in question was convicted, shall be admissible in evidence for that purpose.

(3) Nothing in this section shall prejudice the operation of section 13 of this Act or any other enactment whereby a conviction or a finding of fact in any criminal proceedings is for the purposes of any other proceedings made conclusive evidence of any fact.

(4) Where in any civil proceedings the contents of any document are admissible in evidence by virtue of subsection (2) above, a copy of that document, or of the material part thereof, purporting to be certified or otherwise authenticated by or on behalf of the court or authority having custody of that document shall be admissible in evidence and shall be taken to be a true copy of that document or part unless the contrary is shown.

12.—(1) In any civil proceedings—

> (*a*) the fact that a person has been found guilty of adultery in any matrimonial proceedings; and
> (*b*) the fact that a person has been adjudged to be the father of a child in affiliation proceedings before any court in the United Kingdom,

shall (subject to subsection (3) below) be admissible in evidence for the purpose of proving, where to do so is relevant to any issue in those civil proceedings, that he committed the adultery to which the finding relates or, as the case may be, is (or was) the father of that child, whether or not he offered any defence to the allegation of adultery or paternity and whether or not he is a party to the civil proceedings; but no finding or adjudication other than a subsisting one shall be admissible in evidence by virtue of this section.

(2) In any civil proceedings in which by virtue of this section a person is proved to have been found guilty of adultery as mentioned in subsection (1) (*a*) above or to have been adjudged to be the father of a child as mentioned in subsection (1) (*b*) above—

> (*a*) he shall be taken to have committed the adultery to which the finding relates or, as the case may be, to be (or have been) the father of that child, unless the contrary is proved; and
> (*b*) without prejudice to the reception of any other admissible evidence for the purpose of identifying the facts on which the finding or adjudication was based, the contents of any document which was before the court, or which contains any pronouncement of the court, in the matrimonial or affiliation proceedings in question shall be admissible in evidence for that purpose.

(3) Nothing in this section shall prejudice the operation of any enactment whereby a finding of fact in any matrimonial or affiliation proceedings is for the purposes of any other proceedings made conclusive evidence of any fact.

(4) Subsection (4) of section 11 of this Act shall apply for the purposes of this section as if the reference to subsection (2) were a reference to subsection (2) of this section.

(5) In this section—

> "matrimonial proceedings" means any matrimonial cause in the High Court or county court in England and Wales or in the High Court in Northern Ireland, any consistorial action in Scotland, or any appeal arising out of any such cause or action;
> "affiliation proceedings" means, in relation to Scotland, any action of affiliation and aliment;

and in this subsctioen "consistorial action" does not include an action of aliment only between husband and wife raised in the Court of Session or an action of interim aliment raised in the sheriff court.

Notes

1. Under s. 11, the court in the second case will require proof of the prior conviction; it may be necessary to identify the convicted person with the person against whom that conduct is alleged, and a witness of the incident may be needed for this purpose. Under s. 12 the process of identification may be carried out by reference to the pleadings, decree and transcript of judgment in the earlier case: *Sutton* v. *Sutton*, [1969] 3 All E.R. 1348, [1970] 1 W.L.R. 183.

2. Where the defendant seeks to argue that a prior conviction or finding of adultery or paternity was wrong, the Court, in considering exercise of its discretion to admit the statements of witnesses in the prior proceedings under R.S.C. Ord. 38, r. 28 will be more likely to admit the statements at the instance of the plaintiff. This will avoid the plaintiff having to call the witnesses and the defendant being able to cross-examine them. If the defendant denies the relevance of the conviction, finding of adultery or paternity, the position may be different, for the burden of proof of relevancy lies on the plaintiff. The statements might only be admissible on terms that the witnesses are called at the second trial.

3. The presumption under s. 11 does not arise in the case of convictions subject to appeal: though they are "subsisting" it would be wrong for the civil court to act on a conviction which was liable to be quashed. The correct course is to adjourn the civil trial (*Re Raphael*, [1973] 3 All E.R. 19; [1973] 1 W.L.R. 998).

Stupple v. Royal Insurance Co., Ltd.
[1971] 1 Q.B. 50; [1970] 3 All E.R. 230, C.A.

The plaintiff was convicted of armed robbery of a bullion van owned by a bank. The main evidence against him was the finding of some stolen money in his flat. In these proceedings the plaintiff and his wife claimed the money from the insurance company who had paid off the bank. Stupple sought to show he was not guilty of the robbery. Paull, J. gave judgment for the defendants. The Court of Appeal dismissed the plaintiff's appeals.

LORD DENNING, M.R.: Mr. Hawser, for Mr. Stupple, submitted that the only effect of the Act was to shift the burden of proof. He said that, whereas previously the conviction was not admissible in evidence at all, now it was admissible in evidence, but the effect was simply to put on the man the burden of showing, on the balance of probabilities, that he was innocent. He claimed that Mr. Stupple had done so.

I do not accept Mr. Hawser's submission. I think that the conviction does not merely shift the burden of proof. It is a weighty piece of evidence of itself. For instance, if a man is convicted of careless driving on the evidence of a witness, but that witness dies before the civil action is heard (as in *Hollington* v. *F. Hewthorn & Co. Ltd.*, [1943] 1 K.B. 587, [1943] 2 All E.R. 35, C.A.), then the conviction itself tells in the scale in the civil action. It speaks as clearly as the witness himself would have done, had he lived. It does not merely reverse the burden of proof. If that was all it did, the defendant might well give his own evidence negativing want of care, and say: "I have discharged the burden. I have given my evidence and it has not been contradicted." In answer to the defendant's evidence, the plaintiff can say to him: "But your evidence is contradicted. It is contradicted by the very fact of your conviction."

In addition, Mr. Hawser sought, as far as he could, to minimize the effect of shifting the burden. In this, too, he did not succeed. The Act does not merely shift the evidential burden, as it is called. It shifts the *legal* burden of proof. I explained the difference long ago, in 1945, in an article in the Law Quarterly Review 61 L.Q.R. 379. Take a running-down case where a plaintiff claims damages for negligent driving by the defendant. If the defendant has not been convicted, the legal burden is on the plaintiff throughout. But if the defendant has been convicted of careless driving, the legal burden is shifted. It is on the defendant himself. At the end of the day, if the judge is left in doubt the defendant fails because the defendant has not discharged the legal burden which is upon him. The burden is, no doubt, the civil burden. He must show, on the balance of probabilities, that he was not negligent ... But he must show it nevertheless. Otherwise he loses by the very force of the conviction.

How can a man, who has been convicted in a criminal trial, prove his innocence in a subsequent civil action? He can, of course, call his previous witnesses and hope that the judge will believe them now, even if they were disbelieved before. He can also call any fresh witnesses whom he thinks will help his case. In addition, I think he can show the witnesses against him in the criminal trial were mistaken. For instance, in a traffic accident he could prove that a witness who claimed to have seen it was miles away and committed perjury. This would not, of course, prove his innocence directly, but it would do so indirectly by destroying the evidence on which he was convicted. So in this case Mr. Stupple could prove that Mr. Ford was mistaken.

In any case, what weight is to be given to the criminal conviction? This must depend on the circumstances. Take a plea of guilty. Sometimes a defendant pleads guilty in error: or in a minor offence he may plead guilty to save time and expense, or to avoid some embarrassing fact coming out. Afterwards, in the civil action, he can, I think, explain how he came to plead guilty.

Take next a case in the magistrates' court when a man is convicted and bound over or fined a trifling sum, but had a good ground of appeal, and did not exercise it because it was not worth while. Can he not explain this in a civil court? I think he can. He can offer any explanation in his effort to show that the conviction was erroneous; and it is for the judge at the civil trial to say how far he has succeeded.

In my opinion, therefore, the weight to be given to a previous conviction is essentially for the judge at the civil trial. Just as he has to evaluate the oral evidence of a witness, so he should evaluate the probative force of a conviction.

If the defendant should succeed in throwing doubt on the conviction, the plaintiff can rely, in answer, on the conviction itself; and he can supplement it, if he thinks it desirable, by producing (under the hearsay sections) the evidence given by the prosecution witnesses in the criminal trial, or, if he wishes, he can call them again. At the end of the civil case, the judge must ask himself whether the defendant has succeeded in overthrowing the conviction. If not, the conviction stands and proves the case.

Such being the principles, I turn to apply them to the present case. We have the conviction of Stupple for armed robbery. We have the circumstances from which it arises. They were:—(1) the fact that a bullion van was ambushed on September 27, 1963, and £87,000 in notes were stolen from it; (2) the fact that four days later Stupple was found in possession of nearly £1,000 of the stolen notes; (3) the fact that he gave no acceptable explanation of how he came by them; (4) the fact that he put forward an alibi which was not acceptable.

On those facts it was open to the jury, at the criminal trial, to find that he was guilty, not merely of receiving but of the robbery itself. I remember well that at one time it was thought that recent possession of stolen goods, without more, justified only a conviction for receiving and not for the theft itself. But Lord Goddard, C.J. scotched that fallacy in R. v. *Loughlin* (1951), 35 Cr. App. Rep. 69 and R. v. *Seymour*, [1954] 1 All E.R. 1006, [1954] 1 W.L.R. 678. It is open to the jury to convict of the theft itself. And in this regard recent possession of stolen *money* bears a stronger colour than recent possession of stolen *goods*. "Hot money" travels fast: but usually into the hands of those who have helped to get it. Phillimore, J. put it thus to a jury in a robbery case:

"When it comes to money, what is the natural view, the ordinary view, where somebody has got £100, the proceeds of a robbery, within a few hours of the robbery?

I suppose it is possible that a thief may have come to him and said: 'This is hot money, and if you give me £20 for it, I will give you £100.' But the natural thing would be, you may think, that a man who has got proceeds in the shape of money, when it is a money snatch, was probably involved in the actual robbery . . ." see R. v. *Fallon* (1963), 47 Cr. App. Rep. 160, at p. 165, C.C.A.

He may not have been present at the robbery itself but he may have been the brains behind it, he may have helped organize it, or he may have provided the tools with which to do it. It matters not which. The money gets to him as his share. In any of those cases he would be an accessory before the fact and as much guilty of robbery as if he had been at the scene itself: see R. v. *Bainbridge*, [1960] 1 Q.B. 129; [1959] 3 All E.R. 200, C.C.A.

I regard the conviction of Stupple in these circumstances, after a four and a half weeks trial, by a jury who were unanimous, as entitled to great weight in this civil action. It is not conclusive. It can be rebutted. But how does Stupple seek to prove that he was innocent of the robbery? He adduces some fresh material. In particular, evidence to show that Mr. Ford may have been mistaken in his identification of the notes; and evidence of the other convicted men, who say that Stupple was not present at the robbery and had nothing to do with it. Otherwise the evidence was little more than a repetition of the evidence at the criminal trial, plus Mr. Allpress and Mr. Cappuccini, who did not count for much. All of this fell far short of discharging the burden on Stupple to prove that he was innocent of the robbery. The conviction stands firm.

WINN, L.J. I do not myself think that it was any requisite, or, indeed, any proper, part of the function of the judge to consider what view he himself might have taken of the case had he sat on it either as juryman or judge: nor was it on a correct view relevant to his decision whether there had been an unsuccessful application to the Court of Appeal for leave to appeal against the conviction.

BUCKLEY, L.J. There remains . . . the problem of what weight, if any, should be accorded to the proved fact of conviction in deciding whether any other evidence adduced is sufficient to discharge the onus resting on B. In my judgment no weight is in this respect to be given to the mere fact of conviction.

If, as seems to be the case, I differ from Lord Denning, M.R. in this respect, I do so with the greatest diffidence.

The effect of the bare proof of conviction is, I think, spent in bringing section 11 (2) (*a*) into play. But very much weight may have to be given to such circumstances of the criminal proceedings as are brought out in the evidence in the civil action. Witnesses called in the civil proceedings may give different evidence from that which they gave in the criminal proceedings. Witnesses may be called in the civil proceedings who might have been but were not called in the criminal proceedings, or vice versa. The judge may feel that he should take account of the fact that the judge or jury in the criminal proceedings disbelieved a witness who is called in the civil proceedings, or that the defendant pleaded guilty or not guilty, as the case may be. Many examples could be suggested of ways in which what occurred or did not occur in the criminal proceedings may have a bearing on the judge's decision in the civil proceedings: but the judge's duty in the civil proceedings is still to decide that case on the evidence adduced to him. He is not concerned with the evidence in the criminal proceedings except so far as it is reproduced in the evidence called before him, or is made evidence in the civil proceedings under the Civil Evidence Act, 1968, section 2, or is established before him in cross-examination. He is not concerned with the propriety of the conviction except so far as his view of the evidence before him may lead him incidentally to the conclusion that the conviction was justified or is open to criticism; but even if it does so, this must be a consequence of his decision and cannot be a reason for it. The propriety or otherwise of the conviction is irrelevant to the steps leading to his decision.

It was suggested in argument that so to view section 11 would result in the issues in the criminal proceedings being retried in the civil proceedings, and that this would be contrary to an intention on the part of the legislature to avoid this sort of duplication.

I do not myself think that this would be the result in most cases, and I do not discern any such general intention in the section. If the fact of conviction were meant to carry some weight in determining whether the convicted man has successfully discharged the onus under section 11 (2) (*a*) of proving that he did not commit the offence, what weight should it carry? I cannot accept that this should depend on such considerations as, for instance, the status of the court which convicted, or whether the decision was a unanimous or a majority verdict of a jury. I cannot discover any measure of the weight which the unexplored fact of conviction should carry. Although the section has made proof of conviction admissible and has given proof of conviction a particular statutory effect under section 11 (2) (*a*), it remains, I think, as true today as before the Act that mere proof of conviction proves nothing relevant to the plaintiff's claim, and it clearly cannot be intended to shut out or, I think, to mitigate the effect of any evidence tending to show that the convicted person did not commit the offence. In my judgment, proof of conviction under this section gives rise to the statutory presumption laid down in section 11 (2) (*a*), which, like any other presumption, will give way to evidence establishing the contrary on the balance of probability, without itself affording any evidential weight to be taken into account in determining whether that onus has been discharged.

With respect to the judge, I think that he was unnecessarily alarmed at the possiblity of his reaching a different conclusion from the conclusion reached at the criminal trial, where both the burden of proof and the standard of proof differed from those in the action, and by the Court of Criminal Appeal.

Notes

1. The standard of proof is the balance of probabilities: see also *Sutton* v. *Sutton*, [1969] 3 All E.R. 1348, [1970] 1 W.L.R. 183.

2. In *Taylor* v. *Taylor*, [1970] 2 All E.R. 609; [1970] 1 W.L.R. 1148, C.A., Davies, L.J. appeared to share Lord Denning, M.R.'s view.

Zuckerman (1971), 87 L.Q.R. 21) has argued that both Lord Denning, M.R. and Buckley, L.J. were wrong. His view is that s. 11 permits the convicted person to prevent the presumption of guilt based on the conviction from applying by attacking the propriety of the conviction. Its propriety could be attacked either by introducing new evidence or by showing some defect in the proceedings or faulty reasoning. "A distinction should be drawn between proving that a conviction is not justifiable, on the one hand, and between positively proving that the convicted person did not, in reality, commit the offence for which he has been convicted, on the other hand. For proving that a conviction is unjustified it would be sufficient to show that the proceedings leading to it were improper, or that the conclusion of guilt does not follow from the evidence produced, or that the witnesses committed perjury. But this is to say nothing about the question of guilt or innocence" (p. 24). He concludes from this view that the conviction therefore has no intrinsic weight. But the premise, though arguable, seems false; for s. 11 (1) refers to "subsisting" convictions, not "justifiable" ones, and s. 11 (2) (*a*) refers to "a person . . . proved to have been convicted" not "properly convicted". Further, the conclusion does not seem to follow from the premise. The idea of the conviction having weight may be wrong as a matter of statutory interpretation but it is given some support by the common-sense view that jury decisions in favour of guilt are very likely to be correct. If a conviction were improper, it would have less weight; but it must be proved to be improper.

Question

What weight does the conviction have under s. 11?

B. A conclusive presumption

The Civil Evidence Act 1968, s. 13 provides:

13.—(1) In an action for libel or slander in which the question whether a person did or did not commit a criminal offence is relevant to an issue arising in the action, proof that, at the time when that issue falls to be determined, that person stands convicted of that offence shall be conclusive evidence that he committed that offence; and his conviction thereof shall be admissible in evidence accordingly.

(2) In any such action as aforesaid in which by virtue of this section a person is proved to have been convicted of an offence, the contents of any document which is admissible as evidence of the conviction, and the contents of the information, complaint, indictment or charge-sheet on which that person was convicted, shall, without prejudice to the reception of any other admissible evidence for the purpose of identifying the facts on which the conviction was based, be admissible in evidence for the purpose of identifying those facts.

(3) For the purposes of this section a person shall be taken to stand convicted of an offence if but only if there subsists against him a conviction of that offence by or before a court in the United Kingdom or by a court-martial there or elsewhere.

This prevents convicted persons using defamation actions in a gold-digging manner; such cases as *Hinds* v. *Sparks*, [1964] Crim. L.R. 717, cannot recur. It also prevents convicted persons proving that they were unjustly convicted, but there are other methods of doing that. It does not apply to acquittals, contrary to the recommendation of the Law Reform Committee's 15th Report, para. 29.

A statement of claim for defamation alleging that the plaintiff was not properly convicted may not be struck out as an abuse of the process of the Court if defamatory matter other than that relating to the convictions is alleged, even though the effect on the plaintiff's reputation of his convictions may be such as to destroy his chance of recovering more than nominal damages (*Levene* v. *Roxhan*, [1970] 3 All E.R. 683; [1970] 1 W.L.R. 1322 C.A.). Normally the statement of claim would be struck out to prevent the plaintiff using the terror of protracted litigation to get some settlement from the defendant even though he would not succeed at the final hearing.

Is anything left of *Hollington* v. *Hewthorn*? So far as the rule prevents proof of convictions in later criminal cases, it continues; the 1968 Act only applies to civil cases. Acquittals have no probative value in later civil cases. A finding of adultery in a magistrate's court would not be admissible under s. 12: see s. 12 (5). And a civil judgment other than in matrimonial or affiliation proceedings is inadmissible evidence in later civil proceedings: s. 11 applies only to convictions.

The 11th Report of the Criminal Law Revision Committee states that at common law *Hollington* v. *Hewthorn* applies in criminal cases. They recommend that the law be changed so that convictions of persons other than the accused should be made admissible in criminal proceedings as evidence of the convicted person's guilt. This will assist the prosecution where the accused's guilt depends on another person's having committed an offence, e.g. handling stolen goods. The accused will bear the burden of proving the convicted person's innocence on the balance of probabilities, which will be an exception to the normal regime for the burden of proof established by cl. 8 of the draft Criminal Evidence Bill. No equivalent to s. 13 of the Civil Evidence Act 1968 is proposed, for libel prosecutions are rare, are different from civil libel cases, are unlikely to be used by the convicted person as a means of reopening his case, and are unlikely to be permitted by the courts for this purpose (paras. 217–20).

Reading

15th Report of the Law Reform Committee, Cmnd. 3391.

PART FIVE

Witnesses

16

Competence, Compellability and Oaths

I COMPETENCE AND COMPELLABILITY

A. Civil cases

If a person is a competent witness, he may give evidence at the instance of the party calling him if he wishes. If he is a compellable witness, he must give evidence.

The general rule in civil cases is that all persons are competent and compellable witnesses.

To the general rule there are some exceptions. Persons who have sovereign or diplomatic immunity are competent but not compellable. Children or mentally diseased persons who understand the nature and consequences of an oath may give sworn evidence; if they cannot they are not competent or compellable.

B. Criminal cases

The rules are the same in criminal cases as in civil, except as follows.

The Children and Young Persons Act 1933, s. 38, provides that a child may give unsworn evidence even though it does not understand the duty of speaking the truth. The Criminal Law Revision Committee (para. 206) recommends that children aged fourteen or over should always give sworn evidence; other children should give unsworn evidence if the court considers that the child "is possessed of sufficient intelligence to justify the reception of his evidence and understands the importance of telling the truth in [the] proceedings".

The accused is not a competent prosecution witness, so that one co-accused cannot be called by the prosecution to give evidence against another (*R. v. Payne* (1872), L.R. 1. C.C.R. 349). The sole exception is in public nuisance cases under the Evidence Act 1877, where the accused is always competent and compellable for the prosecution. There are various courses open to the prosecution for rendering competent persons who might be caught by this rule. The prosecution might file a *nolle prosequi* (an undertaking by the Attorney-General to stay proceedings against an accused person, which is not binding but is in practice kept). A *particeps criminis* may simply not be prosecuted. A co-accused may be acquitted after a decision not to offer evidence against him. A co-accused may plead guilty, so that his case is no longer an issue for the jury and he can testify for the prosecution; in general he should be sentenced before testifying, so that he will not be tempted to give false evidence in the hope of a lighter sentence. The prosecution may have two accused tried separately so that one can testify at the other's trial. In *R. v. Pipe* (1967), 51 Cr. App. Rep. 17, C.A., it was held to be irregular to call the witness until proceedings against him had been completed.

The accused has been a competent witness for himself since the Criminal Evidence Act 1898, s. 1. Though an accused's out-of-court statements or unsworn evidence are not evidence against a co-accused, his sworn evidence is "evidence for all the purposes of the case including the purpose of being evidence against his co-defendant" (*R. v. Rudd* (1948), 32 Cr. App. Rep. 138, at p. 140). If one co-accused does give evidence against another, he exposes himself to cross-examination on his record under the Criminal Evidence Act 1898, s. 1 (f) (iii), by the co-accused and the prosecution. Further the prosecution may cross-examine a co-accused and his testimony under cross-examination is evidence against his co-accused. The judge has a discretion to limit the cross-examination, but opinions differ on its scope: cf. *R. v. Paul* [1920] 2 K.B. 183, C.C.A. and *Young v. H.M. Advocate*, 1932, J.C. 63, at p. 74, where it was said: "a prosecutor is not entitled, under the cloak of cross-examination, to examine an accused upon matters irrelevant to the question of his own guilt, and extraneous to any evidence he has given, in order to make him an additional witness against his co-accused." It may be difficult to draw the distinction at the time. (See Gooderson (1953), 11 C.L.J. 209; Heydon, [1971] Crim. L.R. 13, at pp. 14–20).

The accused is a competent but not compellable witness for his co-accused. An accused who has pleaded guilty is not a "person charged" and has therefore ceased to be a co-prisoner within the Criminal Evidence Act 1898; he is therefore competent and compellable for a co-accused (*R. v. Boal*, [1965] 1 Q.B. 402, at p. 415; [1964] 2 All E.R. 269, at p. 275, C.C.A.). An accused is also compellable at the instance of a co-accused under the Evidence Act 1877 in public nuisance cases.

The position of the accused's spouse is complicated.

She is not generally a competent or compellable prosecution witness. However, she is competent and compellable in cases falling within the Evidence Act 1877, which concerns prosecutions relating to public highways and other criminal proceedings instituted for the purpose of trying or enforcing civil rights. She is competent at common law on charges that violence against herself or injury to her liberty or health has been committed by the accused: this includes buggery (*R. v. Blanchard*, [1952] 1 All E.R. 114; cf. *R. v. Yeo*, [1951] 1 All E.R. 864 n.). At common law competence includes compellability (*R. v. Lapworth*, [1931] 1 K.B. 117, C.C.A.). The spouse is probably competent and compellable on a charge of treason (*Director of Public Prosecutions v. Blady*, [1912] 2 K.B. 89, at p. 92). The spouse is competent but not compellable (*Leach v. R.*, [1912] A.C. 305, H.L.) in a number of cases provided by statute. These include neglect to maintain or desertion of wife or family, bigamy, most sexual offences, offences against children, national insurance offences and any offence "with reference to" the spouse or committed against the spouse's property (see Theft Act 1968 s. 30 (3); *R. v. Noble*, [1974] 2 All E.R. 811; [1974] 1 W.L.R. 894).

Provided the accused consents, the wife is competent but not compellable as a witness for the co-accused (Criminal Evidence Act 1898, s. 1 (c)). The exceptions listed in the preceding paragraph apply here too: when they apply, the wife testifies without the accused's consent being necessary.

The accused's spouse is a competent, but not compellable witness for the accused. However, she is compellable in the cases covered by the Evidence Act 1877, on charges of violence or injury to the spouse's health or liberty and in treason. The prosecution is prohibited from commenting on the failure of the accused's spouse to testify (Criminal Evidence Act 1898, s. 1 (b)).

A divorced spouse is as incompetent to testify to matters occurring during the marriage as one who has not been divorced (R. v. *Algar*, [1954] 1 Q.B. 279; [1953] 2 All E.R. 1381, C.C.A.).

The Criminal Law Revision Committee have proposed: repealing the Evidence Act 1877; making the wife competent for the prosecution in all cases; making her compellable for the prosecution only in offences of sex and violence towards children under sixteen belonging to the same household as the accused; making her compellable for the accused in all cases; repealing the prohibition on comment by the prosecution on the failure of the accused's spouse to testify; repealing the need for the accused's consent to the wife testifying for a co-accused; making the wife compellable by a co-accused in all cases where she is compellable by the prosecution; and making spouses who are no longer married compellable in the same way as if they had never been married. The reasons for these proposals, which would simplify and render much more rational a very tangled area, are below.

Criminal Law Revision Committee, 11th Report
1972. Paras. 147–56

147. How far the wife of the accused should be competent and compellable for the prosecution, for the accused and for a co-accused is in these days essentially a question of balancing the desirability that all available evidence which might conduce to the right verdict should be before the court against (i) the objection on social grounds to disturbing marital harmony more than is absolutely necessary and (ii) what many regard as the harshness of compelling a wife to give evidence against her husband. Older objections, even to competence, based on the theoretical unity of the spouses or on the interest of the accused's wife in the outcome of the proceedings, and in particular on the likelihood that his wife will be biased in favour of the accused, can have no place in the decisions as to the extent of competence and compellability nowadays. But the question of the right balance between the considerations of policy mentioned is one on which different opinions are inevitably—and sometimes strongly—held. The arguments relate mostly to compellability for the prosecution but . . . not entirely so. The argument for more compellability for the prosecution is the straightforward one that, if it is left to the wife to choose whether to give evidence against her husband, the result may be that a dangerous criminal will go free. The argument to the contrary is that, if the wife is not willing to give the evidence, the state should not expose her to the pitiful clash between the duty to aid the prosecution by giving evidence, however unwillingly, and the natural duty to protect her husband whatever the circumstances. It has been argued strongly in support of this view that the law ought to recognize that, as between spouses, conviction and punishment may have consequences of the most serious economic and social kind for their future and that neither of them should in any circumstances be compelled, against his or her will, to contribute to bringing this about. It is also pointed out that there is at least a considerable likelihood that the result of more compellability will be either perjury or contempt by silence. The

CME—N

particular provisions which we recommend are intended (in addition to simplifying the law) as a compromise between these views.

148. We have no doubt that the wife should be made competent as a witness for the prosecution in all cases. If she is willing to give evidence, we think that the law would be showing excessive concern for the preservation of marital harmony if it were to say that she must not do so. There is only one argument of any substance which we can think of against making the wife competent in all cases. This is that, as we are not proposing to make her compellable for the prosecution in all cases, it would be a mistake to make her competent without being compellable. The argument is that compellability saves her from the embarrassing choice between her duty to the public to give the evidence and her loyalty to her husband. It is said that, if her husband is convicted on her evidence, she can answer his reproaches by saying that she could not have avoided giving the evidence. But we do not think that much can be made of this argument. It may perhaps have some force in the case of a minor offence, but in the case of a serious offence it seems to us too subtle to be likely to be advanced by the wife or appreciated by her husband. We therefore do not think that competence and compellability on behalf of the prosecution should coincide. Moreover the great majority of those whom we consulted agree that the wife should be competent in all cases; and there seems little if any reason why she should be comptent in the case of some offences and not in that of others. Therefore clause 9 (1) makes the wife competent for the prosecution (unless she is being tried jointly with her husband) in all cases.

149. How far the wife should be compellable for the prosecution is a more difficult question. We are in favour of maintaining the existing rule that she is compellable on a charge against her husband of violence to her. We considered an argument that in these days, when wives are so much less under the domination of their husbands, a wife should be made competent only, so that the choice whether to give evidence would be left to her. The result would no doubt be that in many cases it would depend on her whether there was a prosecution or not. We recognize the force of the argument that this would be right in policy, especially because the wife might think that by refraining from giving evidence she would have a better hope that her husband would treat her well in future. But on the whole we think that the public interest in the punishment of violence requires that compellability should remain. It is true that the wife may still refuse to give evidence even though compellable; but the fact that there is compellability should make it easier to counter the effect of possible intimidation by her husband and to persuade her to give evidence. In any event there does not seem to us to be any evidence that the present rule of compellability does any harm, so it seems safest to preserve it.

150. We in fact favour going further and making the wife compellable in the case of offences of violence towards children under the age of sixteen belonging to the same household as the accused. The seriousness of some of these cases seems to us to make it right to strengthen the hand of prosecuting authorities by making the wife compellable, especially as the wife may be in fear of her husband and therefore reluctant to give evidence unless she can be compelled to do so. In the case of violence towards the children compellability seems to us even more important than in cases of violence towards the wife herself. For although violence towards children may be easier to detect than violence towards the wife, it is likely to be harder to prove it in court against the spouse responsible, especially if the child is unable to give evidence. Another reason for giving the wife no choice whether to give evidence is that she may have been a party to the violence or at least have acquiesced in it, although it is not proposed to prosecute her. For similar reasons we think that the wife should be compellable on a charge of a sexual offence against a child under sixteen belonging to the accused's household. We considered an argument that this would be unnecessary because some of these offences may not be serious and it may be better for all those concerned, parent or child, that the offence should be overlooked than that it should be exposed in court and the offender punished, especially as the marriage might as a result be broken up. It has been argued that for this reason it is better to leave it to the wife to judge whether she should give the evidence. On the other hand some sexual offences may have worse effects than all but the most serious offences of violence. On balance we concluded that it was right to draw no distinction in relation to compellability between sexual offences and offences of violence.

151. Our decision to recommend limiting compellability in respect of offences against children under sixteen to children of the same household as the accused was taken after a good deal of consideration as to whether compellability should apply to offences against any child under that age even if unconnected with the spouses. This would have the desirable effect of giving further protection to children, and the proposed limitation would exclude some cases where compellability might be thought desirable in any event—for example, if the offence was against a neighbour's child visiting the spouses' house or against a nephew or niece of the offender. But on the whole we think it excessive to extend compellability so far and to apply it, for example, to a common assault on a boy of fifteen having nothing to do with the family. Short of this it would be difficult to draw the line satisfactorily without great complication. Besides, part of the reason for applying compellability to offences against children of the household is that offences committed in the family may be harder to prove if the unoffending spouse is free to choose whether to give evidence, where as in the case of an offence outside the family other evidence is likely to be available.

152. We do not think that the wife should be compellable for the prosecution in the case of offences other than those mentioned above. We need waste no time on the doubtful compellability under the present law in treason and abduction. It might be argued that the wife should be compellable in very serious cases such as murder and spying or perhaps in all serious cases of violence; but the law has never, except perhaps in treason, made the seriousness of an offence by itself a ground for compellability, and we do not favour doing so now. Therefore clause 9 (3) provides expressly that the wife shall not be compellable except in the cases (mentioned above) specified in the subsection.

153. We have no doubt that the accused's wife should be made compellable for him in all cases. It is surprising that she should not be so now. The only possible argument against this seems to be that the wife ought not to be put into a position where she may have to choose between incriminating her husband and committing perjury. But this argument seems to us quite unacceptable in these days and in any event to have very little weight compared with the argument that the husband might feel a great grievance if he could not compel his possibly estranged wife to give evidence for him. No doubt the accused would prefer, if possible, to avoid calling his wife, if she was reluctant to give evidence, for fear that her evidence would be unfavourable to him because of the compulsion; but if she could in fact give true evidence which would be in his favour, he would probably think that, however reluctant she was to give evidence, the truth would emerge if she did so. Clause 9 (2) makes the accused's wife compellable on his behalf in all cases (unless she is jointly charged and tried with him). This is contrary to proviso (a) to s. 30 (3) of the Theft Act 1968 in the cases to which s. 30 applies; but ... the corresponding provision in the draft Bill annexed to that report was included as an interim measure and pending our consideration of the general question of policy on this reference.

154. The prohibition in s. 1 (b) of the 1898 Act of comment by the prosecution on the failure of the accused's spouse to give evidence should in our opinion be lifted. The case for this is not so obvious as is that for lifting the prohibition of comment on failure of the accused himself to give evidence. In favour of lifting the former prohibition it is argued that, if the accused puts forward a defence which, if true, his wife would be able to corroborate by her evidence, and she is not called, it is natural that the prosecution should be able to comment on this just as they may on the failure of the defence to call somebody else who would have been able to corroborate his evidence if it was true. Also the prohibition is not one which one would expect to exist, especially in a reformed and modernized law of evidence, and there would be the danger that it might be forgotten and that a conviction might have to be quashed in consequence. Moreover in any event it seems right to continue to allow comment by the judge, because in a proper case the judge might think it right to advise the jury that in the circumstances they should not hold the failure against the accused although it might have seemed right to them to do so; and we are not in favour of prohibiting comment by the prosecution when comment by the judge is allowed. In favour of the present prohibition it is argued that inexperienced prosecutors might use their new freedom without sufficient discrimination (though the effect of this should be counteracted by the court). Another argument is that the real reason for the failure to call the wife might have been that the accused was afraid that, because she was being compelled to give evidence, she might deliberately be unhelpful to him. It was also pointed out that a practice might grow up of calling the wife unnecessarily in order to avoid adverse comment on failure to call her. We think that the arguments in favour of lifting the prohibition are the stronger. Clause 9 (6) provides accordingly.

155. We recommend that the wife of accused A should be competent to give evidence on behalf of his co-accused B whether or not A is willing. At present A's consent is necessary under s. 1 (*c*) of the 1898 Act. We do not think that A should have any right to prevent Mrs. A from giving evidence on behalf of B if she is willing. A more difficult question seems to be whether she should be compellable on behalf of B in all cases. In favour of making her so it is argued that the interests of justice require that B should be able to compel anybody not being tried with him to give evidence on his behalf and that the fact that the witness happens to be A's wife should make no difference even though the result might be her incriminating A. Against this it is argued that, since the prosecution cannot call Mrs. A as a witness in order that she may incriminate A, it is wrong that they should be able to compel her to incriminate him by cross-examination if she is called by B. We think that the argument against compellability is the stronger. We considered a possible compromise by which Mrs A. should be compellable on behalf of B only if A consented. Then A could give his consent if Mrs. A could help B's defence without incriminating A. But on the whole we are opposed to this, because it might be procedurally awkward, and embarrassing for A's defence, if it were necessary to ask him in court whether he consented to his wife's giving evidence, especially if he agreed at first that she should do so but changed his mind before the time came to call her because of evidence given meanwhile. But we propose that Mrs. A should be compellable on behalf of B in any case where she would be compellable on behalf of the prosecution even though the result might be that she would incriminate A. Here the argument mentioned above against making her compellable for B in general does not apply; and although the general arguments for compellability on behalf of the prosecution (in particular the possibility of intimidation by the witness's husband) do not apply either, it seems wrong to deny to the co-accused a right which is given to the prosecution. Clause 9 (3) provides accordingly.

156. We considered whether to provide that, if the spouses were judicially separated or were not cohabiting, they should be treated for the purpose of competence and compellability as if they were unmarried. There is clearly a case for this, at least where they are judicially separated, for the law recognizes that for many purposes this is equivalent to a divorce. But it is difficult to draw a line for this purpose without complicating the clause (and the other provisions in the draft Bill where a similar question arises). For if there is to be an exception from the general rule in cases of judicial separation, it would seem logical to apply the exception to cases where there is a matrimonial order under the Matrimonial Proceedings (Magistrates' Courts) Act 1960 (c. 48) containing a provision under s. 2 (1) (*a*) that the spouses should no longer be bound to cohabit, as this provision has the same effect as a judicial separation. But the inclusion or non-inclusion of such a provision in a matrimonial order depends very much on the circumstances of the case in question and may therefore be an inappropriate test for the purpose of compellability. Moreover, the parties often resume cohabitation even when there is a provision of the kind mentioned in the order; and, although this causes the order to cease to have effect under s. 7 (2) of the 1960 Act, the provision would involve the side issue whether the spouses had resumed cohabitation. Again, if such a provision as suggested were to be included, it would be necessary to consider whether it should apply to orders made by courts outside England. We considered providing that the spouses should be treated as unmarried for the purpose of compellability if there were in existence any judicial order relating to the marriage and they were not cohabiting or if, irrespective of whether there was such an order in existence, they were in fact not cohabiting. But again this would involve the question whether they were cohabiting. On the whole we think that it is unnecessary to complicate the clause by any provision for these purposes.

II OATH AND AFFIRMATION

A. General

In general oral evidence is given by witnesses who have sworn a religious oath to tell the truth. An oath administered in a form which a witness accepts without objection or declares to be binding on him is valid even though he in fact has no religious belief. A witness may sometimes "declare and affirm" that he will speak the truth if his religious beliefs forbid swearing judicial oaths, or he has no religious beliefs, or it is impracticable to administer an oath in the manner appropriate to the witness's religious belief. (See the Oaths Acts 1888, 1909 and 1961.)

Criminal Law Revision Committee
1972. Paras. 279–81

279. We considered whether to recommend that witnesses in criminal proceedings should no longer take the oath but should make a declaration in the appropriate form undertaking to tell the truth. The great majority are strongly of the opinion that this change should be made. Their reasons are given in paragraph 280. A minority are strongly opposed to the change for the reasons given in paragraph 281. The reason why we have not included a provision to this effect in the draft Bill is that the question is obviously an important one of general policy going beyond the criminal law. In particular it would hardly be thought right to abolish the oath in criminal proceedings only while keeping it in civil proceedings. We were informed that the Law Reform Committee decided to make no recommendation about the oath in civil proceedings because they regarded the question as a social rather than a legal one. We agree that this is a good reason for not making a recommendation, but we think it right to express our opinion for two reasons. First, assuming that it is in fact right to replace the oath, this is one of those kinds of reform which may never happen unless bodies in favour of making it express their opinion on appropriate occasions, and a general review of criminal evidence is in our opinion an appropriate occasion. Second, three of our recommendations directly concern the oath. These are the abolition of the accused's right to make an unsworn statement, the provision for calling on the accused to give evidence and the fixing of fourteen as the lowest age for giving evidence on oath. If the witness's oath is replaced by a declaration, the law of perjury would be applied to false evidence given after a declaration as it applies to false evidence on oath or affirmation; and it might be thought right that the declaration should include an acknowledgment by the witness of his liability to be prosecuted for perjury if he told an untruth in giving his evidence.

280. The reasons why the majority consider that the oath should be replaced by an undertaking to tell the truth are given below:

(i) The oath is a primitive institution which ought not to be preserved unless there is a good reason for preserving it. Its use has been traced back to times when man believed that a verbal formula could itself produce desired results, as in the case of the curse. Curses were operative magic performances, and the oath was a conditional self-curse. With the growth of religious belief it was thought that God was the executor of man's oath. He was believed to respond to its magic. The oath was an imprecation to heaven calling upon the supernatural powers to bring disaster on the speaker if he uttered falsehood. This was the basis of the Anglo-Saxon system of compurgation, which rested on the belief that the taking of a false oath brought automatic supernatural punishment. This view of the oath lasted for a surprisingly long time. A judicial expression of the traditional view of the oath is to be found as late as 1786 in *White* (Leach 430), where at a trial at the Old Bailey for horse-stealing a man was rejected as a witness because he "acknowledged that he had never learned the catechism, was altogether ignorant of the obligations of an oath, a future state of reward and punishment, the existence of another world, or what became of wicked people after death". The court said "that an oath is a religious asseveration, by which a person renounces the mercy, and imprecates the vengeance of heaven, if he do not speak the truth; and therefore a person who has no idea of the sanction which this appeal to heaven creates, ought not to be sworn as a witness in any court of justice". However, in 1817 Bentham attacked the traditional view with his usual vigour. He pointed to the "absurdity, than which nothing can be greater", of the supposition that "by man, over the Almighty, *power* should be exercised or exercisable; man the legislator and judge, God the sheriff and executioner; man the despot, God his slave" (*Swear Not at All*, pp. 3–4).

(ii) It might be said that, although the original purpose of the oath is no longer relevant, it nevertheless has value now in that it serves to call the attention of a witness who believes in God to the fact that, if he tells a lie, he will incur the divine displeasure. But if this is its justification, it is curious that it is only in the case of lying in certain official proceedings that the citizen has his attention called to his assumed belief in divine retribution. We do not draw attention to this possibility for any other purpose of law enforcement.

(iii) There have already been large inroads into the practice of taking the oath. Originally, non-believers were prevented from taking the oath because this would have involved practising a kind of deception on the state. Eventually, however, concern for the promotion of trade brought about a change of attitude and infidels were allowed to take the oath and so to testify in legal proceedings. The Oaths Act 1838 (c. 105) for the first time allowed persons other than Christians and Jews to be sworn in such form as the witness might declare to be binding on him. In effect this involved an abandonment for these persons of an inquiry into their beliefs as to the hereafter. Section 3 of the Oaths Act 1888 (c. 46) declares that, where an oath has been duly administered, "the fact that the person to whom the same was administered had, at the time of taking such oath, no religious belief, shall not for any purpose affect the validity of such oath". The same Act introduced the affirmation as an alternative to the oath. But affirmations were allowed only for those who declared that they had no religious belief or that their religious belief prevented them from taking an oath. Cases have occurred in which persons who could not bring themselves within either of these requirements, nor state what form of oath was binding on them, had their evidence rejected altogether. It is no longer considered a fatal objection to receiving the evidence of a child that he does not understand the nature of an oath. The last stage has been the Oaths Act 1961 (c. 21), which empowers the court to require a witness to affirm instead of taking the oath if it would not be "reasonably practicable without inconvenience or delay" to administer the oath to him in the way appropriate to his religion. In passing this Act Parliament recognized that there is nothing wrong in requiring a person to give evidence without being sworn even though he has a religious belief and it is not contrary to this to take an oath. It seems difficult, therefore, to see why this should not apply to all witnesses.

(iv) To many people it is incongruous that the Bible should be used, and the Deity invoked, in giving evidence of such matters as, for example, a common motoring offence. In evaluating evidence, little attention is paid to the mere fact that it has been given on oath. In any case it is probable that many witnesses who in fact have no religious belief take the oath because they do not wish to call attention to themselves or because they fear that the impact of their evidence will be weakened if they depart from the customary oath.

(v) If it is right to regard it as incongruous to require ordinary witnesses to take the oath, this is specially inappropriate in the case of the accused. The accused, if guilty (and sometimes even if not), is under an obvious temptation to lie. Our proposals involve putting pressure on him to give evidence, and it may seem to many excessive to require him to take a religious oath as well.

(vi) There would be a good case for keeping the oath if there were a real probability that it increases the amount of truth told. The majority do not think that it does this very much. For a person who has a firm religious belief, it is unlikely that taking the oath will act as any additional incentive to tell the truth. For a person without any religious belief, by hypothesis the oath can make no difference. There is value in having a witness "solemnly and sincerely" promise that he will tell the truth, and from this point of view the words of the affirmation are to many at least more impressive than the customary oath. The oath has not prevented an enormous amount of perjury in the courts. A witness who wishes to lie and who feels that the oath may be an impediment can easily say that taking an oath is contrary to his religious belief.

We need hardly say that we have no wish to offend any religious feelings, nor do we see why anything said above should do so. Moreover, the replacement of the oath by some form of declaration has been advocated several times recently in legal periodicals and in two of the observations sent to us, and the arguments in the periodicals do not seem to have provoked any arguments to the contrary. In 1968 the Magistrates' Association at their annual meeting voted by a narrow majority (140–130) that the oath sworn in magistrates' courts should be replaced by a simple promise to tell the truth, *The Times*, 12 October 1968. In July 1970 the Memorandum of the Council of the Law Society on Oaths, Affirmations and Statutory Declarations recommended that "the present forms of oaths, affirmations and statutory declarations should be abolished and replaced by a single, non-religious form of promise or declaration for use on all occasions where formality is required". In any event, whether the oath is kept or replaced, we hope that steps will be taken to ensure greater solemnity when a witness swears or makes the declaration. In our opinion it may be desirable that the oath or declaration should always be administered by the judge or presiding magistrate, as is the practice in Scotland. If it is decided to abolish the witness's oath, the question of the jurors' oath will require consideration; for if the jurors took the oath and the witnesses made a declaration, this might suggest that the witnesses' duty was less important than the jurors'. We express no opinion as to the abolition or preservation of other oaths.

281. The minority are strongly opposed to the replacement of the witness's oath by a declaration. They recognize that there is force in the arguments for this as set out in the previous paragraph; but they do not find any of them convincing. In their opinion there are many persons to whom the oath, administered properly and in complete silence, serves to bring home most strongly the solemnity of their obligation to tell the truth and to be careful about what they say in giving their evidence.

B. The accused's right to make an unsworn statement

Before the accused was allowed legal representation or the right to testify on oath, he was given the right to make an unsworn statement. The Criminal Evidence Act 1898 granted the right to testify on oath to the accused but rather anomalously preserved the right to make an unsworn statement (s. 1 (h)). The trier of fact may treat the statement as evidence (R. v. Frost (1964), 48 Cr. App. Rep. 284, C.C.A.). Because it is not open to cross-examination, it will not often be very weighty evidence, but it confers the advantage of avoiding cross-examination on the accused's record under the Criminal Evidence Act 1898, s. 1 (f). The Criminal Law Revision Committee strongly recommended abolition of the right (paras. 104–5). It regarded the immunity from cross-examination as an unfair advantage. "The present rule has another disadvantage in that, if the accused is unrepresented, the court should explain to him that he has the choice between giving evidence on oath or unsworn and the differences between these courses. Since in the great majority of cases the accused, if he intends to give evidence, intends to do so on oath, the explanation is mostly unnecessary anyhow; and it has the practical disadvantage in the case of an accused who is at all nervous, that just at the time when he has to make his defence and should be concentrating on this, he may be put off by the legal technicality of an invitation to consider doing something which he had no thought of doing." He will continue to have the right to address the court if he is unrepresented.

The right to make an unsworn statement does little harm, but it is hard to discover any good in it. It is therefore strange that its proposed abolition was one of the most strongly attacked parts of the Criminal Law Revision Committee's 11th Report.

17

Private Privilege

Privilege is said to exist when one is not obliged to answer particular questions or produce particular documents. It is distinct from the non-competence or non-compellability of a witness: these phrases refer to the incapacity of a witness or his right to refuse to testify at all.

Private privilege may be waived by its possessor; the matters it relates to may be proved by other evidence; no adverse inference should be drawn from a claim to it; and the wrongful refusal of a claim by a witness is not a ground of appeal by the party who called that witness, for the privilege is personal to the witness.

The modern tendency is to restrict existing privileges and only reluctantly to create new ones. The privilege against self-incrimination (Chap. 6, *ante*) was recently narrowed by the Civil Evidence Act 1968, a statute which abolished several other privileges in civil cases. There are in fact only two private privileges of major importance.

I LEGAL PROFESSIONAL PRIVILEGE

Communications between a lawyer and his client made in confidence for the purpose of pending litigation or for the purpose of obtaining professional advice may not be disclosed without the client's consent. The privilege cannot be waived by the lawyer. The privilege also extends to communications between lawyer or client and a third party for the purposes of litigation.

A. Rationale

The privilege is usually said to exist for the following reasons. Human affairs and the legal rules governing them are complex. Men are unequal in wealth, power, intelligence and capacity to handle their problems. To remove this inequality and to permit disputes to be resolved in accordance with the strength of the parties' cases, lawyers are necessary, and the privilege is required to encourage resort to them and to ensure that *all* the facts will be put before them, not merely those the client thinks favour him. If lawyers are only told some of the facts, clients will be advised that their cases are better than they actually are, and will litigate instead of compromising and settling. Lawyer-client relations would be full of "reserve and dissimulation, uneasiness, and suspicion and fear" without the privilege; the confidant might at any time have to betray confidences. (See *Pearse* v. *Pearse* (1846), 1 De

393

G. & Sm. 12, at p. 28, *per* Knight Bruce V.-C. See also *Annesley* v. *Earl of Anglesea* (1743) 17 State Tr. 1139, at pp. 1225–40; *Greenough* v. *Gaskell* (1833), 1 My. & K. 98, at p. 103; [1824–34] All E.R. Rep. 767, at p. 770; *Anderson* v. *Bank of British Columbia* (1876) 2 Ch.D. 644, at p. 649, and C., "On the Production of Cases prepared for the Opinion of Counsel" (1837), 17 Law Magazine 51, at p. 68). Bentham, consistently with his general policy of removing obstacles to the discovery of truth, used two main arguments against the privilege. One was that its abolition would enhance professional standards by removing any power to hide the accused's guilt. But professional standards are surely not influenced so much by the law of evidence as by prevailing moral standards and the operation of internal professional discipline and criminal punishment. Secondly, Bentham argued that if abolition meant that clients repose less confidence in their lawyers "wherein will consist the mischief? The man by the supposition is guilty; if not, by the supposition there is nothing to betray" Book IX, Pt. IV, c. 5; and see *Flight* v. *Robinson* (1844) 8 Beav. 22, at p. 36. But both sides in civil cases will tend to have strong points and weak: "a person who has a partly good cause would often be deterred from consultation by virtue of the bad part or the part that might possibly (to his notion) be bad." (Wigmore, para. 2291). Further, even if in a criminal case the client is wholly guilty, it is wrong to allow the prosecution to use his admissions to his lawyer, for the police might come to rely as far as possible on this kind of evidence to the exclusion of independently obtained evidence. If there were no privilege, the accused would stay silent: the prosecution would gain nothing and the accused would lose in that what he thinks incriminating may not be so in fact. Another argument sometimes put against the privilege is that it increases unfounded claims: "It is common knowledge in the profession that a potential litigant will consult lawyer A and ascertain that he has no cause of action because a certain fact was X instead of Y, and that the same litigant later brings action through lawyer B when he has assumed that the certain fact was Y and not X" (Morgan, Foreword, *American Law Institute Model Code of Evidence* (1942), p. 27). But if the danger exists at all, it is outweighed by the likelihood of bad advice being given because of lack of information. And in civil cases the parties are compellable; in criminal cases the accused usually enters the box. Clients will avoid deliberate lying which if revealed in cross-examination may cause defeat and result in a perjury prosecution. For similar reasons the privilege causes very little harm in modern conditions, since so far as the client is skilfully cross-examined and does not lie, he will have to tell the court anything relevant he told his lawyer.

B. Scope

Wheeler *v.* Le Marchant
(1881), 17 Ch.D. 675

This was an action for specific performance of a building contract to lease building land from the defendants. The defendants claimed privilege for letters passing between their solicitors and their surveyors. The Court of Appeal refused to grant privilege except so far as they were prepared after the dispute arose and with reference to existing or contemplated litigation.

JESSEL, M.R.: . . . What they contended for was that documents communicated to the solicitors of the Defendants by third parties, though not communicated by such third parties as agents of the clients seeking advice, should be protected, because those documents contained information required or asked for by the solicitors, for the purpose of enabling them the better to advise the clients. The cases, no doubt, establish that such documents are protected where they have come into existence after litigation commenced or in contemplation, and when they have been made with a view to such litigation, either for the purpose of obtaining advice as to such litigation, or of obtaining evidence to be used in such litigation, or of obtaining information which might lead to the obtaining of such evidence, but it has never hitherto been decided that documents are protected merely because they are produced by a third person in answer to an inquiry made by the solicitor. It does not appear to me to be necessary, either as a result of the principle which regulates this privilege or for the convenience of mankind, so to extend the rule. In the first place, the principle protecting confidential communications is of a very limited character. It does not protect all confidential communications which a man must necessarily make in order to obtain advice, even when needed for the protection of his life, or of his honour, or of his fortune. There are many communications which, though absolutely necessary because without them the ordinary business of life cannot be carried on, still are not privileged. The communications made to a medical man whose advice is sought by a patient with respect to the probable origin of the disease as to which he is consulted, and which must necessarily be made in order to enable the medical man to advise or to prescribe for the patient, are not protected. Communications made to a priest in the confessional on matters perhaps considered by the penitent to be more important even than his life or his fortune, are not protected. Communications made to a friend with respect to matters of the most delicate nature, on which advice is sought with respect to a man's honour or reputation, are not protected. Therefore it must not be supposed that there is any principle which says that every confidential communication which it is necessary to make in order to carry on the ordinary business of life is protected. The protection is of a very limited character, and in this country is restricted to the obtaining the assistance of lawyers, as regards the conduct of litigation or the rights to property. It has never gone beyond the obtaining legal advice and assistance, and all things reasonably necessary in the shape of communication to the legal advisers are proteted from production or discovery in order that that legal advice may be obtained safely and sufficiently.

Now, keeping that in view, what has been done is this: The actual communication to the solicitor by the client is of course protected, and it is equally protected whether it is made by the client in person or is made by an agent on behalf of the client, and whether it is made to the solicitor in person or to a clerk or subordinate of the solicitor who acts in his place and under his direction. Again, the evidence obtained by the solicitor, or by his direction, or at his instance, even if obtained by the client, is protected if obtained after litigation has been commenced or threatened, or with a view to the defence or prosecution of such litigation. So, again, a communication with a solicitor for the purpose of obtaining legal advice is protected though it relates to a dealing which is not the subject of litigation, provided it be a communication made to the solicitor in that character and for that purpose. But what we are asked to protect here is this. The solicitor, being consulted in a matter as to which no dispute has arisen, thinks he would like to know some further facts before giving his advice, and applies to a surveyor to tell him what the state of a given property is, and it is said that the information given ought to be protected because it is desired or required by the solicitor in order to enable him the better to give legal advice. It appears to me that to give such protection would not only extend the rule beyond what has been previously laid down, but beyond what necessity warrants. The idea that documents like these require protection has been started, if I may say so, for the first time to-day, and I think the best proof that the necessities of mankind have not been supposed to require this protection is that it has never heretofore been asked. It seems to me we ought not to carry the rule any further than it has been carried. It is a rule established and maintained solely for the purpose of enabling a man to obtain legal advice with safety. That rule does not, in my opinion, require to be carried further.

[BRETT and COTTON, L.JJ. delivered concurring judgments.]

O'Rourke v. Darbishire
[1920] A.C. 581; [1920] All E.R. Rep. 1, H.L.

LORD SUMNER: No one doubts that the claim for professional privilege does not apply to documents which have been brought into existence in the course of or in furtherance of a fraud to which both solicitor and client are parties. To consult a solicitor about an intended course of action, in order to be advised whether it is legitimate or not, or to lay before a solicitor the facts relating to a charge of fraud, actually made or anticipated, and make a clean breast of it with the object of being advised about the best way in which to meet it, is a very different thing from consulting him in order to learn how to plan, execute, or stifle an actual fraud. No one doubts again that you can neither try out the issue in the action on a mere interlocutory pro-ceeding, nor require the claimant to carry the issue raised to a successful trial before he can obtain production of documents which are only relevant to that issue and only sought for the purpose of proving it. I am, however, sure that it is equally clear in principle that no mere allegation of a fraud, even though made in the most approved form of pleading, will suffice in itself to overcome a claim of professional privilege, properly formulated.

Butler v. Board of Trade
[1971] Ch. 680; [1970] 3 All E.R. 593

The defendants began a prosecution against the plaintiff. The plaintiff claimed privilege for a copy of a letter written by his solicitor to him. The plaintiff's argument that any privilege was lost because the letter was in preparation for a criminal design by the plaintiff was rejected by Goff, J.

GOFF, J.: It is submitted on behalf of the defendants, however, that as the plaintiff is charged with criminal offences, and the letter is relevant thereto, which it undoubtedly is, the privilege does not apply. Now, it is clear that a sufficient charge of crime or fraud will in certain circumstances destroy the privilege, but there is a dispute between the parties about what it is necessary to show for that purpose. The defendants say that relevance is alone sufficient, and the position is in effect so stated in the Supreme Court Practice 1970, Vol. I, p. 377, para. 24/5/9. The plaintiff submits, however, that it is necessary to go further and to show that the professional advice was in furtherance of the crime or fraud, as is said in Phipson on Evidence, 11th Edn., p. 251, para. 590, and 36 Halsbury's Laws (3rd Edn.) p. 51, para. 72, or in preparation for it: see *R. v. Cox and Railton* (1884), 14 Q.B.D. 153, at p. 165; [1881–5] All E.R. Rep. 68, at p. 70; see *per* the Earl of Halsbury, L.C. in *Bullivant* v. *A.-G. for Victoria* [1901] A.C. 196, P.C. at p. 201; [1900–3] All E.R. Rep. 812, at p. 814; and see also 10 Halsbury's Laws (3rd Edn.) p. 479, para. 877.

As questions of this nature have to be determined on a *prima facie* basis, often without seeing the documents or knowing what was orally communicated, the two tests will, I think, in many and probably most cases be found in practice to produce the same result because in most cases of relevance the proper *prima facie* inference will be that the communication was made in preparation for or in furtherance or as part of the criminal or fraudulent purpose. However, the two tests are not the same and in the present case cannot, I think, possibly produce the same result. On the information before me, the letter was nothing but a warning volunteered, no doubt wisely, but still volunteered by the solicitor that if her client did not take care he might incur serious consequences, which she described. I cannot regard that on any showing as being in preparation for, or in furtherance or as part of, any criminal designs on the part of the plaintiff. I must, therefore, decide which test is correct, and I prefer the narrower view.

First, that appears to me to be the true effect of R. v. *Cox and Railton*. Counsel for the defendants argued to the contrary and he relied on the passage where Stephen, J. said (1884), 14 Q.B.D. 153, at p. 165; [1881–5] All E.R. Rep. 68, at p. 70:

> "We must take it, after the verdict of the jury, that so far as the two defendants, Railton and Cox, were concerned, their communication with Mr. Goodman was a step preparatory to the commission of a criminal offence, namely, a conspiracy to defraud."

That passage, he argues, cannot mean that the criminal trial disclosed that they went to see Mr. Goodman with an already-formed criminal intention, for that the verdict did not show, and, therefore, the true explanation must be, that the evidence was held rightly admitted because it was relevant to the criminal offence subsequently proved to have been committed. I do not so read it. The court by then knew that a criminal offence had been committed and the evidence which had been admitted showed that criminal purpose existed in the minds of Cox and Railton when they saw Mr. Goodman, since ((1884), 14 Q.B.D. 153, at p. 156; (1881–5) All E.R. Rep. 68, at p. 70): "It was expressly arranged that the partnership should be kept secret". As I see it, the court having to decide *ex post facto* whether the evidence had been rightly admitted, inferred that the advice was preparatory to the crime proved, and it will be observed that immediately after the passage in question Stephen, J. went on to say ((1884), 14 Q.B.D. 153, at p. 165; [1881–5] All E.R. Rep. 68, at p. 70):

> "The question, therefore is, whether, if a client applies to a legal adviser for advice intended to facilitate or to guide the client in the commission of a crime or fraud, the legal adviser being ignorant of the purpose for which his advice is wanted, the communication between the two is privileged? We expressed our opinion at the end of the argument that no such privilege existed."

If relevance alone is the test, it follows that privilege could never be claimed in cases of crime or fraud, except as to communications in connexion with the defence. That, in my judgment, is too narrow, and inconsistent with the whole tenor of R. v. *Cox and Railton*. Stephen, J. said that they would first state the principle on which the present case must be decided, then set out in the forefront the nature of the privilege itself and then draw the exception to it in these terms ((1884), 14 Q.B.D. 153, at pp. 166–7; [1881–5] All E.R. Rep. 68, at p. 76):

> "The reason on which the rule is said to rest cannot include the case of communications, criminal in themselves, or intended to further any criminal purpose, for the protection of such communications cannot possibly be otherwise than injurious to the interests of justice, and to those of the administration of justice. Nor do such communications fall within the terms of the rule. A communication in furtherance of a criminal purpose does not 'come into the ordinary scope of professional employment'."

Further, the relevance test is in my judgment negatived by the conclusions of the court (*ibid.*) and in particular the words:

> "We are far from saying that the question whether the advice was taken before or after the offence will always be decisive as to the admissibility of such evidence."

Secondly, in my judgment all the members of the House of Lords in *O'Rourke* v. *Darbishire*, [1920] A.C. 581, H.L.; [1920] All E.R. Rep. 1 with the possible exception of Lord Wrenbury, clearly adopted the narrower test, and that is binding on me. Counsel for the defendants relied very strongly on the decision of Kekewich, J. in *Williams* v. *Quebrada Railway, Land and Copper Co.* That learned judge appears [1895] 2 Ch. 751, at p. 756, to have construed R. v. *Cox and Railton* as laying down the relevance test, but if he did I respectfully beg leave to disagree, and in any case this was long before *O'Rourke* v. *Darbishire*. The actual decision can, I think, be supported on either test since where, as also in R. v. *Cox and Railton*, the alleged criminal or fraudulent purpose consists in endeavouring to defeat another's rights by unlawful means, advice as to the nature and extent of those rights and the limits of one's own lawful powers may well be regarded when considered on a *prima facie* basis as at least in preparation for that unlawful purpose.

Counsel for the defendants also relied on the Canadian cases of *Re Goodman and Carr and Minister of National Revenue* (1968), 70 D.L.R. (2d) 670 and *Re Milner* (1968, 70 D.L.R. (2d) 429. *Re Goodman* does not really assist because the court there found that there was no *prima facie* case of fraud, but it is to be noted that the judge cited passages which support the limited view of the exception, and in particular (1968), 70 D.L.R. (2d) 670, at p. 673 the headnote in R. v. *Cox and Railton*. In *Re Milner* it was assumed that relevance was the basis of the exception, but there was no argument or decision as to the ambit of the exception. The only question before the court was whether there was a sufficient *prima facie* case of fraud. I do not, therefore, find anything in these cases to deflect me from the decision which I have otherwise reached. In my judgment, therefore, on the limited facts before me, the original letter is privileged and the copy confidential.

It thus becomes unnecessary for me to decide the further question which was canvassed, whether in any case the charge of crime is for the purposes of the question in this special case sufficiently averred, in accordance with the principles laid down by Lord Halsbury, L.C. in *Bullivant's* case [1901] A.C. 196, at p. 201; [1900–3] All E.R. Rep. 812, at p. 814, P.C. and by Lord Sumner in *O'Rourke* v. *Darbishire*, [1920] A.C. 581, at pp. 613–14; [1920] All E.R. Rep. 1, at p. 11, H.L. although in my view the answer would be in the negative on the assumed facts because I think that it comes back to the original question. If one rejects the bare relevance test, as I have done, then what has to be shown *prima facie* is not merely that there is a *bona fide* and reasonably tenable charge of crime or fraud but a *prima facie* case that the communications in question were made in preparation for or in furtherance or as part of it. It was then argued that the copy letter having left the care of the solicitor and come into the hands of the defendants, so that one is no longer in the realm of privilege but of confidence, there can be no equity which the plaintiff can set up because of the principle succinctly summed up by Wood V.-C. in *Gartside* v. *Outram* (1856), 26 L.-J. Ch. 113, at p. 114 in the phrase, "there is no confidence as to the disclosure of iniquity". Lord Denning, M.R. cited that in *Initial Services Ltd.* v. *Putterill* [1968] 1 Q.B. 396, at p. 405; [1967] 13 All E.R. 145, at p. 148, C.A. and then said:

> "In *Weld-Blundell* v. *Stephens* [1919] 1 K.B. 520, at p. 527, Bankes, L.J. rather suggested that the exception was limited to the proposed or contemplated commission of a crime or a civil wrong; but I should have thought that that was too limited. The exception should extend to crimes, frauds and misdeeds, both those actually committed as well as those in contemplation, provided always—and this is essential—that the disclosure is justified in the public interest. The reason is because 'no private obligations can dispense with that universal one which lies on every member of the society to discover every design which may be formed, contrary to the laws of the society, to destroy the public welfare'. See *Annesley* v. *Earl of Anglesea* (1743), 17 State Tr. 1139, at pp. 1223–46. The disclosure must, I should think, be to one who has a proper interest to receive the information."

In my judgment, however, that does not apply to the present case. At the trial, the defendants may or may not prove the criminal offences with which the plaintiff is charged, and the letter if received in evidence may or may not help them to do so; but although, if more were known of the facts, one might find some communication falling within this exception, I cannot see in this bare warning any element of vice which the umbrella of confidence may not in general cover.

Notes

1. The client's privilege survives any particular piece of litigation; it comes on to his successors in title (*Minet* v. *Morgan* (1873), 8 Ch. App. 361; *Calcraft* v. *Guest*, [1898] 1 Q.B. 759; [1895–9] All E.R. Rep. 346, C.A.). There may be problems over divided title and compulsory acquisition.

2. The privilege is not to be destroyed by counsel simply because he thinks his client has no case (*Tuckiar* v. *R.* (1934), 52 C.L.R. 335).

3. The privilege applies even in respect of proceedings contemplated in a foreign court (*Re Duncan, Garfield and Fay* [1968] P. 306; [1968] 2 All E.R. 395).

4. The privilege only protects communications made, not facts learnt, e.g. the client's handwriting.

5. The communication must be confidential: if it arises in the presence of strangers it will not be protected.

6. The privilege applies as between the heads of a government department and their internal legal advisers: *Alfred Crompton Amusement Machines, Ltd.* v. *Customs and Excise Commissioners (No. 2)*, [1974] A.C. 405; [1973] 2 All E.R. 1169, H.L. The same is doubtless true of private business.

7. The privilege will not arise unless the lawyer and client either are in fact in a lawyer-client relationship or contemplate it.

8. A common example of legal professional privilege is reports made to company directors which are to be placed before the company's solicitor. However, the client must contemplate obtaining legal advice, so that reports aimed merely at preventing accidents in future are not privileged (*Longthorn* v. *British Transport Commission*, [1959] 2 All E.R. 32; [1959] 1 W.L.R. 530). The obtaining of legal advice need not be the sole or primary aim of the communication (*Birmingham and Midland Motor Omnibus Co., Ltd.* v. *London and North Western Rail. Co.*, [1913] 3 K.B. 850, C.A.; *Seabrook* v. *British Transport Commission*, [1959] 2 All E.R. 15; [1959] 1 W.L.R. 509, see also *Di Pietrantonio* v. *Austin Hospital (Heidelburg)* [1958] V.R. 325).

9. The privilege belongs to the client; it does not protect the maker of any report to the client or the lawyer if the client does not object to production (*Schneider* v. *Leigh*, [1955] 2 Q.B. 195; [1955] 2 All E.R. 173, C.A.).

10. The reason for the exception as to advice sought to enable the commission of a crime or fraud was stated by Stephen J. thus. If the privilege applied in these circumstances, "the result would be that a man intending to commit treason or murder might safely take legal advice for the purpose of enabling himself to do so with impunity, and that the solicitor to whom the application was made would not be at liberty to give information against his client for the purpose of frustrating his criminal purpose. Consequences so monstrous reduce to an absurdity any principle or rule in which they are involved" (*R.* v. *Cox and Railton* (1884), 14 Q.B.D. 153, at pp. 165–6; [1881–5] All E.R. Rep. 68, at pp. 70–1).

11. No legal professional privilege attaches to documents which would

help further the defence of an accused person: *R. v. Barton*, [1972] 2 All E.R.
1192; [1973] 1 W.L.R. 115.

C. Loss of the privilege

Calcraft *v.* Guest
[1898] 1 Q.B. 759; [1895–9] All E.R. Rep. 346, C.A.

Certain documents in respect of which the plaintiff could claim legal professional
privilege by accident fell into the defendant's hands. The Court of Appeal held the
defendant entitled to give secondary evidence of the documents.

LINDLEY, M.R.: It appears that the appellant has obtained copies of some of these
documents, and is in a position to give secondary evidence of them; and the question is
whether he is entitled to do that. That appears to me to be covered by the authority of
Lloyd v. *Mostyn* (1842), 10 M. & W. 478. . . . That was an action on a bond which was
said to be privileged from production on the ground of its having come into the hands
of the solicitor in confidence. . . . The plaintiff then tendered in evidence a copy of the
bond . . . Parke, B. said: ". . . Where an attorney entrusted confidentially with a document communicates the contents of it, or suffers another to take a copy, surely the
secondary evidence so obtained may be produced. Suppose the instrument were even
stolen, and a correct copy taken, would it not be reasonable to admit it?" The matter
dropped there; but the other members of the Court (Lord Abinger, Gurney, B., and
Rolfe, B.) all concurred in that, which I take it is a distinct authority that secondary
evidence in a case of this kind may be received.

[RIGBY and VAUGHAN WILLIAMS, J.J. concurred.]

Lord Ashburton *v.* Pape
[1913] 2 Ch. 469, C.A.

The defendant improperly obtained certain letters written by the plaintiff to his
solicitor. The Court of Appeal upheld the grant of an injunction to restrain the
defendant from disclosing certain privileged letters or making copies of them, and an
exception to the injunction inserted by Neville, J. permitting use of the documents in
certain pending bankruptcy proceedings.

COZENS-HARDY, M.R.: Neville, J. . . . made an order that Pape do forthwith hand over
to Nocton all original letters from the plaintiff to Nocton or his firm in Pape's possession
or control. Pape naturally said "I do not object to that; I will deliver up the originals,
because I have got copies." Then the order goes on in this way: "And it is ordered
that the defendants Edward James Pape, Charles William Langford and Thomas
Howard Redfern their servants and agents be restrained until judgment or further
order from publishing or making use of any of the copies of such letters or any information contained therein except for the purpose of the pending proceedings in
the defendant Edward James Pape's bankruptcy and subject to the direction of the
Bankruptcy Court." Now, the question is raised that that exception is wrong, and that
the injunction ought to go to the full extent until the trial of the action, namely, from
publishing or making use of any of the copies of letters or information contained therein. In my opinion the contention of the appellant is right. Nocton's clerk, of course,
had no right whatever to hand over the originals to Pape nor to make any copies of
any sort or kind, and Pape, who was really a party to this transaction, was quite clearly
under the same obligation, and liable to precisely the same jurisdiction as has long been
exercised by this Court. I do not go back to *Morison* v. *Moat* (1851), 9 Hare 241,
which, although not the first, is probably the leading authority on the point, but one
passage from *Lamb* v. *Evans*, [1893] 1 Ch. 218; at p. 235, C.A., in a judgment of Kay,
L.J., states briefly and, I think, with perfect accuracy what the true law is upon this

subject. He says referring to *Morison* v. *Moat*: "Then the judgment goes on to give several instances, and many of them are of cases where a man, being in the employment of another, has discovered the secrets of the manufacture of that other person, or has surreptitiously copied something which came under his hands while he was in the possession of that trust and confidence, and he has been restrained from communicating that secret to anybody else, and anybody who has obtained that secret from him has also been restrained from using it." Apart, therefore, from these pending or threatened proceedings in bankruptcy, it seems to me to be perfectly clear that the plaintiff can obtain the unqualified injunction which he asks for. Now, can it make any difference that Pape says "I want, by means of these copies, to give secondary evidence in the bankruptcy proceedings?" In my opinion that is no ground for making any distinction. The rule of evidence as explained in *Calcraft* v. *Guest*, [1898] 1 Q.B. 759; [1895–9] All E.R. Rep. 346, C.A. merely amounts to this, that if a litigant wants to prove a particular document which by reason of privilege or some circumstance he cannot furnish by the production of the original, he may produce a copy as secondary evidence although that copy has been obtained by improper means, and even, it may be, by criminal means. The Court in such an action is not really trying the circumstances under which the document was produced. That is not an issue in the case and the Court simply says, "Here is a copy of a document which cannot be produced; it may have been stolen, it may have been picked up in the street, it may have improperly got into the possession of the person who proposes to produce it, but that is not a matter which the Court in the trial of the action can go into." But that does not seem to me to have any bearing upon a case where the whole subject-matter of the action is the right to retain the originals or copies of certain documents which are privileged. It seems to me that, although Pape has had the good luck to obtain a copy of these documents which he can produce without a breach of this injunction, there is no ground whatever in principle why we should decline to give the plaintiff the protection which in my view is his right as between him and Pape, and that there is no reason whatever why we should not say to Pape in pending or future proceedings, "You shall not produce these documents which you have acquired from the plaintiff surreptitiously, or from his solicitor, who plainly stood to him in a confidential relation." For these reasons I think the appeal ought to be allowed so far as it asks, and only so far as it asks, to strike out the exception.

[KENNEDY and SWINDEN EADY, L.JJ. gave concurring judgments.]

Butler *v.* Board of Trade
[1971] Ch. 680; [1970] 3 All E.R. 593

The plaintiff brought a declaration that the defendants were not entitled to produce a copy of a letter written to him by his solicitor in evidence at a prosecution being brought against him by the defendants. Goff, J. refused the declaration.

GOFF, J.: There remains, however, the final question whether the law or equity as to breach of confidence operates in the terms of para. 14 of the special case to give the plaintiff—

"any equity to prevent the Defendants from tendering a copy of the letter in evidence in any of the said criminal proceedings"

where, if tendered it would, as I see it, clearly be admissible: see *Calcraft* v. *Guest*, subject of course to the overriding discretion of the trial court to reject it if it thought its use unfair. The plaintiff relies on the decision of the Court of Appeal in *Lord Ashburton* v. *Pape*, where, a party to certain bankruptcy proceedings having by a trick obtained a copy of a privileged letter, Neville, J. granted an injunction restraining him and his solicitors from publishing or making use of it, save for the purposes of those proceedings, and the Court of Appeal varied the order by striking out the exception, so that the injunction was unqualified.

Before I consider that further, I can dispose briefly of the argument advanced by counsel for the defendants that the plaintiff cannot be entitled to any relief in equity, because he does not come with clean hands. That seems to me to beg the question. If the letter was part of a criminal project then the copy is not protected anyhow. If, however, it was not such a part then the mere fact, if it be so, that it may help the defendants prove their case on the criminal charge does not soil the hands of the plaintiff with respect to his proprietary interests in the copy.

I turn back to *Ashburton* v. *Pape*. In the present case there was no impropriety on the part of the defendants in the way in which they received the copy, but that, in my judgment, is irrelevant because an innocent recipient of information conveyed in breach of confidence is liable to be restrained. I wish to make it clear that there is no suggestion of any kind of moral obliquity on the part of the solicitors, but the disclosure was in law a breach of confidence. Nevertheless, that case does differ from the present in an important particular, namely that the defendants are a department of the Crown and intend to use the copy letter in a public prosecution brought by them. As far as I am aware, there is no case directly in point on the question whether that is merely an immaterial difference of fact or a valid distinction, but in my judgment it is the latter because in such a case there are two conflicting principles, the private right of the individual and the interest of the State to apprehend and prosecute criminals: see *per* Lord Denning, M.R. in *Chic Fashions (West Wales) Ltd.* v. *Jones*, [1968] 2 Q.B. 299, at p. 313; [1968] 1 All E.R. 229, at p. 236, C.A. and in *Ghani* v. *Jones* [1970] 1 Q.B. 693, at p. 708; [1969] 3 All E.R. 1700, at p. 1704, C.A.

In my judgment it would not be a right or permissible exercise of the equitable jurisdiction in confidence to make a declaration at the suit of the accused in a public prosecution in effect restraining the Crown from adducing admissible evidence relevant to the crime with which he is charged. It is not necessary for me to decide whether the same result would obtain in the case of a private prosecution, and I expressly leave that point open.

My reasons for the conclusion I have reached are as follows: first, it is clear that if the copy letter were in the hands of a third party I would in restraining him have to except the power of the trial court to subpoena him to produce the letter and his obligation to comply with that order: see *per* Bankes, L.J. in *Weld-Blundell* v. *Stephens*, [1919] 1 K.B. 520, at p. 527, C.A. It would be strange if the defendants could subpoena a witness to produce this document yet, having it themselves, not be allowed to tender it in evidence. Secondly, and even more compelling, is the effect of the conflict between the two principles to which I have already referred. In *Elias* v. *Pasmore*, 2 K.B. 164, at p. 173; [1934] All E.R. Rep. 380, at p. 384, it was held accordingly by Horridge, J. that the police were justified in retaining and using at the trial of Hetherington, documents belonging to Elias which they had seized irregularly when entering the premises to arrest Hetherington. True it is that in *Ghani* v. *Jones* Lord Denning, M.R. criticized the *dictum* of Horridge, J. as being too wide, in that he gave the police a right to use the documents in the trial of any person, but with that qualification Lord Denning, M.R. accepted what Horridge, J. had said. Thus *Elias* v. *Pasmore* is authority for the proposition that the right and duty of the police to prosecute offenders prevails over the accused's right of ownership. He cannot demand his own goods back. By analogy it seems to me that the interest and duty of the defendants as a department of the State to prosecute offenders under the Companies Act 1948 must prevail over the offender's limited proprietary right in equity to restrain a breach of confidence, and here, of course, the doubt suggested by Lord Denning, M.R. does not arise because the accused and the person entitled to the benefit of the confidence are one and the same.

This view of the matter is further supported by *Ghani* v. *Jones* itself and the statement by Lord Denning, M.R. of the relevant principles, and particularly the second and third, guiding the right of the police to retain and use articles where no man has been arrested or charged, and *a fortiori* where, as here, a criminal prosecution is actually pending. I find some further support for this conclusion in the cases of *Saull* v. *Browne* (1874), 9 Ch. App. 364 and *Kerr* v. *Preston Corporation*, (1876), 6 Ch.D. 463, which say that in general a court of equity will not interfere with a criminal prosecution, although the question there was one of restraining it altogether. For these reasons, in my judgment, the answer to the question proponded in para. 14 of the special case is in the negative and the action must be dismissed.

Before parting with the case, however, I should perhaps comment on the speech of Viscount Radcliffe in *Rumping* v. *Director of Public Prosecutions*, [1964] A.C. 814, at p. 845; [1962] 3 All E.R. 256, at pp. 266–7, H.L. Counsel for the plaintiff, rightly observing that Lord Radcliffe differed from the rest of the House because they held that there was no rule of public policy rendering marital communications inadmissible, relied on Lord Radcliffe's observations in support of his claim that the copy letter was confidential, there being legal professional privilege for the original. As I have said, in my judgment that follows and counsel had no need to support himself with this dissenting judgment or with *Margaret, Duchess of Argyll* v. *Duke of Argyll*, [1967] Ch. 302; [1965] 1 All E.R. 611, on which he also relied. Lord Radcliffe did, however, say this in *Rumping's* case [1964] A.C. 814, at p. 845; [1962] 3 All E.R. 256, at pp. 266–7, H.L.

> "Ought the law to apply a different rule merely because the letter has miscarried and has come into the hands of the police? Considering the history and the nature of the principle that lies behind the special rules governing testimony of husband and wife in criminal trials. I do not think that it should. If it does, we must recognize the implications that, personally, I find overwhelmingly distasteful. A husband may gasp or mutter to his wife some agonized self-incrimination, intended for no ear in the world but hers: yet the law will receive and proceed on the evidence of the successful eavesdropper, professional, amateur or accidental. It is free, I suppose, to entertain the testimony of the listening device, if properly proved. An incriminating letter may be intercepted by any means: it may be snatched from the wife's hand after receipt, taken into custody if she has mislaid it accidentally, withdrawn from her possession by one means or another: in all these cases, it is said, the trophy may be carried into court by the prosecution and, given proof that the prisoner is its author, the law has no rule that excludes it from weighing against him as a confession."

It might be thought at first sight that this is inconsistent with my judgment, but it is not, because there Lord Radcliffe held that communications between husband and wife were not only privileged from disclosure but inadmissible, and therefore his observations about the police intercepting the letter and so forth have no relevance to the question whether they may retain and use in evidence a copy which is admissible but which was supplied to them in breach of confidence.

Notes

1. Reference should be made to a valuable note by Tapper (1972), 35 M.L.R. 83 and Heydon, (1974), 37 M.L.R. 601. The cases are puzzling. One oddity is that Cozens-Hardy, M.R., who led for the successful defendant in *Calcraft* v. *Guest*, was a party to *Ashburton* v. *Pape*. His reconciliation of the decisions at a technical level can be regarded as a success only at that level. There is obscurity in the sentence: "It seems to me that, although Pape has had the good luck to obtain a copy of these documents which he can produce without a breach of this injunction, there is no ground whatever in principle why we should decline to give the plaintiff the protection which in my view is his right as between him and Pape." This appears to contradict what has gone before in suggesting that the copies can be used in later litigation. The problem may be solved by taking "this injunction" to refer to Neville, J.'s

limited injunction (in contrast to the wide injunction granted by the Court of Appeal). Further, other reports remove the contradiction from what Cozens-Hardy, M.R. says, e.g. "although, if Pape has the good luck to obtain a copy of these documents which he can produce without a breach of this injunction. . . .' (82 L.J. Ch. 527, at p. 529; see Tapper, *op. cit.* at p. 86). This implies that Pape could only use copies if he obtained them in some completely innocent way, e.g. in consequence of waiver of the privilege; this is certainly the usual understanding of the effect of *Ashburton* v. *Pape*: see e.g. Phipson, para. 584.

2. Goff, J. in *Butler* v. *Board of Trade* [1971] Ch. 680, at pp. 90–1 appears to misunderstand *Ashburton* v. *Pape* in saying: "if the copy letter were in the hands of a third party I would in restraining him have to except the power of the trial court to subpoena him to produce the letter and his obligation to comply with that order: see *per* Bankes, L.J. in *Weld-Blundell* v. *Stephens*, [1919] I K.B. 520, at p. 527." Bankes, L.J. then says: "No contract would be implied as between a professional man and his client not to disclose communications if required by process of law to do so, whereas a contract might well be implied not to disclose the same communications voluntarily." As Tapper says (*op. cit.*, at p. 87), this is inconclusive since it "envisages the confidence arising out of the supposed obligation not to disclose, and not independently of it". That is, it does not refer to a confidence arising from legal professional privilege or from the duty, enforceable by injunction, not to make copies of privileged documents within the *Ashburton* v. *Pape* doctrine.

3. Whether or not *Calcraft* v. *Guest* and *Ashburton* v. *Pape* are reconcilable at a technical level, they seem to be fundamentally in conflict. If the *Calcraft* doctrine is sound on the basis that it causes more relevant evidence to be put before the court, it is odd that its result can be thwarted by obtaining an injunction in separate proceedings. Alternatively, if *Ashburton* is sound in holding that an injunction is obtainable in separate proceedings, why should not the client be entitled to plead it in the main proceedings to which it is relevant and which he might lose if he cannot? The client's success should not depend on the date at which he found out that he was the victim of a wrong-doer; it should not depend on the chance of whether there is time to institute independent proceedings which may add to costs. It is hard to see that the principal proceedings would be much delayed by determining the issue, admittedly a collateral one, of whether the original was privileged.

4. It should be noted that *dicta* in *Butler* v. *Board of Trade* substantially extend *Ashburton* v. *Pape* in that Goff, J. purports to protect all confidential information: "an innocent recipient of information conveyed in breach of confidence is liable to be restrained" [1971] Ch. 680, at p. 690). If this were correct, it would mean that the long debate about whether priests, doctors, journalists and other professional men should have a privilege similar to that of lawyers has been pointless, since they were already covered as recipients of confidential information. The *dicta* in *Butler* should therefore be confined to the particular context: confidential relationships arising out of information gained by a third party to the lawyer-client relationship. Indeed it would be neater and less likely to cause confusion not to say, as Goff, J. does, that an original document is privileged and a copy confidential, but to say that both are privileged.

5. The third party exception to legal professional privilege seems unjust in

several ways. The exception arose in an age when eavesdropping and the purloining and intercepting of communications was difficult, rare and unfavoured. Similarly, the Law Reform Committee felt that though the exception was bad there was no urgent need to change it, because "the circumstances envisaged seldom occur in practice, and in civil proceedings professional etiquette would militate against unfair advantage being taken of them" (16th Report on Privilege in Civil Proceedings, Cmnd. 3472 (1967), para. 33). Both points are now suspect. For example, though formerly eavesdropping could be guarded against by a proper choice of meeting place and a simple inspection of it, there are now a variety of very efficient mechanical eavesdropping devices. It is not enough to say that the client should take reasonable precautions against disclosure (Wigmore, paras. 2325–6), because even if he does he will not be safe. The increased use of these devices has made them respectable, so that the operation of professional etiquette is unlikely to be a safeguard. It is because of this feature of modern life that the proposed American Federal Rules of Evidence 1971 extend the privilege to cover third parties who learn of a privileged communication (r. 503 (6), Comment).

A related point is that the client is almost certain to be ignorant of the possibility of losing his privilege. His lawyer will doubtless encourage him to speak by telling him of the privilege, but he is unlikely to tell the client of how it can be lost. If the client knows the exception he may be reluctant to speak for fear of eavesdropping, particularly in prison cells, so that the exception conflicts with the policy of the privilege. If he does not know the exception, it is unfair for his admissions to be held against him since he will not have realized that he was in fact putting himself at risk at the very moment when he sought help and thought himself safest. Further, as the Law Reform Committee said, it seems wrong that a party should obtain a procedural advantage as a result of his own or another's wilful misconduct (Cmnd. 3472, para. 32). Ordered legal procedure seeks to overcome the ill-effects of self-help; to permit one litigant to win his case by stealing documents is regressive.

The exception seems out of step with the policy of legal professional privilege from another point of view. The policy demands that privilege attaches to an interview with a person whom the client mistakenly thinks to be a legal adviser, whether the mistake arises as a result of deceit or innocently (*Feuerheerd* v. *London General Omnibus Co., Ltd.*, [1918] 2 K.B. 1565; cf. *Fountain* v. *Young* (1807), 6 Esp. 113). Now if the privilege exists when the client mistakenly trusts in a man whom he thinks to be a lawyer, why should it not exist when the client mistakenly trusts in the confidentiality of communications with the lawyer learnt by a third party? A Canadian case provokes further thought on these lines. In *R.* v. *Choney* a police agent entered the cell of the accused who could speak only Ruthenian, and represented himself to be an interpreter working for the accused's solicitor and mandated by the latter to get the accused to tell him everything about the case. The accused's incriminating admissions were taken down by two persons concealed behind his cell. Perdue, J.A. and the Manitoba Court of Appeal excluded the evidence of both the interpreter and the eavesdroppers. Several reasons were given for the latter decision. First, had the interviewer been a real lawyer or his agent, he might have taken precautions against eavesdropping ((1908), 13 C.C.C. 289, at p. 293, *per* Perdue, J.A.). This point is sound, though neutral on the question of whether the *Calcraft* exception is correct. Secondly, Phippen,

J.A. said "we must treat the whole as an interview with several persons who had fraudulently adopted the character of solicitor's representatives" (*ibid.*, at p. 296; Richards, J.A. agreed at p. 295). This is fictitious: the accused never believed there was more than one representative. Thirdly, the interpreter's evidence was excluded because it was gained by a trick, and "as part of the trick the listeners were placed where they could overhear what passed" (*ibid.*, at p. 296, *per* Phippen, J.A.). This is more convincing, and suggests that all breaches of the privilege should result in exclusion of the evidence.

A further respect in which English law on this point is at odds with its underlying justification is this. The English rule is that the privilege is lost even if the disclosure is made voluntarily by the lawyer in bad faith. The evidence is admissible whether the client's privilege is violated by his lawyer or a third party. The client is only protected against a faithless lawyer if the latter attempts to violate the privilege while in court. This makes the privilege easily capable of being evaded. American decisions have overcome this weakness by a compromise: the privilege continues if a breach of confidence occurs as a result of the lawyer's voluntary conduct (Wigmore, para. 2325, n. 1). As a practical matter this is a step in the right direction, though it lacks the internal consistency of the English position. But it provokes the question: if the privilege survives the lawyer's bad faith why should it not survive the opponent's bad faith?

6. How does the rule under consideration relate to the rule that illegally or improperly obtained evidence is admissible, subject to the discretion of the judge in a criminal trial to exclude evidence the admission of which would operate unfairly against the accused. Now whatever the merits of admitting the ordinary kind of improperly obtained evidence, there are surely stronger arguments against admitting evidence seized in violation of legal privilege. This involves a double impropriety: the client is the victim of wrongful conduct at the very moment when he thought he was safest against it. In any event, there are strong arguments against the rule admitting illegally obtained evidence. The writer favours its admission only if it is required in connexion with crimes which cannot be prosecuted without it, or if it was obtained by accidental or trivial illegality, or in circumstances requiring urgent action. Such a rule has the drawback of uncertainty of operation; any exception to legal privilege, operating in a much narrower area, can be governed by simpler and more clear-cut rules. One compromise might be the Law Reform Committee's proposal that only evidence obtained by crimes or deliberate torts should remain privileged. But in the interests of maintaining the integrity of the policies underlying the legal privilege, and remembering that the privilege will cause little evidence to be lost to the court in cases where the client goes into the witness box, the writer favours the continuance of the privilege no matter how the third party came to learn of the privileged information.

7. It is instructive to observe the changes over the last thirty years in American law reform proposals. In 1942 the American Law Institute's Model Code of Evidence, r. 210 (c) (iii) provided that the privilege only continued when the third person learnt of the confidential communication "as a result of an intentional breach of the lawyer's duty of non-disclosure by the lawyer or his agent or servant". In 1953 the Uniform Rules of Evidence, r. 26 (1) (c) went further in providing that the client could prevent third parties disclosing a

privileged communication "if it came to the knowledge of such witness (i) in the course of its transmittal between the client and the lawyer, or (ii) in a manner not reasonably to be anticipated by the client, or (iii) as a result of breach of the lawyer-client relationship". The 1971 Federal Rules of Evidence, r. 503 (*b*) makes the client's right to prevent third parties testifying unqualified. This trend, at a time when American law reformers, like English, advocate restriction or abolition of most other privileges, is significant.

II WITHOUT PREJUDICE STATEMENTS

If a party to litigation has previously made an offer to compromise it, there may be circumstances in which the offer constitutes an admission because it reveals a consciousness of the unsoundness of his case. However, any offer of a compromise made without prejudice to the maker's rights cannot be admitted into evidence without the consent of both maker and receiver. The purpose of the privilege is to reduce litigation by encouraging the settlement and compromising of disputes.

Whether letters are without prejudice depends not on whether they are so headed but on the intentions of the parties.

Statements made to a mediator by estranged spouses may not be disclosed by him without the consent of the parties (*McTaggart* v. *McTaggart*, [1949] P. 94; [1948] 2 All E.R. 754, C.A.); this is so when only one of the parties has approached a mediator (*Mole* v. *Mole*, [1951] P. 21; [1950] 2 All E.R. 328, C.A.). Mediators would include doctors, clergymen, solicitors, marriage guidance counsellors, probation officers and children's welfare officers. The privilege is joint in the sense that it cannot be waived without the consent of both spouses (*Theodoropoulas* v. *Theodoropoulas*, [1964] P. 311; [1963] 2 All E.R. 772). The statements made may concern reconciliation, the custody of children, or financial arrangements (*Rodgers* v. *Rodgers* (1964), 114 C.L.R. 608).

If an agreement is reached as a result of without prejudice negotiations the privilege ceases to apply, for the parties' rights have been changed. Without prejudice communications may be examined to decide whether an agreement has in fact been reached (*Tomlin* v. *Standard Telephones and Cables Ltd.*, [1969] 3 All E.R. 201; [1969] 1 W.L.R. 1378, C.A.).

Without prejudice communications to which this privilege applies may not be admitted as evidence of the truth of what is asserted, but may be admitted merely to prove that certain statements were made, e.g., as libels, acts of bankruptcy, or threats to sue for patent infringement.

III MISCELLANEOUS

A. Abolition

The Civil Evidence Act 1968, s. 16 abolished a number of privileges in civil cases. One was the rule that a party cannot be compelled to produce any document relating solely to his own case and not tending to impeach that case or support his opponent's (s. 16 (2)). This had no application to criminal cases. Another was the rule that a person other than a party could not be compelled to produce any document relating to his title to land (s. 16 (1) (*b*)). This had virtually no practical application in criminal proceedings. Thirdly, a witness in any proceedings instituted in consequence of adultery, whether party or not, could refuse to answer questions tending to show his or her adultery (s. 16 (5), see *Nast* v. *Nast* [1972] Fam. 142, C.A.; [1972] 1 All E.R. 1171). This never existed in criminal cases. Fourthly, spouses had a privilege not to give evidence of whether marital intercourse did or did not occur during any period (s. 16 (4)). This may remain for criminal cases but in practice can have hardly any scope. Fifthly, a husband or wife had a privilege not to disclose any communication made to him or her by the other spouse during the marriage (s. 16 (3)). This still applies in criminal proceedings (Criminal Evidence Act 1898, s. 1 (d)). The privilege only lasts as long as the marriage continues (*Shenton* v. *Tyler*, [1939] Ch. 620, C.A.; [1939] 1 All E.R. 827).

So far as these privileges continue to exist in criminal cases, their abolition has been recommended in the 11th Report of the Criminal Law Revision Committee (Criminal Evidence Bill, cl. 16).

B. Creation of new principles

The Civil Evidence Act, s. 15, created a privilege for communications between a person and his patent agent for the purpose of pending or contemplated proceedings under the Patents Act 1949 before the comptroller or the Appeal Tribunal.

The Act did not grant any privilege to ministers of religion or medical practitioners; and the Criminal Law Revision Committee in its 11th Report recommended no change. The court has a discretion to disallow questions which unduly embarrass the witness (and see *Broad* v. *Pitt* (1828), 3 C. & P. 518). There is strong authority against journalists having a privilege respecting their sources of information (*McGuiness* v. *A.-G. of Victoria* (1940), 63 C.L.R. 73; *A.-G.* v. *Mulholland*, [1963] 2 Q.B. 477, C.A.; [1963] 1 All E.R. 767).

Criminal Law Revision Committee, 11th Report
1972. Paras. 273–6

273. There are two arguments, both entitled to the highest respect, for conferring a privilege for communications to a minister of religion. The first is that it is in the interests of religion, morality and society generally that a person who is willing to confide in a minister about his wrongdoing or his wicked propensities should be encouraged to do so in the hope that the minister will be able to persuade him to lead a better life and that a person will be more ready to confide in the minister if there is no danger that the minister will be compelled to reveal the confidence in legal proceedings. The second argument is that to confer the privilege would be in accordance with the wish of the church leaders. In particular the Archbishop of Canterbury represented to the Law Reform Committee, and through them to us, that the creation of an absolute statutory privilege for penitential communications might remove a constitutional obstacle to a new canon on confessions which the Convocations of the Church of England desired to make. To confer the privilege would also avoid the possibility of a conflict, such as has very occasionally arisen, between the duty imposed on a priest by the rules of his church to keep secret a confidence (in particular one made during confession) and his legal duty to obey a requirement to reveal the confidence in court. This would ensure that a judge should not be in the embarrassing position of having to decide whether to punish a priest for refusing to disobey a rule of his church.

274. But the great majority of the committee, while fully sympathizing with the arguments above, are opposed to recommending the conferment of a privilege in respect of these communications. Their main reason is that there should be no restriction on the right of a party to criminal proceedings to compel a witness to give any information in his possession which is relevant to the charge, unless there is a compelling reason in policy for the restriction, and that the arguments for the proposal are not strong enough for this purpose. No serious difficulty has arisen for a great many years, and the majority are satisfied that the prosecuting authorities and the courts would always be able to prevent a clash such as mentioned above. In a case where the accused had told a minister of religion that he had committed the offence charged—or, say, that he had a propensity to commit an offence of this kind—it would be exceptional for the prosecution to know of the communication, and there would have to be a strong reason for the prosecution to seek to compel the minister to give evidence about the communication or for the court to insist that he should give the evidence. On the other hand, it might occasionally happen that one of two accused persons had confessed to a minister that he alone, and not his co-accused, committed the offence. Even if any minister of religion felt able to stand by and let a possibly innocent person be convicted when the minister was in a position to exculpate him by giving evidence, we should not wish to recommend legislation which would allow this. It is possible, therefore, that any provision which might be enacted should apply only to information given by the accused about his own conduct. We have no doubt that the legislation would have to secure that the minister should be compellable to give evidence about a disclosure which the person who made it was willing to have disclosed. Whether the minister should be free (so far as the law is concerned) to give the evidence without the consent of the person who made the disclosure is a more difficult question, and the fact that it would arise is an additional reason for our preference for not legislating but for leaving it to the courts and prosecuting authorities to deal with any case which might arise in practice.

275. But in this connexion we should refer to a doubt which has been expressed in the committee about part of the Law Reform Committee's argument for not recommending that a statutory privilege should be conferred. The committee said that it was the policy of the common law "to limit to a minimum the categories of privileges which a person has an absolute right to claim, but to accord to the judge a wide discretion to permit a witness, whether a party to the proceedings or not, to refuse to disclose information where disclosure would be a breach of some ethical or social value and non-disclosure would be unlikely to result in serous injustice in the particular casc in which it is claimed" (16th Report, para. 1). . . . The committee relied a good deal on the argument that conferring a statutory privilege might have the undesirable effect of narrowing the area in which the courts would feel able to exercise their discretion in favour of protecting confidential relations (16th Report, paras. 1, 47). But although some of the statements in *Mulholland* at least are clearly in favour of the existence of a discretion, some members of the present committee have serious doubts whether the statements, if they are right for civil proceedings, have any general application to criminal proceedings. In criminal proceedings it is now established that the court has a general discretion to exclude evidence in order to prevent injustice to the defence; but whether a judge could ever excuse a witness from answering a relevant question asked by the defence in a criminal case on the ground that this would be a breach of a confidence reposed in the witness seems to some members highly questionable. But be this as it may, the majority are confident that any serious difficulties can be avoided, as mentioned above, even in the absence of an exclusionary discretion.

276. The arguments for and against conferring a privilege in relation to communications with a medical practitioner are broadly—though not entirely—similar to those for and against conferring a privilege in relation to communications with a minister of religion. Therefore it is unnecessary to go fully over the ground in relation to medical practitioners. But in their case there is a difficult question as to what should be the scope of the privilege if given. The privilege might be a wide one which would allow the doctor to refuse to give evidence (without the patient's consent) about any communication made to him by the patient in confidence, even one concerning a physical ailment or injury or, perhaps, even about the facts of any treatment given. The argument for this is that the public interest requires that a person should seek medical advice when this is necessary and that he should be able to speak freely to his doctor, even about something embarrassing or discreditable, without the danger that the doctor might have to give evidence about this in court. But we think that, even if any privilege were given, it would be wrong to go as far as this. To do so might exclude information which it was important in the interests of justice to have before the court. For example, it would be a scandal if a criminal who had been injured when blowing a safe or committing a robbery could prevent the doctor who had attended him from revealing what the criminal told him about how he came by his injury. There would be a stronger case for giving a narrower privilege according to which a person who had told a doctor practising psychiatry, in confidence, about an offence which he had committed, or a criminal propensity to which he was subject, for the purpose of obtaining advice or treatment which might help him to avoid committing offences in future, could object to the doctor's giving evidence about this. It is undoubtedly desirable that a person should consult a doctor for this purpose; and it can be argued that the possibility that this would bring about a reform in the conduct of the person in question is a good enough reason for conferring the privilege. The British Medical Association, in a memorandum sent to the Law Reform Committee and ourselves, argued in favour of conferring a medical privilege and said that, while the possibility of a conflict between medical and legal obligations applied to all physicians, "the dilemma is most acute in the field of psychiatry". They added:

> "If a psychiatrist is to assist his patient, and in criminal cases possibly to assist the court to the best of his ability, it is essential that his interviews with his patient should be free and frank. In the course of such frank discussions matters may be brought to light which, whilst relevant to the mental state of the person concerned, will be gravely prejudicial to his interest, if the doctor is, as now, compelled to report them in open court."

When we discussed this question, the general view was that the privilege, if given, should be the narrower one mentioned above, although it might sometimes be difficult to decide whether the case was a psychiatric or an ordinary medical one. For example, an unsophisticated person might consult a general practitioner about a problem about which a more sophisticated person would consult a psychiatrist, or a doctor might see that what a patient thought was a physical condition was in fact the result of psychological disturbance. In any event, we thought that some exceptions would have to be made. An example would be where the accused called the doctor as a witness in order to make out a defence of insanity, diminished responsibility, or some other defence depending on his mental state, and the prosecution wished to cross-examine the doctor in order to rebut the defence. However, in the end we decided, by a large majority, that for reasons similar to those in relation to ministers of religion—in particular the unlikelihood that any difficulty would arise in practice—we should not recommend that any privilege should be conferred in relation to medical practitioners.

18

Public Policy

I STATE INTEREST

Evidence may be excluded on grounds of "public policy" or "Crown privilege". The latter title is a misnomer, because the essence of a privilege is that it can be waived by its holder, whereas if a claim to Crown privilege is not taken by the Crown or one of the parties, it must be taken by the court. The relevant rules are usually applied to the disclosure of documents, but extend also to oral evidence.

The court may uphold a claim to privilege if the contents of a document should not be revealed in the public interest, e.g. because they would assist the nation's enemies in wartime to understand the design of a new submarine: *Duncan* v. *Cammell Laird & Co., Ltd.*, [1942] A.C. 624; [1942] 1 All E.R. 587, H.L. Other examples are military plans: *Asiatic Petroleum Co., Ltd.* v. *Anglo-Persian Oil Co., Ltd.*, [1916] 1 K.B. 822; [1916–17] All E.R. Rep. 637, C.A.; and diplomatic despatches (*M. Isaacs & Sons, Ltd.* v. *Cook*, [1925] 2 K.B. 391). This is usually referred to as a "contents" claim. The court may also uphold a "class" claim, namely that a document should not be disclosed because though its own contents are innocuous, it belongs to a class of documents which should not be produced. Class claims are usually based on the argument that the success of the claim is necessary for the proper functioning of the public service in that if it were not upheld civil servants would communicate with each other less candidly.

The usual method of claiming privilege is for the Minister or permanent head of the relevant department to swear an affidavit or certify that each document to be excluded should be excluded on either class or contents grounds. The Minister or permanent head must himself inspect the documents for which he claims privilege and personally judge whether or not it should be disclosed. The judge has a discretionary power to inspect the documents and judge for himself whether the interests of the administration of justice in full disclosure outweigh the injurious effects of disclosure on the interests of the State. If the former consideration prevails, the judge may order disclosure.

On a number of these points there were differences between the English courts on the one hand and the rest of the common law world and Scotland on the other between 1942 and 1968. This culminated in many critical *dicta* in the Court of Appeal in the middle 1960s. The differences have been resolved by the House of Lords in *Conway* v. *Rimmer*.

411

Conway v. Rimmer
[1968] A.C. 910; [1968] 1 All E.R. 874, H.L.

A probationer police constable was prosecuted for theft by a superintendent. The jury stopped the case. In subsequent proceedings for malicious prosecution brought by the constable against the superintendent the Home Secretary claimed privilege for three probationary reports and a report by a District Police Training Centre on the plaintiff, as well as a report leading to his prosecution. The House of Lords held that the courts had jurisdiction to inspect the document and order production. (Subsequently production was ordered: [1968] A.C. 910, at pp. 996–7; [1968] 2 All E.R. 304.)

LORD REID: The question whether such a statement by a Minister of the Crown should be accepted as conclusively preventing any court from ordering production of any of the documents to which it applies is one of very great importance in the administration of justice. If the commonly accepted interpretation of the decision of this house in *Duncan* v. *Cammell Laird & Co., Ltd.*, [1942] A.C. 624; [1942] 1 All E.R. 587, H.L. is to remain authoritative the question admits of only one answer—the Minister's statement is final and conclusive. Normally I would be very slow to question the authority of a unanimous decision of this House only twenty-five years old which was carefully considered and obviously intended to lay down a general rule. But this decision has several abnormal features. Viscount Simon, L.C. thought that on this matter the law in Scotland was the same as the law in England, and he clearly intended to lay down a rule applicable to the whole of the United Kingdom. In *Glasgow Corporation* v. *Central Land Board*, 1956 S.C. (H.L.) 1, however, this House held that that was not so, with the result that today on this question the law is different in the two countries. There are many chapters of the law where for historical and other reasons it is quite proper that the law should be different in the two countries; but here we are dealing purely with public policy—with the proper relation between the powers of the executive and the powers of the courts—and I can see no rational justification for the law on this matter being different in the two countries. Secondly, events have proved that the rule supposed to have been laid down in *Duncan's* case is far from satisfactory. In the large number of cases in England and elsewhere which have been cited in argument much dissatisfaction has been expressed, and I have not observed even one expression of whole-hearted approval. Moreover, a statement made by Viscount Kilmuir, L.C. in 1956 on behalf of the government, to which I shall return later, makes it clear that that government did not regard it as consonant with public policy to maintain the rule to the full extent which existing authorities had held to be justifiable.

I have no doubt that the case of *Duncan* v. *Cammell Laird & Co., Ltd.* was rightly decided. The plaintiff sought discovery of documents relating to the submarine Thetis including a contract for the hull and machinery and plans and specifications. The first Lord of the Admiralty had stated that "it would be injurious to the public interest that any of the said documents should be disclosed to any person". Any of these documents might well have given valuable information, or at least clues, to the skilled eye of an agent of a foreign power; but Lord Simon took the opportunity to deal with the whole question of the right of the Crown to prevent production of documents in a litigation. Yet a study of his speech leaves me with the strong impression that throughout he had primarily in mind cases where discovery or disclosure would involve a danger of real prejudice to the national interest. I find it difficult to believe that his speech would have been the same if the case had related, as the present case does, to discovery of routine reports on a probationer constable. . . . Summing up towards the end, he said ([1942] A.C. 624, at p. 642; [1942] 1 All E.R. 587, at p. 595, H.L.)

"The rule that the interest of the State must not be put in jeopardy by producing documents which would injure it is a principle to be observed in administering justice, quite unconnected with the interests or claims of the particular parties in litigation . . .''

Surely it would be grotesque to speak of the interest of the State being put in jeopardy by disclosure of a routine report on a probationer. Lord Simon did not say very much about objections ([1942] A.C. 624, at p. 635; [1942] 1 All E.R. 587, at p. 592, H.L.)

". . . based upon the view that the public interest requires a particular class of communications with, or within, a public department to be protected from production on the ground that the candour and completeness of such communications might be prejudiced if they were ever liable to be disclosed in subsequent litigation rather than upon the contents of the particular document itself."

At the end he said that a Minister ([1942] A.C. 624, at p. 642; [1942] 1 All E.R. 587, at p. 595, H.L.)

". . . ought not to take the responsibility of withholding production except in cases where the public interest would otherwise be damnified, e.g. where disclosure would be injurious to national defence, or to good diplomatic relations, or where the practice of keeping a class of documents secret is necessary for the proper functioning of the public service."

I find it difficult to believe that he would have put these three examples on the same level if he had intended the third to cover such minor matters as a routine report by a relatively junior officer. My impression is strengthened by the passage at the very end of the speech ([1942] A.C. 624, at p. 643; [1942] 1 All E.R. 587, at pp. 595–6, H.L.)

". . . the public interest is also the interest of every subject of the realm, and while, in these exceptional cases, the private citizen may seem to be denied what is to his immediate advantage, he, like the rest of us, would suffer if the needs of protecting the interests of the country as whole were not ranked as a prior obligation."

Would he have spoken of "these exceptional cases" or of "the needs of protecting the interests of the country as a whole" if he had intended to include all manner of routine communications? Did he really mean that the protection of such communications is a "prior obligation" in a case where a man's reputation or fortune is at stake and withholding the document makes it impossible for justice to be done?

It is universally recognized that here there are two kinds of public interest which may clash. There is the public interest that harm shall not be done to the nation or the public service by disclosure of certain documents, and there is the public interest that the administration of justice shall not be frustrated by the withholding of documents which must be produced if justice is to be done. There are many cases where the nature of the injury which would or might be done to the nation or the public service is of so grave a character that no other interest, public or private, can be allowed to prevail over it. With regard to such cases it would be proper to say, as Lord Simon did, that to order production of the document in question would put the interest of the state in jeopardy; but there are many other cases where the possible injury to the public service is much less and there one would think that it would be proper to balance the public interests involved. I do not believe that Lord Simon really meant that the smallest probability of injury to the public service must always outweigh the gravest frustration of the administration of justice.

It is to be observed that, in a passage which I have already quoted, Lord Simon referred to the practice of keeping a class of documents secret being "*necessary* (my italics) for the proper functioning of the public interest". But the certificate of the Home Secretary in the present case does not go nearly so far as that. It merely says that the production of a document of the classes to which it refers would be "injurious to the public interest": it does not say what degree of injury is to be apprehended. It may be advantageous to the functioning of the public service that reports of this kind should be kept secret—that is the view of the Home Secretary—but I would be very surprised if anyone said that that was necessary.

There are now many large public bodies, such as British Railways, and the National Coal Board, the proper and efficient functioning of which is very necessary for many reasons, including the safety of the public. The Attorney-General made it clear that Crown privilege is not and cannot be invoked to prevent disclosure of similar documents made by them or their servants, even if it were said that this is required for the proper and efficient functioning of that public service. I find it difficult to see why it should be *necessary* to withhold whole classes of routine "communications with or within a public department", but quite unnecessary to withhold similar communications with or within a public corporation. There the safety of the public may well depend on the candour and completeness of reports made by subordinates, whose duty it is to draw attention to defects. So far as I know, however, no one has ever suggested that public safety has been endangered by the candour or completeness of such reports having been inhibited by the fact that they may have to be produced if the interests of the due administration of justice should ever require production at any time.

I must turn now to a statement made by Viscount Kilmuir, L.C. in this House on 6 June 1956. When counsel proposed to read this statement your lordships had doubts, which I shared, as to its admissibility; but we did permit it to be read, and, as the argument proceeded, its importance emerged. With a minor amendment made on 8 March 1962, it appears still to operate as a direction to, or at least a guide for, Ministers who swear affidavits. So we may assume that in the present case the Home Secretary acted in accordance with the views expressed in Lord Kilmuir's statement. The statement sets out the grounds on which Crown privilege is to be claimed. Having set out the first ground that disclosure of the contents of the particular document would injure the public interest, it proceeds:

> "The second ground is that the document falls within a class which the public interest requires to be withheld from production, and Lord Simon particularised this head of public interest as 'the proper functioning of the public service'."

There is no reference to Lord Simon's exhortation, which I have already quoted, that a Minister ought not to take the responsibility of withholding production of a class of documents except where the practice of keeping a class of documents secret is necessary for the proper functioning of the public service. Then the statement proceeds:

> "The reason why the law sanctions the claiming of Crown privilege on the 'class' ground is the need to secure freedom and candour of communications with and within the public service, so that government decisions can be taken on the best advice and with the fullest information. In order to secure this it is necessary that the class of documents to which privilege applies should be clearly settled, so that the person giving advice or information should know that he is doing so in confidence. Any system whereby a document falling within the class might, as a result of a later decision, be required to be produced in evidence, would destroy that confidence and undermine the whole basis of class privilege, because there would be no certainty at the time of writing that the document would not be disclosed."

But later in the statement, the position taken is very different. A number of cases are set out in which Crown privilege should not be claimed. The most important for present purposes is:

> "We propose that if medical documents, or indeed other documents, are relevant to the defence in criminal proceedings, Crown privilege should not be claimed."

The only exception specifically mentioned is statements by informers. That is a very wide-ranging exception, for the Attorney-General stated that it applied at least to all manner of routine communications and even to prosecutions for minor offences. Thus it can no longer be said that the writer of such communications has any "certainty at the time of writing that the document would not be disclosed". So we have the curious result that "freedom and candour of communication" is supposed not to be inhibited by knowledge of the writer that his report may be disclosed in a criminal case, but would still be supposed to be inhibited if he thought that his report might be disclosed in a civil case.

The Attorney-General did not deny that, even where the full contents of a report have already been made public in a criminal case, Crown privilege is still claimed for that report in a later civil case; and he was quite candid about the reason for that. Crown privilege is claimed in the civil case not to protect the document—its contents are already public property—but to protect the writer from civil liability should he be sued for libel or other tort. No doubt the government have weighed the danger that knowledge of such protection might encourage malicious writers against the advantage that honest reporters shall not be subjected to vexatious actions, and have come to the conclusion that it is an advantage to the public service to afford this protection; but it seems very far removed from the original purpose of Crown privilege.

The statement, as it has been explained to us, makes clear another point. The Minister who withholds production of a "class" document has no duty to consider the degree of public interest involved in a particular case by frustrating in that way the due administration of justice. If it is in the public interest in his view to withhold documents of that class, then it matters not whether the result of withholding a document is merely to deprive a litigant of some evidence on a minor issue in a case of little importance, or on the other hand is to make it impossible to do justice at all in a case of the greatest importance. I cannot think that it is satisfactory that there should be no means at all of weighing, in any civil case, the public interest involved in withholding the document against the public interest that it should be produced. So it appears to me that the present position is so unsatisfactory that this House must re-examine the whole question in light of the authorities.

Two questions will arise: first, whether the court is to have any right to question the finality of a Minister's certificate and, secondly, if it has such a right, how and in what circumstances that right is to be exercised and made effective.

A Minister's certificate may be given on one or other of two grounds: either because it would be against the public interest to disclose the contents of the particular document or documents in question, or because the document belongs to a class of documents which ought to be withheld whether or not there is anything in the particular document in question disclosure of which would be against the public interest. It does not appear that any serious difficulties have arisen or are likely to arise with regard to the first class. However wide the power of the court may be held to be, cases would be very rare in which it could be proper to question the view of the responsible Minister that it would be contrary to the public interest to make public the contents of a particular document. A question might arise whether it would be possible to separate those parts of a document of which disclosure would be innocuous from those parts which ought not to be made public, but I need not pursue that question now. In the present case your lordships are directly concerned with the second class of documents.

[LORD REID discussed the earlier authorities and continued:] The last important case before *Duncan's* case was *Robinson* v. *South Australia State* (*No.* 2). The state government had assumed the function of acquiring and marketing all wheat grown in the state and distributing the proceeds to the growers. A number of actions was brought alleging negligence in carrying out this function. The Australian courts had upheld objections by the state to discovery of a mass of documents in their possession. For reasons into which I need not enter, the Privy Council could not finally decide the matter. What they did was ([1931] A.C. 704, P.C., at p. 723; [1931] All E.R. Rep. 333, at p. 341):

"... to remit the case to the Supreme Court of South Australia with a direction
that it is a proper one for the exercise by that court of its power of itself inspecting
the documents for which privilege is set up in order to see whether the claim is
justified. Their lordships have already given reasons for their conclusion that the
court is possessed of such a power."

This case was of course dealt with in *Duncan's* case, but not, I venture to think, in a
very satisfactory way. Lord Simon said that ([1942] A.C. 624, at p. 641; [1942] 1 All
E.R. 587, at p. 595, H.L.): "Their lordships' conclusion was partly based on their
interpretation of a rule of court ...". In fact it was not. The passage which I have
quoted occurs in the judgment before there is any reference to the rule of court. Beyond that Lord Simon said no more than "I cannot agree with this view". So he thought
that, even where discovery is sought in an action against the State arising out of what
was in effect a commercial transaction, the view of the Minister is conclusive. Lord
Kilmuir's statement, however, promised a considerable relaxation in contract cases.

I shall not examine the earlier Scottish authorities in detail because the position in
Scotland has now been made clear in the *Glasgow Corporation* case, where the earlier
authorities were fully considered. Viscount Simonds said (1956 S.C. (H.L.) 1, at p. 11):

"In the course of the present appeal we have had the advantage of an exhaustive
examination of the relevant law from the earliest times, and it has left me in no
doubt that there always has been and is now in the law of Scotland an inherent power
of the court to override the Crown's objection to produce documents on the ground
that it would injure the public interest to do so."

Now I must examine the English cases since 1942. In *Ellis* v. *Home Office*, [1953] 2
Q.B. 135, [1953] 2 All E.R. 149, C.A.; Crown privilege had been asserted to such an
extent as to cause Devlin, J. and the Court of Appeal to express great uneasiness and this
led to the making of Lord Kilmuir's statement in 1956. In *Broome* v. *Broome* (*Edmundson
cited*), a wife sought divorce on the ground of cruelty. There had been some investigation by a representative of the Soldiers' Sailors' and Airmen's Families Association.
It was sought to recover documents made by that representative. The Secretary of
State for War certified:

"I am of opinion that it is not in the public interest that the documents should be
produced or the evidence of Mrs. Allsop [the representative of S.S.A.F.A.] given
orally."

Admittedly that association and its representatives were neither servants nor agents of
the Crown. Sachs, J. said ([1955] P. 190, at p. 200; [1955] 1 All E.R. 201, at p. 206):

"In relation to the present case the claim involves the extension or development
of Crown privilege in three separate directions, viz., (i) as to the all embracing nature
of the evidence privileged [for previous claims in this form have related only to
documents], (ii) as to the person affected [the claim referred to all witnesses, as
opposed to classes of witnesses], and (iii) as to the heads of public interest [the head
here asserted being the maintenance of the morale of the forces]."

Then he said ([1955] P. 190, at p. 201; [1955] 1 All E.R. 201, at p. 20]):

"It is of obvious importance to ensure generally that claims of Crown privilege
are not used unnecessarily to the detriment of the vital need of the courts to have
the truth put before them; and the facts of the present case well illustrate how easily
it can be sought unnecessarily, albeit in the utmost good faith, to make such a claim."

He allowed Mrs. Allsop to be examined and said:

"On all these points her evidence was of assistance to the court; on none of them
was there any apparent cause for any intervention in the name of Crown privilege."

The position of the same association was considered in *Whitehall* v. *Whitehall*. There the letter which the Minister sought to suppress had already been produced in process. I need not consider the procedural difficulties which emerged. The Lord President (Lord Clyde) said (1957 S.C. 30, at p. 39):

"Public interest may in certain circumstances entitle a Minister to prevent the courts seeing documents which are in his department's possession or have emanated from his department, but it would be a quite intolerable extension of this privilege were he able, where no question of national safety is involved, to intervene in litigations between private individuals . . ."

I think it may be too narrow to limit the exception to "national safety". Lord Russell referred (1957 S.C. 30, at p. 40) to disclosure being injurious to the safety of the realm or affecting diplomatic relations or revealing state secrets or matters of high state policy. Lord Sorn said (1957 S.C. 30, at, p. 43):

"The proposition therefore is that the Crown can select any institution which serves the public, or a section of it, and throw a protective veil of secrecy over its internal communings—and even the letters it writes to individuals—by means of a ministerial certificate."

That was a proposition which he was not prepared to accept.

Gain v. *Gain*, [1962] 1 All E.R. 63; [1961] 1 W.L.R. 1469, was a petition for divorce. A surgeon commander was called to give evidence about the husband's condition five years earlier. The husband's solicitor had a copy of a report about this which the witness had made in the course of his duty. The admiralty claimed Crown privilege for the report. Apparently no objection was made to the witness giving evidence about what he had seen and heard when examining the husband, but, on the motion of counsel for the Crown, the witness was prevented from looking at the copy of his report in order to refresh his memory. This was inevitable as the law stood: if a document is protected by Crown privilege the court is powerless and secondary evidence of its contents cannot be given. But the result is little short of being ridiculous. There was no question of requiring the Admiralty to produce any document in their possession: the contents were already known; and there was no question of its being against the public interest for the witness to give the facts which he had observed. The only result of the attitude taken up by the Admiralty was to deprive the court of the most reliable account of those facts with no profit to anyone. There must be something wrong with a rule which permits Crown privilege to be asserted in this way.

These cases open up a new field which must be kept in view when considering whether a Minister's certificate is to be regarded as conclusive. I do not doubt that it is proper to prevent the use of any document, wherever it comes from, if disclosure of its contents would really injure the national interest, and I do not doubt that it is proper to prevent any witness, whoever he may be, from disclosing facts which in the national interest ought not to be disclosed. Moreover, it is the duty of the court to do this without the intervention of any Minister if possible serious injury to the national interest is readily apparent. In this field, however, it is more than ever necessary that in a doubtful case the alleged public interest in concealment should be balanced against the public interest that the administration of justice should not be frustrated. If the Minister, who has no duty to balance these conflicting public interests, says no more than that in his opinion the public interest requires concealment, and if that is to be accepted as conclusive in this field as well as with regard to documents in his possession, it seems to me not only that very serious injustice may be done to the parties, but also that the due administration of justice may be gravely impaired for quite inadequate reasons.

It cannot be said that there would be any constitutional impropriety in enabling the court to overrule a Minister's objection. That is already the law in Scotland. In Commonwealth jurisdictions from which there is an appeal to the Privy Council the courts generally follow *Robinson's* case, [1931] A.C. 704; [1931] All E.R. Rep. 333, P.C., and, where they do not, they follow *Duncan's* case, [1942] A.C. 624; (1942) 1 All E.R. 587, H.L. with reluctance; and a limited citation of authority from the United States seems to indicate the same trend. I observe that in *United States* v. *Reynolds*, Vinson, C.J. in delivering the opinion of the Supreme Court said (345 U.S. 1, at pp. 9–10 (1952)):

> "Regardless of how it is articulated, some like formula of compromise must be applied here. Judicial control over the evidence in a case cannot be abdicated to the caprice of executive officers. Yet we will not go so far as to say that the court may automatically require a complete disclosure to the judge before the claim of privilege will be accepted in any case. It may be possible to satisfy the court, from all the circumstances of the case, that there is a reasonable danger that compulsion of the evidence will expose military matters which, in the interest of national security, should not be divulged. When this is the case, the occasion for the privilege is appropriate, and the court should not jeopardize the security which the privilege is meant to protect by insisting upon an examination of the evidence, even by the judge alone in chambers."

Lord Simon did not say that courts in England have no power to overrule the executive. He said in *Duncan's case*, [1942] A.C. 624, at p. 642; [1942] 1 All E.R. 587, H.L. at p. 595:

> "The decision ruling out such documents is the decision of the judge . . . It is the judge who is in control of the trial, not the executive, but the proper ruling for the judge to give is as above expressed."

I.e., to accept the Minister's view in every case. In my judgment, in considering what it is "proper" for a court to do we must have regard to the need, shown by twenty-five years' experience since *Duncan's* case, that the courts should balance the public interest in the proper administration of justice against the public interest in withholding any evidence which a Minister considers ought to be withheld.

I would therefore propose that the House ought now to decide that courts have and are entitled to exercise a power and duty to hold a balance between the public interest, as expressed by a Minister, to withhold certain documents or other evidence, and the public interest in ensuring the proper administration of justice. That does not mean that a court would reject a Minister's view: full weight must be given to it in every case, and if the Minister's reasons are of a character which judicial experience is not competent to weigh then the Minister's view must prevail; but experience has shown that reasons given for withholding whole classes of documents are often not of that character. For example a court is perfectly well able to assess the likelihood that, if the writer of a certain class of document knew that there was a chance that his report might be produced in legal proceedings, he would make a less full and candid report than he would otherwise have done.

I do not doubt that there are certain classes of documents which ought not to be disclosed whatever their content may be. Virtually everyone agrees that cabinet minutes and the like ought not to be disclosed until such time as they are only of historical interest; but I do not think that many people would give as the reason that premature disclosure would prevent candour in the cabinet. To my mind the most important reason is that such disclosure would create or fan ill-informed or captious public or political criticism. The business of government is difficult enough as it is, and no government could contemplate with equanimity the inner workings of the government machine being exposed to the gaze of those ready to criticize without adequate knowledge of the background and perhaps with some axe to grind. That must in my view also apply to all documents concerned with policy making within departments including it may be minutes and the like by quite junior officials and correspondence with outside bodies. Further, it may be that deliberations about a particular case require protection as much as deliberations about policy. I do not think that it is possible to limit such documents by any definition; but there seems to me to be a wide difference between such documents and routine reports. There may be special reasons for witholding some kinds of routine documents, but I think that the proper test to be applied is to ask, in the language of Lord Simon in *Duncan's* case, whether the withholding of a document because it belongs to a particular class is really "necessary for the proper functioning of the public service".

It appears to me that, if the Minister's reasons are such that a judge can properly weigh them, he must on the other hand consider what is the probable importance in the case before him of the documents or other evidence sought to be withheld. If he decides that on balance the documents probably ought to be produced, I think that it would generally be best that he should see them before ordering production and, if he thinks that the Minister's reasons are not clearly expressed, he will have to see the documents before ordering production. I can see nothing wrong in the judge seeing documents without their being shown to the parties. Lord Simon said in *Duncan's* case [1942] A.C. 624, at p. 640; [1942] 1 All E.R. 587, at p. 594, H.L. that, where the Crown is a party, this would amount to communicating with one party to the exclusion of the other. I do not agree. The parties see the Minister's reasons. Where a document has not been prepared for the information of the judge, it seems to me a misuse of language to say that the judge "communicates with" the holder of the document by reading it. If on reading the document he still thinks that it ought to be produced, he will order its production.

It is important, however, that the Minister should have a right to appeal before the document is produced. This matter was not fully investigated in the argument before your lordships; but it does appear that in one way or another there can be an appeal if the document is in the custody of a servant of the Crown or of a person who is willing to co-operate with the Minister. There may be difficulty if it is in the hands of a person who wishes to produce it. That difficulty, however, could occur today if a witness wishes to give some evidence which the Minister unsuccessfully urges the court to prevent from being given. It may be that this is a matter which deserves further investigation by the Crown authorities.

The documents in this case are in the possession of a police force. The position of the police is peculiar. They are not servants of the Crown and they do not take orders from the government. But they are carrying out an essential function of government, and various Crown rights, privileges and exemptions have been held to apply to them. . . . It has never been denied that they are entitled to Crown privilege with regard to documents, and it is essential that they should have it.

The police are carrying on an unending war with criminals many of whom are today highly intelligent. So it is essential that there should be no disclosure of anything which might give any useful information to those who organize criminal activities; and it would generally be wrong to require disclosure in a civil case of anything which might be material in a pending prosecution, but after a verdict has been given, or it has been decided to take no proceedings, there is not the same need for secrecy. With regard to other documents there seems to be no greater need for protection than in the case of departments of government.

It appears to me to be most improbable that any harm would be done by disclosure of the probationary reports on the appellant or of the report from the Police Training Centre. With regard to the report which the respondent made to his chief constable with a view to the prosecution of the appellant there could be more doubt, although no suggestion was made in argument that disclosure of its contents would be harmful now that the appellant has been acquitted. As I have said, these documents may prove to be of vital importance in this litigation.

In my judgment this appeal should be allowed and these documents ought now to be required to be produced for inspection. If it is then found that disclosure would not, in your lordships' view, be prejudicial to the public interest, or that any possibility of such prejudice is, in the case of each of the documents, insufficient to justify its being withheld, then disclosure should be ordered.

[LORDS MORRIS OF BORTH-Y-GEST, HODSON, PEARCE and UPJOHN delivered concurring judgments.]

Questions

1. Did the House of Lords in *Conway* v. *Rimmer* distinguish or overrule *Duncan's* case?

2. What is the difference between reasons "which judicial experience is not competent to weigh" and others?

3. How strong is the candour argument? Do you agree with Lord Pearce's words: "What policeman *could* be deterred from candour by the thought that a judge might read his notes? One imagines that he would rather be put on his mettle to make sure that his observations were sound and accurate, and be stimulated by the thought that he might prove to be the one impartial recorder on whom justice between the parties might ultimately turn" ([1968] A.C. 910, at p. 985; [1968] 1 All E.R. 874, at p. 910).

Notes

1. Claims to privilege in criminal cases are unlikely to be made or to succeed: *Re Tunstall, Ex parte Brown* (1966) 67 S.R.N.S.W. 1.

2. Normally the privilege only applies to communications within government departments, but there is one traditional instance of its application to communications from outsiders. In public prosecutions, provided no injustice is caused to the accused, a witness cannot be asked to give answers which would reveal the names of informants: *Marks* v. *Beyfus* (1890), 25 Q.B.D. 494, C.A. It now seems that this exception is not isolated.

Rogers v. Secretary of State for the Home Department
[1973] A.C. 388; [1972] 2 All E.R. 1057, H.L.

A company of which Rogers was a director sought the Gaming Board's consent to the grant of licences in respect of bingo halls to be managed by Rogers. The Board was obliged to take into account Roger's character. They made inquiries of the Sussex Police, and in reply the Assistant Chief Constable of Sussex wrote a letter to the Board, which later refused the consent sought. Rogers began proceedings for criminal libel regarding the contents of the letter. The Home Secretary claimed privilege in respect of the letter and a copy. The House of Lords upheld the claims.

LORD REID: The ground put forward has been said to be Crown privilege. I think that that expression is wrong and may be misleading. There is no question of any privilege in the ordinary sense of the word. The real question is whether the public interest requires that the letter shall not be produced and whether that public interest is so strong as to override the ordinary right and interest of a litigant that he shall be able to lay before a court of justice all relevant evidence. A Minister of the Crown is always an appropriate and often the most appropriate person to assert this public interest, and the evidence or advice which he gives to the court is always valuable and may sometimes be indispensable. But in my view it must always be open to any person interested to raise the question and there may be cases where the trial judge should himself raise the question if no one else has done so. In the present case the question of public interest was raised by both the Attorney-General and the board. In my judgment both were entitled to raise the matter. Indeed I think that in the circumstances it was the duty of the board to do as they have done.

The claim in the present case is not based on the nature of the contents of this particular letter. It is based on the fact that the board cannot adequately perform their statutory duty unless they can preserve the confidentiality of all communications to them regarding the character, reputation or antecedents of applicants for their consent.

Claims for "class privilege" were fully considered by this House in *Conway* v. *Rimmer*. It was made clear that there is a heavy burden of proof on any authority which makes such a claim. But the possibility of establishing such a claim was not ruled out. I venture to quote what I said in that case ([1968] A.C. 910, at p. 952; [1968] 1 All E.R. 874, at p. 888 H.L.):

> "There may be special reasons for withholding some kinds of routine documents, but I think that the proper test to be applied is to ask, in the language of Lord Simon in *Duncan's* case, whether the withholding of a document because it belongs to a particular class is really 'necessary for the proper functioning of the public service' " [1942] A.C. 624, at p. 642; [1942] 1 All E.R. 587, at p. 595 H.L.)

I do not think that "the public service" should be construed narrowly. Here the question is whether the withholding of this class of documents is really necessary to enable the board adequately to perform its statutory duties. If it is then we are enabling the will of Parliament to be carried out.

There are very unusual features about this case. The board require the fullest information they can get in order to identify and exclude persons of dubious character and reputation from the privilege of obtaining a licence to conduct a gaming establishment. There is no obligation on anyone to give any information to the board. No doubt many law abiding citizens would tell what they know even if there was some risk of their identity becoming known, although many perfectly honourable people do not want to be thought to be mixed up in such affairs. But it is obvious that the best source of information about dubious characters must often be persons of dubious character themselves. It has long been recognized that the identity of police informers must in the public interest be kept secret and the same considerations must apply to those who volunteer information to the board. Indeed it is in evidence that many refuse to speak unless assured of absolute secrecy.

The letter called for in this case came from the police. I feel sure that they would not be deterred from giving full information by any fear of consequences to themselves if there were any disclosure. But much of the information which they can give must come from sources which must be protected and they would rightly take this into account. Even if information were given without naming the source, the very nature of the information might, if it were communicated to the person concerned, at least give him a very shrewd idea from whom it had come.

It is possible that some documents coming to the board could be disclosed without fear of such consequences. But I would think it quite impracticable for the board or the court to be sure of this. So it appears to me that, if there is not to be very serious danger of the board being deprived of information essential for the proper performance of their difficult task, there must be a general rule that they are not bound to produce any document which gives information to them about an applicant.

We must then balance that fact against the public interest that the course of justice should not be impeded by the withholding of evidence. We must, I think, take into account that these documents only came into existence because the applicant is asking for a privilege and is submitting his character and reputation to scrutiny. The documents are not used to deprive him of any legal right. The board have a wide discretion. Not only can they refuse his application on the ground of bad reputation although he may say that he has not deserved that reputation; it is not denied that the board can also take into account any unfavourable impression which he has made during an interview with the board. Natural justice requires that the board should act in good faith and that they should so far as possible tell him the gist of any grounds on which they propose to refuse his application so that he may show such grounds to be unfounded in fact. But the board must be trusted to do that; we have been referred to their practice in this matter and I see nothing wrong in it.

In the present case the board told Mr Rogers nothing about the contents of this letter because they say that they had sufficient grounds for refusing his application without any need to rely on anything in the letter. Their good faith in this matter is not subject to any substantial challenge. If Mr Rogers had not by someone's wrongful act obtained a copy of the letter there was no reason why he should ever have known anything about it.

In my judgment on balance the public interest clearly requires that documents of this kind should not be disclosed, and that public interest is not affected by the fact that by some wrongful means a copy of such a document had been obtained and published by some person.

LORD PEARSON: It seems to me that the proper procedure is that which has been followed, I think consistently, in recent times. The objection to disclosure of the document or information is taken by the Attorney-General or his representative on behalf of the appropriate Minister, that is to say, the political head of the government department within whose sphere of responsibility the matter arises, and the objection is expressed in or supported by a certificate from the appropriate Minister. This procedure has several advantages: (1) the question whether or not the disclosure of the document or information would be detrimental to the public interest on the administrative or executive side is considered at a high level; (2) the court has the assistance of a carefully considered and authoritative opinion on that question; (3) the Attorney-General is consulted and has opportunities of promoting uniformity both in the decision of such questions and in the formulation of the grounds on which the objections are taken. The court has to balance the detriment to the public interest on the administrative or executive side, which would result from the disclosure of the document or information, against the detriment to the public interest on the judicial side, which would result from non-disclosure of a document or information which is relevant to an issue in legal proceedings. Therefore the court, although naturally giving great weight to the opinion of the appropriate Minister conveyed through the Attorney-General or his representative, must have the final responsibility of deciding whether or not the document or information is to be disclosed.

Although that established procedure is the proper procedure, it is not essential as a matter of law. It is not always practicable. If the appropriate Minister is not available, some other Minister or some highly-placed official must act in his stead. If it becomes evident in the course of a trial or in interlocutory proceedings that perhaps some document or information ought in the public interest to be protected from disclosure, it must be open to the party or witness concerned or the court itself to raise the question. If such a situation arises in the course of a trial, the court can adjourn the trial for the appropriate Minister or the Attorney-General to be consulted, but the court will be reluctant to adjourn the trial unless it is really necessary to do so, and in some cases that will be unnecessary because the court is able to give an immediate answer.

The expression "Crown privilege" is not accurate, although sometimes convenient. The Crown has no privilege in the matter. The appropriate Minister has the function of deciding, with the assistance of the Attorney-General, whether or not the public interest on the administrative or executive side requires that he should object to the disclosure of the document or information, but a negative decision cannot properly be described as a waiver of a privilege.

[LORDS MORRIS OF BORTH-Y-GEST, SIMON OF GLAISDALE and SALMON delivered concurring judgments.]

Note

The phrase "Crown privilege" was attacked by every member of the House except Lord Morris; the phrase "public policy" was preferred.

Norwich Pharmacal Co. *v.* Customs and Excise Commissioners
[1974] A.C. 133; [1973] 2 All E.R. 943, H.L.

The appellants were owners and licencees of a patent for a chemical called fura-zolidone. The patent was being infringed by illegal imports of the substance. The appellants instituted proceedings against the Commissioners to obtain the names and addresses of the importers. The Commissioners made a claim for privilege in an affida-vit sworn by Sir Louis Petch, the Chairman of the Commissioners. It was upheld by Graham, J., denied by the Court of Appeal, but upheld by the House of Lords.

LORD REID: [W]e have to weigh the requirements of justice to the appellants against the considerations put forward by the respondents as justifying non-disclosure. They are twofold. First it is said that to make such disclosures would or might impair or hamper the efficient conduct of their important statutory duties. And secondly, it is said that such disclosure would or might be prejudicial to those whose identity would be disclosed.

There is nothing secret or confidential in the information sought or in the documents which came into the hands of the respondents containing that information. Those documents are ordinary commercial documents which pass through many different hands. But it is said that those who do not wish to have their names disclosed might concoct false documents and thereby hamper the work of the Customs. That would require at least a conspiracy between the foreign consignor and the importer and it seems to me to be in the highest degree improbable. It appears that there are already arrangements in operation by the respondents restricting the disclosure of certain matters if the importers do not wish them to be disclosed. It may be that the knowledge that a court might order discovery in certain cases would cause somewhat greater use to be made of these arrangements. But it was not suggested in argument that that is a matter of any vital importance. The only other point was that such disclosure might cause resentment and impair good relations with other traders: but I find it impossible to believe that honest traders would resent failure to protect wrongdoers.

Protection of traders from having their names disclosed is a more difficult matter. If we could be sure that those whose names are sought are all tortfeasors, they do not deserve any protection. In the present case the possibility that any are not is so remote that I think it can be neglected. The only possible way in which any of these imports could be legitimate and not an infringement would seem to be that someone might have exported some furazolidone from this country and then whoever owned it abroad might have sent it back here. Then there would be no infringement. But again that seems most unlikely.

But there may be other cases where there is much more doubt. The validity of the patent may be doubtful and there could well be other doubts. If the respondents have any doubts in any future case about the propriety of making disclosures they are well entitled to require the matter to be submitted to the court at the expense of the person seeking the disclosure. The court will then only order discovery if satisfied that there is no substantial chance of injustice being done.

I would therefore allow this appeal.

VISCOUNT DILHORNE: I do not accept the proposition that all information given to a government department is to be treated as confidential and protected from disclosure, but I agree that information of a personal character obtained in the exercise of statutory powers, information of such a character that the giver of it would not expect it to be used for any purpose other than that for which it is given, or disclosed to any person not concerned with that purpose, is to be regarded as protected from disclosure, even though there is no statutory prohibition of its disclosure. But not all information given to a government department, whether voluntarily or under compulsion is of this confidential character and the question is whether the names of the importers of the furazolidone were given in confidence. I do not think that that is established. The names and addresses of the importers had to be given to the master of the ship and made known to all those taking part in securing the transit of the chemicals. Presumably the parcels of furazolidone had on them the names and addresses of the consignees for all to see, though they may, I do not know, have not disclosed that the contents of the parcels were furazolidone. The documents completed for the transit of the chemicals and for Customs which show the names of the consignees and the contents of the parcels do not seem to me more confidential than consignment notes completed for British Railways and British Road Services.

. . . I must confess that I am not in the least impressed by the "candour" argument. I really cannot conceive it to be realistic to suggest that the vast majority of importers who do not infringe patents or do other wrongs, will be in the least deterred from giving proper information to Customs by the knowledge that pursuant to an order of the court the names of the wrongdoers are disclosed by Customs.

LORD CROSS OF CHELSEA: Sir Louis says that he is afraid that the good relations and mutual confidence which usually exist between the officers of the Customs and traders would be seriously impaired if it became known that any information of a confidential character obtained from traders under statutory powers might have to be disclosed by the commissioners otherwise than under the provisions of a statute enabling them to disclose it. The traders whose good relations with the Customs Sir Louis is anxious to maintain are, presumably, honest traders. Any honest trader who was disturbed at the thought that a court could order the disclosure of importers' names in circumstances such as exist here would be a most unreasonable man and I cannot believe that there would be many such. No doubt dishonest traders might be disturbed by the knowledge that such disclosure could be ordered, and Sir Louis gives it as a further ground for the claim of privilege that dishonest traders who now tell the Customs the truth with regard to the character of the goods and the identity of the importers may be driven to giving false information. An argument that one should not try to stop one form of wrongdoing out of fear that some of the wrongdoers may take to committing yet further offences in order to be able to maintain their original course of wrongdoing is not very attractive. But in any case I think that Sir Louis' fears on this head are exaggerated. On the question of public interest I agree with Graham, J. and disagree with the Court of Appeal.

[LORDS MORRIS OF BORTH-Y-GEST and KILBRANDON delivered concurring judgments.]

Notes

1. Had the documents been relevant to litigation between two private parties neither could have claimed any private privilege.

2. In *Conway* v. *Rimmer*, [1968] A.C. 910, at p. 946; [1968] 1 All E.R. 874, at p. 884, H.L., Lord Reid said: "If the State insists on a man disclosing his private affairs for a particular purpose, it requires a very strong case to justify that disclosure being used for other purposes."

Alfred Crompton Amusements Machines Ltd., v. Customs and Excise Commissioners (No. 2)
[1974] A.C. 405; [1973] 2 All E.R. 1169, H.L.

An issue arose between the company and the Commissioners as to the correct assessment for purchase tax on certain machines made by the company. The Commissioners, in an affidavit sworn by their Chairman, Sir Louis Petch, claimed privilege for certain documents containing information supplied by third parties. The House of Lords upheld the claim.

LORD CROSS OF CHELSEA: "Confidentiality" is not a separate head of privilege, but it may be a very material consideration to bear in mind when privilege is claimed on the ground of public interest. What the court has to do is to weigh on the one hand the considerations which suggest that it is in the public interest that the documents in question should be disclosed and on the other hand those which suggest that it is in the public interest that they should not be disclosed and to balance one against the other. Plainly there is much to be said in favour of disclosure. The documents in question constitute an important part of the material on which the commissioners based their conclusion that the appellant sell to retailers. That is shown by the reply which the commissioners made to the request for particulars under paragraph 5 (*h*) of the defence. Yet if the claim to privilege made by the commissioners is upheld this information will be withheld from the arbitrator. No doubt it will form part of the brief delivered to counsel for the commissioners and may help him to probe the appellants' evidence in cross-examination; but counsel will not be able to use it as evidence to controvert anything which the appellants' witnesses may say. It is said, of course, that the appellants cannot reasonably complain if the commissioners think it right to tie their own hands in this way. But if the arbitrator should decide against them the appellants may feel—however wrongly—that the arbitrator was unconsciously influenced by the fact that the commissioners stated in their pleadings that they had this further evidence in support of their view which they did not disclose and which the appellants had no opportunity to controvert. Morever, whoever wins it is desirable that the arbitrator should have all the relevant material before him. On the other hand, there is much to be said against disclosure. The case is not, indeed, as strong as the case against disclosing the name of an informer—for the result of doing that would be that the source of information would dry up whereas here the commissioners will continue to have their powers under section 24 (6) [of the Purchase Tax Act 1963]. Nevertheless, the case against disclosure is, to my mind, far stronger than it was in the *Norwich Pharmacal* case. There it was probable that all the importers whose names were disclosed were wrongdoers and the disclosure of the names of any, if there were any, who were innocent would not be likely to do them any harm at all. Here, on the other hand, one can well see that the third parties who have supplied this information to the commissioners because of the existence of their statutory powers would very much resent its disclosure by the commissioners to the appellants and that it is not at all fanciful for Sir Louis to say that the knowledge that the commissioners cannot keep such information secret may be harmful to the efficient working of the Act. In a case where the considerations for and against disclosure appear to be fairly evenly balanced the courts should I think uphold a claim to privilege on the ground of public interest and trust to the head of the department concerned to do whatever he can to mitigate the ill-effects of non-disclosure. Forbes, J. was so impressed by those possible ill-effects that he failed to appreciate how reasonable Sir Louis' objections to disclosure were and dismissed them with the remark "We are not living in the early days of the Tudor administration". I do not regard Sir Louis as a modern Cardinal Morton. His objections to disclosure were taken in the interests of the third parties concerned as much as in the interests of the commissioners and if any of them is in fact willing to give evidence, privilege in respect of any documents or information obtained from him will be waived.

[LORDS REID, MORRIS OF BORTH-Y-GEST and KILBRANDON and VISCOUNT DILHORNE agreed.]

Questions

1. How can Lord Cross' last sentence be reconciled with the view that the right and duty to object to disclosure on public interest grounds is not a privilege and cannot be waived?

2. Do these decisions unduly exalt state interests above those of priests and doctors?

3. What differences are there between the *Pharmacal* and *Norwich* cases which compelled a different result?

Reading

Clark (1969) 32 M.L.R. 142; Tapper (1974), 37 M.L.R. 92.

II PREVIOUS LITIGATION

It should be noted that on grounds of public policy judges of inferior courts cannot be compelled to testify about the cases they have heard: *R.* v. *Gazard* (1838), 8 C. & P. 595. Arbitrators can be compelled to testify but not to give reasons for their award: *Buccleuch (Duke)* v. *Metropolitan Board of Works* (1872), L.R. 5 H.L. 418, H.L. Evidence will not be received from jurors as to their discussions: *Jackson* v. *Williamson* (1788), 2 Term Rep. 281. There is little authority on advocates.

PART SIX

The Course of the Trial

19

The Course of the Trial

I CIVIL CASES

A. Order

The "right to begin" is the right to make a speech to the court explaining the issues. The right depends on who has the right to begin calling evidence, and this will be the plaintiff if he has the evidential burden on any issue raised by the pleadings, as he almost always does and as we will henceforth assume. After he addresses the court, he begins calling witnesses. After he examines them ("examination in chief") the defendant may cross-examine them and the plaintiff may re-examine them. The plaintiff will make a closing speech if the defendant does not call witnesses; the defendant will then have a right to reply. If the defendant calls witnesses (who may be cross-examined by the plaintiff) the procedure will be: plaintiff's opening, plaintiff's witnesses, defendant's opening, defendant's witnesses, defendant's final speech, plaintiff's reply.

This procedure may be interrupted by arguments about the admissibility of evidence or other points of law. At the close of the plaintiff's case the defendant may submit that there is no case to answer. If this is done before a judge with a jury, the judge must put the maker of the submission to an election; if he adheres to the submission he must not call evidence (*Alexander* v. *Rayson*, [1936] 1 K.B. 169, C.A.; *Storey* v. *Storey*, [1961] P. 63; [1960] 3 All E.R. 279, C.A.). However, the judge has a discretion not to compel an election in civil cases tried by jury. In *Young* v. *Rank*, [1950] 2 K.B. 510, at p. 415; [1950] 2 All E.R. 166, at p. 169 Devlin, J. offered this explanation:

> "[I]n a case tried by judge alone the Court of Appeal has a complete power of rehearing, and if evidence for the defendant has not been taken and the court disagrees with the ruling of the trial judge, it is, in effect, prevented from exercising its power of rehearing and has no alternative but to send the case back for retrial, which will result in additional costs to the parties. In cases of trial by jury, the Court of Appeal has no power of rehearing, and, if the verdict of the jury is set aside for any reason, the court has no power except to send it back for re-trial."

The judge may delay taking his decision on a submission of no case to answer until after the jury's verdict; this avoids the need for a new trial if an appeal against his decision to uphold the submission succeeds. It does produce a slightly unattractive appearance of judicial overruling of juries. An appeal may be dismissed even though the appellate court thinks the submission should have been upheld if subsequent evidence is against the party making it (*Payne* v. *Harrison*, [1961] 2 Q.B. 403, C.A.; [1961] 2 All E.R. 873). In making his decision on a "no case" submission, the judge should assume the plaintiff's witnesses are telling the truth, both on the points on which they are in his favour as well as those on which they favour the defendant. If the judge decides against the submission the case goes to the jury; but even if the defendant gives no evidence they may decide against the plaintiff. This may arise because of the difference between the evidential burden of proof considered by the judge and the legal burden considered by the jury; or because the jury takes a different view of the credibility of the witnesses.

In proceedings before magistrates the doctrine of election applies. If the magistrates hold there is a case to answer, the maker of the submission should be given a further opportunity to address them (*Disher* v. *Disher* [1965] P. 31; [1963] 3 All E.R. 933).

B. Kinds of examination

i *Examination-in-Chief*

The purpose of questions put to a witness in chief is to obtain evidence supporting the case of the party calling the witness. In various respects examination in chief is more restricted than cross-examination. Leading questions can be used less freely; and though an unfavourable witness may be contradicted by other evidence he cannot be discredited unless he proves hostile.

ii *Cross-Examination*

The purpose of cross-examination is to destroy those parts of the witness's testimony which tell in favour of the party calling him and to obtain testimony favourable to the cross-examiner. Both aims are achieved by cross-examination to the issue; only the first aim is achieved by cross-examination which seeks to destroy the witness's credit. The normal rules of admissibility apply, but the cross-examiner has greater freedom than the examiner-in-chief. He may use leading questions, he may ask about previous inconsistent statements and prove them if they are denied, he may ask questions about bad character, previous convictions, unreliability or bias, and prove the convictions, the physical or mental causes of unreliability, or the bias if they are denied. A witness may probably be cross-examined by any party (*Murdoch* v. *Taylor*, [1965] A.C. 574, at p. 584; [1965] All E.R. 406, at p. 409, H.L., *per* Lord Morris of Borth-y-Gest; *R.* v. *Hilston*, [1972] 1 Q.B. 421; [1971] 3 All E.R. 541, C.A.).

However, the witness is to some extent protected even under cross-examination. If it is proposed to contradict him by subsequent evidence on any point, that point must be put to him so that he can explain any misunderstanding. If this is not done the cross-examiner may be taken to accept the evidence. The judge has a discretion to disallow improper or aggressive questions.

iii *Re-examination*

The purpose of re-examination is to rehabilitate the witness's testimony from the effects of cross-examination, if this is necessary. It is generally subject to the same rules as examination-in-chief. Further, re-examination must be confined to matters arising out of the cross-examination, and new material cannot be introduced without the judge's leave. This avoids the danger of the other side being unable to examine the witness on the material.

C. Special problems

i Leading questions

Cross (p. 200) defines a leading question as one which "leads" the witness by suggesting the answer desired or assuming the existence of disputed facts. In examination-in-chief or re-examination such questions are frowned on because they encourage and make too easy the coaching of witnesses, and because the assumption of disputed facts may improperly influence the jury. They are, however, permitted for introductory, formal or undisputed matters, for questioning about identity, and to bring a witness's attention to some special point. The judge has considerable discretion as to how many leading questions may be asked, for they do save time and enable testimony to be given naturally. They are widely permitted in cross-examination so as to focus the attention of witness and court on the points on which his testimony is being challenged and tested.

ii Refreshing memory

A witness may "refresh his memory" by referring to documentary records of the facts in issue. The document must have been made about the time of the facts being testified to; as always, this is a vague question of degree. The document must have been made by or under the supervision of the witness. The document must be handed to the opponent for inspection to enable cross-examination to occur on its contents; the trier of fact has a right to see it. The original must be produced if the document does not actually revive the witness's memory of what he swears to, but instead simply makes him confident as to the truth of what he recorded. (This will often arise with policemen and doctors who record many very similar events that may culminate in litigation; they cannot be expected to remember them in detail but they can swear to the truth of their record.) However, if the document actually causes him to remember the fact, the original need not be produced (*Doe d. Church and Phillips* v. *Perkins* (1790), 3 Term. Rep. 749). Using the document to refresh memory does not make it evidence of the truth of its contents. Nor is it made evidence by the opponent inspecting it and cross-examining on the parts used to refresh memory (*Senat* v. *Senat*, [1965] P. 172; [1965] 2 All E.R. 505). But more extensive cross-examination or reliance on the parts of the document makes it evidence, and is equivalent to calling a witness for the purposes of the order of speeches.

The law relating to refreshing memory has been made of much less practical importance by Part I of the Civil Evidence Act 1968, for the documents are now admissible in their own right under ss. 2 and 4. Section 3 (2) states that when the document is admitted at common law to refresh memory it is admissible "as evidence of any fact stated therein of which direct oral evidence by [the witness] would be admissible".

It has been held that the above rules apply only to the refreshing of memory in court: *R.* v. *Richardson*, [1971] 2 Q.B. 484; [1971] 2 All E.R. 773, C.A.; but this decision may be doubted: Howard, [1972] Crim. L.R. 351.

iii Previous consistent statements

There used to be a general rule that a witness might not be asked in chief whether he has made a prior statement consistent with his present testimony, nor might other witnesses prove it. The rule existed to prevent the manufacture of self-serving evidence by party-witnesses and to prevent the introduction of collateral issues and superfluous testimony. It had the substantial drawback of preventing witnesses telling their stories in a natural way, i.e. by stating facts observed and statements made about them to others. It is also doubtful whether it might not have been better to admit statements made near the time of the facts in issue rather than be limited to those made years later at the trial. In civil cases the rule has been substantially eroded by the Civil Evidence Act 1968, and there are other exceptions. The Civil Evidence Act, s. 2 (1), provides that any statement made by any person "whether called as a witness . . . or not, shall . . . be admissible as evidence of any fact stated therein of which direct oral evidence by him would be admissible". Section 2 (2) requires that the leave of the court be obtained if such statement was made by a witness; and that it should not be given in evidence until the conclusion of the witness's examination-in-chief unless the intelligibility of the witness's testimony would be affected by not being allowed to narrate it earlier in his examination-in-chief, or unless the statement is proved by an earlier witness, to avoid the inconvenience of calling him twice. R.S.C. Ord. 38, r. 21 requires notice of intention to introduce such statements to be given to all parties; the court has a discretion to overlook breach of this requirement (R.S.C. Ord. 38, r. 29). Section 4 (2) enacts a similar system for documentary records admissible under s. 4 (1) (pp. 363–4, *ante*).

Res gestae statements.—At common law previous consistent statements were sometimes admissible as part of the *res gestae*. In future, so far as these statements are tendered as evidence of their truth, the exception will have been swallowed up by the Civil Evidence Act. But so far as they are tendered as evidence of the fact that they were made, they will continue to be admissible; section 1 of the Act which abolishes common law hearsay exceptions will not apply to evidence which is original rather than hearsay in character (e.g. *Milne* v. *Leisler* (1862), 7 H. & N. 786).

Rebutting afterthought.—At common law, if in cross-examination it was suggested to a witness that he had recently fabricated his story, his previous consistent statements could be admitted, not as evidence of the truth of what they asserted, but to show consistency. The Civil Evidence Act 1968, s. 3 (1) (b), provides that a previous statement so proved is admissible as evidence of any fact stated therein of which direct oral evidence by him would be admissible. There are not many reported cases on recent fabrication and it seems difficult to admit previous statements on this ground (see *Fox* v. *General Medical Council*, [1960] 3 All E.R. 225; [1960] 1 W.L.R. 1017, P.C.; *Nominal Defendant* v. *Clements* (1961), 104 C.L.R. 476; *R.* v. *Oyesiku* (1971), 56 Cr. App. Rep. 240, C.A.). The exception would now have little operation independently of the Civil Evidence Act, but it does have the advantage of not being subject to the notice procedure.

Miscellaneous.—Writers have noted that in practice there are other exceptions to the old rule, e.g. the accused's statements favourable to himself at the time of the charge (*R.* v. *Storey* (1968), 52 Cr. App. Rep. 334, C.A.) and pre-trial identifications by identity witnesses (Cross, p. 218; Gooderson, [1968] C.L.J. 64)).

iv Unfavourable and hostile witnesses

A party may be disappointed by the evidence a witness called by him gives. The witness may not "come up to proof"—he may tell a different story to the court from that told outside it. If he merely fails to testify to certain facts or testifies to the opposite of what was expected, he is an "unfavourable" witness. A hostile witness is one who is "unwilling, if called by a party who cannot ask him leading questions, to tell the truth and the whole truth in answer to non-leading questions—to tell the truth for the advancement of justice" (*R.* v. *Hayden*, [1959] V.R. 102, at p. 103, *per* Sholl, J.). The decision as to a witness's hostility is one in the discretion of the judge, and on this issue his decision will only rarely be reversed, depending as it does on observation of demeanour and detailed knowledge of the course of the trial. However, it is probably too much to say it will never be reversed (cf. *Rice* v. *Howard* (1886), 16 Q.B.D. 681).

The normal rule is that a party may not impeach his own witness, i.e. may not treat him as if he is under cross-examination. At common law, an unfavourable witness could be contradicted by calling other evidence (*Ewer* v. *Ambrose* (1825), 3 B. & C. 746); and a hostile witness could also be asked leading questions and challenged regarding his means of knowledge and powers of observation; but no evidence of lack of veracity could be adduced (e.g. proof of convictions). At common law it was doubtful whether previous inconsistent statements could be proved. To remove the doubt the obscure Criminal Procedure Act 1865, s. 3, was enacted. It applies to both civil and criminal cases. It provides: "A party producing a witness shall not be allowed to impeach his credit by general evidence of bad character, but he may, in case the witness shall, in the opinion of the judge, prove adverse, contradict him by other evidence, or, by leave of the judge, prove that he has made at other times a statement inconsistent with his present testimony; but before such last-mentioned proof can be given the circumstances of the supposed statement, sufficient to designate the particular occasion, must be mentioned to the witness, and he must be asked whether or not he has made such statement."

"Adverse" means "hostile". Does it follow that the common law power to introduce evidence contradicting an unfavourable witness is lost? This disastrous result is avoided by one of two means. Cockburn, C.J. preferred to ignore this conclusion as being based on "a great blunder" (*Greenough* v. *Eccles* (1859), 5 C.B.N.S. 786, at p. 806). Williams and Willes, JJ. said: "we think the preferable construction is that in case the witness shall, in the opinion of the judge, prove 'hostile' the party producing him may not only contradict him by other witnesses, as he might heretofore have done, and may still do, if the witness is unfavourable, but may also, by leave of the judge, prove that he has made inconsistent statements" (28 L.J.C.P. 160, at p. 163).

The Civil Evidence Act 1968, s. 3 (1) (*a*), provides that previous inconsistent statements are admissible as evidence of the facts asserted. The notice procedure does not apply. In criminal cases, as in civil cases before 1968, the statement goes only to credibility.

v Previous inconsistent statements

Similar rules apply to previous inconsistent statements put, not to a hostile witness, but to an opponent's witness while he is being cross-examined. They are stated by the Criminal Procedure Act 1865, ss. 4 and 5. These sections apply in both civil and criminal cases: s. 4 concerns oral statements and s. 5 written ones:

> 4. If a witness, upon cross-examination as to a former statement made by him relative to the subject matter of the indictment or proceeding, and inconsistent with his present testimony, does not distinctly admit that he has made such statement, proof may be given that he did in fact make it; but before such proof can be given the circumstances of the supposed statement sufficient to designate the particular occasion, must be mentioned to the witness, and he must be asked whether or not he has made such statement.

> 5. A witness may be cross-examined as to previous statements made by him in writing or reduced into writing relative to the subject matter of the indictment or proceeding, without such writing being shown to him; but if it is intended to contradict such witness by the writing, his attention must, before such contradictory proof can be given, be called to those parts of the writing which are to be used for the purpose of so contradicting him: provided always, that it shall be competent for the judge, at any time during the trial, to require the production of the writing for his inspection, and he may thereupon make such use of it for the purposes of the trial as he may think fit.

The Civil Evidence Act 1968, s. 3 (1) (*a*), makes previous inconsistent statements admissible evidence of the truth of what they assert. In criminal cases the former rule that they go only to show inconsistency applies.

vi Collateral questions

The answers given by a witness to questions put in cross-examination about collateral facts are final. The jury may not believe the answers, but this process cannot be encouraged by the cross-examiner introducing contradictory evidence. The rule is intended to prevent side issues arising.

The usual test for what a collateral fact is was stated by Pollock, C.B. in *A.-G.* v. *Hitchcock* (1847), 1 Exch. 91, at p. 99. "[I]f the answer of a witness is a matter which you would be allowed on your own part to prove in evidence . . . then it is a matter on which you may contradict him." Thus collateral facts are those relevant to credibility rather than to the main issues. (There seems to be an error in Cross, p. 234, in discussing *Piddington* v. *Bennett and Wood Pty., Ltd.* (1940), 63 C.L.R. 533 and *R.* v. *Burke* (1858), 8 Cox C.C. 44. He asserts that evidence that a particular witness was not present at some event he claimed to be at, or that he cannot understand a language he claimed to, is not evidence of collateral facts. He draws the conclusion that Pollock, C.B.'s test is not wide enough. This seems wrong because though the evidence mentioned may be very important, it is still evidence going to credibility and hence collateral to the issues in the case. If anything is wrong, it is not Pollock, C.B.'s test but the rule that test is trying to express. However, the rule is substantially undercut by exceptions.

There are several exceptions, apart from previous inconsistent statements, discussed p. 433, *ante*. In the case of all these exceptions to the collateral answers rule, apart from previous inconsistent statements, the evidence may be introduced without there first being a denial of the fact proved; but it is convenient to treat them together in this way. If the witness denies that he has been convicted, his convictions may be proved to show his lack of credibility; the conviction need not be of a kind relevant to truth-telling (Criminal Proceedure Act 1865, s. 6, which applies to both civil and criminal cases).

Bias. The witness's denials of taking bribes, or of being on very good or bad terms with a party, may be contradicted.

Incapacity to tell the truth. The rules here may be illustrated by two criminal cases, the principles of which apply equally to civil cases.

R. v. Richardson
[1969] 1 Q.B. 299; [1968] 2 All E.R. 761, C.A.

EDMUND DAVIES, L.J.:

1. A witness may be asked whether he has knowledge of the impugned witness's general reputation for veracity and whether (from such knowledge) he would believe the impugned witness's sworn testimony.

2. The witness called to impeach the credibility of a previous witness may also express his individual opinion (based upon his personal knowledge) as to whether the latter is to be believed upon his oath and is *not* confined to giving evidence merely of general reputation.

3. But whether his opinion as to the impugned witness's credibility be based simply upon the latter's general reputation for veracity or upon his personal knowledge, the witness cannot be permitted to indicate during his examination-in-chief the particular facts, circumstances or incidents which formed the basis of his opinion, although he may be cross-examined as to them.

Toohey v. Metropolitan Police Commissioner
[1965] A.C. 595; [1965] 1 All E.R. 506, H.L.

The appellant and two other men were charged with assault with intent to rob Madden, a sixteen year old boy. The police found the accused in an alley with Madden, the latter being dishevelled and hysterical. The defence was that the accused had found Madden in a drunken condition and were trying to help him home when he became hysterical. A police surgeon said in evidence at the first trial that Madden smelt of alcohol, that his hysteria would have been exacerbated by alcohol and that he might be more prone to hysteria than ordinary people. The jury disagreed. At a second trial the doctor's evidence was excluded. The House of Lords held this to be wrong.

LORD PEARCE: It is common knowledge that hysteria can be produced by fear. The hysteria of the victim of an alleged assault may, if he is a person of normal stability, confirm a jury in the belief that he has been assaulted. When, however, the victim is unstable and hysterical by nature, the hysteria can raise a doubt whether in truth an assault ever occurred or whether it was the figment of an hysterical imagination. Here the real question to be determined was whether, as the prosecution alleged, the episode created the hysteria, or whether, on the other hand, as the defence alleged, the hysteria created the episode. To that issue medical evidence as to the hysteric and unstable nature of the alleged victim was relevant. It might be that, on a careful examination of the medical evidence, the predisposition to hysteria and instability was not enough to create an episode of this kind without some assault to provoke it. But, equally, that evidence might have created a real doubt whether there was any assault at all and might have inclined the jury to believe the account given by the accused. On that ground the defence was entitled to have the evidence considered by the jury.

The second question, whether it was permissible to impeach the credibility of Madden, *qua* witness, by medical evidence of his hysterical and unstable nature, raises a wider and more important problem which applies to evidence in criminal and civil cases alike.

The Court of Criminal Appeal held that such evidence was not admissible since they were bound by the case of R. v. *Gunewardene*. Undoubtedly they were right in thinking that on this point the present case is not distinguishable from it. In *Gunewardene's* case, [1951] 2 K.B. 600, at p. 609; [1951] 2 All E.R. 290, at p. 294, C.C.A. the appellant (to quote the words of Lord Goddard, C.J.) "wished to call [Doctor Leigh] to say that he . . . had examined the witness and had come to the conclusion that the man was suffering from a disease of the mind and that therefore he regarded his testimony as unreliable. In our opinion that is exactly what the cases show cannot be done." It was there held that the most that the doctor could have been asked on oath was: "From your knowledge of the witness, would you believe him on his oath?" And although it was open to the other side in cross-examination to probe the particular reasons for the belief, the doctor could not give them in examination in chief. Thus, the only evidence which a doctor could give in chief would seem mysterious or meaningless to the jury; and if it was not amplified by questions in cross-examination (from which opposing counsel might well refrain) it would be liable to be robbed of its proper effect. Moreover, the principle in *Gunewardene's* case would exclude altogether the evidence of a doctor who cannot go so far as to say that he would not believe the witness on oath. It would not allow a doctor to testify (as is desired in the present case) to the abnormality and unreliability of the witness, or (as may happen in some other case) to the fact that the witness, by reason of some delusion, would on some matters not be credible, whereas on others he might be quite reliable.

Throughout *Gunewardene's* case the court dealt with the problem created by the mental disease and mental abnormality of the witness as if it were identical with the problem of moral discredit and unveracity. They referred to many cases dealing with bad character and reputation, but to none which dealt with mental disturbance.

From olden times it has been the practice to allow evidence of bad reputation to discredit a witness's testimony. It is perhaps not very logical and not very useful to allow such evidence founded on hearsay. None of your Lordships and none of the counsel before you could remember being concerned in a case where such evidence was called. But the rule has been sanctified through the centuries in legal examinations and textbooks and in some rare cases, and it does not create injustice. Its scope is conveniently summarized by Professor Cross (Evidence, 2nd Edn. (1963), p. 225):

> "In *Mawson* v. *Hartsink* (1802), 4 Esp. 102 it was held that the witness must be asked whether he is aware of the impugned witness's reputation for veracity and whether, from such knowledge, he would believe the impugned witness on oath. In R. v. *Watson* (1817), 2 Stark. 116, at p. 152 however, it was held that the witness might simply state whether he would believe the oath of the person about whom he was asked, and although R. v. *Rowton* (1865), Le. & Ca. 520 decides that, when asked about a prisoner's character, the witness must speak to the accused's general reputation and not give his personal opinion of the accused's disposition, R. v. *Brown* (1867), L.R. I.C.C.R. 70 sanctions the form of question approved in R. v. *Watson*."

Where a witness's general reputation, so far as concerns veracity, has been thus demolished, it seems that it may be reinstated by other witnesses who give evidence that he is worthy of credit or who discredit the discrediting witness (Taylor on Evidence, 12th Edn., Vol. II, para. 1473; Stephen on Evidence, 12th Edn., Art. 146). Thus far, and no further, it appears, may the process of recrimination go (Taylor, para. 1473, citing R. v. *Lord Stafford* (1680), 7 State Tr. 1293, at p. 1484). How far the evidence is confined to veracity alone or may extend to moral turpitude generally seems a matter of some doubt (see Taylor, para. 1471).

There seems little point, however, for present purposes in exploring these archaic niceties. The old cases are concerned with lying as an aspect of bad character and are of little help in establishing any principle that will deal with modern scientific knowledge of mental disease and its effect on the reliability of a witness. I accept all of the judgment in *Gunewardene's* case in so far as it deals with the older cases and the topic with which they were concerned. But, in my opinion, the court erred in using it as a guide to the admissibility of medical evidence concerning illness or abnormality affecting the mind of a witness and reducing his capacity to give reliable evidence. This unreliability may have two aspects either separate from one another or acting jointly to create confusion. The witness may, through his mental trouble, derive a fanciful or untrue picture from events while they are actually occurring, or he may have a fanciful or untrue recollection of them which distorts his evidence at the time when he is giving it.

The only general principles which can be derived from the older cases are these. On the one hand, the courts have sought to prevent juries from being beguiled by the evidence of witnesses who could be shown to be, through defect of character, wholly unworthy of belief. On the other hand, however, they have sought to prevent the trial of a case becoming clogged with a number of side issues, such as might arise if there could be an investigation of matters which had no relevance to the issue save in so far as they tended to show the veracity or falsity of the witness who was giving evidence which *was* relevant to the issue. Many controversies which might thus obliquely throw some light on the issues must in practice be discarded because there is not an infinity of time, money and mental comprehension available to make use of them.

There is one older case (R. v. *Hill*) in which the Court for Crown Cases Reserved considered how it should deal with the evidence of a lunatic who was rational on some points. Evidence was given by doctors as to his credibility. Alderson, B. in argument made the sensible observation (1851), (20 L.J.M.C. 222, at pp. 224–5):

"It seems to me almost approaching to an absurdity to say that a jury may, by hearing the statement of doctors, be able to say whether a man was insane when he made his will, and yet that they should not be competent to say whether a man be in a state of mind to enable him to give credible evidence when they see him before them."

Lord Campbell, C.J. in giving judgment said (*ibid.*, at p. 225):

"The true rule seems to me to be that it was for the judge to see whether the witness understands the nature of an oath and, if he does, to admit his testimony. No doubt, before he is sworn, the lunatic may be cross-examined, and evidence may be called to show that he labours under such a diseased mind as to be inadmissible; but, in the absence of such evidence he is *prima facie* admissible, and the jury may give such credit as they please to his testimony."

The point was not quite the same as that which is before your Lordships, since the question was whether the lunatic should be allowed to give evidence at all. But there is inherent, I think, in the judgments an intention that the jury should have the best opportunity of arriving at the truth and that the medical evidence with regard to the witness's credibility should be before them.

Human evidence shares the frailties of those who give it. It is subject to many cross-currents such as partiality, prejudice, self-interest and, above all, imagination and inaccuracy. Those are matters with which the jury, helped by cross-examination and common sense, must do their best. But when a witness through physical (in which I include mental) disease or abnormality is not capable of giving a true or reliable account to the jury, it must surely be allowable for medical science to reveal this vital hidden fact to them. If a witness purported to give evidence of something which he believed that he had seen at a distance of 50 yards, it must surely be possible to call the evidence of an oculist to the effect that the witness could not possibly see anything at a greater distance than 20 yards, or the evidence of a surgeon who had removed a cataract from which the witness was suffering at the material time and which would have prevented him from seeing what he thought he saw. So, too, must it be allowable to call medical evidence of mental illness which makes a witness incapable of giving reliable evidence, whether through the existence of delusions or otherwise.

It is obviously in the interest of justice that such evidence should be available. The only argument that I can see against its admission is that there might be a conflict between the doctors and that there would then be a trial within a trial. But such cases would be rare and, if they arose, they would not create any insuperable difficulty, since there are many cases in practice where a trial within a trial is achieved without difficulty. And in such a case (unlike the issues relating to confessions) there would not be the inconvenience of having to exclude the jury since the dispute would be for their use and their instruction.

Mr. Buzzard very fairly expressed himself as unable to support the judgment in the case of *Gunewardene* since, in the Crown's view, the important thing was that the jury should be enabled to arrive at the truth and do justice.

In R. v. *Pedrini*, [1964] Crim. L.R. 719; *Times*, July 28, 29, 1964 before the Court of Criminal Appeal no reliance was placed on *Gunewardene's* case. Without opposition from the Crown, since justice seemed to demand it, the court considered the evidence of three doctors as to the mental condition at the relevant time of a witness who had subsequently become insane. Lord Parker, C.J. said of that evidence:

> "That it is fresh evidence this court is prepared to accept: that it is relevant evidence there is no doubt; that it is credible evidence in the sense that it is capable of belief and of carrying some weight is also clear."

In my view, the court was right in not excluding the medical evidence in that case.

Gunewardene's case was, in my opinion, wrongly decided. Medical evidence is admissible to show that a witness suffers from some disease or defect or abnormality of mind that affects the reliability of his evidence. Such evidence is not confined to a general opinion of the unreliability of the witness but may give all the matters necessary to show, not only the foundation of and reasons for the diagnosis, but also the extent to which the credibility of the witness is affected.

[LORDS REID, MORRIS OF BORTH-Y-GEST, HODSON and DONOVAN agreed.]

vii Evidence in rebuttal

All evidence which one side intends to call should be called before the end of that side's case in chief. One major exception to this is where the exceptions to the rule that answers to collateral questions are final apply. There are few others: new evidence can only be called if the judge gives leave, and he will only do so if it relates to an issue which could not have been foreseen.

II CRIMINAL CASES

A. Order

If the accused pleads not guilty, the Crown has the right to begin because it must bear the evidential burden of proof on some issue unless the accused has made a formal admission on that point. The Crown will make an opening speech, call witnesses, and sum up if the accused proposes to call no witness; the accused will then reply. If the accused submits that there is no case to answer a ruling is given at once without the accused being put to his election whether to call evidence or not. An appeal may be dismissed even though it is the accused's own witnesses who incriminate him so that the submission of no case was wrongfully rejected (R. v. *Power*, [1919] 1 K.B. 572, C.C.A.). The position is different if the submission is wrongfully rejected and the incriminating evidence comes from a co-accused (R. v. *Abbott*, [1955] 2 Q.B. 497; [1955] 2 All E.R. 899).

B. Kinds of examination

No special comment need be made for criminal cases on the general problems of examination-in-chief, cross-examination and re-examination.

C. Special problems

No special comment need be made on leading questions, the refreshing of memory, unfavourable and hostile witnesses, or previous inconsistent statements.

i Previous Consistent Statements: Complaints

There is one special kind of previous consistent statement relevant in criminal cases: the complaint of the victim in a sex case.

Kilby v. R.

(1973), 1 A.L.R. 283

The accused was convicted of rape. The victim had made no immediate complaint. The High Court of Australia refused the accused's application for special leave to appeal.

BARWICK, C.J.: [T]he applicant does not raise or rely on the failure of the judge to instruct the jury as to the effect upon the credibility of the prosecutrix of a failure to complain. His counsel submits that as a matter of law a judge on a trial of an accused for rape is bound in every case to instruct the jury, no matter what the circumstances, that the failure to make such a complaint is evidence of consent by the woman to the intercourse. The submission is founded on the proposition that because evidence of proximate complaint is evidence, as it was said, that the woman had not consented, the lack of complaint must be evidence of consent. But, in my opinion, even granting the premises, the conclusion does not follow. Further, evidence of a complaint at the earliest reasonable opportunity is exceptionally admitted only as evidence of consistency in the account given by the woman claiming to have been raped: that is to say, it is admitted as matter going to her credit (see R. v. *Lillyman,* [1896] 2 Q.B. 167, *per* Hawkins, J. at 170; [1895–9] All E.R. Rep. 586; *Sparks* v. R., [1964] A.C. 964, at p. 979; [1964] 1 All E.R. 727). Because the account with which the complaint is said to show consistency is an account of intercourse without consent, it has often been said that the evidence of the complaint is evidence negating consent. In my opinion, this manner of expressing the function of the evidence of proximate complaint is not correct: though, as it shows consistency in her account of rape, the fact of the complaint buttresses her evidence of no consent or, as it was said in R. v. *Lillyman, supra,* is inconsistent with consent. At times also it is said with technical inaccuracy that the evidence of such a complaint is corroborative of the woman's evidence of the rape. It is quite clearly not so corroborative (see R. v. *Christie,* [1914] A.C. 545; *Eade* v. R. (1924), 34 CLR 154), though it is so spoken of in American literature (see *Wigmore on Evidence,* 3rd Edn., Vol. IV, p. 219, para. 1134 and p. 227, para. 1137; Vol. VI, p. 173, para. 1761).

However, having regard to the importance of the matter and the need to have uniformity of practice and the avoidance of laxity in the use of evidence or lack of evidence of proximate complaint, it is proper that I should examine the course of decision in the courts.

Wigmore, in para. 1134 in Vol. IV of the 3rd edition says as to the admission of evidence of a proximate complaint by a prosecutrix in rape:

> "Down to the beginning of the 1800's, evidence of this sort was received by the courts as a matter of old tradition and practice, with little or no thought of any principles to support it. The tradition went back by a continuous thread to the primitive rule of hue-and-cry: and the precise nature of the survival is more fully explained in dealing with the hearsay exception of *res gestae.* But as more and more attention began to be given, in the early 1800's, to the principles underlying every sort of evidence, there came to be felt a need of explaining on principle this inherited

and hitherto unquestioned practice; and thus the various aspects of its significance began to be thought of" [p. 219].

Wigmore gives the American experience in some detail: but, though this is instructive, we are here concerned with the experience of the common law of England which we have inherited and which in this field we still apply without modification.

A review of the subject begins, in my opinion, with R. v. *Lillyman, supra.* The trial judge at the time of an indictment for rape had admitted, over the objection of counsel for the accused, all that the prosecutrix had said to her mistress very shortly after the commission of the acts of the accused of which the prosecutrix complained. The Court of Crown Cases Reserved (Lord Russell of Killowen, C.J., Pollock, B. Hawkins, Cave and Wills, JJ.) decided that the details of the complaints were admissible and took occasion to state the basis of admissibility and the function of the evidence of a proximate complaint. Prior to that decision there had developed in England a practice of excluding the details of a complaint by a prosecutrix, whilst admitting the fact that she had complained at a time proximate to the occurrence forming the basis of the charge against the accused.

It is worth mentioning in passing that Sir Robert Finlay the Solicitor-General in arguing for the Crown in *Lillyman's Case* submitted that "the principle upon which the fact of the complaint having been made is allowed to be given in evidence is that it is the natural expression of the woman's feelings that as soon as possible after the occurrence she should tell her mother, or her mistress, or some person in a confidential relation, what has happened; it is *further* admissible as evidence of non-consent" ([1896] 2 Q.B., at p. 169). But quite clearly the Court did not accept the whole of that submission. Passages in the judgment delivered for the Court by Hawkins, J. to my mind make this quite plain:

"It is necessary, in the first place, to have a clear understanding as to the principles upon which evidence of such a complaint, not on oath, nor made in the presence of the prisoner, nor forming part of the *res gestae*, can be admitted. It clearly is not admissible as evidence of the facts complained of: those facts must therefore be established, if at all, upon oath by the prosecutrix or other credible witness, and, strictly speaking, evidence of them ought to be given before evidence of the complaint is admitted. The complaint can only be used as evidence of the consistency of the conduct of the prosecutrix with the story told by her in the witness-box, and as being inconsistent with her consent to that of which she complains" (p. 170).

Here the emphasis is that the complaint is not probative but only an aid to the credibility of the prosecutrix. When it is said that the complaint can be used "as being inconsistent with her consent to that of which she complains" the Court, in my opinion, is but stating the obverse of the statement that the complaint tends to show consistency in the evidence of the prosecutrix which, whether consent be an issue in the trial or not, must in the nature of things be an account of an occurrence taking place without her consent.

The passage cited by Hawkins, J. from *Blackstone* shows that the admission of evidence of the complaint is based solely on the effect it has on the credit of a prosecutrix

"... but the credibility of her testimony, and how far forth she is to be believed, must be left to the jury upon the circumstances of fact that concur in that testimony. For instance: if the witness be of good fame; if she presently discovered the offence, and made search for the offender ... these and the like are concurring circumstances, which give greater probability to her evidence. But, on the other side, if she be of evil fame, and stand unsupported by others; if she concealed the injury for any considerable time after she had opportunity to complain; if the place, where the fact was alleged to be committed, was where it was possible she might have been heard, and she made no outcry; these and the like circumstances carry a strong, but not conclusive, presumption that her testimony is false or feigned" (*Lillyman's Case* [1896] 2 Q.B., at p. 171).

Having dealt with the submission that the particulars of the complaint ought not to be admitted and having examined in that connexion a course of decision between 1779 and 1877, the judgment proceeded to express the Court's definitive opinion:

> "After very careful consideration we have arrived at the conclusion that we are bound by no authority to support the existing usage of limiting evidence of the complaint to the bare fact that a complaint was made, and that reason and good sense are against our doing so. The evidence is admissible only upon the ground that it was a complaint of that which is charged against the prisoner, and can be legitimately used only for the purpose of enabling the jury to judge for themselves whether the conduct of the woman was consistent with her testimony on oath given in the witness-box negativing her consent, and affirming that the acts complained of were against her will, and in accordance with the conduct they would expect in a truthful woman under the circumstances detailed by her" (see the report at p. 177).

In my opinion, nothing in this judgment lends any support to the proposition that evidence of the making of the complaint is evidence of any fact other than the fact of the making of the complaint itself and of the terms in which it is claimed to have been made. When Hawkins, J. in the first of the two passages which I have quoted from *Lillyman's Case* spoke of the evidence of a complaint as being inconsistent with consent he was not, in my opinion, intending to place its admissibility upon a second and different ground from that of its tendency to show consistency in the conduct of the prosecutrix. He was merely indicating the extent of its effect on the credit of the prosecutrix.

In my opinion, the error which has been made by text writers and in subsequent decisions is in treating this remark of Hawkins, J. as if it did set up a second and independent ground of admissibility. In my respectful opinion, it did not.

In R. v. *Lillyman*, reference was made to the passage in *Hawkins' Pleas of the Crown* where it is said: "It is a strong, but not a conclusive, presumption against a woman that she made no complaint in a reasonable time after the fact" (at pp. 170–1 of the report). But just as the fact of a proximate complaint tends to support credibility of the complainant so its absence may be a considerable factor where a tribunal of fact is deciding on the credibility of the complainant. The word "presumption", in this connexion, is not, of course, a reference to a presumption of law but is no more, in my opinion, than a statement that a tribunal of fact might well consider that a woman who made no complaint was not to be believed when she gave an account of events to which she gave no consent. This use of the word "presumption" has assisted to give rise to misconception as to the basis of admissibility of a proximate complaint and as to the effect of the absence of such a complaint.

In any case, to say that *Lillyman's Case* recognizes that the evidence of a proximate complaint may be used to negative consent is to make an ambiguous statement. If it means that in so far as a complaint tends to buttress the evidence of the prosecutrix that what occurred did occur without her consent and in so far as belief in the truth of her statement would negative consent, it may be an acceptable statement, though, I think, prone to be, as it has proved to be, misleading. If, of course, it means that the evidence of a complaint is direct evidence negativing consent, I am of opinion that the statement is completely unwarranted, both in point of precedent so far as *Lillyman's Case* is concerned and in point of logic. It is true that Ridley, J. in R. v. *Osborne*, [1905] 1 K.B. 551; [1904–07] All E.R. Rep. 54, treated the evidence of proximate complaint as admissible on two grounds, founding himself on *Lillyman's Case*. He did not intend to depart from the decision or to enlarge its reasoning. But as I have indicated, *Lillyman's Case* does not really warrant the conclusion that there are two distinct grounds of admissibility of evidence of proximate complaint. Always the basic authority for the contrary proposition in the texts and in the decisions has been *Lillyman's Case.*

Phipson in all its editions has stated the rule thus:

"In cases of rape, indecent assault, and similar offences, the fact that the prosecutrix or prosecutor made a complaint, shortly after the outrage, of the matters charged against the prisoner, together with the particulars of the complaint, are admissible as evidence in chief for the prosecution, not to prove the truth of the matters stated, but (1) to confirm her or his testimony, and (2) where consent is in issue, to disprove consent" (para. 355, 11th Edn.).

See also *Archbold's Criminal Pleading Evidence and Practice,* 36th Edn., p. 392, para. 1077:

"In R. v. *Lillyman, supra,* it was held after consideration of the earlier authorities, that upon the trial of an indictment for rape or other kindred offences against women or girls (including indecent assault and sexual intercourse with girls under thirteen and between thirteen and sixteen) the fact that a complaint was made by the prosecutrix shortly after the alleged occurrence, and the particulars of such complaint, may so far as they relate to the charge against the prisoner, be given in evidence by the prosecution, not as being evidence of the facts complained of but as evidence of the consistency of the conduct of the prosecutrix with the story told by her in the witness-box, and as negativing consent on her part. The mere complaint is no evidence of the facts complained of, and its admissibility depends on proof of the facts by sworn or other legalized testimony: R. v. *Brasier* (1779), 1 Leach 199; R. v. *Wood* (1877), 14 Cox C.C. 46;

"In R. v. *Osborne* [1905] 1 K.B. 551, the indictment was for an indecent assault on a girl under thirteen, and consent was therefore immaterial. It was held that in the case of charges of sexual offences against females, evidence of fresh complaint is admissible 'whether non-consent is legally a necessary part of the issue or whether on the other hand it is what may be called a collateral issue of fact' in consequence of the story told by the complainant in the witness-box, and the complaint is not admissible merely as negativing consent, but as being consistent with the sworn evidence of the complainant."

Though Ridley, J. in R. v. *Osborne, supra,* said that evidence was admitted because, if believed, it was consistent with a complainant's story in evidence and also that it was inconsistent with consent, he did not say at any time that it was evidence of the absence of consent. Indeed on neither of the bases of the admissibility which his Lordship expressed is the complaint probative of any fact, not even of the facts made in the complaint.

The definitive passage in the judgment of Hawkins, J. in R. v. *Lillyman,* ([1896] 2 Q.B., at p. 177) finds its echo and endorsement in *Sparks* v. R., [1964] A.C. 964; [1964] 1 All E.R. 727. The conclusion there expressed that the evidence of a complaint is not admissible in the absence of evidence by the prosecutrix is emphatic of the proposition that the evidence of a complaint is not probative of the absence of consent.

Jordan, C.J. in *Smith* v. *Commonwealth Life Assurance Society, Ltd.* (1935), 35 S.R. N.S.W. 552, said at p. 556:

"Such evidence is admissible, not because what was said by way of complaint can be treated as corroborating the evidence of the facts of the alleged happening given by the witness in the witness-box, but, firstly, because absence of complaint is strong evidence of consent in any case in which consent is material, and secondly because the fact that a complaint was made at the time in terms similar to the evidence afterwards given, goes to negative the possibility that what is now said in evidence is an afterthought—an invented story prepared after the event—a possibility which is regarded as existing in a special degree in this class of case."

In support of these propositions the learned Chief Justice cited R. v. *Osborne* and R. v. *Christie, supra.* In my respectful submission neither of these cases lends support for either of these propositions. *Halsbury,* 3rd Edn., Vol. 10, para. 859 at p. 468, in my opinion, puts the matter in proper perspective when it is there said:

> "The admissibility of the particulars of a complaint made soon after the commission of an alleged offence in the absence of the defendant by the person in respect of whom a crime is alleged to have been committed is peculiar to rape, indecent assault and similar offences upon females, and also offences of indecency between male persons. This evidence is not to be taken in proof of the facts complained of, but only as matter to be borne in mind by the jury in considering the consistency, and, therefore, the credibility, of the complainant's story, including the consideration of the question of consent if the prisoner raises that as a defence."

The admission of a recent complaint in cases of sexual offences is exceptional in the law of evidence. Whatever the historical reason for an exception, the admissibility of that evidence in modern times can only be placed, in my opinion, upon the consistency of statement or conduct which it tends to show, the evidence having itself no probative value as to any fact in contest but, merely and exceptionally constituting a buttress to the credit of the woman who has given evidence of having been subject to the sexual offence.

To understand the reasons for the admissibility and the use which can properly be made of the evidence of recent complaint is to deny the validity of the applicant's proposition that lack of complaint is probative of consent. I can see no ground in logic for saying that because evidence of complaint is admitted to show consistency in the story told by the woman, evidence of non-complaint is evidence of her consent to the intercourse. In my opinion, quite apart from the fact that there may be many reasons why a complaint is not made, the want of a complaint does not found an inference of consent. It does tell against the consistency of the woman's account and accordingly is clearly relevant to her credibility in that respect.

I am clearly of opinion, therefore, that a trial judge is not only bound as a matter of law but not entitled to instruct a jury in the trial of an accused on a charge of rape that the failure of the woman claiming to have been raped to complain at the earliest possible opportunity is evidence of her consent to the intercourse. Statements to the contrary in R. v. *Hinton,* [1961] Qd. R. 17 and in R. v. *Mayberry* (unreported) in the Court of Criminal Appeal of Queensland are not, in my opinion, supportable.

[McTiernan, Menzies, Stephen and Mason, JJ. agreed.]

Notes

1. The complaint may be made by male victims as well as female: "probably little attention would or should be paid to a complaint by an abandoned male person of mature years, but perhaps that observation goes rather to the weight, than to the admissibility, of the complaint" (R. v. *Camelleri,* [1922] 2 K.B. 122, at p. 125, C.C.A.).

2. The law on complaints applies whether or not consent is in issue (R. v. *Osborne,* [1905] 1 K.B. 551).

3. The complaint must be made at the first opportunity after the offence which reasonably offers itself. There is little of general value to be said about this difficult question of degree.

4. The complaint must be made voluntarily in the sense that leading or intimidating questions must not be used (e.g. R. v. *Adams,* [1965] Qd.R. 255).

5. The details of the complaint may be given, not merely the fact of the complaint R. v. *Lillyman,* [1896] 2 Q.B. 167).

6. Since complaints only prove consistency and are not evidence of the truth of what they assert, they are not, when proved by someone other than the maker, exceptions to the hearsay rule. For the same reason they do not corroborate the maker, and this conclusion is also supported by the fact that they are not independent of the witness to be corroborated (*Eade* v. R. (1924), 34 C.L.R. 154).

7. Since the only relevance of complaints is to show consistency in testimony, a complaint is inadmissible if the complainant does not testify (*Sparks* v. R., [1964] A.C. 964, at p. 979; [1964] 1 All E.R. 727, at p. 734, P.C.). Not even the fact of complaint may be admitted in these circumstances (cf. R. v. *Wallwork* (1958), 122 J.P. 299, C.C.A.).

8. It is not clear whether the complaint rules apply to sexual allegations in civil cases, or to all allegations of violence in both criminal and civil cases. There is some authority for these extensions (*R.* v. *Wink* (1834), 8 C. & P. 397; *Berry* v. *Berry* (1898), 78 L.T. 688; *Jones* v. *South Eastern and Chatham Rail Co.'s Managing Committee* (1918), 87 L.J.K.B. 775, at p. 778; *Fromhold* v. *Fromhold*, [1952] 1 T.L.R. 1522, at pp. 1526, 1528, *per* Denning and Hodson, L.JJ.). But in *De B.* v. *De B.*, [1950] V.L.R. 242 a wife's complaint of her husband's sodomy was held inadmissible in a divorce case because the intimate nature of marriage made it very unlikely that there could be said to be any lack of consistency on the part of a wife who did not make immediate complaint of her husband's unwanted behaviour but later sued for divorce.

ii Collateral questions

Rape cases provide the usual examples of collateral questions. A complainant of rape who denies intercourse with other men cannot be contradicted. In *R.* v. *Holmes* (1871), L.R. 1 C.C.R. 334, at p. 336, Kelly, C.B. said:

> "If such evidence as that here proposed were admitted, the whole history of the prosecutrix's life might be gone into; if a charge might be made as to one man, it might be made as to fifty, and that without notice to the prosecutrix. It would not only involve a multitude of collateral cases, but an inquiry into matters as to which the prosecutrix might be wholly unprepared, and so work great injustice."

Indeed, it is difficult to see how the question is ever relevant even to credibility, though extreme promiscuity might be relevant to consent. But if she denies previous or subsequent voluntary intercourse with the accused she may be contradicted, for the evidence is relevant to the issue of consent (*R.* v. *Riley* (1887), 18 Q.B.D. 481; *R.* v. *Aloisio* (1969), 90 W.N. (Pt. 1) (N.S.W.) 111). Similarly, her denials of being a prostitute may be contradicted (*R.* v. *Bashir*, [1969] 3 All E.R. 692; [1969] 1 W.L.R. 1303).

iii Evidence in rebuttal

Examples of the judge giving leave for the admission of evidence in rebuttal after the close of a party's case occur most commonly when the accused raises some unexpected last minute defence. One example is a late alibi (*R.* v. *Flynn* (1957) 42 Cr. App. Rep. 15, C.C.A.); but now advance notice of an alibi must be given (Criminal Justice Act 1967, s. 11). Evidence in rebuttal is more likely to be admitted where the evidence which is now clearly relevant to credibility could only have been marginally relevant to guilt in chief (*R.* v. *Levy* (1966), 50 Cr. App. Rep. 198, C.C.A.), or is only made relevant by the accused's attack on the prosecution witnesses' characters (*R.* v. *Milliken* (1969), 53 Cr. App. Rep. 330, C.A.).

D. Reform

The Criminal Law Revision Committee in its 11th Report recommends the following reforms for criminal cases. Cross-examination as to convictions should only be directed to convictions relevant to an issue or to credibility (para. 159). Though the prohibition on proof by a party of his own witness's bad character will continue, such a witness may be cross-examined by a party if he has made a previous inconsistent statement or has given adverse evidence. The witness's attention need not be drawn to the occasion on which he is supposed to have made the previous inconsistent statement (para. 165). Previous consistent and inconsistent statements will be admissible as evidence of the truth of what they assert (para. 257): the effect will, *inter alia*, be to destroy the special rules as to complaints.

Reading

Gooderson, [1968] C.L.J. 64.

Index

IDENTITY, 74
need for corroboration as to, 67, 92–96

ILLEGITIMACY
standard of proof of, 41

IMPROPERLY OBTAINED EVIDENCE,
223–254
admissible, 223, 226, 233, 234, 237, 238,
240, 245
discretion to disallow, 237, 238, 241, 242,
243, 244
exclusionary rule, 245, 246, 249, 250, 251,
252, 253
fact discovery by, 224–227
obtained by crime, tort or breach of contract, 230, 232, 233, 234, 237, 238,
240, 242, 247
relevance test, 234, 235, 237, 238, 240

JUDGE
accomplice, evidence, 78
direction
jury, to, on corroboration, 67–96, 119–
120
discretion to
admit confession, 7
disallow
improper question in cross-examination, 7, 430
improperly obtained evidence, 237,
238, 241, 242, 243, 244
exclude relevant evidence, 7
functions, of, 7
hostile witness, 433
issues of law, 7
leading question, 430
privilege against self-incrimination, 123–
140
public policy, 411, 412, 415, 416, 417, 418,
419
Rules, Judges', 194–207
summing up, 8

JUDICIAL NOTICE, 6
finger prints, 9

JURY
absence of
during *voir dire*, 7
direction on corroboration, 67–96, 119–120
function of, 7, 8
accomplice, 77
standard of proof, explanation of, to, 32–35
weight of evidence, 7

LEADING QUESTION, 430–431
cross-examination, in, 430
definition of, 430
judge's discretion as to, 430

LEGITIMACY
presumption, of, 44, 45, 47, 53–54

NO CASE TO ANSWER
election to give evidence, 429, 430
submission of, 429, 431, 438

OPINION
definition, 369
expert evidence, 360, 370–372
doctor, 371

OPINION—*contd.*
expert evidence—*contd.*
qualification to give, 370, 371, 372
valuation, 371, 372
non-expert, 369, 370
drunkenness, 370, 372
identity, 370
speed, 370
value of objects, 370
question of foreign law, 372
statutory reform, 372–373

PRESUMPTION, 373–380; *see also* BUR-
DEN OF PROOF, 44–64
commorientes, 46–47, 48
conclusive (irrebuttable), 44, 45, 379–380
conflicting, 62–64
continuance, 61
death, 45, 48–53
driver of car authorized by owner, 62
due appointment, 60
evidential, 44, 46, 60–62
general practice, 62
habits, 61
innocence, of, 44, 47
irrebuttable, *see* conclusive
legitimacy, of, 44, 53–54
marriage, validity of, 54–55
mechanical devices, 62
motive, 61
persuasive, 44, 46, 48–60, 373–379
possession, 60
prima facie case, 17
prior convictions, 373, 374
provisional, 44, 46, 60–62, 375, 377
reasons, for, 46–47
res ipsa loquitur, 55–60
rule in *Hollington v. Hewthorn*, 373, 375, 379,
380
sanity, of, 44
spoliation, 62
standard of proof, for, 45
statutory provisions, 373, 377, 378, 379,
380
testamentary capacity, 46

PREVIOUS STATEMENT
complaint of victim in sex case, 439–444
consistent, 431–432, 445
civil cases, 432
general rule as to, 431–432
res gestae, admitted as part of, 432
identification as to, 432
inconsistent, 433–434, 445
hostile witness, by, 433
statutory provisions as to, 434
recent fabrication, 432

PRIVILEGE
adultery
answer tending to show, 407–408
document relating to title to land, 407
legal professional, 3, 393–407
communications to facilitate crime or
fraud, 396, 397, 400, 402
communications to third parties, 394,
395
confidential communication, 399
documents in hands of defendant or
third party, 400–407

Printed in Great Britain by Butler & Tanner Ltd, Frome and London